"Artificial Curiosities"

Captn. James Cook F.R.S.

"ARTIFICIAL CURIOSITIES"

being

An exposition of
native manufactures collected on the
three Pacific voyages of
Captain James Cook, R.N.

at the

Bernice Pauahi Bishop Museum
January 18, 1978-August 31, 1978

on the occasion of the

Bicentennial of the
European Discovery of the Hawaiian Islands
by Captain Cook – January 18, 1778

by

ADRIENNE L. KAEPPLER

Bernice P. Bishop Museum Special Publication 65

BISHOP MUSEUM PRESS
HONOLULU, HAWAII

Printing of this book was made possible through partial financial support from the Atherton Family Foundation; Charles M. and Anna C. Cooke, Ltd.; McInerny Foundation; Frear Eleemosynary Trust; Samuel N. and Mary Castle Foundation; National Endowment for the Arts; National Science Foundation; National Endowment for the Humanities; Bishop Museum Association. To each of these the Trustees of Bishop Museum wish to express their appreciation.

Library of Congress Catalog Card No. 77-91442
ISSN 0067-6179
ISBN 0-910240-24-8

Tahitian women making bark cloth. British Library Add. Ms. 23,921.50.

TO THE MEN AND WOMEN OF THE PACIFIC who made the objects represented in this exhibition – to those for whom these objects were real and functional rather than "artificial curiosities," as they were to their European collectors.

– and –

TO THE DESCENDANTS of these men and women in their search for inspiration in the works of their ancestors.

"Artificial Curiosities"
is the 18th Century term for
Ethnographic Artifacts

Tahitian woman scraping bark, British Library Add. Ms. 23,921.50.

Contents

Ola ka inoa o na Kūpuna

Ola ka inoa o na Kūpuna
E ho'omau ia i ke kahua ho'omana'o

Kūkulu ia e Konia me Paki[1]
Ka Hale Hō'ike'ike a Pihopa
Hō'ike'ike i na mea i hana 'ia
Me ka no'eau a na kāhiko
Na mea hana lima i ho'iho'i ia mai

I ke one hānau o Hawaii nei
Ka 'āina kahua nani o Ka'iwi'ula[2]
Na mea makamae a kāhiko

Ho'omaika'i makou i ka po'e i alu like mai
Nolaila ko makou aloha
E kou lokomaika'i he nui
E ka Wahine-hele-lā o Kaiona[3]
E ola o Pauahi Lani
A kau i ka pūaneane.

Ancestral names live on
Perpetuated at this commemorative
  foundation
Buildings named for Konia and Paki
At the Bishop Museum
Exhibited are unusual objects
Skillfully manufactured by our forebears
Whose ancient artifacts from distant lands
  will return
To Hawaii
The beautiful land, Ka'iwi'ula
Where all may observe these ancient
  treasures
We thank those who made this possible
Therefore our love
For your great goodness
The Lady Kaiona
Long live the Chiefess Pauahi
To the extreme end of life.

MARY KAWENA PUKU'I, LITT.D.

---

[1]Konia and Paki were the mother and father of Mrs. Bishop.

[2]Ka'iwi'ula is the old place name of the area where the Bishop Museum is located.

[3]Bernice Pauahi Bishop was frequently compared in chants to Kaiona, the beneficent goddess of Mt. Ka'ala, on the Wai'anae Mountain range, O'ahu.

Foreword

Hawaii is extremely fortunate to have one of the outstanding cultural and scientific institutions in the world, Bernice P. Bishop Museum, founded in 1889 by Charles Reed Bishop in honor and memory of his beloved wife, Princess Bernice Pauahi.

As Hawaii's oldest scientific institution, its contributions to knowledge over the years have taken many forms, including nearly 1,000 publications. These publications are a significant source of the professional recognition and esteem for Bishop Museum which is held worldwide. It is this high regard for the Museum and for Hawaii's people that played such an important role in the loan of Cook voyage cultural treasures for the Museum's unique exhibition "Artificial Curiosities." It is an honor that may be shared by every citizen of Hawaii.

It has been enlightening for me to realize that in the study of these artifacts, much still may be learned about the heritage of Hawaii and the Pacific, not only in an academic sense, but also in an expansion of our views and an enrichment of our lives.

Whatever our cultural or ethnic origins, people in the Pacific today benefit from a common Pacific heritage, a heritage about which we are ever learning. In Hawaii, we cherish this heritage, at once precious and vigorous. It is the foundation and the inspiration whereby we live harmoniously and creatively together in the spirit of Aloha.

On behalf of the people of Hawaii, I wish to express our gratitude to Bishop Museum and its dedicated staff whose years of cooperative work with governments, institutions, agencies, and individuals have made this exhibition possible.

Through this catalogue, Bishop Museum gives the exhibition an extended life and makes new information available to us all. For the people of Hawaii, I am honored to convey to readers of this beautiful and important publication, our warmest Aloha.

GEORGE R. ARIYOSHI
Governor, State of Hawaii

Honolulu, Hawaii
September, 1977

View of Niihau. Watercolor by William Ellis (70).

Preface

Captain James Cook (1728-1779) of the English Navy rose from humble origins to become the greatest European navigator of the 18th century. Cook made three exemplary voyages into the Pacific. The purpose of the first voyage was to observe scientifically the transit of the planet Venus from the vantage point of Tahiti, only recently discovered for the Western world by his countryman Captain Samuel Wallis; the second was to search for the great Southern Continent that was believed to exist by geographers of the time; and the third was to search for a Northern Passage between the Atlantic and Pacific Oceans. Strictly speaking, then, all three voyages might be considered failures—the observations of Venus were disappointing, a great Southern Continent eluded him, and a Northern Passage between the two oceans was not found. But considering the geographical and scientific information gathered during the voyages, it can only be concluded that the importance of these voyages has never been surpassed, either before Cook's time or since.

Certainly, from the point of view of ethnography, no voyages have been more important in the formulation of ideas about the nature of certain Pacific societies and their material cultures before they were influenced by the Western world. Yet, it is astounding to find that, after 200 years, little is known about the location of the objects collected on the voyages and those that are available remain largely unused in serious studies of change in material culture. Many objects have been attributed to collection on Cook's voyages by hearsay or because "they look right." But such "intuitive scholarship" can have no validity when there is no documented corpus of material to work from. Research on change in material culture and the society it reflects cannot proceed until accurate information about the precise nature of the objects at the time of first European contact is known.

This was my dilemma in 1969 when I attempted to study change in Tongan society and in its material culture since the time of Cook. There simply was no corpus of material documented as of undoubted Cook provenance that I could use. Museum registers suggested tantalizing attributions which all too often turned out to be only half-truths. Curators revealed alarming information such as, "Yes, we have objects from Cook's voyages, but we cannot identify which ones they are." Private collectors, convinced that their objects were from Cook, told me that "certainly it must be from Cook, you can tell by its classic style." I was not convinced.

Indeed, my first four months of research in Europe in 1969 taught me that Cook voyage ethnographic objects were not going to be located by asking Museum personnel or private collectors about their collections. If I wanted documented pieces that could be used as a base line for culture change, I would have to search out the documentation myself. This volume is the result of eight years of such research—which began with inadvertently finding the "Catalogue of Curiosities" that established the identity and provenance of much of the Cook voyage collection at Oxford—and the research may never be finished. However, now I can go back to my study of Tongan material culture convinced that I have documented material with which to work. Perhaps others will find the information presented here useful for their own studies of material culture and society.

Ethnographic collections from Cook's voyages are important because his voyages made the first extensive contact with Pacific peoples. It was not always the first contact, but it is the first contact from which we have collections that can be identified and studied. Although both the British Museum[1] and Cambridge are thought to have objects from Wallis's voyage, they cannot be identified; and traceable to Bougainville are only some pieces of Tahitian bark cloth. Objects from the voyages of Tasman and of Schoten and LeMaire cannot be found, although I have searched in both Europe and Batavia (Jakarta); and no objects can be traced to the voyages of Mendana and Roggeveen.

[1] An entry in the British Museum Register for 3-9 1770 reads, "Several curiosities brought from the newly discovered Islands and other parts of the world by Captains Wallis and Carteret. Lords of the Admiralty."

From Cook's voyages there are more than 2,000 pieces that can be traced and more than 400 have been assembled for this exhibition—the largest assemblage of Cook voyage objects since the sale of the Leverian Museum in London in 1806.

This volume has three aims. First, it accompanies and identifies the "Artificial Curiosities" of the exhibition, while the photographs give the exhibition a more permanent life and make it available to those unable to visit the exhibition itself. Second, it enumerates the artifact types collected on the voyages as far as these can be ascertained today. Artifacts which were considered too breakable (such as Hawaiian gourds), their condition too fragile (such as Marquesan feather headdresses), too difficult to pack (such as Tahitian headdresses), or too large in some dimension (such as Tongan spears), were not sought for the exhibition. A few artifact types could not be found (such as a New Zealand greenstone *mere* or a New Caledonia "ceremonial axe"), others their owners were reluctant to send, and in the final analysis the types were simply too numerous. The missing types, however, are listed and in most cases a photograph of one example is included in order to give as complete a picture as possible of the native manufactures collected on Cook's voyages. Third, there is an inventory of all the documented Cook voyage ethnographic objects that I have been able to find—documented either by actual traceable links or by strong circumstantial evidence. No doubt there are others. Readers may find that some of their favorite "Cook" objects are missing. Although it is possible that I do not know of them, it is more than likely that I find their documentation unconvincing. I will be happy to learn about other objects and will assist their owners in tracing documentation.

In short, this volume is not a summary of Pacific ethnography at the time of the voyages of Cook, but an exposition of objects collected on those voyages. It is not an exhibition of Pacific art, but a gathering of native manufactures that individuals on Cook's voyages managed to obtain. Indeed, it is not an exhibition in honor of Captain Cook the explorer-navigator, but rather, an exhibition that acknowledges and honors the achievements of Pacific peoples as they were before the impact of Cook and others of the Western world irrevocably changed their lives.

ACKNOWLEDGMENTS

It is my pleasant task to acknowledge those who helped make this exhibition and Catalogue possible. Most important, of course, are the lenders to this exhibition listed below. The directors and curators of the museums and the private owners have all been most helpful. I do not wish to list them here simply as a string of names. Rather I wish to acknowledge them not only as colleagues, but also as friends. They have graciously endured my endless visits and letters, and their cooperation and attention to detail has been most rewarding. Among these, I want to especially acknowledge Hans Manndorff, Christian Feest, and John Hewett.

I have been aided by many people at Bishop Museum, especially Roland W. Force, Director Emeritus, and Yosihiko Sinoto, Chairman of the Anthropology Department, who encouraged my research and made it possible to pursue it year after year. Peter Gathercole has helped me in innumerable ways, making available his own unpublished research, helping me to understand the 18th century, and bringing down to earth my sometimes unfounded enthusiasm. I am grateful to researchers on other aspects of Cook's voyages who discussed my research with me, especially Peter Whitehead on natural history and Rüdiger Joppien on Philippe Jacques de Loutherbourg and other artists of the 18th century.

In addition to support by a Federal indemnity from the Federal Council on the Arts and the Humanities, and support from the national and local foundations and private individuals listed below, I wish to acknowledge the granting agencies which made it possible to carry out my research—the Wenner-Gren Foundation for Anthropological Research, the National Endowment for the Arts, and the American Philosophical Society.

The realization of the exhibition and of this Catalogue would have been impossible without the active and moral support of my co-workers at Bishop Museum. In addition to those listed below, I want to particularly acknowledge Eleanor Williamson, Roger Rose, Cynthia Timberlake, Anthony Werner and the Pacific Regional Conservation Center, Kenneth P. Emory, Catherine Summers, Mary Judd, Anita Manning, Joyce Kaaihue, Michael Mueller-Ali, Lynn Davis, Debra Sullivan, David Huffman, and Acting Director Frank Radovsky. The production of this Catalogue could not have been achieved without the careful, painstaking editorial work of Genevieve Highland with the assistance of Sadie Doyle, and of Patience Bacon, whose first name was put to the test in typing these words over and over again. To all of my co-workers, my thanks.

Finally, I wish to acknowledge with fondest felicitations my tireless co-organizer John Cotton Wright, whose photographic and artistic abilities are reflected in this Catalogue. John photographed, packed, and transported priceless, fragile artifacts from around the world and worked endless hours on the organization and execution of this exhibition.

Lenders to the Exhibition

UNITED KINGDOM

Her Majesty Queen Elizabeth the Second

Institutions

British Museum, London, England
Hunterian Museum, University of Glasgow, Scotland
London School of Economics and Political Science, England
Merseyside County Museum, Liverpool, England
National Maritime Museum, Greenwich, England
Pitt Rivers Museum, University of Oxford, England
Royal Albert Memorial Museum, Exeter, England
Royal Scottish Museum, Edinburgh, Scotland
Saffron Walden Museum, Essex, England
University Museum of Archaeology and Ethnology, Cambridge, England

Individuals

Anonymous Private Collection
Michael Emanuel, Southampton, England
William Greene, London, England
John Hewett Collection

IRELAND

Institution

National Museum of Ireland, Dublin, Ireland

EUROPE

Institutions

Etnografiska Museet, Stockholm, Sweden
Institut für Völkerkunde der Universität, Göttingen, Germany
Museum of Anthropology and Ethnography, Leningrad, U.S.S.R.
Museum für Völkerkunde, Vienna, Austria

Individuals

George Ortiz, Geneva, Switzerland
Kenneth Weston Winsor, Camaiore, Italy

AUSTRALIA

Institutions

The Australian Museum, Sydney
Mitchell Library, State Library of New South Wales, Sydney

NEW ZEALAND

Institution

National Museum, Wellington

Individual

A. R. Merritt, Christchurch

SOCIETY ISLANDS

Individual

Jean-Jacques Laurent, Papeete, Tahiti

HAWAII

Institution

Bernice Pauahi Bishop Museum, Honolulu

Individuals

Mr. and Mrs. Leo Fortess, Kaneohe
Mr. and Mrs. Don Severson, Honolulu

UNITED STATES MAINLAND

Institutions

Field Museum of Natural History, Chicago, Illinois
Isaac Delgado Museum, New Orleans Museum of Art, Louisiana
Menil Foundation, Houston, Texas

Individuals

Anonymous Private Collection
Susanne Bennet, Washington, D.C.
David W. Forbes, San Francisco
Fulcher Collection, Florida
John H. Hauberg, Seattle, Washington

Realization of the Exhibition

Research and Selection of Objects
Adrienne L. Kaeppler

Overall Exhibition Coordination
John Cotton Wright

Conception and Design
Adrienne L. Kaeppler
John Cotton Wright

Installation
Hisao Goto
Dora Jacroux
Adrienne L. Kaeppler
David Kemble
Atonio Lilomaiava
John McLaughlin
John Cotton Wright

Preparation of Galleries
Charles Baker
George Bunton
Paul Ellis
Rolf Gantert
Hisao Goto
Tadao Harada
George Mason
Kenneth S. Miyazaki
Michael Mueller-Ali
Vincent Nakano
Donald Sichter
Andres Tabios

Curation of Objects
Roger G. Rose
Dora Jacroux

Registration
Anita Manning

Maps
Lee Motteler

Library Materials
Cynthia Timberlake
Marguerite K. Ashford
Janet A. Short
Janet Ness

Photography
John Cotton Wright
Benjamin W. Patnoi
Lynne Gilliland

The Board of Trustees Bernice Pauahi Bishop Museum

Directors of Bishop Museum
Roland W. Force (until April 30, 1976)
Frank J. Radovsky (Acting Director, May 1, 1976-October 31, 1977)
Edward C. Creutz (from November 1, 1977)

Consultation and Coordination
Yosihiko H. Sinoto

Bishop Museum Association
Dean Ho
Patricia Schattenburg

Senior Docent
Mary Louise Kaleonahenahe Kekuewa

Funding and Support
This Exhibition is supported by a Federal Indemnity from the Federal Council on the Arts and the Humanities
National Endowment for the Arts
National Endowment for the Humanities
National Science Foundation
Architects Hawaii, Ltd.
Association of Hawaiian Civic Clubs
Atherton Family Foundation
Bishop Museum Association
Samuel N. and Mary Castle Foundation
Charles M. and Anna C. Cooke, Ltd.
Committee for the Preservation and Study of Hawaiian Language, Art and Culture
Mary D. and Walter F. Frear Eleemosynary Trust
Hawaiian Airlines
McInerny Foundation
Pan American World Airways
Barbara B. Smith
United States Department of State
J. Watumull Estate
G. N. Wilcox Trust

Introductory Exhibition in the Kahili Room

To attempt some new discoveries in that vast unknown tract . . .
The London *Gazetteer*
August 18, 1768

The 18th century—and particularly the three Pacific voyages of James Cook—opened to the Western world entirely new vistas of geographic and scientific knowledge. These vistas were not only quantitative but qualitative—quantum steps which were not rivaled until man stepped on the moon. The "new discoveries" of Cook and his Gentlemen "in that vast unknown tract" are presented in this exhibition in three sections—natural history, human history, and geography and navigation. Although "new discoveries" to the Europeans, this information had been known to Pacific peoples for hundreds of years—and viewed from the Pacific, the encounter is more aptly described as "fatal impact." Discovery and integration of the discovered into the existing states of knowledge operated in both directions, for Cook and his companions had as much difficulty fitting their new knowledge into 18th century European views of the world as Pacific people had in fitting these strange white men and their curious ships into their Pacific world views.

NATURAL HISTORY

In the 18th century the importance of the "natural curiosities" collected on the voyages was immediately recognized. Shells, birds, fish, insects, and botanical and geological specimens significantly expanded the existing knowledge of these subjects. The specimens collected, described, and depicted during and after the voyages became type specimens for numerous genera and species. The drawings and written works of those who traveled on the voyages, and those to whom the specimens were given for scientific analysis after the voyages, are still basic reference materials for study of Pacific natural history.

Figure 1. — Joseph Banks. Artist unknown (1).

On Cook's first voyage the natural history team included Joseph Banks (Fig. 1), an enthusiastic dilettante;[1] Daniel Carl Solander, a proponent of Linnean nomenclature; Herman Diedrich Spöring, an assistant/draftsman; and Sydney Parkinson (Fig. 2), a

[1]The generally accepted meaning of dilettante, like other words used in this Catalogue and exhibition, has changed during the past two centuries.

natural history illustrator. Cook's second voyage included the natural historians Reinhold and George Forster, father and son, and an assistant, Anders Sparrman. Much of the natural history illustration was done by George Forster. On the third voyage there were no official natural historians, but collections were made by Anderson, Samwell, Bayly, and Clerke, among others. John Webber, the official artist of the voyage, and William Ellis, surgeon's second mate, did the natural history drawings.

EXHIBITED

1. "The R.^{t} Honble S.^{R} J. Banks, B.^{t} &tc &tc &tc." Unknown artist (Fig. 1).

Engraved sketch, unsigned and undated. 23 × 17 cm (plate mark); 33.5 × 25 cm. sheet.

Similar sketch listed in Mitchell Library Bibliography (Beddie, 1970, p. 710). Entry states: "from painting by T. Phillips, R.A., 1816." "Private plate, only 12 impressions made [signed] Dawson Turner."[2]

Fuller collection,[3] Bishop Museum Library.

2. "Sydney Parkinson." Unknown artist (Fig. 2).

Engraving. Oval. Hand col. 25 × 18.5 engr. surface (no plate mark, clipped?).

"Ja^{s} Newton, sculp."

Frontispiece to Parkinson's *Journal of a Voyage to the South Seas*, London: Stanfield Parkinson, 1773.

Fuller collection, Bishop Museum Library.

Figure 2. — Sydney Parkinson. Artist unknown (2).

Botany and zoology as scientific disciplines were in a fairly primitive state at the time. Most important to the natural scientists on Cook's voyages "was a catalogue of nature's storehouse and a system into which the newly discovered material could be slotted" (Whitehead, 1969, p. 244). The scientists on the voyages collected, catalogued, and described the new natural curiosities, using Linnaeus's *Systema Naturae* for the system. It is estimated that on first voyage alone the collections included more than a thousand plants, 500 fish, 500 birds, and hundreds of insects, shells, and other invertebrates (Whitehead, 1969, p. 245). Unfortunately, few studies were completed at the time, and even more distressing, only a fraction of the specimens collected can be located today. According to Whitehead there are "no mammals, reptiles or amphibians . . . perhaps a hundred fish, twice that number of insects, some corals, a single crab, and a single tunicate" (1969, p. 246). Botanical specimens and shells are represented in some numbers, however, in the British Museum (Natural History). Fortunately, also, many of the natural history drawings were preserved. In the wake of the recent interest in the historical aspects of natural history and the history of science, derived, at least in part, from the bicentenary of Cook's voyages, a number of them have been recently published.

EXHIBITED

Botany

3. Botanical specimens collected on Cook's voyages (Bishop Museum Herbarium).

4. Captain Cook's florilegium:

A selection of engravings from the drawings of plants collected by Joseph Banks and Daniel Solander on Captain Cook's first voyage to the islands of the Pacific, with accounts of the voyage by Wilfred Blunt and of the botanical explorations and prints by William T. Stearn. London: Lion and Unicorn Press, 1973 (Bishop Museum Library, purchase).

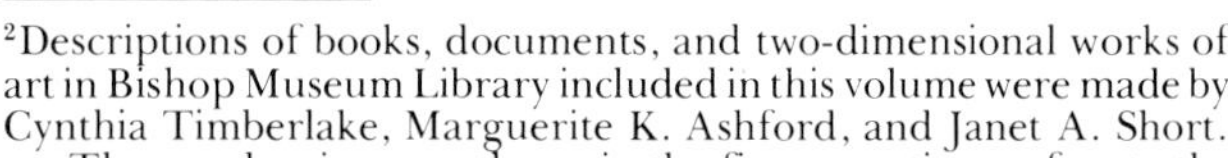

[2]Descriptions of books, documents, and two-dimensional works of art in Bishop Museum Library included in this volume were made by Cynthia Timberlake, Marguerite K. Ashford, and Janet A. Short.
The number in parentheses in the figure captions refers to the Catalogue number listed herein. If not otherwise noted, the object depicted is from the Bishop Museum collections.

[3]Captain A. W. F. Fuller, noted artifact collector and bibliophile, developed his collection of rare Pacific books over a period of sixty years, until his death in 1961. Bishop Museum purchased his collection in 1964 from his widow, Mrs. Estelle Winifred Fuller. Of utmost value in interpreting this remarkable collection are Captain Fuller's own manuscript notes which accompany each item in the collection. Mrs. Fuller has also been a generous donor to the Museum Library in recent years and her many gifts have been assimilated into the "Fuller collection."

Figure 3. — Manuka or Tea Tree, New Zealand, by William Hodges (6).

Figure 4. — Fan palm of Cracatoa by John Webber (7).

The story behind the production of this monumental work on plants collected during Cook's first voyage is detailed in a separate publication by Joy Law: *Captain Cook's Florilegium: A Note on Its Production,* London, Lion and Unicorn Press, 1976. The sketches by Sydney Parkinson, who died en route, were turned into carefully detailed paintings by artists in England, and engravings were made from the drawings under the direction of Joseph Banks. The engravings remained unpublished in the British Museum (Natural History), together with the original copper plates, although some inferior reproductions of some of them were published in 1900-1901. In 1962 the British Museum (Natural History) and the Royal College of Art took the first steps in a cooperative venture which culminated in the production of the present work. Hand-printed from the original plates are 30 heretofore unpublished engravings of plant specimens from Cook's first voyage. The plants had been named and described by the voyage naturalists Joseph Banks and Daniel Solander at the time, but because the plates and notes were not published, the names proposed then are not now used. The descriptive notes had to be translated from Latin, corrected and annotated. To finance its production, the work was distributed by subscription only, in a limited edition of 100 copies, of which the Bishop Museum Library copy is No. 52.

5. Ellis, John (1710?-1776)

A description of the mangostan and the bread-fruit: the first, esteemed one of the most delicious; the other, the most useful of all the fruits in the East Indies. By John Ellis, Esq. To which are added, directions to voyagers, for bringing over these and other vegetable productions, which would be extremely beneficial to the inhabitants of our West India Islands. London: Printed for the author: and sold by Edward and Charles Dilly, 1775 (Fuller collection, Bishop Museum Library).

A description of the two trees, including Cook's observations on the breadfruit. Illustrations and accompanying descriptions of cases used to transport live plants from the South Seas are also included.

6. Manuka or Tea Tree ("tea plant of New Zealand") from Dusky Bay, New Zealand (*Leptospermum scoparium*) (Myrtaceae) by William Hodges (1744-1797) (Fig. 3).

Copper plate engraving after Hodges by unknown engraver. 22 × 18 cm (plate mark); 29.5 × 22 cm sheet.

Published in the official edition of Cook's second voyage, v. 1, plate 22, Feb. 1, 1777 (Bishop Museum Library, purchase 1976).

Cook described the use of this plant for flavoring beer and as a tea substitute. He was probably led to experiment with the plant, because of its aromatic qualities, in his efforts to combat scurvy and beri-beri through the use of native plants. Cook concludes the account with this passage: "It is the business of Voyagers to pass over nothing that may be usefull to posterity and it cannot be denied that this would if ever this Country were settled by a Sevelized people or frequented by shipping" (Beaglehole, 1961, p.137).

7. "The Fan Palm in the Island of Cracatoa" by John Webber, R.A. (1751-1793) (Fig. 4).

Soft-ground etching, with sepia and grey wash added. 43 × 31.5 cm (plate mark).
Watermark: "J. Whatman" [n.d.], lower L. verso.
"J. Webber fecit. 1788."
"London. Pub. Aug[t] 1, 1788 by J. Webber N.° 312 Oxford Street. Vide Cooks last Voyage Vol. 3 Chap. 10"
A later version was published as plate 16 in *Views of the South Seas,* London: Boydell, 1808 [1820-21?]. The exhibited etching was presumably engraved and hand colored by Webber himself (Fuller collection, Bishop Museum Library).

Zoology[4]

8. Martyn, Thomas, 1760-1816

The universal conchologist, exhibiting the figure of every known shell accurately drawn and painted after nature with a new systematic arrangement. [Added title page: Figures of non descript shells collected in the different voyages to the South Seas since the year 1764]. 2d ed. London: Thomas Martyn, 1789 (Bishop Museum Library, purchase 1919).

Among the 18th century works published on shells, Martyn's appears to be the most comprehensive and useful. Although Martyn, noted publisher and artist of natural history, had originally planned an even more exhaustive work, he and his artists beautifully illustrated with great correctness in drawing and coloring, all of the then known, and some hitherto undescribed, species of shells. Martyn did not distinguish between shells collected by Cook's voyages and those of the earlier voyages of John Byron (1764-1766) and Samuel Wallis (1766-1769). However, his explanatory table giving place found, as well as English and Latin names, and in what shell collection they were observed, can offer clues of localities known to have been visited first by Cook. Although no descriptions of the shells are included, and Martyn did not publish his developing scheme of organization for them, his nomenclature was, in time, accepted by scientific authorities, and his work was the basis for a great deal of later work on the subject of shells. His detailed introduction has the added merit of describing shell collections he had seen. Martyn's own shell collection included sizable purchases from Cook's second and third voyages. Two of the superb illustrations depict *Bulla virgata* from the Sandwich Islands and *Heliotropium* from New Zealand (Figs. 5 and 6).

9. Ellis, John (1710?-1776), and Solander, Daniel Carl (1736-1782)

The natural history of many curious and uncommon zoophytes, collected from various parts of the globe by the late John Ellis, Esq., F.R.S. . . . systematically arranged and described by the late Daniel Solander, M.D.F.R.S.&c. London: B. White and Son and P. Elmsly, 1786 (Fuller collection, Bishop Museum Library).

Descriptions and illustrations of various specimens of corals, including some that were brought to England by Cook on his first or second voyage. The work is also of great importance because it is one of the factors which forced Linnaeus and Pallas to admit that corals belonged to the animal kingdom, rather than the vegetable.

10. Whitehead, Peter James Palmer

Forty drawings of fishes made by the artists who accompanied Captain James Cook on his three voyages to the Pacific, 1768-71, 1772-75, 1776-80: some being used by authors in the description of new species. Text by Peter James Palmer Whitehead. London: British Museum (Natural History), 1968 (Bishop Museum Library, purchase 1969).

Before Cook's voyages, naturalists had scarcely touched the Pacific area. Here, beautifully reproduced with full, explanatory introduction, is a unique example of the detailed work that Cook's artists and naturalists did to record Pacific natural history specimens of the 18th century. Some biological specimens from Cook's voyages that have survived are preserved in the British Museum (Natural History). For some specimens, the drawings and paintings produced by Cook's artists are the only known evidence of Pacific species of the time. The 270 known paintings and drawings of fish from Cook's voyages were used by scientists of the 19th century as the basis for description of some 50 new species. Most of the extensive zoological and botanical Cook voyage illustrations are still unpublished, and hence known only to the relatively few who have been to London to study them. While a certain amount has been published on birds and plants from the voyages, less attention has been given to fish. This book, published during the bicentenary of Cook's first voyage, reproduces 40 fish illustrations, all but three published for the first time. The artists represented include Alexander Buchan, Herman Diedrich Spöring, Sydney Parkinson, and George Forster.

11. Latham, John (1740-1837)

A general synopsis of birds. London: printed for B. White, printed for Leigh and Sotheby, 1781-1785. Also Supplement of the General synopsis of birds. London: printed for Leigh & Sotheby, 1787-1801. Index, 1790 (Bishop Museum Library, purchase 1972).

[4]The shells and birds exhibited were not collected on Cook's voyages.

Many of the new species of birds herein described were based on specimens and paintings of specimens collected on Cook's voyages, as seen by Latham in the collections of the Leverian Museum, of Joseph Banks, and in the British Museum, as well as from Latham's own collection. Latham attempted in this general synopsis to describe the then known birds of the world. He noted between 500 and 600 new forms, many of which came from Australia, and he was one of the first to describe birds from the Sandwich Islands. J. F. Gmelin in the thirteenth edition of *Systema Naturae* (1788-1793) supplied Latin names and descriptions to Latham's English names, rendering the descriptions scientifically valid. Because there are few extant bird specimens from Cook's voyages, Latham's work is of prime importance as a record of Pacific birds of the time. Latham himself etched all of the copper plates for the engravings in his original work. One of the famous illustrations depicts the Hawaiian *'apapane* and *'akialoa* (Fig. 7).

12. *Mamo.* Pen and watercolor drawing by F. W. Frohawk, illustrator of *Aves Hawaiienses* 28 × 33 cm. (Fig. 8).

"F.W. Frohawk, 1889."
Watermark upper L. verso: "1887 B" (Bishop Museum Library).

This is an original sketch of *Drepanis pacifica,* the *mamo* which was later published in *Aves Hawaiienses* (Wilson and Evans, 1890-1899). The *mamo* was first described by Latham from two specimens observed in the Leverian Museum; "[It] inhabits the Sandwich Islands in general and is one of the birds whose plumage the natives make use of in constructing their feathered garments . . . the most beautiful coverings of these islanders" (Latham, 1782, Vol. 1, Pt. 2, p. 704).

13. "Sea Horses" by John Webber (Fig. 9).

Engraving 27 × 37.5 cm (plate mark).
"Drawn by Webber. Engraved by E. Scott. The Figures by J. Heath."
Published as Plate 52 in the *Atlas* to Cook's third voyage. The figure holding the gaff has been identified as Lt. Bligh (Bishop Museum Library, gift of Mrs. Robert McKeague).

General

14. Forster, Johann Reinhold (1729-1798)

Observations made during a voyage round the world, on physical geography, natural history, and ethic philosophy. Especially on 1. the earth and its strata, 2. water and the ocean, 3. the atmosphere, 4. the changes of the globe, 5. organic bodies, and 6. the human species. By John Reinold Forster. London: G. Robinson, 1778 (Carter collection,[5] Bishop Museum Library).

An account by one of the naturalists on the second voyage, the majority of which concerns the South Sea Islands. Extensive observations are made concerning the customs of the indigenous peoples.

HUMAN HISTORY

Eighteenth century Europe was greatly influenced, especially in the arts, by peoples of other lands. The earlier influence of China had led to the development of chinoiserie wallpapers, furniture, and other visual arts. With the opening of the Pacific, the publication of Cook's journals, and the distribution of the curiosities collected on the voyages, new influences entered libraries and drawing rooms. A Pacific wallpaper, designed by Charvet and printed by Dufour,[6] vied with chinoiserie, and in "cabinets of curiosities" one or more pieces from Otaheite, New Zealand, or the Sandwich Isles were almost mandatory. If these "artificial curiosities" (as ethnographic specimens were called in the 18th century)[7] had been brought from the South Seas on the voyages of the British folk hero, Captain Cook, so much the better. In the following generations many of these objects lost their association with Cook's voyages, such as those exhibited here from Warwick Castle. Minute historical research is necessary to reestablish links to original collectors of such important pieces. Useful for such research are the journals of the voyages, guides or companions to early museums and private collections, drawings made on the voyages and shortly after, sales catalogues of early collections, and contemporary accounts in letters and newspapers.[8]

EXHIBITED

The following objects are probably from Cook's voyages, but are not traceable by documented links.

15. Hawaiian shark tooth implement, John Hewett collection, formerly in Warwick Castle.[9] Length 75.5 cm. Figure 10.

---

[5]The George R. Carter Library of Hawaiiana collected by former Governor Carter (1903-07) was placed under the Museum's trusteeship in 1946 as a loan. In 1959, Mr. George Robert Carter II generously presented this fine rare book collection to the Museum library as a memorial to his father. Governor Carter, in his capacity as Bishop Museum trustee, was responsible for obtaining many treasures for the Museum and Museum library, including the three original William Ellis watercolors exhibited.

[6]One of these Dufour wallpapers, "Les Sauvages de la Mer Pacifique," based on the Pacific voyages of Cook and other 18th century navigators, is part of the permanent collection of the Honolulu Academy of Arts.

[7]This terminology continued for some time. The term "artefact" was first used in 1834 by Coleridge, deriving, of course, from the same root as "artificial," meaning "man-made." "Curiosities" later developed into "curios." These terms were widely used throughout the 19th century. The Hawaiian Queen Liliuokalani referred to the works of her ancestors as "curiosities" in her autobiography (1898, p. 212).

[8]See below, Ethnography and the Voyages of Captain Cook, for a detailed account of such research.

[9]Objects from Warwick Castle probably descended from Charles Greville, friend of Banks and others who sailed on Cook's voyages. Some of the objects from this collection were certainly from Cook's voyages, but no documents can be found that can identify which objects came from Cook's voyages and which ones did not.

16. New Zealand whalebone *patu paraoa,* William Greene collection, formerly in Warwick Castle. Length 49 cm. Figure 11.

17. Bronze *patu* bearing Joseph Banks's coat of arms. Made in the form of a New Zealand basalt *patu onewa.* Joseph Banks had several such specimens cast by Mathew Boulton of Soho, Birmingham, to take with him on his second voyage with Cook to give to Pacific islanders. However, since Banks did not go on the second voyage, the *patu* remained in England. John Hewett collection. Length 37 cm. Figure 12.

18. Turtle shell bracelet of 18th century style. The bracelet may have been in the Leverian Museum, but documented links cannot be traced. Bishop Museum (1977.206.8), formerly in the Hooper collection (348). Purchased on behalf of Bishop Museum by Mrs. Margaret Ross in memory of her daughter, Alexandra, and her husband, Finlay Ross. Length 16.5 cm.

19. Hawaiian feather *lei* of 18th century style. The *lei* is traditionally thought to have been collected on Cook's voyage, but documentary evidence is lacking. Bishop Museum (1977.206.6), formerly in the Hooper collection (332). Purchased on behalf of Bishop Museum by the Bishop Museum Association. Length 40.6 cm.

Figure 6. — *Heliotropium,* New Zealand (8).

Figure 5. — *Bulla virgata,* Hawaii (8).

20. Leglet of shells, National Museum of Ireland, Dublin (1897.282). Height 21 cm, width 33 cm. Figure 13.

Of the style collected on Cook's voyages and possibly part of the collection given by Captain King to Trinity College, Dublin. However, it is not part of the number series to which other objects in the Cook voyage collections in Dublin belong.

21. Book of bark cloth pieces of 18th century style. Although the pieces were probably collected on Cook's voyages,[10] documentary evidence is lacking. Bishop Museum collection.

22. Tahitian gorget. John Hewett collection. Figure 14. Probably the most superb example extant of a breast gorget. Encased in a fitted 18th century Sheraton frame with the original glass. Having passed through several hands, its history has been lost. Exhibited at the entry to Polynesian Hall.

[10]Some of these have been published by Brigham, 1911, and Kaeppler, 1975.

Figure 7. — *'Apapane* and *'akialoa,* Hawaii (11).

PUBLISHED ACCOUNTS OF COOK'S VOYAGES[11]

First Voyage

23. Hawkesworth, John (1715?-1773), compiler

An / Account / of the / Voyages / undertaken by the / Order of His Present Majesty / for making / Discoveries in the Southern Hemisphere, / And successively performed by / Commodore Byron, / Captain Wallis, / Captain Carteret, / And Captain Cook, / In the Dolphin, / the Swallow, and the Endeavour: / drawn up / From the Journals which were kept by the several Commanders, / And from the Papers of Joseph Banks, Esq; / By John Hawkesworth, LL.D. / In Three Volumes. / Illustrated with Cuts, and a great Variety of Charts and Maps relative to / Countries now first discovered, or hitherto but imperfectly known. / Vol. I [II, III] / (double rule) London: / Printed for W. Strahan; and T. Cadell in the Strand. / MDCCLXXIII.

First edition. Three volumes, quarto, full leather binding with gold tooled spine, red and black label leathers, illustrated with charts and plates (Carter collection, Bishop Museum Library).

The second and third volumes of this set comprise the official account of Cook's first voyage. John Hawkesworth, an eminent London author, was commissioned by the Admiralty to edit this set of voyages, which are written in the first person. Hawkesworth was chosen by Lord Sandwich for the task, and received £6000 from the government for his services. It was felt that, since these voyages were officially organized and sent out by the government for the purpose of adding to England's prestige as a maritime power, they should not be written in the style of men of the sea. The edition was widely criticized, but was reprinted again and again in one form or another, and it became, according to Beaglehole, "a sort of classic unacknowledged by the historians of literature, the indispensable introduction to 'Cook's Voyages,' whether laid out in full, or pillaged and abridged; a classic not of English prose but of English adventure; and for a hundred and twenty years, so far as the first voyage was concerned, Hawkesworth was Cook" (Beaglehole, 1955, p. ccliii).

24. Hawkesworth, John, compiler

An / Account / of the / Voyages / undertaken by the / Order of His Present Majesty / for making / Discoveries in the Southern Hemisphere, / And successively performed by / Commodore Byron, / Captain Wallis, / Captain Carteret, / And Captain Cook, / In the Dolphin, the Swallow, and the Endeavour; / drawn up / From the Journals which were kept by the several Commanders, / And from the Papers of Joseph Banks, Esq; / By John Hawkesworth, LL.D. / In Three Volumes. / Illustrated with Cuts, and a great Variety of Charts and Maps relative to / Countries now first discovered, or hitherto but imperfectly known. / Vol. I [II, III] / (double rule) London: / Printed for W. Strahan; and T. Cadell in the Strand. / MDCCLXXIII.

Figure 8. — *Mamo,* Hawaii (12).

[11]The exhibited volumes of the published accounts of the three voyages are listed in voyage order. Full bibliographic descriptions are supplied in order to distinguish between variant editions and sets. Surreptitious and anonymous accounts follow the official editions for each voyage.

Figure 9. — Sea horses by John Webber (13).

Second edition. Three volumes, quarto, full polished golden calf leather binding with elaborate gold tooling on boards and edges of lining paper and interior board edges, gold tooled spine with red and black label leathers, gilded edges, illustrated with charts and plates (Fuller collection, Bishop Museum Library).

The second edition of this set differs from the first edition only in the inclusion of a bantering preface dated August 2nd, 1773, in which Hawkesworth replies to the charges made against him by Alexander Dalrymple,[12] and in some slight alterations in the errata sheets. "Dalrymple was outraged by Cook's scepticism in the matter of the Great Southern Continent, and his disappointment in being passed over for the voyage joined with his sense of renewed injury to make an attack from him inevitable and terrible in form . . . It was difficult to attack Cook in person, but by direct implication Dalrymple does manage to accuse him of incompetence, neglect of duty, and worse" (Beaglehole, 1955, pp. ccli-cclii). The second edition is considered the best of the various editions of the first voyage. This particular set is unique in that it contains the plates from the French edition of Cook's first voyage as well as those in the standard Hawkesworth edition.

[12]Pamphlet exhibited in Geography and Navigation case (64).

25. Anonymous

A / Journal / of a Voyage round the World, / in His Majesty's Ship Endeavour, / in the years 1768, 1769, 1770, and 1771; / Undertaken in Pursuit of Natural Knowledge, at the / Desire of the Royal Society: / containing / All the various Occurrences of the Voyage, / with / Descriptions of several new discovered Countries in the Southern / Hemisphere; and Accounts of their Soil and Productions; and of / many Singularities in the Structure, Apparel, Customs, Manners, Policy, Manufactures, &c. of their Inhabitants. / To which is added, / A Concise Vocabulary of the Language of Otahitee. / Ornari res ipsa negat, contenta doceri. Hor. / (double rule) London, / Printed for T. Becket and P.A. De Hondt, in the Strand. / MDCCLXXI.

First edition. One volume, quarto, quarter leather morocco binding with green German marbled paper boards, gold tooling at edge of board leather and corners, stamped spine, sprinkled edges (Fuller collection, Bishop Museum Library).

Published anonymously, nearly two years before Hawkesworth's account. The first edition bears a dedication to the Lords of the Admiralty and to Banks and Solander. The dedication was withdrawn on Banks's and Solander's request, and does not appear in later editions. Authorship has been variously attributed to James Magra or Matra, a midshipman on the *Endeavour,* to Banks and Solander, to Richard Orton, to William Perry, and to the publisher, Thomas Becket. Beaglehole favors James Magra, the American mid-

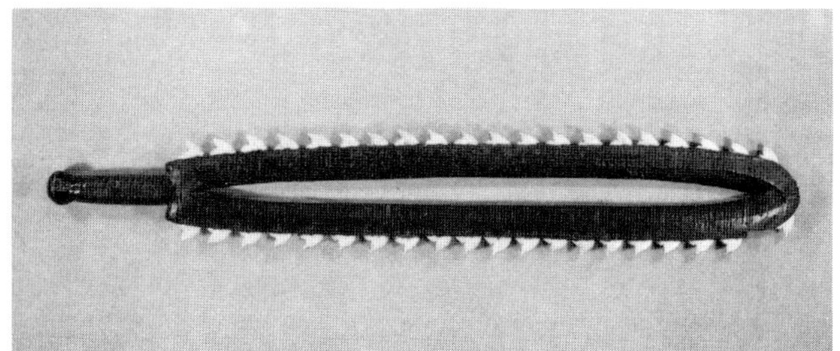

Figure 10. — Shark tooth implement, Hawaii. Hewett collection (15).

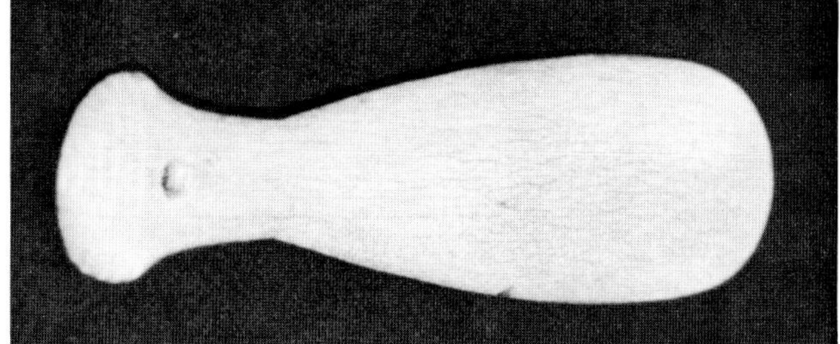

Figure 11. — Whalebone hand club, New Zealand. Greene collection (16).

shipman who, twelve years later, with his name changed to Matra, brought forward after consultation with Banks a noteworthy proposal for the foundation of a colony in New South Wales. This is chronologically the first published account of the first voyage.

26. Parkinson, Sydney (1745?-1771)

A / Journal / of a / Voyage / to the / South Seas, / in His / Majesty's Ship, the Endeavour. / Faithfully transcribed from the Papers of the late Sydney Parkinson, / Draughtsman to Joseph Banks, Esq. on his late Expedition, / with Dr. Solander, round the World. / Embellished with / Views and Designs, / delineated by the Author, and / engraved by capital Artists. / London: / Printed for Stanfield Parkinson, the Editor: / And sold by Messrs. Richardson and Urquhart, at the Royal-Exchange; Evans, in / Pater-noster Row; Hooper, on Ludgate-Hill; Murray, in Fleet-street; / Leacroft, at Charing-Cross; and Riley, in Curzon-street, May-Fair. / M.DCC.LXXIII.

First edition. One volume, quarto, full leather smooth calf binding with single line gold tooling on spine cords, red spine label, illustrated with fronts. and 27 plates (Fuller collection, Bishop Museum Library).

Parkinson was employed by Banks as botanical draftsman at a salary of £80 a year, and as such was exempted from the instruction that the officers and petty officers should deliver up the log books and journals they might have kept, and from the injunction on the whole crew not to divulge where they had been until they were given permission. Parkinson died at sea on January 26, 1771, from malaria and dysentery contracted at Batavia. His brother, Stanfield, to anticipate Hawkesworth's account, hurriedly published this journal. After a few copies had appeared, the further issue was stopped by an injunction in Chancery, on the grounds of infringement of Hawkesworth's rights and of material belonging to Banks. Dr. Fothergill, a friend of the Parkinsons, afterwards bought the remainder, which appeared in 1784 as the reissue, with an appendix added.

Second Voyage

27. Cook, James, 1728-1779

A / Voyage / towards the / South Pole, / and / Round The World. / Performed in / His Majesty's Ships the Resolution and Adventure, / In the Years 1772, 1773, 1774, and 1775. / Written / By James Cook, Commander of the Resolution. / In which is included, / Captain Furneaux's Narrative of his / Proceedings in the Adventure during the Separation of the Ships. / In Two Volumes. / Illustrated with Maps and Charts, and a Variety of Portraits of / Persons and Views of Places, drawn during the Voyage by / Mr. Hodges, and engraved by the most eminent Masters. / Vol. I [II] / (double rule) London: / Printed for W. Strahan; and T. Cadell in the Strand. / MDCCLXXVII.

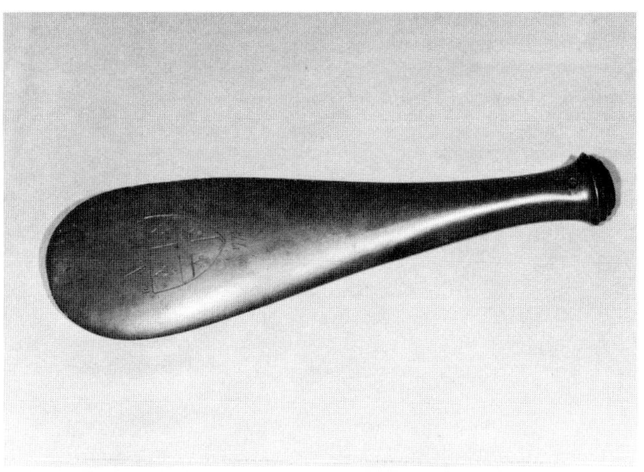

Figure 12. — Bronze *"patu,"* Hewett collection (17).

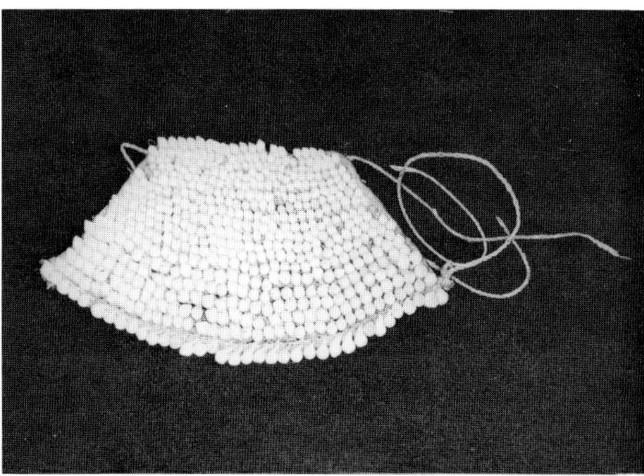

Figure 13. — Shell leglet, Hawaii, National Museum of Ireland, Dublin (20).

Figure 14. — Gorget, Tahiti. Hewett collection (22).

First edition. Two volumes, quarto, full polished golden calf leather binding with elaborate gold tooling on boards and edges of lining paper and interior board edges, gold tooled spine with red and black label leathers, gilded edges, illustrated with charts and plates (Fuller collection, Bishop Museum Library).

This, the official account of the second voyage, was written by Cook himself, but it was not ready for publication before he sailed on his third voyage, and thus it was seen through the press by Dr. John Douglas, Canon of Windsor and afterwards Bishop of Carlisle. Beaglehole has shown that Douglas edited and reworked portions of the journal as well. In a letter dated June 22, 1776, to his friend, Commodore William Wilson, Cook writes:

> The Journal of my late Voyage will be published in the course of next winter, and I am to have the sole advantage of the sale. It will want those flourishes which Dr. Hawkesworth gave the other, but it will be illustrated and ornamented with about sixty copper plates, which, I am of opinion, will exceed every thing that has been done in a work of this kind. . . . As to the Journal, it must speak for itself. I can only say that it is my own narrative, and as it was written during the voyage (Beaglehole, 1961, p. cxliii).

This particular set is unique in that it contains the plates from the French edition of Cook's second voyage as well as those from the official edition.

28. *Atlas* to Cook's second voyage.

[No title page; binder's title: Plates / To / Cook's / Voyages. London: Strahan & Cadell, 1777]. Frontispiece and 63 plates.

Folio, quarter calf binding with Stormont marbled paper boards, gold tooling at board edges and corners and on spine, stamped spine (Fuller collection, Bishop Museum Library).

There was no atlas issued to accompany the account of Cook's second voyage, because all of the plates were included in the quarto volumes. There was, however, a small issue of the plates. These, when bound, comprise the "atlas" to the second voyage. Such bound sets are rare and are not mentioned in standard bibliographies.

29. [Marra, John]

Journal / of the / Resolution's Voyage, / in 1772, 1773, 1774, and 1775. / on / Discovery to the Southern Hemisphere, / by which / The Non-Existence of an undiscovered Continent, / between the Equator and the 50th Degree of Southern Latitude, is demonstra-

A

CATALOGUE

Of a ſmall but choice Collection of

RARITIES,

From the new-diſcovered Places in the SOUTH SEAS;

CONSISTING OF THE

Cloth, Garments, Warlike Inſtruments, and other ſingular Inventions of the Natives (particularly from *Owhyhee*, the Iſland where Captain *Cook* was killed;) ſome Hammer Oyſters, and other curious Shells;

The Property of an OFFICER belonging to His Majeſty's Ship *The Diſcovery*, lately arrived:

Which will be Sold by AUCTION,

By Mr. HUTCHINS,

At his ROOMS in KING-STREET and HART-STREET, COVENT-GARDEN,

On THURSDAY, *June* 14, 1781, and the following Day.

To be viewed on *Wedneſday*, and till the Sale, which will begin each Day at Twelve o'Clock.

CATALOGUES may be had of Mr. HUTCHINS, as above: Who fixes a Valuation on Noblemen's and Gentlemen's Effects of all Sorts, in Town or Country, and the Value, if required, immediately given for the ſame.

Figure 15. — Sale catalogue title page (42).

tively proved, / Also a / Journal / of the / Adventure's Voyage, / In the Years 1772, 1773, and 1774. / With an Account of the Separation of the two Ships, / and the most remarkable Incidents that befel each. / interspersed with / Historical and Geographical Descriptions of / the Islands and Countries discovered in the Course / of their respective Voyages. / Illustrated With a Chart, / In which the Tracks of both Vessels are accurately / laid down, / And Other Cuts. / London: Printed for F. Newbery, at the Corner of / St. Paul's Church-Yard. / 1775.

First edition. One volume, octavo, quarter leather binding with antique spot marbled paper boards, blind tooling and gold tooling at edge of board leather and corners, gold tooled spine with black label leather, illustrated with a folded chart and five plates (Bishop Museum Library).[13]

This rare account of Cook's second voyage was published anonymously and surreptitiously eighteen months before the official narrative of the voyage. It records many incidents omitted by Cook and gives the reasons which caused Sir Joseph Banks and his twelve assistants to withdraw from the expedition at the last moment. Correspondence between Cook and the Admiralty shows that the author was John Marra, one of the gunner's mates on the *Resolution.* He was an Irishman whom Cook had picked up at Batavia during the first voyage. Marra made an unsuccessful attempt to desert at Tahiti on May 14, 1774. The journal is based on his private notes of the voyage, but was substantially enlarged and rewritten by some literary person in the employ of the publisher Newbery, probably David Henry, who ran the *Gentleman's Magazine.*

30. Forster, Johann Georg Adam, 1754-1794

A voyage round the world, in His Britannic Majesty's sloop, Resolution, commanded by Capt. James Cook, during the years 1772, 3, 4, and 5. By George Forster. London: B. White, J. Robson, P. Elmsly, G. Robinson, 1777. Two volumes (Fuller collection, Bishop Museum Library).

An account of Cook's second voyage based on the journal of Johann Reinhold Forster who, together with his son Johann Georg (George), served as the naturalists aboard the *Resolution.* It was originally intended that the elder Forster should write the official record of the voyage, but the offer was withdrawn after a dispute with the Admiralty, and the Forsters hurried to publish this, their own account, which appeared only some six months before the official account written by Cook himself.

31. Anonymous

A / Voyage / Round the World, / in the years / MDCCLXXII, LXXIII, LXXIV, LXXV. / by / Captain James Cook, / Commander of His Majesty's Bark The Resolution. / Undertaken by Order of the King, and encouraged by a / Parliamentary Grant of Four Thousand Pounds. / Drawn up from Authentic Papers. / By an Officer on Board. / (rule) Magnum Maris Aequor Arandum. / (double rule) London, / Printed for W. Lane, Leadenhall Street: (rule) MDCCLXXXI.

Remainder issue of first edition. One volume, quarto, quarter leather morocco binding with green German marbled paper boards, gold tooling at edge of board leather and corners, stamped spine, sprinkled edges (personal copy of Charles Reed Bishop, Bishop Museum Library).

A surreptitious, anonymous account of Cook's second voyage from the journal of one of the officers published a year before the official accounts. In the prospectus of George Forster's account of Cook's second voyage, it is stated that the author of the account was a student of Cambridge University. The unknown author was severely castigated for sensationalism and falsehoods in the *Monthly Review* (Oct., 1776, pp. 270-273). The reviewer gave a list of fifteen alleged incidents described in the book, prefacing the list with the statement: "The passages contained in the following selection are, on the authority of Capt. Cook, all pronounced to be false." Despite the statement that this work was printed for W. Lane, it is a remainder issue of the first edition, the only new matter being the title page.

Third Voyage

32. Cook, James (1728-1779) and King, James (1750-1784)

A / Voyage / to the / Pacific Ocean. / Undertaken, / By The Command Of His Majesty, For Making / Discoveries in the Northern Hemisphere. / To Determine / The Position and Extent of the West Side of North America; / its Distance from Asia; and the Practicability of a / Northern Passage to Europe. / Performed Under The Direction Of / Captains Cook, Clerke, and Gore, / In his Majesty's Ships the Resolution and Discovery. / In the Years 1776, 1777, 1778, 1779, and 1780. / In Three Volumes. / Vol. I and II. written by Captain James Cook, F.R.S. / Vol. III. by Captain James King, LL.D. and F.R.S. / Illustrated with Maps and Charts, from the Original Drawings made by Lieut. Henry Roberts, / under the Direction of Captain Cook; and with a great Variety of Portraits, Views / of Places, and Historical Representations of Remarkable Incidents, drawn by Mr. / Webber during the Voyage, and engraved by the most eminent Artists. / Published by Order of the Lords Commissioners of the Admiralty. / Vol. I. [II, III] / (double rule) London: / Printed By W. And A. Strahan: / For G. Nicol, Bookseller To His Majesty, In The Strand; / And T. Cadell, In the Strand. / MDCCLXXXIV.

First edition. Three volumes, quarto, full polished golden calf leather binding with elaborate gold tooling on boards and edges of lining paper and interior board edges, gold tooled spine with red and black label leathers, gilded edges, illustrated with charts and plates (Fuller collection, Bishop Museum Library).

This, the official account of Cook's third voyage, did not appear until some four years after the return of the ships to England. Demand for it was so great, despite earlier surreptitious accounts, that the edition was sold out on the third day after publication. The set consists of three volumes and a folio atlas (herein listed separately), the whole of which was edited by John Douglas, editor of the second voyage account. James King, second lieutenant on the *Discovery,* who suc-

[13] Bishop Museum Library also has a rare untrimmed copy in temporary pasteboards.

ceeded to the command of the *Discovery* on Clerke's death, wrote the third volume of the set which covers the period from January 17, 1779, until the end of the voyage. There is a variant impression of the first edition, in which the only alterations are the omission of the words "printed by W. & A. Strahan" and the addition of a medallion to the title page. This particular set is unique in that it contains the French edition of those folio plates usually bound in the atlas.

33. *Atlas* to Cook's third voyage.

[No title page; binder's title: Cook's / Voyages / Plates. London: Nicol and Cadell, 1784]. 2 charts and 61 plates.

Folio, full polished golden calf leather binding with elaborate tooling on boards and edges of lining paper and interior board edges; gold tooled spine with red and black label leathers, gilded edges (Fuller collection, Bishop Museum Library).

The folio atlas accompanying the official account of Cook's third voyage was designed to accommodate the larger plates listed in Volume 1 of the text. In most atlases, 61 plates and 2 charts are found. In some copies a 62nd plate, by Bartolozzi after Webber, representing the death of Cook is found, and quarto size portraits of Cook and/or King may also be included. Very few volumes contain the complete set of plates for the third voyage, 87 in all. It is this atlas which includes the well-known engravings after Webber, which were the first illustrations published of Hawaii and the Hawaiian people.

34. [Rickman, John]

Journal / of / Captain Cook's / last / Voyage / to the / Pacific Ocean, / on / Discovery; / performed in the / Years 1776, 1777, 1778, 1779, / illustrated with / Cuts, and a Chart, shewing the Tracts of / the Ships employed in this Expedition. / (rule) Faithfully Narrated from the original MS. / (double rule) London: / Printed for E. Newbery, at the Corner of / St. Paul's Church Yard. / (rule) MDCCLXXXI.

First edition. One volume, octavo, quarter leather binding with brown French shell marbled paper boards, gold tooled spine with red and green label leathers, burnished gold chalk edges, illustrated with fronts., chart, and four additional plates (Bishop Museum Library).

A surreptitious and anonymous account of the third voyage which preceded the authorized account by more than two years. It has been attributed to William Ellis and to John Ledyard, the latter as late as 1930, but the question of authorship was finally established by Howay (1921, pp. 51-58). The text, especially as regards Cook's death, differs substantially from other accounts, and is highly romanticized. Beaglehole dismisses it with the phrase: ". . . on the whole it is a fanciful and ridiculously exaggerated production, done exclusively for the market" (1967, p. ccv).

COMPANIONS, SALE CATALOGUES AND DRAWINGS

Among the late 18th century museum collections of natural and artificial curiosities in England, two collections are of particular significance in relation to the voyages of Captain Cook: Ashton Lever's Museum, and William Bullock's Museum. The Leverian Museum, thriving well before its move to London in 1774, was the recipient in 1781 of a large collection resulting from Cook's third voyage. Unfortunately, museum expenses could not be met, government and public financial assistance were not forthcoming, and the government could not be persuaded to purchase the collection at a greatly reduced cost for the British Museum. In 1786 the Leverian collection was disposed of by lottery. The museum's new owner, Mr. James Parkinson, moved it to Albion Street. In 1806 the collection was dispersed, sold by King and Lochee in a sixty-five day sale, comprising over 7,800 lots. Two publications about the Leverian collection were crucial in documenting many objects in this exhibition.

35. A Companion to the Museum

(Late Sir Ashton Lever's) Removed to Albion Street, the Surry End of Black Friars Bridge. London: [s.n.], 1790 (Fuller collection, Bishop Museum Library).

36. Catalogue of the Leverian Museum, Part I.

Including the first eight days' sale. The remaining parts will be published with all possible speed. The Sale of The Entire Collection (By Messrs. King and Lochee), will commence On Monday, the 5th of May, 1806, at Twelve o'Clock, In the Building now occupied by The Museum. [London: G. Hayden, Printer, 1806]. (Carter collection, Bishop Museum Library).

The volume contains the catalogue of all sixty-five days of the sale of the Leverian Museum, as well as a list of the prices for which each lot was sold.

37. Great Britain. Parliament. 16th. 1st Session.

An act for enabling Sir Ashton Lever to dispose of his Museum, as now exhibited at Leicester House, by way of chance. Chapter 22. London: Charles Eyre and William Strahan, printers, 1784 (Fuller collection, Bishop Museum Library).

The Act includes a schedule which enumerates the contents of the Leverian Museum collection. As noted therein by Captain Fuller, the Sandwich Island Room of the Museum contained more than 1,860 objects, mostly from Captain Cook's voyages. Unfortunately many cannot be located and identified today.

Most important in identifying objects that were once in the Leverian Museum was a series of three sketchbooks by Miss Sarah Stone, an artist who for several years sketched objects in the Leverian collection. After the dispersal of the collection, many of the artifacts lost their association with Captain Cook and the Leverian Museum, but with the help of such aids as Miss Stone's detailed sketches, many have since been located.

38. Objects in the Leverian Museum as depicted by Sarah Stone.

Sketch Book / Volume the Second.
Sketch Book / Vol. the Third.[14]
[Cover titles; unpublished]
Vol. 2: [2 blank leaves], 85 pencil numbered leaves [numbered at later date?] Leaf 21 has part of sketch cut out. 33 × 21 cm.
Vol. 3 [3 blank leaves], 78 pencil numbered leaves. Leaf 12 has part of sketch cut out, and Capt. Fuller notes 10 pages cut out. 32.5 × 20.5 cm.
Fuller collection, Bishop Museum Library. Gift of Mrs. A. W. F. Fuller.

Both volumes are vellum bound. The sketches, some with several objects on a leaf, are on paper bearing watermarks of a variety of designs and sizes. One leaf is autographed by Sarah Stone, and others bear notes attributed to her.

In Volume 2, Fuller noted that he saw the two volumes in Quaritch's catalogue priced at £50 in 1932 and that he purchased them from this dealer March 15, 1940. From newspaper clippings inserted in the volumes, Fuller dated the sketch books "before, or shortly after, 25 March 1783, and, therefore must show 'Cook' specimens." Volume 3 includes sketches of Hawaiian, Eskimo, Tahitian, Chinese, and other artifacts, with penciled notes by Fuller.

Sarah Stone's sketch books, Volumes 2 and 3, have been published as *Art and Artifacts of the 18th Century: Objects in the Leverian Museum as Painted by Sarah Stone*, by Roland W. Force and Maryanne Force (Bishop Museum Press, 1968).

Sarah Stone and Chevalier de Barde each made zoological drawings of exhibits in the Leverian Museum. Miss Stone's "Drawings for Sir Ashton Lever's Museum, 1781-85," including some signed drawings and references to Lever's Museum, are now in the Library of the British Museum (Natural History). The drawings of Chevalier de Barde are in the Louvre; a photograph of his shell drawing is included in the section on natural history in this exhibition.

About 1790 Sarah Stone married and her later drawings are in her married name, Mrs. Smith. One of her latest drawings is exhibited here.

39. Hawaiian chief in feather helmet and cape.

Original watercolor. Dimensions 29 cm × 38 cm.
Signed "Sarah Smith."
Watermark 1830.
Severson collection, Hawaii.

William Bullock's museum, originally in Liverpool, was moved to London in 1809, where, from 1812 it was housed at the Egyptian Temple, Piccadilly. This private museum also had significant 18th century natural history and ethnological specimens from the Pacific. Bullock added to his collection of Cook voyage curiosities by purchasing from the 1806 auction of the Leverian Museum collection. In 1819, although his museum was operating successfully, Bullock auctioned off the collection and ventured into other areas. Two of the many "Companions" to his museum are exhibited here.

40. Bullock, William

A Companion to the Liverpool Museum, containing a brief description of two thousand of its Curiosities; the natural history arranged according to the System of Linnaeus. and now open for the inspection of the public, at The Shop of W. Bullock, Church-Street, nearly opposite the Post-Office. Intended principally for the Information of those who visit this Cabinet of Rarities, and to enable them to describe it afterwards to their Friends. 4th edition. Liverpool: Printed for the Proprietor by J. Nuttall, 1805 (Fuller collection, Bishop Museum Library).

41. Bullock, William

A Companion to the London Museum, and Pantherion, containing a brief description of upwards of fifteen thousand natural and foreign curiosities, antiquities, and productions of the fine arts; now open for public inspection in The Egyptian Temple, Piccadilly, London, by William Bullock. 16th edition. London: Printed for the Proprietor, by Whittingham and Rowland, 1814 (Fuller collection, Bishop Museum Library).

42. Anonymous

A catalogue of a small but choice collection of rarities, from the new-discovered places in the South Seas; consisting of the cloth, garments, warlike instruments, and other singular inventions of the natives (particularly from Owhyhee, the island where Captain Cook was killed); some hammer oysters, and other curious shells; the property of an officer belonging to His Majesty's ship *The Discovery*, lately arrived: which will be sold by auction, by Mr. Hutchins, at his rooms in King-Street and Hart-Street, Covent Garden, on Thursday, June 14, 1781, and the following day (Carter collection, Bishop Museum Library) (Fig. 15).

A unique catalogue of Pacific Islands, and particularly Sandwich Islands, artifacts belonging to an officer who participated in Cook's third voyage. It is the only known copy of the first ethnological catalogue of the South Seas ever printed. Sir Ashton Lever was one of the buyers at this auction, and there is no doubt that a number of the Cook voyage objects at the Leverian Museum came from this sale.

43. Missionary Museum

Catalogue of the Missionary Museum, Blomfield Street, Finsbury; including specimens in natural history, various idols of heathen nations, dresses, manufactures, domestic utensils, instruments of war, &c. &c. &c. London: Reed and Pardon, printers, [1890?] (Fuller collection, Bishop Museum Library).

The articles in this collection were given to the Museum chiefly by missionaries employed by the London Missionary Society. The mission to the South Sea Islands was the first undertaken by this Society, the first party of missionaries arriving in Tahiti in 1797. Images from the Orient, Africa, and the Pacific are among the chief items described in this rare catalogue

[14] The first volume of the sketch books is in the Australian Museum, Sydney.

Figure 16. — Leverian Museum. Artist unknown (45).

of the Missionary Museum collection, but a number of other artifacts from the Sandwich Islands and the Pacific are noted as well, some formerly in the Leverian Museum. When the Missionary Museum collection disbanded ca. 1912, the British Museum acquired many of the items. Captain Fuller purchased some of the remainders, as noted in the catalogue.

44. Anonymous

A catalogue of the genuine & entire museum of curious subjects of natural history, &c. including the whole stock in trade of Mr. Jacob Forster, late of Gerard Street, Soho, deceased; consisting of a numerous collection of well-chosen specimens of minerals; most of them remarkable either for figure or crystallization, particularly those of the gold and silver genera. Among the former will be found most of the different species of gems, polished stones; and ores afford all the known kinds and varieties of the metals, particularly those of the latest discovery. Great choice of marine, terrestrial, and other curious shells, of great diversity in respect to colour and form; elegant madrepores and other corals, echini, petrifactions, &c. presumed to be one of the largest and best assemblages of the kind ever offered to the public. Also, a choice assortment of artificial rarities, from the various countries in the Southern Hemisphere, collected during the voyages of the celebrated Capt. Cook, among which are many singular and uncommon articles: together with the magnificent glazed cases, tables, and mahogany cabinets. Which will be sold by auction, by Messrs. King & Lochee, at their Great Room, No. 38, King-street, Covent-Garden, on Monday, May 2, 1808, and nine following days, at twelve o'clock. May be viewed on Saturday, preceding the sale, and catalogues then had at the Room. [London]: J. Barker, Printer, [1808] (Carter collection, Bishop Museum Library).

This sales catalogue, typical of those of the 18th and 19th centuries, was not by any means restricted to items of natural history. The sale, which lasted 46 days, included many lots of ethnographic items, such as numerous samples of bark cloth from Polynesia and "artificial curiosities from the Southern Hemisphere." Lot 1921 included "a bow, from Owhyhee, four singular arrows, from different islands, a tabooing, or forbidding rod, several of which, when fixed in the ground, prescribe bounds for the populace, from Otaheite, and a fish-gig; from Nootka Sound."

45. Drawing of Leverian Museum exterior. Unknown artist (Fig. 16).

Pen and watercolor 23.5 × 7.5 cm.
Penciled in l. rt. "Leverian. Pennant."
Verso: Notes by Fuller give details about the Museum, date of purchase (7 Oct. 1947 £5), and that "another drawing of this set by the same hand and on similar paper bears the watermark '1794 J. Whatman.' They came from the notable coll[n] of Londiniana of Arthur Boney" (Fuller collection, Bishop Museum Library).

The paper used in this drawing is the type of watercolor paper used exclusively by artists of the late 18th century, and is therefore believed to have been done at that time.

46. "Mr. Bullock's Exhibition of Laplanders": by Thomas Rowlandson (1756-1827) (Fig. 17).

Engraving, Handcol. 30 × 45 cm (plate mk.).
London. Pub[d] Feb[y] 8th 1882 by R. Ackermann. 101, Strand.
Watermark 1821 (Fuller collection, Bishop Museum Library).

Thomas Rowlandson was a celebrated caricaturist of the day who included among his subjects Smollett, Goldsmith, Sterne, and Swift. Most of his drawings were done first in ink with a reed pen and then given a delicate wash of color. For reproduction he etched them himself on copper, the printer later coloring them by hand.

Figure 17. — Bullock Museum exhibition by Thomas Rowlandson (46).

47. "John Hawkesworth" by Joshua Reynolds (1723-1792) (Fig. 18).

Mezzotint. 38.5 × 28 cm (plate mk.).
"Sir Jos.[a] Reynolds pinx[t]
James Watson Fecit.
Publish[d] According to Act of Parliament Aug[t] 1st 1773" (Fuller collection, Bishop Museum Library).

It is indicative of the importance of the official account of Cook's first voyage that Joshua Reynolds, Britain's most famous portrait painter, chose to paint its editor.

Cook's voyages, mainly through the published accounts and the objects collected on them, were influential in generating interest in the study of man and his culture. Anthropological museums, which seek to record and interpret the cultural history of mankind, owe their origins in part to early explorers such as Cook who were impressed with the diversity and dignity of man. The elegance of many of the objects seen and collected, and the infinite patience required in the many stages of manufacture, was quite overwhelming to Europeans who immediately appreciated their beauty. "Artificial curiosities"—manmade objects of wonder—are now sold on the international art market along with Chinese porcelains, Japanese swords, and European paintings by famous artists. Apparently, in the 18th century the objects were considered by Pacific peoples to be appropriate gifts and trade articles (see Figs. 19 and 64).

Today they are considered priceless symbols of identity and heritage. The objects themselves have not changed, but changes in the values of men—both in Europe and the Pacific—have made these objects what they are today.

Figure 18. — John Hawkesworth by Joshua Reynolds (47).

GEOGRAPHY AND NAVIGATION

Perhaps most significant to Europeans of the time was the geographic and navigational knowledge generated by Cook's voyages. The intervening two centuries have witnessed changes in modes of transportation that have taken us from masted ships to Boeing 747's. Cook's ships *Endeavour, Resolution, Adventure,*

Figure 19. — View of Kauai after John Webber.

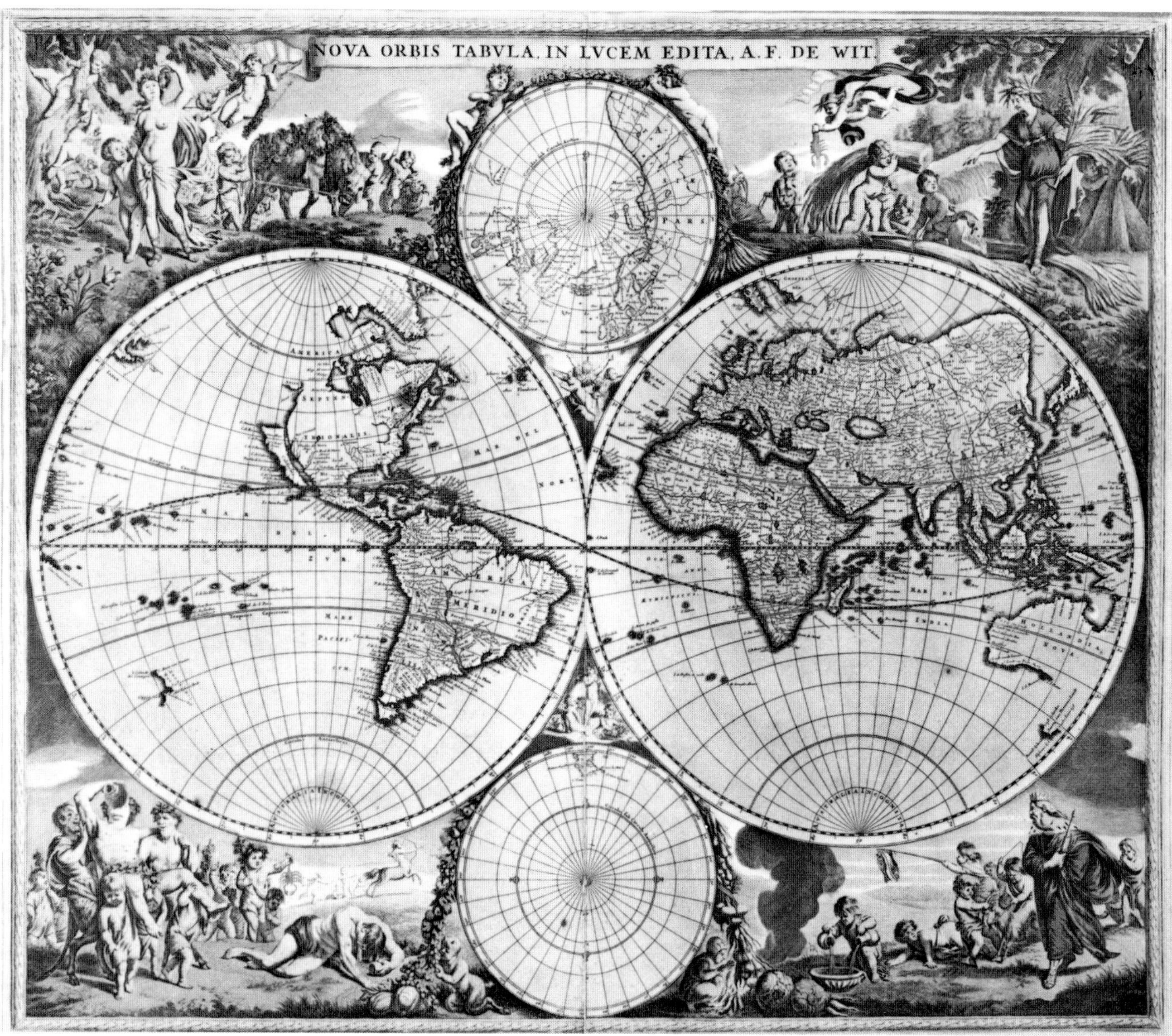

Figure 20. — Map of the Pacific in the 17th century (49).

and *Discovery* were manned by skillful navigators, astronomers, and cartographers, using the most sophisticated instruments of their day. Navigational instruments, telescopes, clocks, and charts, perhaps inaccurate by today's standards, only emphasize the skill of their users. The cartographic and written results of these men form the basis of much scientific knowledge still relevant today. The importance of Cook's voyages to geographical knowledge can be instantly recognized by comparing maps and charts of the Pacific before and after Cook.

EXHIBITED[15]

The Pacific Before Cook

Four maps illustrate the growth of geographical knowledge about the Pacific Ocean from the 16th to 18th centuries, before the three voyages of its great European explorer and navigator.

48. Sixteenth Century

Two hundred years before Cook, the Pacific had been crossed by the earliest circumnavigators, who entered through the Strait of Magellan and thus were at the mercy of winds and currents which deflected them northward. Few discoveries were made because they were obliged to sail a route which bypassed most islands, just as did the Spanish voyages between Mexico and the Philippines. This map depicts *Terra Australis,* also known as *Terra Incognita,* the great southern continent believed to exist by geographers for centuries, and persisting on maps and in the minds of men right up to Cook's day (Ortelius, 1589 copy, PSIC).

49. Seventeenth Century (Fig. 20).

About a century before Cook, the western Pacific was considerably better known. Dutch explorations had added much of Australia (named *Hollandia Nova* or "New Holland" here) to the map, and Tasman had discovered the west coast of New Zealand (*Zelandia Nova*), thought by many to be part of the great southern continent.

[15] Descriptions of maps and charts in this volume were made by Lee S. Motteler of the Pacific Scientific Information Center (PSIC), Bishop Museum.

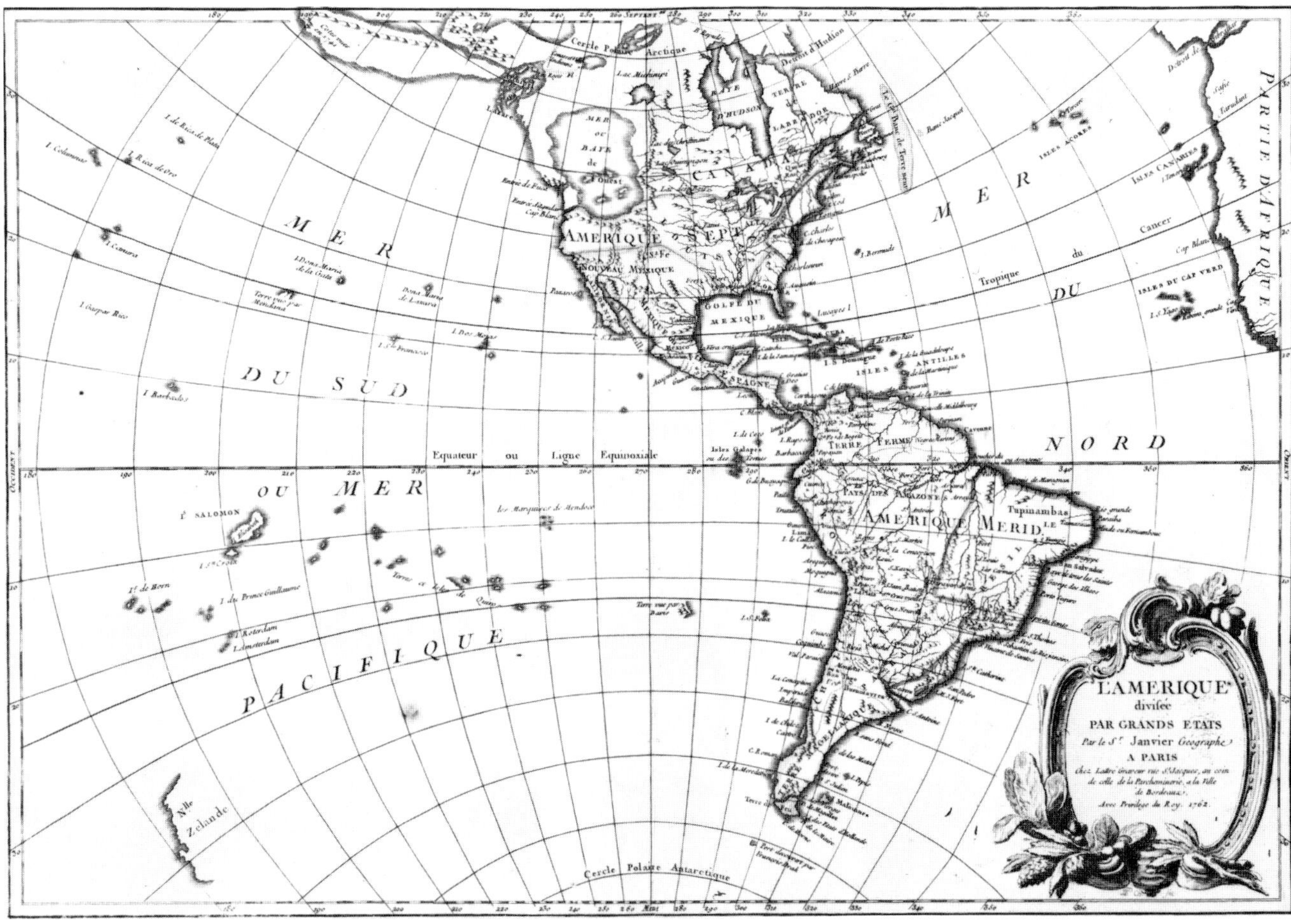

Figure 21. — Map of the Pacific in the 18th century (50).

Though not shown in its suspected dimensions as on earlier maps by De Wit, *Australia Incognita* is named near the South Pole. The central and eastern parts of the Pacific were still very little known at this period (De Wit, Terrarum Orbis Pl. 1, 1688 original, Bishop Museum Library).

50. Eighteenth Century (Fig. 21).

Knowledge of Pacific geography was advanced very little in the hundred years prior to Cook, as comparison of this map with that of the 17th century shows. This map was published in 1762, too early to record the discoveries of Byron, Wallis, and Carteret, Cook's immediate predecessors, though, except for Wallis' great find of Tahiti, their contributions were comparatively small (Janvier, 1762 original, PSIC).

51. Bougainville's Chart of 1771, Hand-annotated by Cook (Fig. 22).

The French circumnavigator Louis de Bougainville sailed in 1766 and did not return until 1769, when Cook had already embarked on his first voyage. Bougainville's account, *Voyage autour du Monde*, appeared soon after and Cook, visiting Dr. Burney in England in 1772, perused Bougainville's chart with interest. At Dr. Burney's request, Cook took a pencil and retraced the route of the *Endeavour* on the voyage just completed. Burney's priceless copy of Bougainville's chart is now in the British Library. Bougainville's track is the more northerly of the two in the Pacific (Bougainville Pl. 1, 1771 photographic copy).

The Pacific After Cook

Cook's voyages and discoveries, seen here in a series of maps and charts, managed in a brief ten years to obliterate the geographic delusions and oversights of more than two centuries.

52. Roberts's Chart of Cook's Voyages (Fig. 23).

This famous chart was published shortly after the end of Cook's third voyage, and represented for the first time the Pacific in all its major features. On his first voyage, Cook sought the elusive southern continent according to secret instructions, after observation of the transit of Venus at Tahiti. Not finding land, he turned west at 40° South Latitude, and eventually fell in with the uncharted eastern coast of New Zealand. Proving New Zealand to be two separate islands and not part of a large continent, he sailed on to chart the eastern coast of the "island continent," Australia, and passed through lately rediscovered Torres Strait separating Australia from New Guinea. If Cook had retired from the sea after this one epic voyage, his place in history would have been well assured. But with his second voyage he once and for all put to rest the ageless idea of "Terra Incognita" by circling the globe at extreme southern latitudes, three times passing south of the Antarctic Circle, where he encountered "Vast Mountains of Ice." On his third voyage, from which Cook never returned to receive his just accolades, his ships *Resolution* and *Discovery* crossed the Pacific from south to north for the first time and discovered Hawaii, the last great chain of islands to completely elude Western man (Nicol & Cadell, 1784 original, Donald Angus collection, Bishop Museum Library).

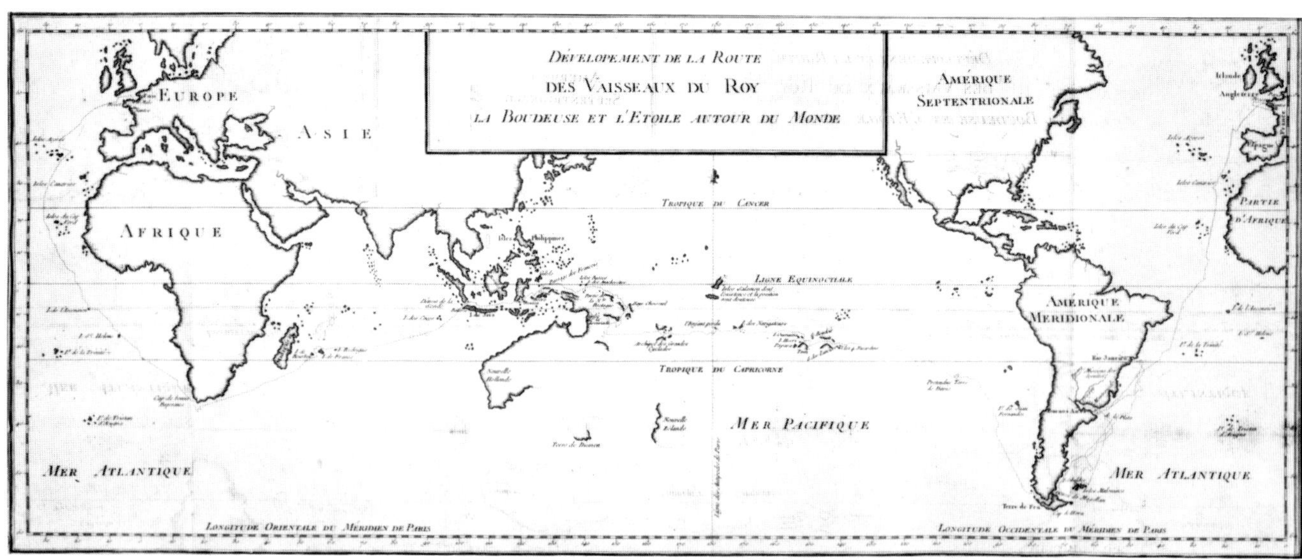

Figure 22. — Chart of the tracks of Bougainville and Cook. British Library (51).

Eight local maps exhibited with the Roberts chart are only a small part of Cook's contribution to Pacific geography.[16]

53. Easter Island 1774 (Fig. 314).

Cook visited Easter Island in March, 1774 on the Second Voyage, returning north from his deepest penetration of Antarctic seas. The island was long associated with and thought part of the great south land (Strahan & Cadell, 1777 original, Bishop Museum Library).

[16] They are illustrated in this volume in the sections below dealing with each specific area.

54. Tahiti (Otaheite) 1769 (Fig. 205).

Discovered to the Western World in 1767 by Wallis, Tahiti was chosen for an observation of the transit of Venus in 1769. The *Endeavour* anchored in Matavai Bay on the north coast, where the nearby promontory was named Point Venus (Hogg, ca. 1773 original, Fuller collection, Bishop Museum Library).

55. Dusky Bay, New Zealand 1773.

On his second voyage, Cook sailed into the Pacific from the west and charted Dusky Bay and little Pickersgill Harbour on the southwest coast of New Zealand. Resolution Island was named for his flagship on this and the third voyage (Strahan & Cadell, 1777 original, PSIC).

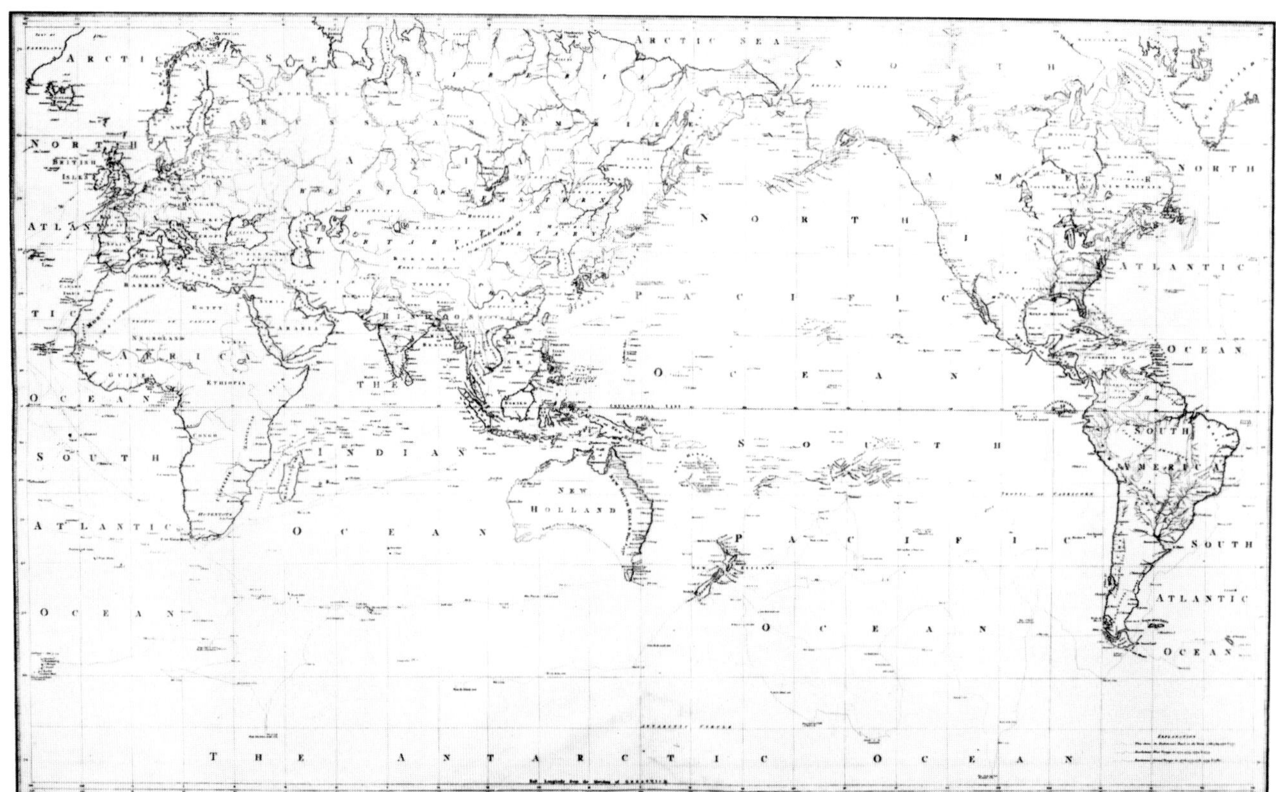

Figure 23. — Chart of Cook's Voyages (52).

56. New Caledonia & New Hebrides (Great Cyclades) 1774 (Fig. 521).

Although the New Hebrides (here named *Great Cyclades*) had been partially known since 1606, Cook on his second voyage explored their full extent. He went on to discover New Caledonia and Norfolk Island, as shown on this map (*Gentleman's Magazine,* n.d. original, Bishop Museum Library).

57. Tonga (Isles des Amis) 1777 (Fig. 412).

The Friendly Isles (present-day Tonga) were known since Tasman's voyage in 1643, whence the Dutch names. This hand-colored French chart is a composite from the second and third voyages, showing the tracks of both through Tonga. North is toward the left. Added is a plan of Tongataboo (Tongatapu) Harbor, with north toward bottom, and insets of the Cook Islands, Wateeoo (Atiu), Wenooa Ette (Takutea), and Mangeea (Mangaia) and Toobouai (Tubuai) in the Australs. These islands were all discovered on Cook's third voyage (Bonne, *Atlas encyclopédique* Pl. 129, 1787 original, Anon. private collection).

58. Christmas Island 1777 (Fig. 24).

After sighting it the previous day, Cook spent Christmas here and charted the western part of the island (North is toward the left). After observing a solar eclipse on December 30, he sailed north, unsuspecting, toward Hawaii (Nicol & Cadell Pl. 32, 1784 original, Bishop Museum Library).

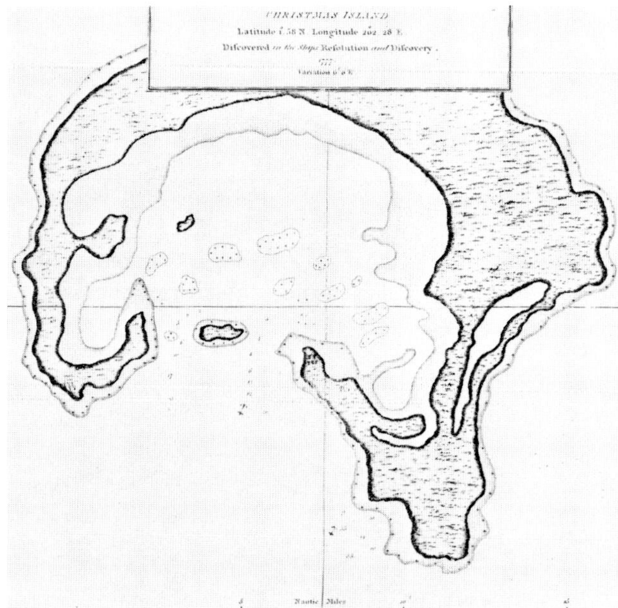

Figure 24. — Map of Christmas Island (58).

59. Hawaii (Sandwich Islands) 1778-79 by William Bligh (Fig. 53 and inside Catalogue covers).

This is the famous and much-copied engraving of the Hawaiian Islands, named the Sandwich Islands by Cook to honor the Earl of Sandwich. It shows his track in January, 1778, when he landed at Waimea (Wymoa), on Kauai (Atooi), and Niihau (Oneeheow), then sailed toward the coast of North America. After returning from Arctic seas, Cook landed at Kealakekua Bay (Karakakooa Bay, inset) on the island of Hawaii (Owhyhee) (Butler engr., ca. 1784 original, Donald Angus collection, Bishop Museum Library).

60. Nootka Sound 1778 (Fig. 547).

Sailing up the northwest coast of America, Cook surveyed Nootka Sound. He went on to explore the coast of Alaska and Siberia, entering Bering Strait and crossing the Arctic Circle before returning to Hawaii (Hogg, 1785? original, Donald Angus collection, Bishop Museum Library).

61. The World in 1830 (Fig. 25).

Cook's successors filled in various details of the Pacific map, mostly along the fringes (Australia's south coast and Bass Strait, separating it from Tasmania, and the Pacific coast of the Americas), but the configuration remained largely Cook's. This French map, published fifty years after Cook's last voyage, indicates his routes on all three voyages. The first voyage is shown by a dashed line, the second by a dash-dot line (not to be confused with Surville's route, indicated by a dotted line), and the third by a solid line (Hérisson, 1830 original, PSIC).

ALSO EXHIBITED

62. Telescope made by Dollond, London.

Said to have belonged to Captain Cook. Fulcher collection, Florida.

63. Terrestrial globe "exhibiting the different tracks of Captain Cook" (Fig. 26).

London, January 1, 1800 (Bishop Museum 1970.330.01, gift of Alfred Castle).

64. Dalrymple, Alexander (1737-1808)

A letter from Mr. Dalrymple to Dr. Hawkesworth, occasioned by some groundless and illiberal imputations in his account of the late voyages to the south. London: J. Nourse, T. Payne, Brotherton and Sewell, B. White, J. Robson, P. Elmsly, T. Davies, and S. Leacroft, 1773 (Fuller collection, Bishop Museum Library).

A rare pamphlet published in response to the official account of Cook's first voyage. Dalrymple, who had been passed over for Cook as commander of the voyage, attacked Cook obliquely through Hawkesworth, principally over the matter of Cook having sailed over a substantial portion of Dalrymple's supposed Great Southern Continent. Hawkesworth replied to this attack in a bantering fashion in his second edition of Cook's first voyage.

Included in the pamphlet is Dalrymple's rare "Chart of the South Pacifick Ocean, Pointing out the Discoveries made therein Previous to 1764. Publish'd according to Act of Parliament Octo[r] 1767." The chart well illustrates Dalrymple's obsession with the existence of a Great Southern Continent. Near "Davis's Land or Easter I." he has a line labeled "Signs of Land"; farther west, again, "Signs of Continent"; and east of Tonga, another "Signs of Land." In the pamphlet, Dalrymple states that he gave a copy of his "Discoveries" to Banks, "with the *Chart,* which I had printed several months before, though I did not publish it till after Bougainville's return." The Chart was published in Dalrymple's *An Historical Collection of the Several Voyages and Discoveries in the South Pacific Ocean,* being chiefly a literal translation from the Spanish writers (London: printed for the author, 1770).

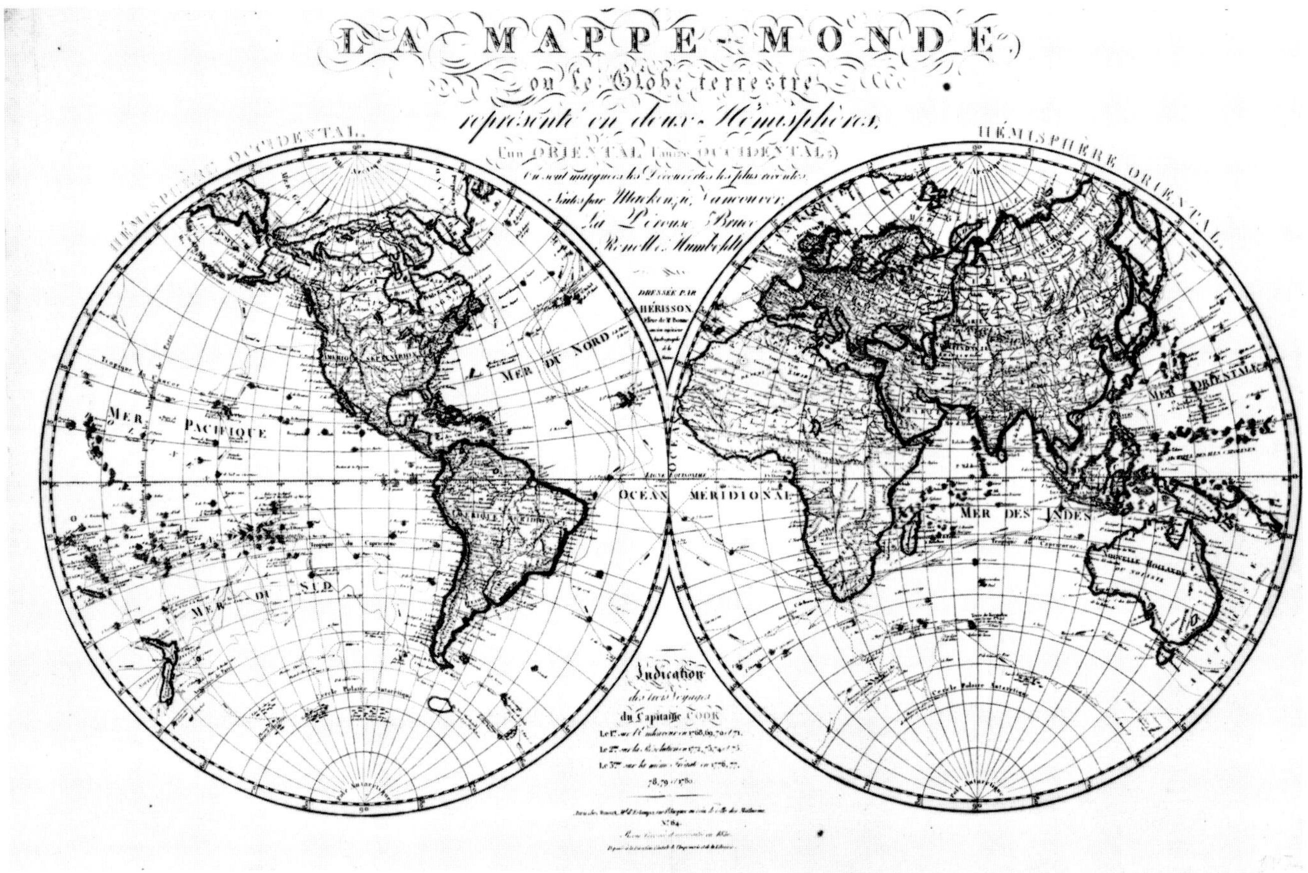

Figure 25. — Map of the world in 1830 (61).

65. Winthrop, John (1714-1779)

Observations of the transit of Venus over the sun, June 3, 1769. In a letter to the Reverend Nevil Maskelyne, F.R.S. Astronomer Royal, from John Winthrop, Esquire, F.R.S. Hollisian Professor of Mathematics at Cambridge in New England. [Extracted from the Proceedings of the Royal Society, 1770?] (Fuller collection, Bishop Museum Library).

The transit of Venus was observed by numerous astronomers at various points around the world at the same time as the observations by Cook and Charles Green in Tahiti. This is one of many reports received by The Royal Society which supposedly would enable a calculation of the distance of the earth from the sun.

66. Cook, James

Transit of ♀ Sat. : June 3rd : 1769 [Facsimile of Captn. Cook's observations of the transit of Venus. Engraved for the Edinburgh Cabinet Library, n.d.] (Fuller collection, Bishop Museum Library).

A facsimile of Cook's own observations at Tahiti on the occasion of the passage of Venus across the face of the sun.

67. Wales, William and Bayly, William

The original astronomical observations, made in the course of a voyage towards the South Pole, and round the world, in his Majesty's ships the *Resolution* and *Adventure*, in the years 1772, 1773, 1774, and 1775. London: Board of Longitude (W. and A. Strahan, printers), 1777 (Fuller collection, Bishop Museum Library).

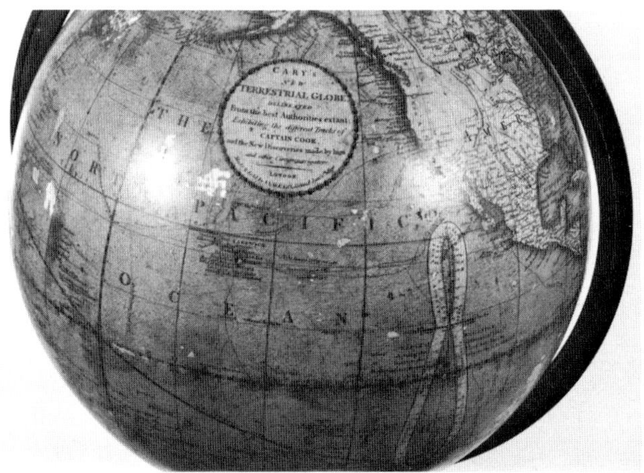

Figure 26. — Terrestrial globe of 1800 (63).

While one of the main aims of Cook's second voyage was to settle once and for all the question of the existence of a Great Southern Continent in temperate latitudes through searching the South Pacific, South Atlantic, and Indian Ocean, an important secondary aim was to try out four marine timekeepers for determining longitude at sea. The Board of Longitude, which undertook the scientific supervision of this voyage, appointed two professional astronomers, William Wales and William Bayly, to this purpose. Through a system of recording and comparing the rates of the clocks in different latitudes, assuming other constants, theoretically the longitude at sea could be determined. Through Cook's and a succession of later voyages, these chronometers were to prove equal to the task, and were the forerunners of the chronometers which finally replaced the rival lunar-distance method of finding longitude.

68. View of Morea (added in pencil below) by John Cleveley[17] (Fig. 27).

Variant state from aquatint set. Either (a) "proof state," as Fuller notes, or (b) faint impression after aquatint engraving with color added.
"Drawn on the spot by J^s Clevely. Painted by Jno Clevely, London" (no other letter-press).
51.5 × 66 cm (plate mk.).
Fuller collection, Bishop Museum Library.

This view of Moorea was painted by John Cleveley, one of the foremost marine artists of his day, from "on the spot" sketches by his brother James, who travelled on Cook's voyages as carpenter.

70. View of Oneehow, one of the Sandwich Islands, South Sea (Niihau), by William Ellis (illustrated on p. xii, this volume).

Original watercolor 18.5 × 38 cm.
"W. Ellis delin:^t pinz: 1778."
Penciled on verso "No. 48" [?].
Carter collection, Bishop Museum Library.

William Ellis' charming view of the approach to Niihau conveys some sense of the vastness of the Pacific, and the smallness of men's ships.

71. "Captain Cook Taking Possession of the Australian Continent on behalf of the British Crown, A.D. 1770" (Fig. 28).

"From a Painting by Gilfillan, in the possession, of the Royal Society of Victoria. Calvert [sculp.] [Botany Bay]."
Colored lithograph. 37.5 × 48 cm.
Reproduced in Supplement to Illus. Melbourne Post, Dec. 1865.
Bishop Museum Library, purchase 1977.

[17] Although apparently spelled "Clevely" in the 18th century, usually spelled "Cleveley" today.

72. "Admiral Bligh, J. Chapman, sc." Unknown artist (Fig. 29).

Stipple engraving. Oval port. 12 × 9.5 cm. No plate mk. (clipped and mounted).
"Published as the Act directs Oct. 1st, 1801."
Fuller collection, Bishop Museum Library.

Bligh, then a lieutenant and master of the *Resolution,* was chief cartographer of many of the maps and charts of Cook's third voyage, despite credit often being given to Lt. Henry Roberts.

THE DEATH OF COOK

Cook was initially thought by the Hawaiians to be an incarnation of Lono, god of peace and agriculture, because of the similarity of the ship's masts to the Hawaiian representation of Lono. An original pen, wash, and watercolor drawing by Webber of the "Boxing Match," in Bishop Museum, (Fig. 30) depicts the games celebrating the *makahiki* season. In the left background is the image of Lono—an upright pole with a crossbar hung with bark cloth strips. The depicted occasion took place on January 28, 1779, but in a few short weeks Cook, several of his men, and several Hawaiians were killed after an unfortunate misunderstanding.

73. [Boxing Match before Captain Cook, Sandwich Islands] by John Webber (Fig. 30).

Pen, wash, and watercolor. 56 × 98.5 cm.
Bishop Museum Library, purchase 1922.

Cook's death generated numerous accounts of the skirmish by individuals on the voyages. In addition to these "eyewitness" accounts, literary productions inspired by the event included elegies, pantomimes, and dramas.

EXHIBITED

74. Roberts, Lt. Henry

Eye witness account of the death of Cook: facsimile from the log of Henry Roberts mate of the "Resolution" and officer in charge of the pinnace in which Captain Cook went ashore for the last time [London: F. Edwards, 1930?].

Only fifty copies were printed of this reproduction of two pages of an original manuscript of 144 pages. The facsimile features the events of February 14, 1779, and the two days following from the viewpoint of an officer who was devoted to his commander, describing him in part as a man "justly stiled father of his people from his great good care and attention, honored, & beloved by them . . ." (Carter collection, Bishop Museum Library).

Figure 27. — View of Moorea by John Cleveley (68).

75. Samwell, David (1751-1798)

A narrative of the death of Captain James Cook. To which are added some particulars, concerning his life and character. And observations respecting the introduction of the venereal disease into the Sandwich Islands. By David Samwell, surgeon of the Discovery. London: G. G. J. and J. Robinson, 1786.

An extremely rare, beautifully bound copy of the pamphlet by the surgeon of the *Discovery* on Cook's third voyage. The pamphlet is of particular importance because it fills in gaps of suppressed information lacking from the official accounts, such as the responsibility for Cook's death (Bishop Museum Library).

76. Seward, Anna

Elegy on Captain Cook. To which is added, an ode to the sun. By Miss Seward. 3d ed. London: J. Dodsley, 1781.

Beautifully bound poem of 238 lines, with numerous footnotes referring to passages in the official accounts of the voyages. This was one of the first posthumous tributes to Cook, the first edition being published several months after news of his death reached England (Fuller collection, Bishop Museum Library).

77. Arnould, Jean François Mussot

La mort du Capitaine Cook, à son troisième voyage au nouveau monde. Pantomime quatre actes; représenté, pour la première fois sur le Théâtre de l'Ambigu-Comique, au mois d'octobre 1788. Paris: Chez Lagrange, Libraire, 1788.

This pantomime illustrates some of the imaginative but completely unhistorical accounts that resulted. Cook, who has helped the King of Hawaii defeat his enemies, intercedes for the lives of the prisoners, only to be murdered by them for his role in their defeat (Carter collection, Bishop Museum Library).

78. Société de Géographie, Paris.

Centenaire de la mort de Cook célébré le 14 février 1879 à l'hotel de la Société de Géographie. Paris. Extrait du Bulletin de la Société de Géographie, May 18 (Fuller collection, Bishop Museum Library).

The events organized by the Société on the centenary of the death of Captain Cook are highlighted in this publication. Speeches about Cook, his voyages and contributions to geography, a bibliography including maps, and a most interesting catalogue of the exposi-

Figure 28. — Cook Taking Possession of Australia (71).

Figure 29. — Admiral Bligh. Unknown artist (72).

Figure 30. — The Boxing Match by John Webber (73).

Figure 31. — The Death of Cook by Johan Zoffany, National Maritime Museum, Greenwich.

tion held for eight days are herein presented. Overwhelming public response to solicitation for Cook-related articles to be presented to the exposition resulted in a collection of some 355 items, ranging from personal effects (particularly those relating to Cook's death), manuscripts, maps, art, and published works of Cook and collaborators, to ethnological objects and latter-day photographs.

Cook's death stirred the imagination of the British and a series of drawings, paintings, and lithographs depicted Cook as martyr, arbitrator, hero, and saint. One of the most famous depictions is the oil painting by Johan Zoffany (Fig. 31) in the National Maritime Museum, Greenwich, done in classical style—the Hawaiian Chief modeled after a sculpture of the Greek athlete Discobolus, and Cook an abstract tragic figure (Mitchell, 1944, p. 60)—but having little basis in reality.

EXHIBITED

George Carter (1737-96), a British painter of historical events presented a popular, if imaginary, representation of the event. Carter's intention was to produce a companion painting to Benjamin West's "The Death of General Wolfe"—both being landmark paintings in which classical costume was replaced by dress appropriate to the historical event depicted.[18] There are several versions of this famous painting, some made by Carter himself, and others which, although attributed to Carter, were apparently done by others. Known versions include the following: the B. F. Dillingham II collection, Hawaii; the W. D. Child collection, Hawaii; the Nan Kivell collection, National Library of Canberra, Australia; Captain Cook's Landing Place Museum, Botany Bay, Australia; Papeete Museum, Tahiti; UCLA Library, Los Angeles, California; Peabody Museum, Salem, Massachusetts; John Judkyn Memorial, Bath, England.

[18]The two paintings were part of a series of nine historical paintings made "to celebrate good men and brave actions" (Mitchell, 1944, p. 59n).

79. The Death of Cook by George Carter (Fig. 32).
Oil on canvas ca. 1783. 76 × 91 cm.
Carter collection, Bishop Museum Library.

John Cleveley (1747-86), was a marine painter, and brother to James Cleveley, who was carpenter aboard the *Resolution* during Cook's third voyage. James is the only illustrator of the death scene who may have been present at the event.

80. The Death of Cook by John Cleveley (Fig. 33).
Watercolor, ca. 1784. Dimensions 42 × 57.5 cm.
Painted from a sketch by his brother and published in similar form as an aquatint.
G. R. Merritt collection, New Zealand.

81. The Death of Cook by John Cleveley (Fig. 34).
Aquatint with watercolor.
Barely legible below view "Drawn on the spot by Ja.s Clevely."
Watermark verso upper rt. "J. Whatman." Pencil "953" on verso, 51.5 × 66 cm.
One of set of four in the Fuller collection, Bishop Museum Library.

82. John Webber, official artist on the third voyage, painted this view probably based on Cleveley's "on the spot" version (Fig. 35).
"To the Right Honourable the Lord Commissioners for executing the Office of Lord High Admiral of Great Britain, &c. This Plate representing The Death of Captain Cook is humbly inscribed. By their Lordship's most obedient and devoted Servant, John Webber. Drawn by J. Webber. The Figures Engraved by F. Bartolozzi, R.A. Engraver to His Majesty. The Landscape by W. Byrne. Published . . . Jan. 4 1787, by J. Webber, . . . and W. Byrne . . . London."
Copper plate engraving. 47.5 × 59.5 cm (plate mark).
Fuller collection, Bishop Museum Library.

83. Hamilton (Fig. 36).
"The Death of Capt.n Cook, at O'-why-hee, near Kamschatka, whose discoveries in His Last Voyage, as well as those of his First and Second, will be included in this New & Improved System of Geography."
"Hamilton delin." "Thornton sculp." 31 × 20 cm (plate mark).
Engraved for Millar's New Complete & Universal System of Geography (London: A. Hogg, 1782, p. 216). Bishop Museum Library, purchase 1977.

84. Loutherbourg, Philippe Jacques de (1740-1812), R.A. was a Swiss artist who went to London in 1771 and became a notable painter and stage designer for David Garrick (Fig. 37).
The Apotheosis of Captain Cook. From a Design of P. J. De Loutherbourg, R.A. The View of Karakakooa Bay Is from a Drawing by John Webber, R.A. (the last he made) in the Collection of Mr. G. Baker. Lond. Pub.d Jan.y 20, 1794 by J. Thane . . ."
Engraving. 26.5 × 22 cm. (plate mark).
Fuller collection, Bishop Museum Library.

85. Ramberg, H. (Fig. 38).

"Neptune raising Capt.ⁿ Cook up to Immortality, a 'Genius' crowning him with a Wreath of Oak, and Fame introducing him to History. In the Front Ground are the Four Quarters of the World presenting to Britannia their various Stores." "Designed by H. Ramberg, Engraved by J. Neagle and Ornamented by W. Grainger. Published as the Act directs by J. Cooke . . ." n.d.
Published as frontispiece to Bankes New System of Geography. London, 1798, C. Cooke.
Engraved surface: 36.5 × 20.5 cm. No plate mark, trimmed?
Fuller collection, Bishop Museum Library.

86. "Captain Cook's Monument, at Owhyhee, Sandwich Islands."

From *Gleason's Pictorial Drawing-Room Companion.* Feb. 28, 1852, p. 137. Hand colored woodcut. 6.5 × 20 cm. (Fig. 39) Published first as Plate 47 in Voyage autour du monde . . . by Capt. A. N. Vaillant, who commanded the corvette *La Bonite* (1836-7) ("Monument élevé à Hawaii au Capitaine Cook, lithograph after Admiral Fisquet, by Louis-Phillippe-Alphonse Bichebois with the figures by Adolphe-Jean-Baptiste Bayot).
Bishop Museum Library, purchase 1976.

The monument depicted was located at Kealakekua Bay erected by Vice-Admiral Lord Byron of HMS *Blonde* on its voyage to Hawaii (1825-26) to return the bodies of Liholiho (King Kamehameha II) and his wife Kamamalu who died of measles in 1824 while on a visit to London. The inscription reads: "In memory of Captn. James Cook, R.N., who discovered these islands in the year of our Lord 1778. This humble monument is erected by his fellow countrymen in the year of our Lord 1825."

87. Fabric printed with a scene of the death of Cook. Date and use unknown. (David W. Forbes collection.)

88. A copper marker left by HMS *Imogene* is now in Bishop Museum (1965.55.01) and is exhibited here. The inscription reads "Near this spot / Fell / Captain James Cook, R.N. / the / Renowned Circumnavigator / Who / Discovered these Islands / A.D. 1778 / His Majesty's Ship / Imogene / October 17th 1837."

The illustrations by Carter, Webber, and Cleveley are well-known depictions of Cook's death. The engravings by Hamilton, Loutherbourg, and Ramberg illustrate the florid style and romantic spirit of the time and the reverence paid to Cook by artists of the era. Versions of the death scene similar to these were reprinted over and over again in contemporary literature.

Numerous weapons are said to have been "the one" used to kill Cook—one is exhibited here. Many pieces of shot and trees with shot are said to have come from the very spot on that fatal day. Bishop Museum (along with many other museums) has such mementos.

EXHIBITED

89. Swordfish dagger (which has a good claim to having been used in Cook's death, [Kaeppler, ms., "*L'Aigle* and HMS *Blonde:* The Use of History in the Study of Ethnography"]). Bishop Museum (1977.206.13), formerly in the Hooper collection (366). Purchased on behalf of Bishop Museum by Thurston Twigg-Smith. Length 76.9 cm. Figure 40.

90. Iron fragment said to have been fired by Cook's men at Kealakekua. Bishop Museum (B 8803). Gift of Ralph Kearns.

91. Coconut tree husk from a coconut tree growing at Kaawaloa, the trunk of which was perforated with a ball at the time of Capt. Cook's death. Bishop Museum (7871), ABCFM collection, 1895.

LITERATURE AND ART

Cook's voyages contributed not only in content, but philosophically, to the serious and satirical literature of the late 18th century. Coleridge's *The Rime of the Ancient Mariner,* for example, owes much of its inspiration to Cook's second voyage (Smith, 1956). Satire was often at the expense of Joseph Banks—usually elevating Pacific Islanders and exposing the ill effects of Europeans on indigenous peoples. Omai, the Tahitian taken to England by Captain Furneaux on Cook's second voyage and who returned to his homeland on Cook's third voyage, became the hero and theme of many literary works. One of the most ambitious dramatic events of late 18th century England was the production of the pantomime, *Omai, or a Trip Round the World* (O'Keeffe, 1785), based on Cook's voyages. Philippe Jacques de Loutherbourg designed the stage scenery and costumes of this pantomime, working from drawings by Webber and Hodges made on Cook's voyages, and artificial curiosities brought back on them—along with a bit of artistic license and fancy (Figs. 41 and 42).

EXHIBITED

92. Coleridge, Samuel Taylor, 1772-1834

The rime of the ancient mariner. In seven parts. By Samuel Taylor Coleridge. New York: Pollard & Moss, 1887 (Bishop Museum Library, gift of Mrs. F. Gregory Troyer).

A beautifully illustrated edition of the famous poem.

Figure 32. — The Death of Cook by George Carter (79).

Figure 33. — The Death of Cook, by John Cleveley
Merritt collection, New Zealand (80).

Figure 34. — The Death of Cook aquatint by John Cleveley (81).

93. [Scott-Waring, John]

An epistle from Oberea, Queen of Otaheite, to Joseph Banks, Esq. Translated by T.Q.Z., Esq., Professor of the Otaheite language in Dublin, and of all the languages of the undiscovered islands in the South Seas; and enriched with historical and explanatory notes. 2d ed. London: J. Almon, 1774 (Fuller collection, Bishop Museum Library).

An anonymous poem of 172 lines purported to be from Oberea, in which Banks is twitted for alleged amorous incidents at Tahiti. A reply from "Banks" and a second letter from "Oberea" were published later.

94. [Perry, James]

Mimosa: or, the sensitive plant; a poem. Dedicated to Mr. Banks, and addressed to Kitt Frederick, Dutchess of Queensberry, Elect. London: Printed for W. Sandwich, near the Admiralty, and sold by all the booksellers within the Bills of Mortality, 1779 (Fuller collection, Bishop Museum Library).

An anonymous, erotic poem of 318 lines. The dedication draws anthropometric comparisons between the natives of the South Seas and the inhabitants of England. The publisher's name is undoubtedly fictitious, and taken from that of the First Lord of the Admiralty at the time, who was one of the patrons of Cook's voyages and for whom the Sandwich Isles were named.

95. [Courtney, John]

An epistle (moral and philosophical) from an Officer at Otaheite to Lady GR*S**N*R. With notes, critical and historical. By the author of The Rape of Pomona. London: T. Evans, 1774 (Fuller collection, Bishop Museum Library).

An anonymous, somewhat scandalous poem of 294 lines in which the amorous customs of the Tahitians are depicted, with notes from the Hawkesworth edition of Cook's first voyage added for explanatory purposes.

96. [Fitz-gerald, Rev. Gerald]

The injured islanders; or, the influence of art upon the happiness of nature. Dublin: T. T. Faulkner, 1779 (Fuller collection, Bishop Museum Library).

An anonymous poem of 472 lines written from the viewpoint of Oberea, Queen of Tahiti, in which she dwells on the disastrous effects on the Tahitians of the visits of the Europeans.

Figure 35. — The Death of Cook by John Webber (82).

97. Anonymous
Marvels of savage art: comedy in the cannibal islands. [Extracted from the Brighton Herald, May 1st, 1909] (Fuller collection, Bishop Museum Library).

A broadside reprinting the report of a lecture given by Mr. H. S. Toms, curator of the Brighton Museum, in which the point is made that "civilization is not responsible for all the good things of this world." Mr. Toms used the native cultures of various Pacific people, particularly the Maoris, to demonstrate the ill effects of discovery by the Europeans on indigenous peoples.

98. Anonymous
An historic epistle, from Omiah to the Queen of Otaheite; being his remarks on the English Nation. With Notes by the editor. London: T. Evans, 1775 (Fuller collection, Bishop Museum Library).

An anonymous poem of 746 lines, purported to be the work of Omai, in which he is represented as depicting the public and private life in England in a very unfavorable light, as compared with the simple pleasures of Tahiti.

99. [Baston, Rev. Guillaume André René]
Narrations d'Omai, insulaire de la mer du sud, ami et compagnon de voyage du Capitaine Cook. Ouvrage traduit de l'O-Taïtien, par M. K.***, & publié par le Capitaine L. A. B. [i.e., G. A. R. Baston]. Rouen: Le Boucher, le jeune; Paris: Buisson; 1790 (Bishop Museum Library).

In this multivolume, imaginary autobiography, Captain L. A. B., docked at the Cape of Good Hope, is entrusted by a long-lost former classmate, Monsieur K***, now on his deathbed, with a box of manuscripts: Omai's story. The Captain is to publish it, so that, as Omai explains within the account, "it will pass to all people eager for literary curiosities" [translation]. Sections of the account are dedicated to persons of importance, including Captain Cook, and the last section addresses Christianity. Omai hopes that his account can instruct, or at least amuse.

Figure 36. — (Above, left) The Death of Cook by Hamilton (83).

Figure 37. — (Below, left) The Apotheosis of Captain Cook by P.J. de Loutherbourg (84).

Figure 38. — (Above, right) Neptune raising Capt. Cook to Immortality, by H. Ramberg (85).

Figure 39. — Captain Cook's Monument, after Admiral Fisquet (86).

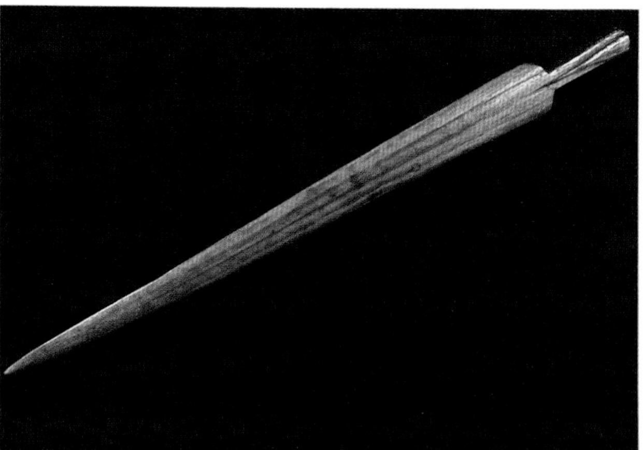

Figure 40. — Swordfish dagger possibly used in Cook's death (89).

Figure 41. — Tahitian woman bringing presents, by P. J. de Loutherbourg, National Library of Australia, Canberra.

Figure 42. — A man of New Zealand, by P. J. de Loutherbourg, National Library of Australia, Canberra.

Figure 43. — A young woman of Tahiti bringing a present, by John Webber (100).

Figure 44. — View in Queen Charlotte Sound by John Webber (101).

Artists became famous for their oil paintings, drawings, water colors, and lithographs based on the voyages. Webber, official artist on Cook's third voyage, was one of the first artists to take full advantage of newly developed papers that made the use of water colors feasible and practical. These early artistic works constitute one of the most valuable resources for the study of natural and cultural history of the areas visited, as well as the history of techniques and artistic styles in the Western tradition.[19]

EXHIBITED

100. Webber, John, R. A.

"A YOUNG WOMAN of OTAHEITE, bringing a PRESENT" (Fig. 43).
Engraving from *Atlas* to Cook's 3d voyage, Plate 27, 57 × 42.5 cm.
Bishop Museum Library, gift of Mrs. Robert McKeague (compare with the drawing by Loutherbourg, Fig. 41).

101. Webber, John, R. A.

"View in Queen Charlotte's Sound, New Zealand" (Fig. 44).
Soft-ground etching, with sepia and gray wash added [by Webber?].
Plate mark 33 × 46 cm., sheet 43 × 60 cm.
"J. Webber fecit."
"London. Pub.[d] Oct.[R] 1, 1790 by J. Webber N° 312 Oxford Street, Vide Cook's last Voyage Vol. 1. Chap. 7."
Captain Fuller believed this impression to be a first state because all other copies known have initials "R.A." engraved after artist's signature. [Webber received this honor in August, 1791].
Published in *Views of the South Seas*, London: Boydell, 1808 [1820-21?], Pl. 1.
Fuller collection, Bishop Museum Library.

102. Webber, John, R. A.

"A View in ANNAMOOKA, one of the FRIENDLY ISLES" (Fig. 45).
Unpublished early engraving [first state?]. Plate mark intact only partially along lower edge. Engr. surface 25 × 40 cm.
"Drawn & Etchd by J. Webber. Aquatinta by M. C. Prestel. London. Pub[d] [blank] 1787 by I Webber N° 312 Oxford Street. Vide Cook's last Voy. Vol. 1 Chap IV."

In disagreement with letter press, Capt. Fuller believed "a very lt. impression, handcolored, probably by Webber and not an aquatint at all. In fact it might be termed an original Webber watercolor" (A. W. F. Fuller ms. notes). Mary Catherine Prestel arrived in London in 1786 and did do aquatints of Webber's work later, such as in the published work by Webber *Views of the South Seas* London: J. Boydell, 1808 [1820-21?]. This same "View" in another state was hand-colored in sepia and gray but apparently never published. (Fuller collection, Bishop Museum Library.)

103. Webber, John, R. A.

"A View in Oheitepeha [Vaitepiha] Bay, in the Island of Otaheite" (Fig. 46).
Soft-ground etching, with sepia and gray wash added [by Webber].
Plate mark 32.5 × 45 cm., sheet 43 × 60 cm.
"J. Webber, R. A. fecit"
"London. Pub.[d] Aug[t] 1, 1791 by J. Webber. N° 312 Oxford Street. Vide Cook's last Voyage. Vol. 2. Chap. 1"
Published in *Views of the South Seas*, London: Boydell, 1808 [1820-21?], Pl. V.
Fuller collection, Bishop Museum Library.

Another view of the same scene by a different artist follows:

104. Ellis, William (d. 1785).

"View in Oitapeeah [Vaitepiha] Bay, in the Island Otaheite" (Fig. 47).
Watercolor. 31 × 49 cm.
"W. Ellis fec[t] 1777" lower rt. drawing.
"6" lower left mount.
Published in Ellis, 1784, v. 1, pl. 16.
Carter collection, Bishop Museum Library.

105. Ellis, William, Surgeon

"Part of the West-Side of Owhaow, one of the Sandwich Islands." [Waimea Bay, Oahu] (Fig. 48).
Watercolor. 14 × 37.5 cm.
"W. Ellis fec[t] 1779" lower rt.
"Owhyhee" lower rt. below title. Title penned below view in different hand?
Verso "18"
Carter collection, Bishop Museum Library.

MEMORABILIA

Cook's voyages have generated a surprising amount of genuine and spurious memorabilia. Sea chests, Bibles, and other mementos are attributed to Cook in large numbers—some with quite legitimate, but nevertheless undocumented, claims. Letters, diaries, seals, and medals of Cook, his sailing companions, and his patrons have become "collectables" and 20th century cabinets of curiosities abound in Cook-related objects and papers. The persistence of the legend of Cook can be seen in recent productions of sculpture and literature.

---

[19] Bishop Museum is fortunate to have in its collection nine original works by John Webber. They are illustrated here as Figures 30, 54, 64, 89, 90, 98, 130, 164, 194. Figure 90 was a gift of Mrs. A. W. F. Fuller. The others were purchased by Bishop Museum in 1922.

Three original works by William Ellis are also part of Bishop Museum's collections given by George R. Carter. They are illustrated here on page xii, and in Figures 47 and 48.

EXHIBITED

106. Medals struck by the Royal Society in commemoration of Captain Cook (two silver, two bronze), Fortess collection, Hawaii.

107. Engraving of both sides of Royal Society's medal in commemoration of Capt. Cook (Fig. 49.)
8.5 × 15 cm (plate mk.) Shows obverse and reverse medal joined by a thin line.
"Engrav[d] from a Model of M[r] Pingo's by T. Trotter"
"Publish[d] as the Act directs by G. Kearsley, Fleet Street London July 27th, 1784"
Fuller collection, Bishop Museum Library.

108. Seal impression with Cook's coat of arms. Emanuel collection, England.

109. Letters and miscellaneous documents, Fortess collection, Hawaii.

110. Letters and miscellaneous documents. Fuller collection, Bishop Museum Library.

111. Memorabilia attributed to Cook, Fulcher collection, Florida. Including: vanity chest, snuff boxes, rum flask, pouches, needle case, bag, other containers, card holder, game set, serviette ring, flint box, boot lacer, pocket sextant log, dingy reeve pulley, miniature Bible and whale teeth—all said to have belonged to Captain Cook.

112. Memorabilia attributed to Cook's voyages, Bishop Museum.
Ivory fan handle, said to have been left by the *Discovery* (1910.18.17). Liliuokalani collection.
Bone handle, said to have been left by the *Discovery* (1910.18.16). Liliuokalani collection.
Ring said to have belonged to Captain Cook (1971.96). Gift of Mrs. Wilfred Crossling.
Piece of wood from a tree said to have been planted by Cook at Point Venus, Tahiti (5014). Eric Craig collection.

113. Modern abstract sculpture (model for a proposed monumental sculpture) inspired by the square sail form of Cook's vessels and the bark cloth hangings of the image of Lono. Italian marble, 1977, Kenneth Weston Winsor, Camaiore, Italy.

114. *The Return of Lono.* Novel of Captain Cook's last voyage, by O. A. Bushnell, 1956.

And what was the impact on Pacific peoples of these encounters with strangers who brought new tools, powerful weapons, jealous gods, different perceptual categories, unknown diseases, and different value systems? That is another story—a story not to be told in an exhibition of the works of their ancestors—but in the people who have descended from those touched by these encounters. Indeed, this exhibition is not an end, but a beginning—an invitation to examine the past in order to understand the present and prepare for the future.

Figure 45. — A View in Annamooka by John Webber (102).

Figure 47. — A View in Vaitepiha Bay by William Ellis (104).

Figure 46. — A View in Vaitepiha Bay by John Webber (103).

Figure 48. — View of Oahu by William Ellis (105).

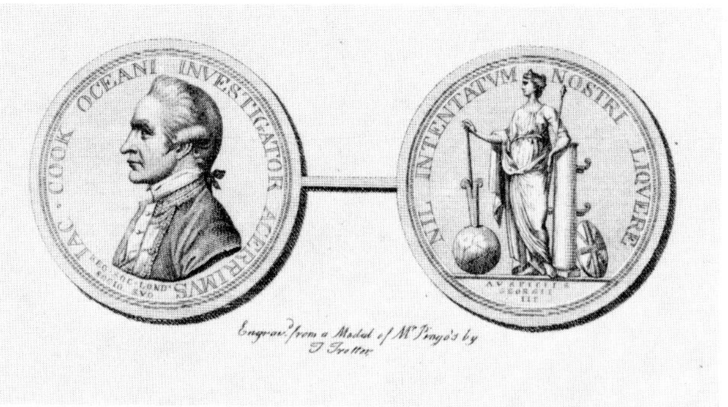

Figure 49. — Engraving of Cook Commemorative Medal (107).

REFERENCES FOR INTRODUCTORY EXHIBITION

Beaglehole, J. C.
1955-1967. *The Journals of Captain James Cook on His Voyages of Discovery*. 3 vols. Cambridge.
1970. "Cook the Navigator." *Explorer's J.* 48(4): 264-273.

Beddie, M. K., Editor
1970. *Bibliography of Captain James Cook, R. N., F.R.S., Circumnavigator.* 2nd ed. Sydney: Library of New South Wales.

Brigham, William T.
1911. "Ka Hana Kapa: The Making of Bark-Cloth in Hawaii." *Mem. B. P. Bishop Mus.* 3: 1-276.

Cole, Douglas
1975. "John Webber: Etchings and Aquatints." *Turnbull Library Rec.* 8(2): 25-27.

Dall, W. H.
1905. "Thomas Martyn and *The Universal Conchologist*." *Proc. U. S. National Mus.* 29: 415-432.

Dance, S. Peter
1971. "The Cook Voyages and Conchology." *J. Conchology* 26: 354-379.

Hill Collection
1974. *The Hill Collection of Pacific Voyages.* R. L. Silveira de Braganza and C. Oakes (eds.). Annotations by J. A. Hill. San Diego: University Library, Univ. California San Diego.

Holmes, Maurice
1952. *Captain James Cook, R.N., F.R.S.: A Bibliographical Excursion.* London: Edwards.

Howay, F. W.
1921. "Authorship of the Anonymous Account of Captain Cook's Last Voyage." *Washington Historical Quart.* 12(1): 51-58.

Kaeppler, Adrienne L.
1975. *The Fabrics of Hawaii: Bark Cloth.* World's Heritage of Woven Fabrics, Vol. 14. Leigh-on-Sea, England.

Liliuokalani
1898. *Hawaii's Story by Hawaii's Queen.* Boston: Lee and Shepherd.

Mitchell, Charles
1944. "Zoffany's Death of Captain Cook." *Burlington Mag.* 84: 56-62.

Murray-Oliver, A. A. St. C. M.
1969. "John Webber and His Aquatints." *Turnbull Library Rec.* 2(2): 74-79.

O'Keeffe [Mr.]
1785. *Omai or, A Trip Round the World.* London: Cadell.

Robertson, W. H.
1970. "James Cook and the Transit of Venus." *J. Proc. Royal Soc. New South Wales* 103 (1): 5-9.

Smith, Bernard
1956. "Coleridge's *Ancient Mariner* and Cook's Second Voyage." *J. Warburg and Courtauld Insts.* 19 (1-2): 117-154.

Whitehead, P. J. P.
1969. "Captain Cook's Role in Natural History." *Australian Natural History* 16(8): 241-246.

Wilson, Scott, and H. H. Evans
1890-1899. *Aves Hawaiienses.* London: Porter

Ethnography and the Voyages of Captain Cook

Instruments of warr and dresses of the Natives seem'd the only Cargo they had brought . . .

At the time of the historic voyages of discovery of Captain James Cook, ethnography as a scientific discipline did not exist. Indeed, it was not until decades later that the social and cultural life of man was considered, except by philosophers, worthy of serious study. Yet the results of the three voyages of Captain Cook are of the greatest importance for the scientific study of certain Pacific peoples, as well as for the development of method and theory in ethnohistory. Hundreds of ethnographic specimens were collected on Cook's voyages and hundreds of pages were filled with accounts of native customs. In fact, if one looks closely at the written accounts and collections of some of the voyagers, such as those of Joseph Banks on Cook's first voyage, Reinhold and George Forster on the second voyage, and William Anderson and David Samwell on the third voyage, one might consider these individuals the first Pacific ethnographers.

Officers, crew, and supernumeraries wrote comments and collected ethnographic specimens. Often these were only curious mementos of their voyages; sometimes they were gifts to the great patrons of the voyages and to private collectors of Britain; or, at a more mundane level, many were simply acquired to be sold at a profit. Ethnographic specimens at this time were for the most part unimportant appendages to the great collections of specimens of natural history, which for centuries had been sought to adorn the "cabinets of curiosities" of the leisured. By the last quarter of the 18th century, it was a seller's market for natural history specimens, with competitive buying among scientists such as Joseph Banks, John Fothergill, and John and William Hunter; dilettantes such as the Duchess of Portland, the Duke of Calonne, and the Alströmer brothers; private museums such as those of Sir Ashton Lever, Anna Blackburne, William Bullock, and Daniel Boulter; as well as natural history dealers such as George Humphrey and Jacob Forster.

Natural history specimens, sought after as they were, must have been difficult for the ordinary seaman to procure—especially such things as birds, insects, and fish—and even more difficult to preserve, especially if one were a novice. Storage, particularly in the crew's quarters, must also have been a problem. Shells and geological specimens[1] were easier for an amateur to collect, but ethnographic specimens must have been easiest of all to obtain, particularly if one were not overly discriminating. The natives showered these visitors with gifts and were eager to trade. Objects which may have taken many hours to produce were given to the personnel of the ships for relatively worthless beads and cloth. The more valuable iron nails and hatchets were often reserved by the ship's officers for official trade for provisions. In some areas, however, such as Tahiti and the Marquesas, the more valuable ethnographic specimens, such as Tahitian mourning dresses and Marquesan ornaments, would be parted with only for the red feathers which were procured in Tonga on the second and third voyages. One is forced to wonder where all these ethnographic specimens were stored, especially such items as ten Tahitian mourning dresses, which were said by George Forster to have been collected on the second voyage (1777, Vol. 2, p. 72).

Most of the natural history collectors had a few "artificial curiosities" (as they were called) in their cabinets of curiosities and showed some interest in these "arms and dresses of savage nations." But because there was no *Systema Naturae* (Linnaeus, 1735) by which to arrange them and no precise terminology with which to discuss them, few took them seriously. Even the museums of the time were unprepared to

[1] It appears that few geological specimens were actually brought back on the voyages, and geologists of the time collected ethnographic specimens of jade, basalt, and so forth, in lieu of the raw materials.

deal with them. William Bullock, for example, in the preface to the *Companion* to his museum puts it this way:

> The articles of Natural History have been carefully compiled from those authors, who have given the most authentic and pleasing relation of the article; whilst in the descriptions of the artificial curiosities, all that has been aimed at is an accurate delineation of the subject, described in simple and intelligent language (1809, pp. vi-vii).

However, because these curiosities were associated with Captain Cook (often quite erroneously, for he did not necessarily collect them) they seemed to acquire a supernatural quality appropriate to the memory of the folk hero he had become. Nevertheless, some of the collectors on the voyages were no doubt disappointed when they attempted to sell their artificial curiosities on their return to England. It is probably no accident that large collections given to museums by their collectors were often ethnographic collections, for example the collections of J. R. Forster (who was a naturalist) in Oxford, and of Anders Sparrman (also a naturalist) in Stockholm. On Cook's third voyage it was an ethnographic collection (possibly made by William Anderson) that was given to the Russians.[2] Anderson, who died at sea, willed his papers and natural history specimens to Joseph Banks[3] (Keevil, 1933, pp. 515-517, 523), but his artificial curiosities were not mentioned in the will, and were thus available to be used as a gift. David Samwell, surgeon's mate on the *Discovery* on Cook's third voyage, was pursued by natural history collectors and agents, but offered to sell "a good collection" of artificial curiosities to Anna Blackburne for £100[4] and finally sold the bulk of his collection at public auction in June, 1781 (Anon., 1781).

Perhaps it is because the ethnographic specimens were not considered particularly valuable 200 years ago and were not traded so often that many of them are identifiable today. The natural history specimens seem to have disappeared at an even more alarming rate than the ethnographic ones.[5] Ethnographic specimens are perhaps easier to identify because of their one-of-a-kind quality, especially if early illustrations of them exist, and because either the style of making many of these items changed rapidly, or they ceased to be manufactured shortly after contact with Europeans. Natural history specimens, on the other hand, continued to be collected in relatively the same form so that descriptions or even illustrations are not diagnostic of one specimen only. Still, if one takes into account the large number of ethnographic specimens that must have been taken to Europe on the three voyages of Cook, the number with precise documentation was really quite small, and many specimens were erroneously attributed to Cook's voyages or documented only by hearsay.[6]

The importance of identifying and documenting ethnographic specimens from Cook's voyages cannot be overemphasized. Only with a large number of dated specimens will it be possible to place the study of material culture of the Pacific at the time of European contact, and its subsequent changes, on any scientific foundation. As more dated specimens are identified, one is forced to question the validity of previously accepted notions about "classic" precontact cultures, which, often because of lack of evidence, have been based on the impressionistic ideas of the analysts. Ethnographic specimens from Cook's voyages—because they are early, extensive, and documentable—are potentially one of the most valuable resources for study of 18th century material culture in the Pacific area.

Identification of specimens often rests on the use of documents which make it possible to follow the routes of specific items from collector to collector, and also on the use of illustrations of specimens known to have come from a particular voyage. Such documents include sale catalogues of specimens, guides, or "companions" to early collections, correspondence of collectors, drawings made in early museums and collections, published and unpublished drawings made on the voyages, and engravings made for the official accounts of the voyages. Identifying a specimen from a drawing, however, is only the beginning, because often a number of objects of the same type are similar enough so that a drawing alone is often not conclusive. In order for the specimen to be "documented" it must be traced step by step back to its original collection.

As a case in point, the Rurutu fly whisk illustrated in Hawkesworth (1773, Pl. 12, [Fig. 50, below]) has long been thought to be the one now in the Cook collection in the Museum für Völkerkunde, Vienna (Moschner, 1955, p. 223), because of the seeming similarity between the illustration and the Vienna specimen. Work-

[2] This collection is now in Leningrad, see Kaeppler, 1977.

[3] Sir Joseph Banks (1743-1820) sailed on Cook's first Pacific voyage; President of the Royal Society (1778-1820).

[4] Correspondence between Samwell and Mathew Gregson, Liverpool Public Library, letter dated November 1, 1780. Evidently Anna Blackburne did not buy it. Her obituary states that her collection was of birds, insects, corals, and shells, and was inherited by her nephew, John Blackburne (Anon., 1794, p. 180).

[5] See Whitehead, 1969, Dance, 1971, 1972 and Medway, 1976, for the difficulties in tracing zoological specimens from Cook's voyages.

[6] The early works of Brigham (1898, 1913) and the preliminary inventory of Dodge (1969, p. 88) are useful as a starting point for research on Cook voyage ethnographic collections. However, these studies should not be relied upon for total numbers of objects in the various collections nor for the provenances to which the various artifacts are assigned.

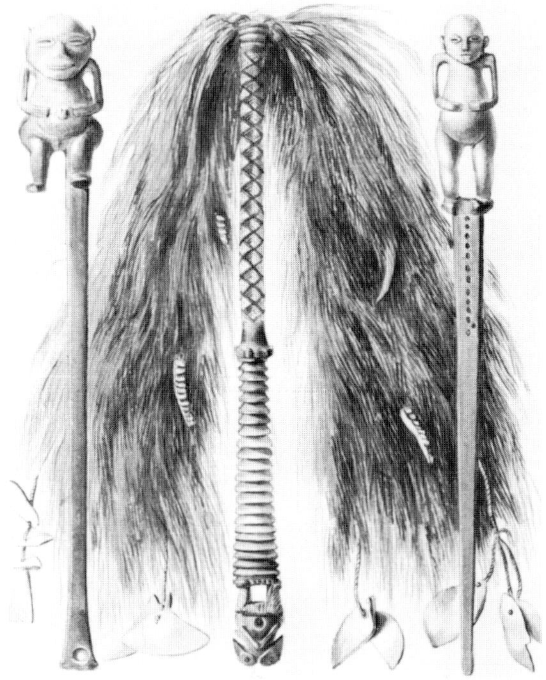

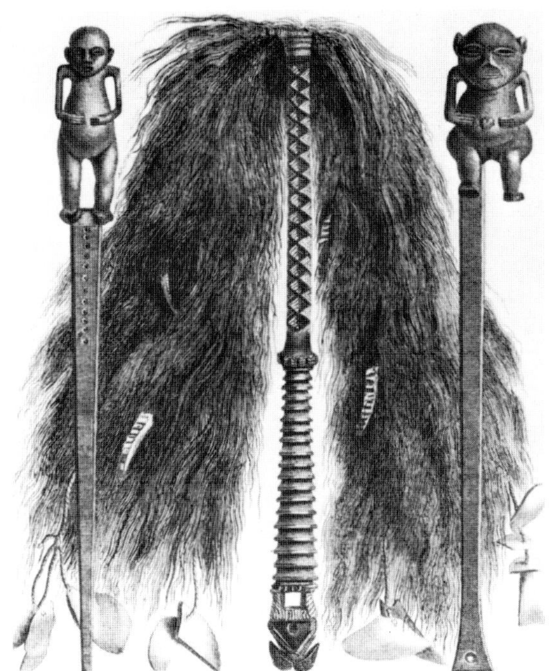

Figure 50. — Fly whisks. British Library Add. Ms. 23,921.53.

ing backward from the fly whisk in Vienna, however, there was no logical way to trace it to the Hawkesworth illustration. There is, however, a similar fly whisk in the British Museum (TAH 27) and if one examines, in turn, the Hawkesworth lithograph, a drawing made in the Leverian Museum in the 1780's (Kaeppler, forthcoming), the British Museum specimen, and the Vienna specimen, along with other documentary evidence on the collections in the British Museum and Vienna, one easily concludes that the Vienna specimen is the one depicted in the 1780's in the Leverian Museum, while the fly whisk in the British Museum is undoubtedly the one depicted in the Hawkesworth plate, as well as in the original drawing for the Hawkesworth plate done by J. F. Miller, and now in the British Library Manuscript Department (Add. Ms. 23,921.53 [Fig. 50, above]).

Little ethnohistoric research of this kind has yet been undertaken, and the fact is that many specimens are incorrectly reputed to have been collected on Cook's voyages, based on assumptions that easily crumble when subjected to closer scrutiny. Specimens "documented" by sound criteria have been few and one of the purposes of this Catalogue is an inventory of the ethnographic objects collected on Cook voyages. The exhibition and this Catalogue are arranged by area and by artifact type. All types of "native manufactures" collected on Cook's voyages are included in the exposition and many are included in the exhibition. A list of every known example of each artifact type that has a reasonable claim to collection on Cook's voyages is also included. Preceding the Catalogue is a summary of the dispersal of the ethnographic objects collected on the three voyages.

COLLECTORS AND COLLECTIONS FROM COOK'S VOYAGES

First Voyage on the Endeavour *(1768-1771)*

Ethnographic specimens that can be traced to Cook's first voyage with any certainty are few. A collection in the University Museum of Archaeology and Ethnology, Cambridge, was received in 1914 from Trinity College, which received it from Lord Sandwich,[7] presumably in two parts, the first of which was in October, 1771 (Trinity College Library, Add. Ms. a106). Until recently all the objects in this gift were thought to have come from Cook's first voyage. But an examination of the labels indicates that some of the objects were brought from the South Seas in 1775, while labels belonging to other objects seem to authenticate a first voyage provenance.[8] It is likely that Cook gave much of his collection of "artificial curiosities" to his patron, Lord Sandwich, who in turn gave two large sections of it to Trinity College, Cambridge (where he had been a student) and to the British Museum, in his

[7]John Montagu, 4th Earl of Sandwich (1718-1792), First Lord of the Admiralty and Patron of Cook.

[8]Shawcross (1970) attributes the whole collection to Cook's first voyage, but he did not know of the existence of the original Trinity College labels, which have recently come to light.

official capacity as First Lord of the Admiralty, while he retained a few pieces himself at his home in Hinchingbrooke.[9] The accession information in Trinity College and the British Museum suggests that the objects and information came from the same person and both are dated October, 1771. The Trinity College list is entitled, "An Inventory of the Weapons, Utensils and Manufactures of various kinds collected by Capt.ⁿ Cook on his majesty's ship the Endeavour in the years 1768, 1769, 1770 and 1771 in the newly discovered South Sea Islands and New zealand and given to Trinity College by the Earl of Sandwich." The second part of the collection was given to the British Museum on October 18, 1771, where it is noted in the Register as "A curious collection of weapons, utensils, and manufactures of various sorts, sent from the Hota Hita [i.e. Otahita] and other newly discovered islands in the South Seas, and from New Zealand made by Captain Cook: from the Lords of the Admiralty." Unfortunately these specimens cannot be individually identified in the British Museum collection because they seem not to have been catalogued or numbered until some years afterward, along with many later objects.

Cook probably also gave objects to his Royal Patron, George III. Some of these (along with a few objects from areas first visited on Cook's second voyage) were apparently inherited in the Royal line. A *heitiki* much like the drawing of a *heitiki* now in the British Library (Add. Ms. 23,920.76), noted "Hawkes Bay, New Zealand, October 18, 1769," is still in the Royal collection (on loan to the Commonwealth Institute). Associated information indicates that it was Captain Cook's personal *heitiki* given to King George III. Some objects that may have been given by Cook to King George may form the basis of the collection once in the possession of Queen Victoria and given to the Imperial Institute (now Commonwealth Institute) by King Edward VII.[10] A paper with the collection said, "This box contains articles brought by Captain Cook from Otaheti." The collection is now in Wellington (see Appendix III).

Besides Cook, Joseph Banks was probably the greatest collector of the first voyage, but because he obtained through other means objects from Cook's second and third voyages, as well as objects from the voyages of others, it is virtually impossible to tell which items were actually collected by Banks in the field. Even objects that come from islands visited by Banks cannot be attributed to his own field collection unless independent evidence of this exists, because Banks was the recipient of many gifts, and he also made purchases. A second group of objects now in Cambridge University Museum were said to have been given to Thomas Pennant[11] by Banks. Inherited by the Earl of Denbigh, the objects were deposited on loan to the Museum in 1912,[12] and finally given to Cambridge in 1925. A collection in Stockholm is also attributed to Joseph Banks (Rydén, 1965). Although the Pennant/Denbigh collection in Cambridge and the "Banks collection" (as it will be called in this Catalogue) in Stockholm may include some specimens that were collected by Banks himself (who was on the first voyage only), other items must surely have come from later voyages because they derive from islands not visited on the first voyage.[13] Shawcross attributes the Maori items in the Pennant/Denbigh collection in Cambridge University Museum to Banks and the first voyage (Shawcross, 1970, p. 305), but this cannot be verified. Indeed, one of these specimens (a conch shell trumpet) is depicted in the official account of Cook's second voyage and never belonged to Banks (Gathercole, 1976). Although it is possible that pieces in the Pennant collection came from Banks's field collection from the first voyage, it is equally likely that they came from the second or third voyage. Three drawings pasted in Pennant's copy of the published account of Cook's voyages (now in the Dixson Library, Sydney) depict objects from Tahiti and Tonga. One of the pieces depicted is now in Cambridge and some possibly in the British Museum. The Tongan pieces, of course, could not have been collected by Banks.

Banks certainly had natural history specimens from Cook's second and third voyages, for example, those left to him by William Anderson, those given to him by the Forsters and others (Whitehead, 1969, p. 163), and, according to David Samwell, most of those from the third voyage. Samwell says in a letter to Gregson, "believe me when I tell you that very few Natural Curiosities have been brought home in our two ships—the whole of those few have in a Manner been monopolized by Mr. Banks" (letter dated November 1, 1780, Gregson correspondence, Liverpool Public Library). Banks's artificial curiosities could have come from the same and additional sources. Banks gave

[9] Including two New Zealand trumpets *(pu kaea)* which were given to Cambridge Museum in 1922.

[10] Although a Lady Elizabeth Noel of Gainsbrough is also associated with the collection (Betty McFadgen, pers. comm.).

[11] Thomas Pennant (1726-1798), an English naturalist and traveler.

[12] See *Cambridge Annual Report* for 1912.

[13] The Australian Museum, Sydney, also has a collection purchased from a Mr. Calvert and said to derive from Banks. This seems doubtful enough, but even if true, the specimens are probably not from Cook's voyages (Kaeppler, 1972, p. 196). Indeed, a letter dated October 1, 1887, from Maudslay to von Hügel, in the Cambridge Museum, mentions this so-called Capt. Cook find: "If it is the same Calvert he is an accomplished swindler and the find may be a bogus one." Another letter of September 28, 1887, describes Calvert as a dealer in eggs and minerals who once lived in the Strand and whose dealings were known to Newton, Professor of Zoology in Cambridge. Unfortunately his dealings were not known in Australia, where the collection was subsequently sold. The objects from this collection are not included in this Catalogue.

some of these to William Bullock's London Museum, including part of a Tahitian mourning costume (Bullock, 1810, p. 11). This was not brought to England by Banks, for, according to Forster, no mourning dresses were collected on the first voyage, but ten were collected on the second (Forster, 1777, Vol. 2, p. 72). Although the mourning dress part that Banks gave to Bullock is probably from Cook's second voyage, it may not have been acquired by Banks until some years later. The Banks mourning dress addition is not mentioned in Bullock's *Companions* until 1810, when it joins another part of a mourning dress which had been in Bullock's Museum at least since 1801 (Bullock, 1801, p. 9). Other items in Bullock's Museum which probably came from Banks are a Hawaiian feather cloak and helmet (purchased—not by Banks—at the sale of the Leverian Museum in 1806), a hook from a Tongan "rat safe," a double *putorino* (wind instrument) from New Zealand, and a *kotiate* (hand club) from New Zealand (see Kaeppler, 1974a).

Whether Banks gave any ethnographic objects that he collected while on Cook's first voyage to the British Museum is unknown. The first entry in the British Museum Register of such objects from Banks is not until 1778. This "collection of artificial curiosities from the South Sea Islands, from Joseph Banks, Esq." could include objects given to him by individuals who had been on Cook's second voyage, his own and those of others (such as his draftsman, Sydney Parkinson) from first voyage, or both. Again, there is no list of these objects, making it impossible to know how many there were, or which ones they are.

It is likely that Banks also gave individual objects that he or others brought back from the South Seas to various friends. One such recipient was probably Charles Greville, a son of the Earl of Warwick, who formed a collection at Warwick Castle. When this collection was sold in 1969, it included a number of early Pacific objects, including some from Hawaii. Although it is probable that at least some of these objects came from Cook's voyages, it is not possible to document them with certainty. Two pieces from the Warwick Castle sale are included in the introductory section of this exhibition, rather than in the main part of the exhibition, because a Cook voyage connection cannot be documented. The pieces included here have counterparts in known Cook voyage collections; however, other pieces that formed part of the Warwick Castle collection appear to be in a style later than that of the 1770's (Sotheby, 1969).

Cook and Banks, then, were the important ethnographic collectors of the first voyage. Their collections can be traced to Cambridge, Stockholm, and the British Museum. Objects in the British Museum cannot be identified by museum documentation alone,

Figure 51. — Joseph Banks, lithograph after a painting by Benjamin West.

but a number of them can be identified on the circumstantial evidence of drawings. A group of drawings by John Frederick Miller, some of which were subsequently engraved for the official account of the voyage (Hawkesworth, 1773), appear to depict specific objects now in the British Museum collection, and perhaps some in Cambridge. J. F. Miller is said to have been a draftsman employed by Banks, but it is not known whether he depicted objects that belonged to Banks or to the "official collection" of Cook (and perhaps Banks) that went to Lord Sandwich and, through the Lords of the Admiralty, to the National Collection. There is a similar problem with the objects depicted in the painting of Joseph Banks by Benjamin West (Fig. 51). The Tahitian chief's headdress painted by West is certainly the one now in the British Museum. The same headdress was depicted by Miller in Add. Ms. 15,508.18, and other objects of the same types as in the West painting are now also in the British Museum. In this case it is really unimportant whether they were collected by Cook or by Banks, because the first voyage provenance seems certain enough. Objects identified solely by depictions (of which there are also some from the first voyage in Wellington) will be so noted in the Catalogue.

Second Voyage on the Resolution *and the* Adventure *(1772-1775)*

Ethnographic collections from Cook's second voyage were larger and more systematic. It is likely that the curious nature of native manufactures was, by this time, more widely appreciated, and objects can be traced to a number of individuals on board both ships.

The British Museum received several collections. On October 6, 1775, Captain Cook gave to the Museum "a collection of artificial curiosities from the South Sea Islands." On June 7, 1776, the Museum was given "a collection of natural and artificial curiosities from the newly discovered islands in the South Sea, by Capt. James Cook and Charles Clerke." But even before Cook returned aboard the *Resolution*, a collection from the commander of the *Adventure* was given to the British Museum. This "collection from New Zealand and Amsterdam in the South Seas, consisting of 18 articles, Domestic and Military, brought by Captain Furneaux" was given by the Lords of the Admiralty on October 6, 1775. These three groups of items are even more difficult to isolate in the British Museum collection than those from the first voyage because there is no large series of drawings to which they can be compared—and most of the objects depicted in the engravings for the official account of the voyage belonged to the Forsters[14] and went elsewhere. It is not known if the collection given by Banks to the British Museum in 1778, mentioned above, included objects from first or second voyage, or both. Two other entries in the British Museum Register, because of their 1777 dates, must surely have also come from Cook's voyages: "Several utensil's manufactures, etc. from Otaheite and New Zealand: from Thomas Pell, Esq. of Wellclose Square" and "Two oars from New Zealand from Mr. Charles Smith of Woolwich." Who these individuals were and from whom their objects derived is unknown. The only hope of identifying the objects is by independent evidence for individual pieces.

Happily, independent evidence for identifying some objects from second voyage in the British Museum collection does exist. For example, that the Tahitian mourning dress was given by Cook was stated by George Forster in his published account of the voyage (1777, Vol. 2, p. 72). A Tongan panpipe in the British Museum (without accession information) can be traced to Cook's second voyage because it is described in a 1775 publication. This panpipe, as stated by Steele (1775) was given to him for analysis by Sir John Pringle, President of the Royal Society, who received it from Joseph Banks, along with a Tahitian nose flute. This panpipe is noted on an old label "Cook Coll." and it is likely that one of the nose flutes in the British Museum collection is the one described by Steele, but it cannot be identified.

A few other objects in the British Museum collection are certainly those depicted in a group of drawings done by Cleveley, an artist employed by Banks, including two Tongan baskets (British Library Add. Ms. 23,920.106 and 23,920.107) having no accession information. It is likely that this group of objects belonged to Banks because another object depicted by Cleveley (British Library Add. Ms. 23,920.110), a Tongan food hook, now in the National Museum, Wellington, was given by Banks to Bullock's London Museum and subsequently sold in 1819 to a Mr. Winn, whose descendant, Lord St. Oswald, gave it to Wellington in 1912 (Kaeppler, 1974a, p. 79). It is likely that the objects in the British Museum depicted by Cleveley were part of Banks's 1778 gift.

In addition to the objects Cook gave to the British Museum, contemporary accounts state that he gave a collection to Ashton Lever for his private museum, called the Holophusicon, located in Leicester Square (Kaeppler, forthcoming). Cook also must have again given collections to Lord Sandwich and King George III. Lord Sandwich again gave objects to Trinity College, at least some of which can be separated from his earlier gift from first voyage by labels dated 1775. This collection is now in the Cambridge Museum of Archaeology and Ethnology. Cook's gifts to George III joined the Royal collection and apparently some were transferred to the Imperial Institute, London (now Commonwealth Institute) and eventually to Wellington.

Some objects in the Hunterian Museum, Glasgow, are said to have been given to William Hunter[15] by Capt. Cook. The so-called Cook voyage collection in the Hunterian Museum, however, is yet another problem. The list of 30 objects drawn up by Anne Robertson[16] includes 16 objects which by style or provenance simply cannot be from Cook's voyages. Also in this group are two objects from Hawaii and two from the Northwest Coast of America which, because

[14]Reinhold and George Forster, father and son, were the official natural historians on Cook's second voyage.

[15]William Hunter (1718-1783) was an anatomist and owner of a large museum of anatomical and pathological collections as well as coins, medals, minerals, shells, and corals. The collection of Dr. Fothergill was added to Hunter's Museum in 1781, which contained Cook voyage material, including shells collected by Sydney Parkinson on first voyage.

[16]Former keeper of the Hunterian Museum, who catalogued the collection, but where this information came from is unknown.

of the third voyage provenances, could not have been given to Hunter by Cook. At least one of these last four, and perhaps others, came from Samwell's sale of 1781. Samwell, after sailing on Cook's third voyage, was a student at the Hunterian school in 1780-1781 (letter dated February 5, 1781, Gregson correspondence, Liverpool Public Library) and sold the remains of his collection in 1781—during which some objects were bought by William Hunter's brother John. In addition, a Captain Laskey was said to have purchased items for the Hunterian Museum at the 1806 sale of the Leverian Museum.[17] Laskey wrote an account of the Hunterian Museum (1813) in which he attributes a number of objects to Cook's voyages, which were keyed to his guide with letter labels. One such label was recently found on a Tongan paddle-shaped club marked "N," but this item was not on the Robertson list. Other Cook voyage objects in the Hunterian Museum may have come from the Forsters, for there is correspondence between the Forsters and William Hunter, and one of the New Caledonian clubs in the Hunterian Museum looks remarkably like one depicted in an engraving of New Caledonia objects in the official account. As will be seen below, these objects apparently belonged to the Forsters.

Finally, four objects, also not on the Robertson list, were given by a Captain King—two of which are from areas visited only on the second voyage, while King was only on third voyage. There would have been little difficulty for King to obtain objects from second voyage so it would seem that a Cook voyage provenance for these four pieces is possible. In the *Dictionary of National Biography* it is stated that "a manuscript was left by Hunter giving full details of his purchases for the Museum; a copy is in the department of antiquities in the British Museum." Unfortunately, the manuscript cannot be located. Taking account of the details above, I have drawn up a list of 19 objects in the Hunterian Museum that I feel reasonably sure can be attributed to Cook's voyages (see Appendix III). These are included in this Catalogue and eleven are in the exhibition.

Still other objects were said to have been given by Cook to William H. Pepys,[18] whose collection was sold in 1861 and several items from it are now in the British Museum, including some Tongan clubs and a New Zealand bone *patu*. Ten weapons now in the National Maritime Museum, Greenwich, were said to have been presented by Capt. Cook to Neil Malcolm of Poltalloch (Anon., 1958). Cook also kept a collection himself, which was inherited by his widow, including objects from the third voyage. Some of these she is said to have given away, for example, a group of nine objects given to Sir John Pringle[19]—given by him in 1781 to the Society of Antiquaries of Scotland, and now in the Royal Scottish Museum, Edinburgh. Other objects were given by Mrs. Cook to friends and to Ashton Lever, and still others were inherited by her relatives. Some of these latter specimens (including some from the third voyage) are now in the Australian Museum, Sydney; National Museum, Wellington; the British Museum; and the collections of John Hewett, London, and J. J. Laurent, Tahiti.

Reinhold and George Forster, besides collecting natural history specimens including a herbarium of "6-700 extremely rare species" (Misc. Mss. 1169, Turnbull Library, Wellington), systematically collected ethnographic specimens, and in their written accounts the Forsters tell of the actual collection of many of the items. It seems that, whenever possible, they collected two or more of each kind of item, just as they did with botanical specimens. From this large field collection of ethnographic specimens, a comprehensive museum collection was given by the elder Forster to the Ashmolean Museum and is now in the Pitt Rivers Museum, University of Oxford (Gathercole, n.d. [1970]). Some of the collection was retained by Forster until his death in 1798 and then was sold to the forerunner of the Institut für Völkerkunde, Göttingen, in 1799. Other pieces were acquired by museums in Berlin, Wörlitz, Danzig, Mitau (Latvia), a few additional pieces by Göttingen, and perhaps some by Florence (Kaeppler, 1977). Some specimens were also given to the British Museum by the Forsters, including the unique human hand carved of wood from Easter Island (EP 32), but if or how they are listed in the British Museum Register is unknown.

From objects so far identified, it appears that the pieces depicted in the engravings for the official account of Cook's second voyage belonged to the Forsters. Reinhold Forster had hoped to write the official account, but after a misunderstanding with the Admiralty, this did not occur. One drawing, presumably by George Forster although not credited to him, was probably finished before the misunderstanding, and was engraved and included in the official account. The engraving of the New Zealand artifacts, for example, includes the *toki pou tangata* and the scarifier now in the Forster collection in Oxford (both included in this exhibition), as well as the shell trumpet given by the Forsters to Thomas Pennant, and now in Cambridge. Pieces depicted in the Tongan, Marquesan,

[17] Part of Laskey's collection was sold at auction in July, 1808 (Chalmers-Hunt 1976, p. 71). The only artificial curiosity included was one club from the South Seas (Anon., 1808).

[18] Pepys (1775-1856), scientist and maker of surgical instruments, was a buyer at the Leverian sale of 1806 and his Cook voyage pieces could well have come from sales or from individuals who had been on any of the voyages, not necessarily the second.

[19] Sir John Pringle (1707-1782) was an influential physician and President of the Royal Society until 1778.

and New Caledonian plates are also in Oxford, probably including the New Caledonia cap, which, unfortunately, is now missing.

Furneaux, Captain of the *Adventure*, seems not to have collected extensively. In addition to the 18 pieces given to the Lords of the Admiralty and now in the British Museum, and possibly some given to the Royal Society, now also in the British Museum, the only specimens that can be traced to him today with certainty are four now owned by one of his collateral descendants[20] (Furneaux, 1960, p. 180). Previous to his voyage with Cook, Furneaux had visited Tahiti in 1767 as 2nd lieutenant under Captain Wallis on the *Dolphin*, and he could have collected Tahitian specimens at that time as well. Captain Furneaux may also have been the recipient of specimens brought by Omai, the Tahitian who traveled to England with Captain Furneaux, for the Tahitian stool in the Furneaux collection appears to be the one depicted with Omai in the portrait by Nathaniel Dance (Fig. 52). There was also a collection exhibited in "Mr. Pinchbeck's Repository . . . lately brought home with Omia . . . In His Majesty's Ship, The Adventure, Captain Furneaux" (see Anon., 1774). None of these items, however, can be located today. Omai may also have given Tahitian objects as gifts to his English hosts. For example, Omai was painted with Banks and Solander[21] by William Parry, at whose estate Omai was a guest. Indeed, it may be that objects from Omai (or Banks or Solander) were included in the sale of the estate of Gambier-Parry in 1971.[22]

Anders Sparrman,[23] scientific assistant to the Forsters, gave a collection of ethnographic specimens to Stockholm which are easily identifiable today (Söderström, 1939) and may also have given the second voyage objects now in Cape Town. James Patten, Surgeon on the *Resolution*, gave his collection to Trinity College, Dublin, which was later transferred to the National Museum of Ireland. However, because of the lack of precise documentation, and the existence of a third voyage collection given to the same institution by James King, it is difficult to tell which specimens were actually given by Patten.

Study of the collectors and collections made on Cook's second voyage leaves one with the uncomfortable feeling that he has been left with more questions than answers. For example, if there were ten Tahitian mourning dresses collected on second voyage, as stated by George Forster, who collected them and what happened to them? A nearly complete one collected by the Forsters went to Oxford and parts of another to Göttingen. According to George Forster, one collected by Cook went to the British Museum (1777, Vol. 2, p. 72), and the one in the Leverian Museum probably also came from Cook. In addition Cook retained a pearl shell chest apron from a mourning dress for himself, which is now in Sydney. Patten gave a nearly complete one to Dublin (now in Bishop Museum). This leaves at least five that cannot yet be associated with existing mourning dresses.[24]

Also noteworthy is the museum of George Humphrey, which was sold in 1779, that is, before the ships returned from third voyage. This museum included "the best and most extensive Collection of the Cloths, Garments, Ornaments, Weapons of War, Fishing Tackle, and other singular inventions of the Natives of Otaheite, New Zealand, and other new discovered Islands in the South Seas" (Humphrey, 1779, title page). The sale catalogue listed 182 lots of artificial curiosities from the South Seas. One of these gives us a clue as to where Humphrey obtained some of his collections. Lot 110 was "a cocoa nut, most elaborately carved, with the following inscriptions cut round the middle, 'John Frazier, on board the *Resolution*,[25] at present in the South seas 1774'" (Humphrey, 1779, p. 143). In a letter of September 29, 1775, Humphrey states, "I have laid out with the people of the *Resolution* principally for shells near £150" (Pulteney Correspondence, British Museum [Natural History]). It would appear that Humphrey simply went to the *Resolution* when it docked and bought whatever he could from whomever he could. He also may have made purchases from the *Adventure*, for it is said that he purchased an Imperial Sun shell from an officer of that ship which he sold to Ashton Lever for £10.10s (De Barde, 1814, p. 48). Humphrey was primarily a collector and dealer in shells and unfortunately he does not make direct reference to his ethnographic specimens. He must have obtained one of the Tahitian mourning costumes from the second voyage, however, because lots 119,

[20] A Tahitian stool, a New Zealand *patu*, and two Tongan clubs.

[21] Daniel Solander (1733-1782), a Swedish scientist who worked with Banks and traveled on Cook's first voyage.

[22] For example, a carved object from the Australs and a Tahitian food pounder now in the Ortiz collection, Geneva.

[23] Sparrman (1748-1820), a Swedish naturalist resident in Cape Town, traveled on Cook's second voyage.

[24] There are relatively complete mourning dresses whose history cannot be precisely documented in Exeter, and Florence; and mourning dress parts of unknown provenance in Cambridge, Oxford (in addition to the Forster one), British Museum (in addition to Cook's gift, including a shell chest apron from the London Missionary Society), Wellington, Perth (Scotland), and the Hooper Collection. There are also parts in Berne and Leningrad from Cook's third voyage. In Saffron Walden, given by Joseph Tickell in 1836, is a part which may have come from a James Tickle who sailed on the third voyage (Beaglehole, 1967, Part 2, p. 1475). A complete mourning dress in Berlin is attributed—on unreliable evidence—to Bougainville. A nearly complete one from Humphrey's museum was broken up in five lots and sold in 1779. Humphrey also sold one to Göttingen in 1782, but its origin is unknown. Some of these may account for the five "missing" from Cook's second voyage.

[25] Frazier (or Frazer) was ship's corporal (Beaglehole, 1961, p. 882).

Figure 52. — Portrait of Omai by Nathaniel Dance.

120, 121, 123, and 125 of the thirty-first day of the sale comprise a nearly complete costume (1779, p. 144).

Most of the ethnographic specimens from Humphrey's museum have not been traced. Twenty-two of the lots were thought by Fox and Sherborn to have been purchased by George Allan and become part of the Hancock Museum, Newcastle.[26] But the annotated version of the Humphrey sale catalogue in the Kroepelien Collection, Oslo University Library, shows that this is incorrect. This important annotated catalogue indicates that Ashton Lever purchased at least seven lots of ethnographic specimens from Humphrey's sale. This is verified by Humphrey in his notes in his own copy of the Leverian Museum sale catalogue now in the Newton Library, University of Cambridge. Many of the lots in the annotated 1779 Humphrey catalogue do not have purchaser's names, and these are almost impossible to identify today.

Humphrey and Ashton Lever (among others) purchased a large number of artificial curiosities at the March, 1776, sale of Samuel Jackson, probably collected by George Jackson, carpenter's mate on the *Resolution* (Anon., 1776). Some of Humphrey's purchases were probably sold in the 1779 sale of his museum. Lever's purchases became part of his museum (sold in 1806). The others are so far untraceable.

Finally, two collections sold in 1777 must have included second voyage material. One of these, the collection of Mr. Joshua Platt, included objects from New Zealand, New Amsterdam, New Caledonia, and Tahiti. The other included "singular inventions of the Otaheitians." The fate of these sale catalogues or the collections that were sold is unknown.[27]

There is still much work to be done on the ethnographic collections from Cook's second voyage.

Third Voyage on the Resolution *and the* Discovery *(1776-1780)*

On the third voyage there were no official natural scientists, yet even more collections were made. On the return of the third voyage, the demand was again for natural history specimens, but the supply was in ethnographica, as admitted by Samwell in a letter to Gregson:

> . . . most people I daresay have been disappointed for very few natural Curiosities have been brought home, there were not above 3 or 4 persons in the two ships who made any collection of that sort, from the great length of the voyage great part of those have been destroyed one way or other—as to artificial Curiosities we were not so badly off (letter dated October 23, 1780, Liverpool Public Library).

John White,[28] also in a letter to Gregson registers his disappointment.

> When I came on board was never more Disappointed—as I saw but one baskett of shells and not a Single bird—Instruments of warr and dresses of the Natives seem'd the only cargo they had brought not an Insect, or animal could I find Except one Starved Monkey (letter dated October 18, 1780, Liverpool Public Library).

---

[26] Sherborn (1905, p. 263) states "It [Humphrey sale catalogue now in the British Museum (Natural History)] was no doubt the copy marked by George Allan himself when purchasing from Humphrey's Museum, as there are lines in the margin as mentioned by Mr. Fox."

[27] These two sale catalogues are listed in the book catalogue of the Edge-Partington Library (1934). The bookseller, Francis Edwards, Ltd., does not have a record of to whom they were sold. Any information about them would be appreciated.

[28] Possibly the Rev. John White, brother of the naturalist, the Rev. Gilbert White.

Of all the ethnographic collections made on third voyage, the only ones traceable as a separate series are a collection now in Leningrad, possibly made by Anderson, and one in Berne made by John Webber (Kaeppler, 1977). Besides the collection given to his ancestral home city, Webber also gave pieces to the British Museum and, it appears, to P. J. de Loutherbourg, who staged the pantomime "Omai: or A Trip round the World" (O'Keeffe, 1785) at Covent Garden. These latter pieces were sold with other objects from Loutherbourg's estate by Mr. Coxe in 1812 and are today untraceable.

Banks was again the recipient of several collections. Surgeon Anderson had willed only his natural history specimens and papers to Banks; however, if there were any artificial curiosities left after the possible gift to the Russians, they probably went to Banks as well. Indeed, Samwell says that Anderson's "curiosities," both "natural and artificial," were left to Banks (Beaglehole, 1967, Pt. 2, p. 1130). Also according to Samwell, one of his friends, the surgeon's mate on the *Resolution* (probably Davies), had promised his collection to Banks (letter from White to Gregson dated October 18, 1780, Liverpool Public Library). Clerke, commander of the expedition after Cook's death, died at sea and left "all curiosities natural and artificial" to Banks (Beaglehole, 1967, Pt. 1, p. clxv). These collections, and particularly those of Clerke, must be the nucleus of Joseph Banks's 1780 gift to the British Museum; "A collection of artificial curiosities from the South Sea Islands, the West coast of North America and Kamchatka; lately brought home in His Majesty's ships *Resolution* and *Discovery*." Some of these objects, notably the Hawaiian bowl with human images (HAW 46), are mentioned by King in the third volume of the official account of the voyage (Beaglehole, 1967, Part 2, p. 1084) as a gift to Captain Clerke from a chief of Kauai.

At the same time, but with a separate entry, were listed "Several natural and artificial curiosities from the South Seas: from John Gore, Esq. Commander of the *Resolution,* James King, Esq. Commander of the *Discovery,*[29] James Burney, Lieut. Phillips, Lieut. Roberts, Mr. William Pickover and Mr. Robert Anderson, gunners, and Mr. Thomas Waling, quartermaster." A few days later there was another gift to the British Museum, "Several artificial curiosities from the South Sea from Captain Williamson, Mr. John Webber, Mr. Cleveley, Mr. William Collett and Mr. Alexander Hogg." I suggest that these two latter groups of objects, along with Cook's gift from the second voyage, constitute the so-called "Cook Collection" in the British Museum. While the Banks gift of 1780 may constitute the so-called "Banks collection" at the British Museum, it is also possible that this designation was assigned to a later collection given by Banks to the British Museum, to separate it from objects from Cook's voyages.

Unfortunately, these collections have never been sorted out—there are only random labels and varied notes on registration slips made much later, such as four Hawaiian feather necklaces (HAW 112), noted "Banks No. 15," and a Hawaiian boar tusk bracelet (HAW 156), noted "Cook Collection No. 26." There are no known catalogues or lists to which these numbers correspond, and all of the pieces may no longer be in the British Museum.[30] All of these specimens, along with others not from Cook's voyages, were catalogued in the British Museum much later in an areal/numerical series, and inclusion or omission in this series is no guide to a Cook voyage provenance. The specimens from the Northwest Coast of America catalogued as NWC 1-117 have traditionally been known as the "Banks Cook Collection." However, as seen above, they probably constitute at least two separate series and, indeed, some of the objects included in NWC 1-117 came from Capt. Dixon, who collected them on the Northwest Coast and gave them to Banks, who gave them to the British Museum in 1789, and some others from Menzies who sailed on Vancouver's voyage. To add to the confusion, in 1781 "A large collection of natural and artificial curiosities being the Museum of the Royal Society" was given to the British Museum—at that time Joseph Banks was president of the Royal Society. And finally, in 1782 Banks gave "A vest and a pair of boots, which belonged to the King of Tsutsky." The 1781 and 1782 dates suggest that these were from Cook's third voyage.

Still other items attributed to Banks and others found their separate ways to the British Museum. Some Hawaiian and Tahitian bark cloth (British Museum specimen number +6896, No. 18 of the Bateman collection) was "given to White Watson of Bakewell by Sir Joseph Banks who brought them from thence when he accompanied Capt. Cook in his first voyage round the world" (British Museum Registration slips). A Hawaiian barbed wooden spear (1946. Oc.1.1) was said to have been "thrown into the boat when Captain Cook was murdered." It was brought to England by Thomas Bean (who sailed on the *Discovery,* see Beaglehole, 1967, Pt. 2, p. 1473), "whose wife was nurse to Thomas Green and gave it to her master." A hook ornament for a Hawaiian necklace from the Beasley Collection (1944.Oc.2.715) "was brought from the South Seas by Mr. Alex Dewar, who accompanied

[29] At the death of Capt. Clerke, John Gore (an American) became Commander of the expedition and Capt. King became Commander of the *Discovery.*

[30] Some objects may have been exchanged.

Capt. Cook as clerk to the ship on two voyages and witnessed his death at Owhyee, 14 Feb. 1779." His inclusion on two voyages as clerk is confirmed by Beaglehole (1967, Pt. 2, p. 1461). On October 12, 1896, Sydney H. Tonks, Esq., gave a "little specimen of native cloth brought home by Capt. Cook from the Sandwich Islands of Owhyee and Otaheite. My dear mother, who was very intimate and in some distant way related to the widow of Captain Cook, used to call it 'Otaheitee cloth.' M. J. Adams, 3 April 1889." Mrs. Adams[31] gave the cloth to Mrs. Tonks.

I have attempted to sort this all out. The tentative results are listed in this Catalogue. Details on the Hawaiian objects will be elaborated in a forthcoming article in the British Museum yearbook.

The most important collection of the third voyage, however, was doubtless that of Cook himself. With no special provision in his will for such objects, one would suggest that these items might go to his Patron, Lord Sandwich, and to his widow. Indeed, in a letter addressed to Lord Sandwich by the Hon. Daines Barrington,[32] it is clear that, although Lord Sandwich might be the rightful recipient, Cook had, in fact, meant his collection for Ashton Lever's Museum. Barrington says:

> I take the liberty of informing your Lordship that the specimens of Natural History collected in this last voyage were destin'd both by Capt. Cook and the late Capt. Clerke for Sr. Ashton Lever's Museum, the strongest proof of which Capt. Cook had shewn by sending six Birds from the Cape to Leicester Fields. As the Captains Gore & King may therefore be expected almost daily, may I beg that they may be directed to give such specimens at least were collected during the lives of Capt. Cook & Capt. Clerke . . . [that] they may not be misus'd after their reaching an English Port. The Specimens can no where receive such complete justice as Leicester House, which from the vast additions lately made, may be truly said to be a national honour (Beaglehole, 1967, Pt. 2, p. 1558).

Clerke's specimens probably went to Banks because of the provision in Clerke's will, but Lever was doubtless the recipient of Cook's Collection, for Lever made a public announcement to this effect in a newspaper dated January 31, 1781:[33]

> Sir Ashton Lever has the pleasure to inform the public, that through the patronage and liberality of Lord Sandwich, the particular friendship of Mrs. Cook, and the generosity of several of the Officers of the voyage, particularly Captain King and Captain Williamson, besides many considerable purchases he himself has made, he is now in possession of the most capital part of the curiosities brought over by the Resolution and Discovery in the last voyage. These are now displayed for public inspection; one room, particularly, contains magnificent dresses, helmets, idols, ornaments, instruments, utensils, etc. etc. of those islands never before discovered, which proved so fatal to that able navigator, Captain Cook, whose loss can never be too much regretted.

This clipping indicates that some objects from the collections of King, Williamson, and Mrs. Cook also went to Lever's museum, the Holophusicon. These collectors are acknowledged again in the *Companion* to the Leverian Museum (1790). Lever is also said to have had first choice of the astronomer Baily's collection before the balance was sold by an advertisement in the newspaper.[34]

Engravings for the official account of the third voyage appear to depict objects that were at one time in the Leverian Museum, and thus were primarily things that belonged to Cook himself. The drawings for the engravings were done by Webber, who also made a large number of drawings of objects that were not engraved. Some of these drawings appear to have been used by Loutherbourg for the costumes for his stage play about Omai and some of them were kept throughout Webber's lifetime and sold at auction in 1793 (Christie's, 1793). Many of Webber's drawings are now in the British Library Manuscript Room, included in folios with drawings from the first and second voyages. All of the objects depicted in these drawings that I have been able to trace so far appear to have been at one time in the Leverian Museum.

George Humphrey again went to the ships when they docked and bought whatever he could.[35] No doubt, at least some of the ethnographic specimens he bought became part of the collection he sold to Göttingen in 1782.

Samwell sold his large collection by public auction in June, 1781.[36] This sale included approximately 400 ethnographic specimens, 56 lots of natural history specimens, including 9 birds, 2 ostrich eggs, one lot of geological specimens, and more than 100 shells and corals. Among buyers of ethnographica at the sale were Ashton Lever, George Humphrey, and John

[31] There were several Adams descendants, apparently related to Mrs. Cook through her cousin, Mrs. Ursula Cragg, whose daughter Mary married Dr. P. James Adams (McFadgen, pers. comm.).

[32] A lawyer and antiquary who was on the Council of the Royal Society and a friend of Lord Sandwich.

[33] The clipping without the name of the newspaper is in the Perceval Bequest in the Fitzwilliam Museum, Cambridge, England.

[34] "Mr. Baily whom you mention was astronomer on board the Discovery, as he had a salary of £400 a year no one had the least Idea that he would have disposed of his collection in the manner he did—therefore I never thought of applying to him and when he advertised them in the newspaper neither Mr. White nor I had the good Luck to see the advertisement tile the 2d day of sale" (Letter from Samwell to Gregson dated November 1, 1780, Liverpool Public Library). Unfortunately we do not know who bought them.

[35] Including at least 87 shells which he sent to Mr. Seymer on December 9, 1780 (Pulteney correspondence, British Museum [Natural History]).

[36] Samwell was the "Discovery Officer" mentioned by Whitehead, 1969, p. 176 and Fig. 1; and Dance, 1971, p. 368.

Hunter.[37] It may have been at this sale that Alexander Shaw obtained some of the tapa for his catalogues of bark cloth specimens (Shaw, 1787). Humphrey's purchases became part of the collection he sold to Göttingen and Hunter's probably went to his brother William's collection, now the Hunterian Museum, Glasgow (perhaps through their nephew Dr. Matthew Baillie). Samwell is also said to have given a collection to the writer Anna Seward, who passed at least some of it on to Doctor Richard Greene of Litchfield for his private museum. After Greene's death the arms and armor in his collection were purchased by William Bullock and the balance by W. H. Yate. At a later date the collection came into the hands of Richard Wright, grandson of Dr. Greene, who dispersed the contents in 1823, and these are now untraceable. Also in Greene's museum there were objects from Cook's voyages given by the Earls of Uxbridge and Donegall (Greene, 1786, p. 77).

Three items collected by William Griffin, cooper of the *Resolution,* are now in the National Maritime Museum, Greenwich. Lt. James Burney did not give all his objects to the British Museum because Mrs. Thrale, a friend of the Burney family, had a court dress which "was copied in a Spitalfields loom from one of Captain Burney's specimens from Owhyee" (Ellis, 1907, p. 266). What happened to the rest of Burney's objects is unknown.

Occasionally other individual pieces are traceable to one of the voyages, such as a Maori whale bone comb now in the collection of John Hewett engraved on the inside "James King, Newszealand, Feb. 12, 1777." A Hawaiian feather image from the Fuller collection and now in the Field Museum is said to have come from a "Bate family." William Bates of Yorkshire sailed on Cook's third voyage, but a connection between the two Bateses cannot be established.

There is also the problem of other reputed, but undocumented, "Cook collections," such as the one in Florence and the Worden Hall collection. The provenance of the Florence specimens indicate mainly a third voyage collection; however, there is no precise documentation on how the collection got to Florence or who collected it. At least some of it was in Florence by 1785 when it is referred to in print in an Elegy of Captain James Cook (Gianetti, 1785, p. 87). A detailed account of this collection and its history can be found in Kaeppler, 1977. Likewise, the Worden Hall collection has traditionally been thought to be from Cook's voyages, but the collector is not known. An old document entitled "Some Account of the Curiosities" lists 25 objects which by style and type could all be from Cook's third voyage—the objects from Hawaii and Northwest Coast of America being noted as "new discovered." Some of these objects are now in Christchurch and are included in this Catalogue, since the evidence seems strong enough. The entire list is included in Appendix II.

Some of the information about the collectors and subsequent owners of Cook ethnographica is still confused. It should be emphasized that the documentation of many so-called Cook specimens is still sketchy and this becomes progressively worse as it becomes more and more fashionable to attribute ethnographic specimens to Cook's voyages. Anything remotely connected with Cook can be sold at a high price, even if the connection is logically impossible. For example, in 1972 Christie's auction house in London sold a club which was "traditionally held to be the weapon which gave Captain James Cook the fatal blow" (Christie's, March 27, 1972, p. 15) with a manuscript "setting out the history of the club." According to the *Sun Herald* of Sydney, February 13, 1972, Banks "took possession of the club immediately after the killing." This club is a Tongan club, and by its style probably 19th century. It is rather unlikely that Cook would be killed with a Tongan club, and outright impossible that Banks could have taken possession of it when he was several thousand miles away. The club, sold for 1,000 guineas, has now joined the roster of weapons that purportedly killed Cook—one of which is included in the introductory section to this exhibition.

It is time to take a fresh look at the specimens and journals of Cook's voyages for what they are—some of the most important documents for scientific knowledge of the Pacific—and to examine each and every specimen individually. Before objects are attributed to Cook's voyages they must be traced to the voyages by documentation or, if the documentation is lacking, it must be stated on what logical grounds the attribution is made. In many cases the specimens and their documentation are widely separated and the owners of the objects do not know of the existence of helpful documentation. For example, the pieces collected by William Griffin in the National Maritime Museum, Greenwich, are referred to in a bookseller's catalogue now in the Dixson Library, Sydney (Griffin Papers); and the photographs that relate specimens in the Australian Museum to Cook's voyages are in a private collection in England. Only by painstaking examination of hearsay evidence, objects, drawings, and other forms of documentation will erroneous attributions be eliminated and the ethnohistory of Cook's voyages be advanced. The information on all Cook voyage objects known, as far as I have been able to sort it out, is included here. Not all detail or conclusions on significance are included and the reader is referred to my past and forthcoming studies.

[37]John Hunter (1728-1793) anatomist and surgeon, brother of William Hunter (mentioned above) and owner of a museum on health and disease. Originally located in Leicester Square, it formed the basis of the Museum of the Royal College of Surgeons in 1800.

Exposition of the Native Manufactures Collected on the Three Pacific Voyages of Captain Cook

More than 2,000 ethnographic artifacts—"artificial curiosities"—were collected on the three Pacific voyages of Captain Cook. Of some artifact types there are many examples; of others there is only one known example; while of still others there are depictions but no known surviving examples. It is the task of this Catalogue to list all artifact types known to have been collected on the voyages and to inventory the known examples of each artifact type. It is, in effect, a "Catalogue Raisonné" of ethnographic objects with a Cook voyage provenance. Not all of the artifact types could be included in the exhibition—though an attempt was made to include as many as possible—and it is hoped that this exposition will not only give a reliable picture of the present location of authenticated Cook voyage materials, but also indicate the extent and scope of ethnographic types collected on Cook's voyages.

In this Catalogue objects are listed by area, and within each area, by artifact type. Their present location is given along with accession numbers and appropriate dimensions, if known. Most of the objects I have examined myself, with the exception of some that were not readily available in Göttingen or Stockholm, or all possible ones in the British Museum. I have not seen the objects in Cape Town, or a few that are in private collections. I have carefully weighed all the documentary evidence for Cook voyage attribution associated with the collections and elsewhere. Summary evidence for Cook voyage provenance is given for each object. Those with circumstantial connections to Cook's voyages are so noted, and in passing, some remarks are made about objects which have been attributed to Cook's voyages on the basis of unreliable evidence. References to 18th century depictions are given and literature is cited which is relevant to Cook voyage attribution. Some of the detail for Cook voyage attribution is given in my earlier and forthcoming publications and it would be superfluous to repeat it here. The reader is referred to past publications for details. The information for all objects noted "Leverian Museum" will be included in my forthcoming volume, *Captain James Cook, Sir Ashton Lever, and Miss Sarah Stone* to be published by Bishop Museum Press.

The task of assembling comparable data on more than 2,000 objects has been, to say the least, a bit difficult, especially as some objects were consistently unavailable. It is hoped that the reader will forgive minor inconsistencies, and the lack of detail on the objects in Göttingen, which Dr. Manfred Urban did not wish me to publish.

Please note that the objects exhibited are identified by the symbol .

The collections from which the objects come are referred to in a shortened form. The full citations for the shortened forms are listed here.

Abbotsford = Abbotsford House, Galashields, Melrose, Roxburghshire, Scotland.
Auckland = Auckland Institute and Museum, Auckland, New Zealand.
Susanne Bennet = Susanne Bennet, Washington, D.C.
Berlin = Museum für Völkerkunde, Berlin-Dahlem, Germany.
Berne = Bernisches Historisches Museum, Berne, Switzerland.
Bishop Museum = Bernice Pauahi Bishop Museum, Honolulu, Hawaii.
British Museum = Museum of Mankind, The Ethnography Department of the British Museum, London, England.
Cambridge = University Museum of Archaeology and Ethnology, Cambridge, England.
Cape Town = South African Museum, Cape Town, South Africa.
Chicago = Field Museum of Natural History, Chicago, Illinois.
Christchurch = Canterbury Museum, Christchurch, New Zealand.
Cuming Museum = Cuming Museum, Southwark District Library, London.
Dublin = National Museum of Ireland, Dublin, Ireland.
Dunedin = Otago Museum, Dunedin, New Zealand.
Edinburgh = Royal Scottish Museum, Edinburgh, Scotland.
Exeter = Royal Albert Memorial Museum, Exeter, England.
Florence = Museo Nazionale di Antropologia e Etnologia, Florence, Italy.
Furneaux = Furneaux collection, England.
Glasgow = Hunterian Museum, University of Glasgow, Glasgow, Scotland.
Göttingen = Institut für Völkerkunde der Universität, Göttingen, Germany.

Greenwich = National Maritime Museum, Greenwich, England.
John Hauberg = John H. Hauberg, Seattle, Washington.
John Hewett = John Hewett collection, England.
Hooper = Hooper collection, England.
Laurent = Jean-Jacques Laurent, Papeete, Tahiti.
Leipzig = Museum für Völkerkunde, Leipzig, German Democratic Republic.
Leningrad = Peter the Great Museum of Anthropology and Ethnography, Leningrad, U.S.S.R.
Liverpool = Merseyside County Museum, Liverpool, England.
London School of Economics = London School of Economics and Political Science, London, England.
de Menil = Menil Foundation, Houston, Texas.
Mitchell Library = Mitchell Library, State Library of New South Wales, Sydney, Australia.
New Orleans = Isaac Delgado Museum, New Orleans Museum of Art, New Orleans, Louisiana.
George Ortiz = George Ortiz collection, Geneva, Switzerland.
Oxford = Pitt Rivers Museum, University of Oxford, England.
Rome = Museo Nazionale Preistorico Etnografico "Luigi Pigorini," Rome, Italy.
Saffron Walden = Saffron Walden Museum, Saffron Walden, Essex, England.
Salem = Peabody Museum, Salem, Massachussetts.
Severson = Mr. and Mrs. Don Severson, Honolulu, Hawaii.
Stockholm = Etnografiska Museet, Stockholm, Sweden.
Sydney = Australian Museum, Sydney, Australia.
Truro = Truro County Museum and Art Gallery, Truro, Cornwall, England.
Vienna = Museum für Völkerkunde, Vienna, Austria.
Wellington = National Museum, Wellington, New Zealand.
Whitby = Whitby Museum, Whitby, Yorkshire, England.
Wörlitz = Staatliche Schlösser und Gärten, Wörlitz, German Democratic Republic.

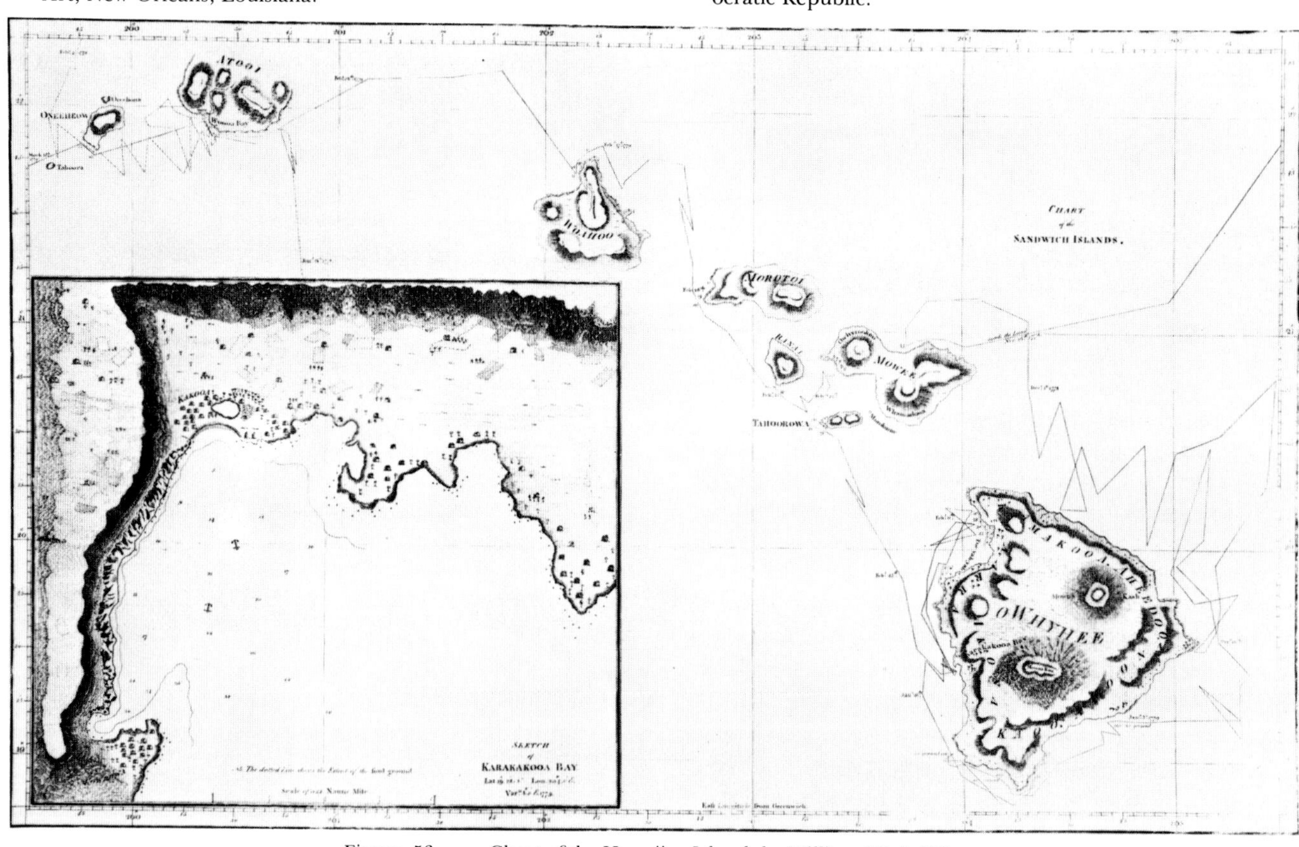

Figure 53. — Chart of the Hawaiian Islands by William Bligh (59).

OWHYHEE OR THE SANDWICH ISLES (THE HAWAIIAN ISLANDS)

European discovery of the Hawaiian Islands was made on January 18, 1778, on Captain Cook's third voyage. During the course of the voyage, the ships spent more than three months in the islands, primarily off Kauai and Hawaii (Fig. 53). Cook considered the Hawaiian Islands one of his most important discoveries and named the archipelago in honor of his patron, Lord Sandwich, First Lord of the Admiralty. Cook was initially treated as a god by the Hawaiians and was given offerings and gifts appropriate to his assumed station (Fig. 54). In addition, a thriving trade between Hawaiians and Cook's officers and men developed. Gifts and trade resulted in an enormous number of Hawaiian artifacts being taken to England, and these objects are crucial in establishing the style and scope of Hawaiian material culture at the time of European contact. Unlike other Pacific island groups, which often had contact and trade among themselves, before European contact the Hawaiian Islands may have been isolated from outside influence for as long as 500 years, when oceangoing voyages between Hawaii and southern Polynesia appear to have ceased.

Figure 54. — An offering before Captain Cook, by John Webber.

Thus, the objects collected in Hawaii on Cook's third voyage exhibit an end point in the evolution of a material culture that is rare in world ethnography—having evolved from ancestral styles probably derived from the Society Islands and the Marquesas Islands without further outside influence. Every Hawaiian object that can be traced to collection on Cook's voyage adds important information to the emerging picture of this society, in which material culture was a visual symbol of status, rank, and power.

Although Hawaii was visited only on the third voyage, there is a large number of objects from Hawaii and a plate of Hawaiian artifacts was engraved for the official account of the voyage (Fig. 55). The objects collected are primarily those of a spectacular nature, or objects significantly different from their counterparts in southern Polynesia. For example, although there are numerous pieces of featherwork, there are no stone food pounders (which abound in Tahitian collections). Although there are numerous pieces of bark cloth, there is only one bark cloth beater. There are several daggers and shark tooth implements, but no nose flutes. There are bowls with human images, but few baskets. One wonders if the Europeans consciously collected things that were different from those they had collected in other places; if Hawaiians were loath to trade things they needed every day; or if the items traded are related to where the interaction between Hawaiians and Europeans took place. If a food pounder or bark cloth beater was traded, everyday activities would be interrupted, whereas, if the bark cloth itself was traded, more could easily be made the next day. Feathered objects could be given away or traded (by chiefs)—they were not needed often and new ones could be made. Household objects are rare—no pillows, no *lomilomi* massage sticks—while fishhooks and weapons are relatively abundant. In short, the objects traded were primarily those things that were carried or worn, or those appropriate to Cook's status as a god.

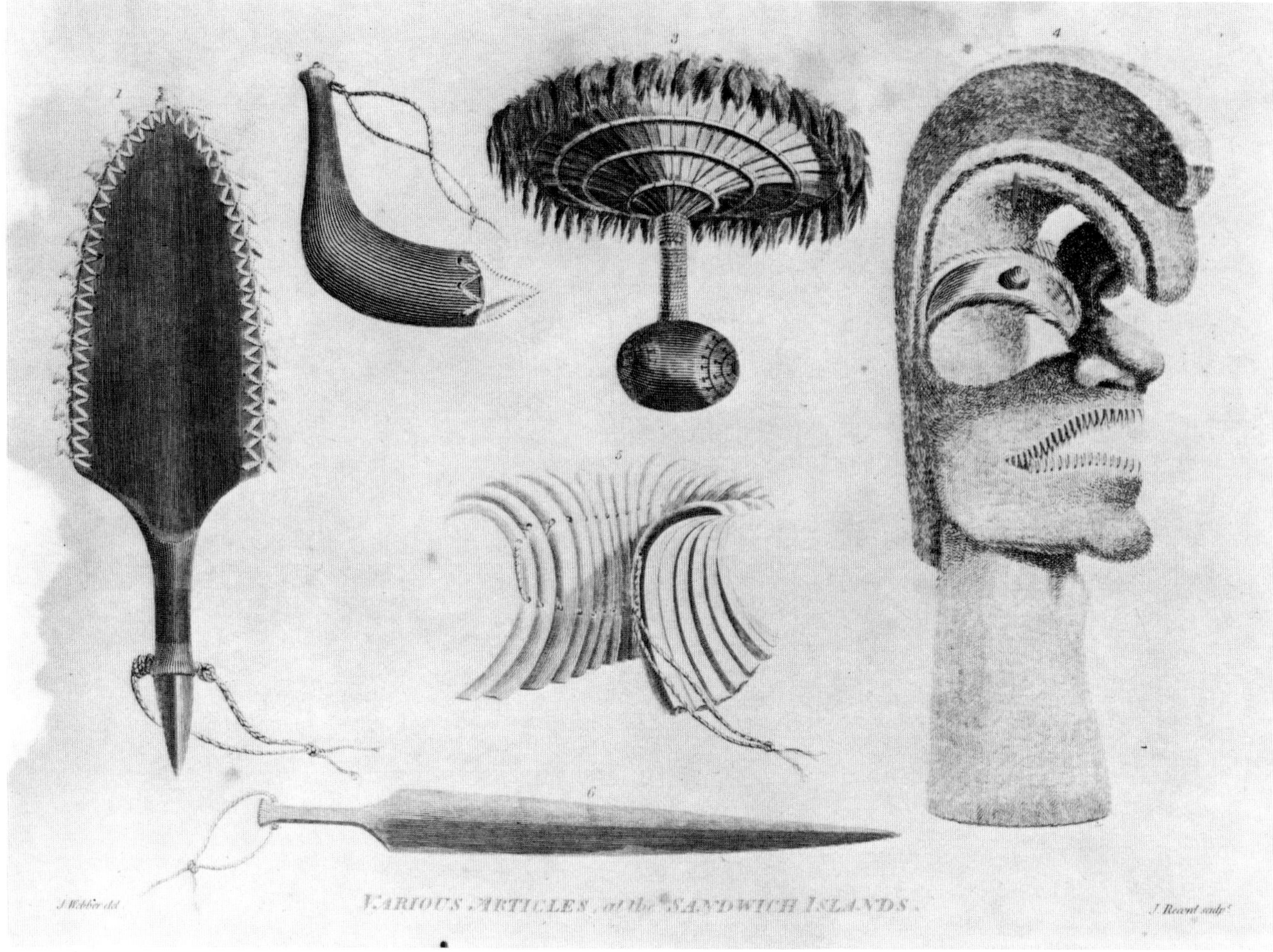

Figure 55. — "Various Articles, at the Sandwich Islands." Plate 67 of *Atlas* to Cook's third voyage.

In view of this apparently selective collecting, a general inventory of Hawaiian material culture cannot be derived from objects collected on Cook's voyage. The objects are, however, crucial to our understanding of the style and scope of certain kinds of material culture at the time of first contact with Europeans. In general terms, it should be noted that the range of variation within an artifact type was greater during Cook's visits, and that some of the variants that existed at the time became almost standardized by the end of the 18th century, while other variants disappeared—this being particularly apparent in featherwork. The question of absence of certain artifact types cannot be elaborated here, nor can we explore the reasons why some artifact types are found only in Cook voyage collections. Rather, it is hoped that this inventory will be useful as data for future studies of the social and economic roles of material culture in Hawaiian society, and of the history of taste in 18th century European society among collectors of such "artificial curiosities."

One of the revelations of research on Hawaiian collections from Cook's voyages is the extent and variation of Hawaiian featherwork. Eight feather images, at least 30 feather cloaks and capes, numerous feather *lei*, plus rare or unique feathered objects about which little is known, extend our knowledge of pre-European Hawaiian featherwork. If these pieces had not been collected at the time, they would have been used and worn out, and knowledge of them today would be nonexistent. The specialized skill necessary for fabrication, and the aesthetic genius of Hawaiians in making use of this colorful part of their environment, speak eloquently of the artistic mastery employed by Hawaiians in fashioning objects of sacred and ceremonial use. The perfection of technique and the variation in form and design are unsurpassed by any Pacific peoples and emphasize the long separation of Hawaii from its parental featherworking techniques in the Society and Marquesas Islands. The use of feather coverings on basketry foundations and flexible netted backings is known in southern Polynesia, notably in the Society Islands, where feather-covered basketry headdresses and breast gorgets, as well as the feather capes and tassels from mourning costumes, can be considered as suitable prototypes for Hawaiian images, helmets, capes, and *lei*. The more numerous birds of colorful plumage found in Hawaii provided possibilities for extending and developing these ancestral forms.

Feather Images

At least eight feather images were collected on Cook's third voyage. Five of these can be traced to the voyage without question, while for two of the others there is circumstantial evidence of Cook voyage provenance.[1] A subtype, of which there are two specimens, has human hair. Feather images are usually referred to as Kūkā'ilimoku, a representation of the god of war. As this appears unlikely for those images collected on Cook's voyages (see Kaeppler forthcoming), they are not here described with this term.[2]

⛵ 1. Feather image, Vienna (202). Height 56 cm. Figures 56 and 57.
Evidence for Cook voyage attribution: Leverian Museum.
Literature: Brigham, 1899, p. 38; Moschner, 1955, pp. 230-231.

2. Feather image (with hair), Berlin (VI 253). Height 62 cm. Figure 58.
Evidence: Leverian Museum
Depiction: Sarah Stone drawing in Force and Force, 1968, p. 27.
Literature: Kaeppler, 1971, p. 199; 1974a, pp. 75, 81.

3. Feather image, British Museum (VAN 231). Height 1 m, 2 cm.
Evidence: Leverian Museum
Depictions: *Atlas* to Cook's Third Voyage (Cook and King, 1784), Plate 67 (Fig. 55); British Library Add. Ms. 15,514.27. Force and Force, 1968, p. 23.
Literature: Force and Force, 1968, p. 22; Kaeppler, 1971, p. 198.

4. Feather image (with hair), British Museum (HAW 78). Height 63 cm.
Evidence: Leverian Museum
Depiction: Force and Force, 1968, p. 25.

5. Feather image, Göttingen (OZ 254).
Evidence: Purchased from London dealer George Humphrey in 1782.[3]
Literature: Plischke, 1929.

6. Feather image, Chicago (272591). Height 26.5 cm.
Evidence: Circumstantial. Tradition of Bate family (from whom it was purchased by A.W.F. Fuller) that it came from Cook's voyage. A "Bates" sailed on Cook's third voyage and a "Bates" was a purchaser at the sale of the Leverian Museum, but no direct links can be traced.
Literature: Force and Force, 1971, p. 82.

7. Feather image, British Museum (LMS 221). Height 104 cm.
Evidence: Circumstantial. Accession information from London Missionary Society notes that it was in the Leverian Museum.

8. Feather image. Lost.
Evidence: Leverian Museum.

"Idol's Eyes"

The use of the so-called idol's eyes is unknown. Made of a flat *'ie'ie* base with a shell eye-white and seed pupil, the eyes are sometimes in pairs. Three pairs of idol's eyes were entered in the Leverian Museum sale catalogue, but have not been located.[4]

⛵ 1. "Idol's eyes," Dublin (1885.189). Diameter 13.5 cm. Figure 59.
Evidence: Circumstantial. Thought to be part of the collection given by Captain King to Trinity College, Dublin. Noted "Cook collection."
Literature: Freeman, 1949, p. 8; Ball, 1894 [1895], p. vi.

2. "Idol's eye." Present location unknown. Formerly in the collection of James Backhouse, York; later in Beasley collection. Diameter about 15 cm.
Evidence: Circumstantial. Said to have been given by Mrs. Cook to Ann Gates, who gave it to Ann Smith, who gave it to Jane Backhouse.
Literature: Brigham, 1903, p. 8.

[1]Other feather images have been attributed to Cook's voyage without proper assessment of the documentary evidence. For example, the feather image in Wellington (FE 325) is regularly attributed to Cook (Brigham, 1918, p. 45; Barrow, 1972, p. 153; Murray-Oliver, 1975, p. 132) but it has been shown that this attribution cannot be confirmed (Kaeppler, 1974a, pp. 69, 76, 77).

[2]Native names used for most Hawaiian artifacts today are usually derived from 19th century specimens or literature. In many cases the 18th century derivation of these terms is not understood and most of them will not be used in this catalogue so that misunderstandings of this sort will not be perpetuated. No attempt has been made to describe the objects in detail, the emphasis here being the evidence that associates the objects with Cook's voyages. For descriptions, uses, and methods of manufacture, see Buck, 1957.

⛵ Objects included in the exhibition.

[3]After Cook's visits no ships called in Hawaii until 1786.

[4]Two sets of idol's eyes in the British Museum (each with five disks—HAW 109 and 110) have no accession information. Although a Cook voyage provenance is possible, no evidence can be found to confirm this.

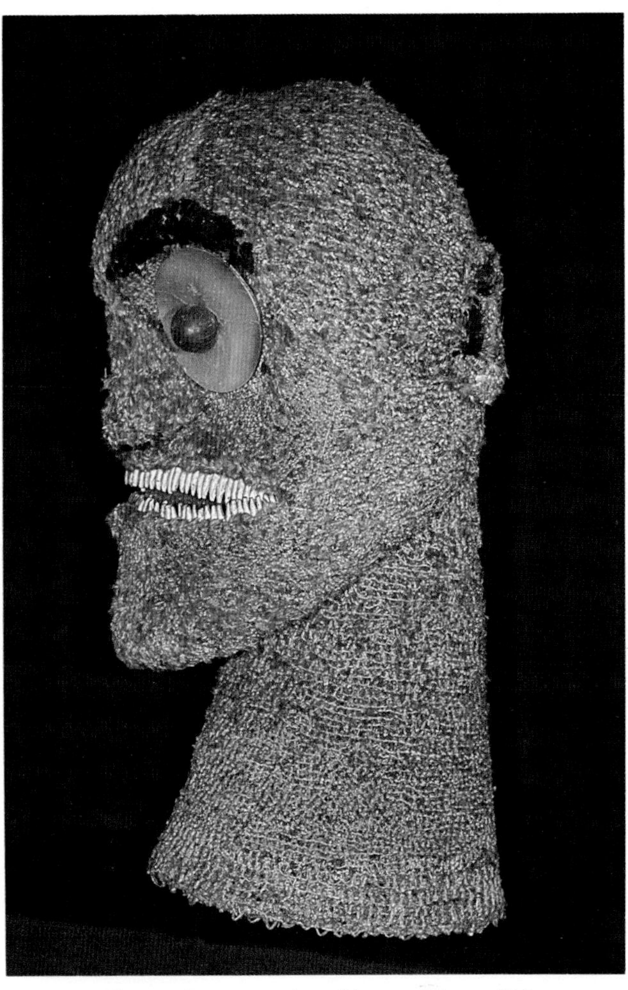

Figure 57. — Feathered image, Vienna 202.

Figure 58. — Feathered image, Berlin VI 253.

Figure 56. — (Opposite page) Feathered image (detail), Vienna 202.

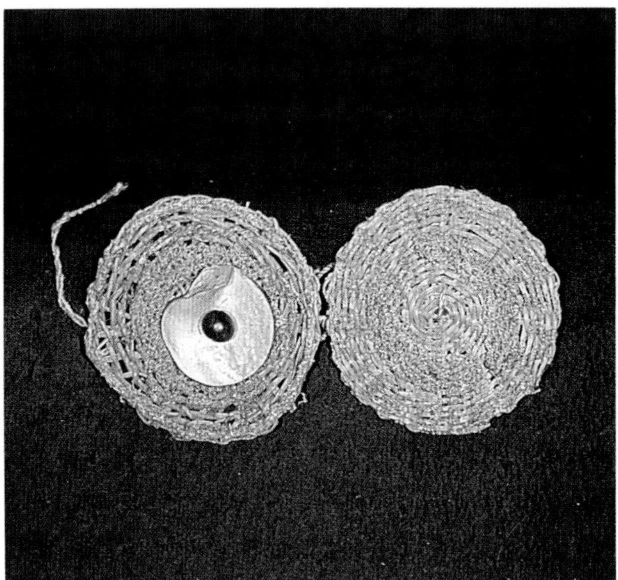

Figure 59. — Idol's eyes, Dublin 1885.189.

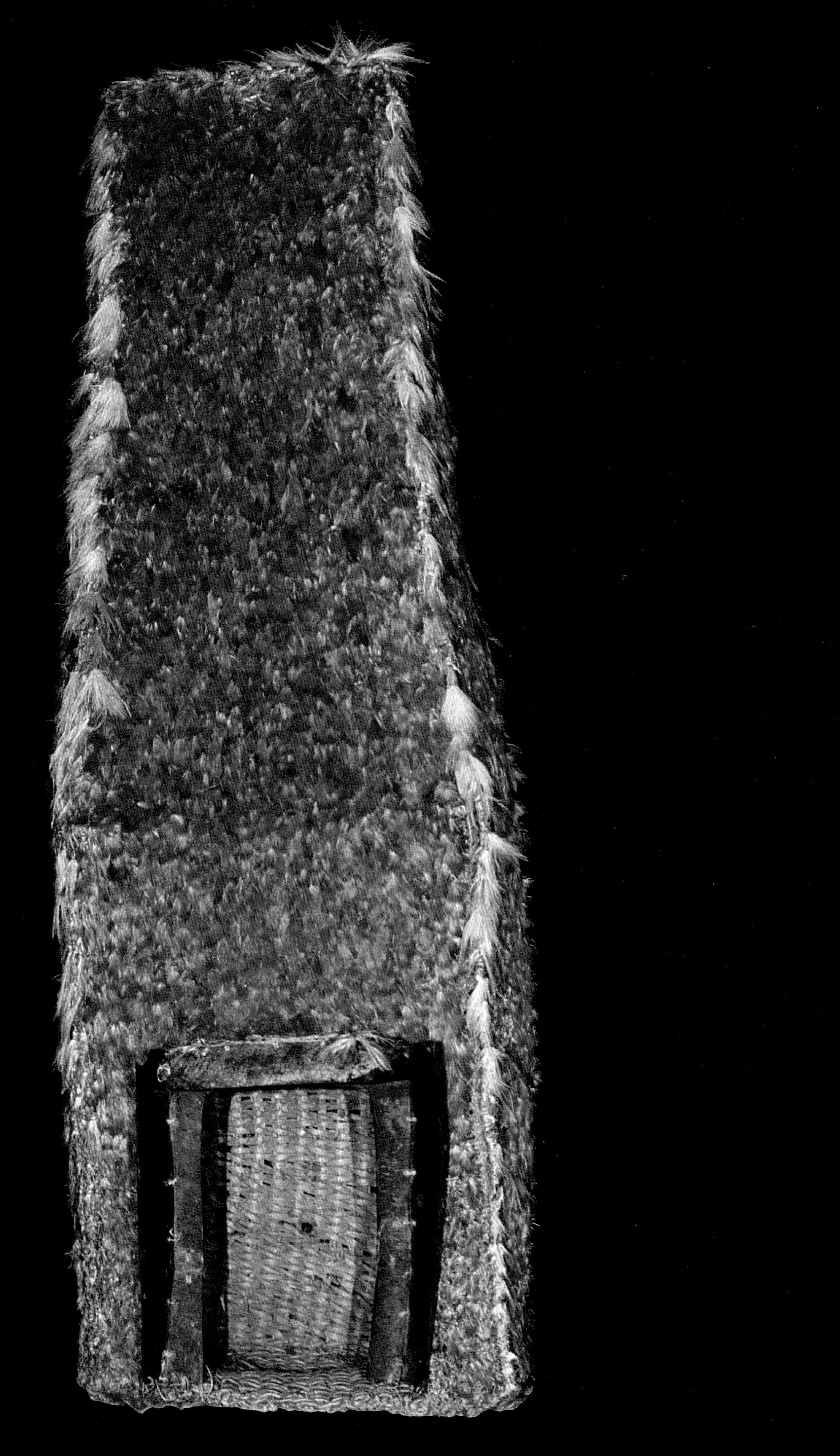

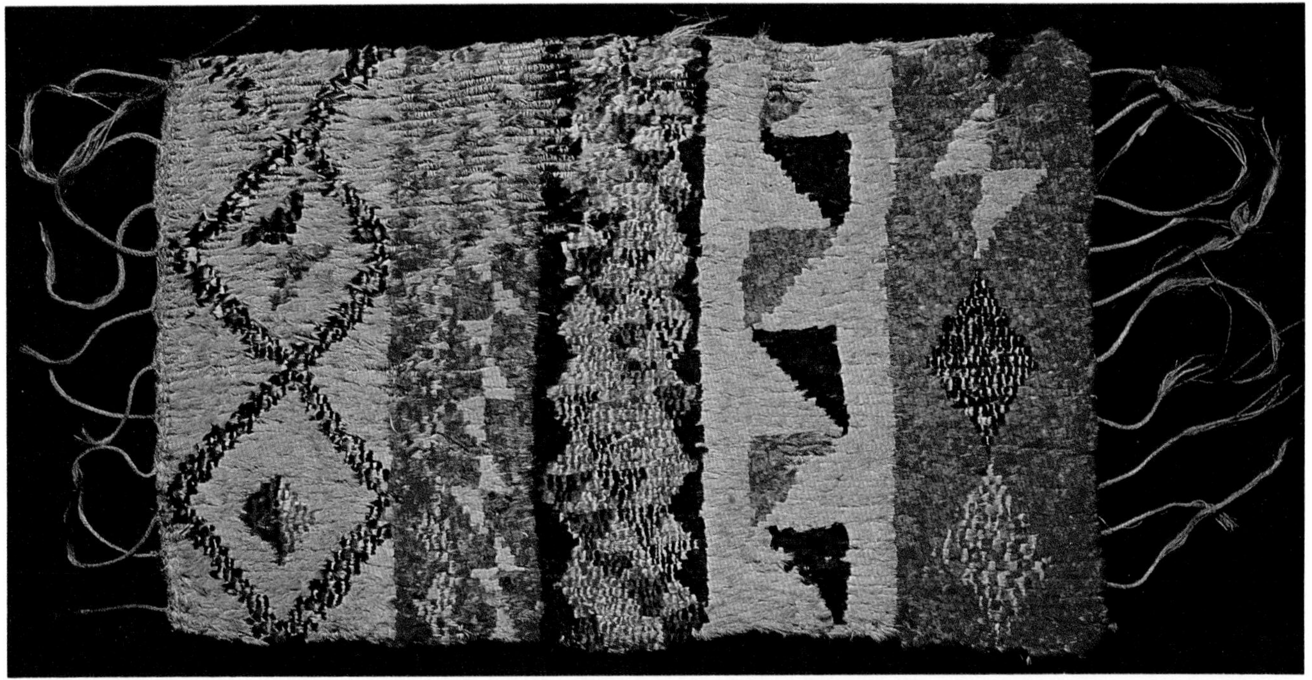

Figure 61. — Feathered apron, British Museum (NN).

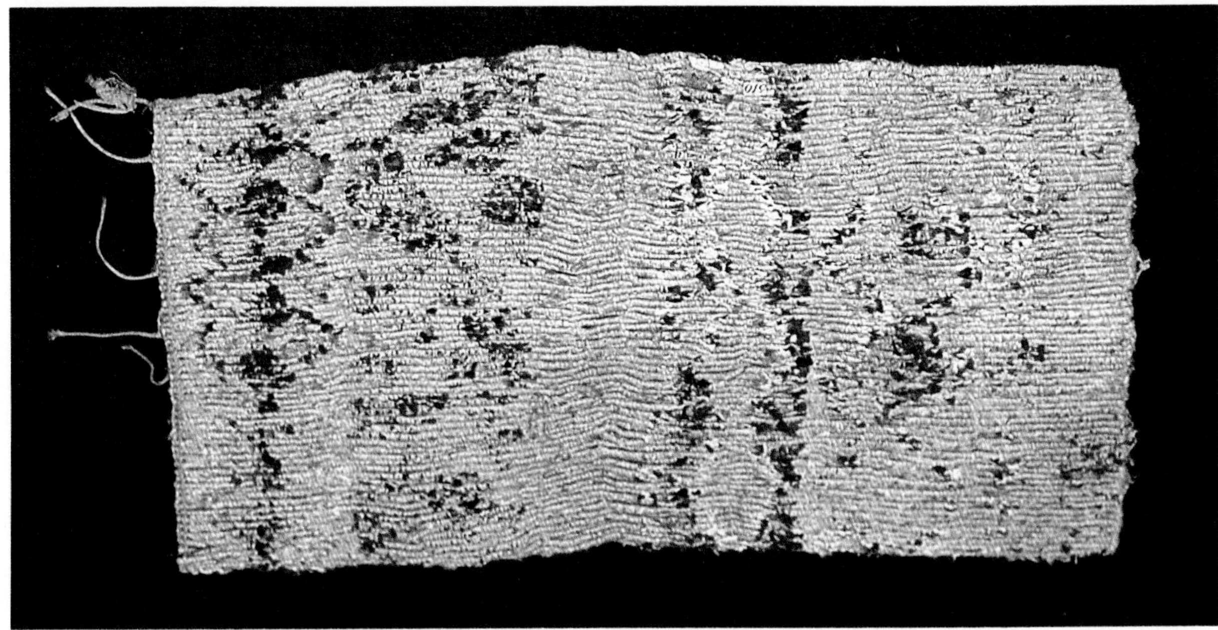

Figure 62. — Feathered apron, Dublin 1882.3904.

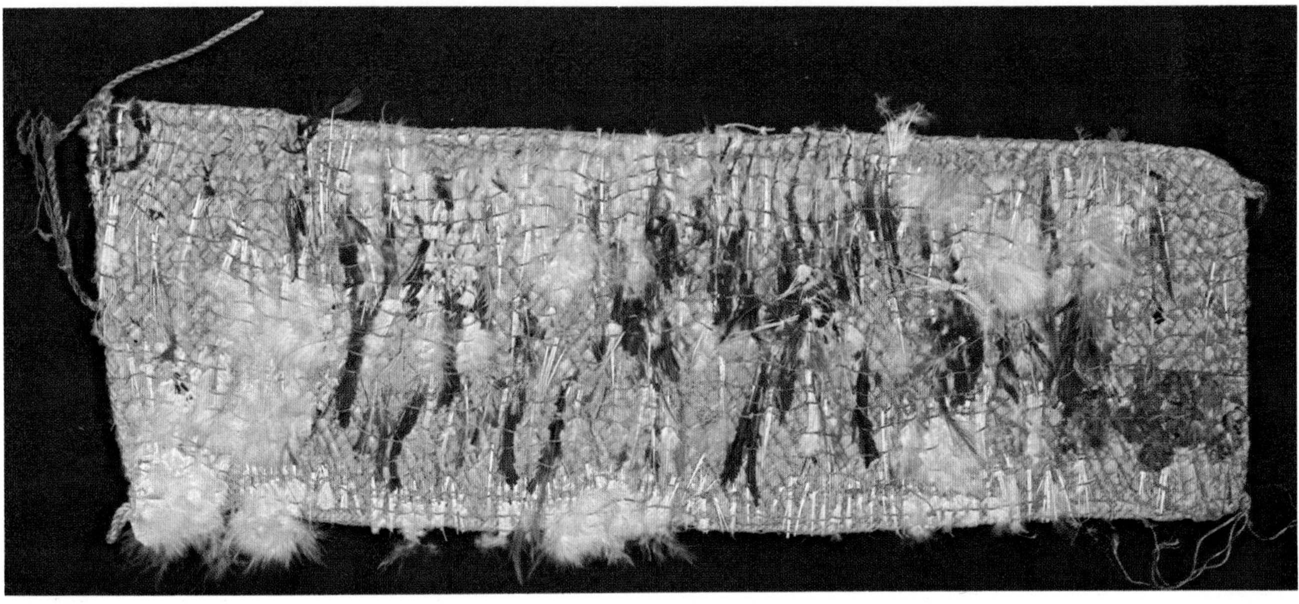

Figure 63. — Feathered apron, Leningrad 505-15.

'igure 60. — (Opposite page) Feathered temple, Vienna 203.

Figure 64. — Kalani'opu'u Bringing Presents to Cook, by John Webber.

Figure 65. — Feathered cloak, Wellington FE327.

Figure 66. — Feathered cape, Sydney H104.

Feathered Temple

A feathered temple collected on Cook's voyage is unique. Its use is unknown, but the similarity in construction to feather images may indicate a similar function, that is, a dwelling place to which gods could be called by prayers or offerings. The *'ie'ie* foundation covered with red and yellow feathers has a turtle shell door frame.

1. Feathered temple, Vienna (203). Height 58 cm. Figure 60.
   Evidence: Leverian Museum
   Depiction: Force and Force, 1968, p. 29.
   Literature: Brigham, 1899, pp. 29-30; Force and Force, 1968, p. 28.

Feathered Aprons

Another artifact type collected on Cook's voyage has not been satisfactorily explained. Usually known as feathered mats, these objects seem likely to have been worn, because they have loops and lacings reminiscent of Hawaiian ankle ornaments. Two of these feathered objects were in the Leverian Museum (Force and Force 1968, pp. 62-63) but cannot now be traced.[5] The specimen in the Dublin collection is called an "apron," a term that will be used here. It is possible that they

[5] Two such objects, similar in design, are in the British Museum. They are unnumbered and have no accession information to associate them with Cook or the Leverian Museum. One is illustrated here in Figure 61.

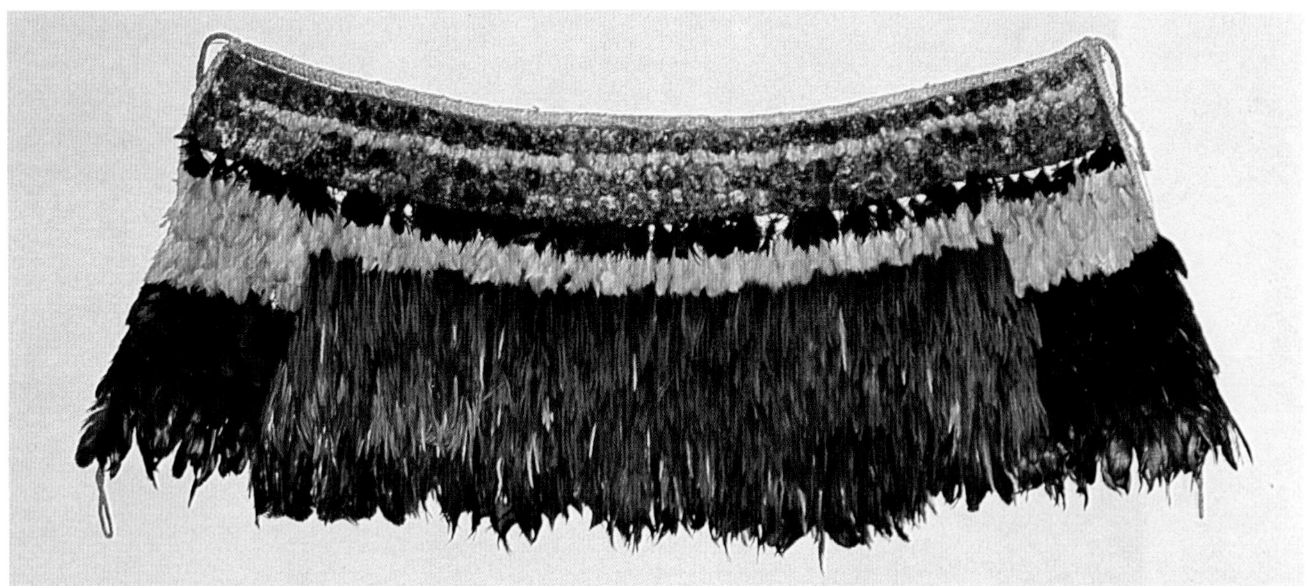

Figure 67. — Feathered cape, Vienna 180.

served as protective garments worn across the chest or stomach with feather cloaks.

1. Feathered "apron," Dublin (1882.3904). Length 53 cm. Figure 62.
   Evidence: Circumstantial. Thought to be part of the collection given by Captain King to Trinity College, Dublin. An old label "510" is attached.
   Literature: Freeman, 1949, p. 8.
2. Feathered "apron," Leningrad (505-15). Length 42 cm. The apron consists of a piece of matting overlain with threads and feathers on both sides. Figure 63.
   Evidence: Given by Captain Clerke to the Governor of Kamchatka.
   Literature: Rozina, 1966, p. 242; Kaeppler, 1977.

Feathered Cloaks and Capes

Feathered cloaks and capes collected on Cook's third voyage are surprisingly varied in color, form, and method of manufacture when compared with those collected in later times. The large number collected on the voyage indicates that they were relatively abundant in the 18th century and may suggest that they were sought after because they were significantly different from anything previously encountered on the voyages. At least 30 were collected on Cook's voyage.[6] On one occasion, the "official reception" of Cook by Kalaniʻopuʻu, six or seven cloaks and capes were given to Cook along with other important feather pieces,

> At Noon Terreeoboo in a large Canoe attended by two others set out from the Village, & paddled towards the Ships in great state. In the first Canoe was Terreeoboo, In the Second Kao with 4 Images, the third was fill'd with hogs & Vegetables, as they went along those in the Center Canoe kept Singing with much Solemnity; from which we concluded that this procession had some of their religious ceremonys mixt with it; but instead of going on board they came to our side, their appearance was very grand, the Chiefs standing up drest in their Cloaks and Caps, & in the Center Canoe were the busts of what we supposed their Gods made of basket work, variously covered with red, black, white, & Yellow feathers, the Eyes represent'd by a bit of Pearl Oyster Shell with a black button, & the teeth were those of dogs, the mouths of all were strangely distorted, as well as other features; we drew out our little guard to receive him, & the Captn observing that the King went on shore, followd him. After we had got into the Markee, the King got up & threw in a graceful

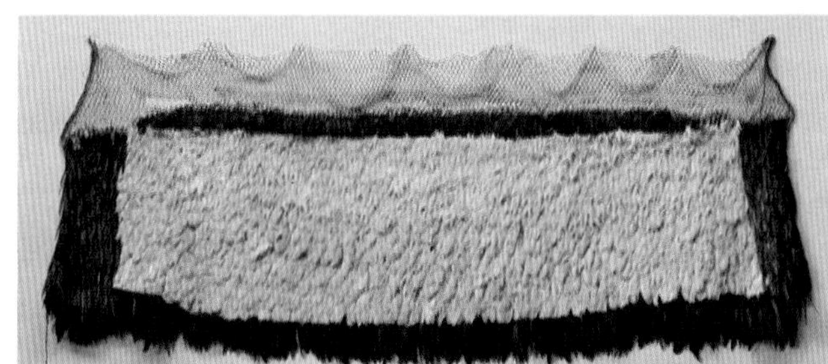

Figure 68. — Feathered cape, Vienna 181.

[6] Several others are known to have been in the Leverian Museum, but they cannot be traced.

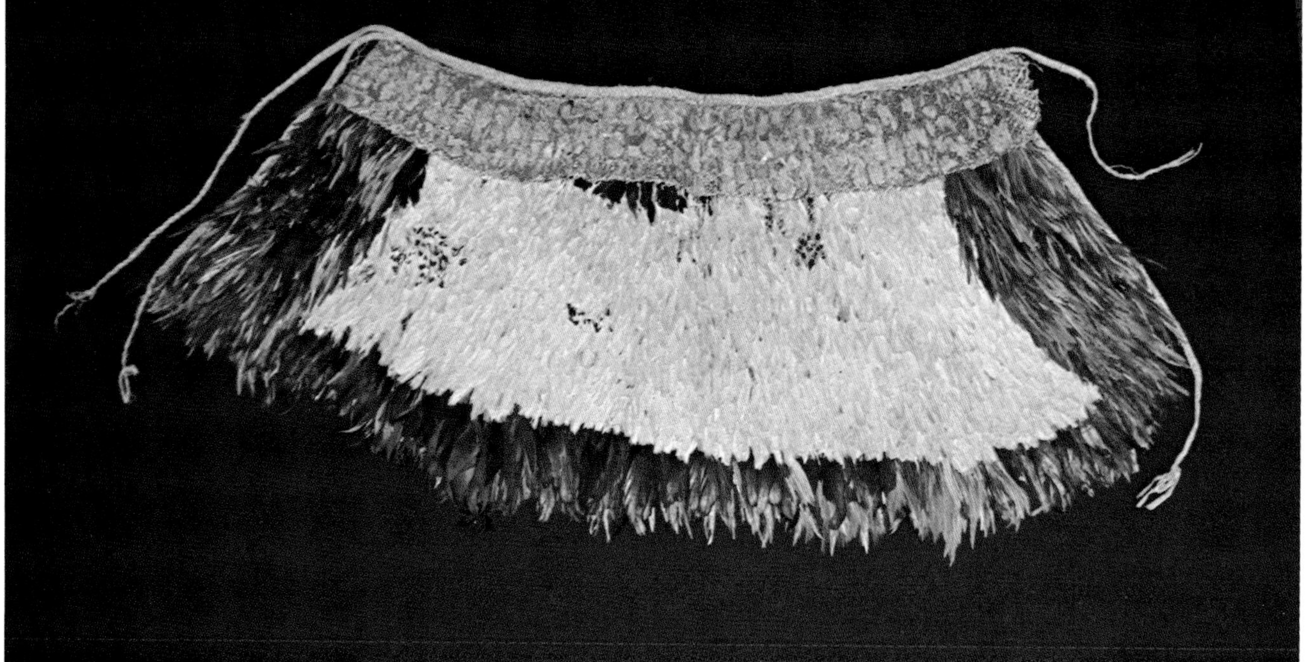

Figure 69. — Feathered cape, Leningrad 505-9.

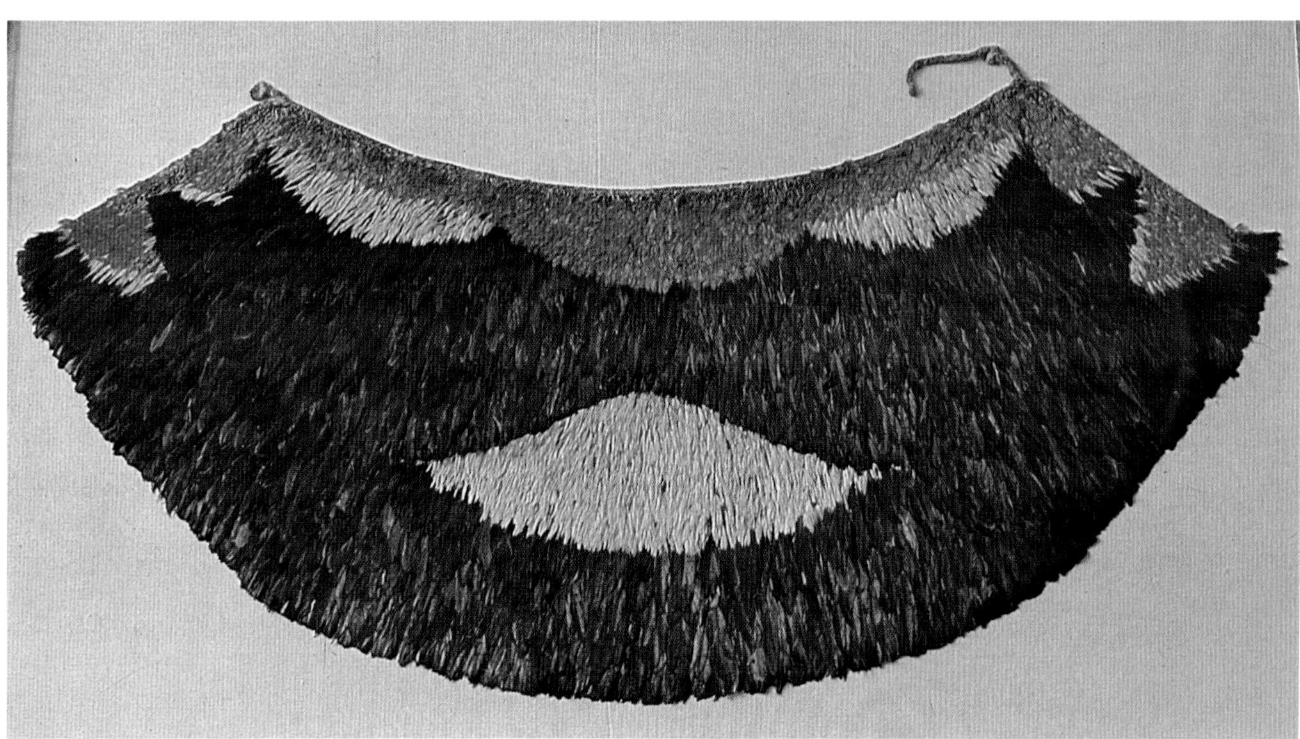

Figure 70. — Feathered cape, London School of Economics.

Figure 71. — Feathered cape, Vienna 179.

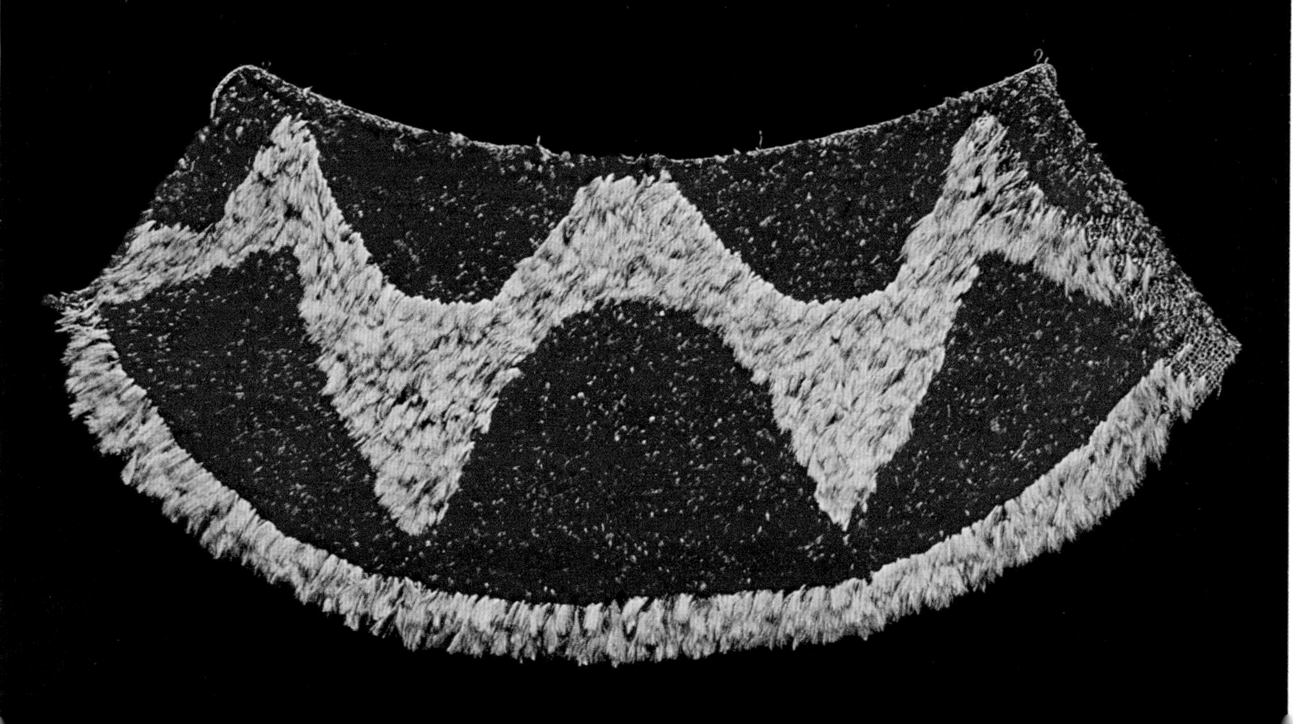

Figure 72. — Feathered cape, Bishop Museum 1977.206.04.

Figure 73. — Hawaiian man in cape and helmet, engraving after John Webber.

manner over the Captns Shoulders the Cloak he himself wore, & put a featherd Cap upon his head, & a very handsome fly flap in his hand: besides which he laid down at the Captains feet 5 or 6 Cloaks more, all very beautiful, & to them of the greatest Value; his attendant brought 4 large hogs, with other refreshments which were also presented.

The occasion was depicted by Webber (Figure 64).

1. Feathered cloak (long with straight neckline), Wellington[7] (FE 327). Length 152 cm. Figure 65.

   Evidence: Leverian Museum. Given by Kalani'opu'u to Captain Cook on January 26, 1779, on the occasion described and depicted.

   Depictions: Force and Force, 1968, p. 41. Possibly the cloak depicted by Johan Zoffany[8] in his painting, *The Death of Captain Cook,* ca. 1795 (Fig. 31).

   Literature: Brigham, 1918, p. 42; Kaeppler, 1971, p. 200; 1974a, pp. 75, 78.

[7] A feather cloak and cape in Wellington (FE 326 and FE 6380) have also been attributed to Cook (Brigham, 1918, pp. 42-44), but it has been shown that the attributions cannot be confirmed (Kaeppler, 1974a, pp. 73, 76, 77).

[8] Johan Zoffany (1733-1810) was born in Germany, but became an important painter of Georgian England.

2. Feathered cloak (long with straight neckline), Berne (HAW 1). Length 150 cm, width 182 cm.
   Evidence: Collected by Webber, official artist on Cook's third voyage.
   Literature: Brigham, 1899, p. 64; Henking, 1957, pp. 361-362; Kaeppler, 1977.

3. Feathered cloak (long). Lost.
   Evidence: Leverian Museum.
   Depiction: Force and Force, 1968, p. 43.

4. Feathered cape (medium length with straight neckline), Sydney (H 104). Length 61 cm; width 129 cm. Figure 66.
   Evidence: Cook collection exhibited at the Colonial and Indian Exhibition (see Appendix I for an account of this exhibition). The cape is unique in that the *'i'iwi* feathers are overlaid by the long tail feathers of red and white tropic birds and black cock feathers.
   Literature: Mackrell, 1886; Brigham, 1899, p. 76, 1918, p. 12.

5. Feathered cape (medium length with straight neckline), Leningrad (505-12). Length 71 cm, width 188 cm.
   Evidence: Given by Captain Clerke to the Governor of Kamchatka.
   Literature: Rozina, 1966, pp. 235-236; Kaeppler, 1977.

6. Feathered cape (straight neckline). Lost. Length 60 cm, base 129 cm. Formerly in Göttingen, stolen in 1932.
   Evidence: Purchased from London dealer Humphrey in 1782.
   Literature: Brigham, 1899, p. 76.

7. Feathered cape (medium length with straight neckline). Lost. Formerly in the Staatliches Museum für Völkerkunde, Dresden. Length 122 cm, width 319 cm. The main color of the cloak was green.
   Evidence: Leverian Museum.
   Depiction: Force and Force, 1968, p. 51.
   Literature: Kaeppler, 1971, p. 199; 1974a, pp. 76, 85.

8,9,10. Feathered capes (medium). Lost.
   Evidence: Leverian Museum.
   Depictions: Force and Force, 1968, pp. 45, 49, 53.

11. Feathered cape (trapezoidal with bark cloth band at top edge covered with pieces of bird skin with feathers adhering), Vienna (180). Length 42 cm, width 112 cm. Figure 67.
   Evidence: Leverian Museum.
   Depiction: Force and Force, 1968, p. 55.
   Literature: Brigham, 1899, p. 76; Moschner, 1955, p. 234.

12. Feathered cape (trapezoidal, formerly with a band at the top, now missing), Vienna (181). Length 45 cm, width 126 cm. Figure 68.
   Evidence: Leverian Museum.
   Depiction: Force and Force, 1968, p. 57.
   Literature: Brigham, 1899, p. 76; Moschner, 1955, p. 234.

13. Feathered cape (trapezoidal with mat band at top edge covered with pieces of bird skin with feathers adhering), Leningrad (505-9). Length 44 cm, width 124 cm. Figure 69.
   Evidence: Given by Captain Clerke to Governor of Kamchatka.
   Literature: Brigham, 1918, p. 9; Rozina, 1966, pp. 238-239; Kaeppler, 1977.

14. Feathered cape (trapezoidal with bark cloth band at top edge covered with pieces of bird skin with feathers adhering), British Museum (VAN 234). Length 38 cm, width 117 cm.
   Evidence: Leverian Museum.
   Literature: Kaeppler, 1971, p. 198.

15-16. Two feathered capes (trapezoidal). Lost.
   Evidence: Leverian Museum.
   Depiction: Force and Force, 1968, pp. 53,[9] 61.

17. Feathered cape (straight neckline), London School of Economics. Length 40 cm, width 103 cm. Figure 70.
   Evidence: Leverian Museum.
   Depiction: Force and Force, 1968, p. 56.

18. Feathered cape (straight neckline), Vienna (179). Length 27 cm, width 92 cm. Figure 71.
   Evidence: Leverian Museum.
   Depiction: Force and Force, 1968, p. 57.
   Literature: Brigham, 1899, pp. 75-76; Moschner, 1955, pp. 233-234.

[9] A feather cape in the British Museum (NN) without accession information is much like this drawing; however, no evidence can be found to confirm an association between it and the Leverian Museum.

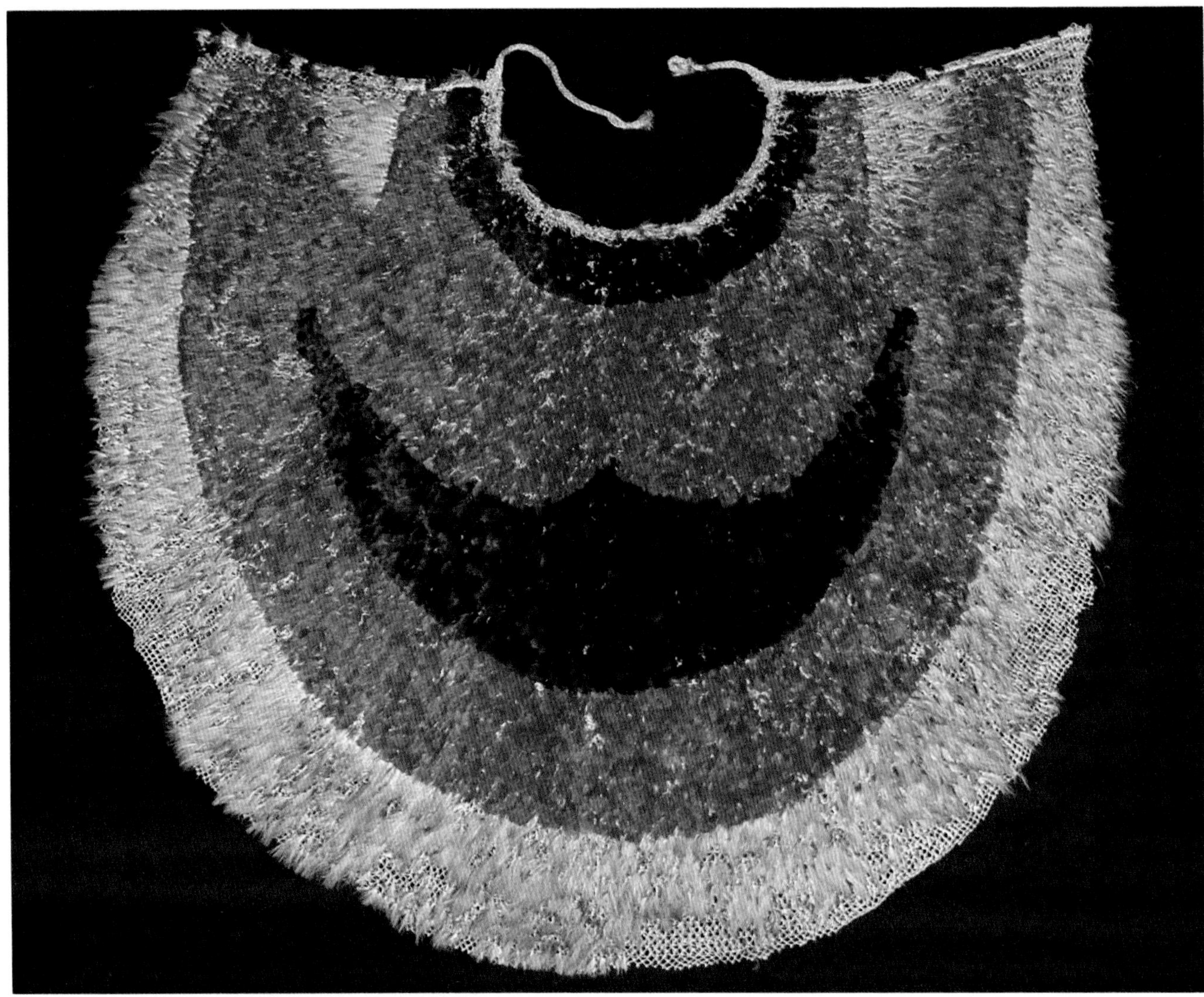

Figure 74. — Feathered cape, Leningrad 505-17.

19. Feathered cape (straight neckline), Bishop Museum (1977.206.04). Length 38 cm, width 79 cm. Figure 72.

Evidence: Circumstantial. Probably from Leverian Museum. Formerly in the Hooper collection[10] and purchased on behalf of Bishop Museum by Thurston Twigg-Smith.

Depiction: Force and Force, 1968, p. 61.

20. Feathered cape (straight neckline), British Museum (NN). Length 58 cm, width 105 cm.

Evidence: Leverian Museum.

Depictions: Force and Force, 1968, p. 59. This cape style, but with different coloring, was depicted by Webber (Fig. 90) and engraved for the official account of the voyage (Fig. 73).

21. Feathered cape (straight neckline), Florence (236). Length 58 cm.

Evidence: Circumstantial. Cook voyage collection from various sources.

Literature: Giglioli, 1895, pp. 76-78; Kaeppler, 1977; Brigham, 1899, p. 75.

22. Feathered cape (straight neckline), Florence (258). Length 40 cm, width 138 cm.

Evidence: Circumstantial. Cook voyage collection from various sources.

Literature: Giglioli, 1895, pp. 76-78; Kaeppler, 1977; Brigham, 1899, p. 75.

23. Feathered cape (straight neckline), Christchurch (E 147.107). Length 33 cm, width 75 cm.

[10] Attributed by Phelps to HMS *Blonde* (1976, p. 417), but it has been shown that this is unlikely (Kaeppler, forthcoming).

Figure 75. — Netting sample for feather cape, Sydney H114.

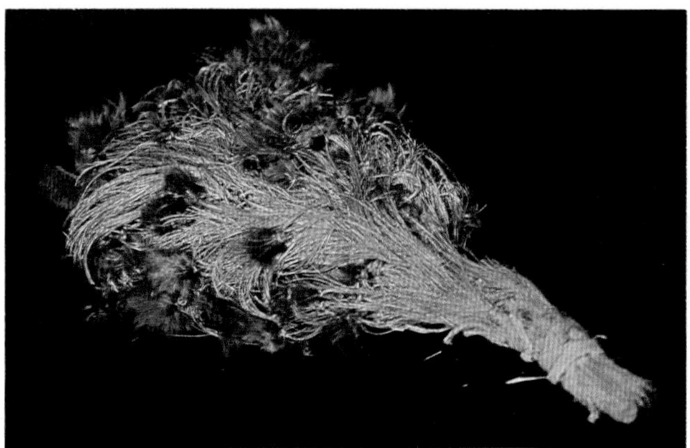

Figure 76. — Feathers prepared for use, Leningrad 505-3.

Evidence: Circumstantial. Probably Leverian Museum.

Depiction: Force and Force, 1968, p. 60.

24-26. Three feather capes (straight necklines). Lost.

Evidence: Leverian Museum.

Depictions: Force and Force, 1968, pp. 55, 59.

27. Feathered cape (shaped neckline), Leningrad (505-17). Length 50 cm, width 67 cm. Figure 74.

Evidence: Given by Captain Clerke to the Governor of Kamchatka.

Literature: Rozina, 1966, p. 238; Kaeppler, 1977.

28. Feathered cape (shaped neckline), Leningrad (505-18). Length 42 cm, width 87 cm.

Evidence: Given by Captain Clerke to the Governor of Kamchatka.

Literature: Brigham, 1918, p. 9; Rozina, 1966, p. 238; Kaeppler, 1977.

29. Feathered cape (shaped neckline), Leningrad (505-19). Length 41 cm, width 74 cm.

Evidence: Given by Captain Clerke to the Governor of Kamchatka.

Literature: Brigham, 1918, p. 12; Vaughan and Murray-Oliver, 1974, pp. 92-93; Rozina, 1966, p. 238; Kaeppler, 1977.

Figure 77. — Feathers probably prepared for use in a *kahili*, Cambridge 25369.

30. Feathered cape (size or style unknown). Lost, formerly in Dublin (possibly disintegrated and discarded).

Evidence: Referred to in the *Dublin Penny Journal* for 16 October, 1835, "No. 5 [case] Cloak made of Feathers from the Sandwich Isles." Thought to be part of collection given by Capt. King to Trinity College, Dublin.

Literature: Ball, 1894 [1895], p. vi; Freeman, 1949, p. 5.

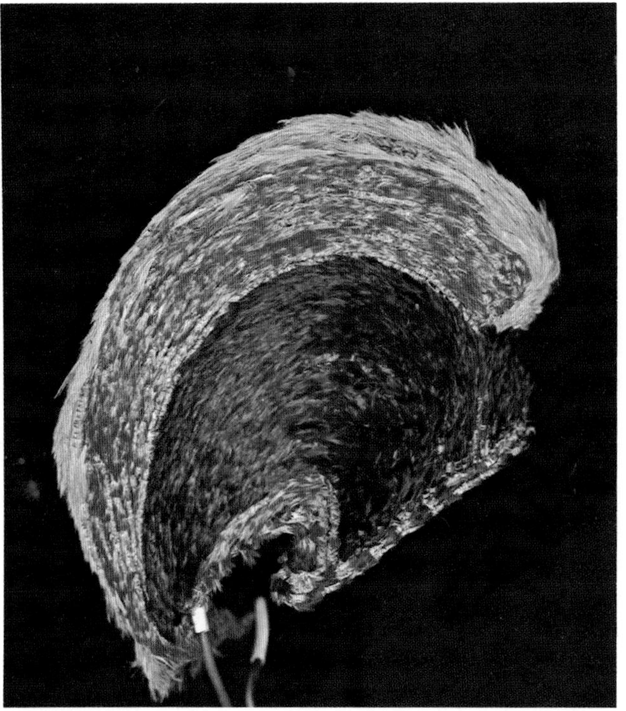

Figure 78. — Feathered helmet, British Museum VAN 236.

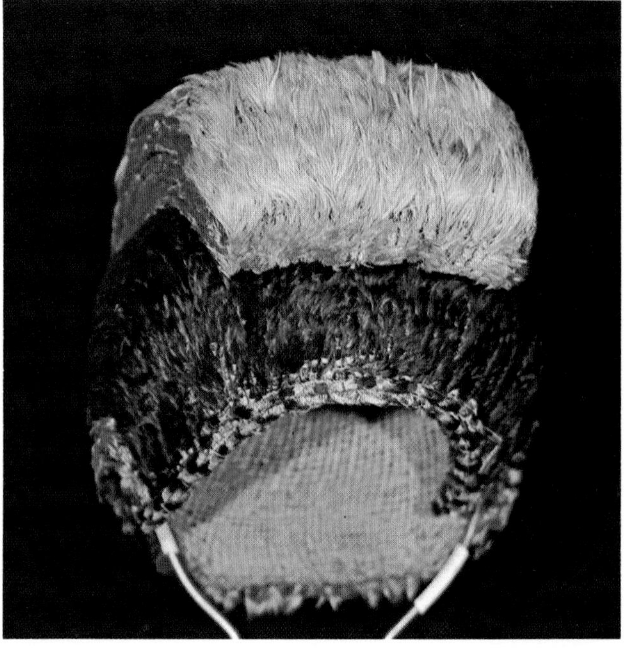

Figure 79. — Feathered helmet, British Museum VAN 236.

Figure 80. — Feathered strips from a feathered helmet, British Museum VAN 253a and b, VAN 258.

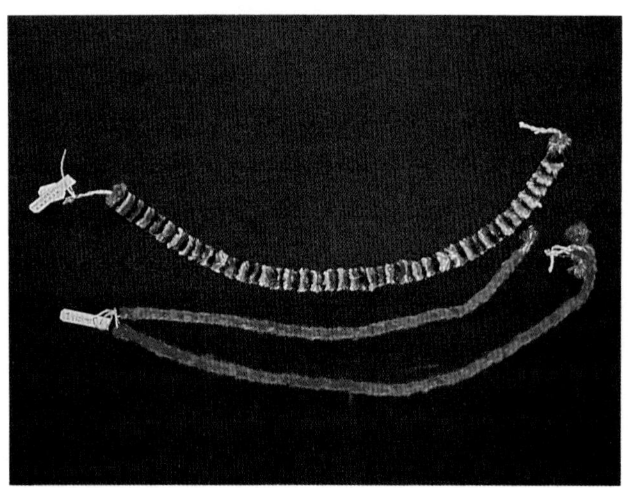

Netting and Feathers[11]

1. Netting sample for feather cape, Sydney (H114). Dimensions 43.5 cm by 40 cm. Figure 75.
   Evidence: Cook collection exhibited at Colonial and Indian Exhibition.
   Literature: Mackrell, 1886; Appendix I, this volume.
2. Feathers prepared for use. Leningrad (505-3). Length 28 cm. Figure 76.
   Evidence: Given by Captain Clerke to the Governor of Kamchatka.
   Literature: Rozina, 1966, p. 247; Kaeppler, 1977.
3. Tuft of yellow and red feathers. Cambridge (25369). Probably prepared for use in a *kahili.* Figure 77.
   Evidence: Pennant collection of Cook voyage objects from various sources.

[11]Two pieces of netting and bunches of feathers were sold in the Leverian Museum sale, but cannot be located. Two tufts of feathers in the British Museum (HAW 103 and 104) may have come from Cook's voyages but their history cannot be traced.

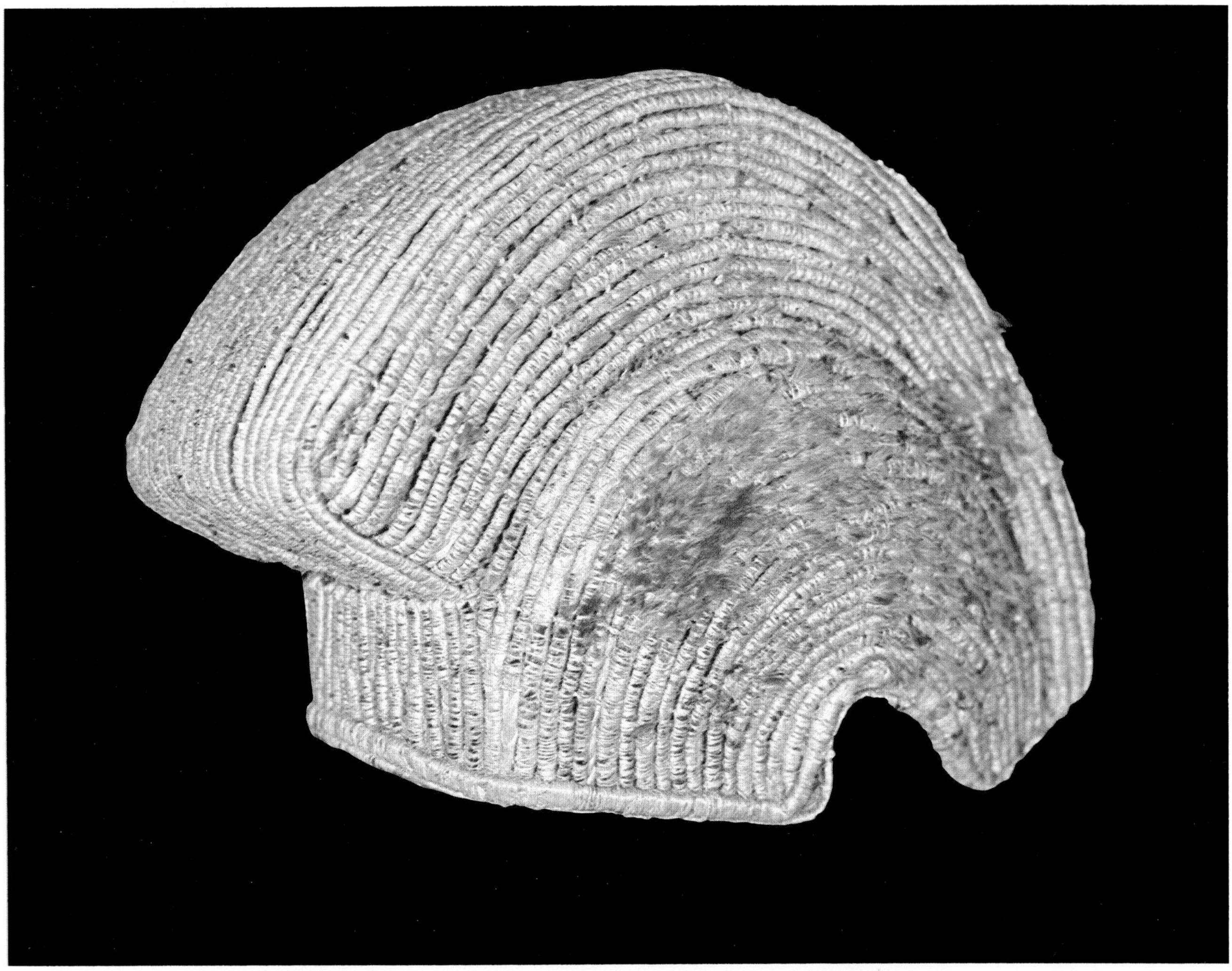

Figure 81. — Feathered helmet with wide crest, Leningrad 505-11.

4. Two tufts of red feathers. Location unknown. Formerly in the collection of James Backhouse, York; later in Beasley collection; probably sold at auction in 1975 by Palmeira Auction Room as part of lot 190.
   Evidence: Circumstantial. Said to have been given by Mrs. Cook to Ann Gates, who gave it to Ann Smith, who gave it to Jane Backhouse.

Feathered Helmets

Feathered helmets collected on Cook's voyage are of two styles and of several colors—variations that shortly changed in favor of a more standardized type which appears to be the style associated with the chiefs of the island of Hawaii, that is, a high narrow crest, the whole covered primarily with red feathers. The other style collected on Cook's voyage appears to be mainly from Kauai, having a lower and wider crest and the

Figure 82. — Feathered helmet with wide crest, Dublin 1880.1676.

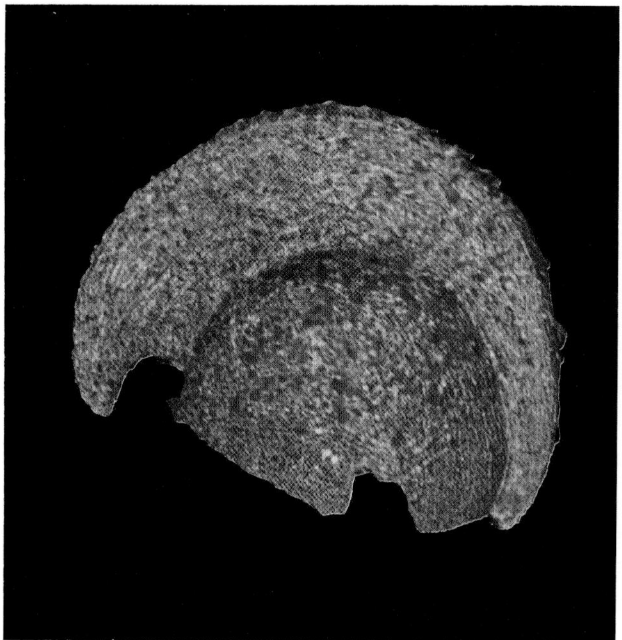

Figure 83. — Feathered helmet with narrow crest, Vienna 189.

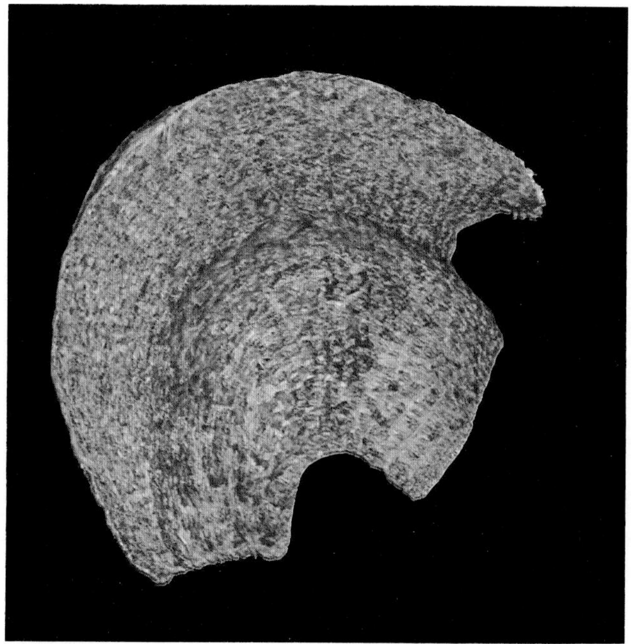

Figure 84. — Feathered helmet with narrow crest, Vienna 190.

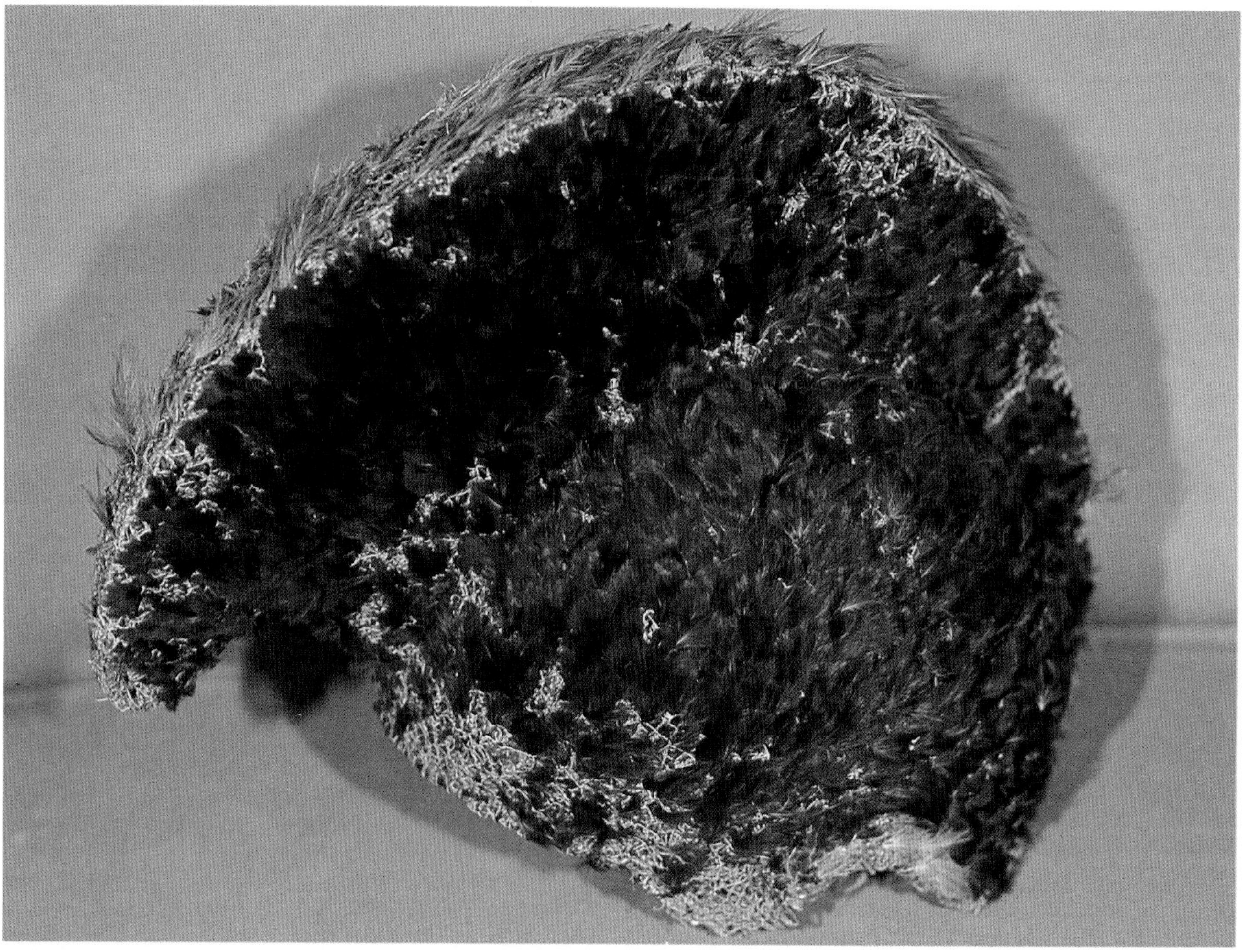

Figure 85. — Feathered helmet with narrow crest, Leningrad 505-7.

Figure 86. — Feathered helmet with narrow crest, Dublin 1882.3686.

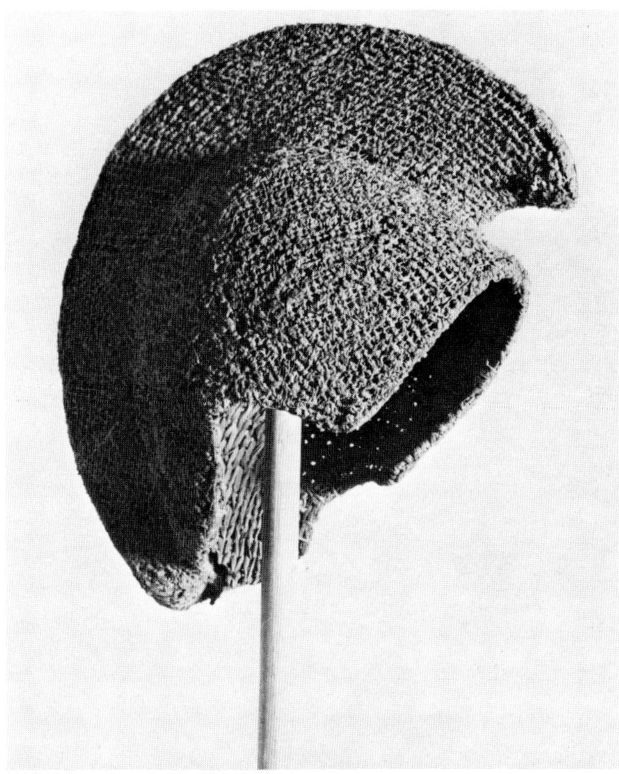

Figure 87. — Feathered helmet with narrow crest, Cape Town SAM 5167.

'ie'ie foundation covered with long strips to which feathers were attached in much the same manner as on the feathered aprons in Dublin and the British Museum.

1. Feathered helmet (wide crest), British Museum (VAN 236). Height 23 cm, length 22 cm, width 21 cm. Figures 78 and 79. The feather strips once attached have come away and are numbered VAN 258 and 253a and b. Figure 80. Lengths 40 cm, 34 cm, 44 cm.
   Evidence: Leverian Museum.
   Depiction: Force and Force, 1968, p. 33.
   Literature: Kaeppler, 1971, p. 198.
2. Feathered helmet (wide crest), Leningrad (505-11). Height 20 cm, length 29 cm. Figure 81.
   Evidence: Given by Captain Clerke to the Governor of Kamchatka.
   Literature: Brigham, 1918, p. 8; Rozina, 1966, p. 239; Kaeppler, 1977.
3. Feathered helmet (wide crest), Dublin (1880.1676). Feathers gone. Height 21.5 cm, length 27 cm. Figure 82.
   Evidence: Circumstantial. Thought to be part of the collection given by Captain King to Trinity College, Dublin. An old label "511" is attached.
4. Feathered helmet (wide crest), Berlin VI 364.
   Evidence: Leverian Museum.
   Depiction: Force and Force, 1968, p. 35.
   Literature: Kaeppler, 1974a, pp. 76-77, 81-82.
5. Feathered helmet (wide crest), Florence.
   Evidence: Circumstantial. Cook voyage collection from various sources.
   Literature: Giglioli, 1895, p. 61; Kaeppler, 1977.
6. Feathered helmet (wide crest). Lost.
   Evidence: Leverian Museum.
   Depiction: Force and Force, 1968, p. 33.
7. Feathered helmet (narrow crest), Vienna (189). Height 27 cm, length 29 cm. Green feathers once covered one side of the cap section, while red feathers covered the other side. Figure 83.
   Evidence: Leverian Museum.
   Depiction: Force and Force, 1968, p. 31.
   Literature: Brigham, 1899, p. 43;[12] Moschner, 1955, p. 233.

[12] Brigham (1899, p. 43) attributes three helmets in Vienna to the Cook collection—there are only two.

Figure 88. — Wicker helmet, Sydney H141.

8. Feathered helmet (narrow crest), Vienna (190). Height 26 cm, length 34 cm. Figure 84.
Evidence: Leverian Museum.
Literature: Brigham, 1899, p. 43; Moschner, 1955, pp. 232-233.

9. Feathered helmet (narrow crest), Leningrad (505-7). Height 26 cm, length 32 cm. Figure 85.
Evidence: Given by Captain Clerke to the Governor of Kamchatka.
Literature: Brigham, 1918, p. 8;[13] Rozina, 1966, p. 239; Kaeppler, 1977.

10. Feathered helmet (narrow crest), Dublin (1882.3686). Height 24 cm, length 32 cm. A hibiscus fiber "padding" is evident between the *'ie'ie* foundation and the net overlay to which the feathers were attached. Figure 86.
Evidence: Circumstantial. Thought to be part of the collection given by Captain King to Trinity College, Dublin.
Literature: Freeman, 1949.

11. Feathered helmet (narrow crest), Wellington[14] (FE 328).
Evidence: Leverian Museum.
Literature: Kaeppler, 1974a, pp. 75, 78.

12. Feathered helmet (narrow crest), Göttingen (OZ 911).
Evidence: Purchased from London dealer Humphrey in 1782.

[13] Brigham (1918, p. 62) attributes four helmets in Leningrad to the Cook collection—there are only two.

[14] A second feather helmet in Wellington (FE 376) has been attributed to Cook's voyage by Brigham (1918, pp. 45, 62) and Duff (1969, pp. 72-73), but this attribution cannot be confirmed (Kaeppler, 1974a, pp. 73, 76, 77). Brigham (1918, p. 13) also attributes two European-style hats in Wellington and Vienna to Cook's voyages. His information is incorrect—the Wellington hat has the same non-Cook provenance as the helmet (FE 376) and the Vienna hat is not part of the Cook collection.

Figure 89. — Hawaiian canoe with the rowers masked, by John Webber.

13. Feathered helmet (narrow crest), Berne (HAW 2).
    Evidence: Webber collection.
    Literature: Brigham, 1899, pp. 44, 46; Henking, 1957, pp. 262-264; Kaeppler, 1977.
14. Feathered helmet (narrow crest), British Museum (HAW 108).[15]
    Evidence: Circumstantial. Noted "Banks collection." Probably inherited by Banks from Captain Clerke who died on the voyage and bequeathed his natural and artificial curiosities to Banks.
15. Feathered helmet (narrow crest), Cape Town (SAM 5167). Height 24 cm. Figure 87.
    Evidence: Circumstantial. Thought to have arrived in Cape Town in 1780.
    Literature: Bax, 1970, p. 146.
16. Feathered helmet (narrow crest), Florence.[16]
    Evidence: Circumstantial. Cook voyage collection from various sources.
    Literature: Giglioli, 1895, p. 62; Kaeppler, 1977.

Wicker Helmets

1. Helmet of *'ie'ie,* Sydney (H141). Height 31 cm. Figure 88.
   Evidence: Part of Cook collection exhibited at the Colonial and Indian Exhibition.
   Literature: Mackrell, 1886; Brigham, 1899, p. 44; Appendix I, this volume.

Hair Helmets

At least one hair helmet was taken to England on Cook's third voyage, but it cannot be located. It was depicted by Sarah Stone in the Leverian Museum (Force and Force, 1968, p. 39).

Gourd Helmets

Whether a gourd helmet was actually collected on Cook's voyage is unknown. No gourd helmet can be traced to the voyage and, indeed, there are no extant examples of authentic gourd helmets.[17] Our only knowledge of these helmets is from the drawings made by Webber, artist on Cook's third voyage (Figure 89). It is thought that gourd helmets were worn by priests of the god Lono and may have been worn only in the presence of these outsiders because Cook was thought to be a representation of Lono.

[15] Several other helmets in the British Museum were attributed to Cook's voyage by Brigham (1918, p. 62). There is no evidence that would confirm these attributions.

[16] Possibly the helmet depicted in Force and Force, 1968, p. 31. At least three other feather helmets were in the Leverian Museum sale but cannot now be identified. The helmet depicted by Webber in the wash drawing in Bishop Museum has not been identified (see Fig. 90).

[17] The gourd helmet in Bishop Museum is a replica made by Stokes after a drawing by Webber, and the gourd helmet in the Tenri Museum, Tenri, Japan, is a replica either of the replica in Bishop Museum, or after the drawing by Webber.

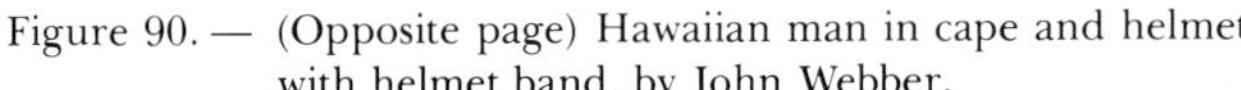

Figure 90. — (Opposite page) Hawaiian man in cape and helmet with helmet band, by John Webber.

Figure 91. — Helmet band, Leningrad 505-8.

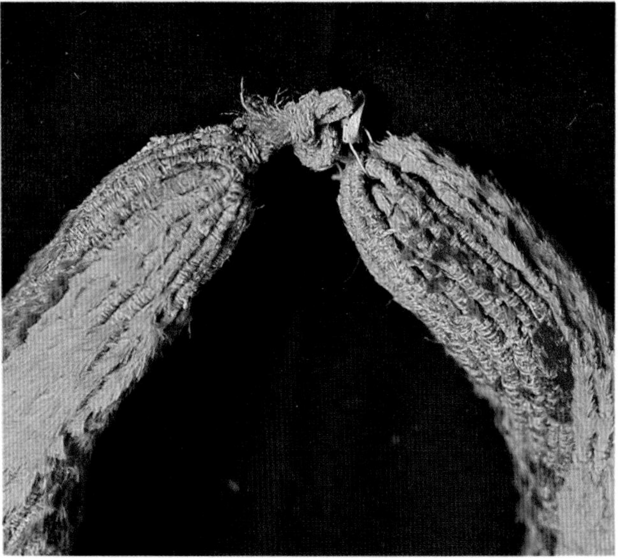

Figure 92. — Helmet band (detail), Leningrad 505-8.

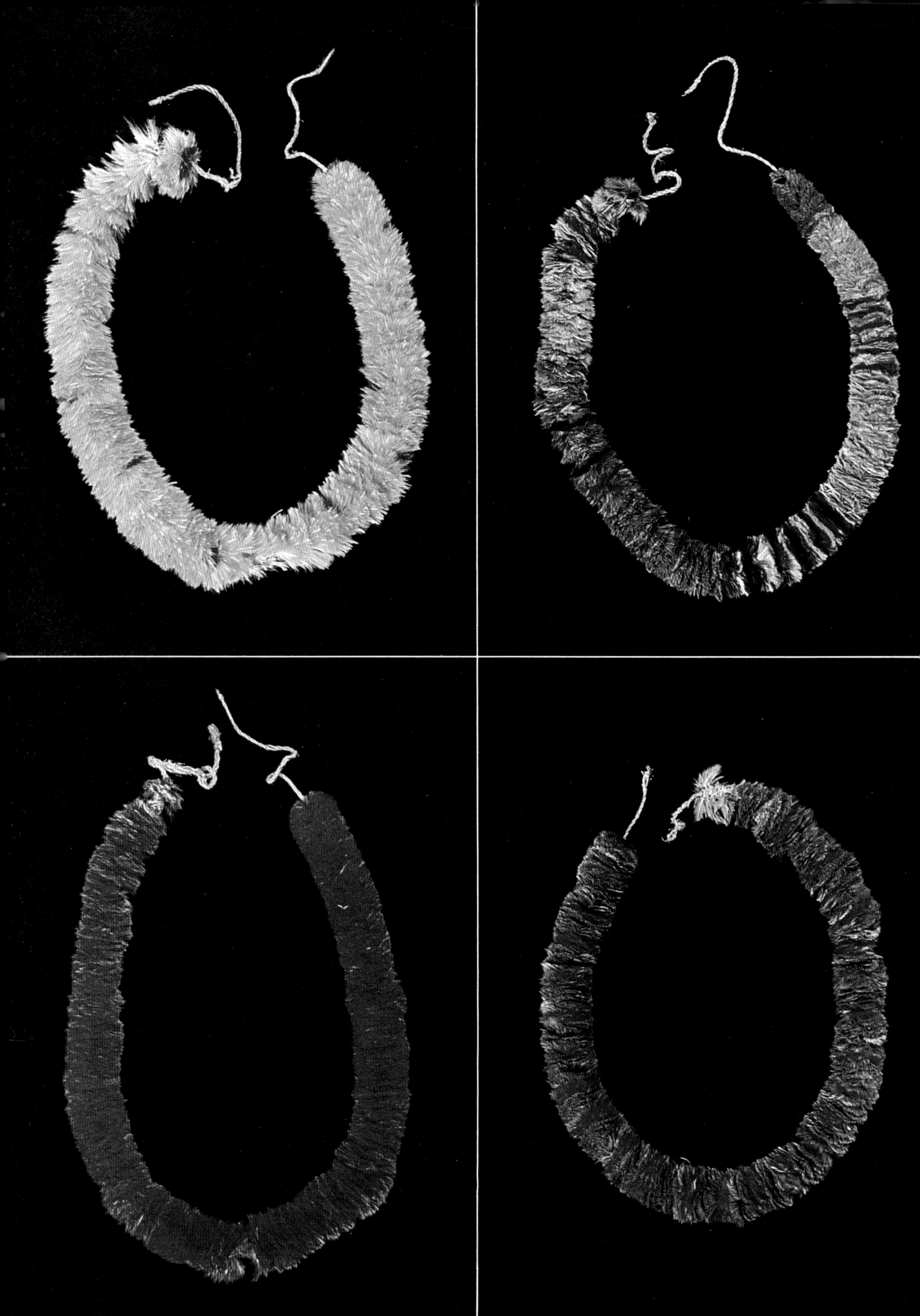

Feathered Helmet Bands

Helmet bands are rare objects of which there are only about five known specimens.[18] These were worn around the feathered helmets (Fig. 90), and, as Samwell notes, give "the whole headdress the appearance of a rich and elegant Turband" (Beaglehole 1967, p. 1231).

1. Feathered helmet band, Leningrad (505-8). Length 77 cm, diameter 28 cm. Figures 91 and 92.
   Evidence: Given by Captain Clerke to the Governor of Kamchatka.
   Literature: Rozina, 1966, p. 239; Kaeppler, 1977.

2. Feathered helmet band, Leningrad (505-13). Length 65 cm, diameter 22 cm.
   Evidence: Given by Captain Clerke to the Governor of Kamchatka.
   Literature: Rozina, 1966, pp. 239-242; Kaeppler, 1977.

3-4. Feathered helmet bands. Lost.
   Evidence: Leverian Museum.
   Depictions: Force and Force, 1968, pp. 35 and 39.

Feathered Ornaments for Hair and Neck (Lei)

Although a large number of feather *lei* appear to have been collected on Cook's third voyage, only a small number of these can be located today.[19] Of some 50 entered in the sale catalogue of the Leverian Museum only seven can be identified with certainty. It is likely that many of the *lei* simply disintegrated through lack of care and were thrown away. Some of those that have been found are too fragile for exhibition.

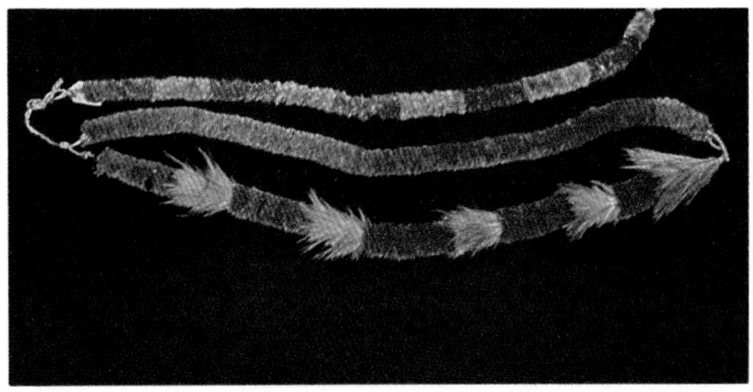

Figure 97. — Three feathered ornaments *(lei)*, British Museum HAW 114.

1-4. Four feathered ornaments (*lei*), Sydney (H 87). Lengths 45.5 cm, 43 cm, 42 cm, 42 cm. Figures 93, 94, 95, and 96.
   Evidence: Cook collection exhibited at the Colonial and Indian Exhibition.
   Literature: Mackrell, 1886; Appendix I, this volume.

5-7. Three feathered ornaments (*lei*), British Museum (HAW 114). Lengths ca. 41 cm. Figure 97.
   Evidence: Circumstantial. Apparently from the Leverian Museum, where one of them was depicted.
   Depiction: Force and Force, 1968, p. 65.

8-11. Four feathered ornaments (*lei*), Vienna (185 [lost], 186, 187, 188). Lengths ca. 46 cm.
   Evidence: Leverian Museum.
   Depiction: Force and Force, 1968, p. 71.
   Literature: Moschner, 1955, p. 237.

12-13. Two feathered ornaments (*lei*), Berne (HAW 14a/b). Lengths 42 cm, 44.5 cm.
   Evidence: Webber collection.
   Literature: Henking, 1957, p. 364; Kaeppler, 1977.

14. Feathered ornament (*lei*), Göttingen (OZ 253). Length 39 cm.
   Evidence: Purchased from London dealer Humphrey in 1782.

15-18. Feathered ornaments (*lei*), British Museum (HAW 112). Length ca. 42 cm.
   Evidence: Noted "Banks No. 15," possibly among the collection inherited by Banks from Captain Clerke.

19. Feathered ornament (*lei*), British Museum (VAN 243). Length ca. 39 cm.
   Evidence: Leverian Museum.
   Depiction: Force and Force, 1968, p. 65.
   Literature: Kaeppler, 1971, p. 198.

---

[18] A feathered helmet band in the British Museum (HAW 116) has no accession information. Although a Cook voyage provenance is possible, no evidence can be found for confirmation.

[19] Among those lost may be a small *lei* formerly in the Hooper collection (332) and now in Bishop Museum, which was reputed by Hooper to have a Cook voyage provenance based on an old label (Phelps, 1976, p. 417); and one possibly once in the Museum für Völkerkunde, Berlin (Kaeppler, 1974a, p. 82).

Figures 93, 94, 95, 96. — (Opposite page) Four feathered ornaments *(lei)*, Sydney (H87).

Figure 98. — "A girl of the Sandwich Islands," by John Webber.

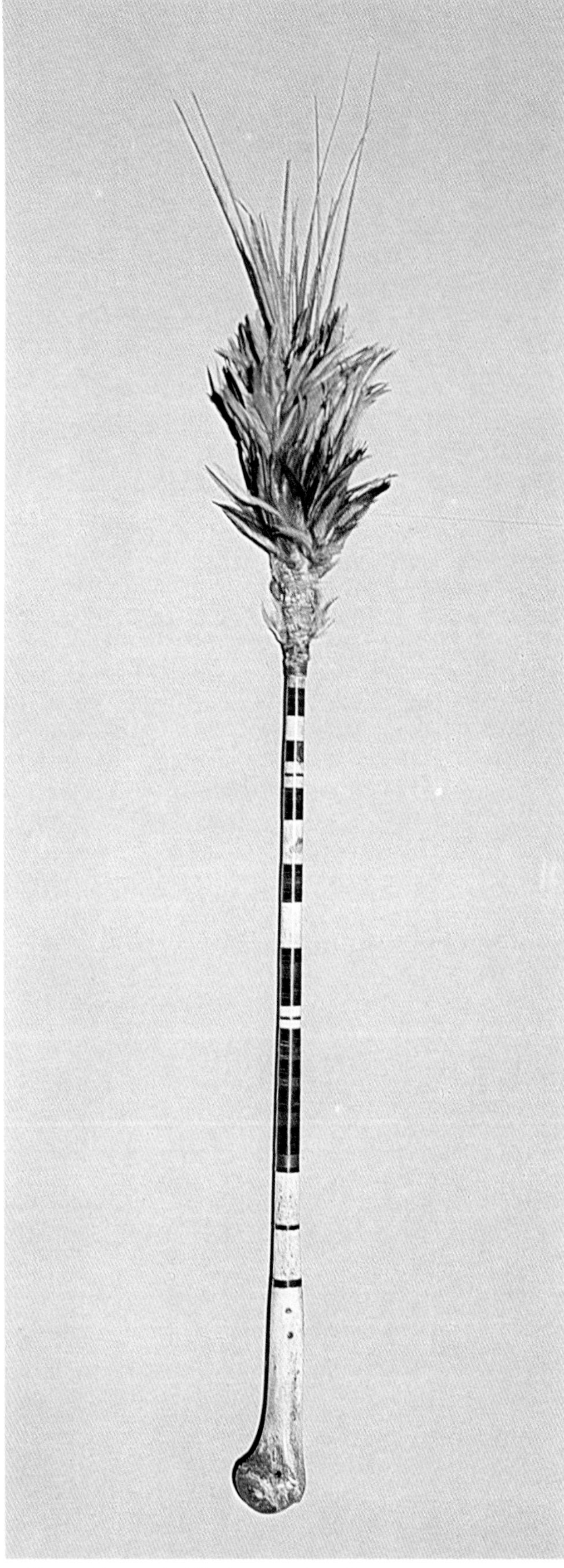

Figure 99. — *Kahili* with bone handle, Wellington FE 329.

The *lei* depicted by Webber in the watercolor drawing in Bishop Museum (Fig. 98) have not been located.

Feather Standards (Kahili)

Writers on Cook's voyage usually referred to *kahili* as fly-flaps, a term derived from their southern Polynesian counterparts. Although quite a number were collected on Cook's voyage, only four can be traced. There were 22 in the Leverian Museum, but only two of these can be found.

Figure 100. — *Kahili*, Vienna 204.

Figure 101. — Two *kahili*, Dublin 1882.3692 and 3693.

1. *Kahili* with bone handle, Wellington (FE 329). Length 90 cm. Figure 99.
   Evidence: Leverian Museum. Collected by Samwell on Kauai March 3, 1779.
   Literature: Beaglehole, 1967, Pt. 2, p. 1224; Kaeppler, 1974a, pp. 73, 79; 1975a, pp. 3-9.

2. *Kahili* with bone handle, British Museum (HAW 167). Length 89 cm.
   Evidence: Circumstantial. Noted "Cook collection 23." Probably collected by Clerke on Kauai, March 4, 1779.
   Literature: Beaglehole, 1967, Pt. 1, p. 577; Kaeppler, 1975a, p. 5.

3. *Kahili* with wood handle, Vienna (204). Length 67 cm. Figure 100.
   Evidence: Leverian Museum.
   Literature: Moschner, 1955, p. 235.

Figure 102. — Feathers from a *kahili*, Leningrad 505-2.

⛵4-5. Two *kahili* with wood handles, Dublin (1882.3692, 1882.3693). Lengths 56 cm and 72 cm. Figure 101.
Evidence: Circumstantial. Thought to be part of the collection given by Captain King to Trinity College, Dublin.
Literature: Freeman, 1949.

6. *Kahili*, Vienna. Lost.
Evidence: Leverian Museum.

7. Feathers for a *kahili*, and section of handle with bone and turtle shell segments, Leningrad (505-2). Figure 102.
Evidence: Given by Captain Clerke to the Governor of Kamchatka.
Literature: Rozina, 1966, pp. 246-247; Kaeppler, 1977.

Wooden Images

Hawaiian wooden images collected on Cook's third voyage are relatively small in size and unpretentious in contrast to the larger and more highly finished images collected near the end of the 18th century. Only four images have convincing Cook voyage associations—one of which is circumstantial.

⛵1. Wooden image, Delgado Museum of Art, New Orleans. Height 78.5 cm. Figures 103 and 104.
Evidence: Leverian Museum.
Depiction: Force and Force, 1968, p. 97.
Literature: Cox and Davenport, 1974, p. 130.

⛵2. Wooden image, Edinburgh (1950.230). Height 76 cm. Figures 105 and 106.
Evidence: Leverian Museum.
Depiction: Force and Force, 1968, p. 171.
Literature: Cox and Davenport, 1974, p. 139.

⛵3. Wooden image, Cambridge (22.917). Height 21.5 cm. Figure 107.
Evidence: Leverian Museum.
Depiction: Force and Force, 1968, p. 101.
Literature: Cox and Davenport, 1974, p. 156.

4. Wooden image, British Museum (HAW 74). Height 76 cm.
Evidence: Circumstantial. This is almost certainly the mate to the image now in New Orleans. The latter probably belonged to Cook, making it likely that its mate might go to the second in command, Capt. Clerke. The collections of Clerke went to the British Museum through Banks, who inherited Clerke's curiosities. HAW 74 has no accession information; thus the circumstantial evidence is based solely on style.
Literature: Cox and Davenport, 1974, p. 157.

5-6. Two wooden images. Lost.
Evidence: Leverian Museum.
Depictions: Force and Force, 1968, pp. 97, 101.

7. Bark cloth covered head. Lost.
Evidence: Leverian Museum.
Depiction: Force and Force, 1968, p. 101.[20]

[20] A similar head is in the British Museum (HAW 77). However, it has no documentation and one cannot be sure that it is the object depicted.

Figure 103. — Wooden image, New Orleans.

Figure 104. — Reverse of Figure 103.

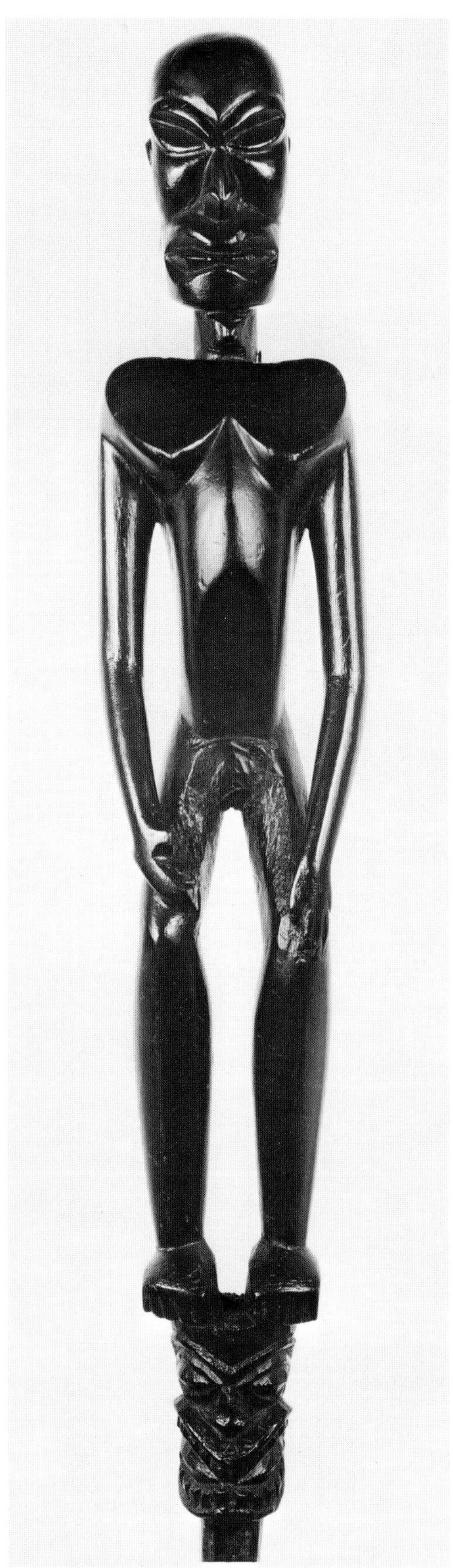

Figure 105. — Wooden image, Edinburgh 1950.230.

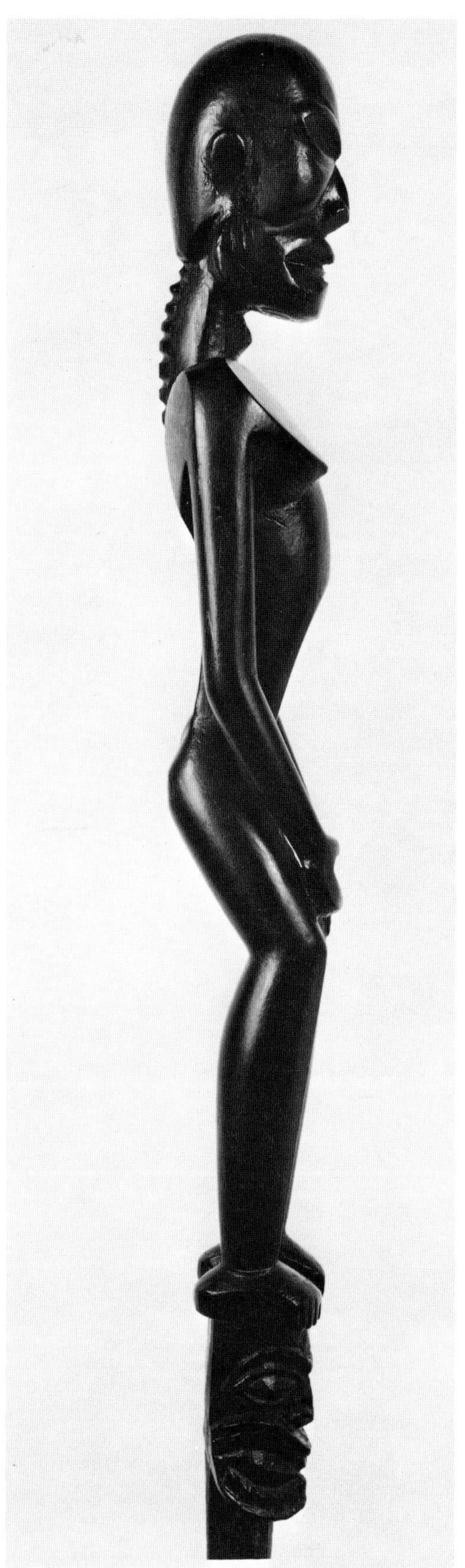

Figure 106. — Side view of Figure 105.

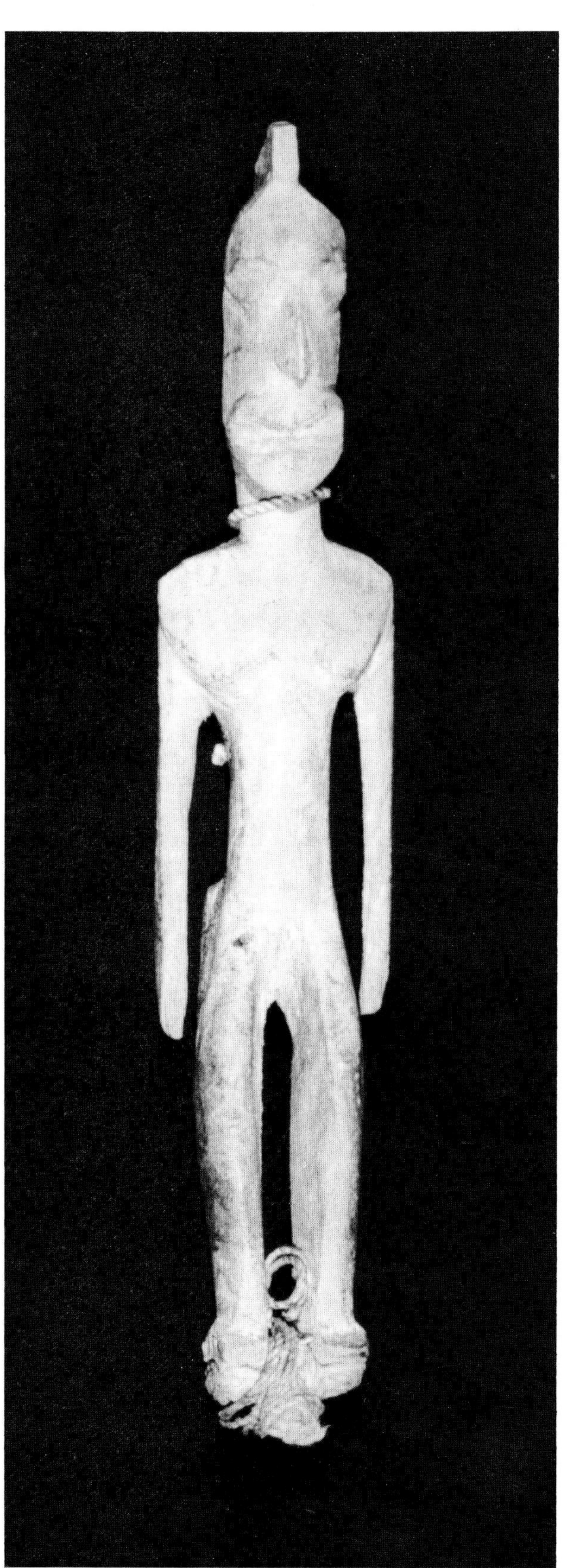

Figure 107. — Wooden image, Cambridge 22.917.

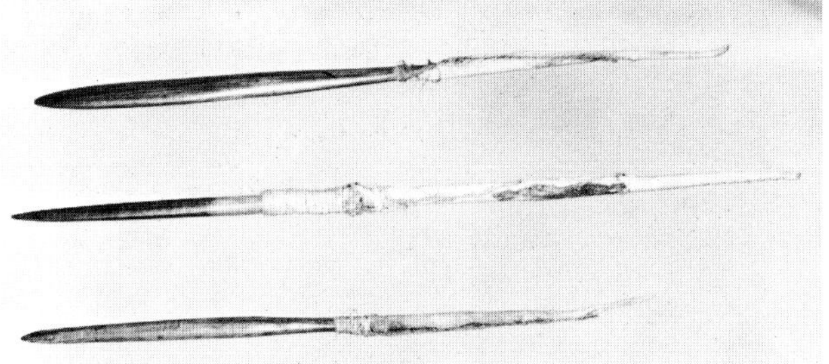

Figure 108. — Three tabooing wands, Vienna 157, 158, 159.

Tabooing Wands

Of the seven tabooing wands known in Museum collections, all can be traced to Cook's voyage and are thus especially important. In the literature they are either ignored or called such misnomers as dance wands or head ornaments. They were described by Capt. King as "wands tipt with dogs hair" (Beaglehole, 1967, pp. 504, 622). Apparently they were used to indicate taboo places and made of pointed wood decorated with dog hair and bird feathers.

1-4. Tabooing wands, Vienna (156 [exhibited], 157, 158, 159). Lengths 55.5 cm; 57 cm; 58.5 cm; 49.5 cm. Figure 108.
Evidence: Leverian Museum.
Depictions: Force and Force, 1968, p. 75.
Literature: Moschner, 1955, pp. 214-216.

5. Tabooing wand, Leningrad (505-6). Length 63 cm. Figures 109 and 110.
Evidence: Given by Capt. Clerke to the Governor of Kamchatka.
Literature: Rozina, 1966, p. 247; Kaeppler, 1977; Vaughan and Murray-Oliver, 1974, p. 93.

6. Tabooing wand, Cuming Museum, London (3505). Length 48 cm.
Evidence: Leverian Museum.

7. Tabooing wand, Göttingen.
Evidence: Purchased from London dealer Humphrey in 1782.

Figure 109. — Tabooing wand (Leningrad 505-6) and truncheon dagger.

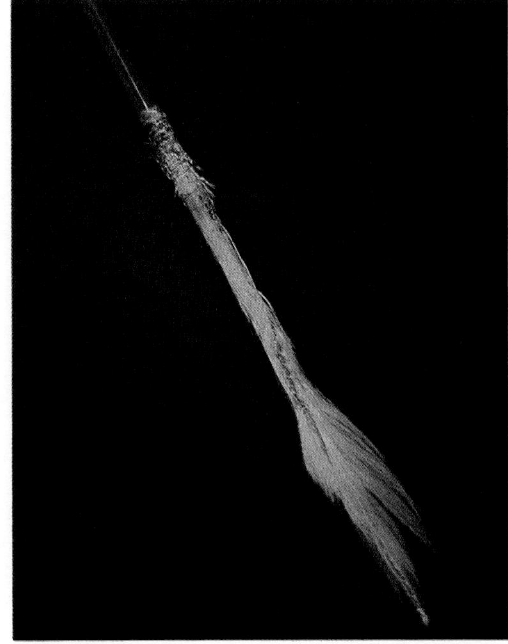

Figure 110. — Tabooing wand (detail), Leningrad 505-6.

Bowls with Human Images

Small bowls with human images collected on Cook's voyage apparently were used for preparing or drinking *'awa*. Beautifully carved and highly finished, these bowls demonstrate the highly developed woodworking techniques of Hawaiians at the time of European contact. They were probably personal bowls of the *ali'i*, made by specialist carvers.

1. Bowl with human images, anonymous private collection.[21] Length 42 cm, height 24 cm, diameter of bowl 24.5 cm. Height of figures 24 cm, width of figures 28 cm. Figures 111 and 112.
   Evidence: Leverian Museum. Collected by Samwell, probably on Kauai.
   Literature: Beaglehole, 1967, Pt. 2, p. 1183; Cox and Davenport, 1974, p. 171.

2. Bowl with human images, British Museum (HAW 46). Length 45.5 cm; height 25 cm.
   Evidence: Circumstantial. Probably made by the same carver as the last bowl, and given to Captain Clerke by a chief of Kauai on January 23, 1778. Clerke's collection was inherited by Banks who gave it to the British Museum.
   Literature: Beaglehole, 1967, Pt. 1, p. 281, Pt. 2, p. 1084; Cox and Davenport, 1974, p. 169.

3. Bowl with human image, Vienna (175). Length 22.5 cm; height of image 7.5 cm. Figures 113 and 114.
   Evidence: Leverian Museum.
   Depiction: Force and Force, 1968, p. 99.
   Literature: Moschner, 1955, pp. 176-177; Cox and Davenport, 1974, p. 174.

4. Bowl with human image, Cambridge (22.916). Length 18 cm, height 7.5 cm, diameter 14.5 cm. Figures 115, 116, and 117.
   Evidence: Circumstantial. Apparently from the Leverian Museum. Probably made by the same carver as the last bowl.[22]
   Literature: Cox and Davenport, 1974, p. 175.

[21] Exhibited during only part of the exhibition.

[22] A bowl with three human images in the British Museum (HAW 48) has similar stylistic features to these two bowls, especially in the facial features of the images. It is likely that this bowl also came from Cook's voyage, but no evidence can be found for confirmation.

Figure 111. — Bowl with human images, anonymous private collection.

Figure 112. — Bowl with human images (top), anonymous private collection.

Figure 113. — Bowl with human image, Vienna 175.

Figure 114. — Bowl with human image (detail), Vienna 175.

Figures 115, 116, 117. — Bowl with human image, Cambridge 22.916.

Figure 118. — Wooden bowl, Vienna 173.

Wooden Bowls

Bowls without images are equally as rare in Cook collections as those with images. Only five can be traced.

1. Wooden bowl (deep), Vienna (173). Height 17 cm, diameter 12.5 cm. Figure 118.
   Evidence: Leverian Museum.
   Literature: Moschner, 1955, pp. 175-176.
2. Wooden bowl (shallow), Vienna (174). Height 8 cm; diameter 21 cm. Figure 119.
   Evidence: Leverian Museum.
   Literature: Moschner, 1955, pp. 175-177.
3. Wooden bowl (shallow), Florence (268). Height 10 cm; diameter 23.5 cm.
   Evidence: Circumstantial. Cook voyage collection from various sources.
   Literature: Giglioli, 1895, pp. 90-92; Kaeppler, 1977.
4. Wooden bowl (shallow), Florence (269). Height 7.4 cm; diameter 20 cm.
   Evidence: Circumstantial. Cook voyage collection from various sources.
   Literature: Giglioli, 1895, pp. 90-92; Kaeppler, 1977.

Figure 119. — Wooden bowl, Vienna 174.

5. Wooden bowl (shallow), Dublin (1882.3662). Height 6 cm; diameter 18.5 cm. Figure 120.
   Evidence: Circumstantial. Thought to be part of the collection given by Capt. King to Trinity College. An old label is attached, "67 A Yawa bowl of Sandwich Islands . . . the Natives have no Tool to Manufacture with but shells & stones."
   Literature: Freeman, 1949.

Gourd Containers

Gourd containers are rare in Cook voyage collections, perhaps because of their fragility (for this reason none were borrowed for this exhibition). Gourd containers from Cook's voyage are of two types—decorated water bottles and storage bowls. Although long gourds used for fishing equipment are mentioned in the accounts of the voyage, none can be traced.

1. Gourd water bottle (decorated), Vienna (176). Height 30 cm. Figure 121.
   Evidence: Leverian Museum.
   Literature: Moschner, 1955, pp. 174-176.

2. Gourd water bottle (decorated), Saffron Walden Museum (LN 190). Height 26 cm, diameter 21 cm. Figure 122.
   Evidence: Circumstantial. Probably from the Leverian Museum.

3. Two gourd water bottles (decorated and undecorated), British Museum (HAW 51, HAW 51a). Height 33 cm, 22 cm, respectively.
   Evidence: Circumstantial. Noted "Cook collection" and remnants of a "Cook collection" label still exist on HAW 51.

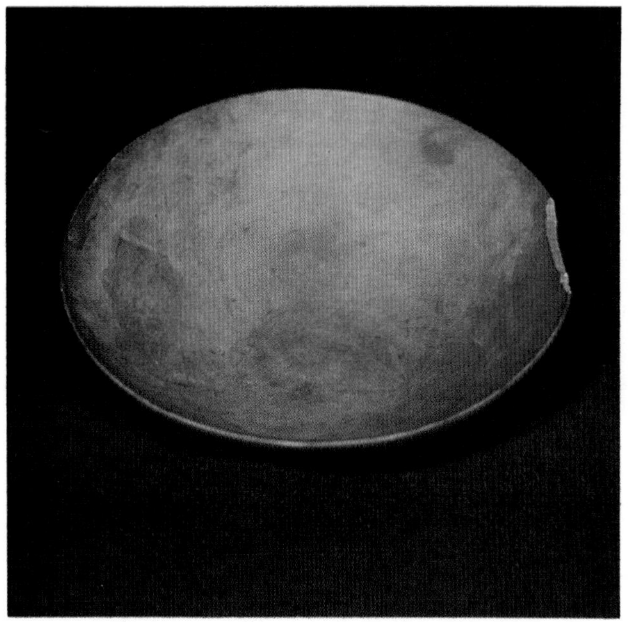

Figure 120. — Wooden bowl, Dublin 1882.3662.

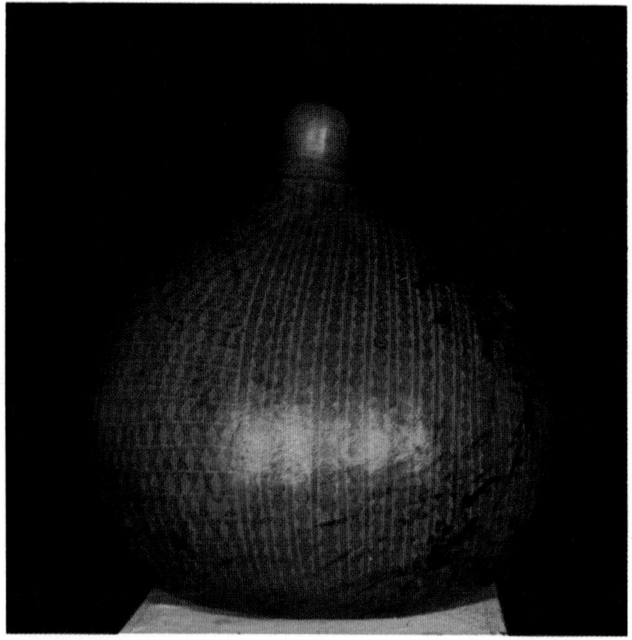

Figure 121. — Gourd water bottle, Vienna 176.

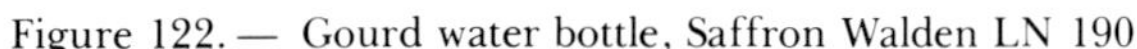

Figure 122. — Gourd water bottle, Saffron Walden LN 190.

4. Small gourd bowl with cover, Vienna (177). Height 13 cm; diameter 12 cm. Figure 123.
   Evidence: Leverian Museum.
   Literature: Moschner, 1955, pp. 175-176.

Other Containers

Small bowls made of coconut shell are mentioned in early Museum catalogues, usually as salt dishes or *'awa* cups. Only one such cup can be located.

1. Coconut shell *'awa* cup, Göttingen.
   Evidence: Purchased from the London dealer Humphrey in 1782.

Baskets

Hawaiian baskets are among the rarest artifact types from Cook's voyage. None have clear documentation that would trace them to Cook's voyage and only one has even circumstantial evidence.

1. Basket of twined *'ie'ie* with cover, British Museum (HAW 50). Height 56 cm, diameter at top 15 cm.
   Evidence: Circumstantial. Noted "Cook collection."

Figure 123. — Gourd container with cover, Vienna 177.

Mats

Hawaiian *makaloa* sedge mats were described in the journals of Cook's voyages and in early Museum catalogues, but only three can be located.

1. *Makaloa* mat, Leningrad (505-30). Length 253 cm, width 210 cm. Figure 124.
   Evidence: Given by Captain Clerke to the Governor of Kamchatka.
   Literature: Rozina, 1966, pp. 247-248; Kaeppler, 1977.
2. *Makaloa* mat, Berne (TAH 17). Length 218 cm, width 190 cm.
   Evidence: Webber collection.
   Literature: Henking, 1957, pp. 381-382; Kaeppler, 1977.
3. *Makaloa* mat, Florence (186c). Length 150 cm, width 98 cm.
   Evidence: Circumstantial. Cook voyage collection from various sources.
   Literature: Giglioli, 1895, p. 73; Kaeppler, 1977.

Figure 124. — *Makaloa* mat, Leningrad 505-30.

Loincloths

Two long and narrow *makaloa* pieces appear to be loincloths.

1-2. Two *makaloa* loincloths, Florence (186a and b).
Evidence: Circumstantial. Cook voyage collection from various sources.
Literature: Giglioli, 1893, pp. 208-209;[23] Kaeppler, 1977.

Cordage

It is likely that a large amount of cordage was collected in Hawaii on Cook's ships—most of it now lost, mislabeled, or perhaps used on the ships.[24]

1-2. Two hanks of cordage, Göttingen.
Evidence: Purchased from London dealer Humphrey in 1782.

Sandals

At least one pair of Hawaiian sandals was collected on Cook's voyage. Depicted in the Leverian Museum (Force and Force, 1968, p. 169). Apparently they went to Vienna but cannot now be located.

Bark Cloth Beaters

Only one Hawaiian bark cloth beater from Cook's third voyage has been located. It is round in cross section and grooved lengthwise, in contrast to the two types of beaters known from later times—a first stage beater which was round and often smooth and a second stage beater which was square with its faces grooved and/or incised with designs. It is possible that at the time of Cook's visit one style of beater served both purposes, or perhaps the one traded was atypical.

1. Bark cloth beater, Leningrad (505-29). Length 39 cm, circumference 18 cm. Figure 125.
Evidence: Given by Captain Clerke to the Governor of Kamchatka.
Literature: Rozina, 1966, p. 252; Kaeppler, 1977.

[23] Described by Giglioli as Tongan house dividers.

[24] Several hanks of cordage in the British Museum (HAW 54, 55, 56) are attributed to the "Banks collection." Although it is possible that these came from Cook's voyage, it is more likely that they came through Menzies, botanist on Vancouver's voyage, who is known to have given a collection to Banks which went to the British Museum.

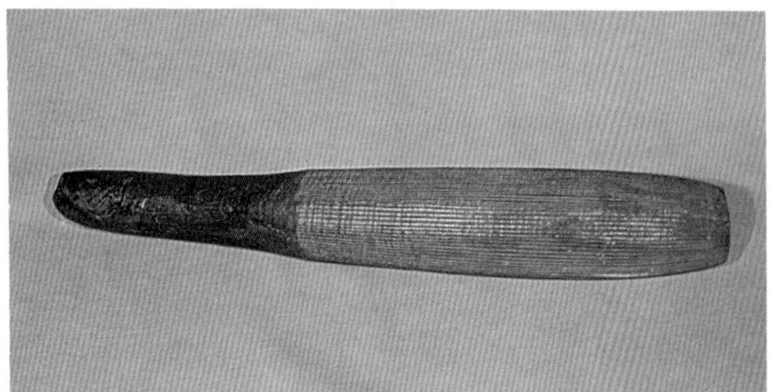

Figure 125. — Bark cloth beater, Leningrad 505-29.

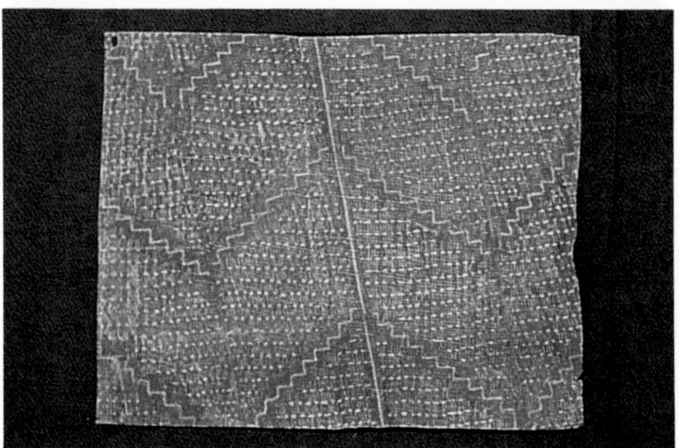

Figures 126, 127, 128. — Three bark cloth pieces, Vienna.

Figure 129. — (Opposite page) Bark cloth piece, Vienna

Bark Cloth

A large amount of bark cloth was collected in Hawaii on Cook's third voyage. Much of it was cut into small pieces and bound or pasted into books, such as the series of volumes by Shaw (1787).

An inventory of Hawaiian bark cloth collected on Cook's voyage would require a separate book and extensive research. Included here are only quite obvious pieces that are not part of books. Hawaiian bark cloth from Cook's voyage is significantly different from that made in postcontact times (Kaeppler, 1975b). Several books and collections of bark cloth samples are included in the exhibition—they are listed below.

1. Florence. Sixteen bark cloth pieces.
   Evidence: Circumstantial. Cook voyage collection from various sources.
   Literature: Giglioli, 1895, pp. 64-73; Kaeppler, 1977. A number of samples were cut from these pieces and given or exchanged by Giglioli to other collections. Bishop Museum has several such pieces which are in this exhibition; Cambridge has at least one (Z5030), and it is likely that there are others.

2. Berne. Six bark cloth pieces (HAW 15, 107, 108, 109, 110, 111).
   Evidence: Webber collection.
   Literature: Henking, 1957, pp. 357-358, 383-387; Kaeppler, 1977.

3. Göttingen. Fourteen bark cloth pieces.
   Evidence: Purchased from London dealer Humphrey in 1782.

4. Vienna. Fifty-eight bark cloth pieces, including several large pieces and a series of 40 cut to approximately 32 cm × 25 cm. Figures 126, 127, 128, and 129.
   Evidence: Leverian Museum.
   Literature: Moschner, 1957, pp. 144-171.

5. Anonymous private collection. Two small pieces.
   Evidence: Exhibited with Cook voyage curiosities in 1785.

6. Chicago. Several pieces in the Fuller collection attributed to Cook's voyage.

7. Sydney. Fifteen small pieces of bark cloth from the Colonial and Indian Exhibition. See Appendix I, this volume.

8. Christchurch, New Zealand. Several pieces from the Worden Hall collection attributed to Cook's voyage on circumstantial evidence.
   Literature: Duff, 1969, p. 79; Appendix II, this volume.

9. Wellington. Two pieces (FE 5246-5247) in the Adams collection. Mrs. P. James Adams was the daughter of Mrs. Cook's cousin, Mrs. Ursula Cragg.

10. British Museum. Unknown number of pieces apparently from Cook's voyage.
    Also (1) + 6896. Bark cloth pieces said to have been given by Banks to White Watson.
    (2) 96.10-12-1 and -3. Two pieces said to have been given by Mrs. Cook to Mrs. M. J. Adams, to Mrs. Tonks.

Ornamentation

Ornamentation used by Hawaiians was extensive. In addition to ornamenting the skin itself with tattooing (Fig. 130), and the "bracelets, necklaces and amulets, which are made of shells, bone or stone" mentioned by Cook (Beaglehole, 1967, p. 280), there were leglets of dog teeth, shells, and seeds, as well as long strands of hair.

Figure 130. — Hawaiian man with tattoo, by John Webber.

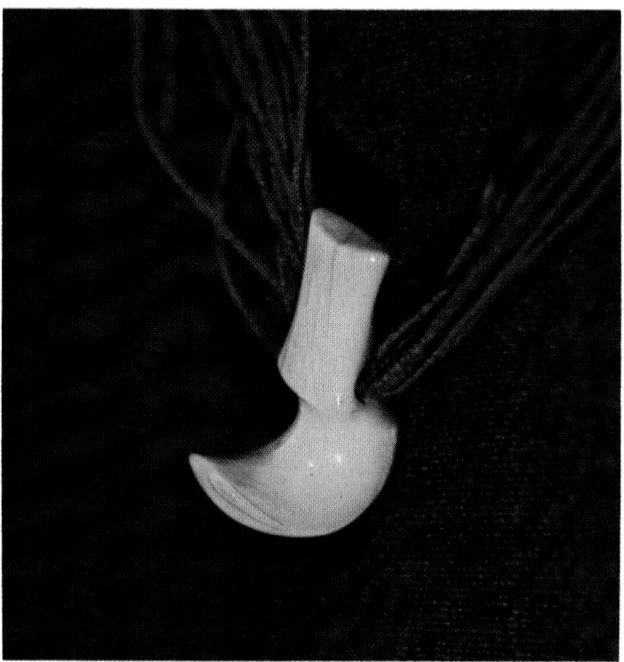

Figure 131. — Ivory hook pendant on human hair (detail), Cambridge 22.924.

Hook Pendant Ornaments

It is significant to note the variation of size and materials in necklaces with hook pendants collected on Cook's voyage. Hooks of ivory, bone, shell, and wood were of small size and hung on twisted hair or strings of tiny shells. Cook and other early European visitors to Hawaii felt that these hook "amulets" had supernatural significance and in early museums they are called idols. It is not clear, however, whether this idea derived from the hook form, or referred to the whale tooth material *(niho palaoa)* from which some of them were made. Many of the hook ornaments collected on Cook's voyage, as will be seen below, were not made of whale tooth and, strictly speaking, were not *lei niho palaoa.* A variant form, known today as *lei 'opu'u,* was also collected.

1. Ivory hook pendant on human hair, Cambridge (22.924). Length of hair (without ties) 41 cm, length of pendant 3.5 cm. Figure 131.
   Evidence: Leverian Museum.

2. Bone hook pendant on human hair, Vienna (184). Length of pendant 4.5 cm. Figure 132.
   Evidence: Leverian Museum
   Literature: Moschner, 1955, pp. 210-212.

3. Bone hook pendant on human hair. Göttingen (OZ 234). Length of pendant 3 cm. Figures 133 and 134.

Figure 132. — Bone hook pendant on human hair, Vienna 184.

   Evidence: Purchased from London dealer Humphrey in 1782.

4. Six ivory hook pendants, on human hair, British Museum (2008).[25] Length of hair (without ties) 28 cm, length of pendants 2.5 cm. Figure 135.
   Evidence: Leverian Museum.

[25] A similar ornament with four ivory hooks, in the British Museum (HAW 117), may also come from Cook's voyage, but its history cannot be traced.

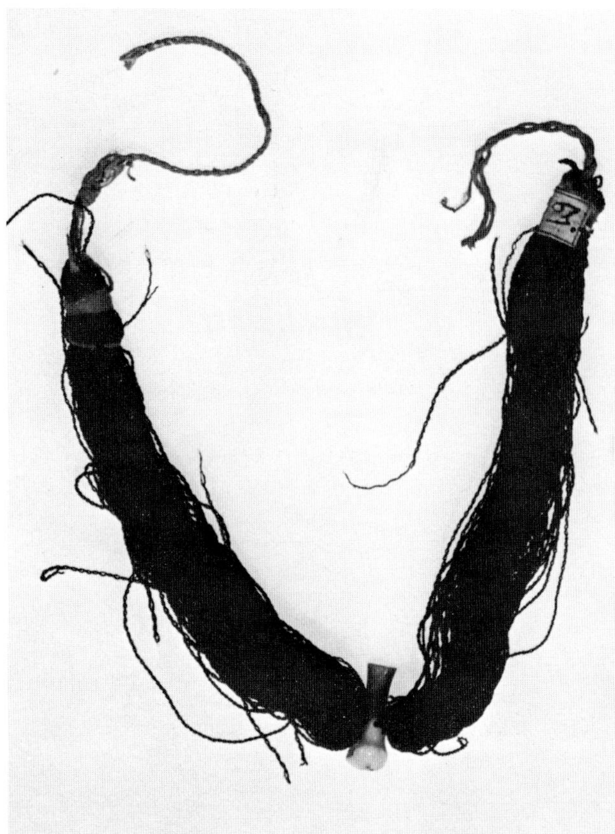

Figure 133. — Bone hook pendant on human hair, Göttingen OZ 234.

Figure 134. — Bone hook pendant on human hair (detail), Göttingen OZ 234.

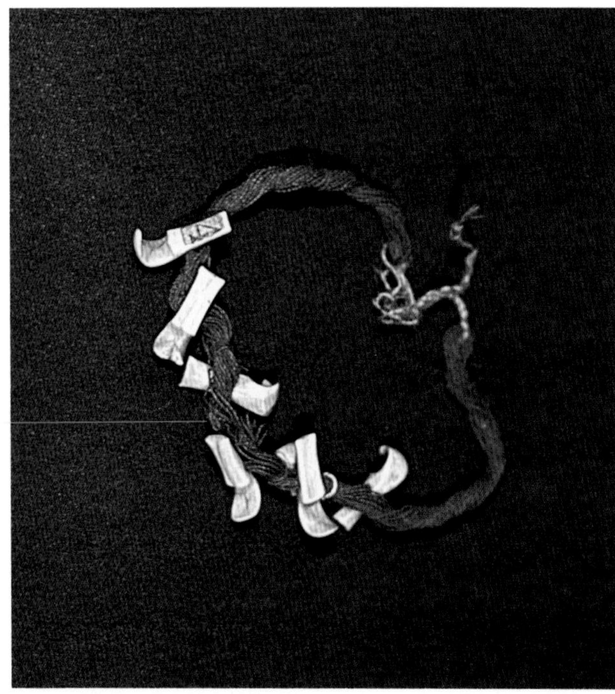

Figure 135. — Six ivory hook pendants on human hair, British Museum 2008.

Figure 136. — Shell hook pendant on shell necklace, British Museum HAW 122.

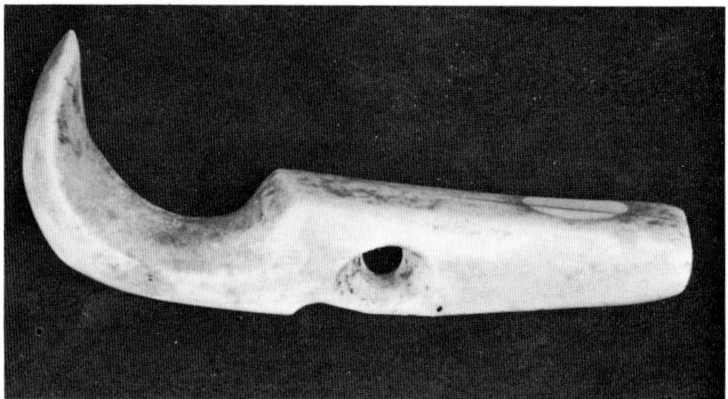

Figure 137. — Shell hook pendant, Göttingen OZ 436.

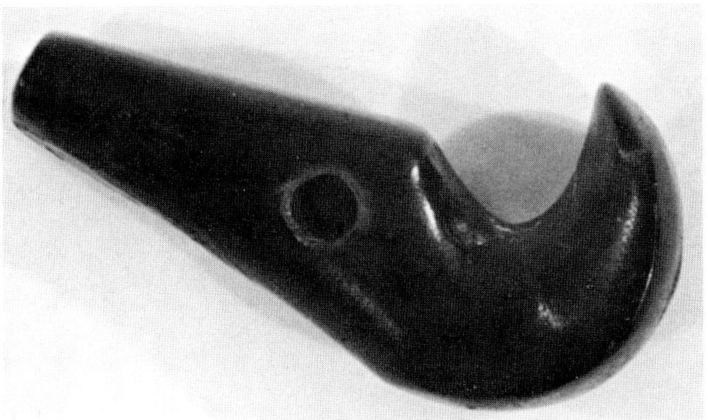

Figure 138.— Black coral hook pendant, Göttingen OZ 235.

5. Three ivory pendants on human hair, Cambridge (22.925). Length of hair (without ties) 29 cm, length of pendants 2.5 cm.
   Evidence: Leverian Museum.

6. Shell hook pendant on strings of tiny shells, British Museum (HAW 122). Length 41 cm, length of pendant 3 cm. Figure 136.
   Evidence: Circumstantial. Probably from the Leverian Museum.

7. Shell hook pendant on strings of tiny shells, Dublin (NN).
   Evidence: Circumstantial. Thought to be part of the collection given by Captain King to Trinity College, Dublin.

8. Shell hook pendant, Göttingen (OZ 436). Length 4 cm. Figure 137.
   Evidence: Purchased from London dealer Humphrey in 1782.

9. Shell hook pendant, British Museum (2009a). Length 5 cm.
   Evidence: Circumstantial. Probably from the Leverian Museum.

10. Shell hook pendant with turtle shell base, British Museum (1944.Oc.2. 715). Length 2.5 cm.
    Evidence: Collected by Alex Dewar, crew member on Cook's third voyage.

11. Shell hook pendant on human hair, Rome (1198). Length 7 cm.
    Evidence: Circumstantial. Cook voyage collection from various sources.
    Literature: Giglioli, 1895, pp. 74-76; Kaeppler, 1977.

12-13. Two shell hook pendants on human hair, Berne (HAW 10 a and b).
    Evidence: Webber collection
    Literature: Henking, 1957, p. 360; Kaeppler, 1977.

14. Calcite hook pendant on human hair. Florence (192). Length 7 cm.
    Evidence: Circumstantial. Cook voyage collection from various sources.
    Literature: Giglioli, 1895, pp. 74-76; Kaeppler, 1977.

15. Black coral (?) hook pendant, Göttingen (OZ 235). Length 3 cm. Figure 138.
    Evidence: Purchased from London dealer Humphrey in 1782.

16. Black coral (?) hook pendant, British Museum (2009b). Length 3.5 cm.
    Evidence: Circumstantial. Probably from the Leverian Museum.

17-18. Two ivory hook ornaments of *"lei 'opu'u"* form, British Museum (2010). Width 2 cm, height 1.5 cm.
    Evidence: Circumstantial. Probably from the Leverian Museum.
    Depictions: Force and Force, 1968, p. 83.

Other Necklaces

In addition to hook pendants strung on human hair and strings of shells, necklaces of various kinds of shells and seeds in single and multiple strands were collected.

1. Necklace of one strand of limpet shells, Göttingen (OZ 243). Length 25 cm. Figure 139.
   Evidence: Purchased from London dealer Humphrey in 1782.

Figure 139.— Shell necklace, Göttingen OZ 243.

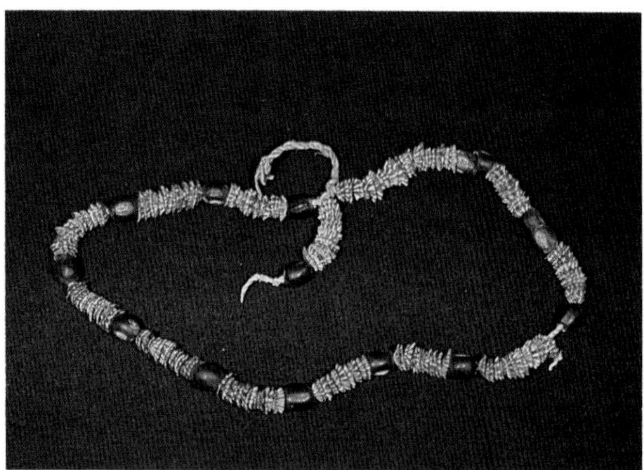

Figure 140. — Seed and shell necklace, British Museum Q77.Oc.2.

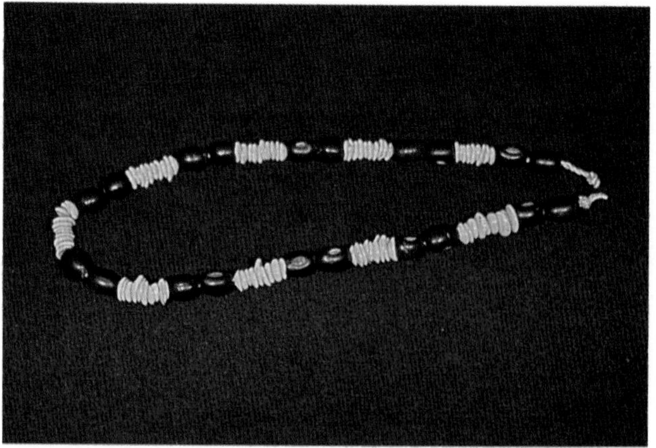

Figure 141. — Seed and shell necklace, British Museum Q77.Oc.3.

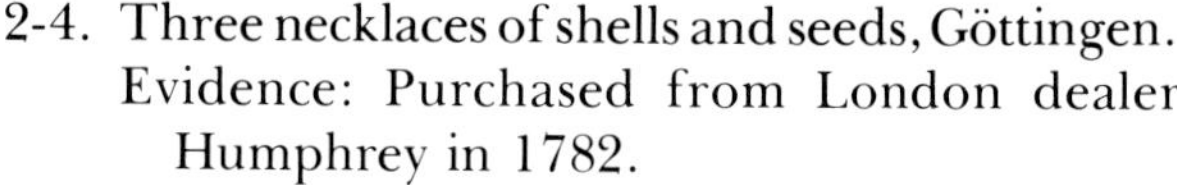

2-4. Three necklaces of shells and seeds, Göttingen.
Evidence: Purchased from London dealer Humphrey in 1782.

5-7. Three necklaces of shells and seeds, British Museum (Q77.Oc.2,3,4). Figures 140, 141, and 142.
(a) Large seeds and limpet shells. Length 54 cm.
(b) Large seeds and *"puka"* shells. Length 45 cm.
(c) "Niihau" shells. Length 40 cm.
Evidence: Circumstantial. Probably from the Leverian Museum.

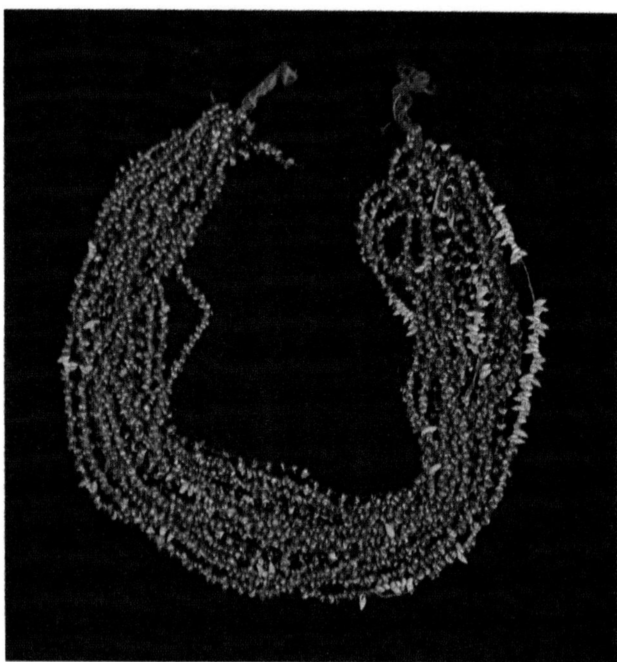

Figure 142. — Niihau shell necklace, British Museum Q77.Oc.4.

8-9. Two necklaces of shells and seeds, Cambridge (27.1638, 27. 1639).
Evidence: Leverian Museum.

10. Necklace of tiny black seeds and *"puka"* shells, Berne (TAH 45).
Evidence: Webber collection.
Literature: Kaeppler, 1977.

11. Necklace of large seeds and *"puka"* shells, Dublin (1880.1680). Length 44 cm. Figure 143.
Evidence: Circumstantial. Thought to be part of the collection given to Trinity College, Dublin, by Captain King.

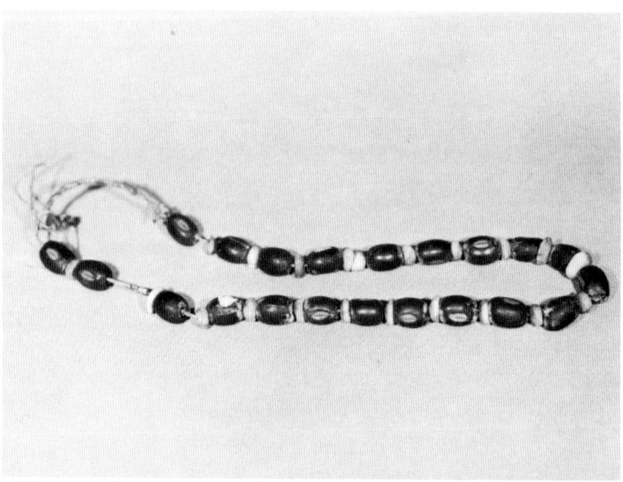

Figure 143. — Seed and shell necklace, Dublin 1880.1680.

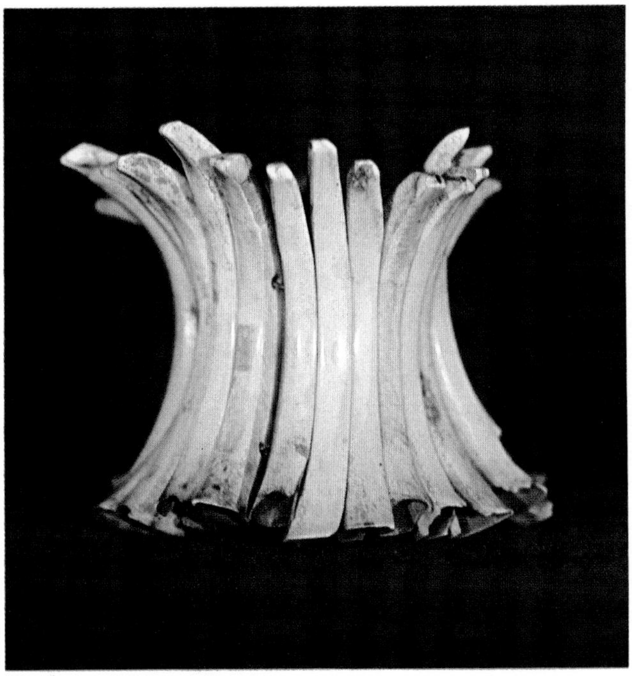

Figure 144.— Boar tusk bracelet, Exeter E1278.

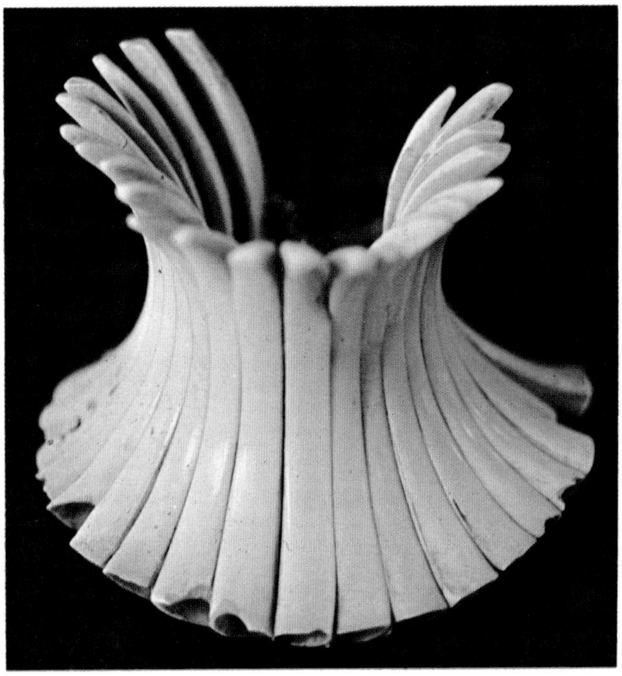

Figure 145.— Boar tusk bracelet, Leningrad 505-16.

Bracelets of Boar Tusks

1. Boar tusk bracelet, Exeter (E1278). Height 9.5 cm. Figure 144.
   Evidence: Leverian Museum.

2. Boar tusk bracelet, Cambridge (22.919). Height 9.5 cm.
   Evidence: Leverian Museum.

3. Boar tusk bracelet, Vienna (196). Height 10 cm.
   Evidence: Leverian Museum.
   Literature: Moschner, 1955, pp. 210-212.

4. Boar tusk bracelet, Leningrad (505-16). Height 10 cm. Figure 145.
   Evidence: Given by Capt. Clerke to the Governor of Kamchatka.
   Literature: Rozina, 1966, p. 242; Kaeppler, 1977.

5. Boar tusk bracelet, Göttingen (OZ 239).
   Evidence: Purchased from London dealer Humphrey in 1782.

6. Boar tusk bracelet, British Museum (HAW 156). Height 8.5 cm.
   Evidence: Circumstantial. Noted "Cook coll. No. 26."

7-8. Two boar tusk bracelets. Edinburgh (1956.1018 a and b). Heights 7.5 cm.
   Evidence: Given by Mrs. Cook to Sir John Pringle.

9. Boar tusk bracelet, Berne (HAW 11). Length of tusks 10.5-14 cm.
   Evidence: Webber collection.
   Literature: Henking, 1957, p. 358; Kaeppler, 1977.

10. Boar tusk bracelet, Florence (165). Height 10 cm.
   Evidence: Circumstantial. Cook voyage collection from various sources.
   Literature: Giglioli, 1895, pp. 78-79; Kaeppler, 1977.

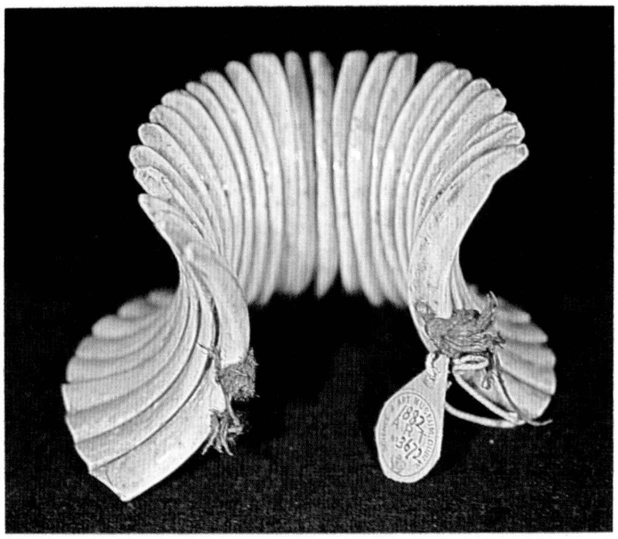

Figure 146.— Boar tusk bracelet, Dublin 1882.3672.

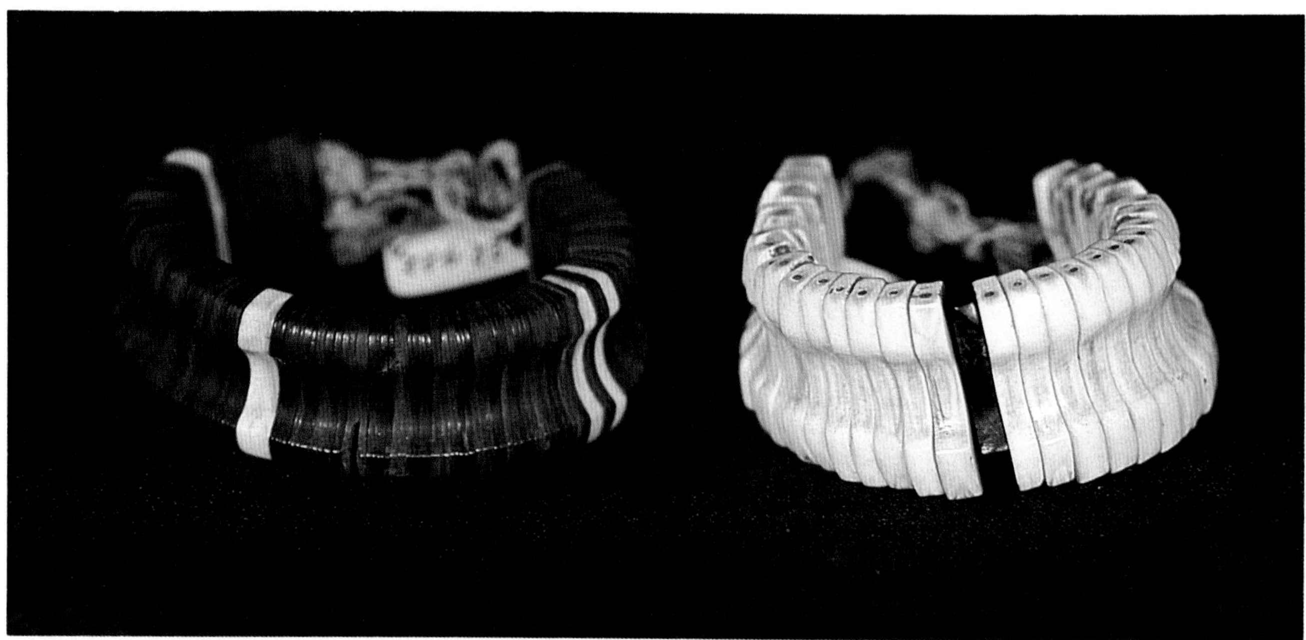

Figure 147.— Two bracelets of turtle shell, dog teeth and ivory, Cambridge 22.922a, 22.922b.

11. Boar tusk bracelet, Rome (2423). Height 9 cm.
    Evidence: Circumstantial. Cook voyage collection from various sources.
    Literature: Giglioli, 1895, pp. 78-79; Kaeppler, 1977.

12. Boar tusk bracelet, Dublin (1882.3672). Height 8 cm. Figure 146.
    Evidence: Circumstantial. Thought to be part of the collection given by Captain King to Trinity College, Dublin.
    Literature: Freeman, 1949, p. 8.

13. Boar tusk bracelet, Wellington (FE 333).
    Evidence: Original Cook collection in Bullock's Museum.
    Literature: Kaeppler, 1974a, p. 78.

14-15. Two boar tusk bracelets, Berlin (VI 369, 372).
    Evidence: Circumstantial. Probably from Humphrey's Cook collection or Leverian Museum.
    Literature: Kaeppler, 1974a, p. 82.

16. Boar tusk bracelet, Christchurch (162).
    Evidence: Circumstantial. Worden Hall collection. See Appendix II, this volume.

In addition, there were about four other boar tusk bracelets from the Leverian Museum, now lost.

Bracelets of Turtle Shell and Ivory

A second type of bracelet collected in some numbers on Cook's voyage was composed of shaped pieces of turtle shell combined with carved pieces of ivory, or dog teeth.[26]

1. Bracelet of dog teeth and turtle shell, Cambridge (22.922a). Length 14 cm; height 2.2 cm. One central piece of turtle shell and 37 carved dog teeth. Figure 147.
   Evidence: Leverian Museum.
2. Bracelet of dog teeth and turtle shell, Göttingen (OZ 240). Length 15 cm; height 2 cm. Two pieces of turtle shell and 47 carved dog teeth. Figure 148.
   Evidence: Purchased from London dealer Humphrey in 1782.
3. Bracelet of turtle shell and ivory, Vienna (197). Height 1.8 cm. Five pieces of carved ivory and hundreds of pieces of turtle shell. Figure 149.
   Evidence: Leverian Museum.
   Literature: Moschner, 1955, pp. 211-212.
4. Bracelet of turtle shell and ivory, Vienna (198). Height 1.2 cm. Pieces of carved ivory and hundreds of pieces of turtle shell. Figure 149.
   Evidence: Leverian Museum.
   Literature: Moschner, 1955, pp. 211-212.

[26] Three bracelets of this type in the British Museum (HAW 151, 152, 153) unfortunately have no accession information.

Figure 148. — Bracelet of dog teeth and turtle shell, Göttingen OZ 240.

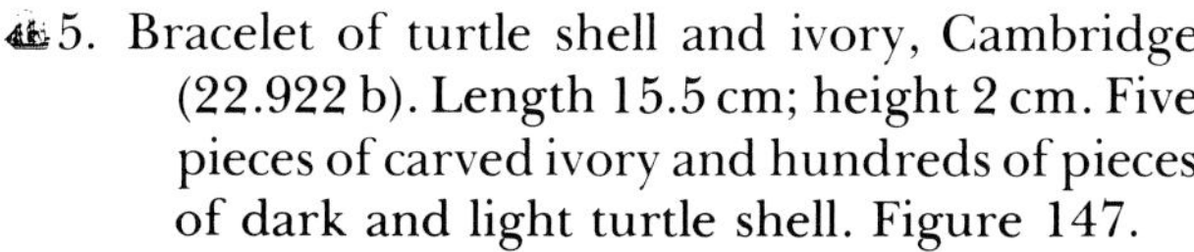

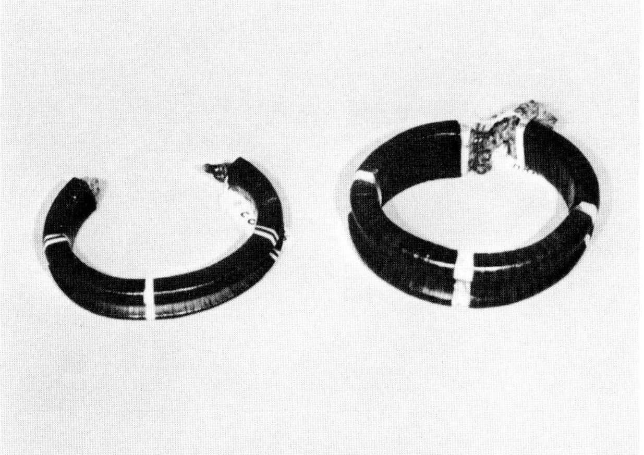

Figure 149. — Two bracelets of turtle shell and ivory, Vienna 197, 198.

5. Bracelet of turtle shell and ivory, Cambridge (22.922 b). Length 15.5 cm; height 2 cm. Five pieces of carved ivory and hundreds of pieces of dark and light turtle shell. Figure 147.
   Evidence: Leverian Museum.
6. Bracelet of turtle shell and ivory, Berne (HAW 12). Length 19 cm. Five pieces of carved ivory and 215 pieces of turtle shell.
   Evidence: Webber collection
   Literature: Henking, 1957, p. 358; Kaeppler, 1977.
7. Bracelet of turtle shell and other substances, Florence (2849). Length 16 cm; height 2.5 cm. Hundreds of pieces of turtle shell with tridacna shell and bone dividers.
   Evidence: Circumstantial. Cook voyage collection from various sources.
   Literature: Giglioli, 1895, pp. 77-78; Kaeppler, 1977.
8. Bracelet of turtle shell and tridacna shell (?), Rome (2498). Length 16.5 cm; height 2.5 cm.
   Evidence: Circumstantial. Cook voyage collection from various sources.
   Literature: Giglioli, 1895, pp. 77-78; Kaeppler, 1977.
9. Bracelet of turtle shell and ivory, Christchurch (E 149.162).
   Evidence: Circumstantial. Worden Hall collection. See Appendix II, this volume.
10. Sections from a turtle shell and ivory bracelet, Jean-Jacques Laurent, Tahiti.
   Evidence: Part of Cook collection exhibited at Colonial and Indian exhibition.
   Literature: Mackrell, 1886. Appendix I, this volume.

There was also at least one more similar bracelet in the Leverian Museum which has not yet been located.

Shell Ornaments

Ornaments of single or multiple shells strung on fiber cord and probably worn as bracelets were also collected during Cook's visit to Hawaii, but none can be located. The shells probably became part of collections of "natural" rather than "artificial" curiosities. Three such ornaments were depicted in the Leverian Museum (Force and Force, 1968, pp. 86, 95, 97).

Turtle Ornaments

Carved ornaments of bone or ivory in the shape of turtles strung on fiber cord were also said to be worn as bracelets or rings. At least two of these were at one time in the Leverian Museum.[27]

1-3. Three carved turtles, Sydney (H151). Lengths 2.2 cm. Figure 150.
   Evidence: Part of Cook collection exhibited at Colonial and Indian Exhibition.
   Literature: Mackrell, 1886; Appendix I, this volume.

[27]Two such ornaments are in the British Museum, but their lack of accession information makes it impossible to confirm an association with Cook's voyage.

Figure 150. — Three ivory turtles, Sydney H151.

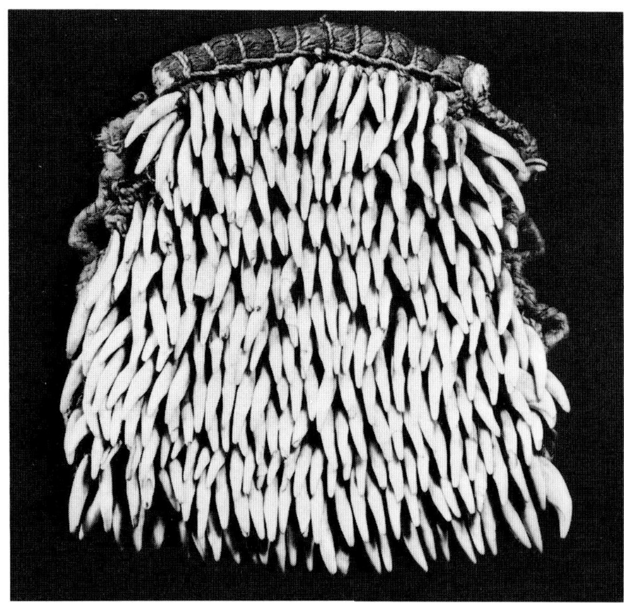

Figure 151.— Leglet of dog teeth, Vienna 194.

Ornaments for the Lower Leg

Leg ornaments collected during Cook's voyage were made of dog teeth, shells, and seeds, while in 19th century collections anklets appear to have been made almost exclusively of dog teeth.

1. Leglet of dog teeth, Vienna (194). Height 15 cm; width 19 cm. Figure 151.
   Evidence: Leverian Museum.
   Literature: Moschner, 1955, pp. 213 and 215.

2. Leglet of dog teeth, British Museum (HAW 158).
   Evidence: Circumstantial. Noted "Cook coll." because of its similarity to that depicted in British Library Add. Ms. 23.921.76.

3. Leglet of shells, Vienna (193). Height 23.5 cm; width 35 cm. Figure 152.
   Evidence: Leverian Museum.
   Literature: Moschner, 1955, p. 213.

Figure 152.— Leglet of shells, Vienna 193.

Figure 153.— Leglet of shells and seeds, Vienna 192.

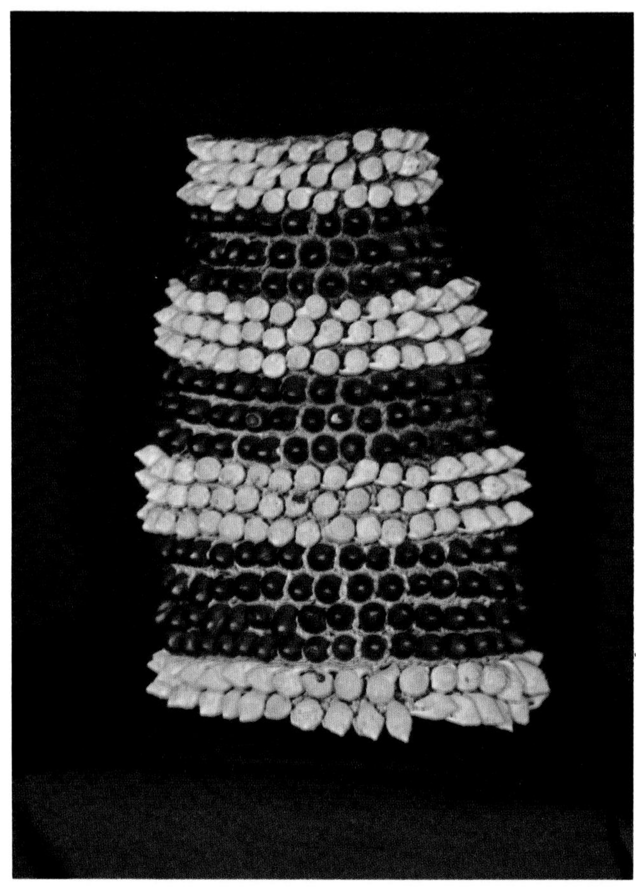

Figure 154.— A view in Kauai by John Webber, British Library Add. Ms. 15,513.30.

4-5. Two leglets of shells, Berne (HAW 106 a and b). Heights 20 cm; widths 32 cm, 37 cm.
Evidence: Webber collection
Literature: Henking, 1957, pp. 358-359; Kaeppler, 1977.

6. Leglet of shells, Florence (217). Height 21 cm; width 40 cm.
Evidence: Circumstantial. Cook voyage collection from various sources.
Literature: Giglioli, 1895, pp. 79-80; Kaeppler, 1977.

7. Leglet of shells and seeds, Vienna (192). Height 23.5 cm; width 38 cm. Figure 153.
Evidence: Leverian Museum.
Literature: Moschner, 1955, pp. 213-215.

8. Part of a leglet of shells and seeds, Cambridge (22.923). Length 34 cm; height 3 cm.
Evidence: Leverian Museum.

9. Dog teeth prepared for use, Florence (53). Thirteen dog teeth strung together probably for safekeeping prior to being made into a leglet.
Evidence: Circumstantial. Cook voyage collection from various sources.
Literature: Giglioli, 1895, p. 79; Kaeppler, 1977.

10. Dog teeth prepared for use, Vienna (200). Fifty dog teeth strung together, probably for safekeeping prior to being made into a leglet.
Evidence: Leverian Museum.
Literature: Moschner, 1955, pp. 211-212.

11. Dog teeth prepared for use, Göttingen (OZ 240). Dog teeth strung together, probably for safekeeping prior to being made into a leglet.
Evidence: Purchased from London dealer Humphrey in 1782.

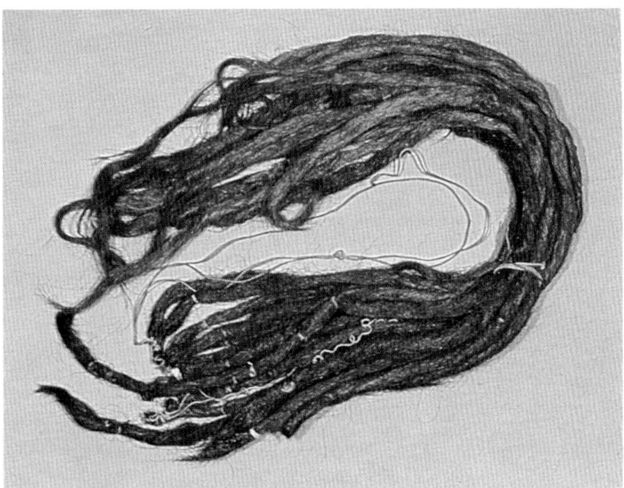

Figure 155. — Ornament of hair, Vienna 191.

Ornaments of Strands of Human Hair

These hair pieces, described as "quantities of false hair . . . it flows down their backs in distinct cords twisted" (Samwell in Beaglehole, 1967, p. 1179), are among the rarest of all Hawaiian artifacts. Only one such hair piece can be traced to Cook's voyage. A drawing by Webber depicts such a hair piece (British Library Add. Ms. 15,513.30). Figure 154.

1. Ornament of human hair, Vienna (191). Eighteen strands of human hair. Length 80 cm. Figure 155.
   Evidence: Leverian Museum.
   Literature: Moschner, 1955, p. 230.

Figure 156. — Four stone mirrors, Vienna 169-172.

Mirrors

Basalt mirrors were used for their obvious function as looking glasses, and some were apparently worn as ornaments hung from a cord around the neck. All five that have been located were once in the Leverian Museum—no doubt there were others but such things can easily lose their historical associations.

1-4. Four mirrors, Vienna (169-170 [exhibited], 171, 172). Diameters 7.6 cm; 6.4 cm; 6.6 cm; 5.7 cm. Figure 156.
   Evidence: Leverian Museum.
   Literature: Moschner, 1955, pp. 227-229.

5. Mirror, Cambridge (22.920). Diameter 7 cm.
   Evidence: Leverian Museum.

Figure 157. — Feather fan, Leningrad 505-4.

Figure 158. — (Opposite page) Wicker fan, Vienna 142.

Fans

Fans collected on Cook's voyage are also rare. Three styles have been isolated, but only one of each can be traced.

1. Feather fan, Leningrad (505-4). Length 46 cm; width 22 cm. The framework of sticks is covered with bark cloth, to which are pasted pieces of bird skin with feathers adhering. Long feathers as fringe. Figure 157.
   Evidence: Given by Captain Clerke to the Governor of Kamchatka.
   Literature: Rozina, 1966, p. 247; Kaeppler, 1977.
2. Wicker fan, Vienna (142). Height 40 cm; width 25 cm. Decorated with human hair and coconut fiber. Figure 158.
   Evidence: Leverian Museum.
   Literature: Moschner, 1955, pp. 220 and 222.
3. Pandanus fan, Institut für Völkerkunde, Göttingen (OZ 140). Length 24.8 cm; width 21.6 cm.
   Evidence: Purchased from London dealer Humphrey in 1782.

Figure 159. — Drum *(pahu)*, Hewett collection.

Musical Instruments

Only drums, gourd rattles, and a gourd nose whistle *(hōkiokio)* can be traced to Cook's voyages. Strangely enough no nose flutes appear to have been collected, or at least cannot be located today.

1. Drum *(pahu)* John Hewett collection. (The membrane has been replaced). Height 53 cm; diameter 41 cm. Figures 159 and 160.
   Evidence: Leverian Museum.
2. Drum *(pahu)*, Vienna (201). Height 29 cm; diameter 19 cm. Figure 161.
   Evidence: Leverian Museum.
   Literature: Moschner, 1955, pp. 246-247.
3. Drum with human images, British Museum, formerly in the Hooper collection (272). Height 29.2 cm.
   Evidence: Leverian Museum.
   Literature: Phelps, 1976, p. 416 (not attributed to Cook).
4. Drum *(pahu)*, Cambridge (22.915). Height 22 cm; diameter 19 cm.
   Evidence: Circumstantial. Apparently from the Leverian Museum.
5. Drum *(pahu)*, Florence (260). Height 30 cm; diameter 28 cm.
   Evidence: Circumstantial. Cook voyage collection from various sources.
   Literature: Giglioli, 1893, pp. 234-235; Kaeppler, 1977.
6. Drum *(pūniu)*, Hunterian Museum, Glasgow (E 367). Height 20.5 cm; height of stand 11 cm; diameter 12 cm. Figure 162. Skin-covered coconut shell drum is bound to a wooden base with fiber cords. A rare piece, indeed—only two being known.[28]
   Evidence: Purchased at Samwell's sale in 1781.

Gourd Rattles

Gourd rattles were depicted by Webber from different views (Fig. 163) and in use (Fig. 164).

1. Gourd rattle, British Museum (HAW 93). Diameter of top 45.5 cm; height 33 cm. Figure 165.
   Evidence: Circumstantial. Noted "Cook coll."

[28]A similar drum in the British Museum (HAW 94) has no accession information and therefore cannot be associated with Cook's voyage.

Figure 160. — Drum (detail), Hewett collection.

Figure 161. — Drum *(pahu)*, Vienna 201.

Figure 162. — Drum *(pūniu)*, Glasgow E 367.

Figure 163. — Drawing of gourd rattles, by John Webber. British Library Add. Ms. 15,514.28.

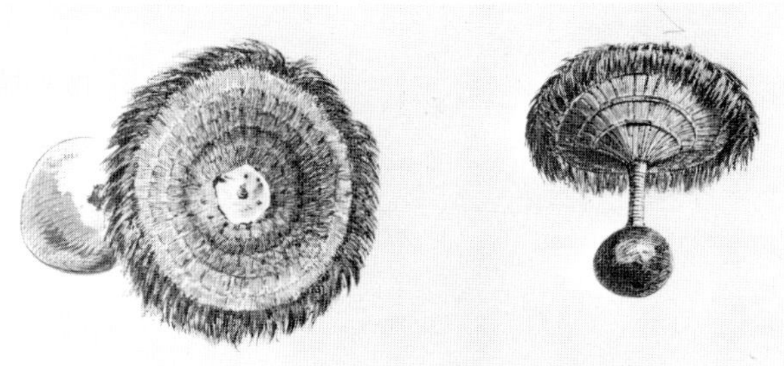

Figure 164. — Three views of a Hawaiian man with a gourd rattle, by John Webber.

Figure 165. — Gourd rattle, British Museum HAW 93.

Figure 166. — Head of a gourd rattle, Vienna 183.

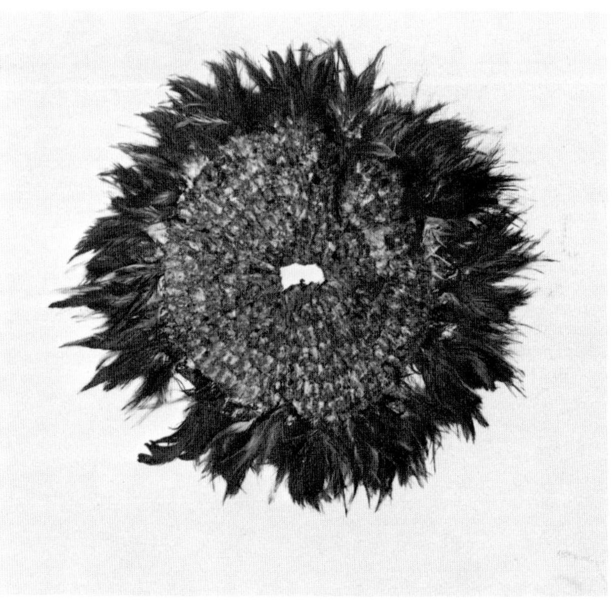

2. Gourd rattle, Lost.
   Evidence: Leverian Museum.
   Depictions: *Atlas* to Cook's Third Voyage, Plate 67 (Fig. 55). Probably the same rattle depicted by Sarah Stone in Leverian Museum, Force and Force, 1968, pp. 79, 81.

3. Feathered head of a gourd rattle, Vienna (183). Diameter of top 28 cm; diameter with feather fringe 47 cm. Figure 166.
   Evidence: Leverian Museum.
   Literature: Moschner, 1955, p. 247.

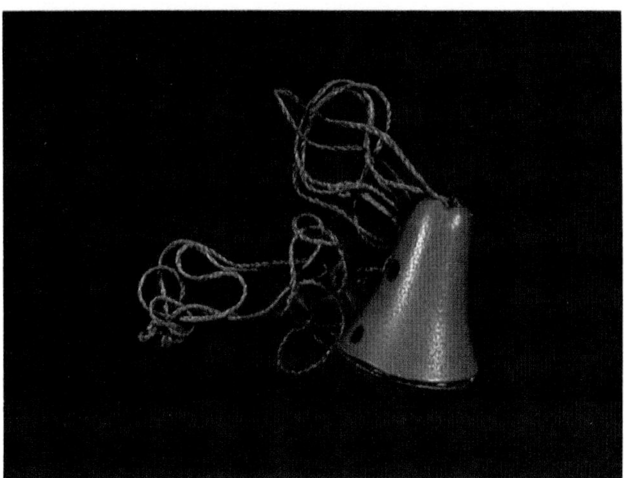

Figure 167.— Gourd nose whistle, Sydney H 118.

Gourd Nose Whistle

1. Nose whistle, Sydney (H 118). Height 6 cm, diameter 4 cm. Figure 167.
   Evidence: Cook collection exhibited at the Colonial and Indian Exhibition.
   Literature: Mackrell, 1886; Appendix I, this volume.

Game Stones

Although a large number of *'ulu maika,* game stones, were collected during Cook's voyage only seven can be located. In the Leverian Museum there were at least 22, but such objects could easily lose their historical associations.

1-5. Five game stones (white sandstone, limestone, and basalt), Vienna (164-168). Diameters 9 cm; 8.2 cm; 7.5 cm; 6.8 cm; 6.8 cm.
   Evidence: Leverian Museum.
   Literature: Moschner, 1955, pp. 248-249.

6. Game stone (white calcareous limestone), Berne (HAW 9). Diameter 8.5 cm.
   Evidence: Webber collection.
   Literature: Henking, 1957, p. 361; Kaeppler, 1977.

7. Game stone (white calcareous limestone), British Museum.
   Evidence: Circumstantial. Possibly Leverian Museum.

8-9. Two game stones (white calcareous limestone), Cambridge (25367-8).
   Evidence: Pennant collection of Cook voyage objects from various sources.

10. Game stone (white calcareous limestone), Göttingen (221). Diameter 8 cm.
   Evidence: Purchased from London dealer Humphrey in 1782.

Wooden Game Implements

An object of unknown use is hypothesized to be a *maile* wand. The long thin stick tufted with dog hair may have been used for the Hawaiian games of *pūhenehene* or *'ume.*[29]

1. Game stick,[30] Florence (272). Length 120 cm.
   Evidence: Circumstantial. Cook voyage collection from various sources.
   Literature: Giglioli, 1895, pp. 99-101; Kaeppler, 1977.

2. Implement for game *pahe'e* (?). Truro Museum.
   Evidence: Circumstantial. Labeled from Cook's voyages and probably from sale of Bullock's Museum (see Kaeppler, 1974a).

Bows and Arrows

Bows and arrows were mentioned in accounts of Cook's voyage and early museums, but none can be located.

---

[29]A feathered staff, formerly in the Hooper collection (331), and now in Bishop Museum, may also be a game stick. It has been attributed to Cook's voyage (Phelps, 1976, p. 417) but this association cannot be confirmed.

[30]A similar object in the British Museum (1978) unfortunately has no accession information.

Weapons

Weapons seen in Hawaii during Cook's voyage were described by Samwell (see Beaglehole, 1967, Pt. 2, p. 1182),

> Their Arms consist of Spears, Daggers, short Clubs, bows & Arrows & Slings; of the Spears there are two Sorts, one long & small like that of New Zealand, the other made of red wood called koa or toa and pointed & barbed at one end, this is for throwing but the other they do not part with; their Daggers are made of fine polished black wood, and of different sizes from a foot & ½ to half a foot long, they put a string through the Handles of them which they turn round their Wrists that they may not be wrenched from them. Their Clubs are about a foot long with round heads and strings through the handles of them. As to their bows and Arrows they never use them in fighting; being very slender & weak, seemingly intended for diversion, tho' we never saw them make use of them. Their Slings are made of twine platted and they are dexterous at the use of them.

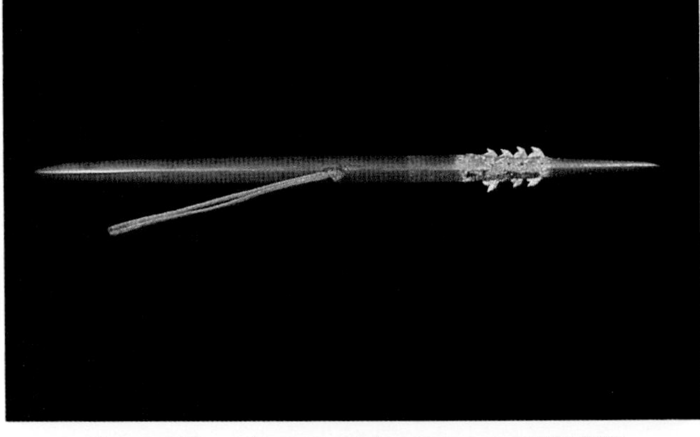

Figure 168.— Dagger, Bishop Museum 1973.275.

Daggers

⛵1. Wooden dagger with shark teeth and feathers, Bishop Museum (1973.275). Purchased on behalf of Bishop Museum by Mrs. Helen Goo Carter. Length 62.5 cm; width 3 cm. Figure 168.
Evidence: Leverian Museum.
Depiction: Force and Force, 1968, p. 83.

2. Wooden dagger, double ended with a single shark tooth (Hawaii?), Greenwich (L15(93)). Length 33 cm. Figure 169.
Evidence: Circumstantial. Belonged to Charlotte Cook who married T. Bradley ca. 1812.

⛵3. Wooden dagger, Cambridge (22.918). Length 33 cm. Figure 170.
Evidence: Leverian Museum.
Depictions: Engraved in *Atlas* to Cook's third voyage, Plate 67 (Fig. 55). British Library Add. Ms. 23,921.79; Force and Force, 1968, p. 111.

4. Wooden dagger, Berne (HAW 7). Length 43.5 cm.
Evidence: Webber collection.
Literature: Henking, 1957, p. 367; Kaeppler, 1977.

5. Wooden dagger, British Museum (HAW 182).[31] Length 60 cm.
Evidence: Circumstantial. Noted "Cook coll."

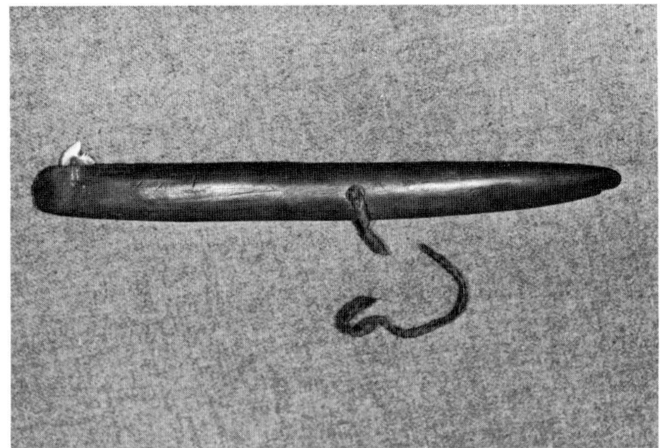

Figure 169.— Dagger, Greenwich L15(93).

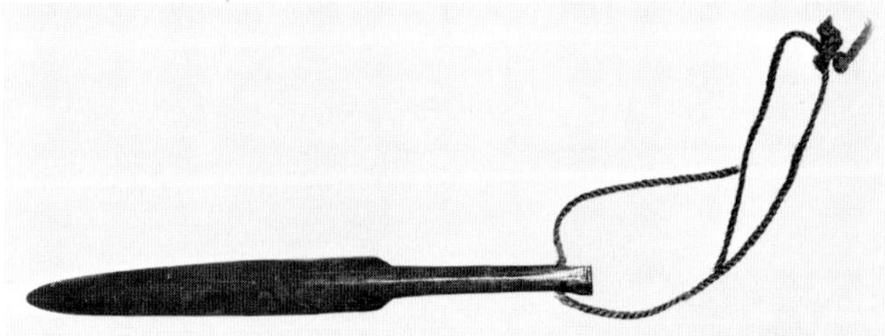

Figure 170.— Dagger, Cambridge 22.918.

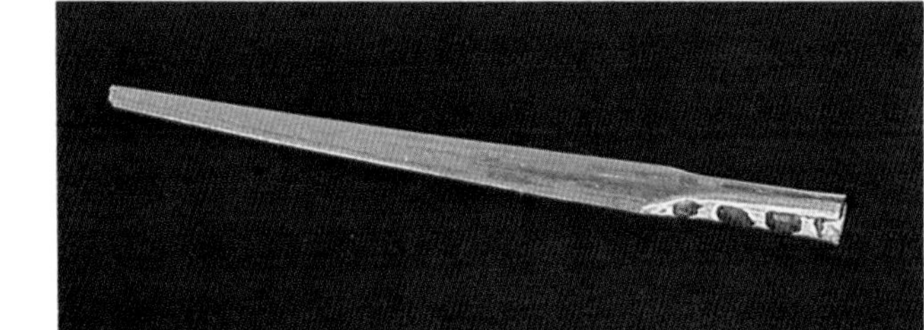

Figure 171.— Swordfish dagger, Hewett collection.

[31] Another object in the British Museum listed as a "spear dagger" (40.5-9.1) is attributed to Cook's voyage. It cannot be located so it is impossible to comment on what it is, or whether a Cook voyage provenance can be confirmed.

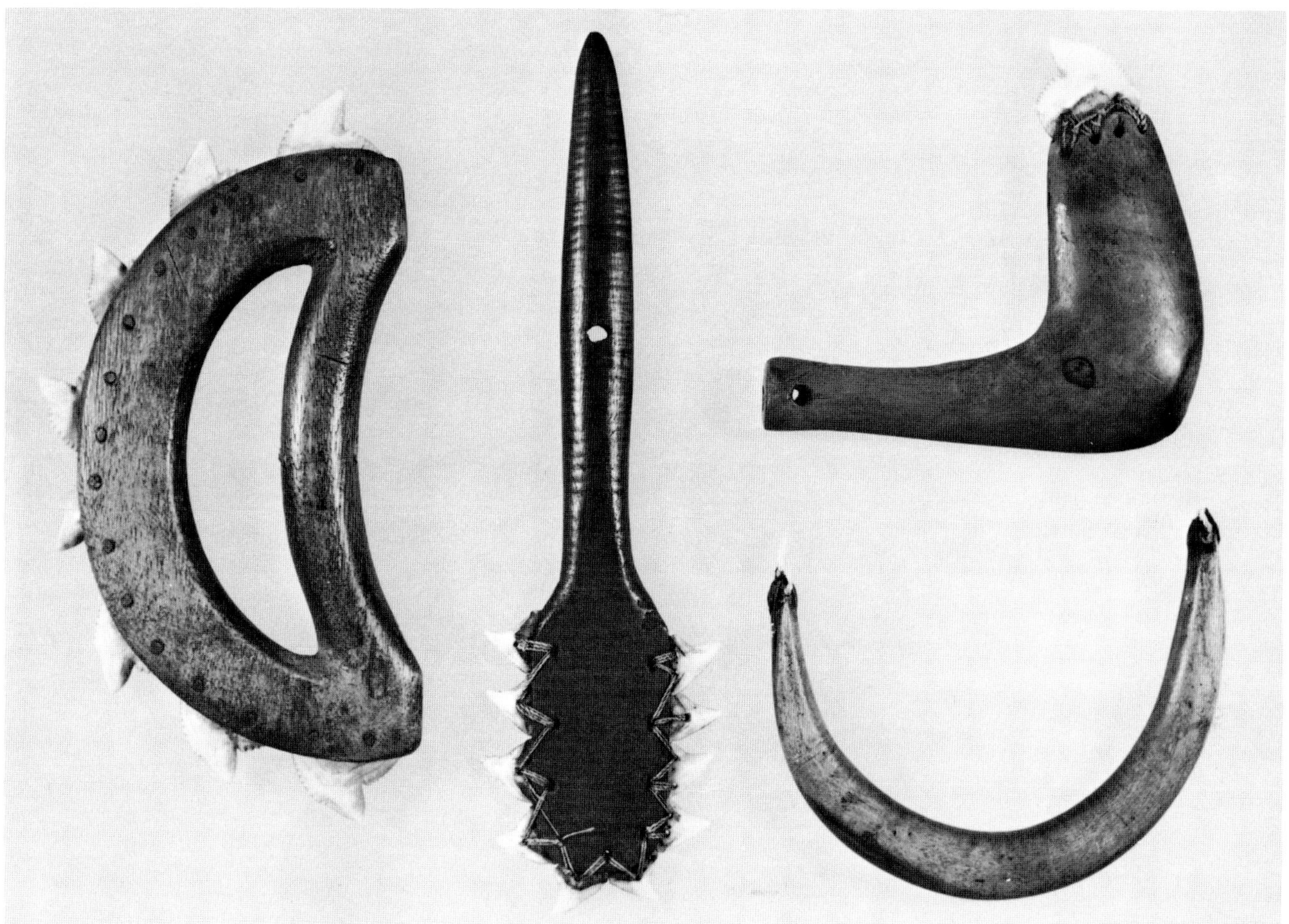

Figure 172. — Four shark tooth implements, Vienna 161, 162, 41, 42.

6. Truncheon dagger,[32] Leningrad (505-33). Length 48.5 cm. Figure 109.
   Evidence: Given by Captain Clerke to Governor of Kamchatka.
   Literature: Rozina, 1966, p. 252; Kaeppler, 1977.
7. Swordfish dagger, John Hewett collection. Length 71 cm. Figure 171. To be presented to Bishop Museum by John Hewett on the occasion of the opening of this exhibition.
   Evidence: Leverian Museum.
8. Swordfish dagger. Lost.
   Evidence: Leverian Museum.
   Depiction: Force and Force, 1968, p. 111.[33]

There were at least 11 other daggers in the Leverian Museum which are now lost.

[32] See Buck, 1957, pp. 425-426.

[33] A dagger in the British Museum (9059) is very much like this drawing. According to accession information it was given by John Davidson, but it cannot be linked to Cook's voyage or the Leverian Museum. A swordfish dagger in Rome (1189) is attributed to Cook's voyage by Giglioli (1895, pp. 95-96), but this attribution is questionable (Kaeppler, 1977).

Shark Tooth Implements

Shark tooth implements collected on Cook's voyage were of several types. Some are of spatulate shape, some of knifelike forms, some crescent-shaped, some attached to a cord binding, and some are finger rings.

1. Shark tooth implement (spatulate), Vienna (161). Length 23 cm; width 6.5 cm. Figure 172.
   Evidence: Leverian Museum.
   Literature: Moschner, 1955, pp. 161 and 163.
2. Shark tooth implement (spatulate), Exeter (E1226). Length 29 cm. Figure 173.
   Evidence: Leverian Museum.
3. Shark tooth implement (spatulate), Leningrad (505-5). Length 32 cm, width 7 cm. Figure 174.
   Evidence: Given by Captain Clerke to the Governor of Kamchatka.
   Literature: Rozina, 1966, pp. 252-253; Kaeppler, 1977.

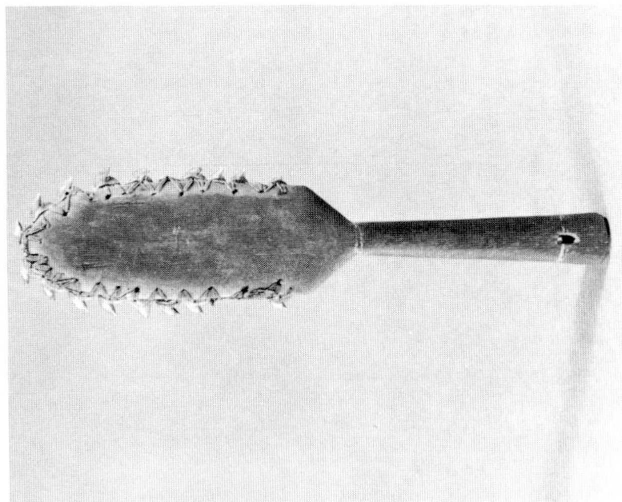

Figure 173. — Shark tooth implement, Exeter E1226.

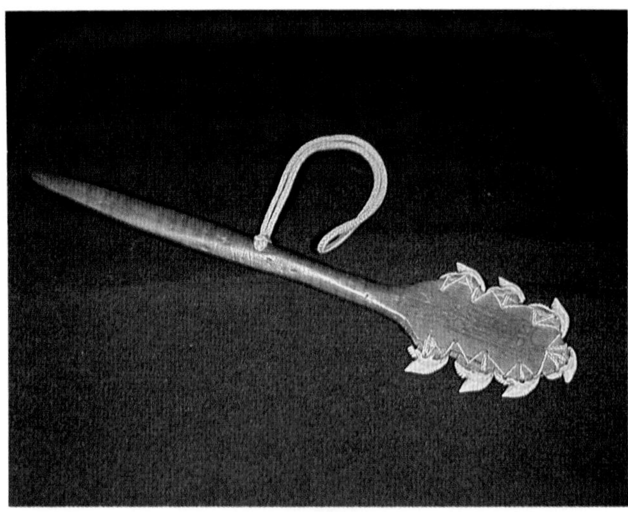

Figure 174. — Shark tooth implement, Leningrad 505-5.

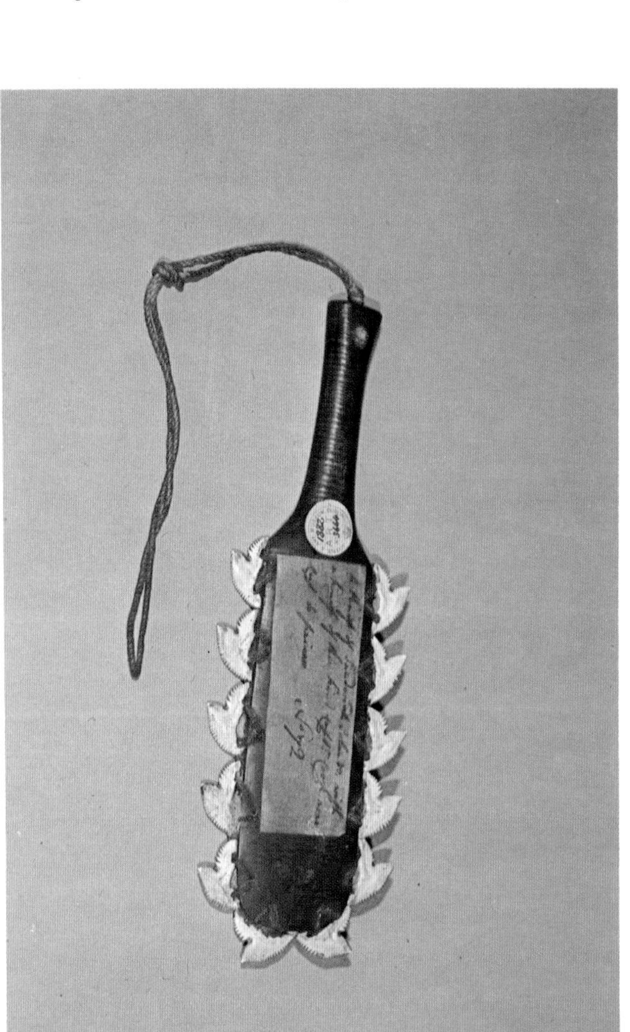

Figure 175. — Shark tooth implement, Dublin 1882.3664.

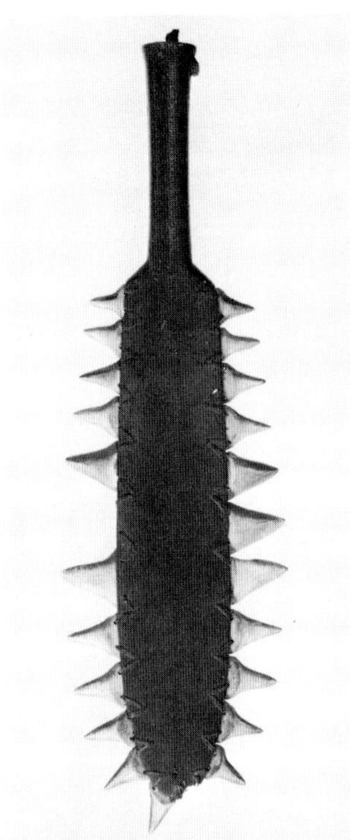

Figure 176. — Shark tooth implement, Cambridge 25.366.

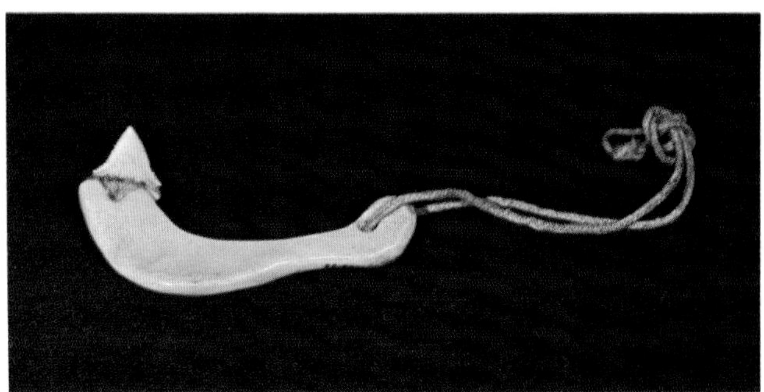

Figure 177. — Shark tooth implement, Cambridge 22.921.

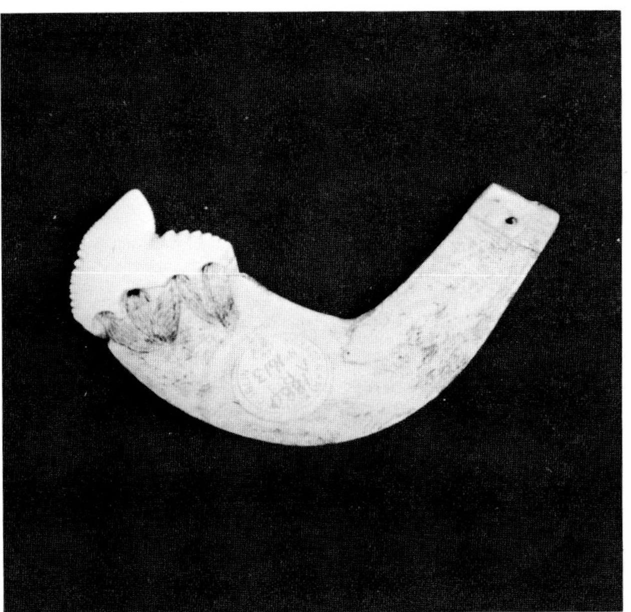

Figure 178.— Shark tooth implement, Dublin 1880.1613.

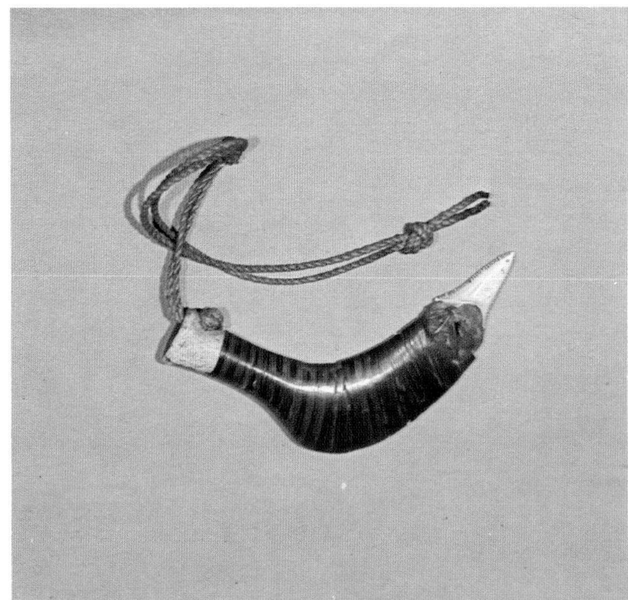

Figure 179.— Shark tooth implement, Dublin 1882.3680.

4. Shark tooth implement (spatulate), Charles Mack collection, Honolulu, formerly in the Hooper collection (368). Length 40 cm.
   Evidence: Leverian Museum.
   Depictions: Cook *Atlas,* Plate 67 (Fig. 55); British Library Add. Ms. 23,921.79. Force and Force, 1968, p. 85.
   Literature: Phelps, 1976, p. 418.
5. Shark tooth implement (spatulate), Florence (157). Length 25.5 cm, width 8 cm.
   Evidence: Circumstantial. Cook voyage collection from various sources.
   Literature: Giglioli, 1895, pp. 97-98; Kaeppler, 1977.
6. Shark tooth implement (spatulate), Dublin (1882.3664). Length 29 cm; width 10 cm. Figure 175.
   Evidence: Circumstantial. Thought to be part of the collection given by Captain King to Trinity College. Label "No. 72" attached.
   Literature: Freeman, 1949.
7. Shark tooth implement (spatulate), Berne (HAW 6). Length 21 cm; width 5 cm.
   Evidence: Webber collection.
   Literature: Henking, 1957, p. 366; Kaeppler, 1977.
8. Shark tooth implement (spatulate), Cambridge (25.366). Length 49 cm. Figure 176.
   Evidence: Pennant collection of Cook voyage objects from various sources.
9. Shark tooth implement (single tooth in bone handle), Cambridge (22.921). Length 10 cm. Figure 177.
   Evidence: Leverian Museum.
   Depiction: Force and Force, 1968, p. 86.
10. Shark tooth implement (single tooth in bone handle),[34] Dublin (1880.1613). Length 8 cm. Figure 178.
    Evidence: Circumstantial. Thought to be part of the collection given by Captain King to Trinity College. Label "500" attached.
    Literature: Freeman, 1949.
11. Shark tooth implement (single tooth in turtle shell and ivory handle), Dublin (1882.3680). Length 9 cm. Figure 179.
    Evidence: Circumstantial. Thought to be part of the collection given by Captain King to Trinity College.
    Literature: Freeman, 1949.
12. Shark tooth implement (single tooth in wood handle), Vienna (162). Length 11 cm. Figure 172.
    Evidence: Leverian Museum.
    Literature: Moschner, 1955, pp. 161 and 163.

[34] Another similar implement is in the British Museum (2045) but has no accession information.

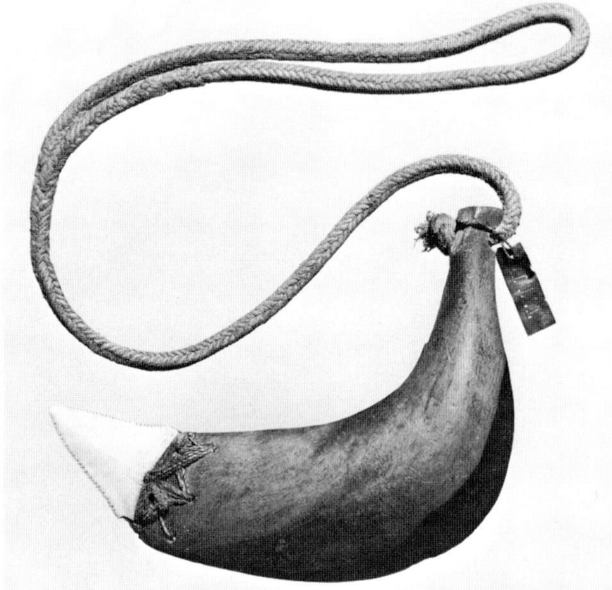
Figure 180. — Shark tooth implement, Sydney H 111.

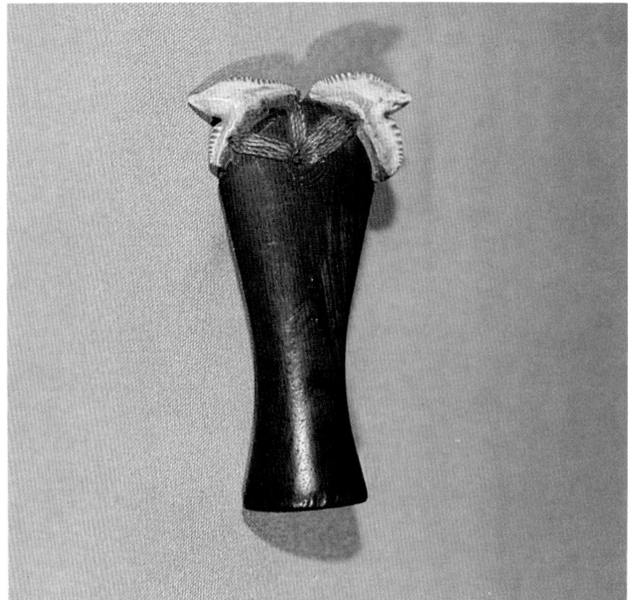
Figure 181. — Shark tooth implement, Edinburgh 1956.1019.

13. Shark tooth implement (single tooth in wood handle), Sydney (H111). Length 12 cm, cord 37 cm. Figure 180.
Evidence: Cook collection exhibited at Colonial and Indian Exhibition.
Literature: Mackrell, 1886; Appendix I, this volume.

14. Shark tooth implement (two teeth in wood handle), Edinburgh (1956.1019). Length 9 cm. Figure 181.
Evidence: Given by Mrs. Cook to Sir John Pringle.

15. Shark tooth implement (single tooth in wood handle), Berne (HAW 4). Length 15.5 cm.
Evidence: Webber collection.
Literature: Henking, 1957, pp. 365-366; Kaeppler, 1977.

16. Shark tooth implement (wood crescent with two teeth), Vienna (41). Width 12.5 cm; depth 10.5 cm. Figure 172.
Evidence: Leverian Museum.
Literature: Moschner, 1955, pp. 162-163.

17. Shark tooth implement ("knuckle-duster"), Vienna (42). Length 19 cm; depth 9 cm. Figure 172.
Evidence: Leverian Museum.
Depiction: Force and Force, 1968, p. 84.
Literature: Moschner, 1955, pp. 160 and 163.

18. Shark tooth implement (three teeth on fiber cord), British Museum (2007). Length of cord 35.5 cm.
Evidence: Circumstantial. Probably Leverian Museum.
Depiction: Force and Force, 1968, p. 87.

19. Shark tooth implement (two teeth on fiber cord), British Museum 2006). Length of cord 12.5 cm.
Evidence: Circumstantial. Probably Leverian Museum.

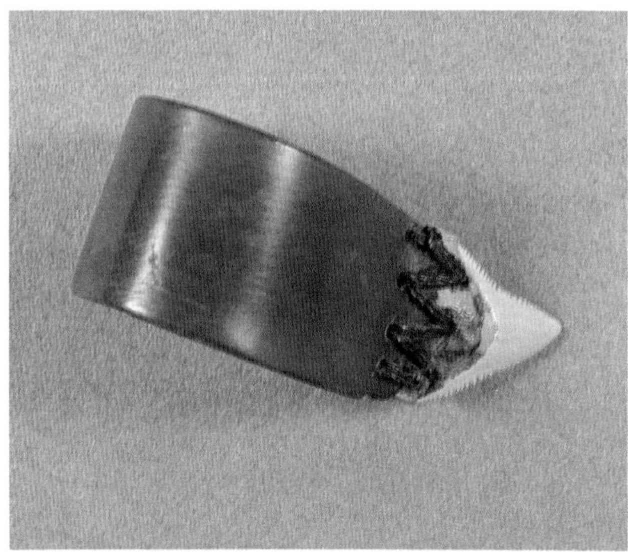
Figure 182. — Shark tooth ring, Sydney H 150.

20. Shark tooth implement (shark jaw bone with teeth in place bound with fiber and feathers). Lost. Formerly in Florence (143).
   Evidence: Circumstantial. Cook voyage collection from various sources.
   Literature: Giglioli, 1895, pp. 116-117, Kaeppler, 1977.

21. Shark tooth ring (single shark tooth on turtle shell ring). Sydney (H 150). Largest dimension 4.5 cm; width 2 cm. Figure 182.
   Evidence: Cook collection exhibited at Colonial and Indian Exhibition.
   Literature: Mackrell, 1886; Appendix I, this volume.

22-23. Two shark tooth rings (single shark teeth on turtle shell bands), Berne (HAW 3 a and b).
   Evidence: Webber collection.
   Literature: Henking, 1957, p. 365; Kaeppler, 1977.

There were several other shark tooth implements in the Leverian Museum which cannot be located. They are depicted in Force and Force, 1968.

Spatulate form, wood handle (p. 85).
Spatulate form, bone handle with feathers (p. 84).
"Knuckle-duster" (p. 84).
Single tooth with wood handle (p. 85).
Crescent with two teeth (p. 86).[35]
Wood handle with teeth on both long sides (p. 86).
Shark jaw bone with teeth in place with feathers (p. 39).

Spears (ihe)

1. Spear (long barbed *ihe*), Greenwich (L15/92/B). Length 216 cm. Figure 183.
   Evidence: Collected by William Griffin on HMS *Resolution*.

2. Spear (long barbed *ihe*), Bishop Museum (1977.206.11) (formerly in the Hooper collection). Length 206.5 cm. Figure 184.
   Evidence: Circumstantial. Probably from the Leverian Museum. Purchased on behalf of Bishop Museum by Grosvenor International.
   Literature: Phelps, 1976, p. 418 (not attributed to Cook).

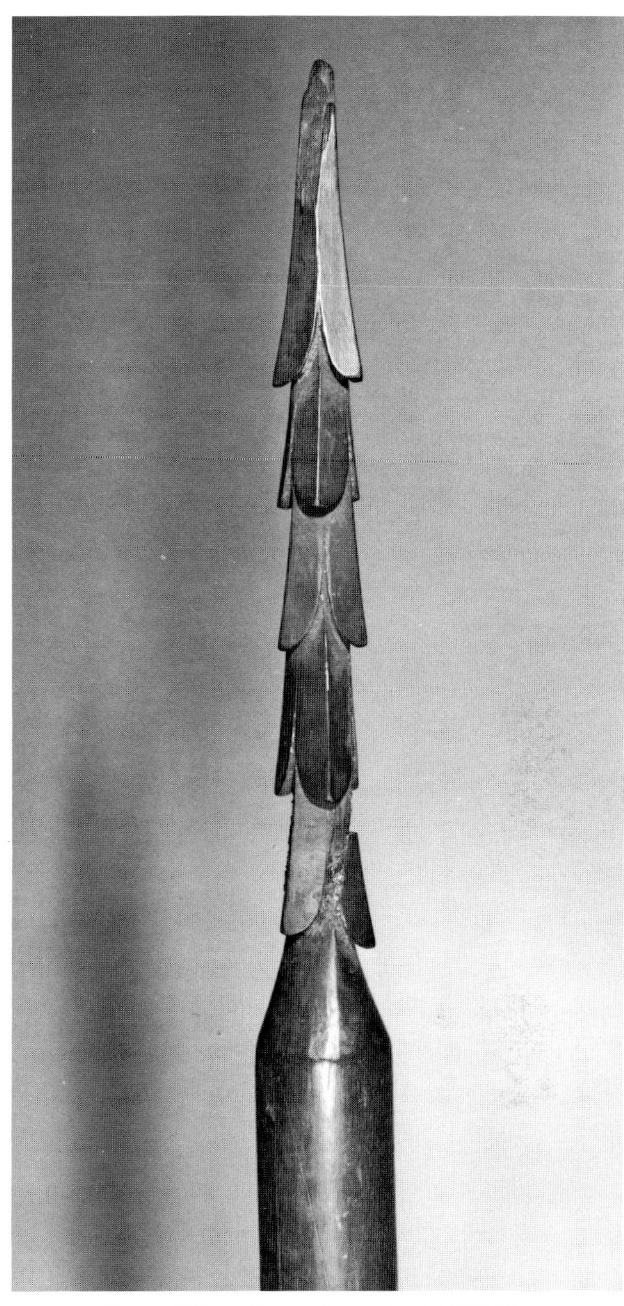

Figure 183. — Spear, Greenwich L15/92/B.

3. Spear (long barbed *ihe*), Cape Town (SAM 2193). Length 245 cm. Figure 185.
   Evidence: Circumstantial. Supposed to have arrived in Cape Town in 1780.
   Literature: Bax, 1970, p. 146.

4. Spear (long barbed *ihe*), Göttingen.
   Evidence: Purchased from London dealer Humphrey in 1782.

[35] Two known implements are very much like this drawing: British Museum 2043 and Oldman collection (310) in Canterbury Museum, Christchurch (E150.1160), but neither can be traced to the Leverian Museum.

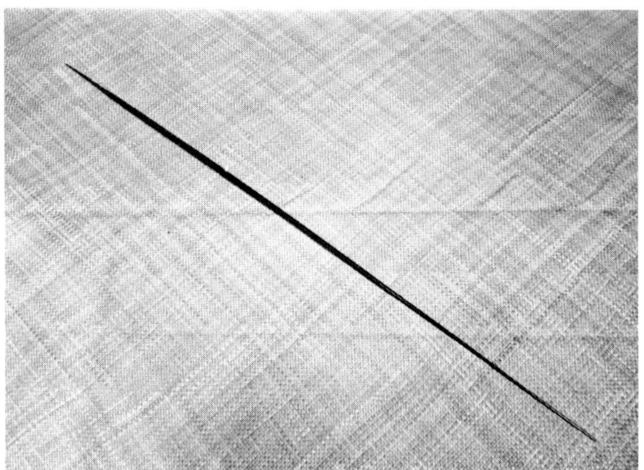

Figure 184. — Spear, Bishop Museum 1977.206.11.

5-7. Three spears (long barbed *ihe*), Florence (279 a,b,c). Lengths 2.28 m, 2.19 m, 1.75 m.
Evidence: Circumstantial. Cook voyage collection from various sources.
Literature: Giglioli, 1895, pp. 94-95; Kaeppler, 1977.

8. Spear (long, barbed *ihe*), British Museum (1946.Oc.1.1). Length 261.5 cm.
Evidence: Collected by Thomas Bean on Cook's voyage.

Adzes

Adz blades are more common than hafts and one might suggest that stone blades were traded for metal ones and replaced on the spot.[36]

1. Hafted adz, Exeter (E 1224). Length of handle 46 cm. Length of blade 20 cm. Figure 186.
Evidence: Leverian Museum.
Depiction: Force and Force, 1968, p. 109.

2. Hafted adz, Leningrad (505-28). Length of handle 59 cm; length of blade 22 cm. Figure 187.
Evidence: Given by Captain Clerke to the Governor of Kamchatka.
Literature: Rozina, 1966, pp. 248 and 252; Kaeppler, 1977.

3. Hafted adz, Wellington (FE 334). Length of handle 51 cm; length of blade 23 cm. Figure 188.
Evidence: Original Cook collection in Bullock's Museum.
Literature: Kaeppler, 1974a, p. 78.

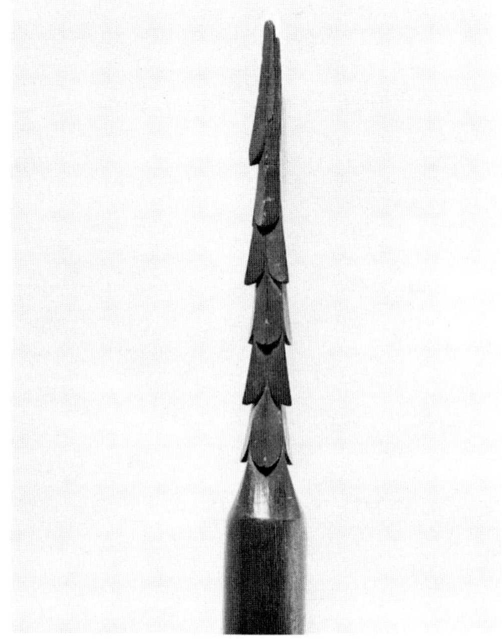

Figure 185. — Spear (detail), Cape Town SAM 2193.

4. Hafted adz, Glasgow (E 366b). Length of handle 66 cm; length of blade 26 cm. Figure 189.
Evidence: Circumstantial. Cook voyage collection from various sources. See Appendix III, this volume.

5. Hafted adz, Berne (TAH 19). Length of handle 65 cm; length of blade 29 cm.
Evidence: Webber collection.
Literature: Henking, 1957, p. 355; Kaeppler, 1977.

6. Hafted adz, Wellington (FE 3667).
Evidence: Bequeathed by Mrs. Cook to her sister Margaret's granddaughter, who gave it to her daughter, Hannah, who married S. J. Long. Given by Mrs. A. G. Long to Wellington.

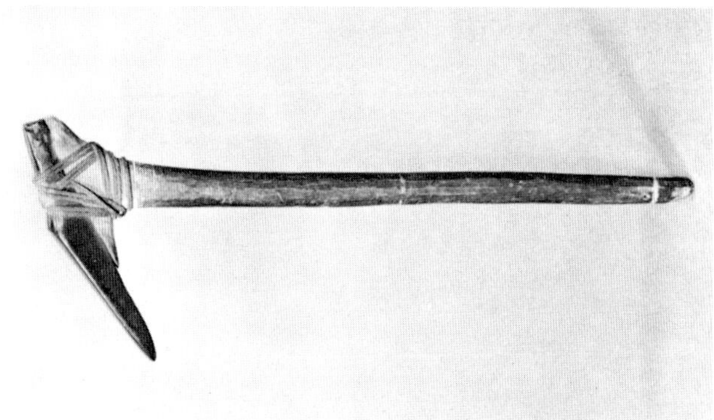

Figure 186. — Hafted adz, Exeter E 1224.

[36] Two hafted adzes in the British Museum (HAW 43, HAW 44) are similar to Cook voyage specimens located, but have no accession information. Two unhafted adzes (72.7-4, 2 and 3) are also similar to those collected—one being white like 8 and 9 below—but they also cannot be associated with Cook.

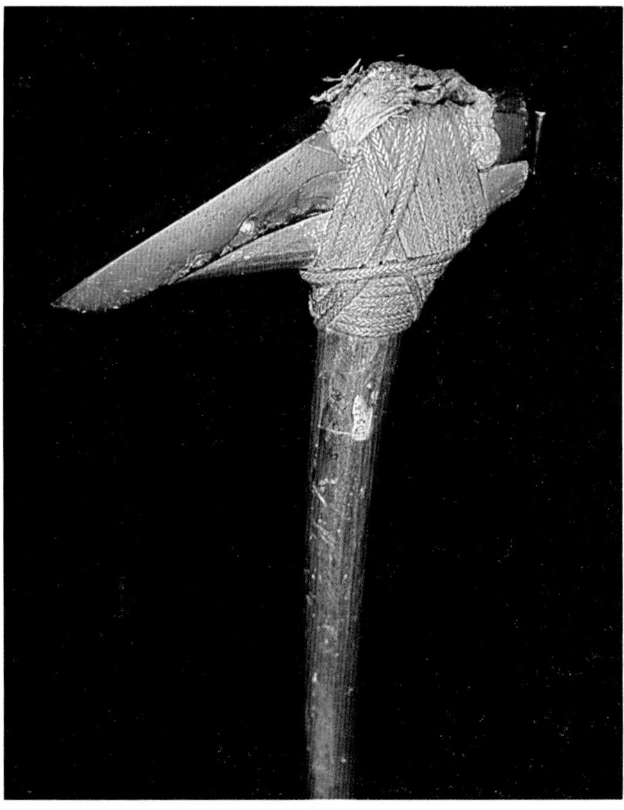

Figure 187. — Hafted adz, Leningrad 505-28.

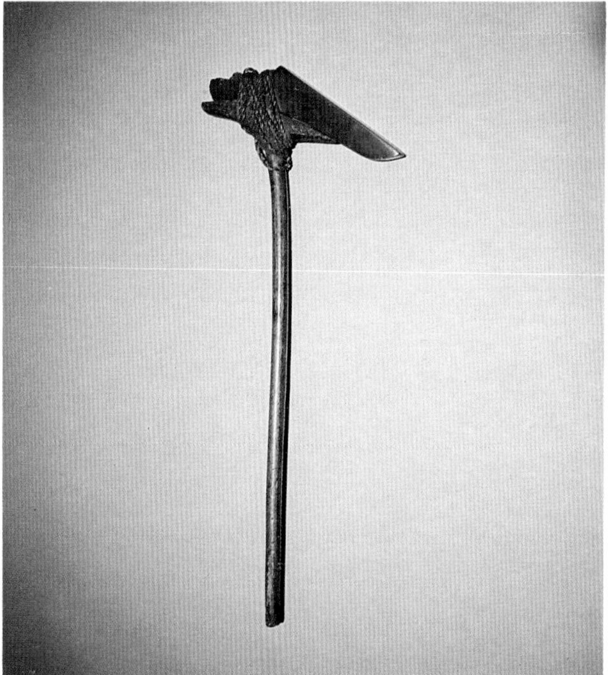

Figure 188. — Hafted adz, Wellington FE 334.

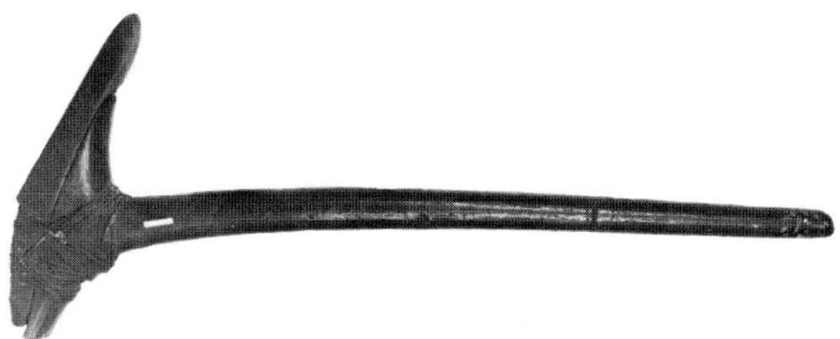

Figure 189. — Hafted adz, Glasgow E 366b.

Figure 190. — Adz blade, Göttingen OZ 273.

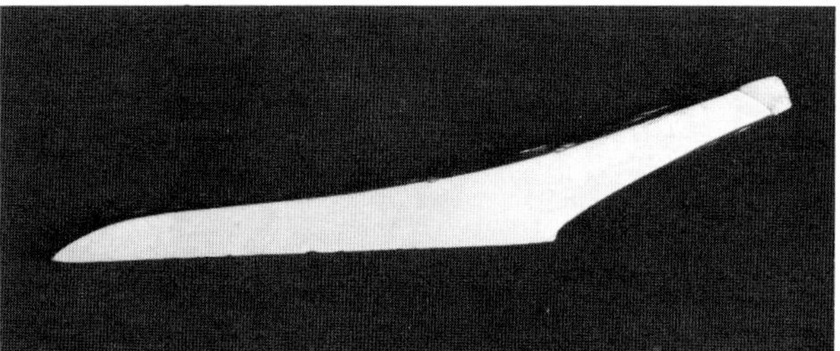

Figure 192. — Adz blade, Vienna 155.

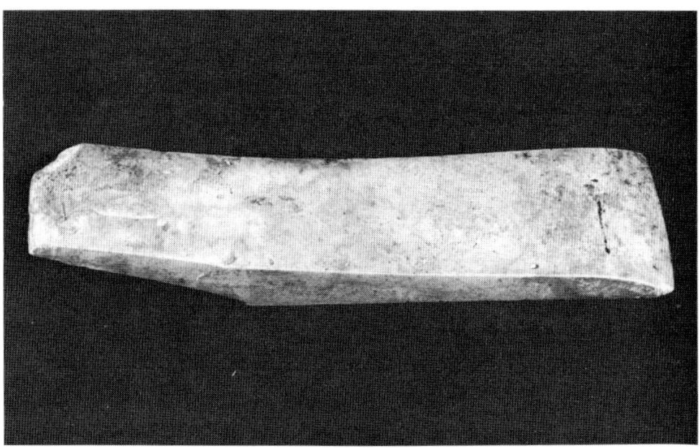

Figure 191. — Adz blade, Vienna 155.

Figure 193. — Black basalt adz blade, Vienna 154.

Figure 194.— Canoes off Niihau, by John Webber.

7. Hafted adz, Florence (179). Length of handle 53 cm; length of blade 30 cm. The haft is unusual and may not be indigenous.
   Evidence: Circumstantial. Cook voyage collection from various sources.
   Literature: Giglioli, 1895, pp. 82-85; Kaeppler, 1977.

⛵8. Adz blade (white calcareous limestone), Göttingen (OZ 273). Length 23 cm. Figure 190.
   Evidence: Purchased from London dealer Humphrey in 1782.

⛵9. Adz blade (white calcareous limestone), Vienna (155). Length 29 cm; width 7 cm. Figures 191 and 192.
   Evidence: Leverian Museum.

⛵10. Adz blade (black basalt), Vienna (154). Length 32 cm. Figure 193.
   Evidence: Leverian Museum.
   Literature: Moschner, 1955, p. 165.

11. Adz blade (black basalt), Göttingen (OZ 364). Length 26 cm.
   Evidence: Purchased from London dealer Humphrey in 1782.

12. Basalt blade in reconstructed haft, Rome (1174). Length of blade 30 cm.
   Evidence: Circumstantial but questionable. Cook voyage collection from various sources.
   Literature: Giglioli, 1895, pp. 82-85; Kaeppler, 1977.

13. Basalt blade in Tahitian haft, Hooper collection (524).
   Evidence: Leverian Museum.
   Literature: Phelps, 1976, pp. 122, 422.

Canoe Paddles

Only one Hawaiian canoe paddle can be traced to Cook's voyage. Although Webber depicted paddles in use (Figs. 89 and 194), no drawings of the paddles can be located for verification of the type.

⛵1. Canoe paddle, Vienna (39). Length 165 cm; width of blade 29 cm. Figure 195.
   Evidence: Leverian Museum.
   Literature: Moschner, 1955, p. 173 (attributed to Tonga).

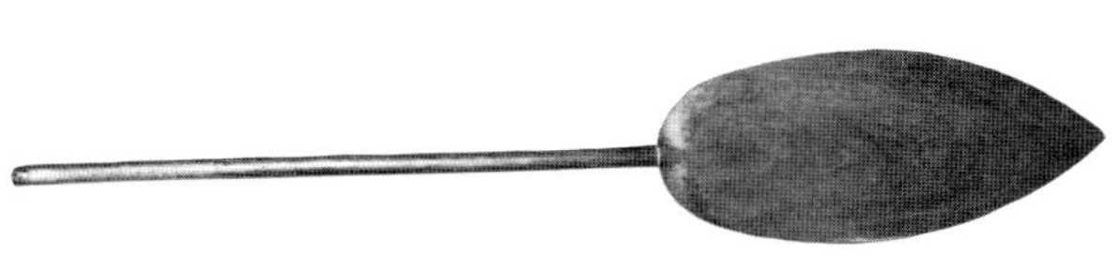

Figure 195. — Canoe paddle, Vienna 39.

Fishhooks

Fishing equipment traceable to Cook's voyage includes shark hooks[37] and one- and two-piece fishhooks of bone and shell.[38] No octopus lures from Hawaii can be traced.

1. Shark hook (wood with bone point), Vienna (45). Length 24 cm. Figure 196.
   Evidence: Leverian Museum.
   Literature: Moschner, 1955, pp. 188, 190.

2. Shark hook (wood with bone point), Leningrad (505-24). Length 36 cm. Figure 197.
   Evidence: Given by Captain Clerke to the Governor of Kamchatka.
   Literature: Rozina, 1966, p. 252; Kaeppler, 1977.

3. Shark hook (wood with bone point), Berne (HAW 5). Length 27 cm.
   Evidence: Webber collection.
   Literature: Henking, 1957, pp. 364-365; Kaeppler, 1977.

4. Shark hook (bone), British Museum (HAW 62).
   Evidence: Circumstantial. Object marked "Captain Cook."

5. Fishhook of bone with stone weight and red feathers (attributed to Hawaii, but probably New Zealand), Cambridge (25.365). Length of hook 2.5 cm. Figure 198.
   Evidence: Pennant collection of Cook voyage objects from various sources.

6. Two-piece bone fishhook, Cambridge (22.926). Figure 199.
   Evidence: Leverian Museum.

7-8. Two two-piece bone fishhooks, Göttingen.
   Evidence: Purchased from London dealer Humphrey in 1782.

9-11. Three one-piece fishhooks (of bone and pearl shell), Göttingen.
   Evidence: Purchased from London dealer Humphrey in 1782.

12-15. Four fishhooks, Vienna (104, 105, 106, 107 [all exhibited]). Figure 200.
   Evidence: Leverian Museum.
   Literature: Moschner, 1955, pp. 181-187.

16. One-piece fishhook of pearl shell, Berne (TAH 27).
   Evidence: Webber collection.
   Literature: Henking, 1957, p. 356; Kaeppler, 1977.

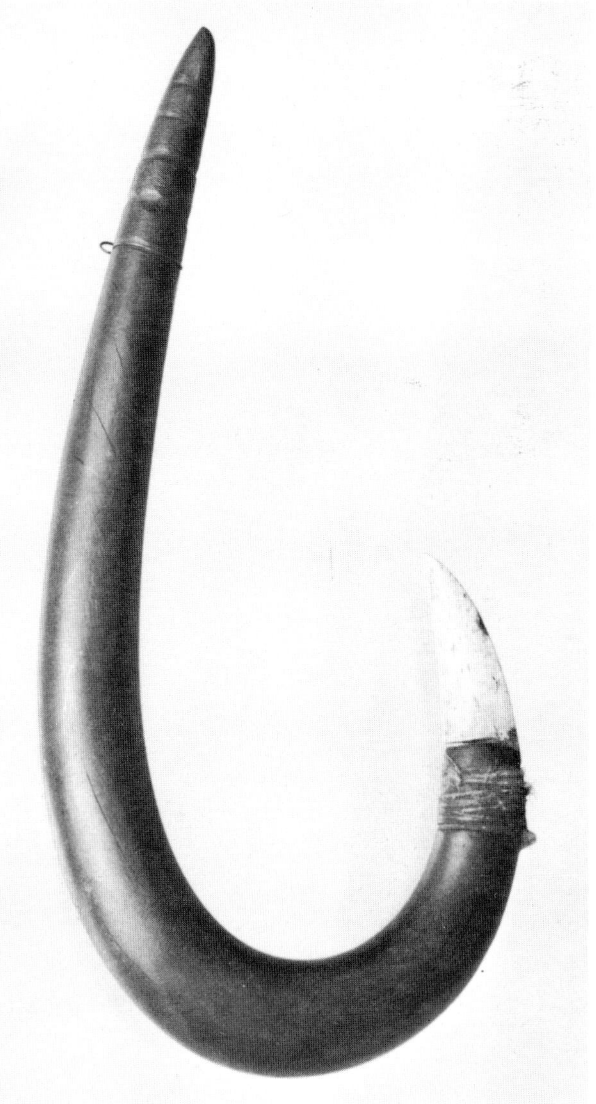

Figure 196. — Shark hook, Vienna 45.

[37] A shark hook in the Hooper collection (287) is attributed by Phelps (1976, p. 416) to the Leverian Museum because of an inked "8" on the shank. This alone, however, is not sufficient to trace it to the Leverian Museum.

[38] Fishhooks in the British Museum (HAW 63-73) may include some from Cook's voyages, but the lack of documentation makes verification impossible.

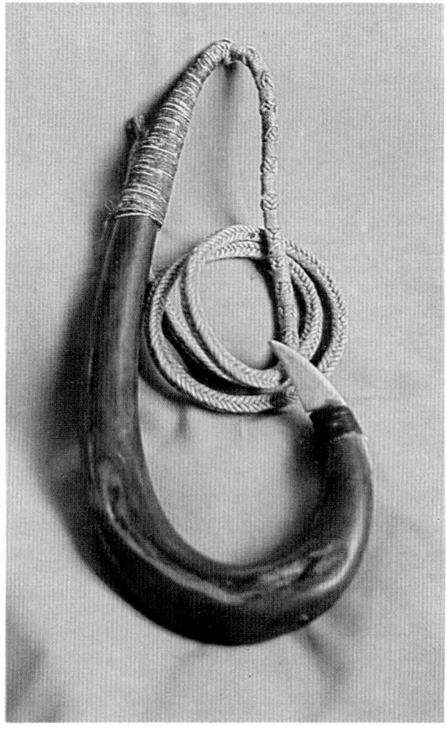

Figure 197. — Shark hook, Leningrad 505-24.

Figure 198. — Fishhook with weight and feathers, Cambridge 25.365 (New Zealand?).

Figure 199. — Two-piece fishhook, Cambridge 22.926.

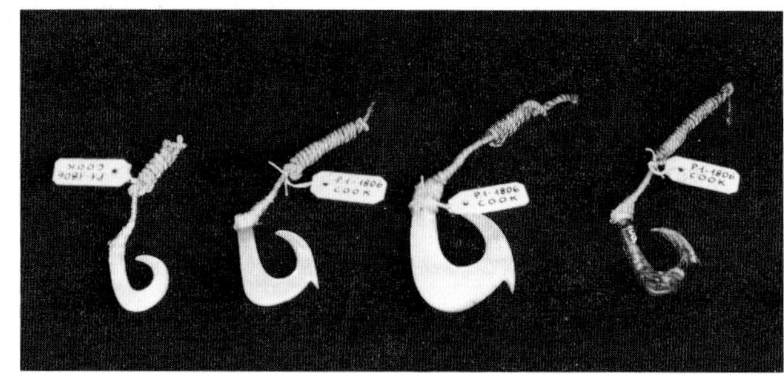

Figure 200. — Four fishhooks, Vienna 104-107.

17. Two-piece fishhook (turtle shell shank, bone point), Florence. Length 5 cm.
    Evidence: Circumstantial. Cook voyage collection from various sources.
    Literature: Giglioli, 1895, pp. 86-87; Kaeppler, 1977.

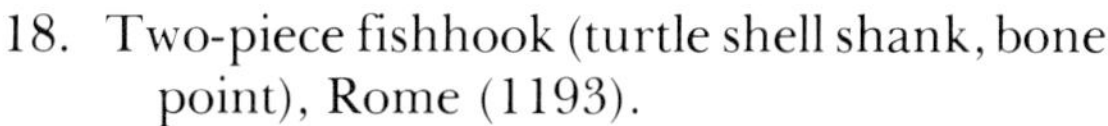

18. Two-piece fishhook (turtle shell shank, bone point), Rome (1193).
    Evidence: Circumstantial. Cook voyage collection from various sources.
    Literature: Giglioli, 1895, pp. 86-87, Kaeppler, 1977.

19-?. Several fishhooks, Wellington.
    Evidence: Circumstantial. Probably part of original Cook voyage collection in Bullock's Museum and/or from sale of the Leverian Museum.
    Literature: Kaeppler, 1974a, p. 80.

Fishhook Parts

1. Bone shank from a two-piece fishhook, Bishop Museum (1970.221.01). Length 5.3 cm.
    Evidence: Leverian Museum.

2. Bone point from a two-piece fishhook, Salem.
    Evidence: Leverian Museum (not from the same fishhook as the above shank).

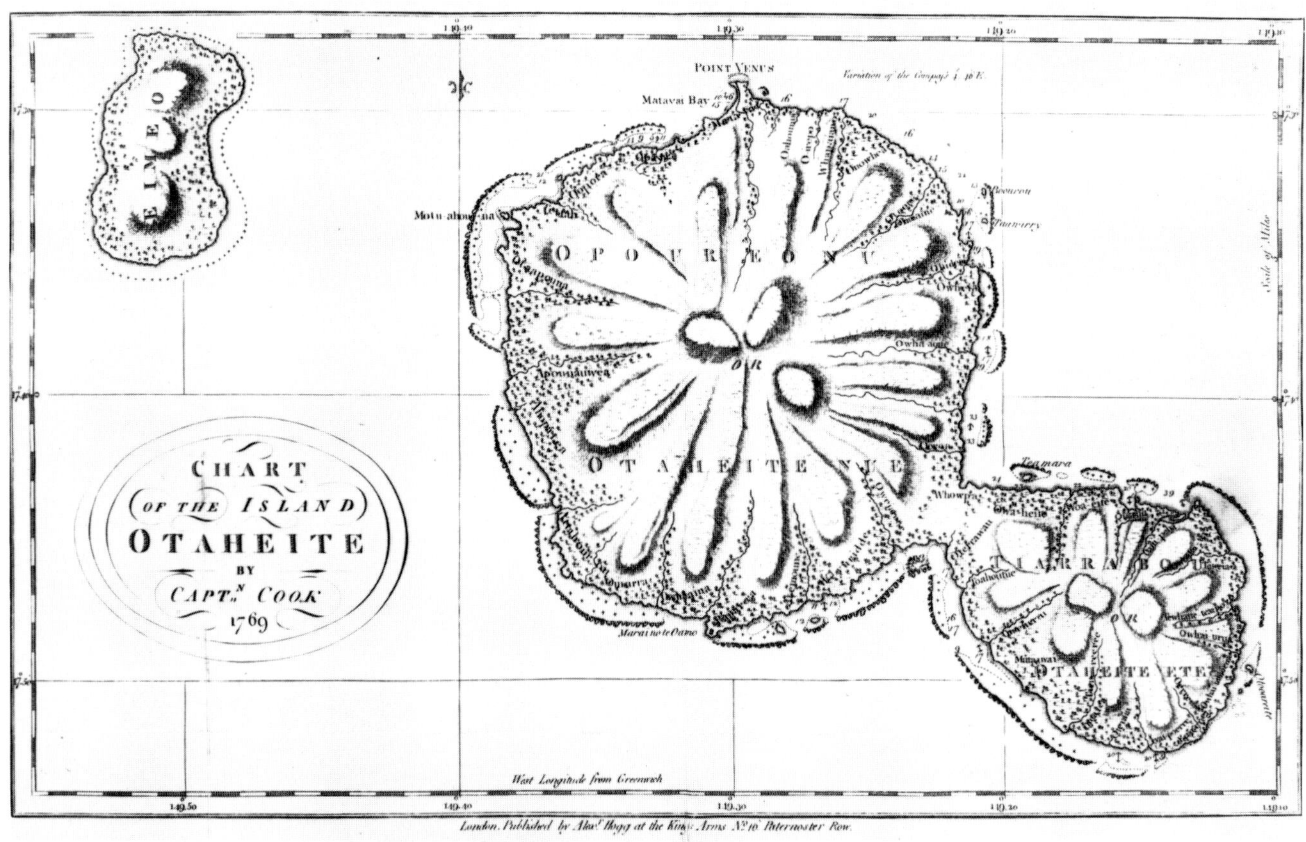

Figure 205. — Chart of Tahiti by James Cook (54).

OTAHEITE OR KING GEORGE III ISLAND (TAHITI AND THE SOCIETY ISLANDS)

European discovery of the Society Islands was made in 1767 on the voyage of H.M.S. *Dolphin* under Captain Samuel Wallis. With Wallis were four men who later served under Captain Cook, including Tobias Furneaux as second lieutenant, John Gore as master's mate,[1] Robert Molyneaux, and Richard Pickersgill. The *Dolphin* was in the Society Islands from June 19 to July 28 and, after several skirmishes between crew and islanders, friendly relations were established. This early voyage, and particularly the presence on it of John Gore, proved to be very useful to Cook two years later. Great quantities of iron nails and spikes from the *Dolphin's* stores (as well as others removed from the ship itself!) were traded for provisions, the favors of the women, and curiosities. In fact, so voracious was this market for nails that it gave rise to Captain Cook's later trading restriction: "No sort of Iron or anything that is made of Iron, or any sort of cloth or other useful or necessary articles, are to be given in exchange for anything but provisions."

The *Dolphin's* sailing master, George Robertson (1948), recorded in his journal some of the curiosities that were traded to that ship. His first such entry was on June 27, when a "peace-offering" included "six large Bales of the Country cloath, from sixt to Eight yards in Each bale" (p. 165). They tried to get the Tahitians to take back their cloth "as it was of very little use to us and certainly a great loss to them" (p. 166), but they would not have it back and eventually it was taken on board the *Dolphin.* The first official purchase of ethnographic specimens recorded by Robertson for Tahiti was on June 30 when the Gunner, who was in charge of trade, purchased a cuttlefish decoy and some mother-of-pearl fishhooks, and on July 1 the Gunner traded for the pearl earrings of some of the young girls. At this time no one else was allowed to trade for anything, but on July 7 Mr. Gore bought "a very fine . . . Shell, and some beautiful Mother of pearl fish hooks and two pearl oyster shells" (p. 180). On July 12 the wooders brought back shells, fishhooks, and "some

[1]John Gore had also previously sailed with Byron.

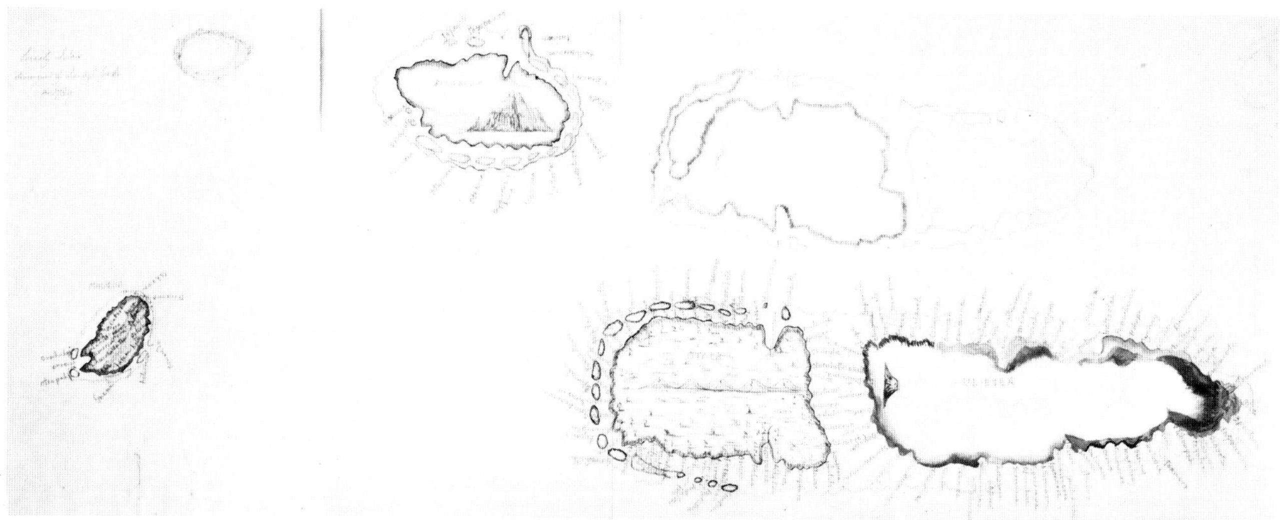

Figure 206. — Chart of Society Islands, British Library Add. Ms. 15,508.16.

lines made of Silk Grass as (neat) as any fishing lines in England" (p. 190). On July 15 the Gunner bought shells, fishhooks, a few pearls, "and several oyther cureous things" (p. 195). On July 16 the Queen "tied round each of the principal officers' necks wreaths of hair knotted together and worked like sennet and she made signs it was her own hair and work."[2]

On July 22 the Queen gave Robertson a garment of cloth 10 feet long and five feet wide with a hole cut in the middle for the head, "and tied it round my west with a Sash of much finer cloth," and also "a piece of very fine cloth made up snug . . . sixteen yards long and three Broad" (p. 214). On July 24 the traders brought back "a great Quantity of . . . shells, Mother of Pearl fish hooks and a few pearls" (p. 217). Finally, on July 26 they purchased pearls, pearl oyster shells, hooks, lines for fishing, stone adzes, stone hammers, several bows and arrows and other curious things (p. 224). And "for several days past our Seamen went into the Woods singley and traded with the natives for all sorts of cureous things" (p. 225).

In short, there were quite a number of objects taken to England from Wallis' voyage and, although none of these pre-Cook objects can be traced, some were supposed to have gone to the British Museum and Cambridge. Objects were also collected on Bougainville's voyage,[3] which visited Tahiti in 1768, and probably also on the Spanish ship *Aguila,* which visited Tahiti between Cook's first and second voyage. More significant to our purposes here than the actual ethnographic specimens traded from the Society Islands by pre-Cook ships are the European iron tools that were traded *to* the Society Islanders. For, unlike the objects collected in the Hawaiian Islands by Cook's ships, which we can be sure are relatively free from European acculturative influence, the objects collected in the Society Islands by Cook's ships, especially by the time of the third voyage, had already been subjected to a decade of European iron tools and ideas. The Society Islanders' sophistication in their trade relations with Europeans mounted with the saturation of the market for iron nails. Even by the time of Cook's second voyage Tahitians were demanding high prices for curiosities, and objects that they considered valuable (such as mourning dresses) would be parted with only for red feathers, which had a traditional value that even iron never attained. Thus, objects collected on Cook's voyages in the Society Islands cannot give us a completely unacculturated picture of the style and scope of material culture in that island group.

Furthermore, the Society Islanders were in contact with other island groups in pre-European times and inevitably there was diffusion of artifacts and ideas between these areas. Objects collected in the Society Islands on Cook's voyages may not necessarily have

[2]This may have been given (or sold) to the Duchess of Portland because at the sale of her Museum in 1786, lot 1372 included a "matted pocket, containing specimens of the body linen made of bark, of Oberea, Queen of Otaheite, with some of her Majesty's hair, braided by herself, a roll of a like plaited hair, and 2 ornaments for the ears, composed of 6 pearls, from Otaheite" (Anon. [Lightfoot?], 1786, p. 59). The name of the purchaser is not recorded, except for "Cash" in the price list bound with some copies of the sale catalogue of the Portland collection (for example, in the Haddon Library, University of Cambridge).

[3]Only a few objects are attributed to Bougainville's voyage today. A piece of bark cloth is in the Museum la Faille of the Musées d'Histoire Naturelle de la Rochelle, France; and two pieces of bark cloth in the Musée de l'Homme, Paris (Wernhart, 1972).

Figure 207. — Society Islands canoes, British Library Add. Ms. 23,921.12.

been made there, but this is useful in itself for demonstrating 18th century interisland contact. In some cases information on artifacts from Cook's voyages is quite specific, for example, the fly whisks with human images (which are today often attributed to Tahiti) were noted as originating in "Oheteroa" (British Museum Add. Ms. 23,921.53), that is, in Rurutu in the Austral Islands.

Using the artifacts and associated information from the voyages of Cook and others to the Society Islands is more complex than using the Hawaiian materials, especially if one desires to form a picture of the material culture as it was known at the time of European contact. However, if we consider Europeans as simply another influence on an already complex society, objects brought back on Cook's voyages are our most important resource for an analysis of Society Island material culture in the 18th century. Being able to separate the materials by voyage is useful, but in some cases this is not possible. In this catalogue Tahitian objects are separated by voyage only if there is some documentary evidence to demonstrate the possibility.

During Cook's three voyages a great deal of time was spent in the Society Islands and in addition to the large number of objects collected, a large number of drawings made by the several artists are an important source for research on canoes (Figs. 207, 208), structures (Fig. 224), and objects not collected or located today. Maps drawn on the voyage show an intimate acquaintance with the geographical features and place names of the various islands (Figs. 205, 206).

Mourning Dresses

Tahitian mourning dresses were described and depicted in the journals of Cook's first voyage (Fig. 209), the Europeans being fascinated not only by the costume itself, but the ritual as well. According to Forster, none were collected until the second voyage,

Figure 208. — Society Islands war canoe, British Library Add. Ms. 23,921.21.

when parts of at least ten were taken to England and more descriptions and depictions were made (Fig. 210).

Complete Mourning Dresses

1. Mourning dress (and additional parts), Bishop Museum (1971.198.Ola-f, 02a-c) Figure 211:
   (a) shell face mask with surmounted headpiece edged with tropic bird feathers;
   (b) turban of bark cloth and matting with tying cords;
   (c) crescentic wood chest piece with mounted pearl shells;
   (d) chest apron of tiny slips of mother-of-pearl shell;
   (e) cape of red brown and natural bark cloth;
   (f) feather tassels;
   (g) bark cloth apron with coconut shell disks;
   (h) feathered cloak;
   (i) second face mask;
   (j) second crescentic wood chest piece;
   (k) second feathered cloak.
   Evidence: Part of the Cook collection formerly in Dublin, labeled "Cook collection." The complete mourning dress was probably given by Surgeon Patten from Cook's second voyage. The additional parts may have come from Patten or Captain King, both of whom gave collections to Trinity College, Dublin.
   Literature: Freeman, 1949, p. 7.

2. Mourning dress, British Museum (TAH 78):
   A watercolor in the British Library purports to depict this mourning dress. It is noted "early Otaheite. The original is in the British Museum" (Add. Ms. 15, 513.18). Figure 212. Note the strings of tiny shells that hang from the chest apron. These were substituted very quickly with trade beads.
   (a) shell face mask with surmounted headpiece edged with tropic bird feathers;
   (b) tying cords for turban (but no turban);
   (c) crescentic wood chest piece with mounted pearl shells;
   (d) chest apron of tiny slips of mother-of-pearl shell;
   (e) cape of red/brown and natural bark cloth;
   (f) feather tassels and extra bunches of feathers;

Figure 209. — Chief mourner, depicted on Cook's first voyage.

Figure 210. — Chief mourner, depicted on Cook's second voyage.

Figure 211.— Mourning dress, Bishop Museum 1971.198.01.

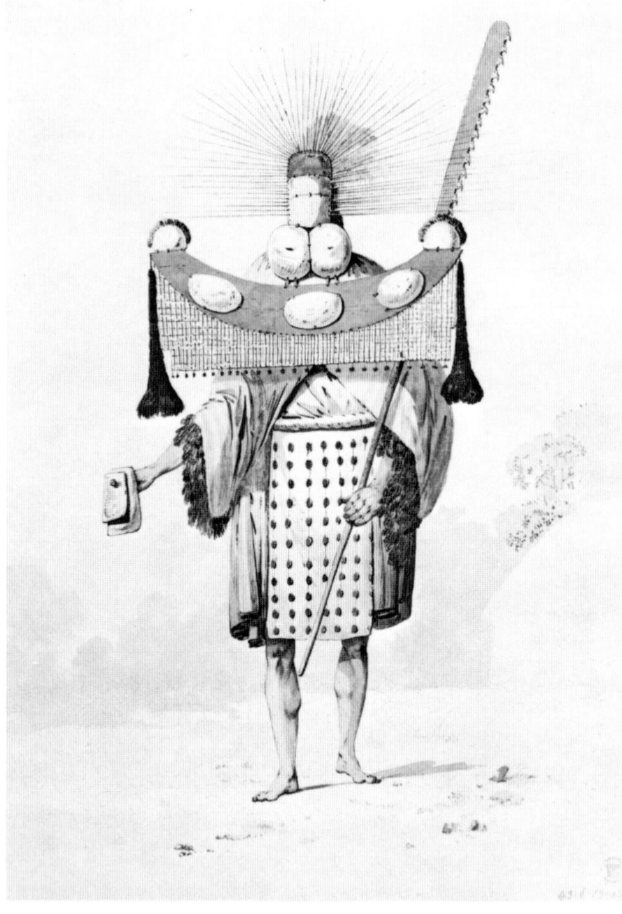

Figure 212.— Mourning dress, British Library Add. Ms. 15,513.18.

(g) bark cloth apron with coconut shell disks;
(h) feathered cloak;
(i) bark cloth sash;
(j) belt of bark cloth and other fibrous materials;
(k) bark cloth piece.

Evidence: Given by Cook to the British Museum. Noted "Cook collection No. 3." Second voyage.

Literature: Forster, 1777, Vol. 2, p. 72; Cranstone and Gowers, 1968.

3. Mourning dress, Oxford (1-4 and 9-11):[4]
(a) shell face mask with surmounted headpiece edged with tropic bird feathers;
(b) turban of bark cloth with tying cords;
(c) crescentic wood chest piece with mounted pearl shells;
(d) chest apron of tiny slips of mother-of-pearl shells;
(e) feather tassels;
(f) bark cloth apron with coconut shell disks;
(g) feathered cloak;
(h) three pieces of bark cloth, white, red, and brown;
(i) bark cloth sash.

Evidence: Forster collection, second voyage.

Literature: Gathercole, n.d. [1970].

[4]The Oxford numbers in this Catalogue refer to the Forster numbers in the Gathercole guide to the collection (n.d. [1970]).

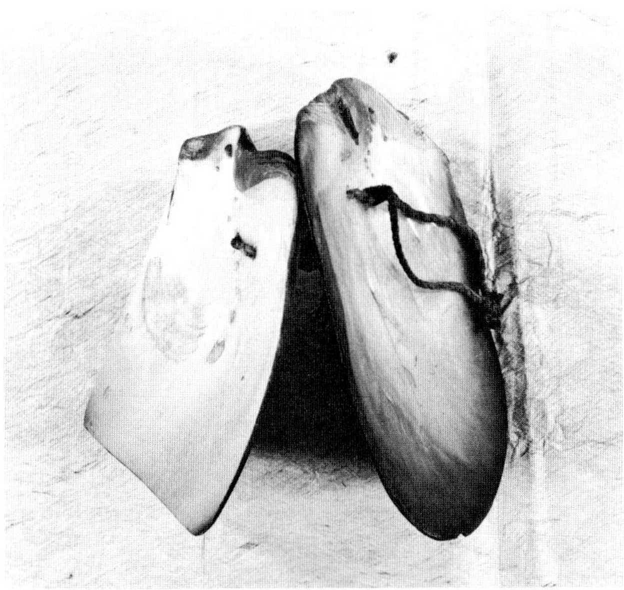

Figure 213.— Mourning dress clappers, Bishop Museum 1971.198.02d.

4. Mourning dress Göttingen:
   (a) shell face mask with surmounted headpiece of black shell edged with tropic bird feathers;
   (b) turban of plaited pandanus and tying cords;
   (c) crescentic wood chest piece with mounted pearl shells;
   (d) chest apron of tiny slips of mother-of-pearl shell;
   (e) bark cloth apron with coconut shell disks;
   (f) bark cloth cape;
   (g) bark cloth sash wound with black fiber and bunches of feathers;
   (h) feather cloak.

   Evidence: Purchased from London dealer Humphrey in 1782. Second and/or third voyage.[5]

   Literature: Plischke, 1931.

5. Mourning dress, Florence (61, 202, 221, 222, 257, 259, 277):
   (a) shell face mask surmounted with black shell headpiece edged with tropic bird feathers;
   (b) turban of bark cloth and tying cords;
   (c) crescentic wood chest piece with mounted pearl shells;
   (d) chest apron of tiny slips of mother-of-pearl shell;
   (e) two bark cloth aprons with coconut shell disks;
   (f) bark cloth sash wound with fiber;
   (g) bark cloth undergarment.

   Evidence: Circumstantial. Cook voyage collection from various sources.

   Literature: Giglioli, 1893, pp. 236-242; Kaeppler, 1977.

6. Mourning dress. Lost.

   Evidence: Leverian Museum—probably second voyage.

   Depictions: Force and Force, 1968, p. 116.

Mourning Dress Parts

1. Shell chest apron, Leningrad (505-20).

   Evidence: Given by Captain Clerke to the Governor of Kamchatka. Third voyage.

   Literature: Rozina, 1966, pp. 243 and 246; Kaeppler, 1977.

Figure 214.— Man in headdress and gorget, Plate 44 of Parkinson's journal.

[5] Humphrey had a nearly complete mourning dress from the second voyage that was sold in five lots at the sale of his Museum in 1779. He may have repurchased some of the pieces to form the Göttingen specimen.

Figure 215. — Headdress, British Museum TAH 9.

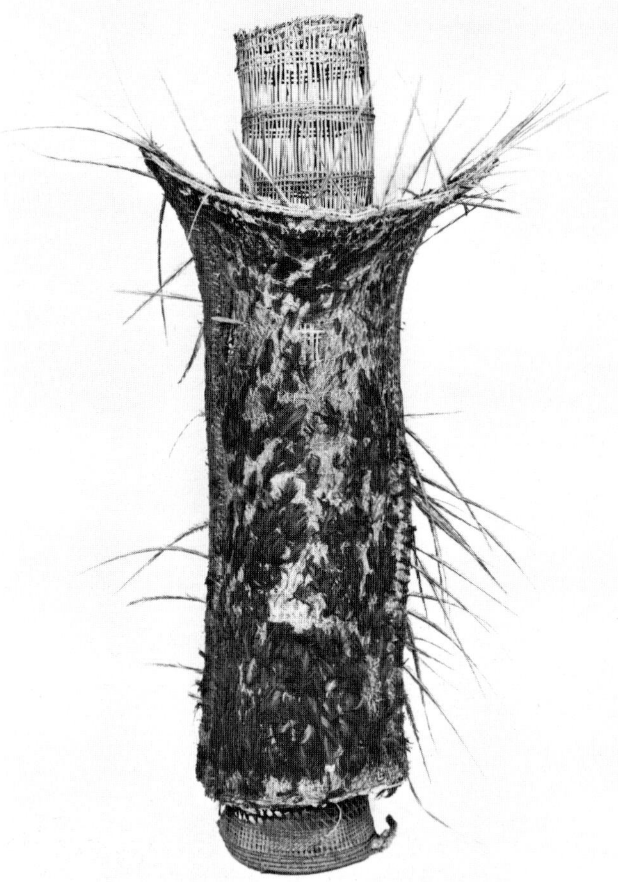

Figure 217. — Headdress, Oxford 5.

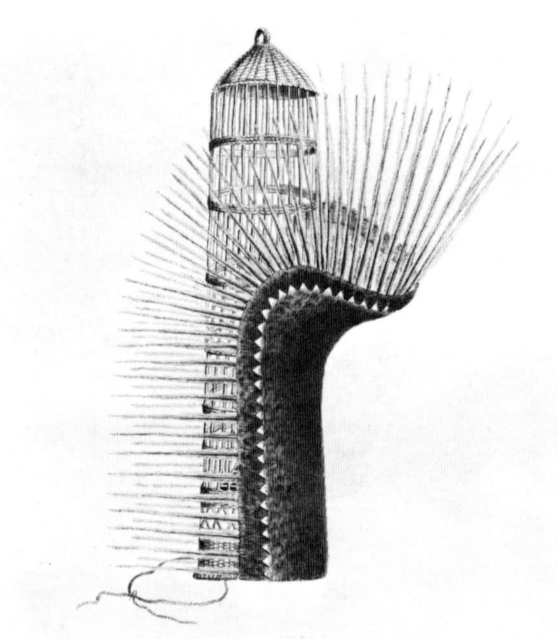

Figure 216. — Headdress, British Library Add. Ms. 15,508.18.

2. Shell chest apron, Sydney (H 149). Depth 20 cm.
   Evidence: Part of Cook collection exhibited at Colonial and Indian Exhibition. Second or third voyage.
   Literature: Mackrell, 1886; Appendix I, this volume.
3. Mask with surmounted headpiece edged with tropic bird feathers, and shell chest apron, Wellington (FE 336).
   Evidence: Circumstantial. Given to Bullock's Museum by Banks.
   Literature: Bullock, 1810, p. 11; Kaeppler, 1974a, pp. 74, 78.
4. Mask with surmounted headpiece, tropic bird feathers, shell chest apron, shells from a crescentic wood chest piece, Berne (TAH 23, 25, 26, 29).
   Evidence: Webber collection. Third voyage.
   Literature: Henking, 1957, pp. 349-351; Kaeppler, 1977.
5. Six parts of a mourning dress, Göttingen.
   Evidence: Forster collection. Second voyage.
   Literature: Plischke, 1931.

Figure 218. — Gorget, Leningrad 505-10.

Mourning Dress Clappers

Six sets of mourning dress clappers can be traced to Cook's voyages. It is likely that more were obtained, but became parts of collections of "natural curiosities" or have lost their connecting cords and are now unidentified as to use.

1. Mourning dress clappers, Bishop Museum (1971.198.02d). Dimensions 16.5 cm by 14.5 cm; 21 cm by 16.5 cm. Figure 213.
   Evidence: Circumstantial. Part of Cook collection formerly in Dublin. Probably collected by Patten on second voyage.

2. Mourning dress clappers, Oxford (27). Dimensions 23 cm.
   Evidence: Forster collection. Second voyage.
   Literature: Gathercole, n.d. [1970].

3. Mourning dress clappers, Göttingen.
   Evidence: Purchased from London dealer Humphrey in 1782. Second or third voyage.
   Literature: Plischke, 1931

4. Mourning dress clappers, Berne (TAH 24 a and b). Largest dimensions 20.5 cm, 16.8 cm.
   Evidence: Webber collection. Third voyage.
   Literature: Kaeppler, 1977.

5. Mourning dress clappers, Sydney (H 46). Missing.
   Evidence: Part of Cook collection exhibited at the Colonial and Indian Exhibition.
   Literature: Mackrell, 1886; Appendix I, this volume.

6. Mourning dress clappers, Florence.
   Evidence: Circumstantial. Cook voyage collection from various sources.
   Literature: Giglioli, 1893, p. 240; Kaeppler, 1977.

Feathered Headdresses

Tahitian headdresses were composed of a basketry foundation partially covered with feathers. They were worn with feather-covered breast gorgets as depicted on Cook's first voyage (Figs. 208, 214). Only two such headdresses appear to have been collected. They are reminiscent of the surmounted head piece of the mourning dress masks, both in shape and in having an edging of tropic bird feathers.

1. Feathered headdress, British Museum (TAH 9). Height 157 cm. Figure 215.
   Evidence: Probably collected by Cook and/or Banks on first voyage. Noted "Cook collection."
   Depictions: British Library Add. Ms. 15,508.18 (Fig. 216). Portrait of Joseph Banks by Benjamin West (Fig. 51).

2. Feathered headdress, Oxford (5). Height 129 cm. Figure 217.
   Evidence: Forster collection. Second voyage.
   Literature: Gathercole, n.d. [1970].

Breast Gorgets

Although feather headdresses were comparatively rare, the breast gorgets were apparently worn in some numbers (Fig. 208), as were the Hawaiian feather capes. Like the latter, they were treasured by their European owners, sometimes framed, as was the superb example in the introductory section of this exhibition (Fig. 14), and treated as a very special artificial curiosity.[6]

[6]From the collection of John Hewett. Unfortunately there is no history attached either to the object or to its 18th century frame.

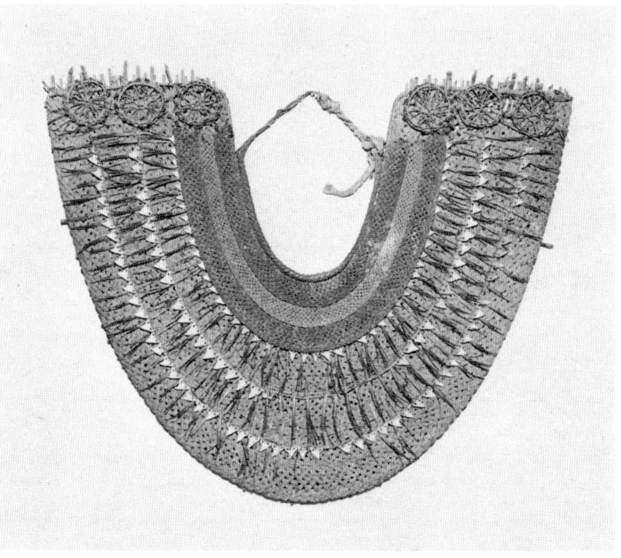

Figure 219. — Gorget, Cape Town SAM 1971.

1-2. Breast gorgets, Leningrad (505-10 [exhibited] 505-14). Height 52 cm, width 63 cm. Height 41 cm, width 54 cm. Figure 218.
   Evidence: Given by Captain Clerke to the Governor of Kamchatka. Third voyage.
   Literature: Rozina, 1966, p. 253; Kaeppler, 1977; Vaughan and Murray-Oliver, 1974, p. 93 [505-14].

3. Breast gorget, Dublin (1885.188). Height 33 cm, width 46 cm.
   Evidence: Circumstantial. Thought to be part of Cook voyage collections given by Patten or King to Trinity College, Dublin. Noted "Cook collection." A paper label attached reads "Gorget Otaheite No. 29." Second or third voyage.
   Literature: Freeman, 1949, p. 8; Ball, 1894 [1895], p. vi.

4. Breast gorget, Vienna (140).
   Evidence: Leverian Museum.
   Literature: Moschner, 1955, p. 209.

5. Breast gorget, Göttingen
   Evidence: Purchased from London dealer Humphrey in 1782.

6. Breast gorget, Stockholm (1799.2.16).
   Evidence: Sparrman collection. Second voyage.
   Literature: Söderström, 1939, p. 33.

7-8. Two breast gorgets, Oxford (6, 45). Missing.
   Evidence: Forster collection. Second voyage.
   Literature: Gathercole, n.d. [1970].

9. Breast gorget, Berne (TAH 50).
   Evidence: Webber collection. Third voyage.
   Literature: Henking, 1957, pp. 347-349; Kaeppler, 1977.

10. Breast gorget, Wellington (FE 335).
    Evidence: Original Cook collection in Bullock's Museum.
    Literature: Kaeppler, 1974a, pp. 70, 78.

11. Breast gorget, British Museum (TAH 57).
    Evidence: Circumstantial. Noted "Cook collection." It is possible that it had a label at one time. A second breast gorget, TAH 537 (now missing), was said to be similar to that depicted in British Library Add. Ms. 15,508.7.

12. Breast gorget, British Museum (1904.255).
    Evidence: Circumstantial. Possibly from the Leverian Museum.[7]

13. Breast gorget, Cape Town (SAM 1971). Height 42 cm, width 53.5 cm. (Fig. 219).
    Evidence: Circumstantial. Thought to have arrived in Cape Town in 1775. Second voyage.
    Literature: Bax. 1970, p. 146.

14-17. Four (?) breast gorgets, Göttingen.
    Evidence: "Three large collars and a smaller one" listed from Forster collection. Second voyage.

18. Breast gorget, Cambridge (1914.10). Width 57 cm, depth 45 cm.
    Evidence: Sandwich collection—probably from Cook from the first voyage.

19. Breast gorget, Sydney (H 105). Width 51 cm, depth 36 cm.
    Evidence: Part of Cook collection exhibited at Colonial and Indian Exhibition.
    Literature: Mackrell, 1886; Appendix I, this volume.

20. Breast gorget, Wörlitz (20).
    Evidence: Forster collection. Second voyage.
    Literature: Germer, 1975, p. 91.

[7]Apparently there were also two others in the Leverian Museum, now lost.

Figure 220. — Young man of Tahiti, Plate 9 of Parkinson's journal.

Other Garments

1. Poncho of hibiscus fiber, Göttingen.
   Evidence: Forster collection. Second voyage. Much like the one depicted by Parkinson (Fig. 220).
2. Hip sections of a dance skirt, Vienna (141).
   Evidence: Leverian Museum.
   Literature: Moschner, 1955, p. 204.
3. Plaited garment (said to be from Tahiti), Stockholm (1848.1.61).
   Evidence: "Banks collection."
   Literature: Rydén, 1965, p. 77.
4. Waist garment of shredded fiber, Göttingen.
   Evidence: Purchased from London dealer Humphrey in 1782.
5. Waist garment of shredded fiber, Oxford (36). Missing.
   Evidence: Forster collection. Second voyage.
   Literature: Gathercole, n.d. [1970].
6. Waist garment of shredded fiber (probably Society Islands), Cambridge (25405).
   Evidence: Pennant collection of Cook voyage objects from various sources.

Figure 221.— Waistcoat pieces embroidered by Mrs. Cook, Mitchell Library R198.

7. Waist garment of shredded fiber, British Museum (TAH 114).
   Evidence: Circumstantial. Noted "Cook Collection No. 71, A Dancing apron Otaheiti."
8. Waist garment, Wörlitz (19).
   Evidence: Forster collection. Second voyage.
   Literature: Germer, 1975, p. 91.

9-10. Two fiber skirts, Wellington (FE 3020).
   Evidence: Circumstantial. From the Imperial Institute from Queen Victoria in a box containing "articles brought by Captain Cook from Otaheti."

11. Plaited fiber garment (said to be a rain garment), Göttingen.
   Evidence: Purchased from London dealer Humphrey in 1782.

Bark Cloth

A great deal of bark cloth was collected in Tahiti and the neighboring islands. As in Hawaii, much of it was cut into pieces, included in books of bark cloth samples, and in many cases lost its association with Cook's voyages. The list that follows is not exhaustive. Some pieces are listed above with mourning dresses. Other pieces were worn as turbans as depicted by Parkinson (British Library Add. Ms. 23,921.21, Fig. 208) or used under the large feather-covered wicker headdresses.

1. Göttingen, 18 pieces purchased from London dealer Humphrey in 1782.
2. Göttingen, four pieces from the Forster collection. Second voyage.
3. Oxford (8-22), 13 pieces from the Forster collection including three pieces belonging to the mourning dress and a turban used to fasten the large helmet.
4. Berne, four pieces from the Webber collection. Third voyage.
5. Bishop Museum (1976.65), one piece exhibited in 1785 as a Cook voyage piece. Gift of John Hewett.
6. Anonymous private collection, two small samples, same source as Number 5.
7. Florence, five pieces of bark cloth.
8. British Museum (96.10-12.3), piece of plain white tapa, from Mrs. Cook to Mrs. Adams to Mr. Tonks to British Museum.
9. Whitby Museum, bark cloth pieces. Said to have been given to friends in Whitby when Cook visited there in January, 1772. Noted "Specimen of Tapa brought by Captain Cook. Presented by R. Ripley." Ripley was one of the founders of the Whitby Literary and Philosophical Society which began the Museum in 1823.
10. Pieces of bark cloth now in the Mitchell Library, Sydney (R198), were embroidered by Mrs. Cook in preparing to make a waistcoat for Captain Cook to wear at Court, had he returned from his third voyage (Fig. 221). Exhibited at the Colonial and Indian Exhibition (Fig. 619).
    Literature: Mackrell, 1886; Appendix I, this volume.
11. Cambridge, large piece of plain white (1914.25). Sandwich collection. Given by Cook, first or second voyage.
12. Cambridge, ten pieces (1924.88a-d, 89-94). Sandwich collection. Probably from Cook from first or second voyage, from Society Islands and other localities in central Polynesia.
13. Brighton (R.3430). Small plain white piece said to be from Cook's second voyage; and (E5/28/70) sixteen pieces bound into a sample book, dated 1769.
14. Sydney. Three large pieces, one with design of red circles and half circles; eleven small white pieces.
15. Christchurch. One piece from the Worden Hall collection. See Appendix II, this volume.
16. Wellington: one piece from the Long collection (FE 3669); three pieces in the Adams collection (FE 5248, 5249); three pieces from the Imperial Institute (FE 3022). See Appendix III, this volume.

Mats

Tahitian mats collected on Cook's voyages were plaited of fine hibiscus or pandanus fiber.

Figure 222. — Hibiscus fiber mat, Göttingen OZ 148.

1-2. Two plaited mats, Göttingen (OZ 148 [exhibited]). Ca. 108 cm × 170 cm. Figure 222.
Evidence: Purchased from London dealer Humphrey in 1782.

3-4. Two plaited mats, Oxford (21, 22). Dimensions 202 cm × 154 cm, 152 cm × 91 cm.
Evidence: Forster collection. Second voyage.
Literature: Gathercole, n.d. [1970].

5. Plaited mat (said to be Tahitian) Göttingen.
Evidence: Forster collection. Second voyage.

6-7. Two plaited mats, Berne (TAH 16a/b).
Evidence: Webber collection. Third voyage.
Literature: Henking, 1957, p. 354; Kaeppler, 1977.

8-9. Two mats, Cambridge (1924.86 and 87). Missing.
Evidence: Given by Cook. First or second voyage.

10. Plaited mat, Wörlitz (18). Dimensions 154 cm by 154 cm.
Evidence: Forster collection. Second voyage.
Literature: Germer, 1975, p. 91.

Sunshades

Objects known as sunshades were apparently worn by women as protection from the sun (see p. vi). They were usually made of fiber stretched on a wooden frame.

1-2. Two sunshades, Dublin (1882.3873 [exhibited] 1882.3874). Height 33.5 cm, width 40.5 cm. Figure 223.
Evidence: Circumstantial. Thought to be part of the Cook voyage collections given to Trinity College by King or Patten. Second or third voyage.
Literature: Freeman, 1949, p. 7.

3. Sunshade, Oxford (136). Length 38 cm.
Evidence: Forster collection. Second voyage.
Literature: Gathercole, n.d. [1970].

4. Sunshade, Berne (TAH 38). Length 35 cm.
Evidence: Webber collection. Third voyage.
Literature: Henking, 1957, pp. 346-347; Kaeppler, 1977.

5. Sunshade, Göttingen. Made of plaited pandanus matting (rather than fiber on a frame).
Evidence: Purchased from London dealer Humphrey in 1782.

6. Sunshade, Wellington (FE 3004).
Evidence: Circumstantial. From the Imperial Institute, from Queen Victoria in a box containing "articles brought by Captain Cook from Otaheti."

Ornaments of Hair

Although few ornaments were collected in the Society Islands on Cook's voyages,[8] the most important of these were long strands of plaited hair, apparently worn by women when dancing (Figure 224).

1. Plaited hair, Stockholm (1799.2.15). Length 500 cm.
Evidence: Sparrman collection. Second voyage.
Literature: Söderström, 1939, p. 33.

2. Plaited hair, Oxford (40). Missing.
Evidence: Forster collection. Second voyage.
Literature: Gathercole, n.d. [1970].

3. Plaited hair, Berne (TAH 18).
Evidence: Webber collection. Third voyage.
Literature: Henking, 1957, p. 346; Kaeppler, 1977.

[8] A feather ornament of unknown use was attributed to the Society Islands from the Forster collection in Oxford. It is missing, thus its use and provenance cannot be confirmed (Gathercole, n.d. [1970], No. 46).

Figure 223. — Sunshade, Dublin 1882.3873.

Figure 224. — Dance at Tahiti, British Library Add. Ms. 15,513.19.

4-5. Plaited hair (two bunches, one unfinished), Göttingen.
Evidence: Purchased from London dealer Humphrey in 1782.

6. Plaited hair, Florence (169).
Evidence: Circumstantial. Cook voyage collection from various sources.
Literature: Giglioli, 1893, pp. 225-226; Kaeppler, 1977.

7. Plaited hair, Cambridge (1914.5).
Evidence: Sandwich collection. Probably from Cook from second voyage.

8. Plaited hair, Cambridge (25424).
Evidence: Pennant collection of Cook voyage objects from various sources.

9. Plaited hair, British Museum (TAH 56).
Evidence: Circumstantial. Noted "Cook collection."

Ear Ornaments

Ornaments for the ear seem to have been the favorite adornment of Tahitian women. Several were collected and depicted (British Library Add. Ms. 23,921.56 [Fig. 225] and 17,277.11 [Fig. 226]).

1-2. Two ear ornaments of seeds, Stockholm (1799.2.22a and b). Figure 227.
Evidence: Sparrman collection. Second voyage.
Literature: Söderström, 1939, p. 32.

3-4. Two ear ornaments of pearls, Göttingen.
Evidence: Purchased from London dealer Humphrey in 1782.

5-9. Five ear ornaments on human hair (one of calcite, two of shells, one of pearls, one of a seed), Cambridge (1914.40, 1914.6-9). Figures 228, 229.
Evidence: Sandwich collection. From Cook from first or second voyage.

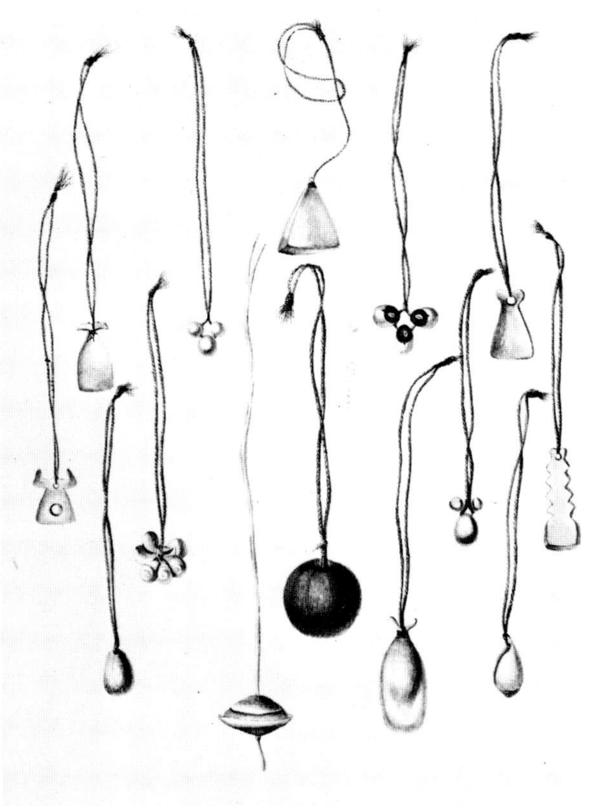

Figure 225. — Ear ornaments, British Library Add. Ms. 23,921.56.

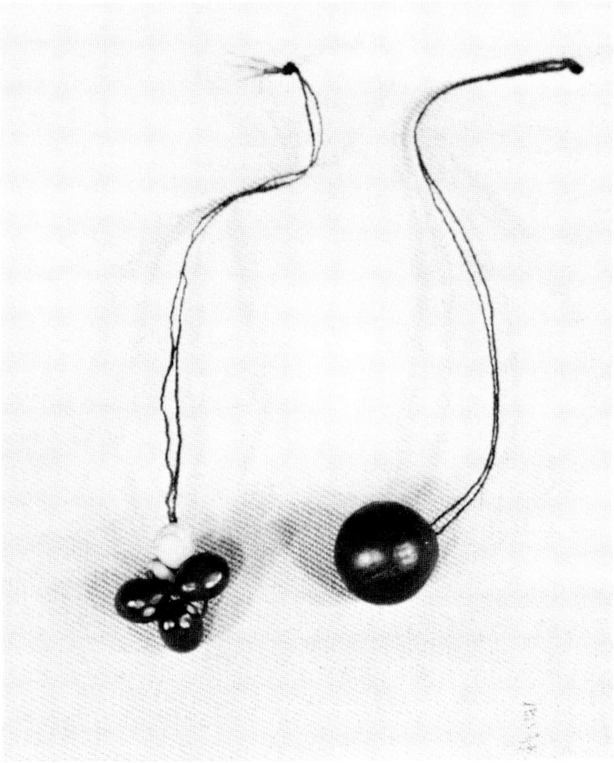

Figure 227. — Ear ornaments, Stockholm 1799.2.22.

Figure 226. — Young lady with ear ornaments, British Library Add. Ms. 17,277.11.

Figure 228. — Ear ornament, Cambridge 1914.40.

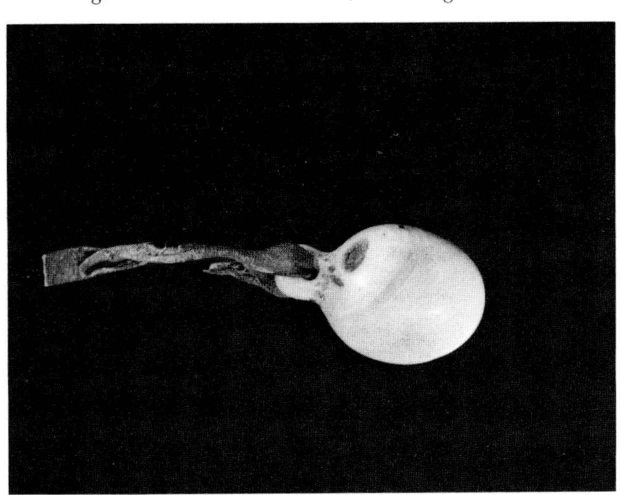

10-15. Six ear ornaments, Wellington (FE 3023).
Evidence: Circumstantial. From the Imperial Institute, from Queen Victoria in a box containing "articles brought by Captain Cook from Otaheti."

Necklaces

Two necklaces of carved pieces of cowry shell laced on braided sennit appear to be from Tahiti—but the provenance cannot be verified because of lack of comparative material.

1-2. Two necklaces, Cambridge (1914.11-12).
Lengths without ties 29 cm, 56 cm. Figure 229.
Evidence: Sandwich collection. From Cook from his first or second voyage.

Tattooing Implements

Tattooing implements collected on Cook's voyages are of two types; the tattooing needles mounted like an adz-blade to a handle of wood, and the mallets for striking them. Several of each were collected and depicted (Figs. 243, 272).

1-2. Two tattooing needles, Vienna (95, 96).
Lengths of handles 16 cm, 17.5 cm. Lengths of needles 3.3 cm, 4.4 cm. Figure 230.
Evidence: Leverian Museum.
Literature: Moschner, 1955, p. 227.

3. Tattooing needle, Stockholm (1799.2.24).
Length of handle 14.4 cm, length of needle 2.5 cm. Figure 231.
Evidence: Sparrman collection. Second voyage.
Literature: Söderström, 1939, p. 32.

Figure 229. — Ear ornaments and necklaces, Cambridge 1914.6-9, 1914.11-12.

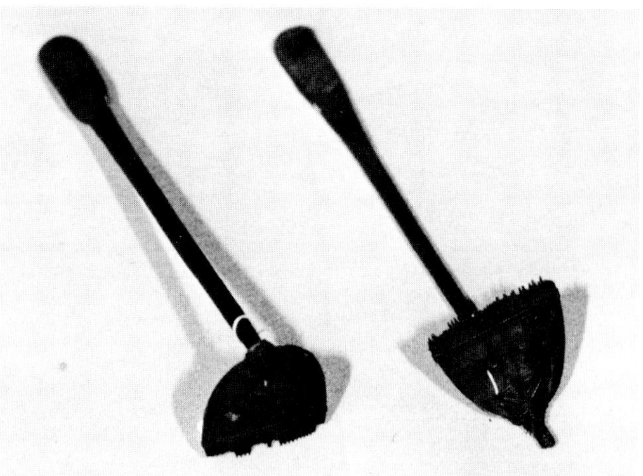

Figure 230. — Two tattooing needles, Vienna 95, 96.

4-5. Two tattooing needles, Dublin (1880.1609).
Lengths of handles 18.5 cm, 15.5 cm. Figure 232.
Evidence: Circumstantial. Thought to be part of the collection given to Trinity College, Dublin, by Patten or King.

6. Tattooing needle, Cambridge (22.928b).
Evidence: Leverian Museum.

7. Tattooing needle, Oxford (37). Length of handle 12.7 cm.
Evidence: Forster collection. Second voyage.
Literature: Gathercole, n.d. [1970].

8-9. Two tattooing needles, Berne (TAH 41 b/c).
Lengths 12.8 cm. and 14.2 cm.
Evidence: Webber collection. Third voyage.
Literature: Henking, 1957, p. 345; Kaeppler, 1977.

10-13. Three tattooing needles, Göttingen.
Evidence: Purchased from London dealer Humphrey in 1782.

14-15. Two tattooing needles, Göttingen.
Evidence: Forster collection. Second voyage.

16-17. Two tattooing needles, Cambridge (1914.47-48).
Evidence: Sandwich collection. From Cook from his first or second voyage.

18. Tattooing needle, Cambridge (25422).
Evidence: Pennant collection of Cook voyage objects from various sources.

19. Tattooing needle, Wellington (FE 3010).
Evidence: Circumstantial. From the Imperial Institute from Queen Victoria in a box containing "articles brought by Captain Cook from Otaheti."

Tattooing Mallets

1. Tattooing mallet, Vienna (97).
   Evidence: Leverian Museum.
   Literature: Moschner, 1955, p. 140.
2. Tattooing mallet, London School of Economics.
   Evidence: Leverian Museum.
3. Tattooing mallet, Cambridge (22.927). Length 48 cm. Figure 233.
   Evidence: Leverian Museum.
4. Tattooing mallet, Oxford (37). Length 46 cm.
   Evidence: Forster collection. Second voyage.
   Literature: Gathercole, n.d. [1970].
5. Tattooing mallet, Berne (TAH 41a). Length 49.5 cm.
   Evidence: Webber collection. Third voyage.
   Literature: Henking, 1957, p. 345; Kaeppler, 1977.
6. Tattooing mallet, Göttingen.
   Evidence: Purchased from London dealer Humphrey in 1782.
7. Tattooing mallet, Göttingen.
   Evidence: Forster collection. Second voyage.
8. Tattooing mallet, British Museum (TAH 118).
   Evidence: Circumstantial. Noted "Cook collection" because of its similarity to that depicted in British Library Add. Ms. 23,921.55[9] (Fig. 272).
9. Tattooing mallet, Wellington (FE 3009).
   Evidence: Circumstantial. From the Imperial Institute from Queen Victoria in a box containing "articles brought by Captain Cook from Otaheti."

Figure 231. — Tattooing needle, Stockholm 1799.2.24.

Treasure Boxes

Three superb wooden treasure boxes can be traced to Cook's voyages and it is likely that one or two in the British Museum (TAH 13, TAH 14) also came from Cook's voyages, but there is, at present, no way to confirm this. Treasure boxes were apparently used to store ornaments and other small valuables, and are reminiscent of Maori feather boxes. The Hawaiian equivalent was a covered basket made of *'ie'ie,* sometimes formed over a large gourd or a pair of large gourds, which served as container and cover, such as the British Museum specimen (HAW 50).

Figure 232. — Two tattooing needles, Dublin 1880.1609.

Figure 233. — Tattooing mallet, Cambridge 22.927.

[9] However, all tattooing mallets are much alike. I have listed it because surely out of all the objects given to the British Museum one must have been included. Whether or not it is TAH 118 cannot be determined.

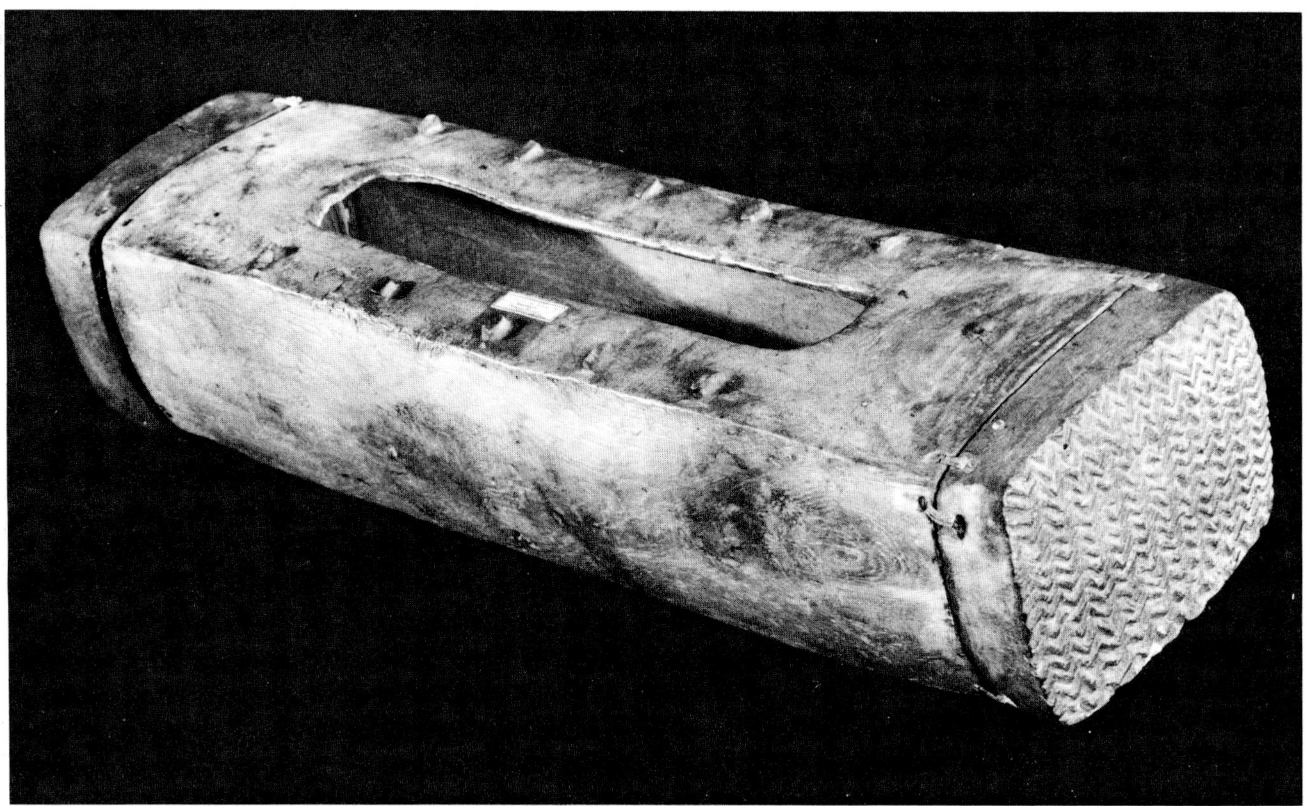

Figure 234. — Treasure box, Vienna 30.

1. Treasure box, Vienna (30). Length 80 cm, width 19 cm, depth 15.5 cm. Figure 234.
   Evidence: Leverian Museum.
   Literature: Moschner, 1955, p. 178.
2. Treasure box, Oxford (33). Length 108 cm.
   Evidence: Forster collection. Second voyage.
   Literature: Gathercole, n.d. [1970].
3. Treasure box, Göttingen (OZ 349). Length 76.2 cm.
   Evidence: Forster collection. Second voyage.

Images

Two types of images were collected during Cook's voyages—carved wooden images in human form known as *ti'i* and pieces of wood covered with braided or plaited sennit known as *to'o*—the latter being the more sacred. It is likely that the wooden images collected on Cook's voyages were canoe carvings.

1-2. Two wooden images, Oxford (38 [exhibited], 39). Heights 30 cm, 33 cm. Figure 235.
   Evidence: Forster collection. Second voyage.
   Literature: Gathercole, n.d. [1970].

3. Wooden image, British Museum (TAH 78a). Height 46.5 cm. Figure 236.
   Evidence: Given by Captain Cook.
   Literature: Cranstone and Gowers, 1968.

4. Sennit image, British Museum (TAH 64). Figure 237.
   Evidence: Circumstantial. Noted "Cook collection" because of its similarity to a depiction in a drawing by John Frederick Miller, British Library Add. Ms. 15,508.26 (Fig. 238).

5. Sennit image. Lost.
   Evidence: Leverian Museum depiction.

6. Wooden object, British Museum (TAH 65). Figure 239.
   Evidence: Depicted by John Frederick Miller in 1771 (British Library Add. Ms. 23,921.57). Figure 240.
   Catalogued as a "staff god" in the British Museum, noted "weapon" in Miller's drawing (in my opinion both are unlikely).

Figure 235. — Wooden image, Oxford 38.

Figure 236. — Wooden image, British Museum TAH 78a.

Figure 237. — Sennit image, British Museum TAH 64.

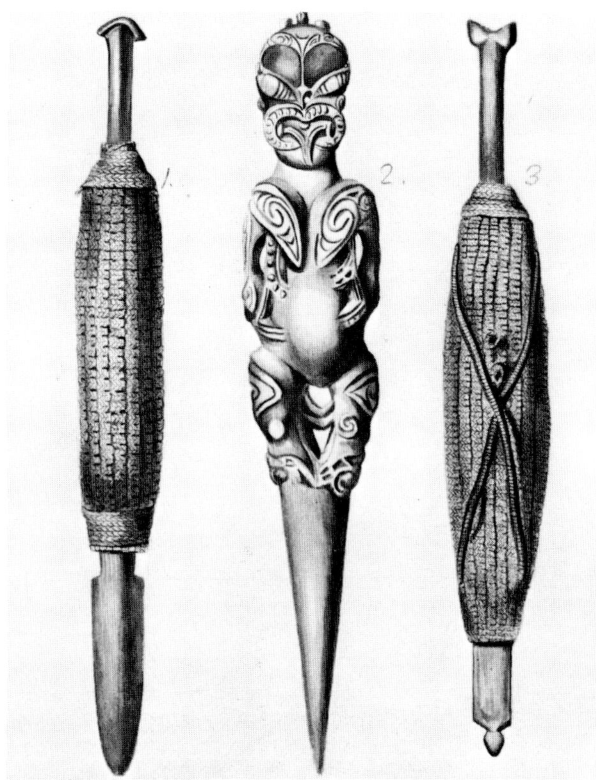

Figure 238. — Images of Tahiti and New Zealand, British Library Add. Ms. 15,508.26.

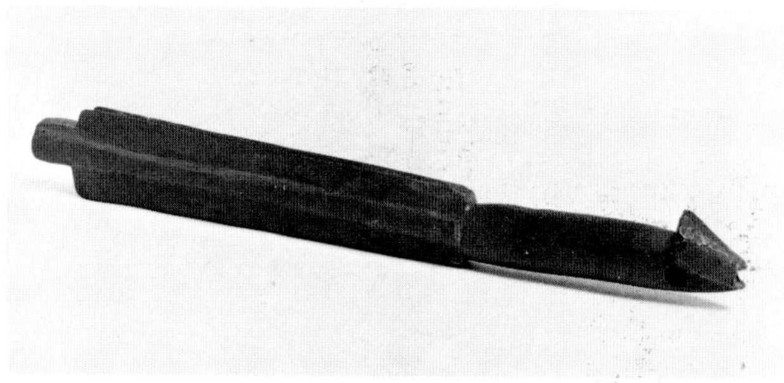

Figure 239. — Wooden object, British Museum TAH 65.

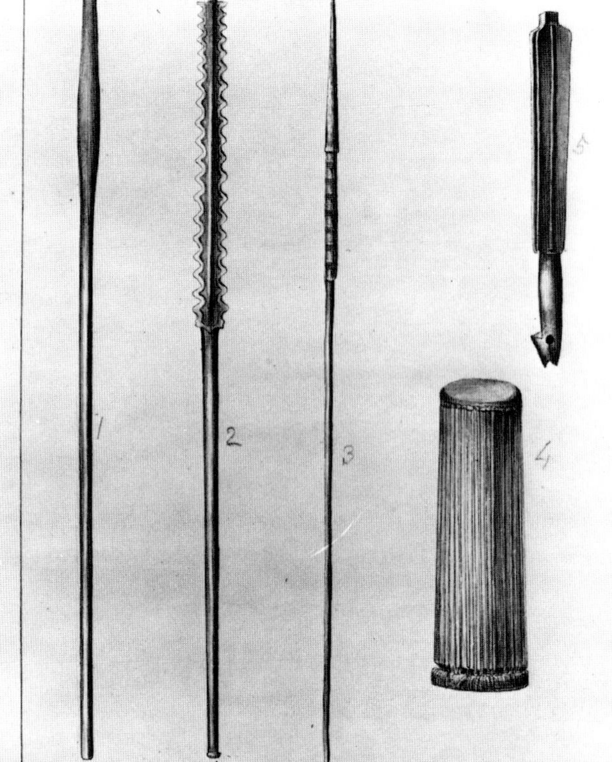

Figure 240. — Artifacts from Tahiti by J. F. Miller, British Library Add. Ms. 23,921.57.

Fly Whisks

Fly whisks from the Society Islands and central Polynesia were often decorated with human images.[10] Two from the Society Islands were depicted by Miller (British Library Add. Ms. 23,921.53), but cannot be identified (Fig. 50).

1. Fly whisk handle with human image, Göttingen (OZ 418). Length 33.5 cm, height of image 10 cm. Figures 241, 242. Similar to the engraving after Parkinson (Fig. 243).
   Evidence: Purchased from London dealer Humphrey in 1782.

2. Image from fly whisk handle, Göttingen (OZ 419). Height 14 cm, width at head 3.5 cm. Figures 244, 245.
   Evidence: Forster collection. Second voyage.

3. Image from fly whisk or canoe, Dublin (1885.190). Height 20.5 cm, width 5.5 cm, depth 7 cm. Figures 246, 247.
   Evidence: Circumstantial. Thought to be part of the Cook collection given to Trinity College by Patten or King.
   Literature: Freeman, 1949, p. 8.

Musical Instruments

Musical instruments collected and depicted on Cook's voyages were drums and nose flutes (Figs. 224, 248). Drums were of various sizes, the larger the size the deeper the tone.

[10] For others see Austral Islands.

Figure 241. — Fly whisk handle, Göttingen OZ 418.

Figure 242. — Fly whisk handle (detail), Göttingen OZ 418.

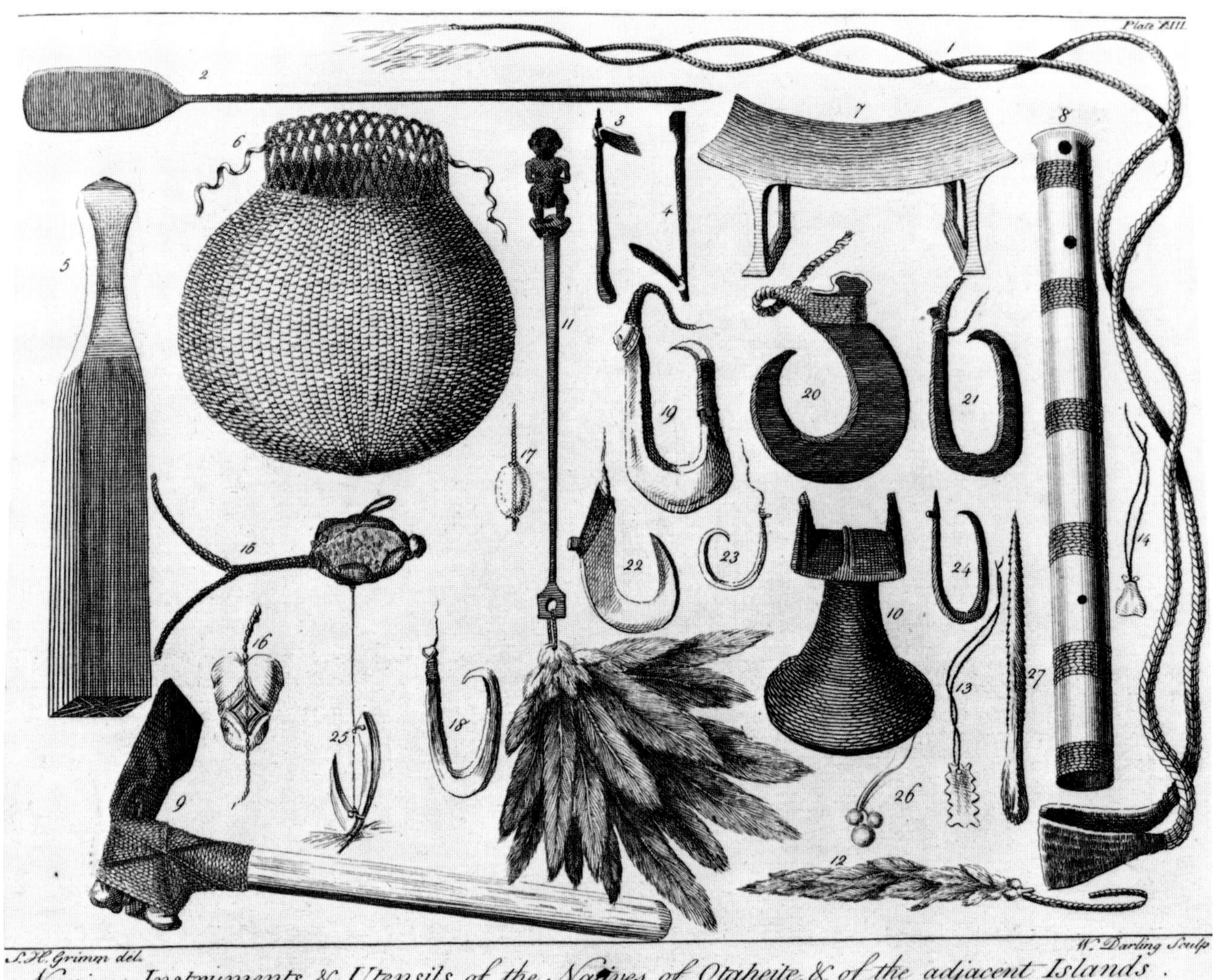

Figure 243. — Artifacts from the Society Islands, from Parkinson's journal.

1. Drum, Vienna (152). Height 64 cm, diameter 14.5 cm. Figure 249.
   Evidence: Leverian Museum.
   Literature: Moschner, 1955, p. 247.

2. Drum, Dublin (1882.3640). Height 40.5 cm, diameter 27 cm. Figure 250.
   Evidence: Circumstantial. Thought to be part of Cook voyage collection given to Trinity College by Patten or King. Noted "Cook collection."
   Literature: Freeman, 1949, p. 7.

3. Drum, Oxford (25). Height 33 cm.
   Evidence: Forster collection. Second voyage.
   Literature: Gathercole, n.d. [1970].

4. Drum, Göttingen (OZ 410). Height 32 cm, diameter 27 cm.
   Evidence: Forster collection. Second voyage.

5. Drum, Berne (TAH 34). Height 30 cm, diameter 16 cm.
   Evidence: Webber collection. Third voyage.
   Literature: Henking, 1957, p. 352; Kaeppler, 1977.

6. Drum, British Museum (TAH 22). Height 63.5 cm.
   Evidence: Circumstantial. Noted "Cook collection" because of its similarity to that depicted in British Library Add. Ms. 23,921.57 (Fig. 240), but this drawing is also much like the following drum.

7. Drum, Cambridge (1914.26). Height 65 cm, diameter ca. 15 cm.
   Evidence: Sandwich collection. Given by Cook. First or second voyage.

Figure 244. — Image from fly whisk handle, Göttingen OZ 419.

Figure 245. — Image from fly whisk handle (side view), Göttingen OZ 419.

Figure 246. — Wooden image, Dublin 1885.190.

Figure 247. — Wooden image (side view), Dublin 1885.190.

1. Nose flute, Sydney (H 143). Length 41 cm. Figure 251.
   Evidence: Cook collection exhibited at Colonial and Indian Exhibition.
   Literature: Mackrell, 1886; Appendix I, this volume.
2. Nose flute, Vienna (151). Length 44 cm.
   Evidence: Leverian Museum.
   Literature: Moschner, 1955, p. 240.
3. Nose flute, Oxford (26). Length 33 cm.
   Evidence: Forster collection. Second voyage.
   Literature: Gathercole, n.d. [1970].
4. Nose flute, Göttingen.
   Evidence: Purchased from London dealer Humphrey in 1782.
5. Nose flute (no twine binding), Cambridge (1914.27). Length 39.5 cm. Figure 252.
   Evidence: Sandwich collection. Given by Cook. Second voyage.
6. Nose flute, Cambridge (25 385). Length 42 cm. Figure 252.
   Evidence: Pennant collection of Cook voyage objects from various sources.

Figure 248. — Musicians, British Library Add. Ms. 15,508.10.

Figure 250. — Drum *(pahu)*, Dublin 1882.3640.

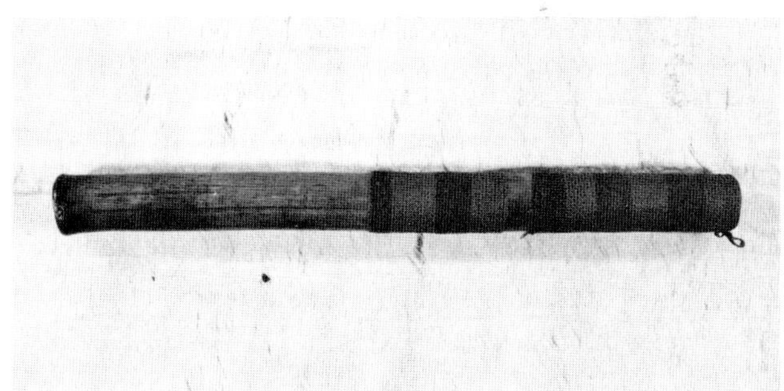

Figure 251. — Nose flute, Sydney H 143.

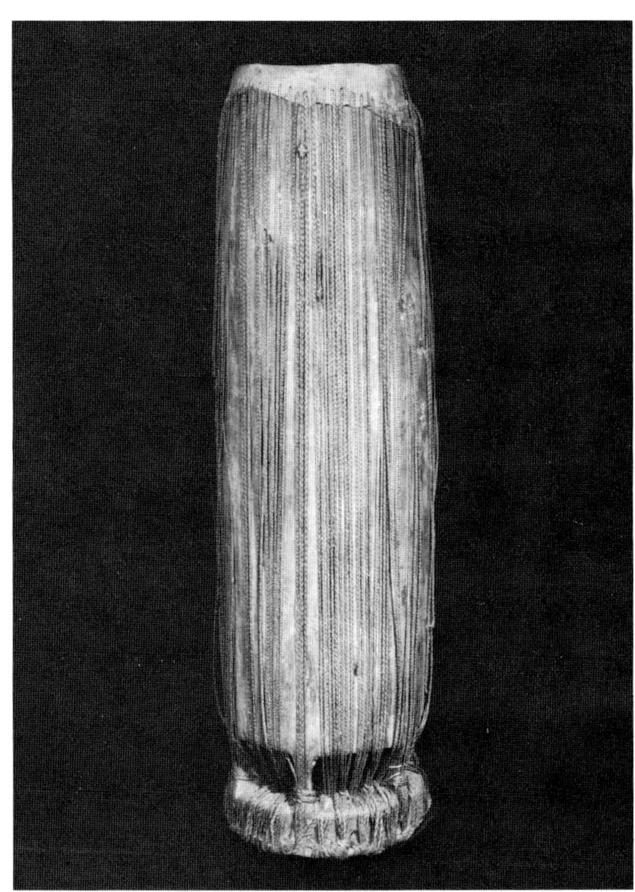

Figure 249. — Drum *(pahu)*, Vienna 152.

Figure 252. — Two nose flutes, Cambridge 1914.27, 25.385.

Figure 253.— Shell trumpet, Cambridge 1914.54.

Shell Trumpets

Shell trumpets in the Society Islands were made of triton shells with a side perforation as a blowing hole. Only one has been located, although another was in the Leverian Museum but is now lost.

1. Shell trumpet, Cambridge (1914.54). Length 35 cm. Side perforation with mouthpiece of gum. Figure 253.
   Evidence: Sandwich collection. Given by Cook, first or second voyage.

Amusements

The most spectacular of the amusements pursued in the Society Islands was the ritualized shooting of bows and arrows. Several, along with their quivers, were collected on Cook's voyages. One set was depicted by J. F. Miller (Add. Ms. 23,921.57). Figure 254.

1-5. Bow (1799.2.20), quiver (1799.2.21a) and three arrows (1799.2.21b, 21c and d). Stockholm. Bow length 152.5 cm, quiver length 85 cm, arrow lengths 82 cm, 80 cm, 80 cm.
Evidence: Sparrman collection. Second voyage.
Literature: Söderström, 1939, pp. 25-28.

6-9. Bow (41), quiver (42), and two arrows, Oxford. Bow length 165 cm, quiver length 93 cm, arrow lengths 71 cm, 81 cm.
Evidence: Forster collection. Second voyage.
Literature: Gathercole, n.d. [1970].

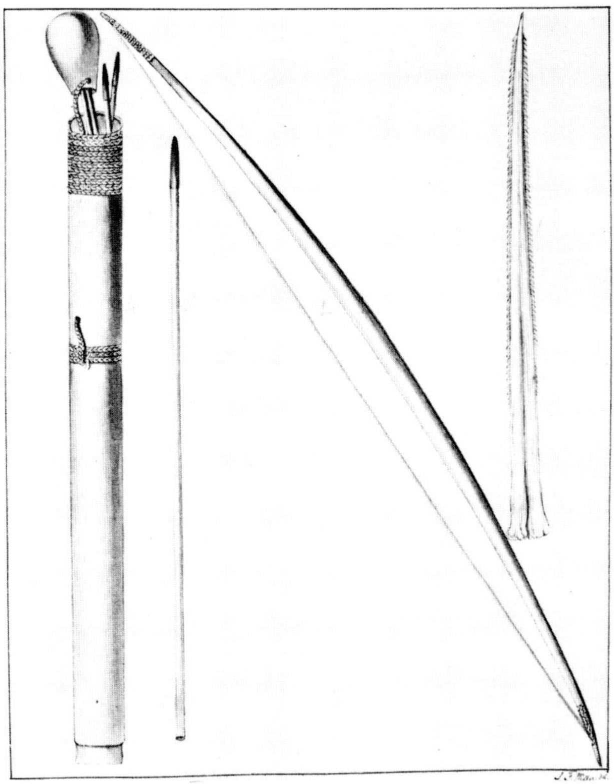

Figure 254.— Artifacts from Tahiti by J. F. Miller, British Library Add. Ms. 23,921.57.

10-17. Bow, quiver, and six arrows, Göttingen.
Evidence: Purchased from London dealer Humphrey in 1782.
Literature: Plischke, 1957, p. 209.

18. Bow, Vienna (93). Missing. Length 165 cm.
Evidence: Leverian Museum.
Literature: Moschner, 1955, pp. 156-158.

19. Arrow, Stockholm (1848.1.27). Length 79 cm.
Evidence: Part of "Banks collection."
Literature: Rydén, 1965, p. 77.

20-21. Two quivers (one made from a Tongan nose flute[11]), Florence (245, 237).
Evidence: Circumstantial. Cook voyage collection from various sources.
Literature: Giglioli, 1893, pp. 230-233; Kaeppler, 1977.

[11]Possibly collected in Tonga and traded to Tahitians on Cook's second voyage, and collected again in Tahiti on Cook's third voyage, if, in fact, it was used as a quiver.

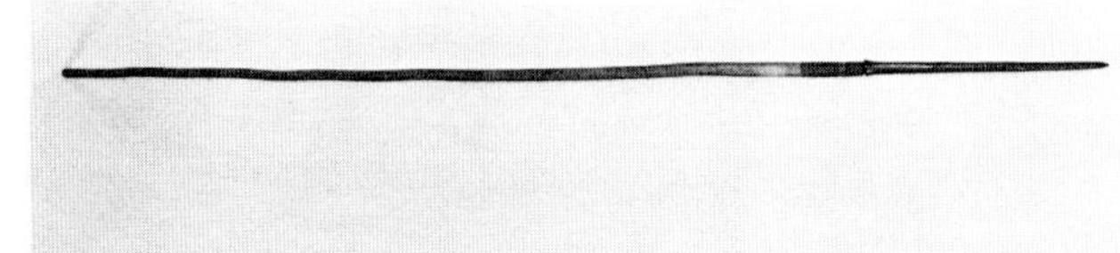

Figure 255.— Javelin, Cambridge 1914.33.

Figure 256.— Neck rest, Stockholm 1799.2.52.

22-35. Bow, quiver, and 12 arrows, Cambridge (1914.97, 1914.83). Length of bow 164 cm, quiver 95.5 cm, arrow ca. 80 cm.
Evidence: Sandwich collection. Given by Cook. First or second voyage.

Another game of skill was throwing a javelin at a target. A lance in the Cambridge collection, made of a shaft of light wood with a long point of hard wood bound with sennit lashing, is said to have been used in this way.

1. Javelin, Cambridge (1914.33). Length 197 cm, length of head 45 cm. Shaft of light wood, head of hard wood, sennit binding. Figure 255.
Evidence: Sandwich collection. Given by Cook. Probably from first voyage and depicted in Miller's drawing (British Library, Add. Ms. 23,921.57). Figure 240.

Tops were used by children for amusement. One has been located.

1. Top, Göttingen. Large seed mounted on a pointed stick.
Evidence: Purchased from London dealer Humphrey in 1782.

Neck Rests

1. Neck rest, Stockholm (1799.2.52). Length 33 cm, height 14 cm. It has an indigenous mend. Figure 256.
Evidence: Sparrman collection. Second voyage.
Literature: Söderström, 1939, pp. 31-32.
2. Neck rest, Stockholm (RM 1404). Length 24.5 cm.
Evidence: Sparrman collection. Second voyage.
Literature: Söderström, 1939, pp. 31-32.
3. Neck rest, Stockholm (1848.1.11). Height 12 cm.
Evidence: "Banks collection."
Literature: Rydén, 1965, p. 73.
4. Neck rest, Cambridge (1914.14). Length 31.5 cm, height 13 cm, width 12 cm.
Evidence: Sandwich collection. Given by Cook. Second voyage.
5. Neck rest, Oxford (30). Height 15 cm.
Evidence: Forster collection. Second voyage.
Literature: Gathercole, n.d. [1970].
6. Neck rest, Furneaux collection.
Evidence: Collected by Captain Furneaux. Second voyage. Probably the neck rest depicted in Dance's portrait of Omai (Fig. 52).
Literature: Furneaux, 1960, p. 180.
7. Neck rest, Göttingen.
Evidence: Purchased from London dealer Humphrey in 1782.

8-9. Two neck rests, Göttingen.
Evidence: Forster collection. Second voyage.

10. Neck rest, British Museum (TAH 1). Length 24 cm, height 11 cm.
Evidence: Circumstantial. Noted "Cook collection" and retaining part of an old paper label evidently used to identify some of the Cook voyage objects, "Pillow Otahaite."
11. Neck rest, Wellington (FE 3018).
Evidence: Circumstantial. From the Imperial Institute from Queen Victoria in a box containing "articles brought by Captain Cook from Otaheti."

Seats

Wooden seats are of two styles—one much like neck rests with joined feet, the other with four separated feet. It is possible that the latter style is from elsewhere in central Polynesia. The former type was depicted (Add. Ms. 15,508.10) Figure 248.

1. Seat, Stockholm (1799.2.54). Length 57 cm, width 22 cm, height at center 19 cm, height at ends 24 cm. Figure 257.
Evidence: Sparrman collection. Second voyage.
Literature: Söderström, 1939, pp. 30-31.
2. Seat, Stockholm (1799.2.8). Length 57 cm, width 21 cm, height of legs 10.5 cm.
Evidence: Sparrman collection. Second voyage.
Literature: Söderström, 1939, pp. 30-31.

Figure 257. — Seat, Stockholm 1799.2.54.

Figure 258. — Wooden bowl, British Museum TAH 4.

Containers

Strangely enough, only one wooden bowl from the Cook voyages can be documented as coming from the Society Islands. Others that have been attributed to the Society Islands seem more likely to be from Tonga and are listed in that section.

1. Wooden bowl, Oxford (29). Missing.
   Evidence: Forster collection. Second voyage.
   Literature: Gathercole, n.d. [1970].
2. Wooden bowl, British Museum (TAH 4). Length 79 cm, height 10 cm, width 22 cm. Figure 258.
   Evidence: Circumstantial. Noted "Cook collection" and retaining its "Cook collection" label, "A trough for their liquid food at Otaheite."
3. Gourd container in a fiber carrier, Oxford (35). Length 23 cm. Said to be for oil. Figure 259.
   Evidence: Forster collection. Second voyage.
   Literature: Gathercole, n.d. [1970].

4-5. Two coconut cups, Berne (TAH 42a/b). Diameters 13 cm, 10 cm.
   Evidence: Webber collection. Third voyage.
   Literature: Henking, 1957, p. 355; Kaeppler, 1977.

6. Coconut shell cups, Cambridge (1914.15).
   Evidence: Sandwich collection. Given by Cook. First or second voyage.

7-8. Two coconut shell cups, Göttingen.
   Evidence: Forster collection. Second voyage.

9. Cowry shell cup, Göttingen.
   Evidence: Purchased from London dealer Humphrey in 1782.

Figure 259. — Gourd container, Oxford 35.

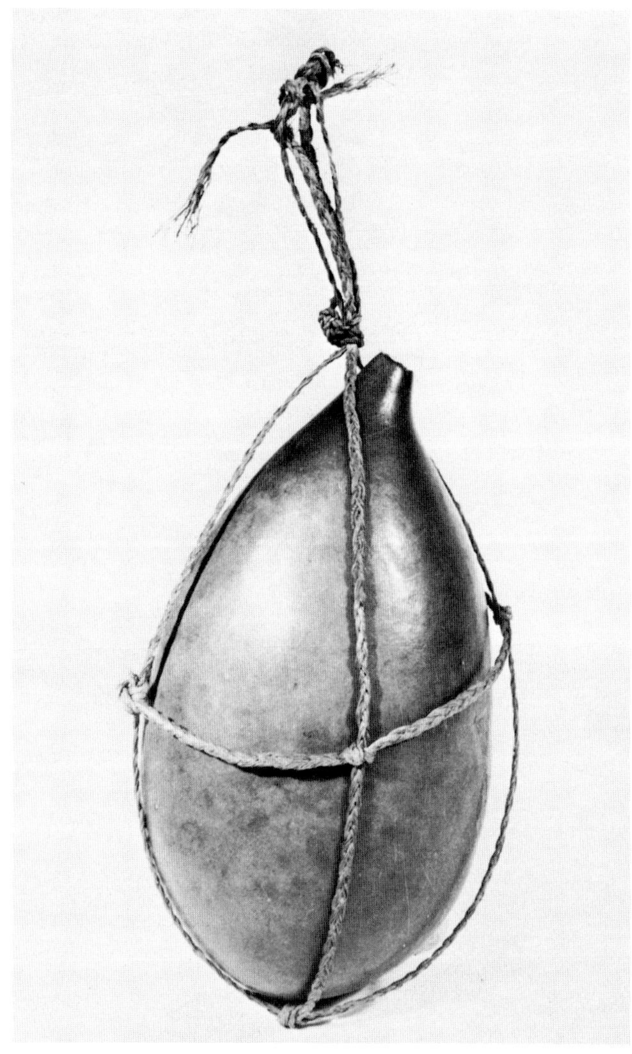

Figure 260. — Basket of wickerwork, Göttingen.

Figure 261. — Basket of sedge, British Museum TAH 35.

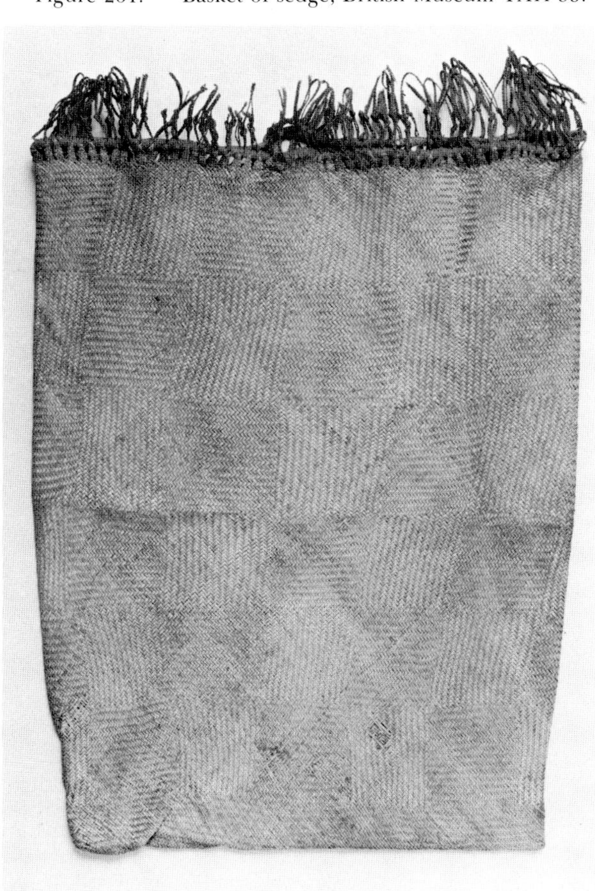

Baskets

Baskets attributed to Otaheite are almost invariably from Tonga and thus it is difficult to confirm their attributed provenances. Those apparently of Society Islands styles are the following:

1. Basket (of wickerwork), Göttingen. Figure 260. Baskets of this type were depicted on canoes (Fig. 207), and may have been used to hold fish.
   Evidence: Purchased from London dealer Humphrey in 1782.
2. Basket (of sedge) plaited in vertical and horizontal designs and with sennit loops around top opening, British Museum (TAH 35). Figure 261.
   Evidence: Circumstantial. Noted "Cook Coll. No. 7."

3-5. Three baskets (of sedge) plaited in vertical and horizontal designs, Stockholm (1848.1.22, 1848.1.18, 1848.1.19).
   Evidence: "Banks collection."
   Literature: Rydén, 1965, pp. 88-89 (attributed to New Zealand).

6. Basket, Cambridge (1914.52). Missing. The basket is variously described as a "fishing basket," a "mat basket" and as a "square bag of ornate plaitwork" (probably like the latter four listed above).
   Evidence: Sandwich collection. Given by Cook, first or second voyage.

7-8. Two baskets, Oxford (31, 32). Missing.
   Evidence: Forster collection. Second voyage.
   Literature: Gathercole, n.d. [1970].

9. Basket, Göttingen.
   Evidence: Purchased from London dealer Humphrey in 1782.

Food Pounders

Food pounders from the Society Islands are of three main types distinguished here as "forked top," "cross bar," and "faceted," which refers to the top of the pounder. Although these may be local styles, gradations, or reworkings, this cannot be confirmed by the present evidence.

⛵1. Food pounder (forked top), Stockholm (1799.2.7). Height 18 cm, width 11.5 cm. Figure 262.
   Evidence: Sparrman collection. Second voyage.
   Literature: Söderström, 1939, p. 29.

Figure 262. — Food pounder, Stockholm 1799.2.7.

Figure 263. — Three food pounders, Vienna 119, 117, 118.

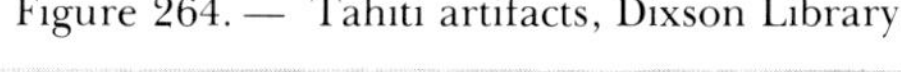
Figure 264. — Tahiti artifacts, Dixson Library.

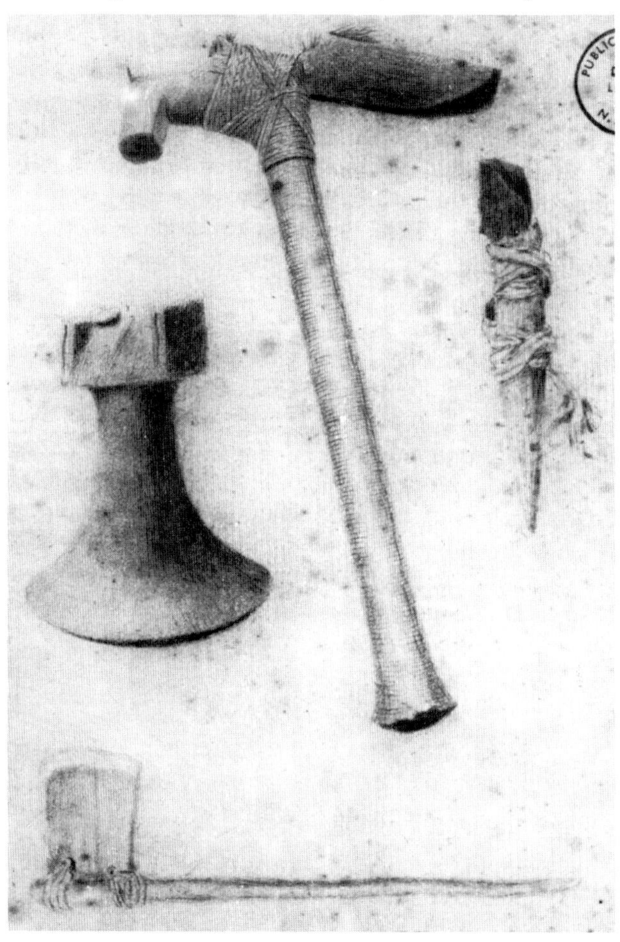

2. Food pounder (forked top), Stockholm (1848.1.9). Height 19 cm.
   Evidence: Circumstantial. "Banks collection."
   Literature: Rydén, 1965, pp. 76-77.
3. Food pounder (forked top), Vienna (117). Height 19 cm. Figure 263.
   Evidence: Leverian Museum.
   Literature: Moschner, 1955, p. 171.
4. Food pounder (forked top), Göttingen.
   Evidence: Purchased from London dealer Humphrey in 1782.
5. Food pounder (forked top), Cambridge (1914.17). Height 18 cm.
   Evidence: Sandwich collection. Probably from Cook from first or second voyage.
6. Food pounder (broken forked top), Cambridge (25.418).
   Evidence: Pennant collection of Cook voyage objects from various sources. Depicted in a drawing pasted in Pennant's copy of the published account of Cook's voyages (Fig. 264).
7. Food pounder (forked top) Oxford (28). Height 16 cm.
   Evidence: Forster collection. Second voyage.
   Literature: Gathercole, n.d. [1970].

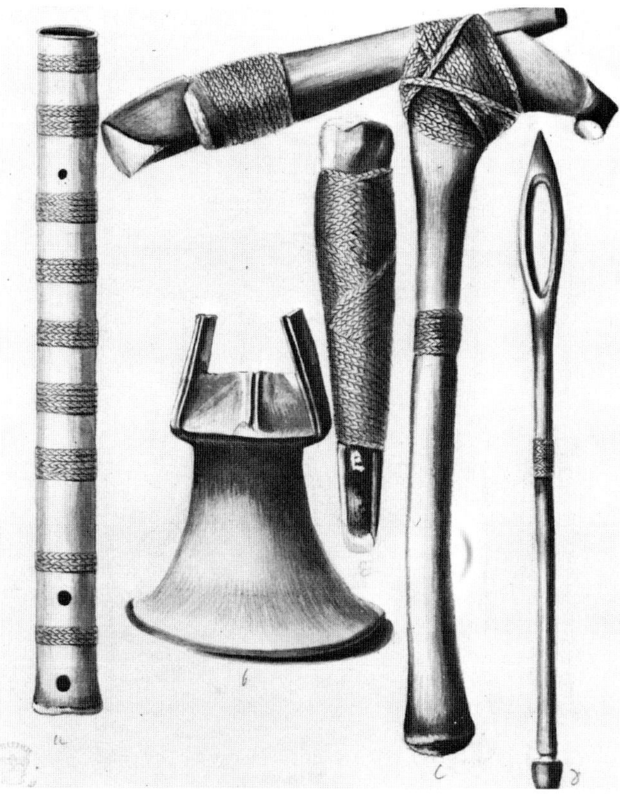

Figure 265. — Tahiti artifacts by J. F. Miller, British Library Add. Ms. 15,508.31.

Figure 266. — Food pounder, Greenwich L15/94/A.

8. Food pounder (forked top), British Museum (TAH 15).
   Evidence: Circumstantial. Noted "Cook collection" because of its similarity to the one depicted in British Library Add. Ms. 15,508.31 (Fig. 265), and retaining a "Cook collection" paper label, "stone pestle, Otaheiti."
9. Food pounder (forked top), Wellington (FE 337).
   Evidence: Original Cook collection in Bullock's Museum.
   Literature: Kaeppler, 1974a, p. 78.
10. Food pounder (faceted), Wellington (FE 3006).
    Evidence: Circumstantial. From the Imperial Institute from Queen Victoria in a box containing "articles brought by Captain Cook from Otaheti."
11. Food pounder (cross bar), Vienna (118). Height 14 cm. Figure 263.
    Evidence: Leverian Museum.
    Literature: Moschner, 1955, p. 171.
12. Food pounder (cross bar), Greenwich (L15/94/A). Height 15.5 cm. Figure 266.
    Evidence: Circumstantial. Said to come from great granddaughter of Cook's sister Margaret.
13. Food pounder (short cross bar), Cambridge (1914.18). Height 16.5 cm.
    Evidence: Sandwich collection. Probably from Cook from first or second voyage.
14. Food pounder (curved cross bar), Vienna (119). Height 15 cm. Figure 263.
    Evidence: Leverian Museum.
    Literature: Moschner, 1955, p. 171.
15. Food pounder (faceted), Cambridge (1914.16). Height 16 cm.
    Evidence: Sandwich collection. Given by Cook. First or second voyage.

Breadfruit Splitters

1. Breadfruit splitter, Cambridge (1914.19). Length of handle 32 cm, length of head 10.5 cm. Figure 267.
   Evidence: Sandwich collection. Collected by Cook on first or second voyage.
2. Breadfruit splitter, Göttingen.
   Evidence: Purchased from London dealer Humphrey in 1782.
3. Breadfruit splitter, Berne (TAH 21). Length of handle 33 cm, length of head 16 cm.
   Evidence: Webber collection. Third voyage.
   Literature: Henking, 1957, p. 383; Kaeppler, 1977.

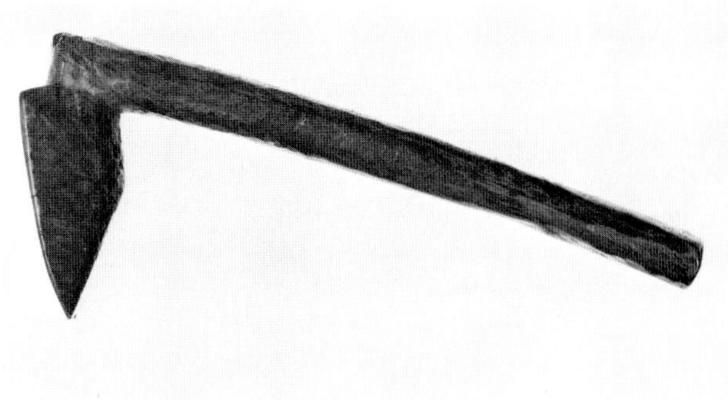

Figure 267. — Breadfruit splitter, Cambridge 1914.19.

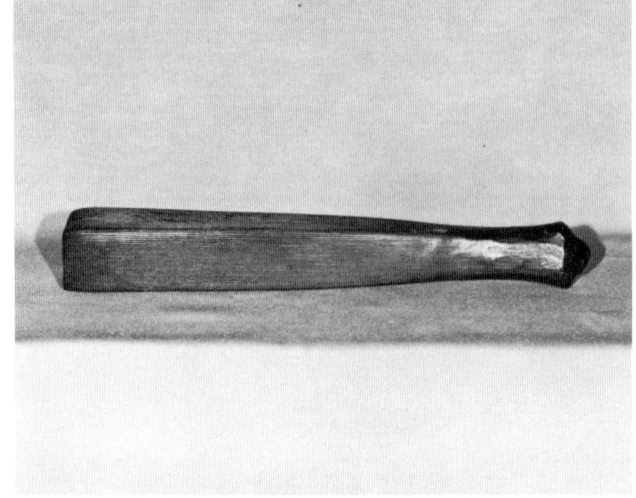

Figure 268. — Bark cloth beater, Vienna 120.

Bark Cloth Beaters

Implements for making bark cloth included beaters and anvils (see p. v). Several beaters have been traced to collection on Cook's voyage and one object, from its description, appears to be an anvil.

1-3. Three bark cloth beaters, Vienna (120 [exhibited], 121, 122). Lengths 40.5 cm, 37 cm, 32.5 cm. Figure 268.
Evidence: Leverian Museum.
Literature: Moschner, 1955, pp. 170-171.

4. Bark cloth beater, Stockholm (1799.2.11). Length 33 cm, width 3.5 cm. Figure 269.
Evidence: Sparrman collection. Second voyage.
Literature: Söderström, 1939, p. 30.

5-8. Four bark cloth beaters, Dublin (1882.3687-3690 [exhibited]). Length 26 cm. Figure 270.
Evidence: Circumstantial. Thought to be part of the Cook voyage collections given to Trinity College, Dublin, by Patten or King. Second or third voyage.
Literature: Freeman, 1949, p. 7.

9. Bark cloth beater, Cambridge (1914.24). Length 38 cm, widths at square end ca. 4.5 cm; 46, 10, 23, and 36 grooves, respectively, on the four sides.
Evidence: Sandwich collection. Collected by Cook on first or second voyage.

10. Bark cloth beater, Cambridge (25.376). Length 34.5 cm, widths at square end ca. 4.5 cm.
Evidence: Pennant collection of Cook voyage objects from various sources.

11. Bark cloth beater, Oxford (24). Length 35 cm.
Evidence: Forster collection. Second voyage.
Literature: Gathercole, n.d. [1970].

12. Bark cloth beater, Göttingen.
Evidence: Forster collection. Second voyage.

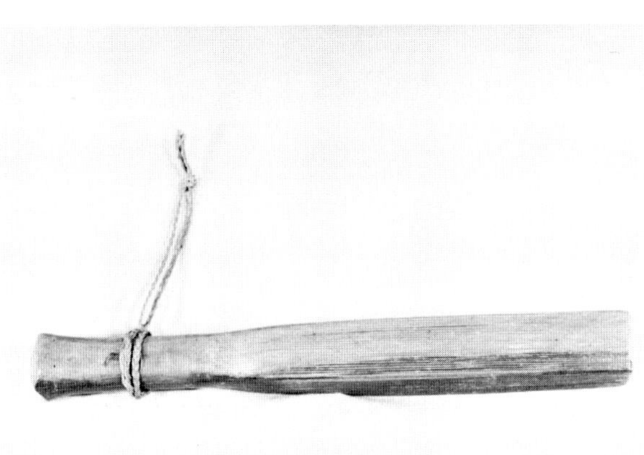

Figure 269. — Bark cloth beater, Stockholm 1799.2.11.

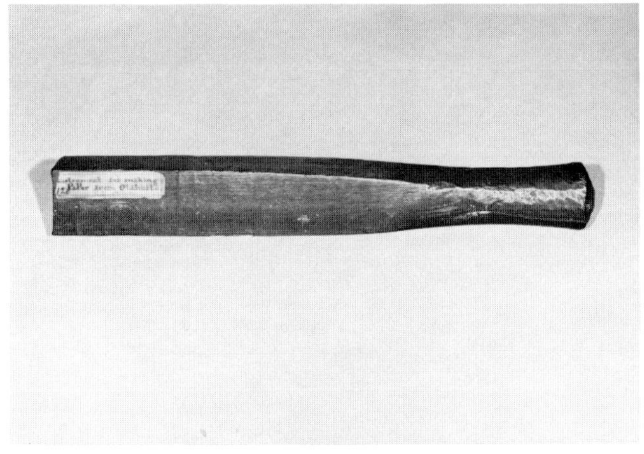

Figure 270. — Bark cloth beater, Dublin 1882.3690.

13. Bark cloth beater, Göttingen.
   Evidence: Purchased from London dealer Humphrey in 1782.
14. Bark cloth beater, British Museum (TAH 20).
   Evidence: Circumstantial. Noted "Cook collection" because of its similarity to the drawing in British Library Add. Ms. 23,921.30.
15. Bark cloth beater, Wellington (FE 3008).
   Evidence: Circumstantial. From the Imperial Institute from Queen Victoria in a box containing "articles brought by Captain Cook from Otaheti."
1. Anvil for beating bark cloth, Göttingen.
   Evidence: Forster collection. Second voyage.

Netting and Thatching Needles

"Needles" for making various kinds of nets and thatching were collected on Cook's voyages. One type was depicted by J. F. Miller from the first voyage (Fig. 265) but cannot be located. A second type was collected with human hair in process of manufacture.[12]

1. Netting needle with human hair, Vienna (127). Length 19.5 cm. Figure 271.
   Evidence: Leverian Museum.
   Literature: Moschner, 1955, p. 169.
2. Netting needle with human hair, Sydney (H 153). Length 40 cm (broken).
   Evidence: Part of Cook collection exhibited at Colonial and Indian Exhibition.
   Literature: Mackrell, 1886; Appendix I, this volume.

[12] It is possible that some of these netting needles are Tongan, but there seems to be no documentary evidence to separate them.

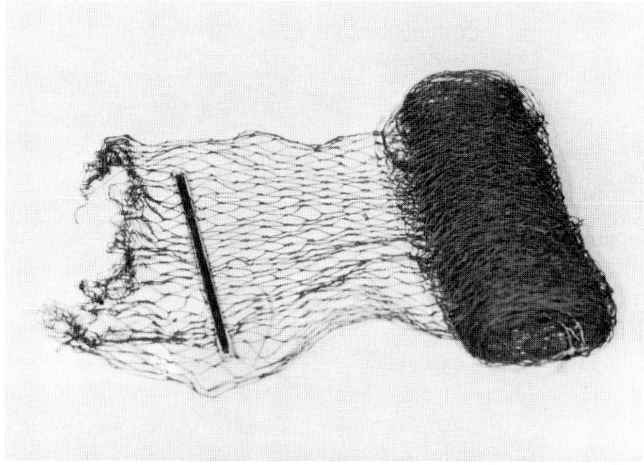

Figure 271.— Netting needle with human hair, Vienna 127.

3-4. Two netting needles, Vienna (124-125). Lengths 34 cm, 29 cm.
   Evidence: Leverian Museum.
   Literature: Moschner, 1955, pp. 168-169.
5. Netting needle, British Museum (TAH 129).
   Evidence: Circumstantial. Noted "Cook collection" and a "Cook collection" label remains, "A Shuttle Otaheiti."
6. Netting needle, Göttingen.
   Evidence: Purchased from London dealer Humphrey in 1782.

Cordage

1. Coconut fiber cordage, Cambridge (1914.13).
   Evidence: Sandwich collection. Collected by Cook on first or second voyage.
2. Coconut fiber cordage, British Museum (TAH 40).
   Evidence: Circumstantial. Noted "Cook collection" and "No. 38."[13]
3. Cordage, Oxford (47). Missing.
   Evidence: Forster collection. Second voyage.
   Literature: Gathercole, n.d. [1970].
4. White leaves (for making cordage ?), Göttingen.
   Evidence: Purchased from London dealer Humphrey in 1782.

Adzes

A large number of hafted adzes from the Society Islands were collected on Cook's voyages. They are of two types—an ordinary hafted style and a style with a removable mounted blade used as a swivel adz. Both were depicted by Miller from objects collected on first voyage (Figs. 265, 272).

1. Hafted adz, Exeter (E 1225). Length of haft 46 cm, length of blade 16 cm. Figure 273.
   Evidence: Leverian Museum.
2. Hafted adz, Stockholm (1799.2.51). Length of haft 53 cm, length of blade 19 cm. Fish scales beneath lashing. Figure 274.
   Evidence: Sparrman collection. Second voyage.
   Literature: Söderström, 1939, p. 28.
3-4. Two hafted adzes, Vienna (91,92). Length of hafts 38.5 cm, 50 cm; length of blades 14.5 cm, 14.5 cm.
   Evidence: Leverian Museum.
   Literature: Moschner, 1955, p. 164.

[13] Perhaps from Menzies on Vancouver's voyage rather than from Cook's voyages.

Figure 272. — Tools from Tahiti, British Library Add. Ms. 23,921.55.

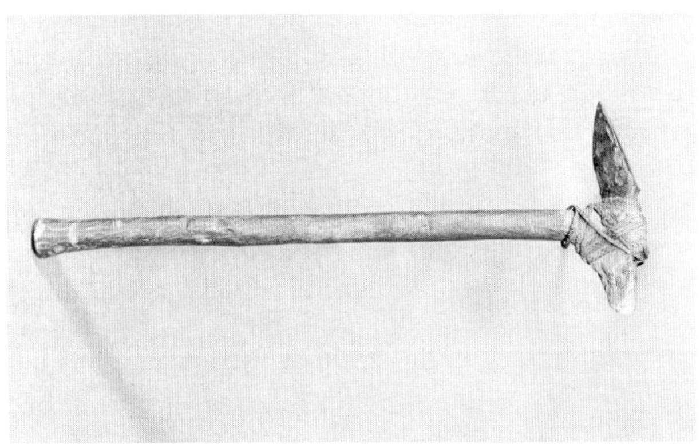

Figure 273. — Hafted adz, Exeter E 1225.

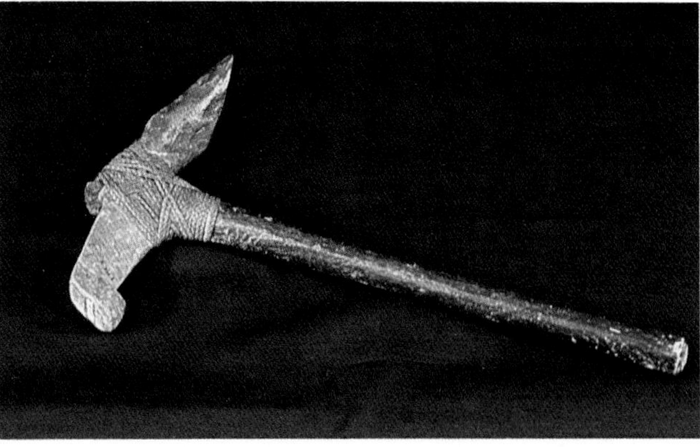

Figure 274. — Hafted adz, Stockholm 1799.2.51.

5-6. Two hafted adzes, Cambridge (22.931, 22.932 [missing]). Length of haft 56.5 cm, length of head 35 cm.
Evidence: Leverian Museum.

7. Hafted adz, Hooper collection (519). Length of haft 66 cm.
Evidence: Leverian Museum.
Literature: Phelps, 1976, p. 422.

8. Haft only, Hooper collection (524). Length 49.5 cm. A Hawaiian blade has been attached (see Hawaiian section).
Evidence: Leverian Museum.
Literature: Phelps, 1976, p. 422.

9. Hafted adz, Stockholm (1848.1.10). Length of haft 60 cm, length of blade 25 cm.
Evidence: "Banks collection."
Literature: Rydén, 1965, p. 74.

10. Hafted adz, Oxford (23). Length of handle 60 cm, length of head 30 cm.
Evidence: Forster collection. Second voyage.
Literature: Gathercole, n.d. [1970].

11. Hafted adz, Berne (TAH 20). Length of handle 40 cm, length of blade 16 cm.
Evidence: Webber collection. Third voyage.
Literature: Henking, 1957, p. 383; Kaeppler, 1977.

12-14. Three hafted adzes, Glasgow (E 366 cde).
Evidence: Circumstantial. Cook voyage collection from various sources. See Appendix III, this volume.

15-16. Two hafted adzes, Cambridge (1914.20, 1914.21).
Evidence: Sandwich collection. Probably from Cook from first or second voyage.

17. Hafted adz, Cambridge (25.377).
Evidence: Pennant collection of Cook voyage objects from various sources.

18. Hafted adz, Sydney (H 146). Handle length 53 cm, blade length 22 cm.
Evidence: Cook collection exhibited at Colonial and Indian Exhibition.
Literature: Mackrell, 1886; Appendix I, this volume.

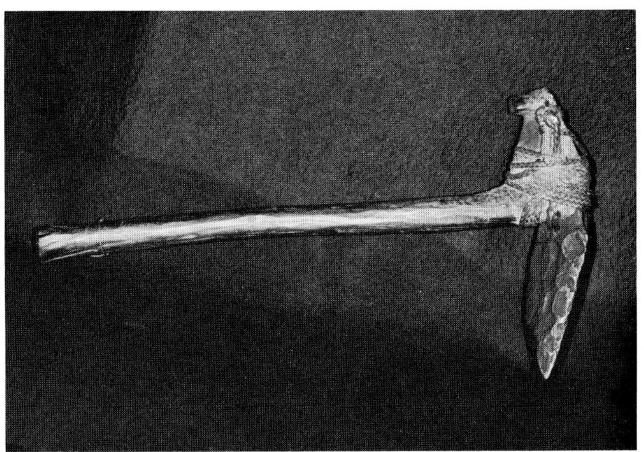

Figure 275. — Hafted adz, Dublin 1894.195.

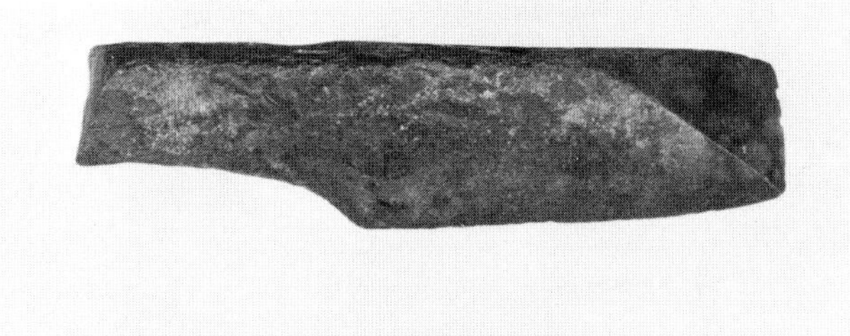

Figure 276. — Adz blade, Vienna.

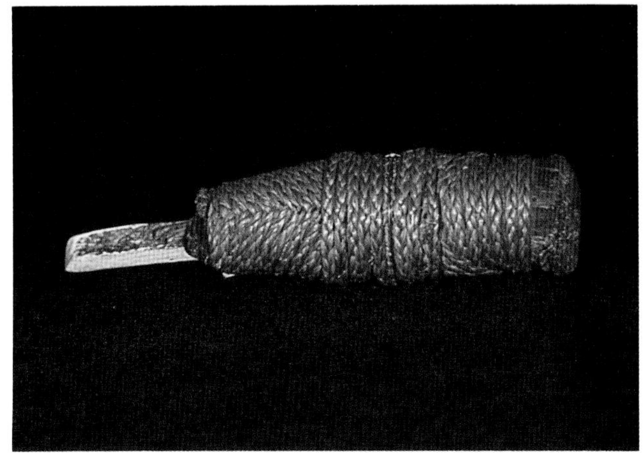

Figure 278. — Bone chisel, Cambridge 1914.22.

Figure 277. — Head of swivel adz, Vienna 18.

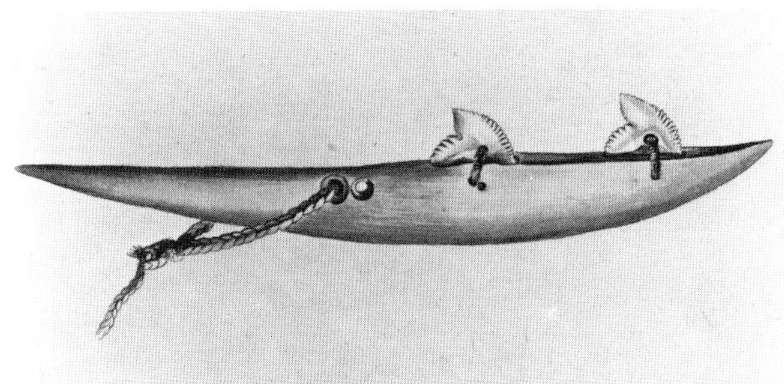

Figure 280. — Shark tooth implement by J. F. Miller, British Library Add. Ms. 23,921.58.

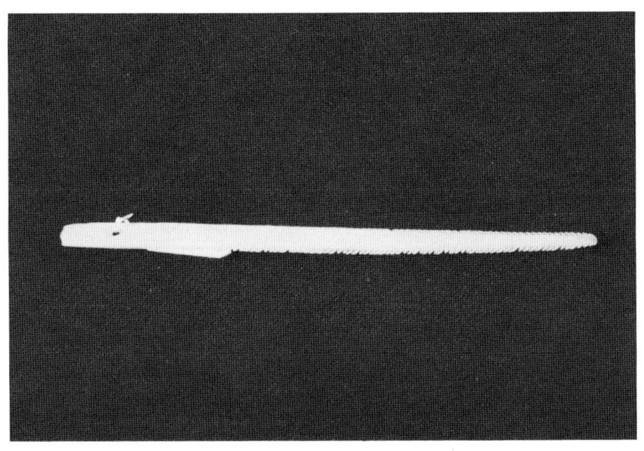

Figure 279. — Implement of stingray point, Vienna 160.

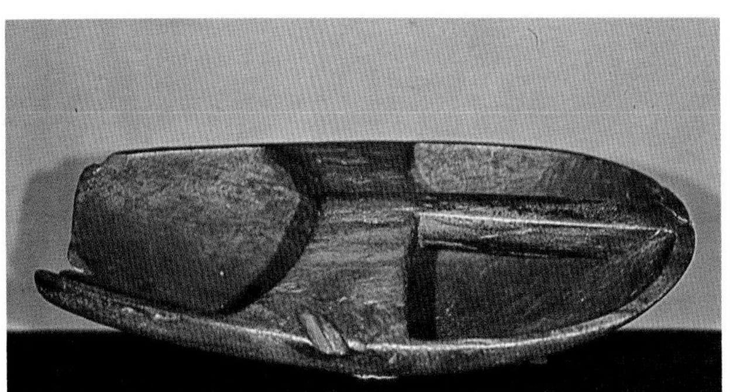

Figure 281. — Canoe bailer, Cambridge 1914.28.

19-21. Three hafted adzes, Dublin (1894.194, 195 [exhibited], 196). Length of haft 50 cm. Figure 275.
Evidence: Circumstantial. Thought to be part of the Cook voyage collection given to Trinity College, Dublin, by Patten or King.
Literature: Freeman, 1949, p. 8.

22-23. Two hafted adzes, Göttingen.
Evidence: Forster collection. Second voyage.

24-25. Two hafted adzes, Göttingen.
Evidence: Purchased from London dealer Humphrey in 1782.

26. Hafted adz, British Museum (St.864). Missing.
Evidence: Circumstantial. Probably purchased at the sale of Pepys's specimens, which were noted that they were brought by Cook.

27. Hafted adz, Wörlitz (14). Length 47.3 cm.
Evidence: Forster collection. Second voyage.
Literature: Germer, 1975, p. 90.

28. Hafted adz, Wellington (FE 3007).
Evidence: Circumstantial. From the Imperial Institute from Queen Victoria in a box containing "articles brought by Captain Cook from Otaheti."

29. Adz blade, Vienna. Figure 276.
Evidence: Leverian Museum.

30. Adz blade, Göttingen.
Evidence: Purchased from London dealer Humphrey in 1782.

31. Hafted adz (with swivel head), British Museum (TAH 88). Length 59.5 cm, head length 34 cm.
Evidence: Circumstantial. Noted "Cook collection" because of its similarity to the one depicted in British Library Add. Ms. 15,508.31 (Fig. 265).

32. Basalt blade bound to a wood handle and probably used for mounting a swivel adz, Vienna (18). Length 19.5 cm. Figure 277.
Evidence: Leverian Museum.
Literature: Moschner, 1955, p. 166.

33. Basalt blade bound to a wood handle and probably used for mounting as a swivel adz, British Museum (TAH 126).
Evidence: Circumstantial.[14] Probably the object depicted in a drawing pasted into Pennant's copy of the printed account of Cook's voyages (Fig. 264).

Chisels

1. Chisel (bone blade bound to a wooden handle with braided sennit), Cambridge (1914.22). Length 18 cm. Figure 278.
Evidence: Sandwich collection. Probably from Cook from first or second voyage.
2. Chisel (bone blade), Cambridge (25.423). Length 18.5 cm.
Evidence: Pennant collection of Cook voyage objects from various sources.
3. Chisel (bone blade), British Museum (NN). Missing. (Listed as New Zealand).
Evidence: Circumstantial. Noted "Cook collection" because of the similarity to that depicted in British Library Add. Ms. 15,508.31 (Fig. 265), (however, the last two listed are also similar to this drawing).

Other Tools

1. Rasp of ray skin,[15] Cambridge (1914.23). Missing.
Evidence: Sandwich collection. Probably from Cook from his first or second voyage.
2. Implement of stingray point (may have been used as a knife, saw, weapon, or spear point [see Fig. 254]), Vienna (160). Length 17 cm. Figure 279.
Evidence: Leverian Museum.
Literature: Moschner, 1955, p. 158.
3. Implement of stingray point, Cambridge (1914.23a). Length 14 cm.
Evidence: Sandwich collection. Probably from Cook from his first or second voyage.
4. Implement of stingray point, Florence (219). Missing.
Evidence: Circumstantial. Cook voyage collection from various sources.
Literature: Giglioli, 1893, pp.232-233; Kaeppler, 1977.

---

[14] A label of the 1920's notes that this chisel was depicted in Volume 1 of Sarah Stone's drawings from the Leverian Museum. It is more likely, however, that the object depicted is Number 32, in Vienna.

[15] See also under Tonga.

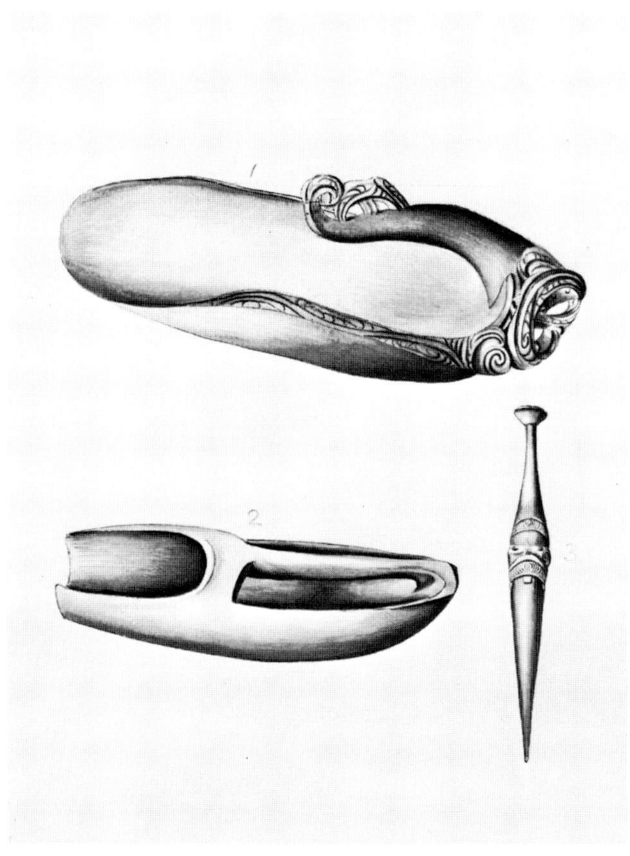

Figure 282. — Artifacts from Tahiti and New Zealand by J. F. Miller, British Library Add. Ms. 15,508.28.

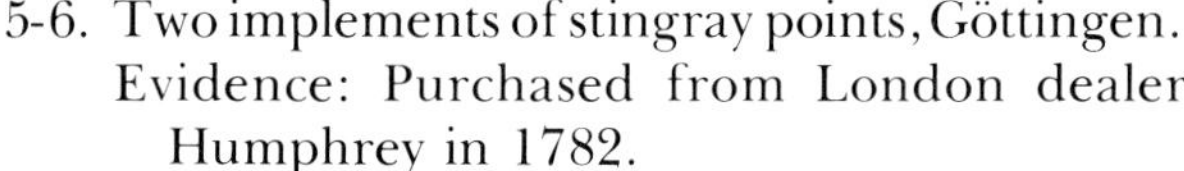

5-6. Two implements of stingray points, Göttingen.
Evidence: Purchased from London dealer Humphrey in 1782.

7. Shark tooth implement. Lost.
Evidence: Depicted by John Frederick Miller, British Library Add. Ms. 23,921.58 (Fig. 280). First voyage.

8. Tool of unknown use (turtle bone? hafted to a wood handle). Lost.
Evidence: Depicted in a drawing of Tahitian artifacts pasted in Pennant's copy of the printed account of Cook's voyages (Fig. 264).

Canoe Equipment

1. Canoe bailer, Cambridge (1914.28). Length 44 cm, width 23.5 cm, height 10 cm. Figure 281.
Evidence: Sandwich collection. From Cook from first or second voyage.

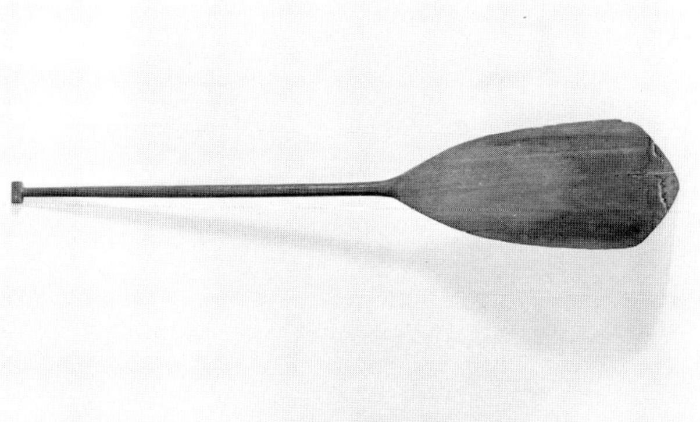

Figure 283. — Paddle, British Museum TAH 87.

2. Canoe bailer, British Museum (TAH 6).
Evidence: Circumstantial. Noted "Cook collection" because of its similarity to the one depicted in British Library Add. Ms. 15,508.28 (Fig. 282), and a "Cook collection" label remains, "Boat Scoop from Otaheitee."
3. Canoe paddle, British Museum (TAH 87). Figure 283.
Evidence: Circumstantial. Noted "Cook collection" because of its similarity to that depicted in British Library Add. Ms. 15,508.29 (Fig. 284).

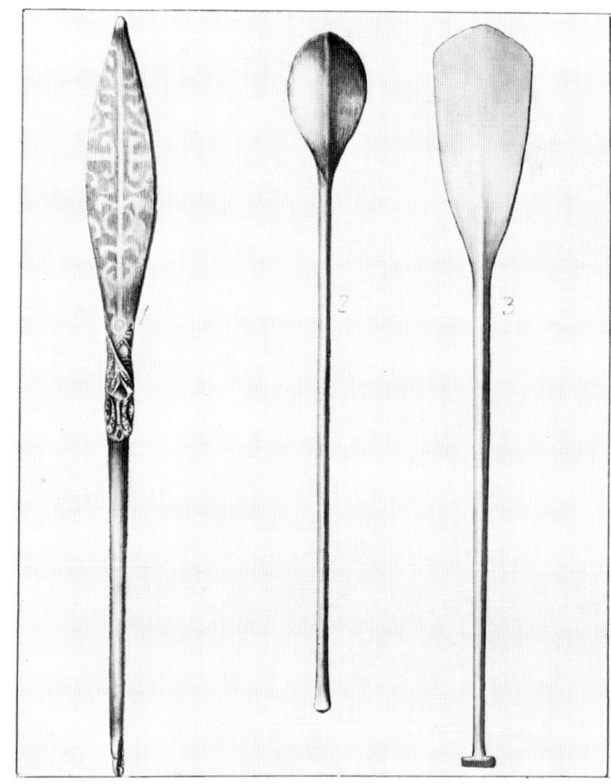

Figure 284. — Paddles from the South Seas, British Library Add. Ms. 15,508.29.

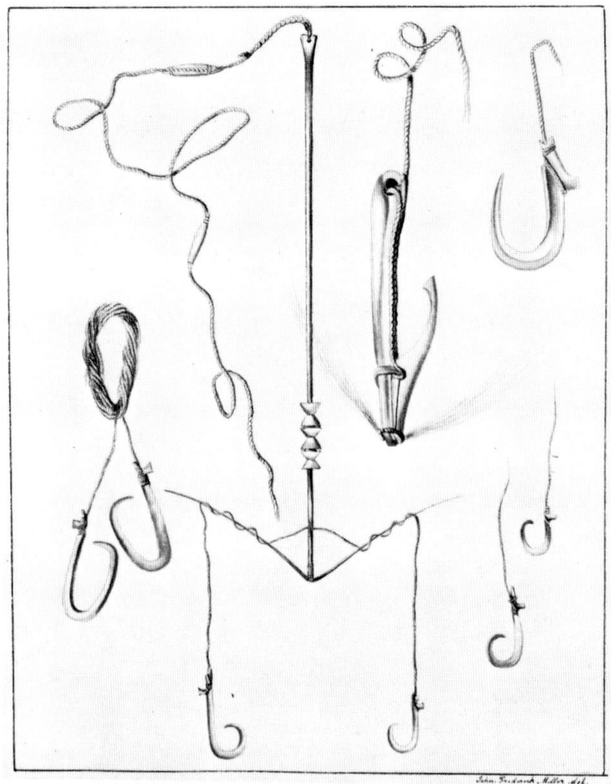

Figure 285. — Society Islands fishhooks, British Library Add. Ms. 23,921.56.

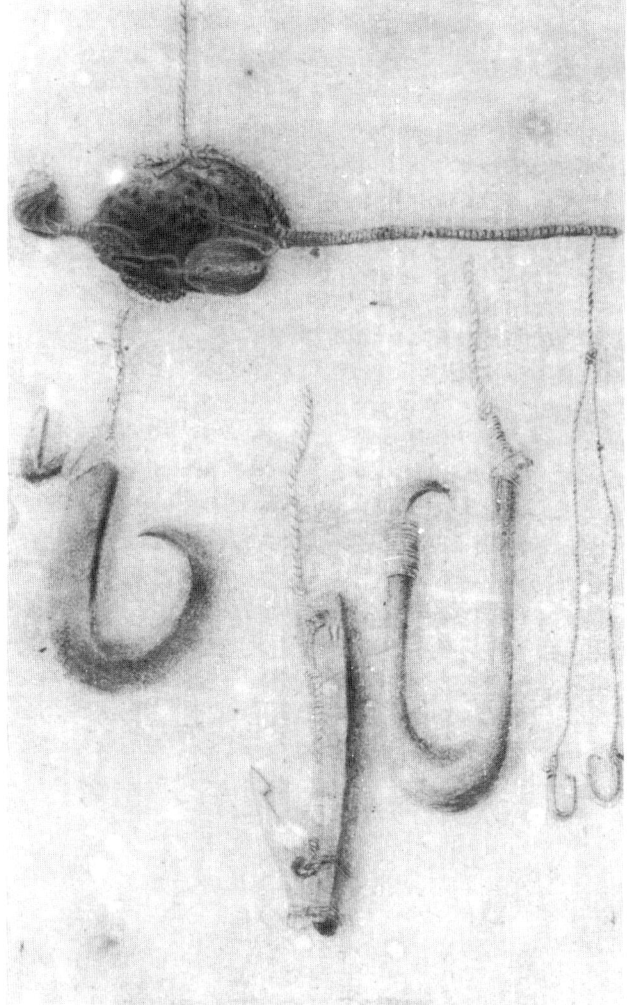

Figure 286. — Society Islands fishhooks, Dixson Library.

Fishing Equipment

Fishing equipment included octopus lures and several kinds of fishhooks, some of which were depicted (see British Library Add. Ms. 23,921.56 [Fig. 285] and the artifact plate from Parkinson's first voyage account [Fig. 243]).

Octopus Lures

1. Octopus lure, Cambridge (22.930). Overall length ca. 45 cm.
   Evidence: Leverian Museum.
2. Octopus lure, Göttingen.
   Evidence: Purchased from London dealer Humphrey in 1782.
3. Octopus lure. Lost.
   Evidence: Depicted in a series of drawings that belonged to Thomas Pennant (Fig. 286).
4. Octopus lure, Dublin (1882.3823). Length 23.5 cm. Figure 287.
   Evidence: Circumstantial. Thought to be part of Cook voyage collection given to Trinity College, Dublin, by Patten or King.
   Literature: Freeman, 1949.

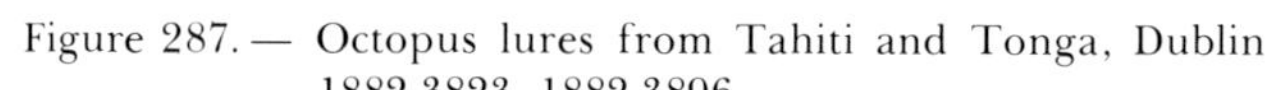

Figure 287. — Octopus lures from Tahiti and Tonga, Dublin 1882.3823, 1882.3896.

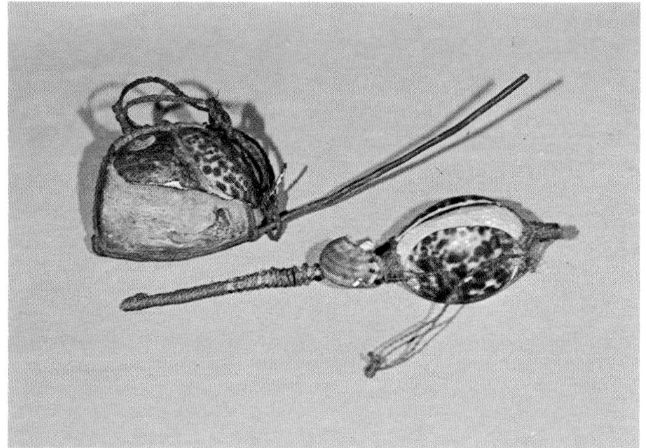

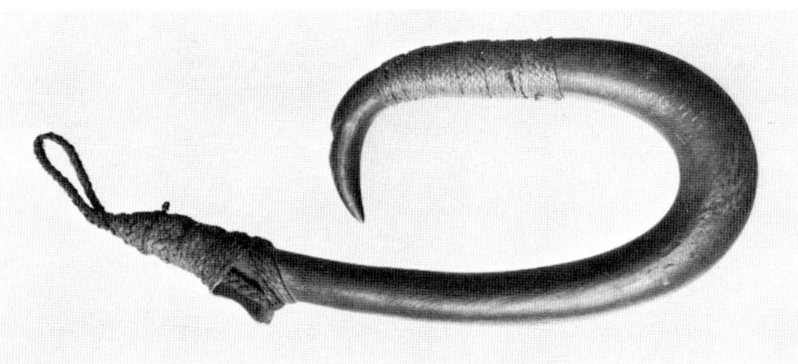

Figure 288. — Shark hook, Vienna 44.

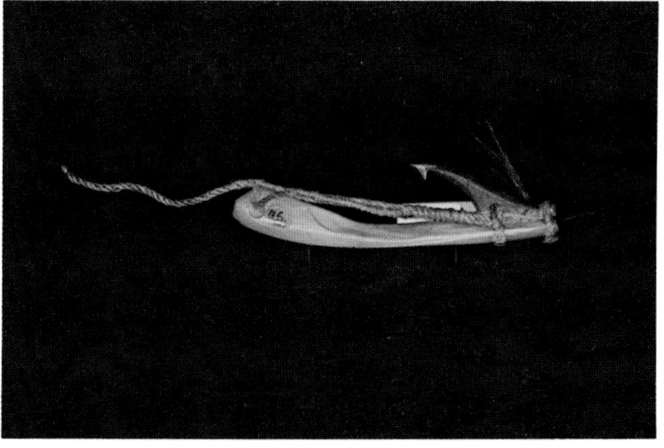

Figure 289. — Fishhook, Vienna 46.

Shark Hooks[16]

1. Shark hook, Vienna (44). Length 34 cm. Figure 288.
   Evidence: Leverian Museum.
   Literature: Moschner, 1955, p. 188.
2. Shark hook, Göttingen.
   Evidence: Purchased from London dealer Humphrey in 1782.
3. Shark hook, Wellington (FE 361).
   Evidence: Circumstantial. Part of Cook collection in Bullock's Museum.
   Literature: Kaeppler, 1974a, p. 80.

Fishhooks

1-3. Three (?) fishhooks,[17] Vienna (46). Lengths 9 cm, 3.2 cm, 2.8 cm. Figure 289.
Evidence: Leverian Museum.
Literature: Moschner, 1955, pp. 182, 186, 187.

4-5. Two fishhooks (one-piece black shell), Leningrad (505-25, 505-26). Lengths 9 cm, 8 cm. Figure 290.
Evidence: Given by Captain Clerke to the Governor of Kamchatka. Third voyage.
Literature: Rozina, 1966, p. 252; Kaeppler, 1977.

6-7. Two fishhooks (one-piece pearl shell; composite) Oxford (34). Lengths 8 cm, 13 cm.
Evidence: Forster collection. Second voyage.
Literature: Gathercole, n.d. [1970].

8-12. Five fishhooks, Cambridge (1914.29-32): two of black shell (1914.31, 1914.32); one of pearl shell (1914.32a); two composite (1914.29 [shell shank, bone point], 1914.30 [shell shank, shell point]).
Evidence: Sandwich collection. Probably from Cook from his first or second voyage.

Figure 290. — Two fishhooks, Leningrad 505-25, 505-26.

[16] A shark hook in the British Museum (+ 248) is noted "Believed by Dodge to be a Cook voyage piece," but there appears to be no documentary confirmation for this attribution.

[17] Although three fishhooks are attributed to Tahiti in the Vienna collection, only No. 46 appears to be Tahitian.

13-15. Three fishhooks, Cambridge (25.419, 20, 21): one of black shell (25.421); one of pearl shell (25.419); one of wood with pearl shell point (25.420).
Evidence: Pennant collection of Cook voyage objects from various sources.

16-19. Four fishhooks, Florence.
Evidence: Circumstantial. Cook voyage collection from various sources.
Literature: Giglioli, 1893, pp. 226-228, 1895, pp. 85-87; Kaeppler, 1977.

20-21. Two fishhooks, Rome.
Evidence: Circumstantial. Cook voyage collection from various sources.
Literature: Giglioli, 1893, pp. 226-228, 1895, pp. 85-87; Kaeppler, 1977.

22. Fishhook, Sydney (H 136). Length 12.5 cm.
Evidence: Cook collection exhibited at Colonial and Indian Exhibition.
Literature: Mackrell, 1886; Appendix I, this volume.

23-38. Sixteen fishhooks, Göttingen.
Evidence: Purchased from London dealer Humphrey in 1782.

Clubs

1. Club, Stockholm (1848.1.17). Length 235 cm.
Evidence: "Banks collection."
Literature: Rydén, 1965, pp. 78-79.
2. Club, British Museum (NN). Length 185 cm. Missing.
Evidence: Circumstantial. Noted "Cook collection" because of its similarity to that depicted in British Library Add. Ms. 23,921.57[18] (Fig. 240).
3. Club, Oxford (7). Missing. "Warriors Battle Axe."
Evidence: Forster collection. Second voyage.
Literature: Gathercole, n.d. [1970].

[18]A similar club in the British Museum (5315) is also much like the drawing. It was given by W.J. Bernhard Smith in 1869 who noted that it had been in England nearly a hundred years.

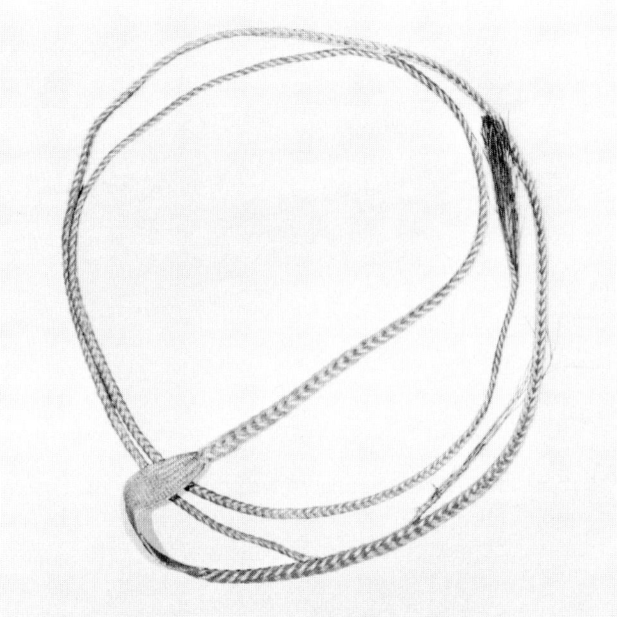

Figure 291. — Sling, Vienna 94.

Slings

1. Sling, Vienna (94). Length 210 cm. Figure 291.
Evidence: Leverian Museum.
Literature: Moschner, 1955, p. 158.

2. Sling, Oxford (176). Length 328 cm.
Evidence: Forster collection. Second voyage.
Literature: Gathercole, n.d. [1970].

3. Sling, Berne (HAW 8). Length 224 cm.
Evidence: Webber Collection. Third voyage.
Literature: Henking, 1957, p. 365; Kaeppler, 1977.

4. Sling, Florence (164). Length 245 cm.
Evidence: Circumstantial. Cook voyage collection from various sources.
Literature: Giglioli, 1893, pp. 233-234; Kaeppler, 1977.

5. Sling, Göttingen.
Evidence: Forster collection. Second voyage.

OHETEROA (RURUTU AND THE AUSTRAL ISLANDS)

On Cook's first voyage the *Endeavour* visited the island of Rurutu, known as Oheteroa, in the group of islands now known as the Australs, and on the third voyage the ships passed close to Tubuai, where some of the islanders came out in canoes. In Rurutu there was trading of "some small trifles . . . for small nails" (Beaglehole 1955, pp. 155-156), and "a small quantity of cloth and some of their weapons" (Beaglehole 1962, p. 331). Yet in Cook voyage collections there are some superb objects from the Austral Islands. Although it is possible that these pieces were collected when the ship was at Rurutu, it is equally likely that they were collected in Tahiti, for the Tahitians were well acquainted with Oheteroa. In the drawing of fly whisks by John Frederick Miller (British Library Add. Ms. 23921.53) one of the whisks is noted Oheteroa (Fig. 50), and in the lithograph after Webber of the *marae* in Tahiti (Fig. 303), the drums are certainly of Austral Islands type rather than Tahitian. Further, Webber depicted "A Man of Oheteroa, Society Islands" (British Library Add. Ms. 15,513.24 [Fig. 292]), which he must have drawn while in the Society Islands, because Webber, who traveled only on the third voyage, did not go to Rurutu. Banks on first voyage describes the tattoo patterns of the men of Rurutu; "they were not tattowed on their backsides, but instead of that had black marks about as broad as my hand under their armpits the sides of which were deeply indented . . . they had also circles of smaller ones round their arms and legs" (Beaglehole, 1962, p. 332); this leaves little doubt that the man depicted by Webber was indeed from Rurutu.

In the collection given by Cook to Lord Sandwich, now in Cambridge, a label identifies an object as from Oheteroa and in an inventory of the collection a piece of bark cloth is attributed to Oheteroa (Trinity College Library Add. Ms. a 106).

1. Wood carving, Cambridge (1914.35). Length 51 cm, height 20 cm, thickness 7 cm. Figure 293. The use of the carving is unknown. It is listed as "an ornamental carving," and identified by a label as from Oheteroa. I suspect that this is a carving from the stern piece of a canoe such as that depicted in British Library Add. Ms. 15,513.26 (Fig. 294) and Add. Ms. 15,513.20 (Fig. 295).[1]
   Evidence: Sandwich collection. Given by Cook. First voyage.

[1]Another drawing in the British Library, Add. Ms. 15,508.8, depicts another canoe carving which may be from the Austral Islands.

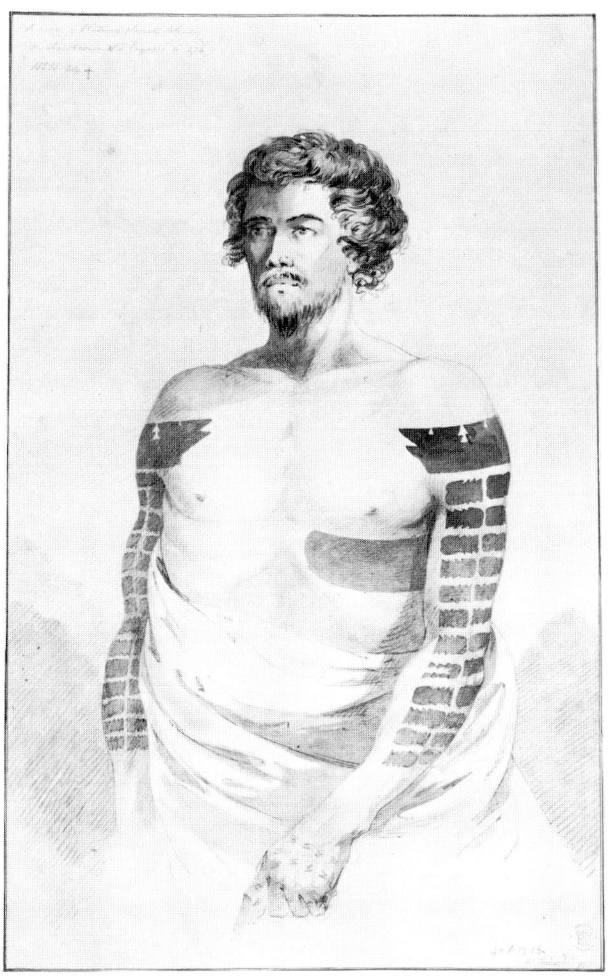

Figure 292.— Man of Oheteroa, British Library Add. Ms. 15,513.24.

2. Canoe paddle. Lost.
   Evidence: Depicted in a drawing of objects from Cook's first voyage in British Library Add. Ms. 15,508.29 (Fig. 284).
3. Carved object (possibly from the Australs), Glasgow (E 349). Length 30.5 cm, width 7 cm. Figure 296.
   Evidence: Circumstantial. Given by Captain King (along with an Easter Island dance paddle). King was on Cook's third voyage only, but he may have obtained objects from the other voyages. Thus, if, in fact, the object is from Cook's voyages, it may be from Rurutu, Tubuai, the Cook Islands, or collected in Tahiti.
4. Fly whisk (with Janus figures), Vienna (143). Length of handle 33.5 cm, length of whisk 39 cm, width of image 3 cm. Figures 297, 298.
   Evidence: Leverian Museum.
   Literature: Moschner, 1955, p. 223; Rose, in press.

5. Fly whisk (with Janus figures), British Museum (TAH 27).[2] Length of handle 33.5 cm. Figure 299.
   Evidence: Depicted by John Frederick Miller, British Library Add. Ms. 23921.53 (Fig. 50).

6-7. Two drums, Dublin (1882.3636, 1882.3637 [exhibited]). Heights 128 cm, 130 cm; diameters 17 cm, 18 cm. Figures 300, 301, 302. The drums are similar to those depicted in the Tahitian *marae* by Webber (Fig. 303) and may have been brought from the Australs for sacred use; whereas drums depicted by Webber for dancing are Tahitian in style (Fig. 224).
   Evidence: Circumstantial. Labeled "Cook collection" and referred to in early descriptions of the Cook collection in Dublin. Given to Trinity College, Dublin, by Patten or King. Second or third voyage.
   Literature: Freeman, 1949, p. 7.

8. Bark cloth, Cambridge (1924.?).
   Evidence: Sandwich collection. Given by Cook. First voyage. Listed in Trinity College, Cambridge, inventory from Oheteroa (possibly 1924.88 a and c).

9. Bark cloth, Exeter (E 1263). Length 530 cm, width 178 cm. Figure 304.
   Evidence: Leverian Museum.

This piece of bark cloth, of unknown provenance, is said to be Tahitian but is unlike any known Tahitian bark cloth.[3] There are small pieces with designs similar to its border design in the Shaw *Catalogues* of bark cloth from Cook's voyages, and in Bishop Museum (1777) and Vienna, also from Cook's voyages (Fig. 305). The designs are reminiscent of the tattoo designs in the depictions by Webber and Banks. A similar piece of bark cloth which might also be from Cook's voyages is in the British Museum (EP 14).[4] Although it has no accession information, its number is within the series which includes Cook voyage specimens.

[2] An unfinished (or broken) image in the British Museum (TAH 128) is reminiscent of Austral Islands carvings. It is attributed to Cook's voyages, but there is no documentation for confirmation.

[3] A very similar piece in the Hooper collection (701) is attributed to Tonga (Phelps, 1976, p. 168) but it is also unlike any known Tongan bark cloth in both design and in the quality of the material (which is more like central Polynesian).

[4] This piece is attributed to the Cook Islands by Kooijman (1972, p. 59), but this is unlikely.

Figure 293. — Wood carving, Cambridge 1914.35.

Figure 294. — Canoe in the Society Islands, British Library Add. Ms. 15,513.26.

Figure 295. — Canoes in the Society Islands, British Library Add. Ms. 15,513.20.

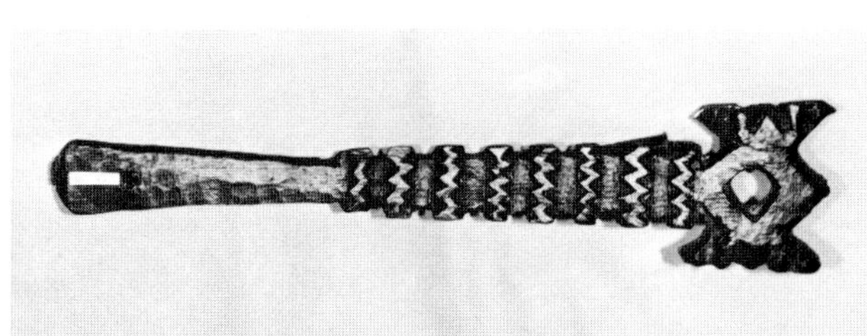

Figure 296. — Carved object, Glasgow E 349.

Figure 297. — Fly whisk, Vienna 143.

Figure 298. — Fly whisk (detail), Vienna 143.

Figure 299. — Fly whisk, British Museum TAH 27.

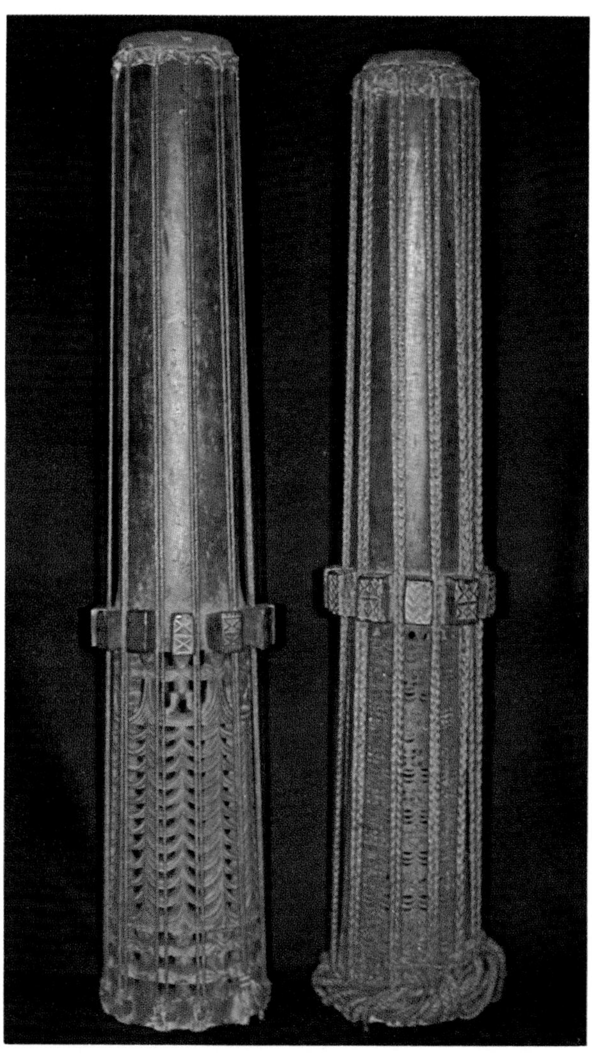

Figure 300. — Two drums, Dublin 1882.3636, 1882.3637.

Figure 301. — Drum detail, Dublin 1882.3637.

Figure 302. — Drum detail, Dublin 1882.3637.

Figure 303. — Marae in Tahiti, British Library Add. Ms. 15,513.16.

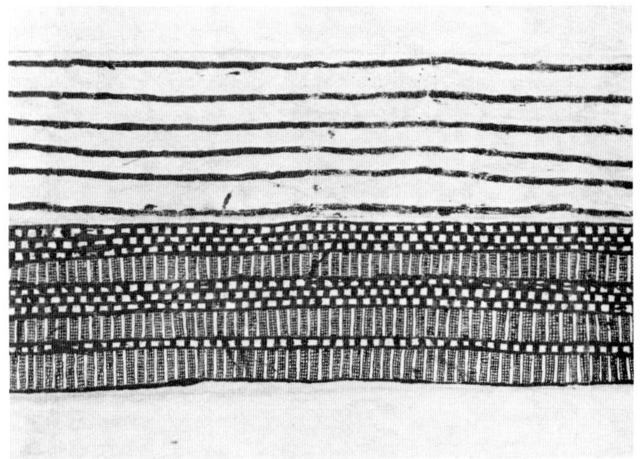

Figure 305. — Bark cloth, Vienna.

Figure 304. — Bark cloth, Exeter E 1263.

COOK ISLANDS

During Cook's second and third voyages several islands in the Cook group were sighted and a landing was made on Atiu, but the only objects that can be localized to these islands are two clubs. One of these must have been collected on Cook's first voyage, probably in Tahiti, because it is depicted with a group of Tahitian objects drawn by John Frederick Miller after the first voyage (British Library Add. Ms. 23921.57 [Fig. 240]).

1. Club, British Museum (NN). Length 510 cm. (?). Missing.
   Evidence: Circumstantial. Noted "Cook collection" because of its similarity to that depicted in British Library Add. Ms. 23921.57.

2. Club. Lost.
   Evidence: Leverian Museum.
   Depiction: Force and Force, 1968, p. 134.

Figure 306. — Man from the Marquesas, *Atlas* to Cook's second voyage (28).

THE MARQUESAS ISLANDS

After Spanish discovery at the end of the 16th century, the Marquesas Islands were not visited by Europeans again until the second voyage of Cook. Although ostensibly the Marquesans had little to trade, a number of valuable ornaments were exchanged, primarily for red feathers obtained in Tonga. The objects collected and depicted were mainly ornaments and weapons (Figs. 306, 307). All are from Cook's second voyage.

Headdresses

1. Headdress of fiber band, shells and feathers, Oxford (134). Length of band without ties (42 cm).
   Evidence: Forster collection.
   Depictions: Cook 1777, Plate 17 (Fig. 307).
   Literature: Gathercole, n.d. [1970], p. 20.

2. Headdress of fiber band, shell and feathers, Stockholm (1799.2.25). Length 41 cm.
   Evidence: Sparrman collection.
   Literature: Söderström, 1939, pp. 22-23.

3. Headdress of fiber band, shells, and feathers, Göttingen.
   Evidence: Purchased from London dealer Humphrey in 1782.

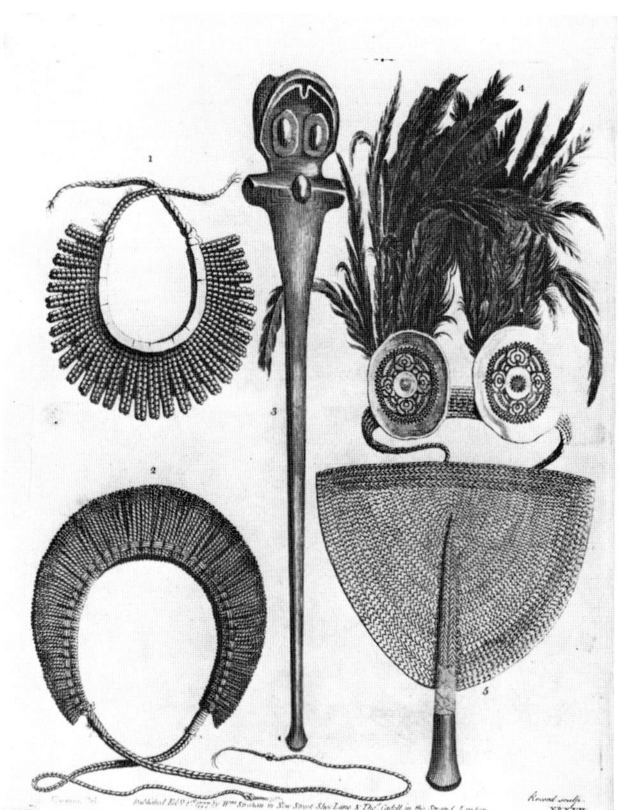

Figure 307. — Marquesan artifact plate, *Atlas* to Cook's second voyage (28).

Figure 308. — Headdress, Cape Town SAM 2577.

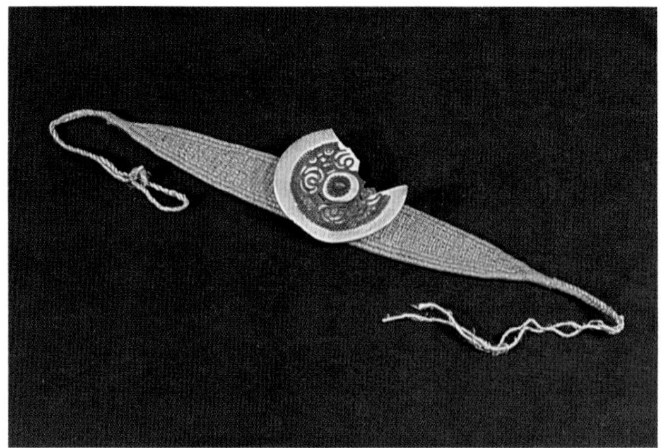

Figure 309. — Headdress, Stockholm 1799.2.26.

4. Headdress of fiber band, feathers (and formerly shells?), Cape Town (SAM 2577). Figure 308.
   Evidence: Circumstantial. Thought to have arrived in Cape Town in 1775.
   Literature: Bax, 1970, p. 146.

5. Headdress of fiber band and shell, Stockholm (1799.2.26). Length 49 cm. Figure 309.
   Evidence: Sparrman collection.
   Literature: Söderström, 1939, pp. 22-23.

Figure 310. — Headdress, Dublin 1882.3682.

6. Headband of fiber, Cambridge (22.1103). Length including ties 82 cm, width 4 cm.
   Evidence: Leverian Museum.

7. Headband of fiber, Göttingen.
   Evidence: Forster collection.

8. Headdress of sennit cords, Dublin (1882.3682). Width 25 cm, height 23 cm. Figure 310.
   Evidence: Circumstantial. Thought to be part of the collection given to Trinity College, Dublin, by Patten.
   Literature: Freeman, 1949, p. 16.

9. Headdress of sennit cords, Oxford (129). Length without ties 42 cm.
   Evidence: Forster collection.
   Depictions: Probably the one depicted in Cook, 1777, Plate 17 (Fig. 307).

Gorgets

1. Gorget of wood and red seeds, Dublin (1882.3875). Dimensions 25.5 cm by 22 cm. Figure 311.
   Evidence: Circumstantial. Thought to be part of the collection given to Trinity College, Dublin, by Patten.
   Literature: Freeman, 1949, p. 16.

2. Gorget of wood and red seeds, Oxford (133). Maximum dimension 26 cm.
   Evidence: Forster collection.
   Depictions: Probably the one depicted in Cook, 1777, Plate 17 (Fig. 307).
   Literature: Gathercole, n.d. [1970].

Figure 311. — Gorget, Dublin 1882.3875.

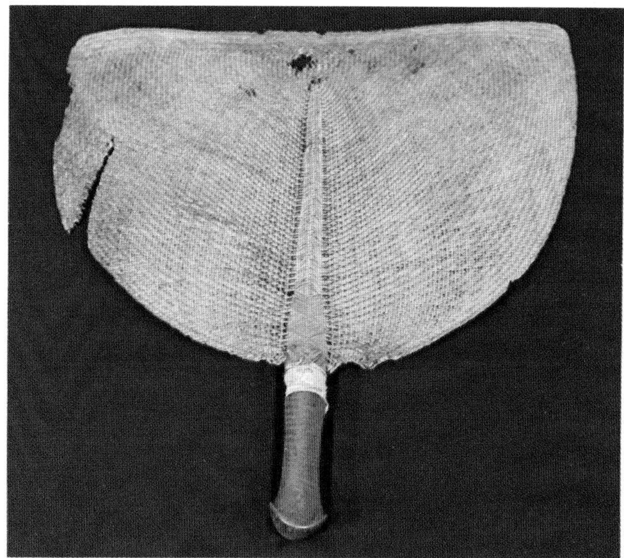

Figure 312. — Fan, Stockholm 1799.2.28.

3. Gorget of wood and red seeds, Stockholm (1799.2.27).
   Evidence: Sparrman collection.
   Literature: Söderström, 1939, pp. 23-24.

4. Gorget of wood and red seeds, Göttingen.
   Evidence: Purchased from London dealer Humphrey in 1782.

Other Ornaments

1. Ornament of feathers and sennit, Oxford (135). Length 14 cm.
   Evidence: Forster collection.
   Literature: Gathercole, n.d. [1970].

2. Ornament of human hair and sennit, Oxford (137). Length 21 cm.
   Evidence: Forster collection.
   Literature: Gathercole, n.d. [1970].

3. Ornament of human hair and sennit, Göttingen.
   Evidence: Purchased from London dealer Humphrey in 1782.

4. Shells carved to resemble whale tooth ornaments, Oxford (139, 140). Lengths 9.5 cm, 8.5 cm. One has a cord of bark cloth.
   Evidence: Forster collection.
   Literature: Gathercole, n.d. [1970].

5. Shells carved to resemble whale tooth ornaments, on bark cloth and fiber cords, Göttingen (OZ 167-169).
   Evidence: Forster collection (?).

6. Ear ornament, Oxford (135). Missing.
   Evidence: Forster collection.
   Literature: Gathercole, n.d. [1970].

Fans

1. Fan (wood handle and plaited blade), Stockholm (1799.2.28). Length 48 cm, width 45 cm. Figure 312.
   Evidence: Sparrman collection.
   Literature: Söderström, 1939, pp. 24-25.

2-3. Two fans (wood handle and plaited blade), Oxford (169-170). Dimensions 55 cm × 58 cm, 46 cm × 41 cm.
   Evidence: Forster collection.
   Depictions: Probably the one depicted in Cook, 1777, Plate 17. Figure 307.
   Literature: Gathercole, n.d. [1970].

4. Fan (wood handle and plaited blade), Göttingen (OZ 108). Dimensions 43 cm × 39.5 cm.
   Evidence: Purchased from London dealer Humphrey in 1782.

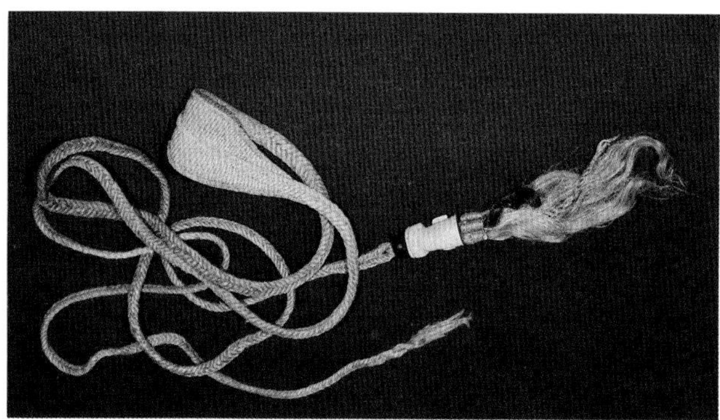

Figure 313. — Sling, British Museum Q77.Oc9.

Thatching Needles

Two thatching needles in the Forster collection are attributed to the Marquesas, but, in view of the lack of other utensils and the similarity of such needles to those of other island groups, the provenance should not be relied upon.

1-2. Two thatching needles, Oxford (141). Lengths 41.5 cm, 33 cm.
Evidence: Forster collection.
Literature: Gathercole, n.d. [1970].

Weapons

1. Club, Göttingen.[1]
Evidence: Purchased from London dealer Humphrey in 1782.

2. Club, British Museum.
Evidence: Circumstantial. Thought to be the club depicted in Cook, 1777, Plate 17 (Fig. 307).

3. "Battle axe" (possibly a *parahu*), Göttingen.
Evidence: Purchased from London dealer Humphrey in 1782.

4. Spear (attributed to the Marquesas), Göttingen.
Evidence: Purchased from London dealer Humphrey in 1782.

5. Sling (with ivory ornament and hair), British Museum (Q77.0c9). Length 245 cm; ivory ornament height 3.5 cm, diameter 2 cm. Figure 313.
Evidence: Leverian Museum depiction.

Bows and Arrows

1-5. Bow and four arrows, Göttingen.
Evidence: Purchased from London dealer Humphrey in 1782.
Literature: Plischke, 1959.

[1]A second club ("knotted war club") in the Göttingen Humphrey collection is also localized to the Marquesas. I have not seen the club, and am thus unable to confirm the provenance.

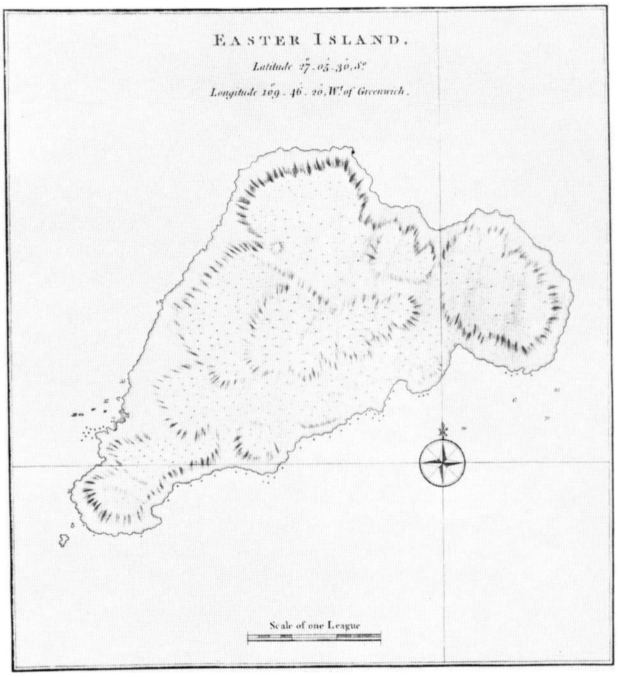

Figure 314. — Map of Easter Island (53).

EASTER ISLAND

Easter Island was first seen by Europeans in 1722 on the voyage of the Dutchman Roggeveen, and was visited at least once after that by a Spanish ship in 1769. On Cook's second voyage, the *Resolution* was in the area for five days, but few ethnographic specimens can be traced to that encounter.

1. Human hand carved of wood, British Museum (EP 32). Length 31 cm, width 10 cm, thickness 3.5 cm. Figures 315, 316.
Evidence: Collected by Forster and given to the British Museum.
Literature: Forster, 1777, Vol. 1, p. 581.

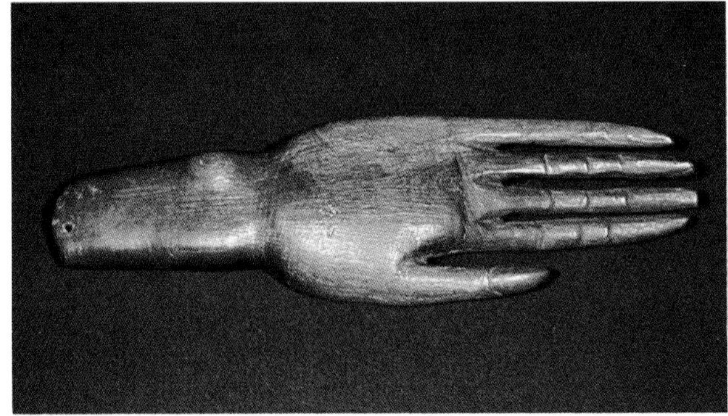

Figure 315. — Hand carved of wood, British Museum EP32.

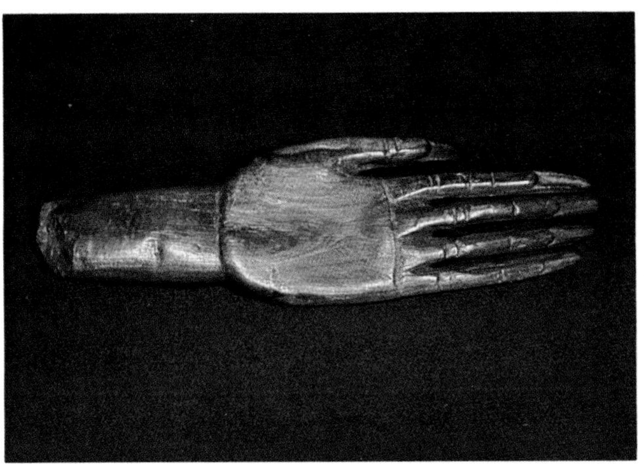

Figure 316.— Hand carved of wood (reverse) British Museum EP32.

⛵2. Stave, Exeter (E 1216). Length 109 cm, width 6 cm. Figures 317, 318.
Evidence: Leverian Museum.

⛵3. Dance paddle, Glasgow (E 348). Length 43.5 cm, width 8 cm. Figure 319.
Evidence: Circumstantial. Given by Captain King, who was not on Cook's second voyage—although it is quite possible that he obtained objects from that voyage.

4. Bark cloth (sewn and quilted), Oxford (128). Dimensions 130 cm by 109 cm.
Evidence: Forster collection.
Literature: Gathercole, n.d. [1970].

5. Feather headdress, Oxford (130). Diameter 37 cm. Figure 320.
Evidence: Forster collection.
Literature: Gathercole, n.d. [1970].

6. Feather headdress. Lost.
Evidence: Leverian Museum depiction.

7-8. Two bone ornaments, Oxford (131-132). Missing. Perhaps neck pendants as depicted by Hodges (Fig. 321).
Evidence: Forster collection.
Literature: Gathercole, n.d. [1970].

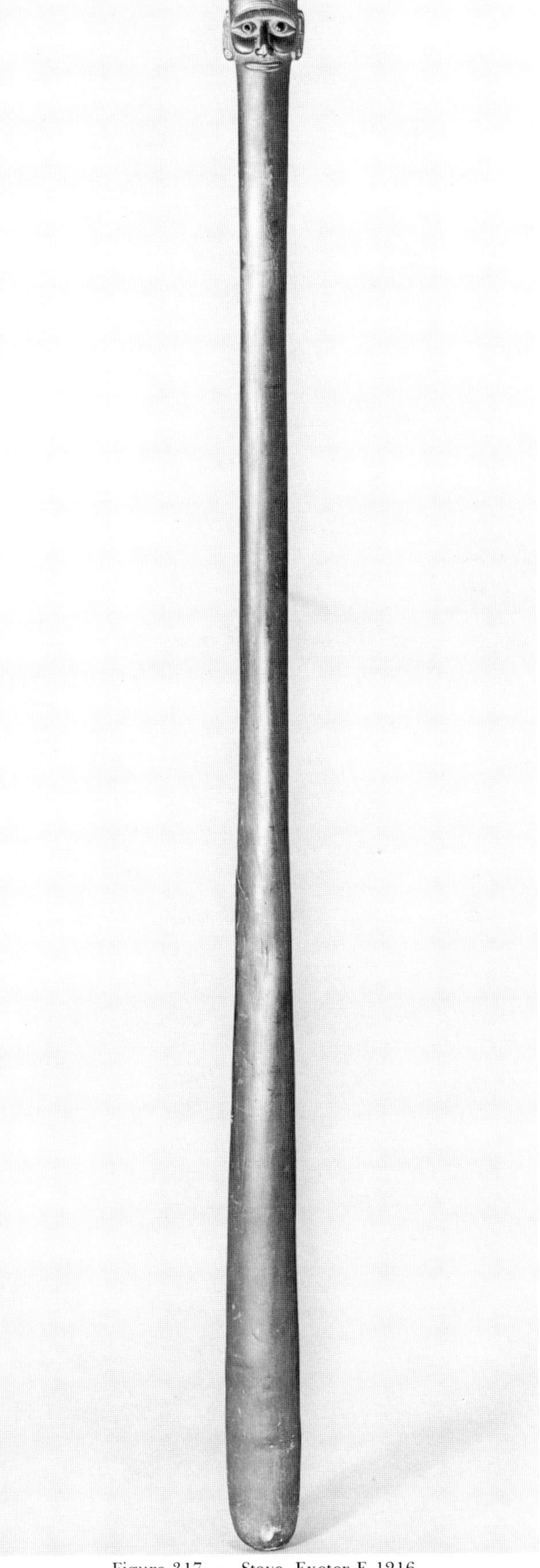

Figure 317.— Stave, Exeter E 1216.

Figure 318. — Stave (detail), Exeter E 1216.

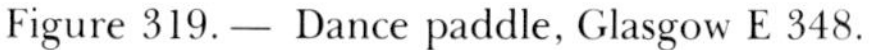

Figure 319. — Dance paddle, Glasgow E 348.

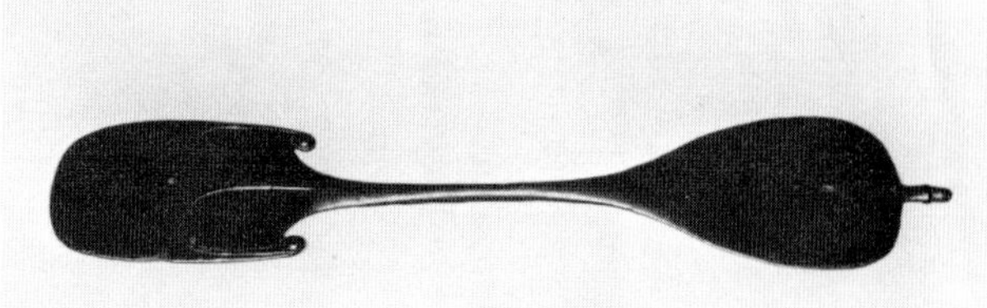

Figure 320. — Feather headdress, Oxford 130.

Figure 321. — Woman of Easter Island, *Atlas* to Cook's second voyage (28).

NEW ZEALAND

European discovery of New Zealand was in 1642 by Tasman, who visited the area now known as Golden Bay. Interaction between the Maoris and Tasman's ships was not only limited, but hostile, and thus for all practical purposes we can disregard significant European influence in New Zealand before Cook. However, as Cook visited New Zealand on all three of his voyages and contacted several groups of Maoris in various locations in both the North and South Islands, there is little doubt that objects collected by the time of the third voyage could have been made with iron tools, and that their nature could have been influenced by European attitudes as to what objects would be most desirable for trade. New Zealand was also visited by DeSurville in 1769, and Du Fresne in 1772, adding yet other groups of European visitors' iron and ideas. For this reason it is useful to be able to separate objects taken to England on Cook's ships according to the voyage on which they were collected.

A second reason for attempting to separate New Zealand artifacts by voyage is the future possibility of localizing the objects and establishing local variations in Maori material culture. Such analyses must proceed with caution because the tribes that traded with Cook's ships were often visiting from other areas, and tribes were relatively mobile, but the pursuit of this information could be quite fruitful. Collections known to have come from specific voyages are most useful for this purpose, for example, the Forster collections in Oxford, Göttingen, and Wörlitz, and the Sparrman collection in Stockholm. It is difficult to do this with Maori materials from many of the collections, but any useful information on possible voyage attribution will be pointed out.

Cloaks

A large number of cloaks were collected in New Zealand on Cook's voyages. At least 40 can be traced with convincing documentation. No attempt is made here to categorize the cloaks by materials or styles—an excellent detailed study has previously been made by Mead (1969).[1] The superb drawing by Parkinson depicts the manner in which cloaks were worn (Fig. 323).

1. Cloak (black and brown *taniko* border, dog hair, dog skin, and feathers), Vienna (25). Length 114 cm, width at lower edge 182 cm. Figures 324, 325.
Evidence: Circumstantial. Probably from Leverian Museum.[2]
Literature: Moschner, 1955, pp. 202-204.

2-6. Five cloaks, Stockholm (1848.1.5, 1848.1.6, 1848.1.7, 1848.1.63 [exhibited], 1848.1.64). Figures 326, 327. Dimensions of cloak exhibited, 125 cm by 135 cm.
Evidence: "Banks Collection."
Literature: Rydén, 1965, pp. 80-84.

7-12. Six cloaks, Cambridge (1924.80-1924.85).
Evidence: Sandwich Collection. Given by Cook, from first and second voyages.
Literature: Shawcross, 1970, pp. 322-325.

13. Cloak, Stockholm (1799.2.2).
Evidence: Sparrman collection. Second voyage.
Literature: Söderström, 1939, pp. 50-54.

14-19. Six cloaks, Oxford (102-107).
Evidence: Forster collection. Second voyage.
Literature: Gathercole, n.d. [1970].

20. Cloak, Wörlitz (22). Dimensions 125 cm by 84 cm.
Evidence: Forster collection. Second voyage.
Literature: Germer, 1975, pp. 72-73, 91.

21. Cloak, Göttingen.
Evidence: Forster collection. Second voyage.

22-26. Five cloaks (including a superb red-brown one), Göttingen.
Evidence: Purchased from London dealer Humphrey in 1782.

27. Cloak, Berne (NS 24).
Evidence: Webber collection. Third voyage.
Literature: Henking, 1957, pp. 379-380; Kaeppler, 1977.

28-30. Three cloaks, British Museum (NZ 137, 135, 125).
Evidence: Circumstantial. Noted "Cook collection," with the numbers 1, 62 and 65. The border of NZ 137 is much like that of the cloak Banks is wearing in his portrait by Benjamin West (Fig. 51).

31. Cloak (dark *taniko* border, brown side edges, body horizontally striped in black and natural). Sydney (H 103).
Evidence: Cook collection from the Colonial and Indian Exhibition. Label "brought by Capt. Cook from Otaheiti, a mantle worn by one of the natives."
Literature: Mackrell, 1886; Appendix I, this volume.

[1] Although I have examined the documentation, I have not personally examined all the cloaks. Several of them could not be located during my visits.

[2] There were about five cloaks from the Leverian Museum which cannot be traced.

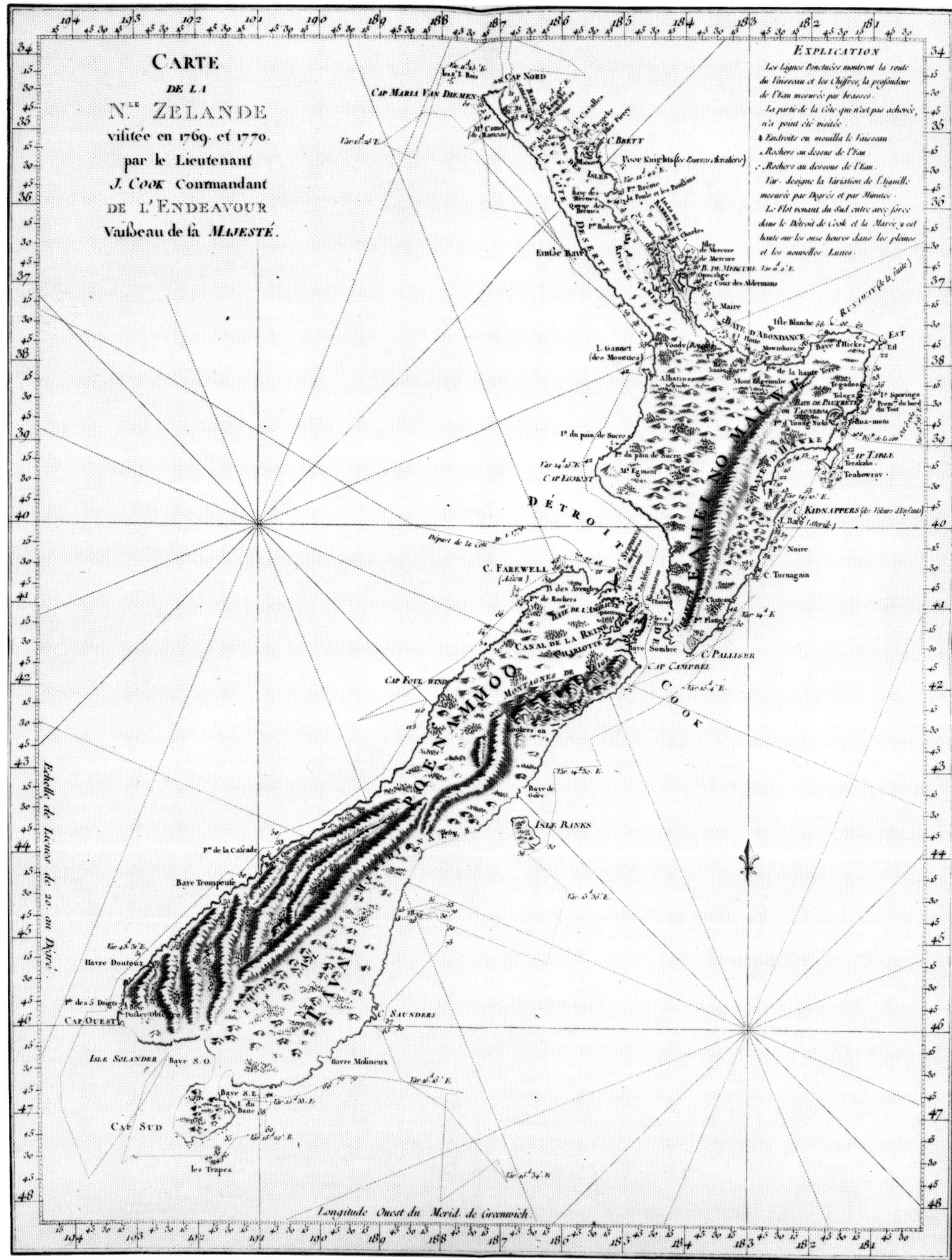

Figure 322. — Chart of New Zealand by James Cook.

Figure 323. — A New Zealand warrior, Plate 15 of Parkinson's journal (26).

Figure 325. — Cloak (detail), Vienna 25.

Figure 324. — Cloak, Vienna 25.

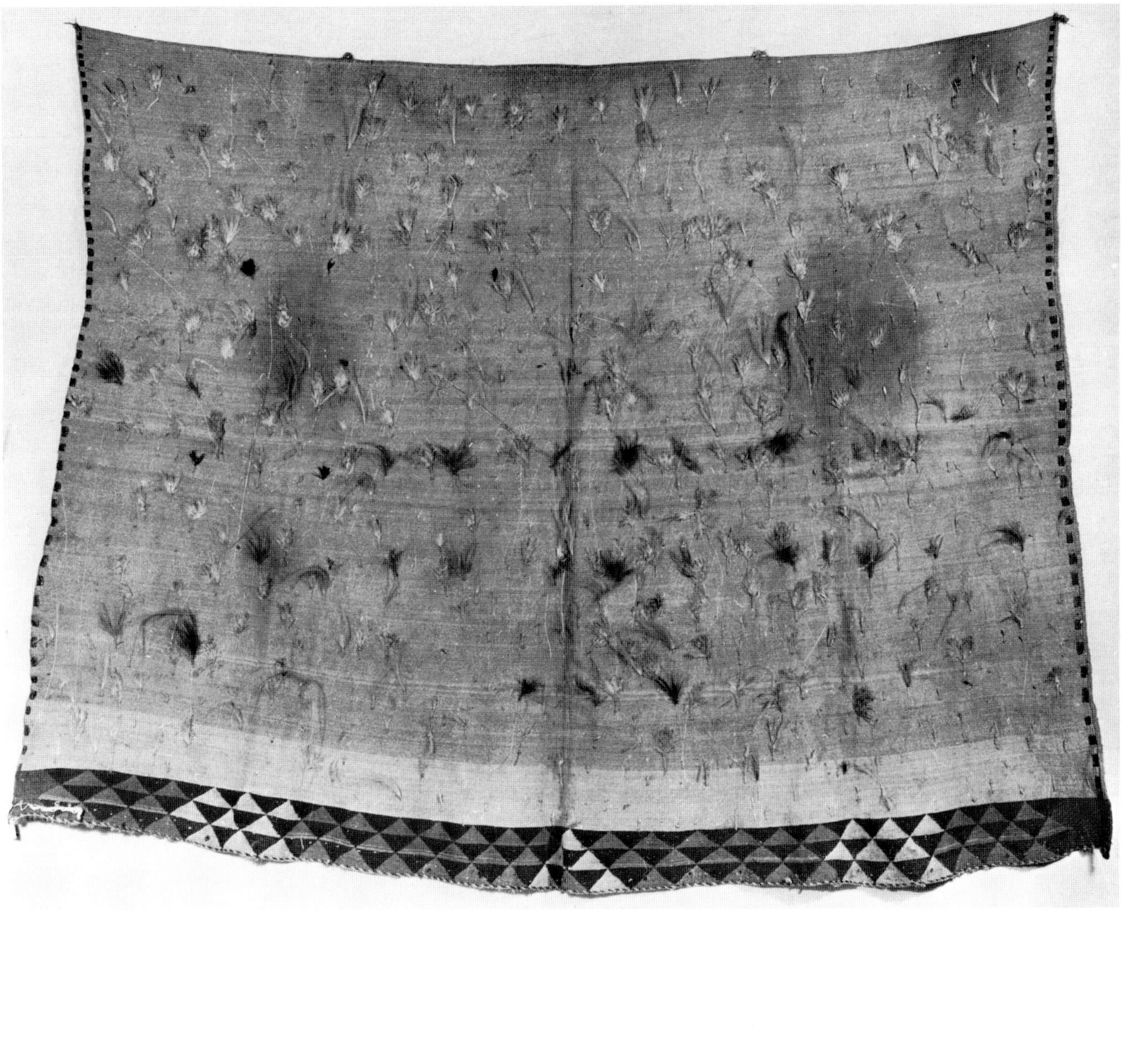

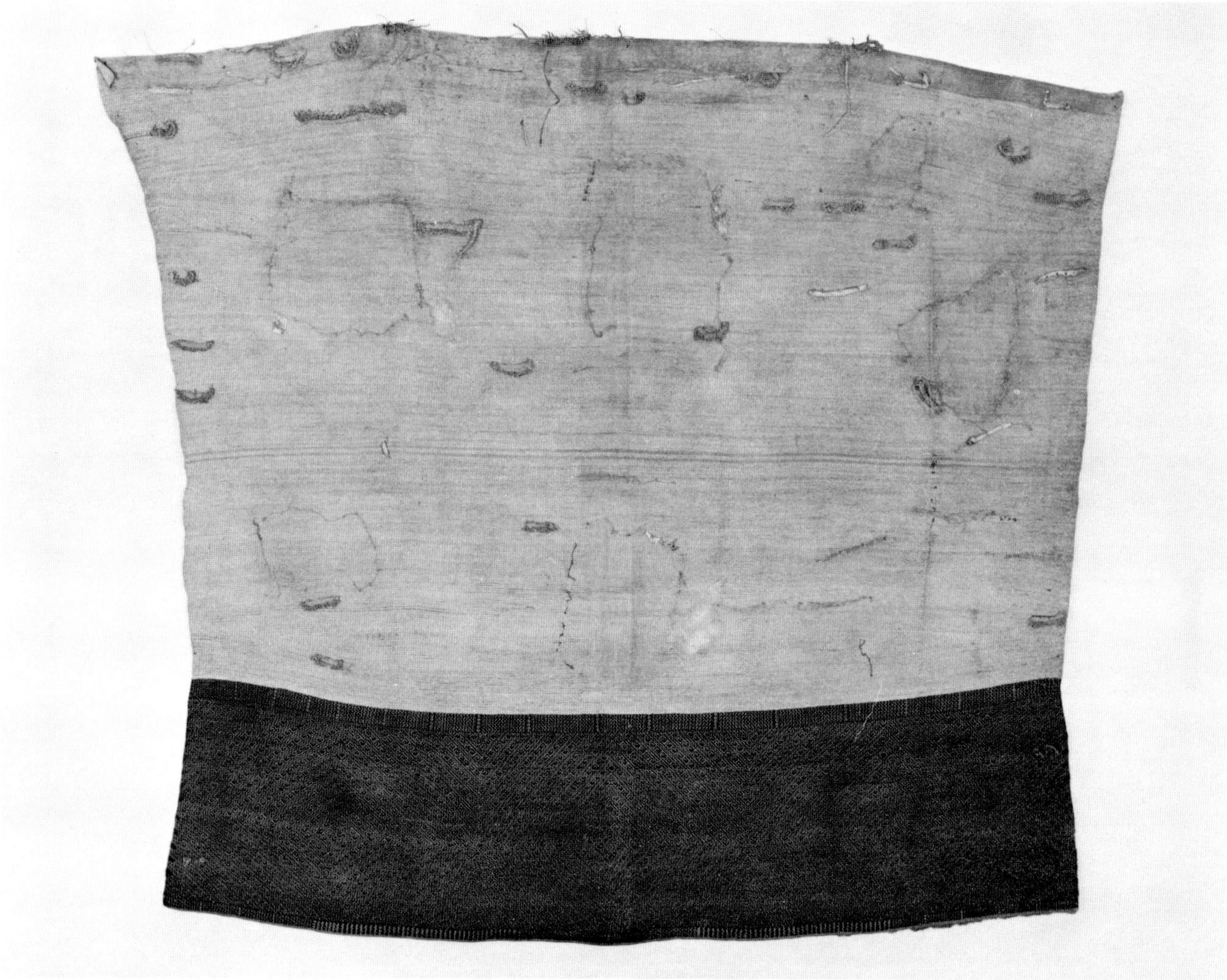

Figure 326. — Cloak, Stockholm 1848.1.63.

Figure 327. — Cloak (detail), Stockholm 1848.1.63.

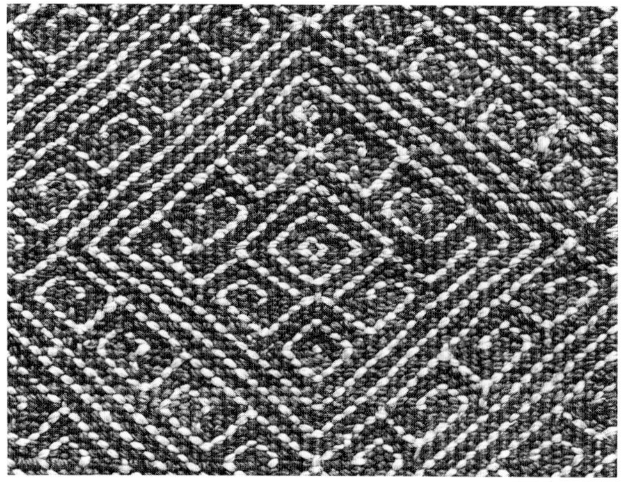

32-37. Six cloaks, Dublin (1882.3729-1882.3734).
Evidence: Circumstantial. Thought to be part of the Cook voyage collections given to Trinity College, Dublin, by Patten and King from the second and third voyages.
Literature: Freeman, 1949, p. 8.

38. Cloak, Florence (244). Dimensions 130 cm × 90 cm.
Evidence: Circumstantial. Cook voyage collection from various sources.
Literature: Giglioli, 1893, pp. 184-185; Kaeppler, 1977.

39-40. Two cloaks, Wellington (ME 7852, 7853).
Evidence: Circumstantial. From the Imperial Institute, from Queen Victoria in a box that contained "articles brought by Captain Cook from Otaheti."

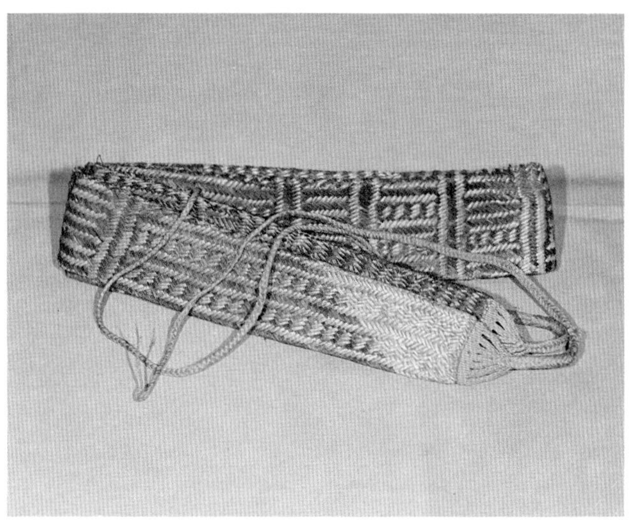

Figure 328. — Belt, Cambridge 22.936b.

Belts

1-2. Two belts, Cambridge (22.936a [lost] & b [exhibited]). Belt length 150 cm; length of ties 81 cm. Figure 328.
Evidence: Leverian Museum.

3-6. Four belts, Cambridge (1914.43-1914.46).
Evidence: Sandwich collection. Given by Cook, from the first or second voyage.
Literature: Shawcross, 1970, pp. 325-330.

7. Belt, Oxford (108). Length without ties 83 cm.
Evidence: Forster collection. Second voyage.
Literature: Gathercole, n.d. [1970].

8-11. Four belts, Stockholm (1848.1.36-40).
Evidence: "Banks Collection."
Literature: Rydén, 1965, pp. 89-90.

12. Belt, Göttingen.
Evidence: Purchased from London dealer Humphrey in 1782.

13-15. Three belts, British Museum (NZ 128, 131, 132).
Evidence: Circumstantial. Noted "Cook collection 69" and "Cook collection."

16-17. Two belts, Florence (258, 481).
Evidence: Circumstantial. Cook voyage collection from various sources.
Literature: Giglioli, 1893, pp. 185-186; Kaeppler, 1977.

Other Clothing

1. Feather penis covering, Göttingen.
Evidence: Purchased from London dealer Humphrey in 1782.

Cordage

1. Cordage, Cambridge (1914.53).
Evidence: Sandwich collection. Given by Cook, first or second voyage.
Literature: Shawcross, 1970, p. 307.

2. Cordage, Oxford (118). Missing.
Evidence: Forster collection. Second voyage.
Literature: Gathercole, n.d. [1970].

3-4. Two hanks of cordage, Göttingen.
Evidence: Forster collection. Second voyage.

5-9. Five hanks of cordage, Göttingen.
Evidence: Purchased from London dealer Humphrey in 1782.

10. Cordage, Stockholm (1848.1.18).
Evidence: "Banks Collection."
Literature: Rydén, 1965, pp. 90-91.

11. Cordage, British Museum (NZ 141).
Evidence: Circumstantial. Noted "Cook Collection 73."

12. Cordage, Berne (NS1).
Evidence: Webber collection. Third voyage.
Literature: Henking, 1957, p. 332; Kaeppler, 1977.

13. Cordage, Wörlitz (22).
Evidence: Forster collection. Second voyage.
Literature: Germer, 1975, pp. 72-73, 91.

14. Cloak sample, Christchurch (E 149.147).
Evidence: Circumstantial. Worden Hall collection. See Appendix II, this volume.

Baskets

1. Basket, Stockholm (1848.1.45).
Evidence: "Banks Collection."
Literature: Rydén, 1965, p. 89.

Ornaments

A large number of Maori ornaments were collected on Cook's voyages, including *heitiki,*[3] other neck ornaments, ear ornaments, cloak pins, and combs (Figs. 323, 329).

[3] Barrow attributes a *heitiki* in Wellington to Cook's voyages (1964, p. 28), but it has been shown that this *heitiki* can only be traced back to 1819 (Kaeppler, 1974a, p. 78).

Figure 329. — A New Zealand warrior, Plate 13 of Hawkesworth (24).

Figure 330. — Greenstone and bone ornaments, Vienna 22, 23, 20, 21, 163.

Figure 331. — *Heitiki,* Chicago 273856.

Figure 332. — *Heitiki,* HM Queen Elizabeth II.

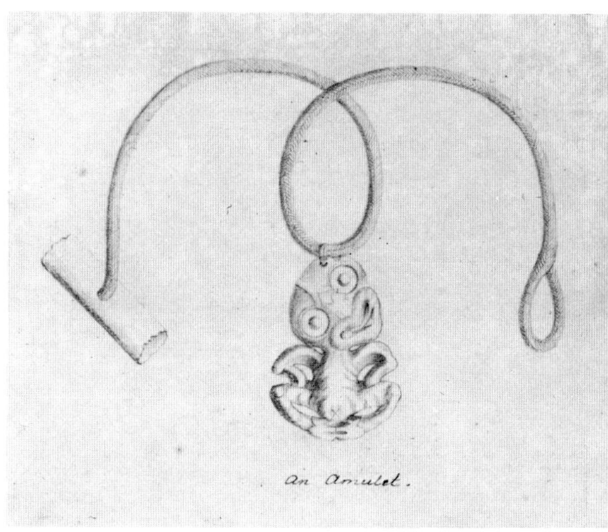

Figure 333. — *Heitiki,* British Library Add. Ms. 23,920.76.

Heitiki

1-2. Two *heitiki* (one with bone toggle), Vienna (22, 23). Dimensions 8.5 cm × 5.5 cm, 6.5 cm × 4 cm. Figure 330.
Evidence: Leverian Museum.
Literature: Moschner, 1955, pp. 204-205.

3. *Heitiki* (with bone toggle), Chicago (273856). Height 21.5 cm. Figure 331.
Evidence: Leverian Museum.[4]
Literature: Force and Force, 1971, pp. 23-24.

4. *Heitiki* (with bone toggle), Her Majesty Queen Elizabeth II, on loan to the Commonwealth Institute, London. Figure 332.
Evidence: Given by Captain Cook to King George III.

5. *Heitiki,* Oxford (120). Height 10 cm.
Evidence: Forster collection. Second voyage.
Literature: Gathercole, n.d. [1970].

6. *Heitiki.* Lost (possibly Number 4 above).
Evidence: Depicted in British Library Add. Ms. 23,920.76, and noted "Hawkes Bay, New Zealand, October 18, 1769" (Fig. 333).

1. Bone toggle (from a *heitiki* ?), Stockholm (1799.2.23). Length 5 cm.
Evidence: Sparrman collection. Second voyage.
Literature: Söderström, 1939, pp. 56-57.

2. Bone toggle (from a *heitiki* ?), Cambridge (1914.42).
Evidence: Sandwich collection. Given by Cook, first or second voyage.
Literature: Shawcross, 1970, pp. 333-334.

[4]Two other *heitiki* from the Leverian Museum have not been located.

Reiputa

1. *Reiputa,* British Museum (NZ 159).[5] Figure 334.
Evidence: Circumstantial. Noted "Cook Collection" because of similarity to that depicted in British Library Add. Ms. 15,508.21, and Add. Ms. 23,920.76. Figures 334, 335.

Necklaces

1. Necklace of flax and dentalium shells, Stockholm (1799.2.31). Length 68 cm. Figure 336.
Evidence: Sparrman collection. Second voyage.
Literature: Söderström, 1939, p. 46 (attributed to Tonga).

2. Necklace of twisted flax, bone toggle, two *paua* shells, Sydney (H 222). Length of fiber ca. 90 cm, bone toggle 3 cm, shells 6.5, 7 cm.
Evidence: Cook collection exhibited at Colonial and Indian Exhibition.
Literature: Mackrell, 1886; Appendix I, this volume.

3-5. Three necklaces, Cambridge (1914.37-39). Missing. A manuscript note by Skinner in the museum suggests that 1914.38 was similar to the Stockholm necklace above.
Evidence: Sandwich collection. Given by Cook, first or second voyage.
Literature: Shawcross, 1970, pp. 331-332.

[5]A *reiputa* formerly in the Hancock Museum, Newcastle, and now on loan to Christchurch, New Zealand, is often attributed to Cook's voyages (Duff, 1969, p. 36), usually on the basis of similarity to the engraving after Parkinson. However, there is no documentation to support this, and in my view it is more likely that an important ornament from Cook's first voyage would have gone to the British Museum.

Figure 334. — *Reiputa,* British Museum NZ 159.

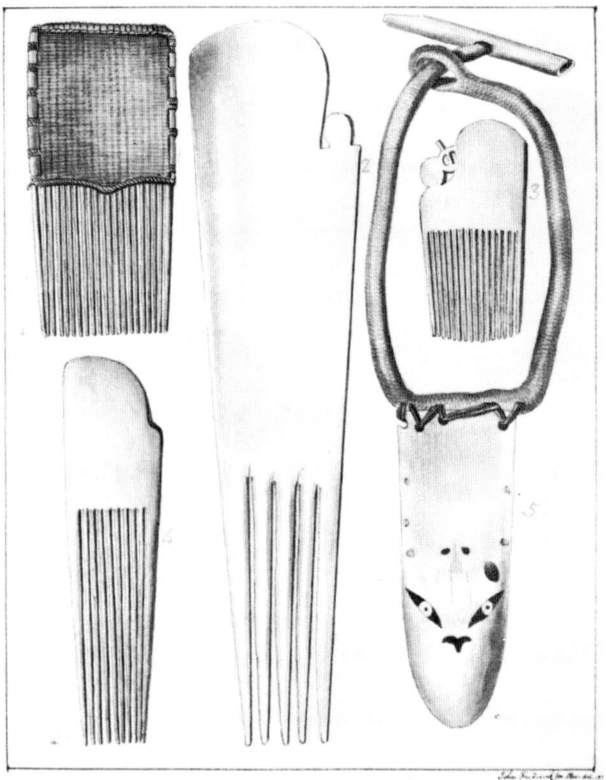

Figure 335. — *Reiputa* and combs, British Library Add. Ms. 23,920.76.

6-7. Necklaces of dentalium shells, Wellington (ME 7855).
Evidence: Circumstantial. From the Imperial Institute from Queen Victoria in a box containing "articles brought by Captain Cook from Otaheti."

8-10. Three necklaces of dentalium shells, bone, and other shells, Oxford (98). Lengths 76 cm, 110 cm, and 165 cm.
Evidence: Forster collection, second voyage.
Literature: Gathercole, n.d. [1970], attributed to Tonga by Forster.

11. Necklace. Lost.
Evidence: Leverian Museum depiction.

Other Ornaments of Greenstone: Ear Ornaments and Cloak Pins

⛵1-2. Two greenstone ornaments, Vienna (20, 21). Lengths 8 cm, 19 cm. Figure 330.
Evidence: Leverian Museum.[6]
Literature: Moschner, 1955, pp. 206-207.

[6]Several other greenstone pendants from the Leverian Museum cannot be located.

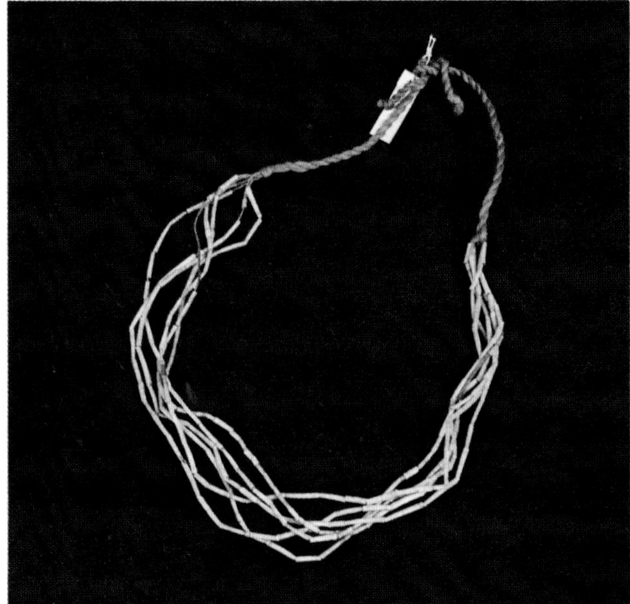

Figure 336. — Necklace, Stockholm 1799.2.31.

⛵3. Bowenite ornament with finely twisted flax fibers, Sydney (H 156). Length 34 cm, fiber 33 cm. Figures 337, 621.
Evidence: Cook collection exhibited at Colonial and Indian Exhibition.
Literature: Raspe, 1791, p. vi; Mackrell, 1886; Thorpe, 1931, p. 181; Appendix I, this volume.

4. Greenstone ornament, Sydney (H 63). Length 12 cm.
Evidence: Cook Collection exhibited at Colonial and Indian Exhibition.
Literature: Mackrell, 1886; Appendix I, this volume.

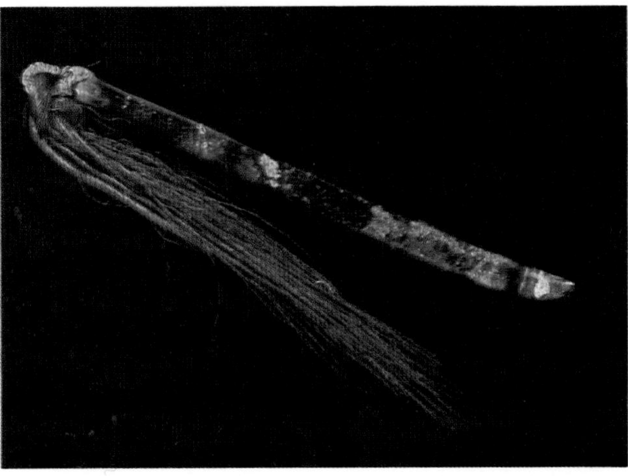

Figure 337. — Bowenite ornament, Sydney H 156.

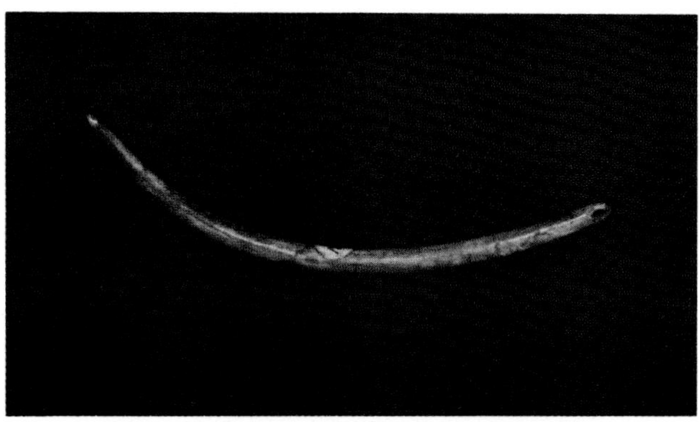

Figure 338. — Cloak pin, Exeter E 1231.

5-6. Two greenstone ornaments, Oxford (122 and 123). Lengths 17 cm, 15.5 cm.
Evidence: Forster collection. Second voyage.
Literature: Gathercole, n.d. [1970].

7-8. Two greenstone ornaments, Göttingen.
Evidence: Purchased by London dealer Humphrey in 1782.

9. Greenstone ornament, Cambridge (1914.36).
Evidence: Sandwich collection. Given by Cook, first or second voyage.
Literature: Shawcross, 1970, p. 333.

10. Greenstone ornament (with two human teeth), British Museum (NZ 162).
Evidence: Noted "Cook collection" because of its similarity to that depicted in British Library Add. Ms. 15,508.21.

11. Greenstone ornament, Wörlitz (25). Length 9.2 cm.
Evidence: Forster collection. Second voyage.
Literature: Germer, 1975, pp. 84, 91.

12. Greenstone ornament. Location unknown.
Evidence: Circumstantial. Said to have been given by Mrs. Cook to Ann Gates, who gave it to Ann Smith, who gave it to Jane Backhouse. Formerly in the Beasley collection.

Cloak Pins

1. Bone cloak pin, Exeter (E 1231). Length 14 cm. Figure 338.
Evidence: Leverian Museum.

2-3. Two cloak pins of bone and seal (?) teeth, Vienna (163 [see Fig. 330] and 43). Length 9.5 cm, 15 cm.
Evidence: Leverian Museum.
Literature: Moschner, 1955, p. 168.

4-5. Two bone cloak pins, Oxford (124-125). Lengths 11.5 cm, 17 cm.
Evidence: Forster collection. Second voyage.
Literature: Gathercole, n.d. [1970].

6-7. Two cloak pins of seal (?) teeth, Göttingen.
Evidence: Forster collection. Second voyage.

8-12. Five cloak pins of bone, ivory, wood, and *paua* shell, Göttingen.
Evidence: Purchased from London dealer Humphrey in 1782.

13-14. Three cloak pins, Berne (NS 3a/b, NS 5).
Evidence: Webber collection. Third voyage.
Literature: Henking, 1957, p. 332; Kaeppler, 1977.

15-17. Two cloak pins of seal (?) teeth, Florence (205).
Evidence: Circumstantial. Cook voyage collection from various sources.
Literature: Giglioli, 1893, pp. 188-189; Kaeppler, 1977.

18. Ivory cloak pin, Cambridge (1914.41).
Evidence: Sandwich collection. Given by Cook, first or second voyage.

19. Bone cloak pin, Dublin (1882.3704).
Evidence: Circumstantial. Thought to be part of Cook voyage collection given to Trinity College, Dublin, by Patten or King, from the second or third voyage.
Literature: Freeman, 1949, p. 8.

20. *Paua* shell cloak pin, Wellington (ME 7854).
Evidence: Circumstantial. From the Imperial Institute, in a box from Queen Victoria said to contain "articles brought by Captain Cook from Otaheti."

Other Ornaments

1. Ornament of 21 human teeth, Oxford (126).
Evidence: Forster collection. Second voyage.
Literature: Gathercole, n.d. [1970].

2. Ornament of five human teeth, Göttingen.
Evidence: Purchased from London dealer Humphrey in 1782.

3. Headdress of feathers, Oxford (127). Missing.
Evidence: Forster collection. Second voyage.
Literature: Gathercole, n.d. [1970].

4. Ear ornament of leaves, Oxford (172). Missing.
Evidence: Forster collection. Second voyage.
Literature: Gathercole, n.d. [1970].

5. Red ocher, Cambridge (1914.74).
Evidence: Sandwich collection. Given by Cook, first or second voyage.
Literature: Shawcross, 1970, p. 331.[7]

---

[7] Shawcross does not describe the red ocher, probably because it was exhibited in the Tahitian case. The tag of dog hair that he describes (1970, p. 334) is not Maori, but an element which has come away from the Tahitian gorget (1914.10).

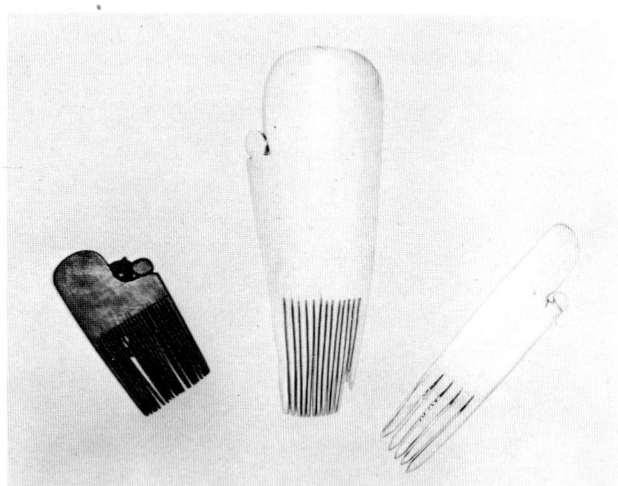

Figure 339. — Wood and whalebone combs, Vienna 28, 26, 27.

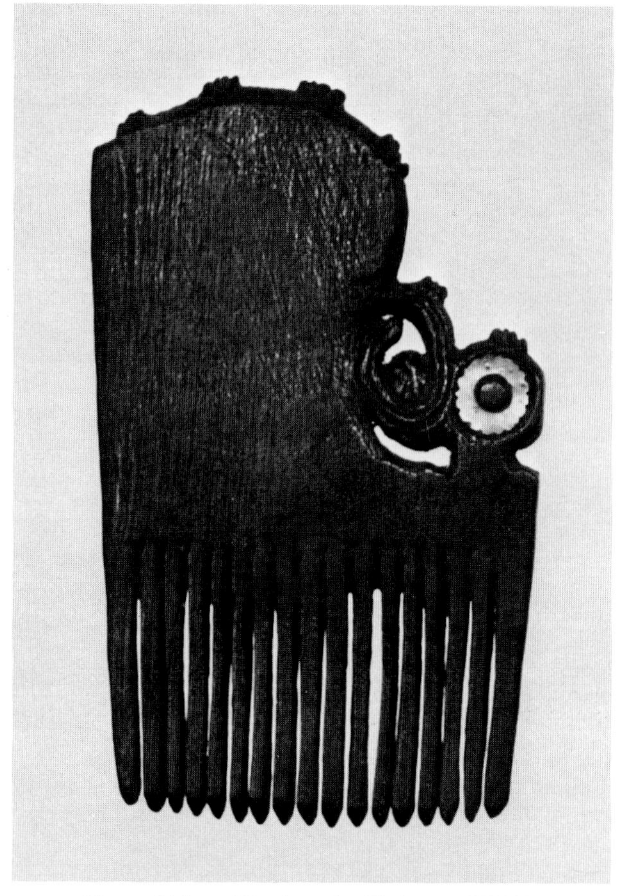

Figure 340. — Wood comb, Göttingen OZ 292.

Combs

Besides being used to comb the hair, combs also served as ornaments. The two major types were made of wood and whalebone, while a third type of wooden teeth with fiber binding was also depicted (British Library Add. Ms. 23,920.76 [Fig. 335]).

1. Wooden comb, Vienna (28). Length 12 cm, width 5.8 cm. Figure 339.
   Evidence: Leverian Museum.
   Literature: Moschner, 1955, p. 216.

2. Wooden comb, Göttingen (OZ 292). Length 10.1 cm, width 6.2 cm. Figure 340.
   Evidence: Purchased from London dealer Humphrey in 1782.

3. Wooden comb, Cambridge (1914.35). Length 9.5 cm.
   Evidence: Sandwich collection. Given by Cook, first or second voyage.
   Literature: Shawcross, 1970, pp. 332-333.

4. Wooden comb, Florence (158).
   Evidence: Circumstantial. Cook voyage collection from various sources.
   Literature: Giglioli, 1893, p. 187; Kaeppler, 1977.

1. Whalebone comb, Hewett collection. Length 26 cm, width 9.5 cm. Figure 341.
   Evidence: Incised on the comb "James King, Newszealand, Feb. 12, 1777."

2. Whalebone comb, Stockholm (1799.2.1). Length 32 cm, width 12 cm. Figure 342.
   Evidence: Sparrman collection. Second voyage.
   Literature: Söderström, 1939, p. 57.

3-4. Two whalebone combs, Vienna (26 and 27 [exhibited]). Lengths 22 cm, 17.5 cm; widths 8.5 cm, 4 cm. Figure 339.
   Evidence: Leverian Museum.
   Literature: Moschner, 1955, p. 216.

5. Whalebone comb, Oxford (171). Length 35 cm.
   Evidence: Forster collection. Second voyage.
   Literature: Gathercole, n.d. [1970].

6. Whalebone comb, Göttingen.
   Evidence: Forster collection. Second voyage.

7. Whalebone comb, Florence (161).
   Evidence: Circumstantial. Cook voyage collection from various sources.
   Literature: Giglioli, 1893, pp. 186-187; Kaeppler, 1977.

8. Whalebone comb, British Museum (NZ 163).
   Evidence: Circumstantial. Noted "Cook collection" because of its similarity to that depicted in British Library Add. Ms. 15,508.21. Remains of a "Cook collection" label are still attached ". . . ornaments . . . of New Zealand."

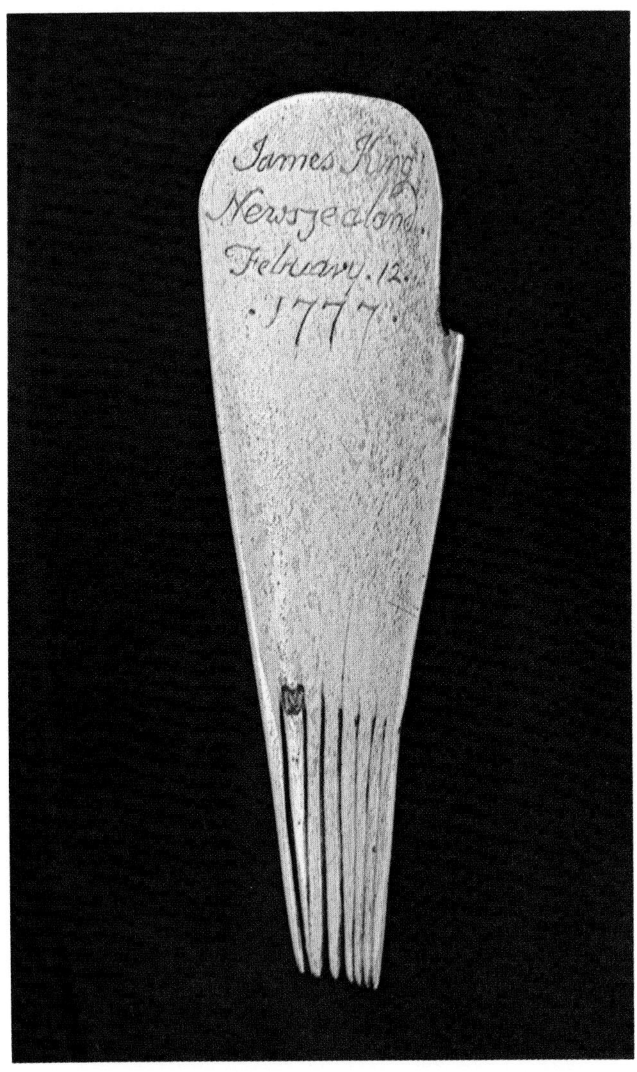

Figure 341. — Whalebone comb, Hewett collection.

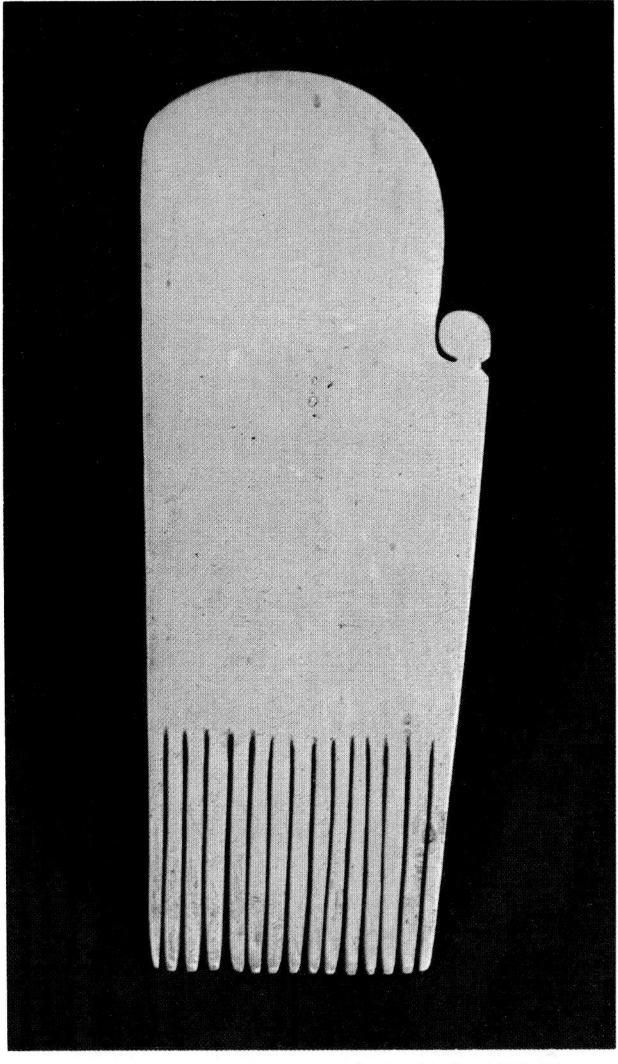

Figure 342. — Whalebone comb, Stockholm 1799.2.1.

9. Whalebone comb, Wellington (ME 7851).
   Evidence: Circumstantial. From the Imperial Institute, from Queen Victoria in a box containing "articles brought by Captain Cook from Otaheti."

Feather Boxes

Although feather boxes abound in later collections, none can be precisely traced to Cook's voyages. Two in the British Museum are attributed to Cook's voyages—one of which appears to be depicted.

1. Feather box, British Museum (NZ 109). Figure 343.
   Evidence: Circumstantial. Noted "Cook collection" because of its similarity to that depicted in British Library Add. Ms. 15,508.22 (Fig. 344).
2. Feather box, British Museum (NZ 113).
   Evidence: Circumstantial. Noted "Cook collection" with no other information.

Musical Instruments

Maori sound-producers for music and ritual are pre-eminently wind instruments. Several types were collected on Cook's voyages and listed here by Maori categories.

1. *Putorino* (double), Dublin (1882.3654). Length 52 cm, width 7 cm. Figures 345, 346.
   Evidence: Circumstantial. Thought to be part of Cook voyage collections given to Trinity College, Dublin, by Patten or King, second or third voyage.
   Literature: Freeman, 1949, p. 8.
2. *Putorino* (double), Wellington (ME 2503).
   Evidence: From Bullock's Museum probably given by Banks. Probably depicted in British Library Add. Ms. 23,920.83.[8]
   Literature: Kaeppler, 1974a, pp. 78-79.

[8]Another similar instrument is in the British Museum.

Figure 343. — Feather box, British Museum NZ 109.

Figure 344. — Feather box, British Library Add. Ms. 15,508.22.

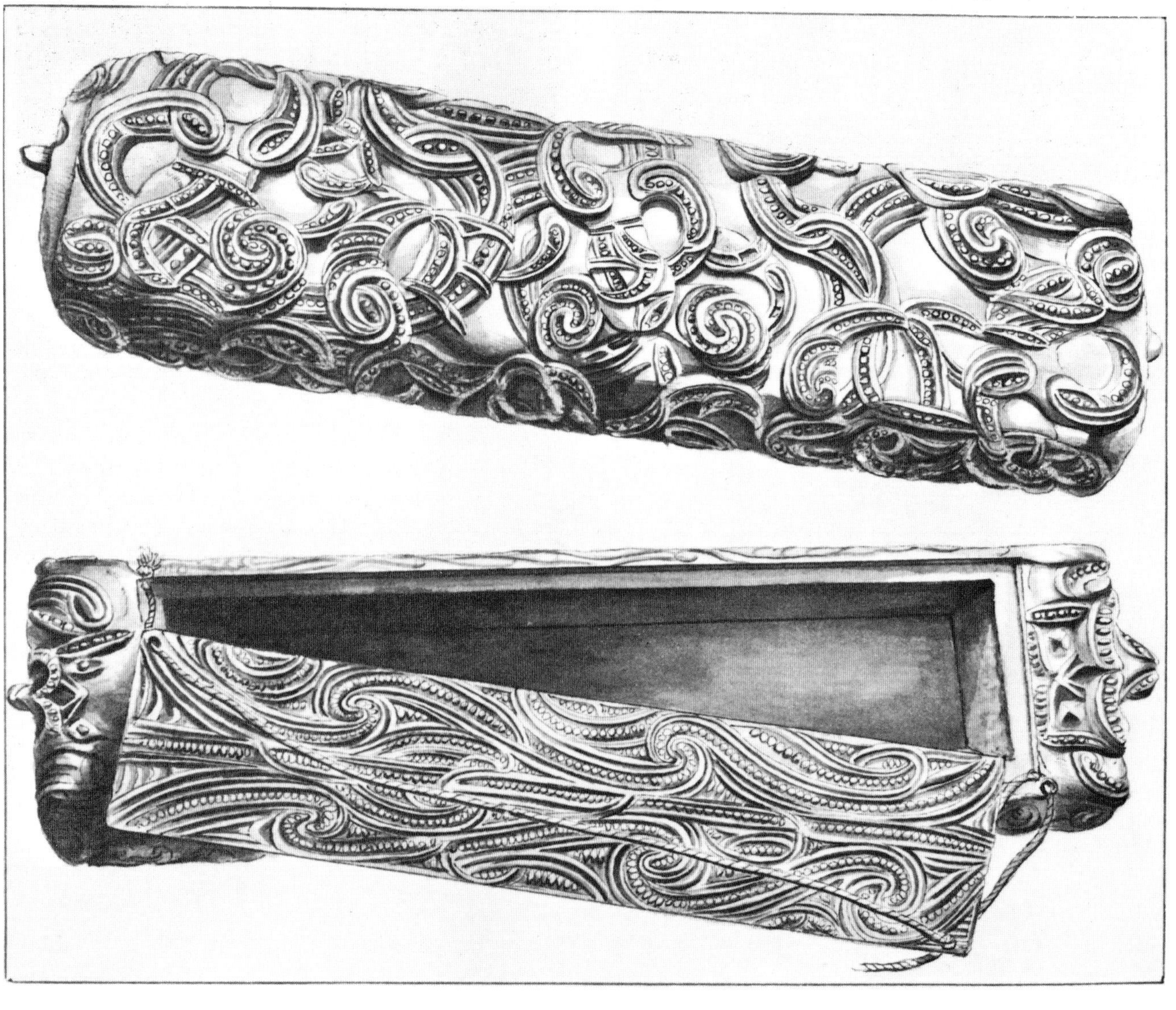

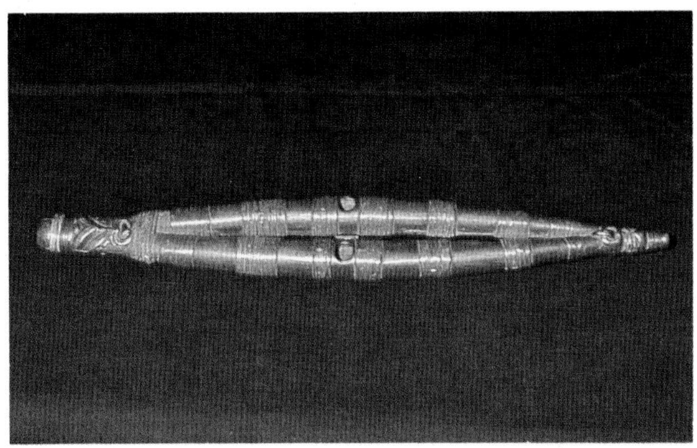

Figure 345. — Double *putorino,* Dublin 1882.3654.

3-4. Two *putorino,* Dublin (1882.3655 and 1882.3656 [exhibited]). Length of exhibited specimen 40.5 cm, width 4 cm. Figures 347, 348.
   Evidence: Circumstantial. Thought to be part of Cook voyage collections given to Trinity College, Dublin, by Patten or King, second or third voyage.
   Literature: Freeman, 1949, p. 8.

5. *Putorino,* Wellington (ME 2502).
   Evidence: Circumstantial. Bullock's Museum, probably given by Banks.
   Literature: Kaeppler, 1974a, pp. 78-79.

6. *Putorino,* Oxford (116). Length 51.5 cm.
   Evidence: Forster collection. Second voyage.
   Literature: Gathercole, n.d. [1970].

7. *Putorino,* Cambridge (22.934).
   Evidence: Circumstantial. Probably from Leverian Museum.

8. *Putorino,* Göttingen.
   Evidence: Purchased from London dealer Humphrey in 1782.

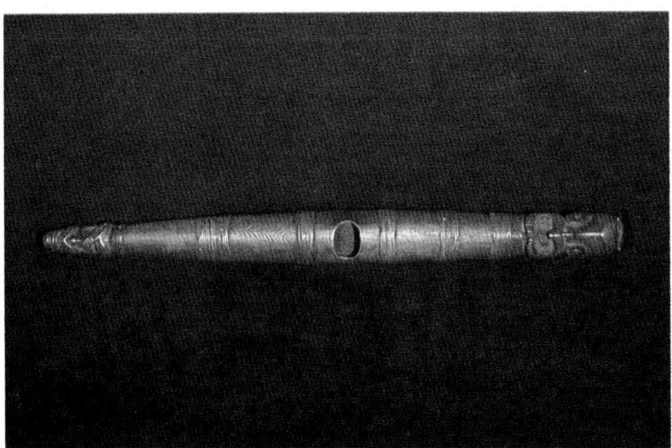

Figure 347. — *Putorino,* Dublin 1882.3656.

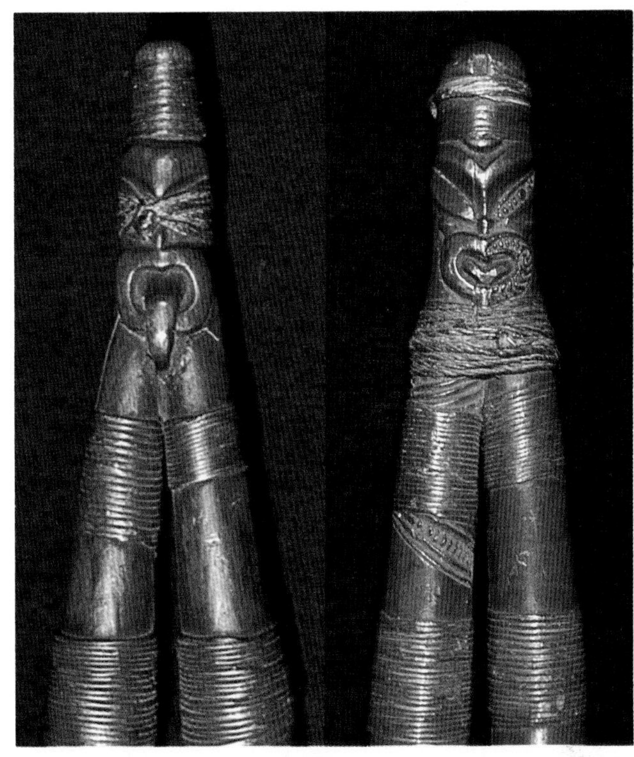

Figure 346. — Double *putorino* (details), Dublin 1882.3654.

Figure 348. — *Putorino* (detail), Dublin 1882.3656.

Figure 349. — *Koauau,* Cambridge 1914.55.

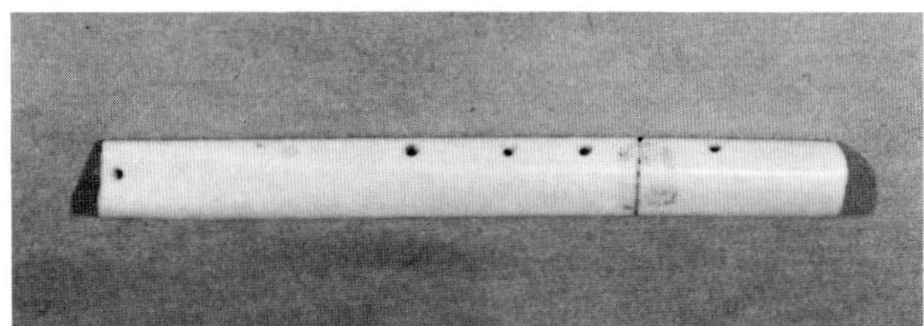

Figure 350. — Bone flute, Vienna 29.

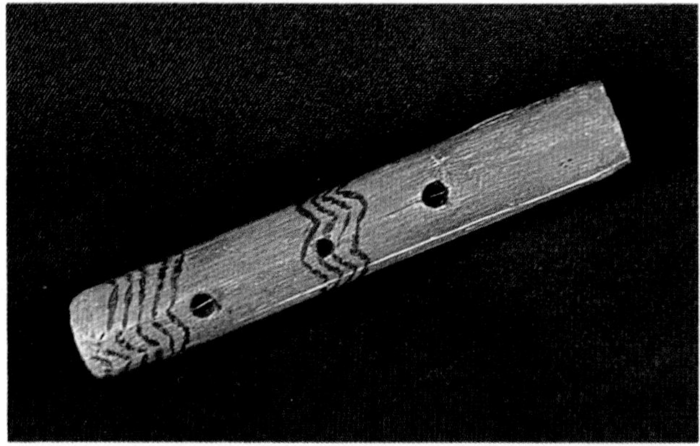

Figure 351. — Wood flute, Stockholm 1799.2.18.

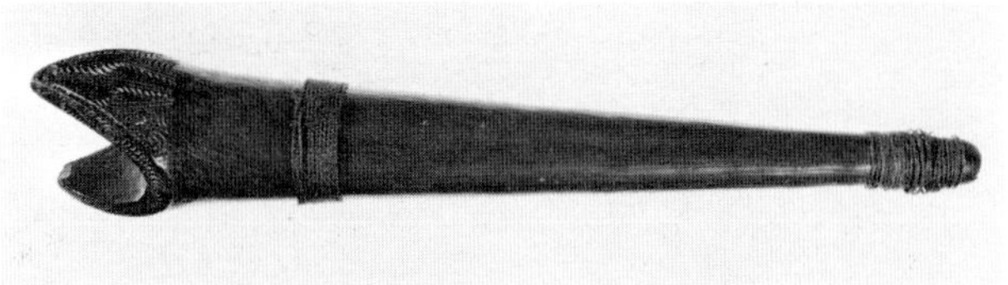

Figure 352. — *Pu kaea,* Cambridge 22.436.

9. *Putorino,* Wellington (ME 7850).
   Evidence: Circumstantial. From the Imperial Institute from Queen Victoria in a box containing "articles brought by Captain Cook from Otaheti."

10. *Koauau,* Cambridge (1914.55). Figure 349.
   Evidence: Sandwich collection. Given by Cook, first or second voyage.
   Literature: Shawcross, 1970, pp. 338-339.

11. *Nguru,* Berne (NS 4).
   Evidence: Webber collection. Third voyage.
   Literature: Henking, 1957, p. 332; Kaeppler, 1977.

12. *Nguru,* Wellington (ME 11809).
   Evidence: Circumstantial. From the Imperial Institute from Queen Victoria in a box containing "articles brought by Captain Cook from Otaheti."

13. Bone flute, Vienna (29). Length 15 cm. Figure 350.
   Evidence: Leverian Museum.
   Literature: Moschner, 1955, p. 244.

14. Wood flute, Stockholm (1799.2.18). Length 13.5 cm. Figure 351.
   Evidence: Sparrman collection. Second voyage.
   Literature: Söderström, 1939, pp. 54-56.

15. Wood flute, Göttingen.
   Evidence: Purchased from London dealer Humphrey in 1782.

1. Short trumpet (*pu kaea*), Cambridge (22.436). Length 53.5 cm, width 10 cm. Figure 352.
   Evidence: Sandwich collection. Given by Cook, first or second voyage.
   Literature: Shawcross, 1970, p. 337.

2. Long trumpet (*pu kaea*), Cambridge (22.435). Length 178 cm.
   Evidence: Sandwich collection. Given by Cook, first or second voyage.
   Literature: Shawcross, 1970, pp. 334 and 337.

3. Shell trumpet (*pu tatara*), Cambridge (25.374). Length 26 cm.
   Evidence: Pennant collection. Given by Forster, second voyage.
   Depictions: Cook 1777, Plate 19; British Library Add. Ms. 15,508.32 (Figs. 353, 354).
   Literature: Gathercole, 1976, pp. 187-199; Shawcross, 1970, pp. 337-338.

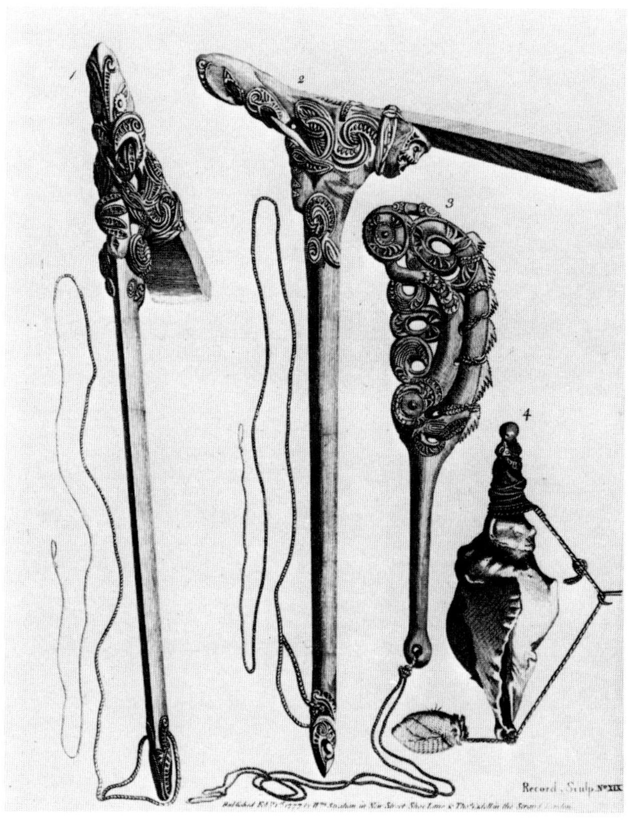

Figure 353. — New Zealand artifact plate, *Atlas* to Cook's second voyage (28).

Weapons

Weapons were the most numerous objects collected on Cook's voyages. Examples of nearly every type were collected. They were known to their European collectors mainly as *patapattoo* and spontoons, but will be separated here, as far as possible, into Maori categories.

Wahaika: Hand Clubs of Wood or Bone

1. *Wahaika* (wood), Exeter (E1220). Length 42 cm, width of blade 17.5 cm, height of figure 6.5 cm. Figures 355, 356.
   Evidence: Leverian Museum.
2. *Wahaika* (wood), Vienna (15). Length 17.5 cm, width 7.5 cm, height of figure 9 cm. Figure 357.
   Evidence: Leverian Museum.
   Literature: Moschner, 1955, pp. 144-145.
3. *Wahaika* (wood), Stockholm (1848.1.1). Length 36 cm, width 11 cm. Figures 358-360.
   Evidence: "Banks Collection."
   Literature: Rydén, 1965, pp. 84-85.

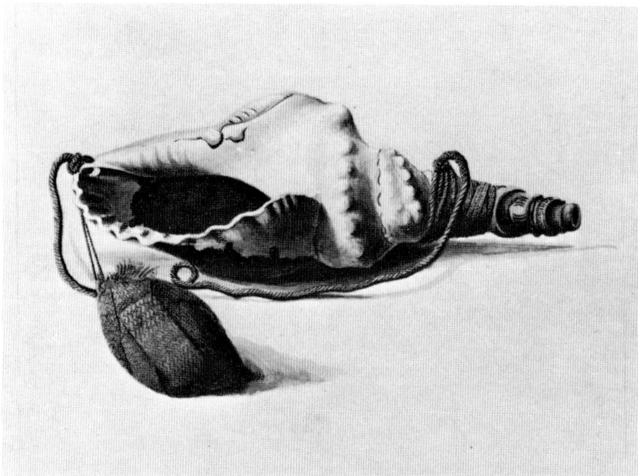

Figure 354. — *Pu tatara,* British Library Add. Ms. 15,508.32.

4. *Wahaika* (wood), Oxford (113). Length 49 cm.
   Evidence: Forster collection. Second voyage.
   Literature: Gathercole, n.d. [1970].

5-7. Three *wahaika* (wood with various degrees of carving), Cape Town (SAM 2031). Figures 361, 362, 363.
   Evidence: Circumstantial. Thought to have arrived in Cape Town in 1775.
   Literature: Bax, 1970, p. 146.

8. *Wahaika* (wood), Wellington.
   Evidence: Circumstantial. Said to be the one depicted in British Library Add. Ms. 15,508.24 and in Hawkesworth, 1773, Plate 14 (Fig. 364). Formerly in the Webster collection, with no history.
9. *Wahaika* (wood), Cambridge (1914.58). Length 41 cm, width 10.5 cm.
   Evidence: Sandwich collection. Given by Cook, first or second voyage.
   Literature: Shawcross, 1970, p. 315.

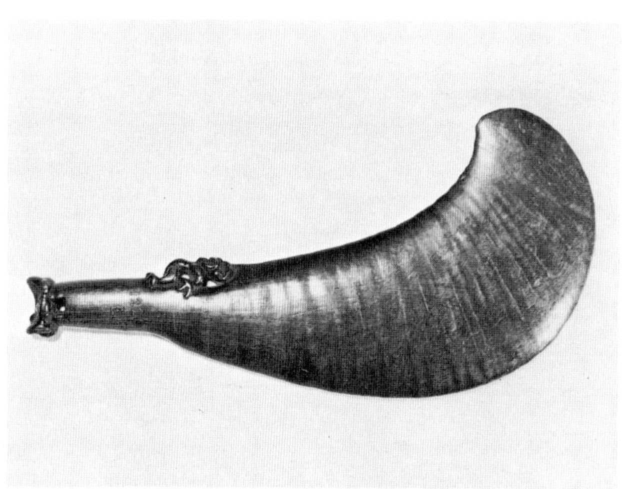

Figure 355. — *Wahaika,* Exeter E 1220.

Figure 356. — *Wahaika* (detail), Exeter E 1220.

Figure 359. — *Wahaika* (detail), Stockholm 1848.1.1.

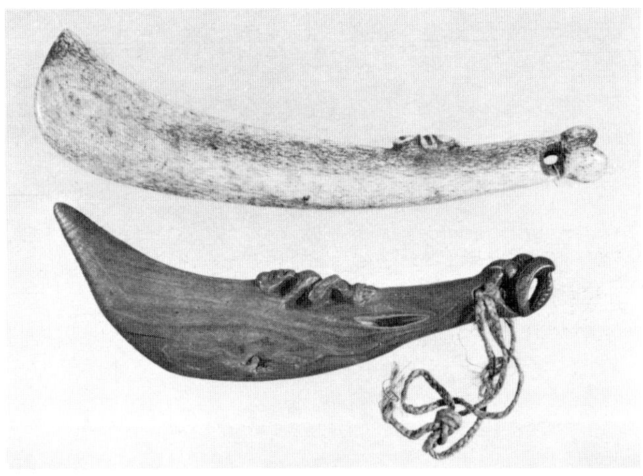

Figure 357. — Two *wahaika*, Vienna 15, 213.

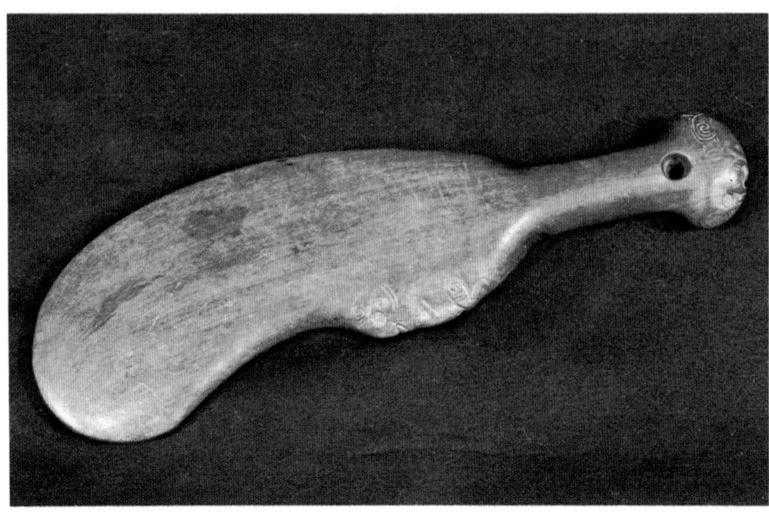

Figure 358. — *Wahaika*, Stockholm 1848.1.1.

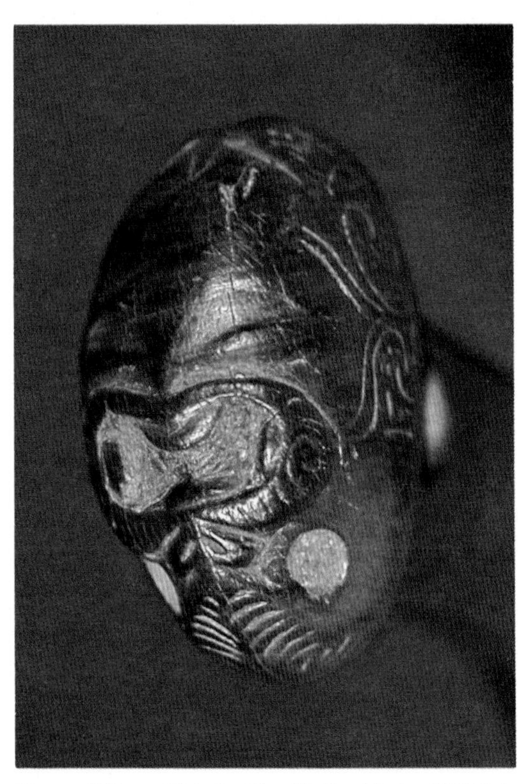

Figure 360. — *Wahaika* (detail), Stockholm 1848.1.1.

Figure 361. — *Wahaika,* Cape Town SAM 2031.

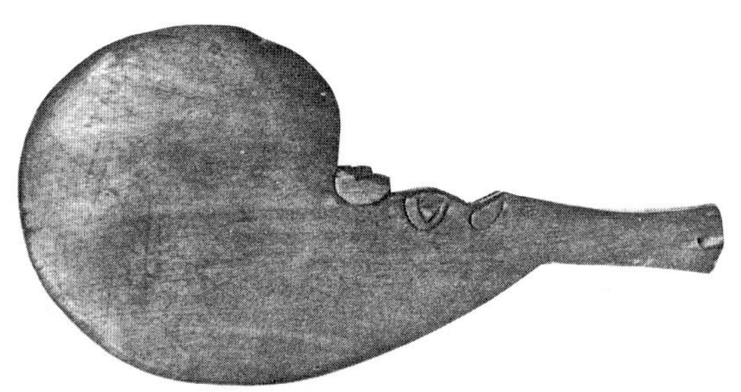

Figure 362. — *Wahaika,* Cape Town SAM 2031.

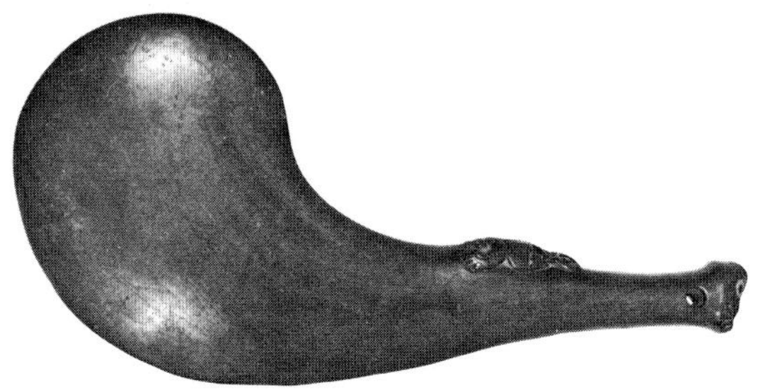

Figure 363. — *Wahaika,* Cape Town SAM 2031.

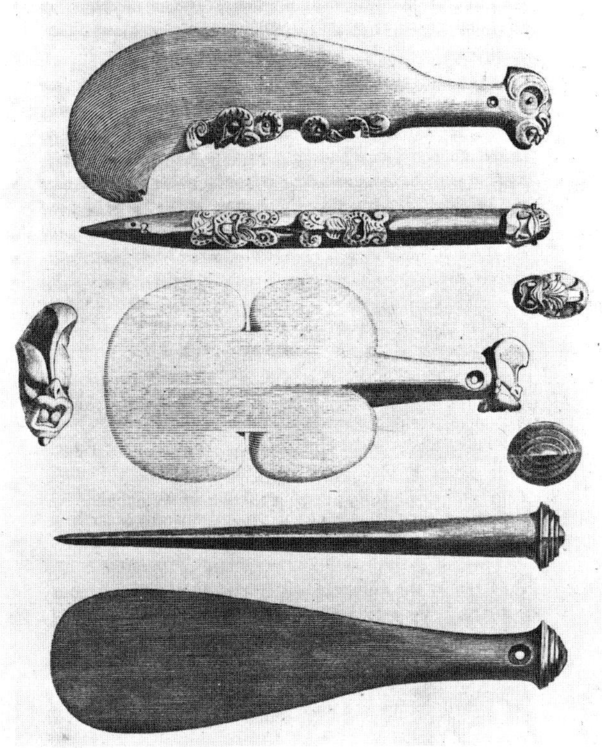

Figure 364. — New Zealand hand clubs, Plate 14 of Hawkesworth (24).

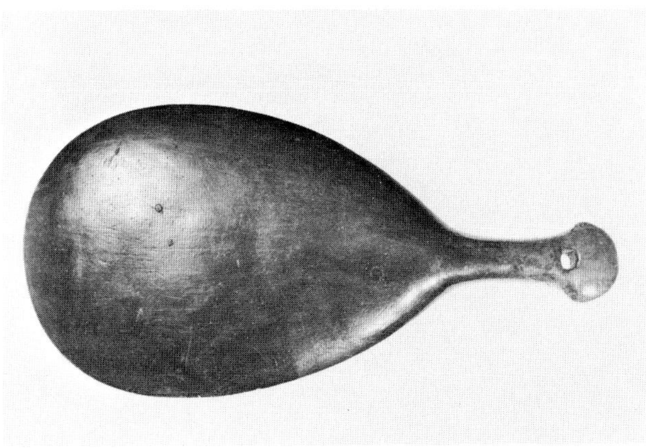

Figure 365. — Wood hand club, Cambridge 22.935.

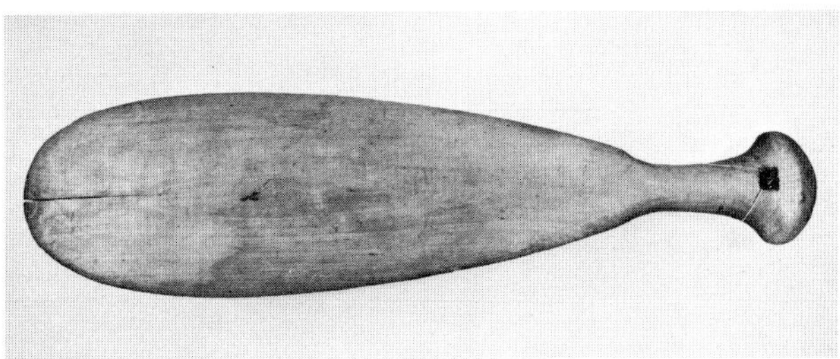

Figure 366. — Wood hand club, Vienna 13.

Figure 367. — Wood hand club, British Museum NZ 91.

10. *Wahaika* (wood), Cambridge (25.373).
    Evidence: Pennant collection of Cook voyage artifacts from various sources.
11. *Wahaika* (wood), Auckland (33640).
    Evidence: Circumstantial. Said to have been given by Cook to a Mr. Skottowe, whose descendant, M. Beverly Sanders, gave it to Auckland Museum.
12. *Wahaika* (bone), Vienna (213). Length 44 cm, width 9 cm. Figure 357.
    Evidence: Leverian Museum.
    Literature: Moschner, 1955, p. 145.
13. *Wahaika* (bone), Cambridge (1914.59). Length 25.5 cm, width 8 cm.
    Evidence: Sandwich collection. Given by Cook, first or second voyage.
    Literature: Shawcross, 1970, p. 315.

Wood Hand Clubs

Several *patu* collected on Cook's voyages are not easily classifiable into the usual Maori categories.

1. Wood hand club, Cambridge (22.935). Length 38.5 cm, width 18.5 cm. In form somewhat like some *wahaika* before the inner curve was cut away, for example, Cape Town SAM 2031a. Figure 365.
    Evidence: Leverian Museum.
2. Wood hand club, Vienna (13). Length 55 cm, width 14 cm. Similar to the above but not so broad in proportion to its length. Figure 366.
    Evidence: Leverian Museum.
    Literature: Moschner, 1955, p. 144.
3. Wood hand club, Göttingen. In form much like a *patu paraoa,* but made of wood.
    Evidence: Purchased from London dealer Humphrey in 1782.
4. Wood hand club, British Museum (NZ 91). In overall form much like a *kotiate* before the "fiddle shape" was carved. Figure 367.
    Evidence: Circumstantial. Noted "Cook Collection" and having a "Cook Collection" label "Wood Bludgeons, Otahaiti."

Kotiate

1. *Kotiate,* Vienna (14). Length 31 cm, width 31.5 cm. Figure 368.
    Evidence: Leverian Museum.
    Literature: Moschner, 1955, p. 146.
2. *Kotiate,* Greenwich (L 15/74). Length 37 cm, width 16 cm. Figure 369.
    Evidence: Said to have been presented by Captain Cook to Neil Malcolm of Poltalloch, shortly before Cook left on his third voyage. Sold as part of Lot 1116 when the contents of Poltalloch House in Argyle, Scotland, were auctioned September 17-19, 1958.
3. *Kotiate,* Cambridge (1914.60). Length 35 cm, width 14.5 cm.
    Evidence: Sandwich collection. Given by Cook, first or second voyage.
    Literature: Shawcross, 1970, pp. 315-316.
4. *Kotiate,* Göttingen.
    Evidence: Purchased from London dealer Humphrey in 1782.
5. *Kotiate,* Berlin (VI 68).
    Evidence: Circumstantial. Probably part of the Cook voyage collection in Bullock's Museum.
    Literature: Kaeppler, 1974a, p. 82.

Figure 368. — *Kotiate*, Vienna 14.

6-7. Two *kotiate*, Wellington (ME 2491-2492). Figure 370.
Evidence: Circumstantial. Probably part of the Cook voyage collection in Bullock's Museum—2491 is very similar to the depiction in Hawkesworth, 1773, Plate 14 (Fig. 364).
Literature: Kaeppler, 1974a, p. 79.

8. *Kotiate*, not located (but may be one of the above).
Evidence: Depicted in British Library Add. Ms. 15,508.23 (Fig. 371).

Patu Paraoa

Patu paraoa are usually described as rounded hand clubs of whalebone. A few whalebone *patu*, however, have further shaping and carving reminiscent of *wahaika* and are listed in that category above.

Besides the specimens listed below, the exhibit includes in the introductory section a *patu paraoa* from the collection of William Greene from the Warwick Castle sale, which probably was given by Banks to his friend Greville.

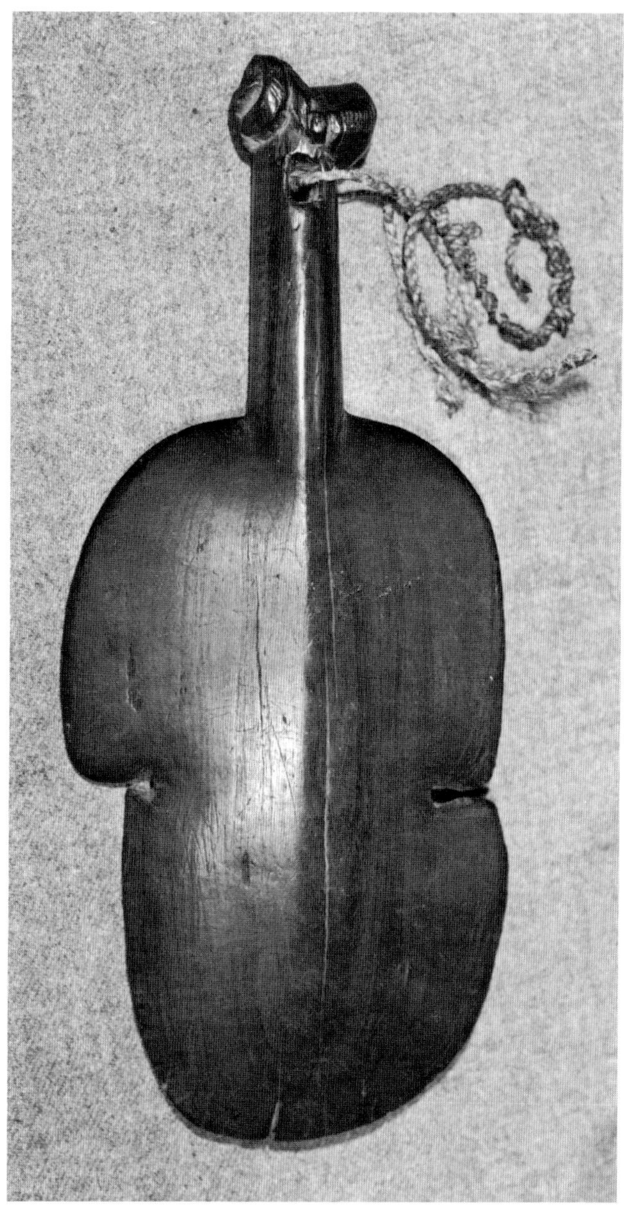

Figure 369. — *Kotiate*, Greenwich L15/74.

⛵1. *Patu paraoa*, Liverpool (R.I. 56). Length 50 cm, width 15 cm. Figure 372.
Evidence: Circumstantial. Probably part of original Cook collection in Bullock's Museum.
Literature: Kaeppler, 1974a, p. 84.

⛵2-3. Two *patu paraoa*, Glasgow (E 563 a [exhibited] and b). Lengths 40 cm, 45 cm; widths 12.5 cm, 12 cm. Figure 373.
Evidence: Circumstantial. Given by Captain King (along with two objects which appear to be from either the first or second voyage, while Captain King was on the third voyage only).

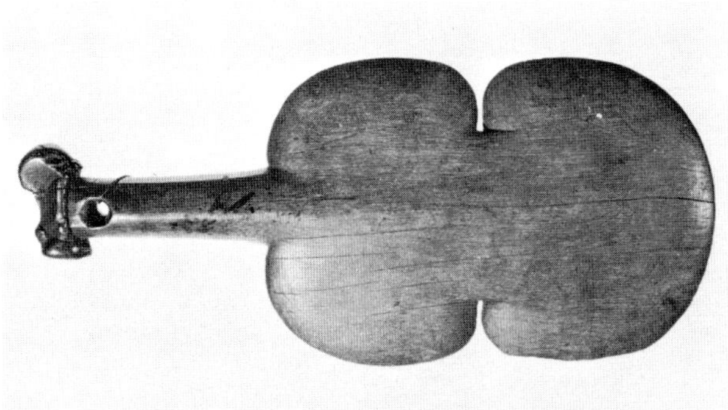

Figure 370. — *Kotiate,* Wellington ME 2491.

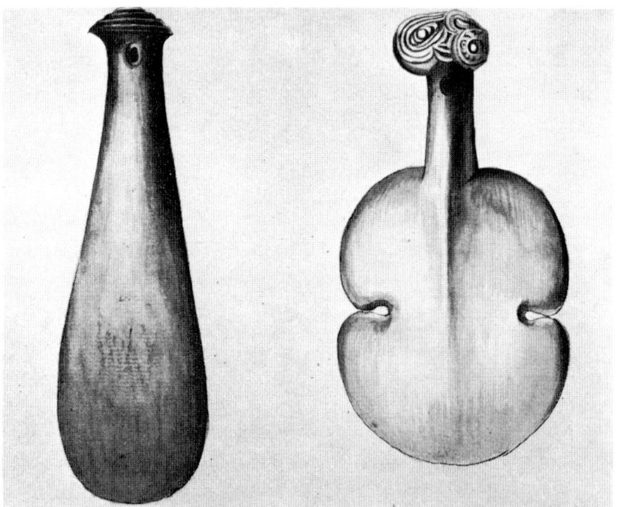

Figure 371. — Two hand clubs, British Library Add. Ms. 15,508.23.

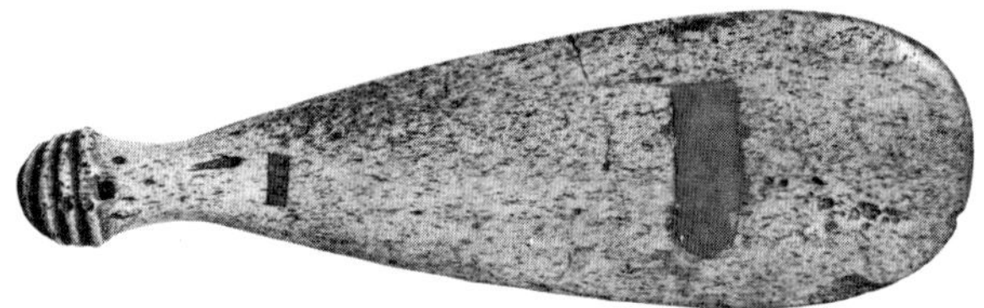

Figure 372. — *Patu paraoa,* Liverpool R.I. 56.

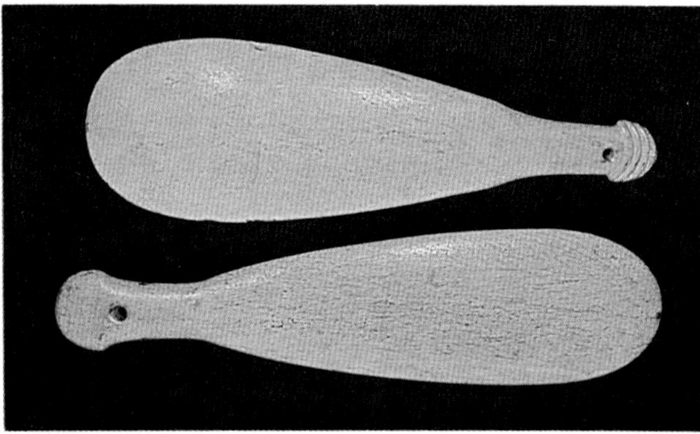

Figure 373. — Two *patu paraoa,* Glasgow E 563a and b.

4. *Patu paraoa,* John Hewett collection. Length 49 cm.
   Evidence: Leverian Museum.
5. *Patu paraoa,* Oxford (114). Length 38.5 cm.
   Evidence: Forster collection. Second voyage.
   Literature: Gathercole, n.d. [1970].
6. *Patu paraoa,* Göttingen.
   Evidence: Purchased from London dealer Humphrey in 1782.
7. *Patu paraoa,* Rupert Furneaux collection, England.
   Evidence: Collected by Captain Furneaux, second voyage.
   Literature: Furneaux, 1960, p. 180.
8. *Patu paraoa,* Cambridge[9] (1914.57). Length 42.5 cm. width 8.5 cm.
   Evidence: Sandwich collection. Given by Cook, first or second voyage.
   Literature: Shawcross, 1970, p. 315.
9. *Patu paraoa,* Cambridge (25.372). Length 44.5 cm, width 12 cm.
   Evidence: Pennant collection of Cook voyage objects from various sources.
   Literature: Shawcross, 1970, p. 316.
10. *Patu paraoa,* British Museum (ST 867).
   Evidence: Circumstantial. Bought at the sale of Pepys, traditionally said to have been brought by Cook and so noted on the specimen.
11. *Patu paraoa,* Wörlitz (24). Length 39.7 cm, width 10.1 cm.
   Evidence: Forster collection. Second voyage.
   Literature: Germer, 1975, pp. 79, 81, 91.

Patu Onewa

Basalt *patu* were greatly admired because of the amount of work necessary to manufacture them with stone tools. Indeed, Banks so admired them that he had replicas made in bronze, with his coat of arms, which he planned to take with him as gifts if he had sailed on Cook's second voyage. One of these Banks bronze *patu* is included in the introductory section of the exhibition—from the collection of John Hewett.[10]

---

[9]Barrow attributes the whalebone *patu* with bird heads in Cambridge to Cook's voyages (Barrow, 1964, p. 40) but there is no justification for this attribution.

[10]There are at least two other examples of these bronze *patu*—in the British Museum and Oxford. They were cast by Matthew Boulton at his Soho Works, Birmingham.

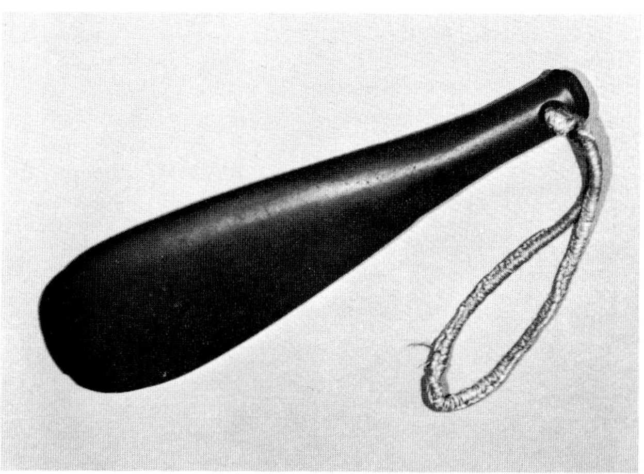

Figure 374. — *Patu onewa,* Stockholm 1799.2.5.

1. *Patu onewa,* Stockholm (1799.2.5). Length 30 cm, width 8 cm. Figure 374.
   Evidence: Sparrman collection. Second voyage.
   Literature: Söderström, 1939, p. 49.
2. *Patu onewa,* Stockholm (1848.1.2). Length 31 cm.
   Evidence: "Banks collection."
   Literature: Rydén, 1965, p. 86.
3. *Patu onewa,* Cambridge (1914.56). Length 32 cm, width 9.5 cm.
   Evidence: Sandwich collection. Given by Cook, first or second voyage.
   Literature: Shawcross, 1970, p. 312.
4. *Patu onewa,* Vienna (16). Length 29.5 cm, width 10 cm.
   Evidence: Leverian Museum.
   Literature: Moschner, 1955, pp. 143-144.
5. *Patu onewa,* British Museum (9006).
   Evidence: Leverian Museum.
6. *Patu onewa,* British Museum (NZ 80).
   Evidence: Circumstantial. Noted "Cook collection" because of its similarity to that depicted in British Library Add. Ms. 15,508,23[11] (Fig. 371).
7. *Patu onewa,* Oxford (112). Length 33 cm.
   Evidence: Forster collection. Second voyage.
   Literature: Gathercole, n.d. [1970].
8. *Patu onewa,* Sydney (H 85). Length 29 cm, width 10 cm.
   Evidence: Part of Cook voyage collection exhibited at the Colonial and Indian Exhibition. The grip has been broken and re-polished.
   Literature: Mackrell, 1886; Appendix I, this volume.
9. *Patu onewa,* Göttingen.
   Evidence: Purchased from London dealer Humphrey in 1782.
10. *Patu onewa,* Berne (NS2).
    Evidence: Webber collection. Third voyage.
    Literature: Henking, 1957, p. 333; Kaeppler, 1977.
11. *Patu onewa,* Florence (144).
    Evidence: Circumstantial. Cook voyage collection from various sources.
    Literature: Giglioli, 1893, pp. 191-192; Kaeppler, 1977.
12. *Patu onewa,* Wellington (ME 2489).
    Evidence: Circumstantial. Probably part of the Cook voyage collection in Bullock's Museum.
    Literature: Kaeppler, 1974a, p. 79.
13. *Patu onewa,* Wellington (ME 7849).
    Evidence: Circumstantial. From the Imperial Institute from Queen Victoria in a box containing "articles brought by Captain Cook from Otaheti."
14. *Patu onewa,* Auckland (33641).
    Evidence: Circumstantial. Said to have been given by Cook to a Mr. Skottowe, whose descendant, M. Beverly Sanders, gave it to Auckland Museum.

Mere Pounamu

These *patu,* of greenstone, are the rarest type of *patu* collected on Cook's voyages. Only two seem to have found their way to known collections, and both of these are missing today.

1. *Mere pounamu,* Exeter (E 1219). Missing.
   Evidence: Leverian Museum.
2. *Mere pounamu,* Oxford (115). Missing.
   Evidence: Forster collection. Second voyage.
   Literature: Gathercole, n.d. [1970].

Patu: Type Unknown

1-4. Four *patu,* Göttingen.
   Evidence: Forster collection. Second voyage.

In addition, there were about seven *patu* in the Leverian Museum that cannot be accounted for today. It is also likely that the Dublin collection included some *patu* from the second and third voyages given by Patten and King, but they cannot be identified in the collection with the available documentation.

[11] However, all *patu onewa* are much alike.

Figure 375. — *Taiaha,* Vienna 17.

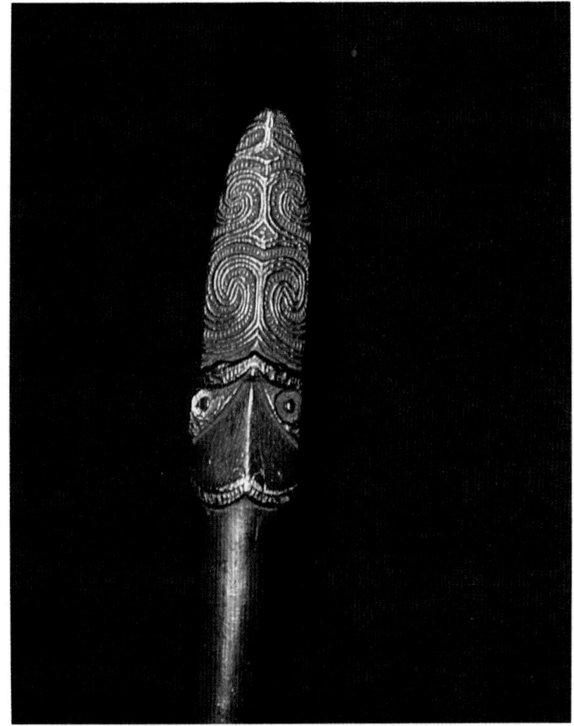

Figure 376. — *Taiaha* (detail), Glasgow E 331.

Long Clubs

Long hand clubs collected on Cook's voyages include *taiaha, pouwhenua,* and *tewhatewha* which were called halberts, spontoons, and battleaxes by 18th century Europeans, although the terms were not applied systematically.[12]

[12]Two *taiaha* and a *tewhatewha* in Wellington in the St. Oswald collection may be from Cook's voyages, but their documentation cannot be traced (Kaeppler, 1974a, p. 79).

1. *Taiaha,* Vienna (17). Length 194 cm. Figure 375.
   Evidence: Leverian Museum.
   Literature: Moschner, 1955, p. 143.

2. *Taiaha,* Glasgow (E 331). Length 145 cm. Figure 376.
   Evidence: Circumstantial. Apparently part of Cook voyage collection from various sources. See Appendix III, this volume.

3. *Taiaha,* Oxford (111). Length 190 cm.
   Evidence: Forster collection. Second voyage.
   Literature: Gathercole, n.d. [1970].

4. *Taiaha* (?), Göttingen (listed as a "long patupatu").
   Evidence: Forster collection. Second voyage.

5. *Taiaha,* Cambridge (1914.61). Length 184.5 cm, width 8.5 cm.
   Evidence: Sandwich collection. Given by Cook, first or second voyage.
   Literature: Shawcross, 1970, p. 317.

6. *Pouwhenua,* Stockholm (1799.2.6). Length 152 cm. Figures 377, 378.
   Evidence: Sparrman collection. Second voyage.
   Literature: Söderström, 1939, p. 48.

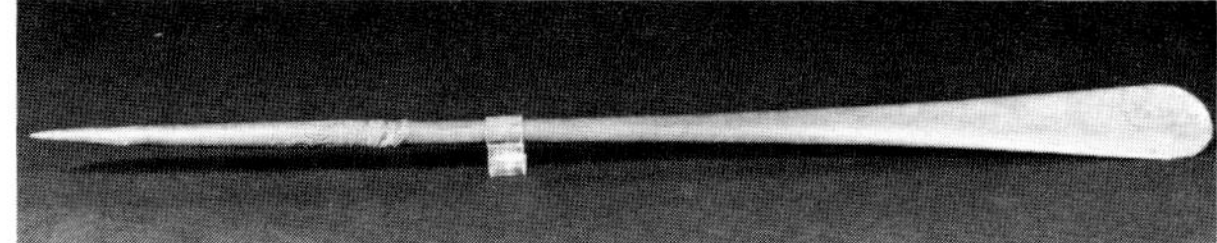

Figure 377. — *Pouwhenua,* Stockholm 1799.2.6.

Figure 378. — *Pouwhenua* (detail), Stockholm 1799.2.6.

7-8. Two *pouwhenua,* Cambridge (1914.62, 1914.63). Lengths 181.5 cm, 171 cm; widths 10 cm, 12 cm.
Evidence: Sandwich collection. Given by Cook, first or second voyage.
Literature: Shawcross, 1970, pp. 317-318.

9. *Pouwhenua,* Göttingen.
Evidence: Purchased from London dealer Humphrey in 1782.

10. *Tewhatewha,* Cambridge (1914.65). Length 137 cm, width of blade, 22.5 cm. Figure 379.
Evidence: Sandwich collection. Given by Cook, first or second voyage.

Figure 379. — *Tewhatewha,* Cambridge 1914.65.

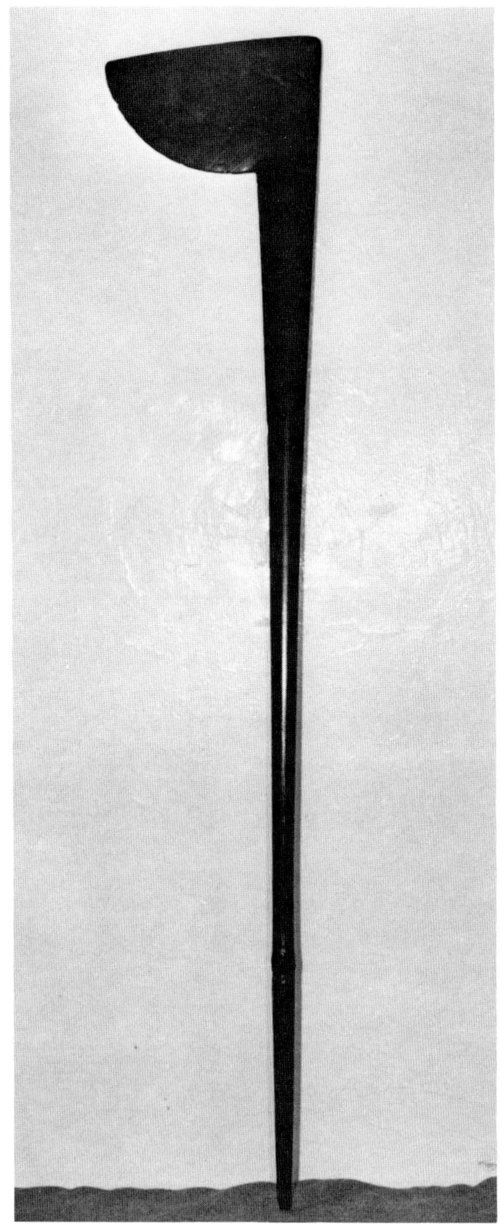

Figure 380. — *Tewhatewha,* Greenwich L15-88.

11. *Tewhatewha,* Stockholm (1848.1.3). Length 122 cm.
    Evidence: "Banks collection."
    Literature: Rydén, 1965, pp. 86-87.

12. *Tewhatewha,* Göttingen.
    Evidence: Purchased from London dealer Humphrey in 1782.

13. *Tewhatewha,* Greenwich (L15-88). Length 133 cm, width of blade 25 cm. Figure 380.
    Evidence: Circumstantial. Part of "Cook collection," but source unknown.

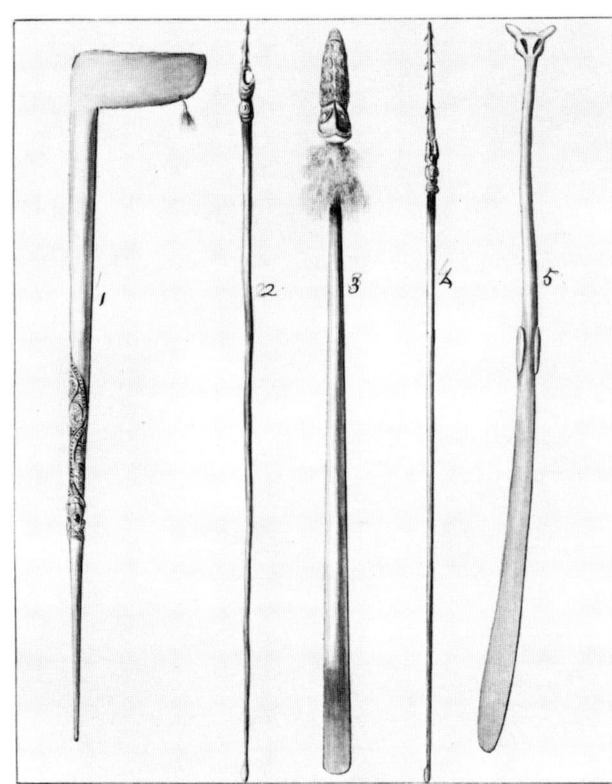

Figure 381. — New Zealand weapons, British Library Add. Ms. 23,920.70.

14. Long club of whale bone. Lost.
    Evidence: Depicted by J. F. Miller in British Library Add. Ms. 23,920.70 (Figure 381). First voyage.

Whipslings and Spears

In contrast to other parts of Polynesia, the Maori sometimes used a whipsling to propel their projectiles.

1. Whipsling *(kotaha),* Stockholm (1848.1.4). Length 143 cm. Figures 382-385.
   Evidence: "Banks collection."
   Literature: Rydén, 1965, pp. 87-88.

2-3. Two whipslings *(kotaha),* British Museum.
   Evidence: Circumstantial. Noted "Cook collection."

4-5. Two spears (one barbed, one unbarbed), Göttingen.
   Evidence: Purchased from London dealer Humphrey in 1782.

6-7. Two spears (one carved with a human figure), British Museum (NZ 72 and 73).
   Evidence: Circumstantial. Noted "Cook collection" because of similarity to that depicted by J. F. Miller in British Library Add. Ms. 23,920.70 (Fig. 381).

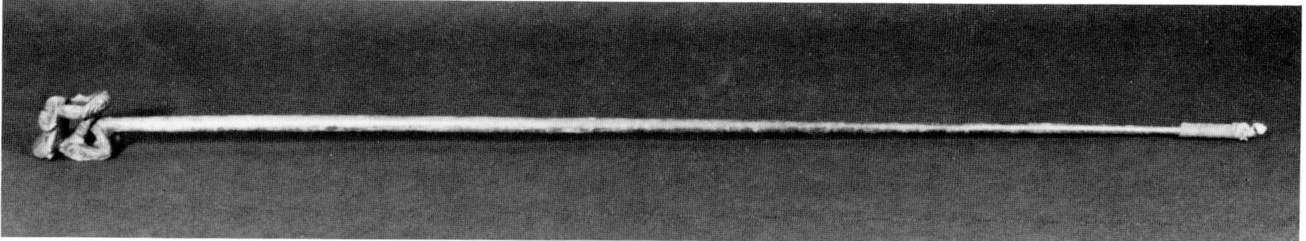

Figure 382. — Whipsling, Stockholm 1848.1.4.

Figure 383. — Whipsling (detail), Stockholm 1848.1.4.

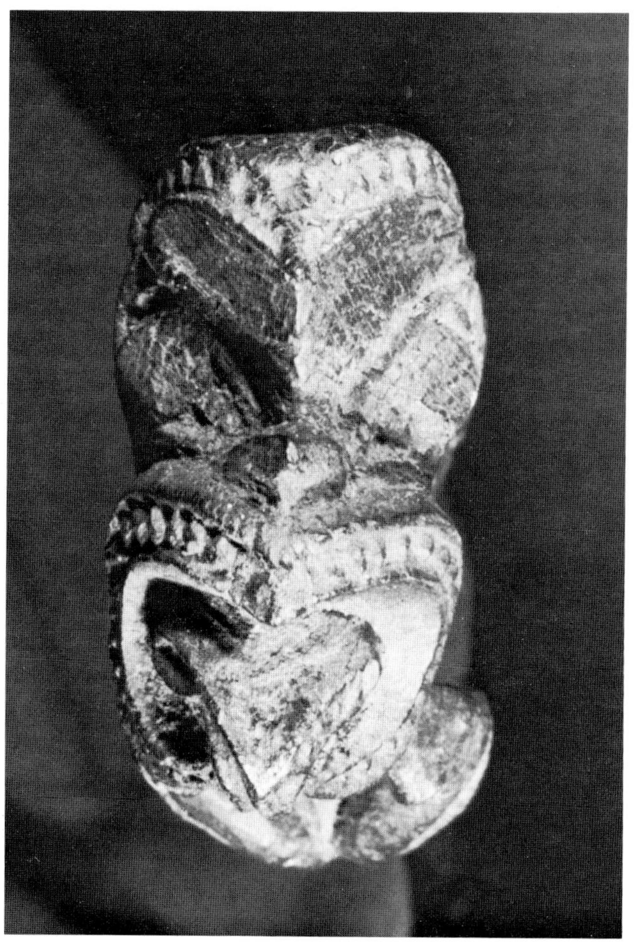

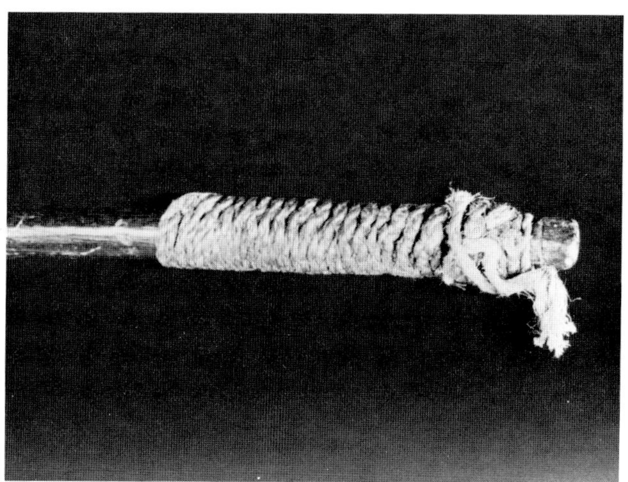

Figure 384. — Whipsling (detail), Stockholm 1848.1.4.

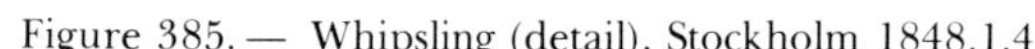

Figure 385. — Whipsling (detail), Stockholm 1848.1.4.

8. Head of a bird spear (carved with barbs), Cambridge (1914.73). Missing.
   Evidence: Sandwich collection. Given by Cook, first or second voyage.
   Literature: Shawcross, 1970, p. 307.

Adzes

Adzes collected on Cook's voyages included ceremonial adzes *(toki pou tangata),* hafted greenstone blades, and unhafted basalt and greenstone blades.

1. *Toki pou tangata* (greenstone blade in a carved haft), Oxford (109). Length of haft 46 cm. Figure 386.
   Evidence: Forster collection. Second voyage.
   Depiction: Cook, 1777, Plate 19 (Fig. 353).
   Literature: Gathercole, n.d. [1970].
2. Hafted adz (greenstone blade in a partly carved haft), Dublin (1894.197). Length of handle 37 cm. Figure 387.
   Evidence: Circumstantial. Noted "Cook collection," given by Patten or King to Trinity College, Dublin.
   Literature: Freeman, 1949, p. 16.
3. Hafted adz (greenstone blade in a plain haft),[13] Stockholm (1799.2.4). Length of handle 40 cm; length of blade 14 cm. Figure 388.
   Evidence: Sparrman collection. Second voyage.
   Literature: Söderström, 1939, pp. 48-49.

[13]A similar adz in Berlin is attributed to Cook's voyages by Barrow (1969, p. 71). This attribution, however, cannot be verified (Kaeppler, 1974a, p. 89). Barrow's drawing makes the Berlin adz appear much thicker than it is—the adz is, in fact, much like the Stockholm specimen.

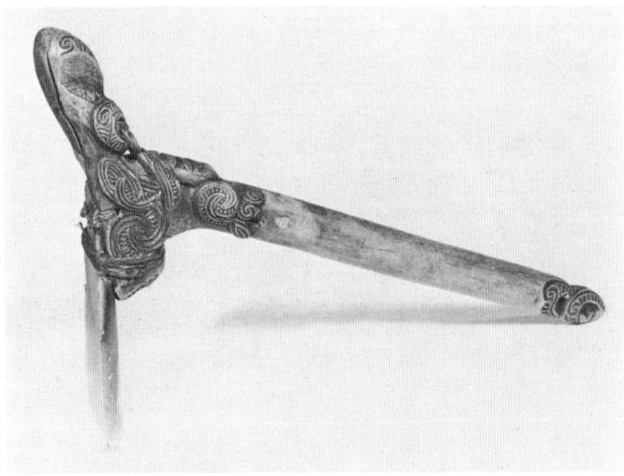

Figure 386.— *Toki pou tangata,* Oxford 109.

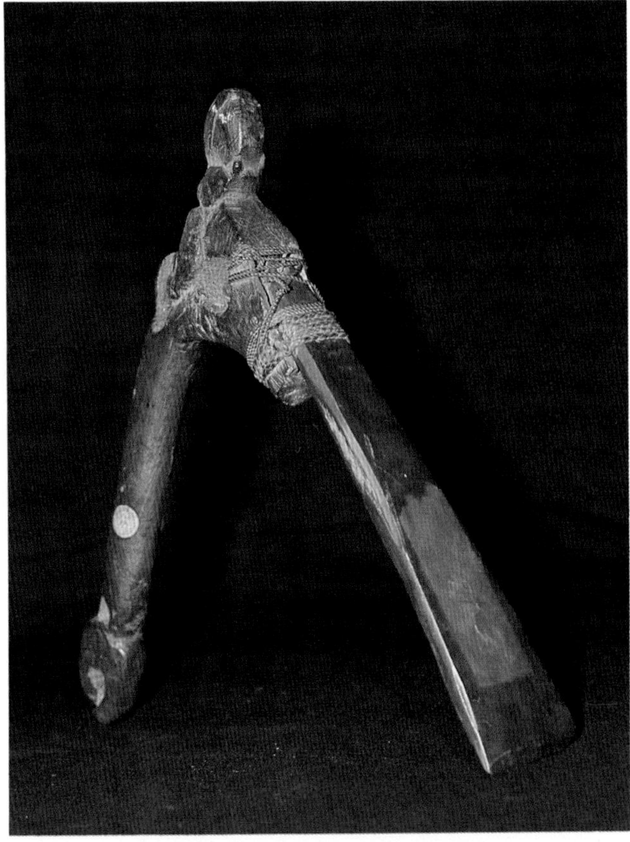

Figure 387.— Hafted adz, Dublin 1894.197.

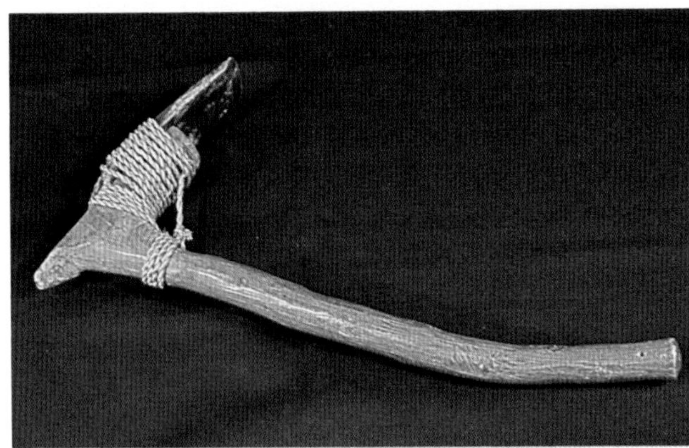

Figure 388.— Hafted adz, Stockholm 1799.2.4.

4. Hafted adz (greenstone blade in a plain haft), Göttingen.
   Evidence: Purchased from London dealer Humphrey in 1782.

5. Greenstone adz blade, Vienna (12). Length 32 cm, width 7 cm. Figure 389.
   Evidence: Leverian Museum.
   Literature: Moschner, 1955, pp. 165-166.

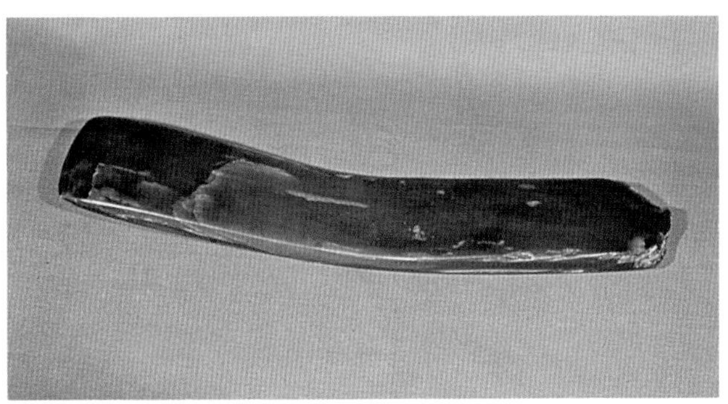

Figure 389. — Greenstone adz blade, Vienna 12.

6-7. Two greenstone adz blades, Cambridge (1914.49, 1914.50). Lengths 4.6 cm, 5.4 cm; widths 4.4 cm, 3.1 cm.
Evidence: Sandwich collection. Given by Cook, first or second voyage.
Literature: Shawcross, 1970, p. 310.

8-9. Two greenstone adz blades, Göttingen.
Evidence: Purchased from London dealer Humphrey in 1782.

10. Greenstone adz blade, Oxford (119). Length 33 cm.
Evidence: Forster collection. Second voyage.
Literature: Gathercole, n.d. [1970].

11. Greenstone adz blade, Wörlitz (21). Length 12.2 cm.
Evidence: Forster collection. Second voyage.
Literature: Germer, 1975, pp. 64, 91.

12-14. Three greenstone adz blades, Sydney (H82, 83, 84).
Evidence: Cook collection exhibited at Colonial and Indian Exhibition.
Literature: Mackrell, 1886; Appendix I, this volume.

15. Basalt adz blade, Göttingen.
Evidence: Purchased from London dealer Humphrey in 1782.

16. Basalt adz blade, British Museum (NZ 153). Missing.
Evidence: Circumstantial. Noted "Cook collection No. 25"

17. Basalt adz blade, Sydney (H 81).
Evidence: Cook collection exhibited at the Colonial and Indian Exhibition.
Literature: Mackrell, 1886; Appendix I, this volume.

Chisels

Greenstone chisels were often hafted in a handle of wood with flax binding. The flax bindings for both chisels and adzes were not done in decorative patterns, as among the Society Islanders.

1. Greenstone chisel, Vienna (19). Length 6.4 cm, width .6 cm.
Evidence: Leverian Museum.
Literature: Moschner, 1955, p. 166.

2. Greenstone chisel, Oxford (121). Missing.
Evidence: Forster collection. Second voyage.
Literature: Gathercole, n.d. [1970].

3. Greenstone chisel, Göttingen.
Evidence: Purchased from London dealer Humphrey in 1782.

4. Greenstone chisel, British Museum (NZ 101).
Evidence: Circumstantial. Noted "Cook collection."

Other Tools

1-4. Four obsidian carving tools, Cambridge (1914.51).
Evidence: Sandwich collection. Given by Cook, first or second voyage.
Literature: Shawcross, 1970, pp. 311-312.

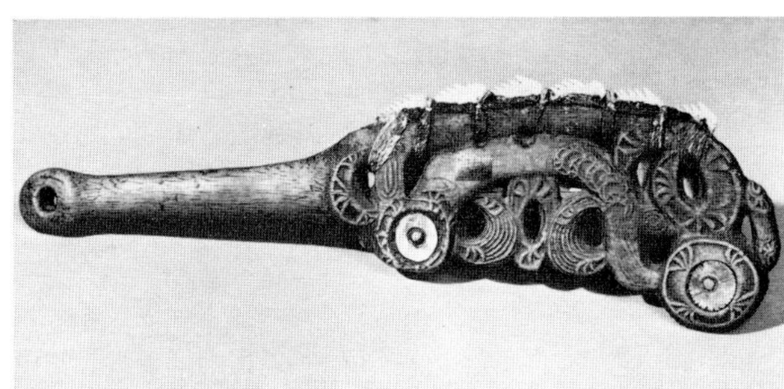

Figure 390. — Shark tooth knife, Oxford 110.

Shark Tooth Knives

Cutting implements with inset shark teeth were usually known as *mira tuatini,* because the teeth come from the *tuatini* shark. Often elaborately carved, they were probably used for ceremonial purposes by persons of high status.[14]

1. Shark tooth knife, Oxford (110). Length 25.5 cm. Figure 390.
   Evidence: Forster collection. Second voyage.
   Depictions: Cook, 1777, Plate 19 (Fig. 353).
   Literature: Gathercole, n.d. [1970].
2. Shark tooth knife, British Museum (NZ 166).
   Evidence: Circumstantial. Noted "Cook collection." Perhaps the knife depicted by Clevely (British Library Add. Ms. 23,920.69).

[14] A shark tooth knife in Glasgow was attributed to Captain King by Barrow (1969, p. 125). The accession records in Glasgow do not confirm the King attribution for this particular piece, although King did give other objects to the Hunterian collection, and the knife is similar in style to the knife in Oxford.

Figure 391.— Fern root beater, Oxford 173.

Figure 392.— New Zealand house with carved lintel, British Library Add. Ms. 17,277.8.

Figure 393.— Inside a *pa* in New Zealand, British Library Add. Ms. 15,513.6.

Figure 394. — House carving, British Library Add. Ms. 23,920.75.

Food Preparation

Few objects used for food preparation or as food containers were collected—perhaps because exchanges usually took place away from the villages.

1. Fern root beater, Oxford (173). Length 43.5 cm. Figure 391.
   Evidence: Forster collection. Second voyage.
   Literature: Gathercole, n.d. [1970].

House Carvings

No house carvings can today be traced to collection on Cook's voyages. A carved lintel was depicted *in situ* by Webber (British Library Add. Ms. 17,277.8 [Fig. 392] and 15,513.6 [Fig. 393]) but apparently was not collected.[15] A carving was depicted by J. F. Miller (British Library Add. Ms. 23,920.75), which apparently was collected on Cook's first voyage (Fig. 394), but unfortunately it cannot be located.

[15]A house carving now in the Nelson Gallery of Art, Kansas City (formerly in the Berlin Museum), is often attributed to Cook's voyages. However, it can only be traced as far back as 1819 when it was sold from Bullock's London Museum—and is with little doubt not from Cook's voyages (Kaeppler, 1974a, p. 82). This piece had been missing from Berlin for some time and has again come to light.

Figure 395. — New Zealand war canoe, British Library Add. Ms. 23,920.49.

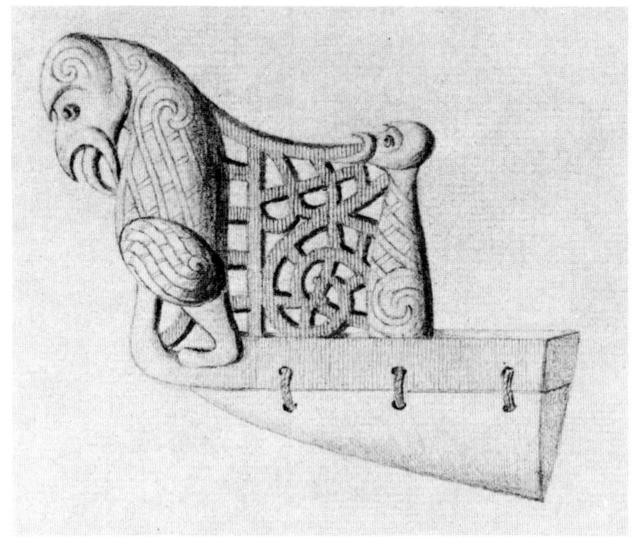

Figure 396.— Canoe ornament, British Library Add. Ms. 23,920.79.

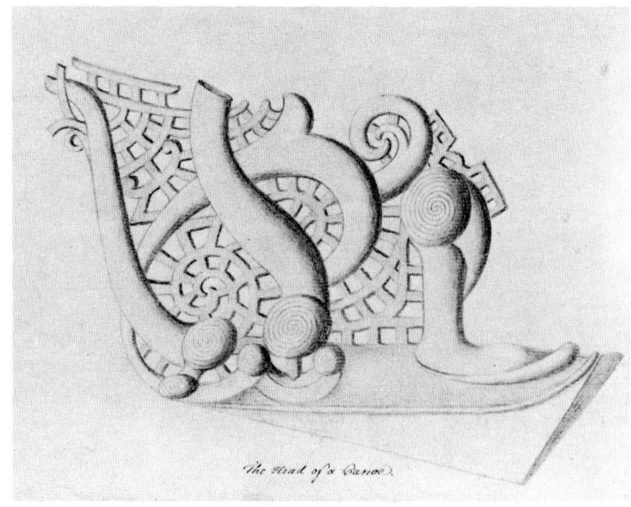

Figure 397.— Canoe ornament, British Library Add. Ms. 23,920.79.

Figure 398.— Artifacts from New Zealand, Tierra del Fuego, and Australia, Plate 26 of Parkinson's journal.

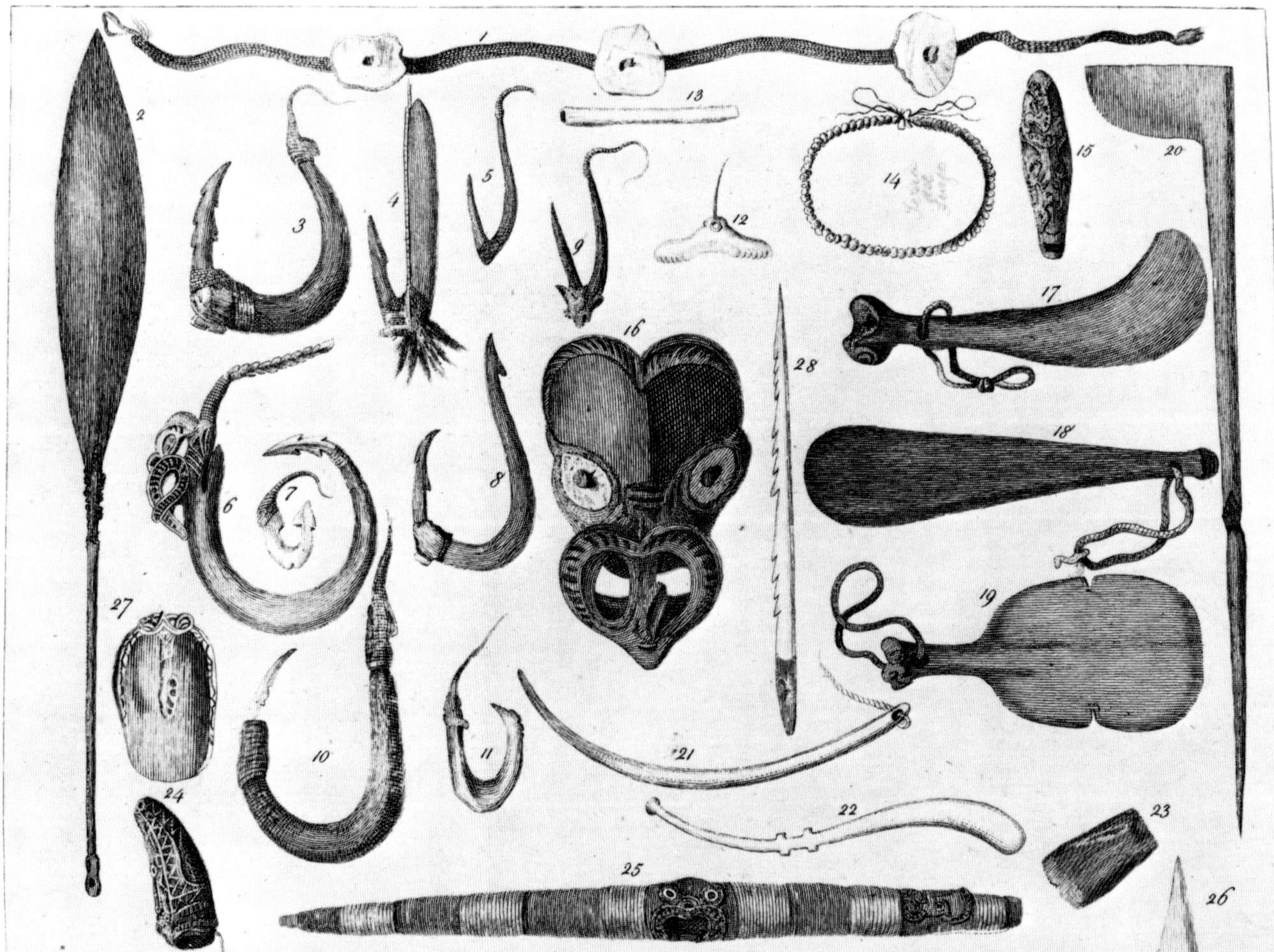

Figure 399. — Wood carving, Göttingen OZ 323.

Figure 400. — Wood carving (side view), Göttingen OZ 323.

Canoe Prow Ornaments

No canoe prow ornaments as depicted during the voyages (see, for example, Figs. 395-397) appear to have been collected—at least none can be traced to a Cook voyage provenance. Two small carvings which may be canoe prow ornaments were collected, and a third was depicted (Fig. 398) but cannot be located.

1. Wood carving (possibly from a canoe), Göttingen (OZ 323). Length 29 cm, width 6.5 cm, height 8.2 cm. Figures 399, 400.
   Evidence: Purchased from London dealer Humphrey in 1782.

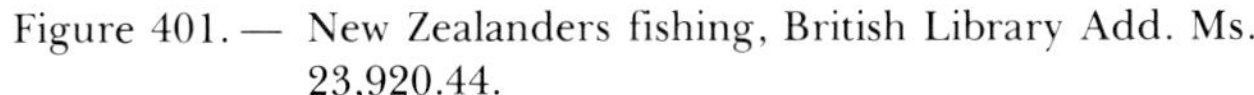

Figure 401. — New Zealanders fishing, British Library Add. Ms. 23,920.44.

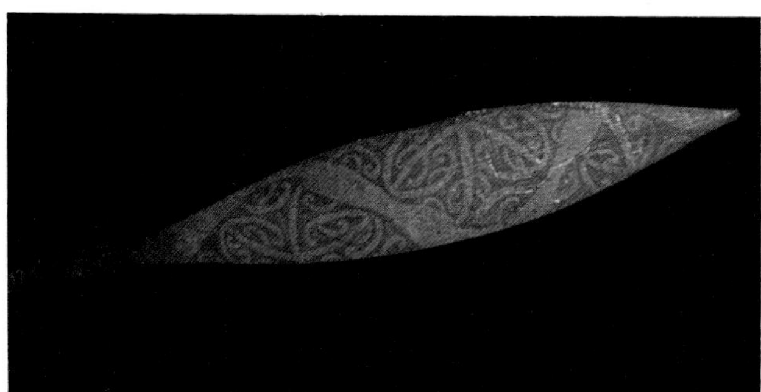
Figure 402.— Paddle blade, Cambridge 1914.66.

2. Wood carving (possibly from a canoe), Cambridge (1914.65). Length 31 cm.
   Evidence: Sandwich collection. Given by Cook, first or second voyage.
   Literature: Shawcross, 1970, pp. 339-341. Shawcross and others have explained these objects as ceremonial bird snares—an argument that seems of doubtful validity when these are compared with other Maori bird snares. A drawing in the British Library (Add. Ms. 23,920.44 [Fig. 401]) depicts a canoe prow ornament somewhat similar.

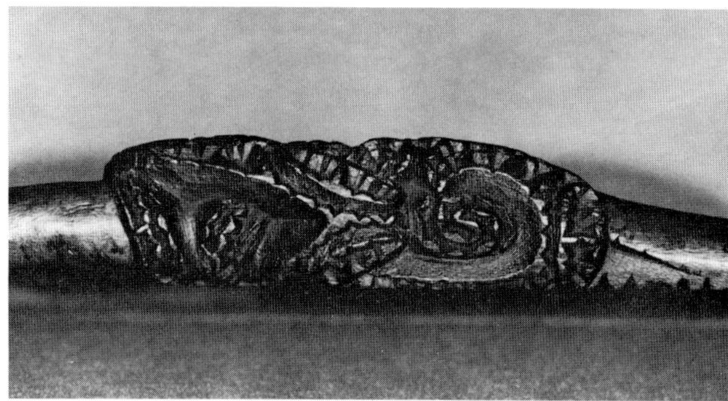
Figure 403.— Detail of paddle carving, Cambridge 1914.66.

Paddles

Some canoe paddles collected on Cook's voyages are beautifully decorated with painting on the blades similar to painting used on house rafters, some with relief carving at midpoint or end,[16] some with images carved on the blades in relief,[17] and some are undecorated.

⛵ 1-2. Two paddles (decorated with painting and carving), Cambridge (1914.66, 67). Lengths 180 cm, width 15 cm. Figures 402-404.
   Evidence: Sandwich collection. Given by Cook, probably from the second voyage.
   Literature: Shawcross, 1970, pp. 320-321.
3. Paddle (decorated with carving), Florence (248). Length 193 cm, width 14 cm.
   Evidence: Circumstantial. Cook voyage collection from various sources.
   Literature: Giglioli, 1893, pp. 189-190; Kaeppler, 1977.

Figure 404.— Detail of paddle carving, Cambridge 1914.66.

[16]A carved and painted paddle in the Hooper collection (50) is thought by Phelps to be from Cook's voyages (1976, pp. 27, 412), but this cannot be confirmed.

[17]Three paddles depicted by Sarah Stone in the Leverian Museum are so decorated (Force and Force, 1968, pp. 114, 128), but they cannot be located.

Figure 405.— Paddle, British Museum NZ 150.

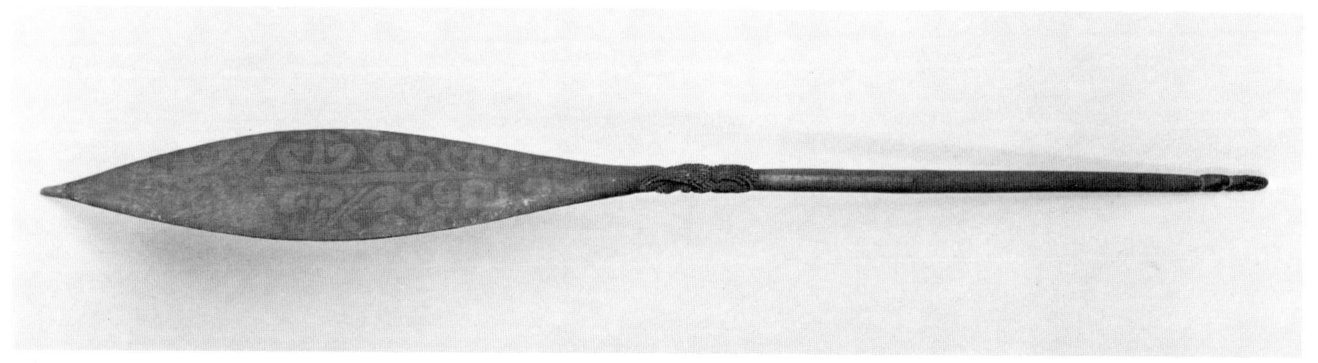

4. Paddle (decorated with carving), Göttingen.
   Evidence: Purchased from London dealer Humphrey in 1782.
5. Paddle (decorated with painting and carving), British Museum (NZ 150). Figure 405.
   Evidence: Circumstantial. Noted "Cook coll." because of its similarity to the one depicted in British Library Add. Ms. 15,508.29 (Fig. 284).
6. Paddle (decorated with a human face carved in relief), Dublin (1894.352). Length 196 cm, width 18 cm. Figure 406.
   Evidence: Circumstantial. Thought to be part of the collection given to Trinity College, Dublin, by Patten or King.
7. Paddle (undecorated), Vienna (24). Length 168 cm, width of blade 13 cm. Figure 407.
   Evidence: Leverian Museum.
   Literature: Moschner, 1955, pp. 172-173.

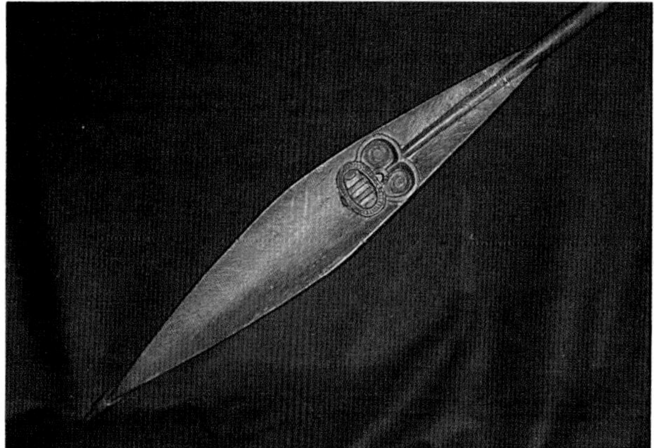

Figure 406.— Paddle blade, Dublin 1894.352.

Figure 407.— Paddle, Vienna 24.

Bailers

Maori bailers collected on Cook's voyages have limited but superb carving. All that have been traced are cracked and have indigenous repairs made with flax fiber.

1. Bailer, Oxford (117). Length 46 cm. Figure 408.
   Evidence: Forster collection. Second voyage.
   Literature: Gathercole, n.d. [1970].
2. Bailer, British Museum (NZ 123). Figure 409.
   Evidence: Circumstantial. Noted "Cook collection" because of its similarity to that depicted in British Library Add. Ms. 15,508.28 (Fig. 282).

Figure 408.— Bailer, Oxford 117.

Figure 409.— Bailer, British Museum NZ 123.

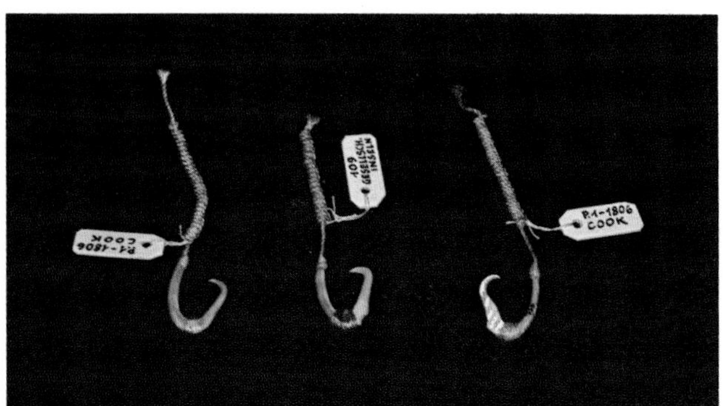

Figure 410. — Three fishhooks, Vienna 109, 111, 112.

3. Bailer, Cambridge (22.933).
Evidence: Circumstantial. Probably from the Leverian Museum.

4. Bailer, Location unknown.
Evidence: Leverian Museum.
Depictions: Force and Force, 1968, p. 130.

Fishing Equipment

1-4. Four fishhooks, Vienna (109, 110, 111, 112). Lengths 2.8 cm, 2.8 cm, 3 cm, 3 cm. Figure 410.
Evidence: Leverian Museum.
Literature: Moschner, 1955, pp. 182-183, 189.

5-9. Four fishhooks and an oval stone sinker, Cambridge (1914.68-72).
Evidence: Sandwich collection. Given by Cook, first or second voyage.
Literature: Shawcross, 1970, p. 309.

10. Fishhook (wood shank with bone point), Cambridge (25.382).[18]
Evidence: Pennant collection of Cook voyage objects from various sources.
Literature: Shawcross, 1970, pp. 309-310.

11-12. Two fishhooks, Florence (36, 198).
Evidence: Circumstantial. Cook voyage collection from various sources.
Literature: Giglioli, 1893, pp. 190-191; Kaeppler, 1977.

13-28. Sixteen fishhooks (attributed to New Zealand), Göttingen.
Evidence: Purchased from London dealer Humphrey in 1782.

29. Fishhook point, Bishop Museum (1970.221.03). Length 7.9 cm.
Evidence: Leverian Museum.

30-31. Two fishhooks with sinkers, Wellington (MÉ 12118, 12119).
Evidence: Circumstantial. From the Imperial Institute, from Queen Victoria in a box containing "articles brought by Captain Cook from Otaheti."

Figure 411. — Wooden image ("planting stick"), British Museum NZ 68.

[18]See also Figure 198 above.

32. Fishhook (wood with bone point), Sydney (H 137).
    Evidence: Cook collection exhibited at Colonial and Indian Exhibition.
    Literature: Mackrell, 1886; Appendix I, this volume.
33. Fishhook, Taranaki Museum (46.832).
    Evidence: Circumstantial. Bullock's Museum, from the Leverian Museum and Banks.
    Literature: Duff, 1969, p. 48; Kaeppler, 1974a, p. 80.
34-39. Six fishhooks, Wellington.
    Evidence: Circumstantial. Bullock's Museum, from Leverian Museum and Banks.
    Literature: Kaeppler, 1974a, p. 80.

Wooden Images

Two objects depicted by J. F. Miller are noted "planting sticks." They are similar to Maori god sticks and weaving pegs.

1. "Planting stick." Wellington.
   Evidence: Circumstantial. Depicted by J. F. Miller in a drawing in the British Library (Add. Ms. 15,508.26) (Fig. 238).

2. "Planting stick." British Museum NZ 68. Figure 411.
   Evidence: Circumstantial. Noted "Cook collection." Possibly the object depicted by J. F. Miller in British Library Add. Ms. 15,508.28 (Fig. 282).

Other artifact types that were depicted but examples cannot be located include a top and a carved bone "thatching needle" (British Library Add. Ms. 23,920.73), and a necklace/belt(?) depicted in the artifact plate published in Parkinson's journal (Fig. 398[1]). Other objects which may not have been collected but were depicted *in situ* include a gourd container and human head (Add. Ms. 23,920.49) Figure 395, and fish trap and hoop net (Add. Ms. 23,920.44) Figure 401.

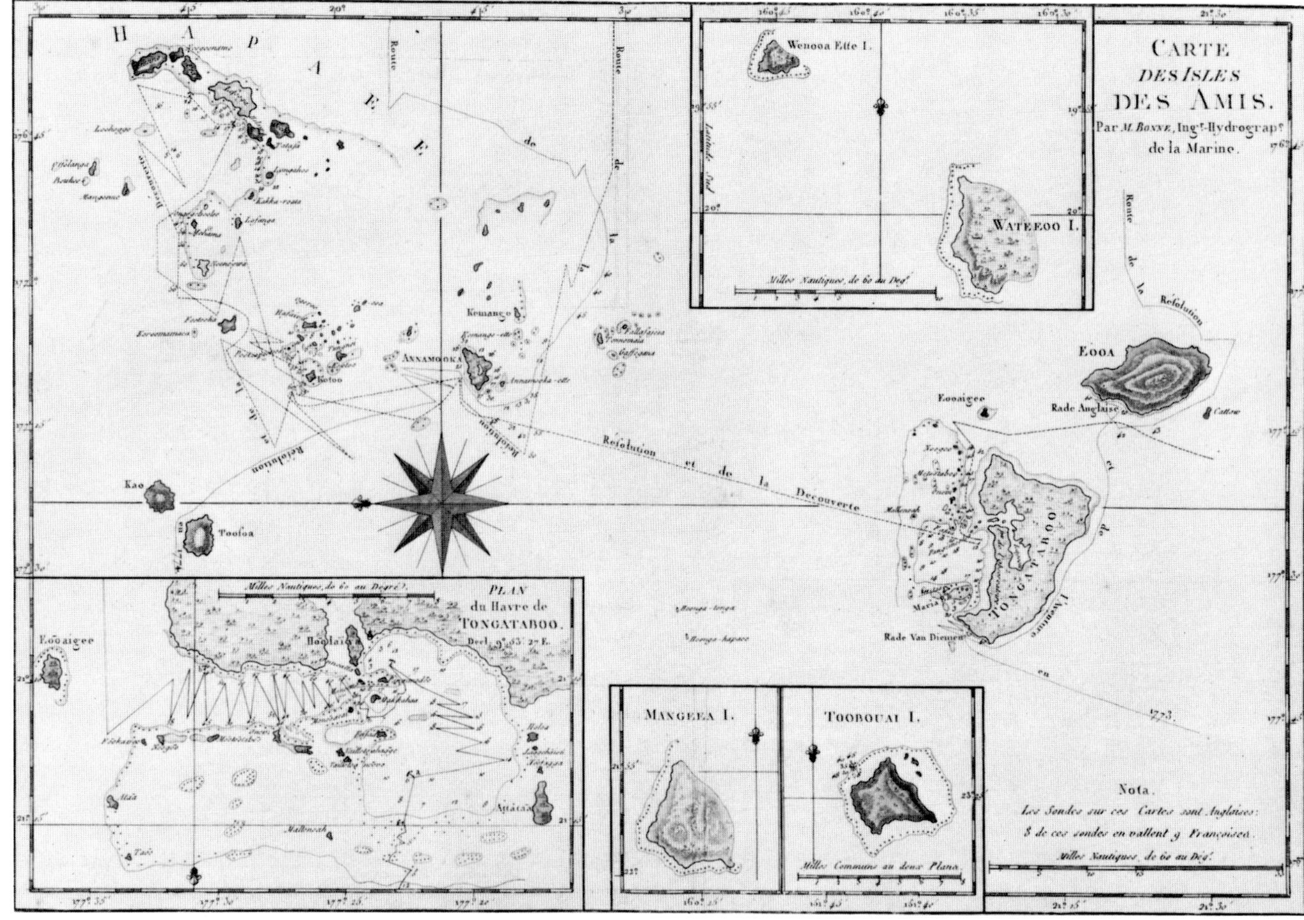

Figure 412. — Map of Tonga from Cook's third voyage (57).

THE FRIENDLY ISLES (TONGA)

The existence of the Tongan Islands had been known to Europeans since the early 17th century when the northern part of the group was discovered by Le Maire in 1616. Tasman visited and described some of the southern islands in 1643, and northern islands were seen by Wallis in 1767. However, no Tongan objects from these voyages can be identified today. Although Tasman records trading for curiosities in his journals, it is unlikely that any of these objects ever reached Europe. The problems at the end of Tasman's voyage are well known (Sharp, 1968), and the objects, if any of them survived, probably went no further than Batavia (Jakarta).[1]

These short, early visits probably had little significant effect on Tongan material culture, and the artifacts collected by Cook's ships during his second voyage (1773-1774) are relatively free of European influence. But even by this time the existence of iron was known to the Tongans, and the Forsters collected a hafted iron nail (now in the Pitt Rivers Museum) which Cook was told was one of five nails traded by Wallis for a club at Niuatoputapu in 1767 (Beaglehole, 1967, p. 162). The iron tools traded to the Tongans during the second voyage stimulated an efflorescence in Tongan carving and, by the third voyage, wooden objects are noticeably different. Thus, when studying Tongan objects from Cook's voyages, it is useful to be able to separate them as to voyage, not only because of the changes in material culture by the time of the third voyage, but also because the rank and status of chiefs met during the two voyages were different, and material culture and social status can be related by a type of verified historic documentation that is unusual in the study of Pacific ethnography (Kaeppler, 1971).

A large number of Tongan specimens were collected on Cook's voyages, and many of these objects can be separated as to voyage. It will be seen that a few objects included here with Tonga are Fijian and Samoan in style. This is extremely useful in the study of Tongan material culture in pre-European times, for as

[1]Although Barrow would have us believe that a club now in the Instituut Voor de Tropen, Amsterdam, came from Tasman's voyage (Barrow, 1972, p. 74), there is no documentation and no reason to believe that this is so. Indeed, the club is with little doubt of 19th century style.

Cook's ships did not visit Fiji (except the small island of Vatoa where the natives fled), or Samoa, it is probable that these objects were collected in Tonga. Thus, trade among Tonga, Fiji and Samoa in pre-European times can be documented by actual objects collected in Tonga as well as by accounts of Tongans.

Tongan objects are often accessioned as from "Otaheite," a catchall phrase which encompassed all of central Polynesia, Tonga, and sometimes even New Zealand and Hawaii. Early museums and collections usually did not separate Tongan materials as a distinct series, and localization is based on those collectors who did separate them, such as the Forsters and David Samwell. Some artifact types are still difficult to separate as to place of origin, and will be so noted in this Catalogue.

Ornaments

A large number of ornaments—necklaces, carved ivory pieces which were hung from necklaces and attached to sennit girdles, elements from decorative girdles, bracelets, and anklets—were collected on Cook's voyages.

Ivory Images

1. Human image of ivory, Vienna (146). Height 6.2 cm, width at shoulders 3.5 cm. Figure 413.
   Evidence: Leverian Museum.
   Literature: Moschner, 1955, p. 228.
2. Human image of ivory, John Hewett collection. Height 3.5 cm, width at shoulders 2 cm. Figure 414.
   Evidence: Cook collection exhibited at the Colonial and Indian Exhibition.
   Literature: Mackrell, 1886; Appendix I, this volume.
3. Human image of ivory, Sydney (H 151). Height 5.3 cm, width at shoulder 2.5 cm. Figure 415.
   Evidence: Cook collection exhibited at the Colonial and Indian Exhibition.
   Literature: Mackrell, 1886; Appendix I, this volume.

Other Carved Ivory Pieces

1-5. Ivory bird and four others, Vienna (81-83 [all exhibited], 84). Length of bird 6.5 cm. Figure 416.

Figure 413. — Ivory image, Vienna 146.

Figure 414. — Ivory image, Hewett collection.

Figure 415. — Ivory image, Sydney H 151.

Evidence: Leverian Museum.
Literature: Moschner, 1955, pp. 209, 214.

6-14. Ivory bird, neck rest, cowry shell and six other ivory pieces, Göttingen. Length of bird 3.5 cm, headrest 3.5 cm, shell 3.2 cm.
Evidence: Purchased from London dealer Humphrey in 1782.
Literature: Plischke, 1939, pp. 137-138.

15. Carved ivory piece of cone shape. Location unknown.
Evidence: Cook collection exhibited at Colonial and Indian Exhibition.
Literature: Mackrell, 1886; Appendix I, this volume.

Figure 416. — Carved ivory pieces, Vienna 81-83.

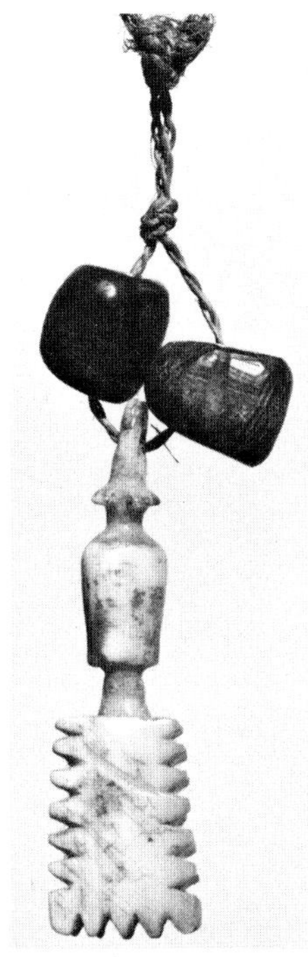

Figure 417. — Ornament of ivory and turtle shell, Sydney H 119.

16. Ornament of carved ivory piece with two turtle shell beads, Sydney (H 119). Ivory piece 4.5 cm. Figure 417.
Evidence: Cook collection exhibited at Colonial and Indian Exhibition..
Literature: Mackrell, 1886; Appendix I, this volume.

17. Ornament of carved ivory piece with beads of shell and turtle shell, Dunedin (D62.998FF). Figure 418.
Evidence: Given by Mrs. Cook to her cousin, who was the great grandmother of a Mrs. Hawker, who gave it to Otago Museum.

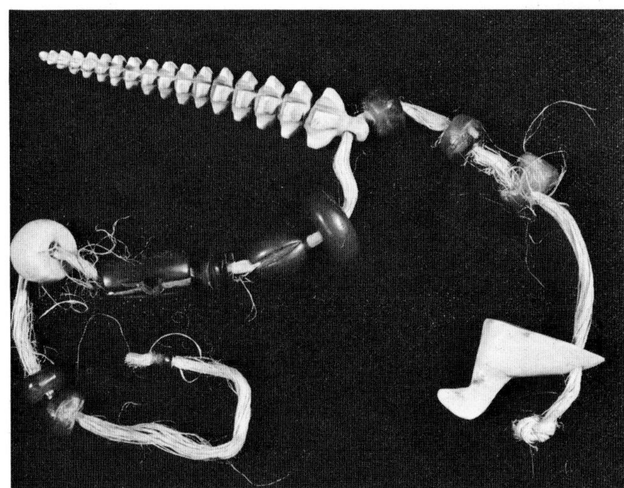

Figure 418. — Tongan ornament with Eskimo bird, Dunedin D62.998FF.

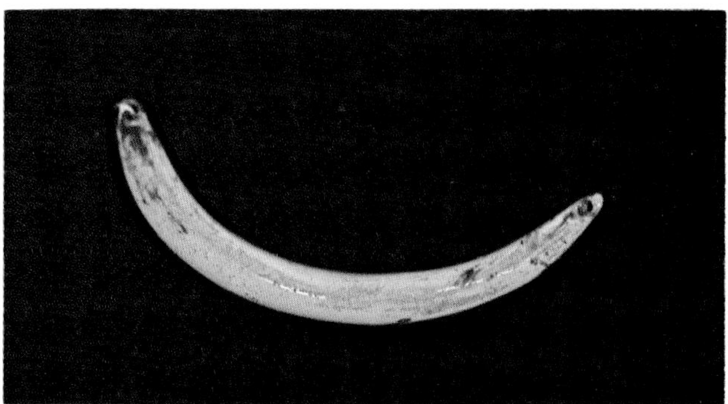

Figure 419. — Ivory ornament, Exeter E 1230.

18. Ivory crescent, Exeter (E 1230). Length 9 cm. Figure 419.
    Evidence: Leverian Museum.

19-20. Two ivory pieces ("earsticks"), Oxford (99). Missing.
    Evidence: Forster collection, second voyage.
    Literature: Gathercole, n.d. [1970].

21. Carved ivory piece, Florence (204).
    Evidence: Circumstantial. Cook voyage collection from various sources.
    Literature: Giglioli, 1893, pp. 187-188; Kaeppler, 1977.

Necklaces and Other Ornaments

1-3. Two necklaces of pearl shell, bird bone, shells, and stone, and a shell leg ornament, Vienna (78, 79, 195, all exhibited). Lengths 78.5 cm, 53 cm, 17.5 cm. Figures 420, 421, 422.
    Evidence: Leverian Museum.
    Literature: Moschner, 1955, p. 207.

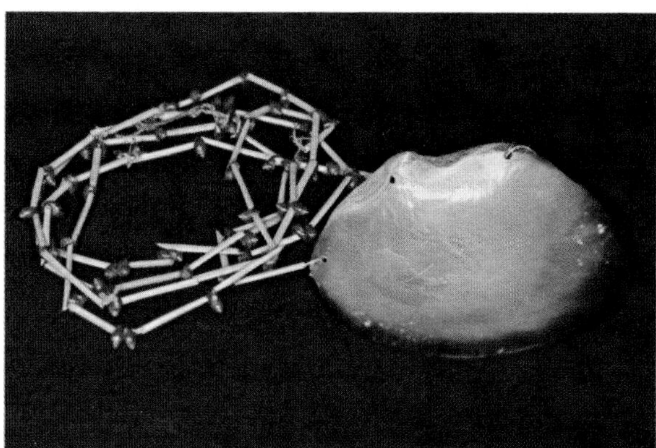

Figure 421. — Necklace, Vienna 79.

Figure 420. — Necklace, Vienna 78.

4-6. Three shell necklaces, Sydney (H116, 117, 152 all exhibited). Lengths 75 cm, 26 cm, 140 cm. Figure 423.
    Evidence: Cook collection exhibited at Colonial and Indian Exhibition.
    Literature: Mackrell, 1886; Appendix I, this volume.

7-9. Three necklaces, Stockholm (1799.2.29 a & b, 1799.2.30 [exhibited]). Lengths 426 cm, 256 cm, 130 cm. Figure 424.
    Evidence: Sparrman collection, second voyage.
    Literature: Söderström, 1939, pp. 45-46.

10-13. Four necklaces, Berne (FR 16, 18, 19, 27).
    Evidence: Webber collection, third voyage.
    Literature: Kaeppler, 1977.

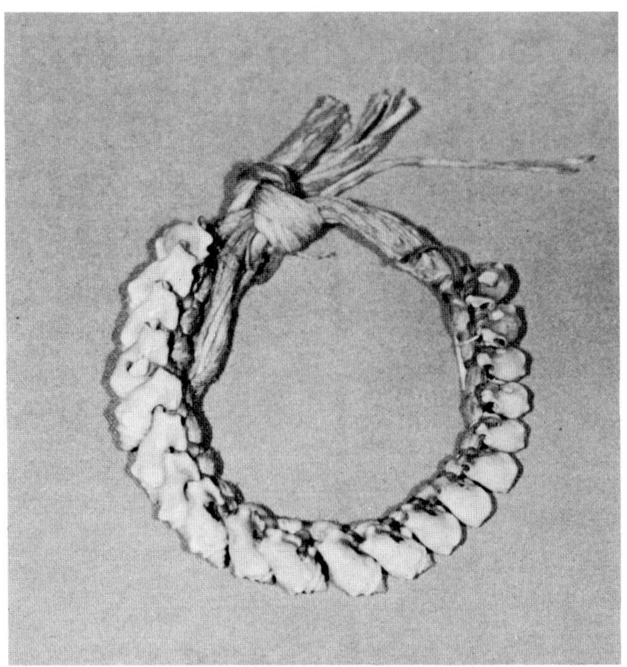

Figure 422. — Leg ornament, Vienna 195.

14-18. Five necklaces of shell, bird bone, coconut shell, ivory pendants, teeth, etc. Oxford (98).
Evidence: Forster collection, second voyage.
Literature: Gathercole, n.d. [1970]; Kaeppler, 1971, p. 217.

19-26. Eight necklaces, Cambridge (22.941-22.945, 27.1641). Figure 425.
Evidence: Leverian Museum.

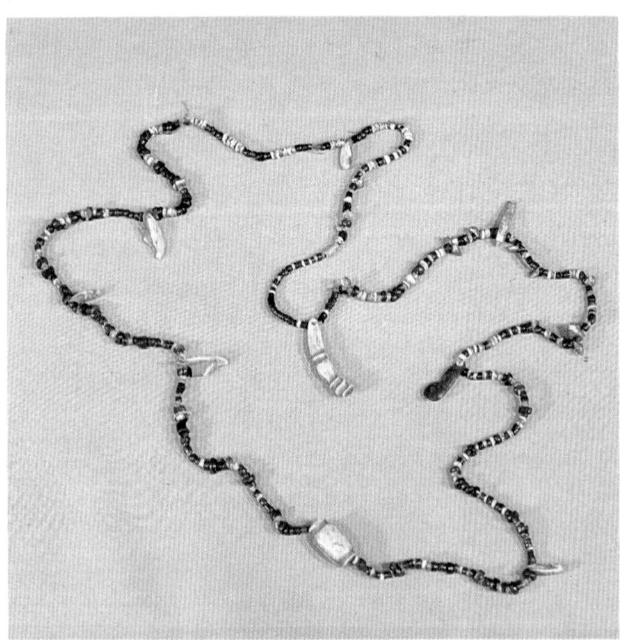

Figure 424. — Necklace, Stockholm 1799.2.30.

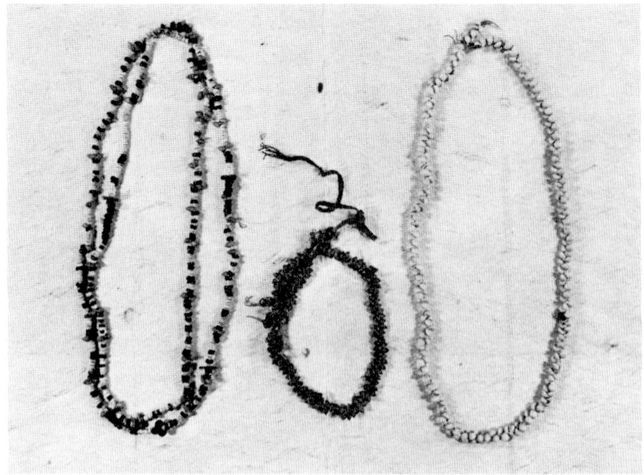

Figure 423. — Three shell necklaces, Sydney H 116, 117, 152.

27-32. Six necklaces of bird bone, shell, coconut shell, and coral, Florence (73b, 54, 81, 213, 207, 65).
Evidence: Cook voyage collection from various sources.
Literature: Giglioli, 1893, pp. 204-206; Kaeppler, 1977.

33-42. Ten necklaces, Göttingen.
Evidence: Purchased from London dealer Humphrey in 1782.

43-44. Two necklaces of shells and bird bone, Wörlitz (10, 11). Lengths 60 cm, 66 cm.
Evidence: Forster collection, second voyage.
Literature: Germer, 1975, pp. 83 and 90.

45-46. Two shell necklaces, Wellington (FE 3024).
Evidence: Circumstantial. From the Imperial Institute from Queen Victoria in a box containing "articles brought by Captain Cook from Otaheti."

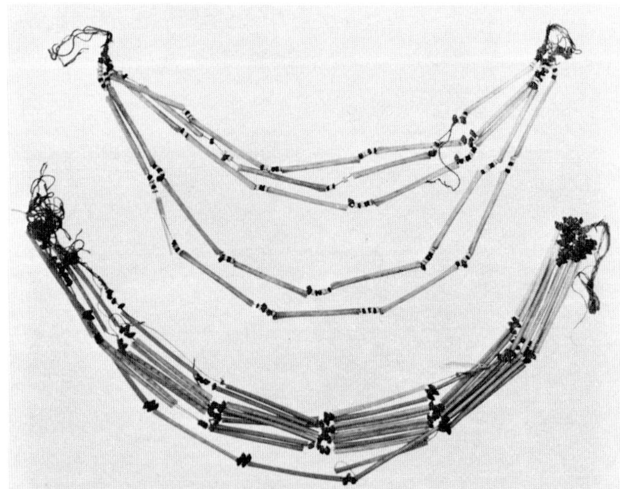

Figure 425. — Two bird bone and shell necklaces, Cambridge 22.944a, 22.944b.

47-50. **Four "gorgets," Göttingen.**
Evidence: Purchased from London dealer Humphrey in 1782.

51-53. Three "mother of pearl shells which hang on the breast," Oxford (98). Missing.
Evidence: Forster collection, second voyage.
Literature: Gathercole, n.d. [1970].

54. Ornament with shell pendant, Stockholm (1799.2.32).
Evidence: Sparrman collection, second voyage.
Literature: Söderström, 1939, p. 46.

55. Two ornaments with shell pendant, Göttingen (OZ 190, 220).
Evidence: Purchased from London dealer Humphrey in 1782.
Literature: Plischke, 1939, pp. 137-138.

56. Ornament with shell pendant, Oxford (100). Missing.
Evidence: Forster collection, second voyage.
Literature: Gathercole, n.d. [1970].

57. Beads and shells for ornaments, Göttingen.
Evidence: Purchased from London dealer Humphrey in 1782.

58. Ornament of yellow shells on sennit (probably part of an ornamental girdle), Cambridge (22.940 a & b).
Evidence: Leverian Museum.

59. Ornament of yellow shells on sennit (probably part of an ornamental girdle), Göttingen.
Evidence: Purchased from London dealer Humphrey in 1782.

60-61. Two ornaments of shells, Berne (FR 17 and FR 25).
Evidence: Webber collection, third voyage.
Literature: Kaeppler, 1977.

62. Bracelet of a shell circlet (attributed to Tonga, but perhaps New Hebrides), Florence (212).
Evidence: Circumstantial. Cook voyage collection from various sources.
Literature: Giglioli, 1893, p. 204; Kaeppler, 1977.

63. Bracelet of a shell circlet (attributed to Tonga, but perhaps New Hebrides), Göttingen.
Evidence: Purchased from London dealer Humphrey in 1782.

64. Breast plate/shield of whalebone, Oxford (62). Diameter 45 cm. Figure 426.
Evidence: Forster collection, second voyage.
Literature: Gathercole, n.d. [1970], p. 14; Kaeppler, 1971, pp. 216-217.

65. Breast plate/shield of whalebone, Göttingen. Diameter 50.5 cm.
Evidence: Forster collection, second voyage.
Literature: Plischke, 1939, pp. 121-136.

Combs

Combs collected on Cook's voyages are invariably made of the midribs of coconut leaflets which are intertwined with sennit in various shades of natural, brown, and black to form decorative patterns. They are either squared off at the top or form an extended triangle.

1-2. Two combs, Stockholm (1799.2.12 and 13). Lengths 13 cm, 10.5 cm. Figure 427.
Evidence: Sparrman collection, second voyage.
Literature: Söderström, 1939, p. 45.

3-8. Six combs, Vienna (10, 11, 85, 86, 87, 88). Lengths 15.6 cm, 14 cm, 13.5 cm, 13 cm, 10.5 cm, 11.6 cm.
Evidence: Leverian Museum.
Literature: Moschner, 1955, pp. 217-219.

9-11. Three combs, Oxford (97). Lengths 12.5 cm, 16 cm, 12.5 cm.
Evidence: Forster collection, second voyage.
Literature: Gathercole, n.d. [1970].

12-13. Two combs, Wörlitz (12, 13). Lengths 14.4 cm, 12.8 cm.
Evidence: Forster collection, second voyage.
Literature: Germer, 1975, pp. 84, 90.

14-19. Six combs, Berne (FR 10 a-f).
Evidence: Webber collection, third voyage.
Literature: Henking, 1957, pp. 336-337; Kaeppler, 1977.

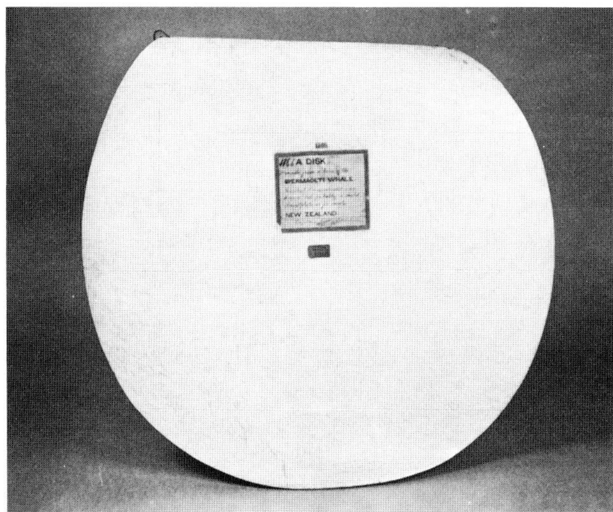

Figure 426. — Whalebone breast plate, Oxford 62.

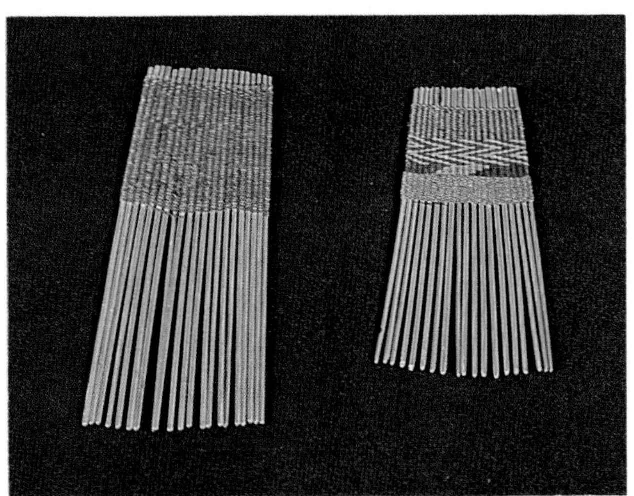

Figure 427. — Two combs, Stockholm 1799.2.12 and 13.

20-21. Two combs, Leningrad (505-22, 505-23). Lengths 16.5 cm and 11 cm.
Evidence: Given by Captain Clerke to Governor of Kamchatka.
Literature: Rozina, 1966, pp. 242-243; Kaeppler, 1977.

22-23. Two combs, Florence (167, 168).
Evidence: Circumstantial. Cook voyage collection from various sources.
Literature: Giglioli, 1893, pp. 202-203; Kaeppler, 1977.

24. Comb, Sydney (109). Length 11.5 cm.
Evidence: Cook collection exhibited at the Colonial and Indian Exhibition.
Literature: Mackrell, 1886; Appendix I, this volume.

25-29. Five combs, Göttingen.
Evidence: Purchased from London dealer Humphrey in 1782.

30. Comb, Wellington (FE 3019).
Evidence: Circumstantial. From the Imperial Institute, from Queen Victoria in a box containing "articles brought by Captain Cook from Otaheti."

Tattooing Needles

Only one Tongan tattooing needle can be traced to Cook's voyages. Although there may have been others now lost, Tongan tattooing was not very common, and much of it took place in Samoa.

1. Tattooing needle, Cambridge (22.928a). Length 12 cm. Figures 428, 429.
Evidence: Leverian Museum.

Feather Headdresses

Although it is likely that the three feather headdresses referred to below were taken to Europe on Cook's voyages, neither the objects themselves nor the documentation can be traced.

1. Feather headpiece depicted in the Tongan plate from Cook's second voyage (Fig. 430). Lost. The style is similar to Fijian feather headpieces and may have been traded from Fiji to Tonga.

2. Feather headpiece, Berne (TAH 43). Lost. The description is similar to the last one. Noted that it was given by Paulaho, King of the Friendly Islands, to Webber.
Evidence: Webber collection, third voyage.
Literature: Henking, 1957, pp. 345-346; Kaeppler, 1977.

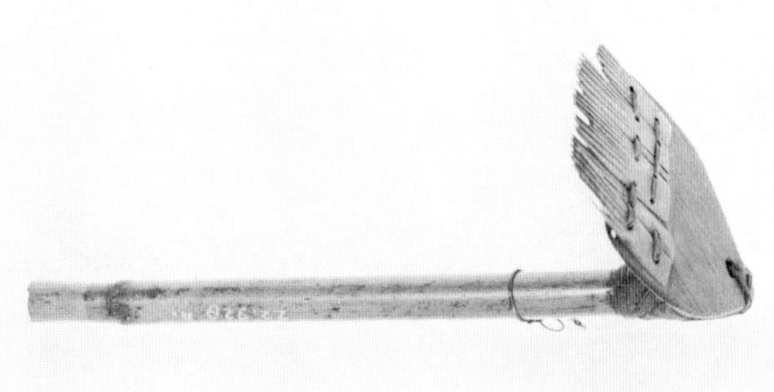

Figure 428. — Tattooing needle, Cambridge 22.928a.

Figure 429. — Tattooing needle (detail), Cambridge 22.928a.

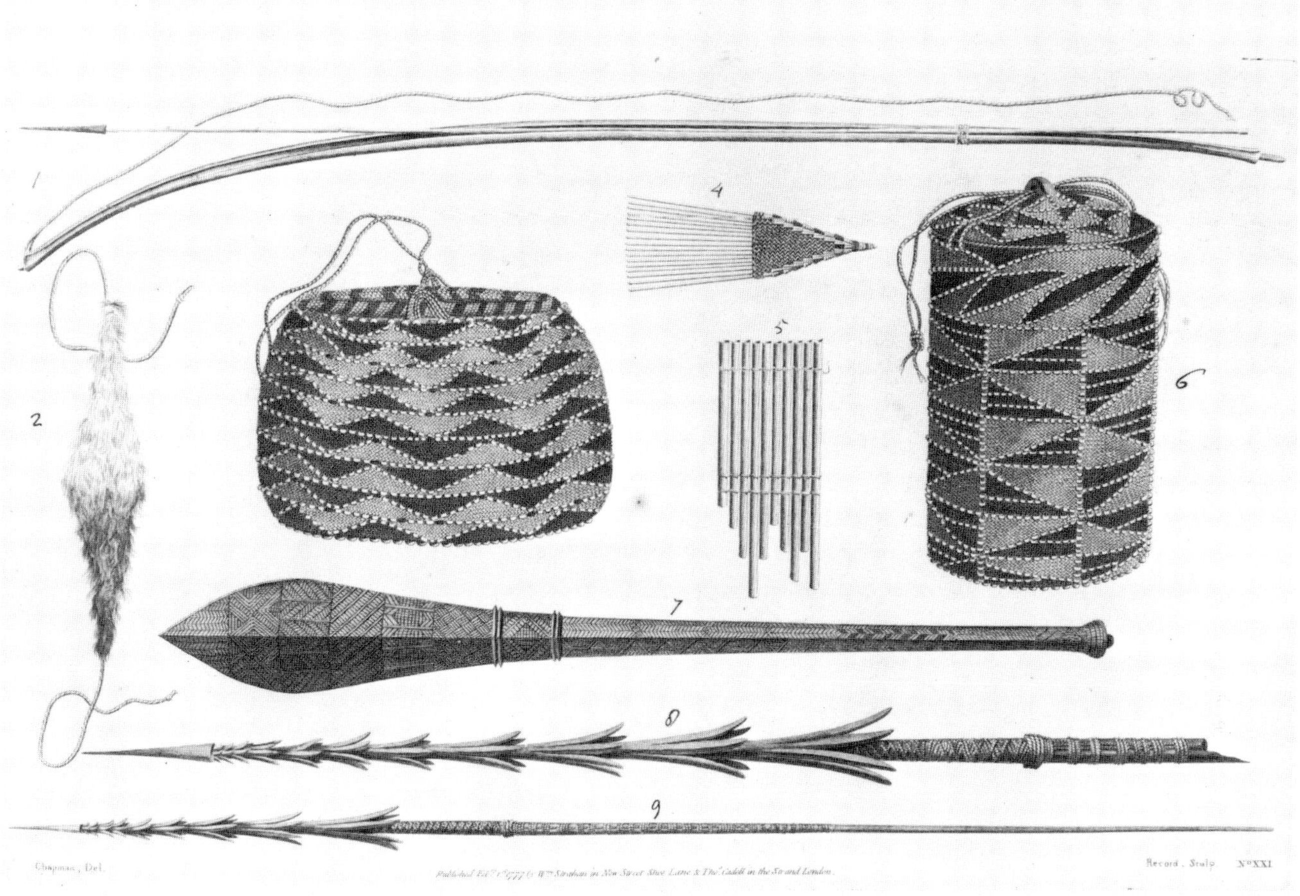

Figure 430. — Tongan artifact plate, *Atlas* to Cook's second voyage (28).

3. Feather headdress depicted by Webber in his portrait of Paulaho (Fig. 431). A similar headdress is in Vienna, but not in the Cook collection obtained from the Leverian Museum. It may have been, however, part of another Cook voyage collection exhibited in Vienna in 1784 and advertised for sale for 600 gildern;[2] but the evidence is, at best, circumstantial.

Decorative Girdles

Decorative girdles collected on Cook's voyages were characteristically made of elements of intertwined sennit covered with red feathers, or knotted from fiber in black and natural designs and covered with red feathers. Of this latter type only two examples are known, both of which were collected on Cook's voyages.

[2] I am indebted to Christian Feest for this reference.

1. Decorative girdle of sennit and red feathers, Vienna (77). Dimensions 36 cm, by 34 cm. Figure 432.
   Evidence: Leverian Museum.
   Literature: Moschner, 1955, p. 201.
2. Decorative girdle of sennit and red feathers, Göttingen (OZ 142). Length 54.5 cm, depth 34.5 cm. Figure 433.
   Evidence: Purchased from London dealer Humphrey in 1782.

3-4. Two decorative girdles, Dublin (1882.3871, 1882.3872 [exhibited]). Heights 35.5 cm, 60 cm, widths 89 cm, 125 cm. Figures 434-435.
   Evidence: Circumstantial. Thought to be part of the collection given to Trinity College, Dublin, by Patten or King.
   Literature: Freeman, 1949.

5. Decorative girdle of sennit and red feathers, Oxford (2). Dimensions 66 cm, by 66 cm.
   Evidence: Forster collection, second voyage.
   Literature: Gathercole, n.d. [1970]; Kaeppler, 1971, pp. 211-212.

Figure 431. — "Paulaho, King of the Friendly Islands," engraving after Webber.

6-8. Parts of four decorative girdles of sennit and red feathers, Florence (302, 235).[3]
Evidence: Circumstantial. Cook voyage collection from various sources.
Literature: Giglioli, 1893, pp. 195-199; Kaeppler, 1977

10. Decorative girdle, British Museum (1971.OC.5.2).
Evidence: Circumstantial. Probably Leverian Museum.

11. Knotted fiber decorative girdle with red feathers, Berne (TAH 46). Dimensions 26 cm, by 108 cm.
Evidence: Webber collection, third voyage.
Literature: Kaeppler, 1977.

12. Knotted fiber decorative girdle with red feathers, Göttingen (OZ 147).
Evidence: Purchased from London dealer Humphrey in 1782.

Other Waist Ornaments

Belts of heavy braided coconut fiber sennit were used to hold up mat or bark cloth skirts and were probably worn by men.

[3] Small pieces of two of these decorative girdles are in Auckland, exchanged from Giglioli from the Florence collection.

Figure 432. — Decorative girdle, Vienna 77.

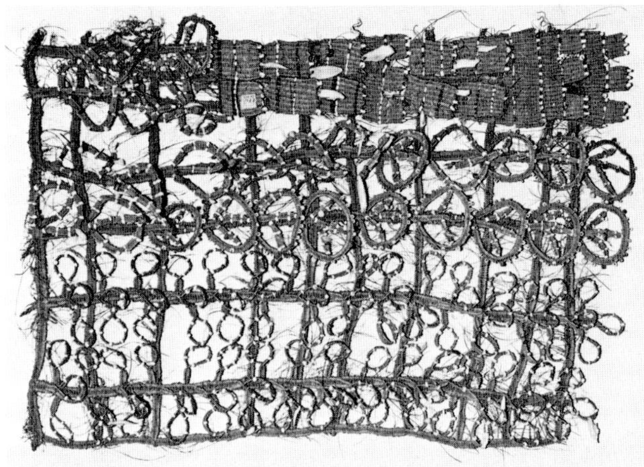

Figure 433. — Decorative girdle, Göttingen OZ 142.

Figure 434. — Decorative girdle, Dublin 1882.3872.

Figure 435. — Decorative girdle (detail), Dublin 1882.3872.

Figure 436. — Sennit belt, Vienna 61.

1-2. Two sennit belts, Vienna (61 [exhibited], 128). Lengths 397 cm, 350 cm. Figure 436.
Evidence: Leverian Museum.
Literature: Moschner, 1955, p. 200.

3. Sennit belt, Oxford (59).
Evidence: Forster collection, second voyage.
Literature: Gathercole, n.d. [1970].

4. Sennit belt, Berne (FR 21). Length 321 cm.
Evidence: Webber collection, third voyage.
Literature: Henking, 1957, pp. 335-336; Kaeppler, 1977.

5-6. Two belts, Florence (196, 243).
Evidence: Circumstantial. Cook voyage collection from various sources.
Literature: Giglioli, 1893, p. 202; Kaeppler, 1977.

7-8. Two "ropes of coconut fiber"—probably belts, Göttingen.
Evidence: Forster collection, second voyage.

Plaited Overskirts

Tongan garments extended from the waist or above to the knee or below and were worn by both men and women. Often plaited garments were worn over garments of bark cloth. Garments made of *fau (Hibiscus tiliaceus)* are among the most remarkable Tongan objects collected on Cook's voyages. They were probably overskirts worn in much the same way as the modern *ta'ovala,* and were usually called "aprons" in contemporary accounts. These overskirts are of two main types—one having a solid backing with projecting tabs plaited out from the backing, the second being plaited into square holes.

1. Overskirt with projecting tabs, Vienna (76). Height 67 cm, length 150 cm. Figure 437.
Evidence: Leverian Museum.
Literature: Moschner, 1955, pp. 200-201.

2. Overskirt with projecting tabs, Göttingen (OZ 143). Width 112 cm, depth 63.5 cm.
Evidence: Purchased from London dealer Humphrey in 1782.

3. Overskirt with projecting tabs, Stockholm (1799.2.23). Dimensions 117 cm, by 55 cm.
Evidence: Sparrman collection, second voyage.
Literature: Söderström, 1939, p. 45.

4-5. Two overskirts with projecting tabs, Florence (299, 300).
Evidence: Circumstantial. Cook voyage collection from various sources.
Literature: Giglioli, 1893, pp. 199-200; Kaeppler, 1977.

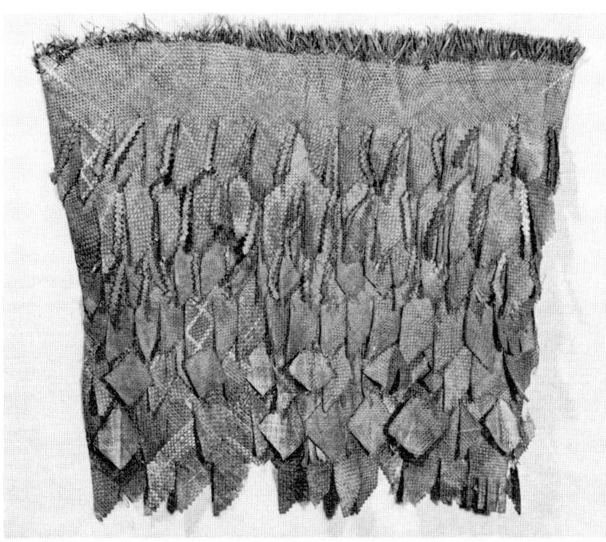

Figure 437. — Overskirt, Vienna 76.

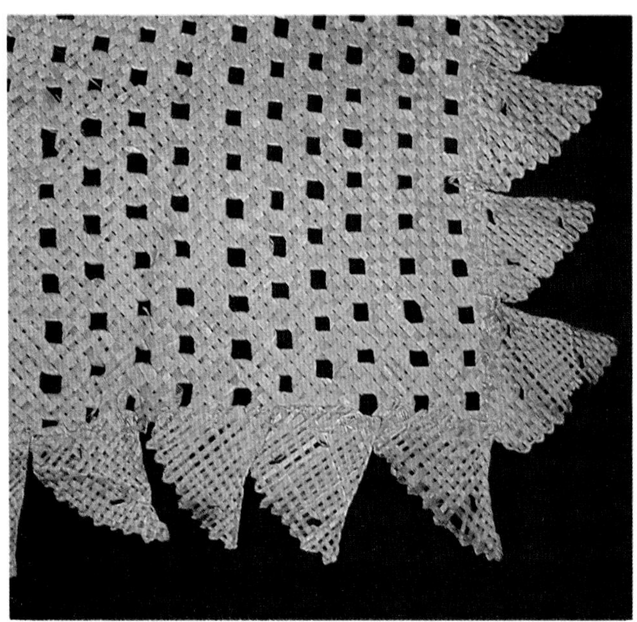

Figure 438. — Overskirt, Leningrad 505-31.

6. Overskirt with projecting tabs, Wellington (FE 3021).
   Evidence: Circumstantial. From the Imperial Institute from Queen Victoria in a box containing articles "brought by Captain Cook from Otaheti."
7. Overskirt with square openwork holes, Leningrad (505-31). Width 85 cm. Figure 438.
   Evidence: Given by Capt. Clerke to Governor of Kamchatka.
   Literature: Rozina, 1966, p. 242; Kaeppler, 1977.
8. Overskirt with square openwork holes, Florence (296).
   Evidence: Circumstantial. Cook voyage collection from various sources.
   Literature: Giglioli, 1893, pp. 200-201; Kaeppler, 1977.
9. Overskirt with square openwork holes, Oxford (56).
   Evidence: Forster collection, second voyage.
   Literature: Gathercole, n.d. (1970), p. 11; Kaeppler, 1971, p. 211.
10. Overskirt with square openwork holes, Göttingen (OZ 151). Width 150 cm, depth 84 cm.
    Evidence: Purchased from London dealer Humphrey in 1782.
11. Overskirt with square openwork holes, dyed black, Berne (TAH 12).
    Evidence: Webber collection, third voyage.
    Literature: Henking, 1957, p. 350; Kaeppler, 1977.

Other Decorative Fiber Objects

Other objects probably collected in Tonga are quite rare in museum collections and their uses can only be conjectured.

1. Skirt (?) of pandanus backing with projecting tufts,[4] Oxford (56a).
   Evidence: Forster collection, second voyage.
   Literature: Gathercole, n.d. [1970].
2. White tufted skirt (?) probably traded from Samoa of the *iesinga* type,[5] Göttingen (OZ 146). Figure 439.
   Evidence: Purchased from London dealer Humphrey in 1782.
3. Grave decoration (?) of plaited band with hanging pandanus strips,[6] Göttingen.
   Evidence: Purchased from London dealer Humphrey in 1782.
4. Belt with hanging fibers (?), probably traded from Fiji, Göttingen (OZ 150).
   Evidence: Purchased from London dealer Humphrey in 1782.

Mats

Tongan mats collected on Cook's voyages were of several kinds, made of different types of pandanus.

1-2. Two mats, Vienna (74 [exhibited], 75). Dimensions 304 cm × 167 cm; 272 cm × 132 cm.
   Evidence: Leverian Museum.
   Literature: Moschner, 1955, pp. 199-200.

3-7. Five mats, Oxford (53, 54, 55, 57, 58).
   Evidence: Forster collection, second voyage.
   Literature: Gathercole, n.d. [1970].

[4] A similar object is in Berlin.

[5] A similar mat was in the Leverian Museum, but is now lost.

[6] Similar grave decorations called *"tapu"* are still used in Tonga.

Figure 439. — White tufted textile, Göttingen OZ 146.

8-12. Five mats, Göttingen.
Evidence: Purchased from London dealer Humphrey in 1782.

13. Mat, Stockholm (1848.1.20). Dimensions 130 cm by 160 cm.
Evidence: "Banks collection."
Literature: Rydén, 1965, p. 93.

14. Mat, Berne (FR 5). Dimensions 337 cm by 190 cm.
Evidence: Webber collection, third voyage.
Literature: Henking, 1957, p. 337; Kaeppler, 1977.

15. Mat, Sydney (H 98). Dimensions 190 cm by 176 cm. Figure 440.
Evidence: Cook collection exhibited at Colonial and Indian Exhibition. Label "This mantle was worn by a chief of Otaheite."
Literature: Mackrell, 1886; Appendix I, this volume.

16-18. Three mats, Wellington (FE 5250-5252).
Evidence: From Mrs. Cook to her cousin's daughter Mary (Mrs. James P.) Adams. (5250 may be part of mat in Sydney [H 98]).

19. Several mats, Dublin (1882.3859-3870).
Evidence: Circumstantial. Thought to be part of the collection given to Trinity College, Dublin by Patten and King.
Literature: Freeman, 1949.

Cordage

1-2. Cordage, Oxford (66, 177).
Evidence: Forster collection, second voyage.
Literature: Gathercole, n.d. [1970].

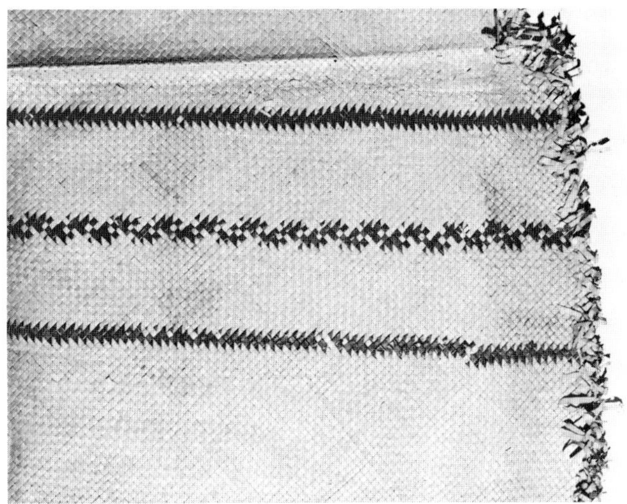

Figure 440. — Pandanus mat, Sydney H 98.

Bark Cloth

The largest pieces of bark cloth collected on Cook's voyages still extant are from Tonga. No large pieces have been brought for the exhibition, but there are several samples in the bound tapa books.

1-4. Four pieces of bark cloth, Oxford (49-52).
Evidence: Forster collection, second voyage.
Literature: Gathercole, n.d. [1970].

5-7. Two large and one small piece of bark cloth, Göttingen.
Evidence: Forster collection, second voyage.

8-9. Two pieces of bark cloth, Wörlitz (16, 17).
Evidence: Forster collection, second voyage.
Literature: Germer, 1975, pp. 69-72, 90.

10. One large piece of bark cloth, Stockholm (1848.1.13).
Evidence: "Banks collection."
Literature: Rydén, 1965, p. 75 (attributed to Tahiti).

11-13. Three pieces of bark cloth, Berne (FR 1, 2, TAH 5).
Evidence: Webber collection, third voyage.
Literature: Henking, 1957, pp. 333-335, 344-345; Kaeppler, 1977.

14-17. Four pieces of bark cloth, Göttingen.
Evidence: Purchased from London dealer Humphrey in 1782.

18-19. Two pieces of bark cloth, Florence (257, 277b).
Evidence: Circumstantial. Cook voyage collection from various sources.
Literature: Giglioli, 1893, p. 201; 1895, p. 66; Kaeppler, 1977.

Baskets

A large number of Tongan baskets were collected on Cook's voyages. Made in several styles from quite diverse raw materials, basketry in Tonga is surely one of the high peaks of craftsmanship in the Pacific area.

1. Basket of rectangular *kato alu* type (a creeper twined around bunches of midribs of coconut leaflet), British Museum (Q 77.0c7). Height 21 cm, length 49 cm, width 16 cm. Figure 441.
Evidence: Leverian Museum.

2. Basket of rectangular *kato alu* type, British Museum (Q 77.0c8). Height 18.5 cm, length 41 cm, width 11 cm. Figure 442.
Evidence: Depicted in a drawing by Cleveley in British Library, Add. Ms. 23,920.106 (Fig. 443); second voyage.

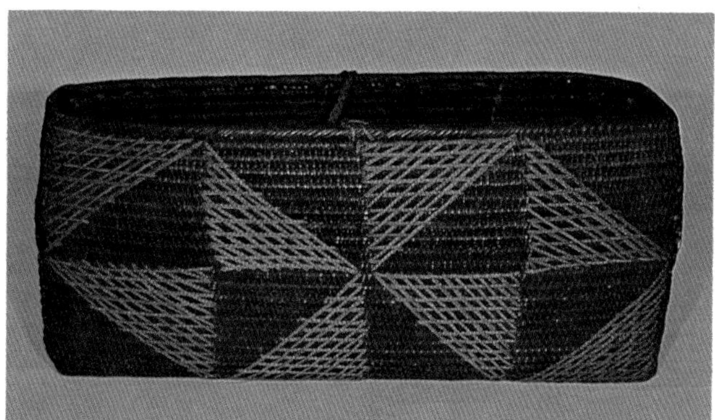

Figure 441. — Basket, British Museum Q77.Oc7.

3. Basket of rectangular *kato alu* type, Vienna (54). Length 53 cm, height 23.2 cm, width 10 cm.
   Evidence: Leverian Museum.
   Literature: Moschner, 1955, pp. 196-197.
4. Basket of rectangular *kato alu* type. British Museum (NN). Height 24 cm, length 53 cm, width 14.5 cm.
   Evidence: Depicted in a drawing by Cleveley in British Library Add. Ms. 23,920.106.
5. Basket of rectangular *kato alu* type, Göttingen.
   Evidence: Purchased from London dealer Humphrey in 1782.
6. Basket of rectangular *kato alu* type, Göttingen.
   Evidence: Forster collection, second voyage.
7. Basket of rectangular *kato alu* type, Berne (FR 2). Length 37 cm, height 18.5 cm, width 8 cm.
   Evidence: Webber collection, third voyage.
   Literature: Henking, 1957, p. 340; Kaeppler, 1977.

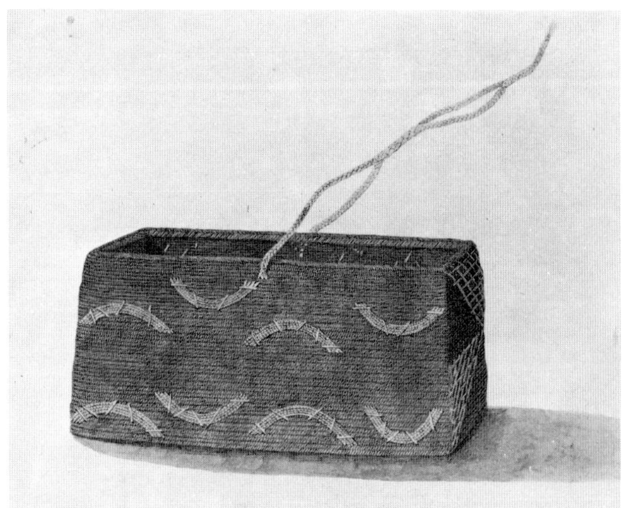

Figure 443. — Drawing by Cleveley, British Library Add. Ms. 23,920.106.

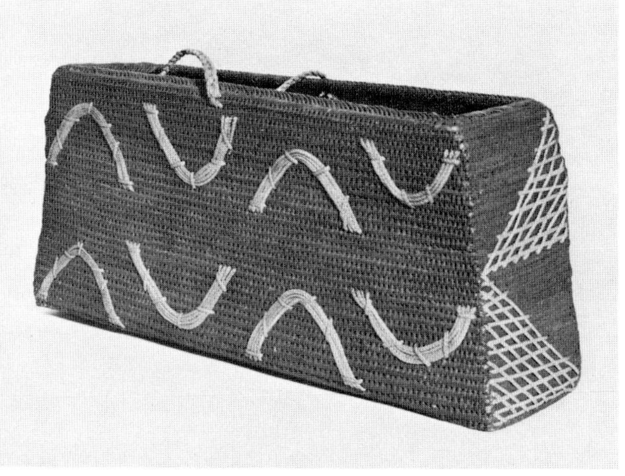

Figure 442. — Basket, British Museum Q77.Oc8.

8. Basket of rectangular *kato alu* type. Lost.
   Evidence: Leverian Museum.
9. Basket of rounded *kato alu* type, Berne (FR 11). Height 14 cm, diameter ca. 13 cm.
   Evidence: Webber collection, third voyage.
   Literature: Henking, 1957, p. 339; Kaeppler, 1977.
10. Basket of oval *kato alu* type, Göttingen (OZ 119). Length 33 cm, height 14 cm.
    Evidence: Purchased from London dealer Humphrey in 1782.
11. Basket of oval *kato alu* type, Oxford (88).
    Evidence: Forster collection, second voyage.
    Literature: Gathercole, n.d. [1970].
12. Basket of sennit twined around coconut leaflet midribs, Göttingen (OZ 115). Length 51 cm, height 28 cm. Figure 444.
    Evidence: Purchased from London dealer Humphrey in 1782.
13. Basket of sennit twined around coconut leaflet midribs, Florence 250.
    Evidence: Circumstantial. Cook voyage collection from various sources.
    Literature: Giglioli, 1893, p. 210; Kaeppler, 1977.

Figure 444. — Basket, Göttingen OZ 115.

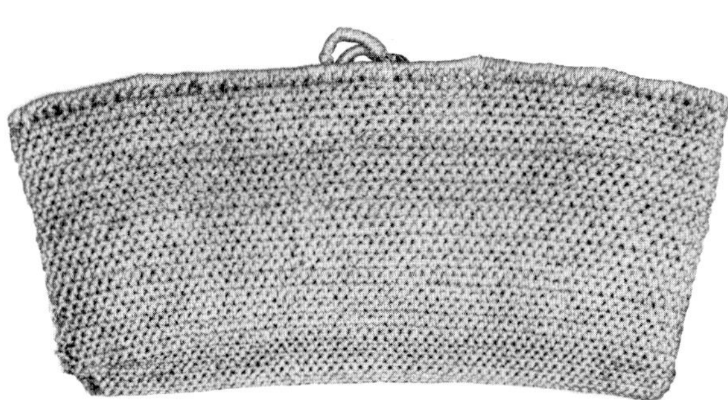

Figure 445.— Basket, Vienna 58.

14-15. Two baskets of knotted sennit, flat, Vienna (58 [exhibited], 59). Lengths 40 cm, 31.5 cm, heights 19 cm, 13.7 cm. Figure 445.
Evidence: Leverian Museum.
Literature: Moschner, 1955, p. 196.

16. Basket of knotted sennit, flat, Wörlitz (6). Height 19 cm, width 30.5 cm.
Evidence: Forster collection, second voyage.
Literature: Germer, 1975, pp. 74, 90.

17. Basket of knotted sennit, flat, Göttingen (OZ 138). Length 39 cm, height 30.5 cm.
Evidence: Purchased from London dealer Humphrey in 1782.

18-19. Two baskets of knotted sennit, flat, Berne (FR 14, 15). Lengths 35.5 cm, 49 cm, heights 23.5 cm, 34 cm.
Evidence: Webber collection, third voyage.
Literature: Henking, 1957, pp. 342-343; Kaeppler, 1977.

20. Basket of knotted sennit, Florence (266).
Evidence: Circumstantial. Cook voyage collection from various sources.
Literature: Giglioli, 1893, p. 209; Kaeppler, 1977.

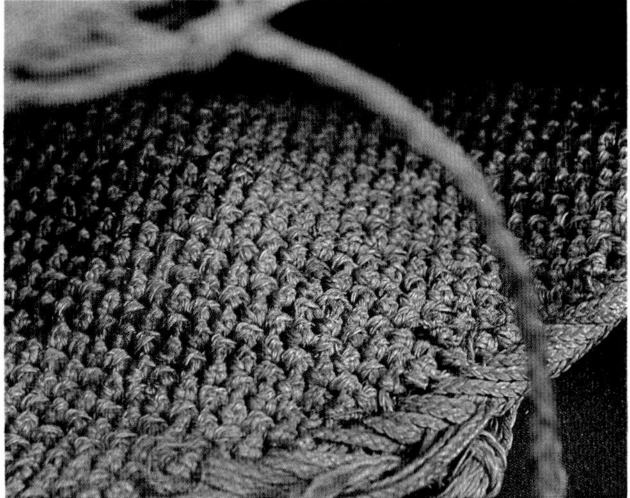

Figure 447.— Basket (detail), Stockholm 1799.2.34.

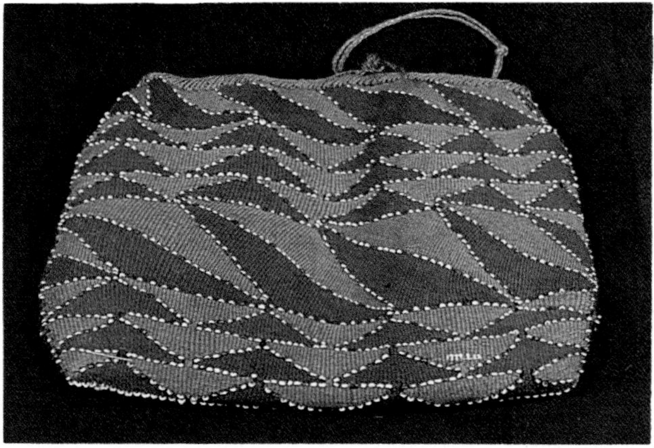

Figure 446.— Basket, Stockholm 1799.2.33.

21-22. Two baskets of *kato mosi kaka* type (twined coconut fibers in two colors and decorated with beads of shell and coconut shell), Stockholm (1799.2.33, 34 [both exhibited]). Lengths 53 cm, 26 cm; heights 37 cm, 18 cm. Figures 446, 447, 448.
Evidence: Sparrman collection, second voyage.
Literature: Söderström, 1939, pp. 46-47.

23. Basket of *kato mosi kaka* type, Stockholm (1848.1.14). Length 60 cm, height 38 cm.
Evidence: "Banks collection."
Literature: Rydén, 1965, pp. 97-98.

24. Basket of *kato mosi kaka* type, Wörlitz (5). Height 27 cm, width 37 cm.
Evidence: Forster collection, second voyage.
Literature: Germer, 1975, pp. 74, 89.

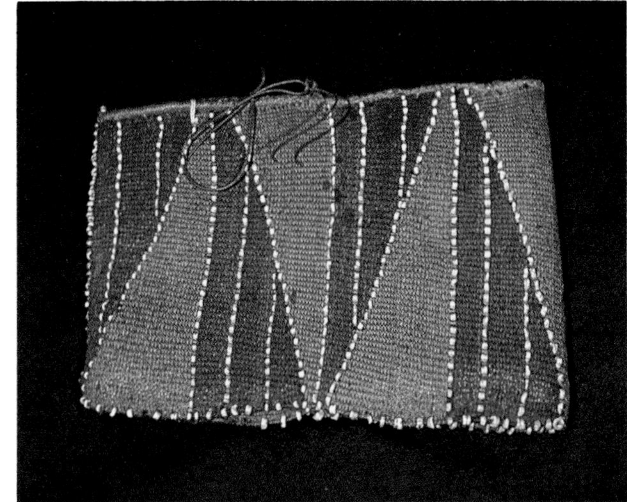

Figure 448.— Basket, Stockholm 1799.2.34.

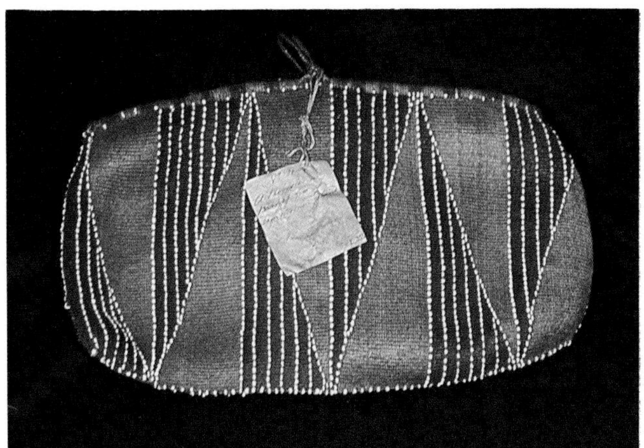

Figure 449. — Basket, Glasgow E 355.

25. Basket of *kato mosi kaka* type, Glasgow (E 355). Length 52 cm, height 30 cm. Figure 449. See Appendix III, this volume.
Evidence: Circumstantial. Cook voyage collection from various sources.

26. Basket of *kato mosi kaka* type, Vienna (56). Length 47 cm, height 29 cm.
Evidence: Leverian Museum.
Literature: Moschner, 1955, p. 192.

27. Basket of *kato mosi kaka* type, Leningrad (505-32). Length 43 cm, height 33 cm. Figure 450.
Evidence: Given by Captain Clerke to Governor of Kamchatka. Third voyage.
Literature: Rozina, 1966, p. 248; Kaeppler, 1977.

28-29. Two baskets of *kato mosi kaka* type, Oxford (89, 90).
Evidence: Forster collection, second voyage.
Literature: Gathercole, n.d. [1970].

30-32. Three baskets of *kato mosi kaka* type, Göttingen.
Evidence: Purchased from London dealer Humphrey in 1782.

33. Basket of *kato mosi kaka* type, Berne (FR 28). Height 21 cm, width 28.5 cm.
Evidence: Webber collection, third voyage.
Literature: Henking, 1957, pp. 341-342; Kaeppler, 1977.

34. Bag of *kato mosi kaka* type basketry, Sydney (H 102). Height 46 cm (X2), width 64 cm. Figure 451.
Evidence: Cook collection exhibited at Colonial and Indian Exhibition. Label, "Brought by Captain Cook from Otaheite. A bag netted with beads, it has been cut open."
Literature: Mackrell, 1886; Appendix I, this volume.

Figure 450. — Basket (detail), Leningrad 505-32.

35. Basket of *kato mosi kaka* type, Florence (251).
Evidence: Circumstantial. Cook voyage collection from various sources.
Literature: Giglioli, 1893, p. 209; Kaeppler, 1977.

36. Basket of *kato mosi kaka* type, Christchurch (E 149.150).
Evidence: Circumstantial. Worden Hall collection. See Appendix II, this volume.

37-41. Five baskets of *kato mosi kaka* type. Lost.
Evidence: Leverian Museum depictions.

42. Basketry (of *kato mosi kaka* type) covered wooden bucket, Vienna (55). Height 27 cm, diameter 17.5 cm. Figure 452.
Evidence: Leverian Museum.
Literature: Moschner, 1955, p. 191.

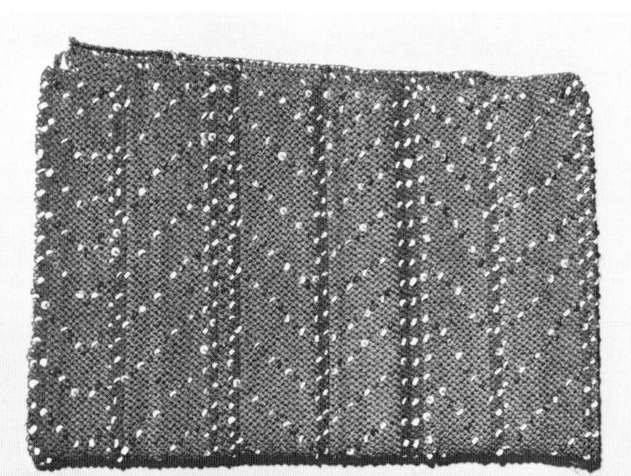

Figure 451. — Basketry bag, Sydney H 102.

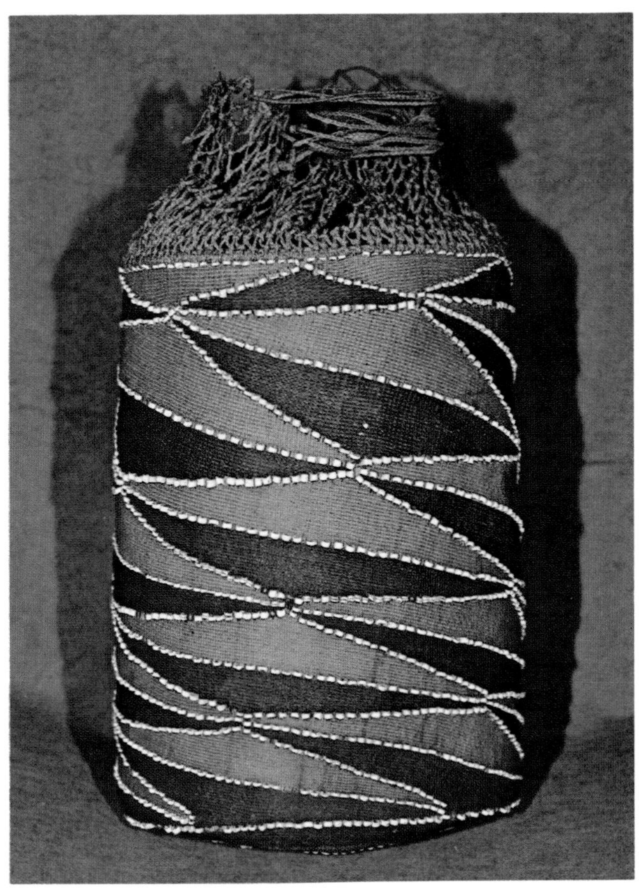

Figure 452.— Basketry-covered wooden bucket, Vienna 55.

43. Basketry-covered wooden bucket, British Museum (NN). Height 43 cm, diameter 21.5 cm. Figure 453.
Evidence: Depicted by Cleveley, British Library Add. Ms. 23,920.107 (Fig. 454); second voyage.

44. Basketry-covered wooden bucket, Oxford (87). Height 36 cm.
Evidence: Forster collection, second voyage. Depicted in the plate of Tongan artifacts in the official account of the voyage (Cook, 1777, Plate 21). Figure 430.
Literature: Gathercole, n.d. [1970].

45. Basket of pandanus (rectangular with cross-pieces at side top), Vienna (60). Length 40 cm, height 24 cm, width 9 cm.
Evidence: Leverian Museum. Figure 455.
Literature: Moschner, 1955, pp. 192-193.

46. Basket of pandanus (rectangular with cross-pieces at side top), Stockholm (1799.2.43). Length 30 cm, height 10 cm, width 4.5 cm. Figures 456, 457.
Evidence: Sparrman collection, second voyage.
Literature: Söderström, 1939, p. 64.

Figure 453.— Basketry-covered wooden bucket, British Museum (NN).

47. Basket of pandanus (rectangular with cross-pieces at side top), Berne (FR 13). Length 18 cm, height 8 cm, width 4.5 cm.
Evidence: Webber collection, second voyage.
Literature: Henking, 1957, p. 341; Kaeppler, 1977.

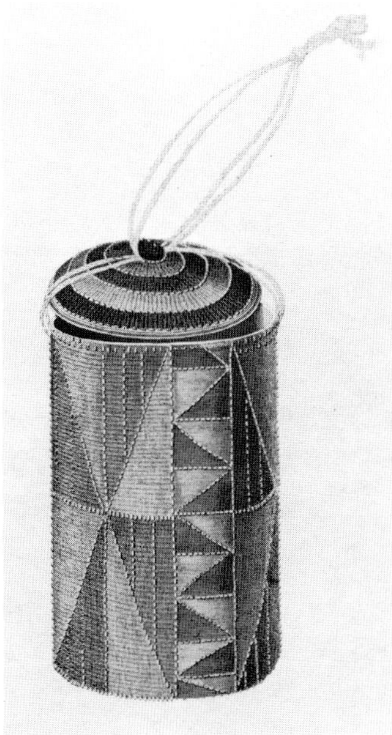

Figure 454.— Drawing by Cleveley, British Library Add. Ms. 23,920.107.

Figure 455. — Basket, Vienna 60.

48. Basket of pandanus (rectangular with cross-pieces at side top), Göttingen.
    Evidence: Purchased from London dealer Humphrey in 1782.

49. Basket of pandanus (rectangular with cross-pieces at side top), Florence (290).
    Evidence: Circumstantial. Cook voyage collection from various sources.
    Literature: Giglioli, 1895, p. 93; Kaeppler, 1977.

50-51. Two pandanus baskets of rectangular form. Lost.
    Evidence: Leverian Museum.

52. Basket of pandanus (square), Oxford (92). Dimensions 36 cm.
    Evidence: Forster collection, second voyage.
    Literature: Gathercole, n.d. [1970].

53. Basket of pandanus (square), Florence (183).
    Evidence: Circumstantial. Cook voyage collection from various sources.
    Literature: Giglioli, 1895, p. 93; Kaeppler, 1977.

54. Basket of pandanus (square), Göttingen.
    Evidence: Purchased from London dealer Humphrey in 1782.

55-56. Two baskets of pandanus (with fold-over flaps), Vienna (129, 130 [exhibited]). Lengths 21 cm, 23.5 cm, heights 17.5 cm, 17 cm. Figure 458.
    Evidence: Leverian Museum.
    Literature: Moschner, 1955, p. 193.

57. Basket of pandanus (with fold-over flap), Oxford (175). Width 23.5 cm.
    Evidence: Forster collection, second voyage.
    Literature: Gathercole, n.d. [1970].

58. Basket of pandanus (with fold-over flap), Berne (TAH 37). Dimensions 25 cm by 21 cm.
    Evidence: Webber collection, third voyage.
    Literature: Henking, 1957, pp. 354-355; Kaeppler, 1977.

59. Basket of pandanus, Vienna (131). Length 23 cm, height 14.5 cm. Figure 459.
    Evidence: Leverian Museum.
    Literature: Moschner, 1955, pp. 193-196.

60. Basket of pandanus (flat with four pockets), Göttingen.
    Evidence: Purchased from London dealer Humphrey in 1782.

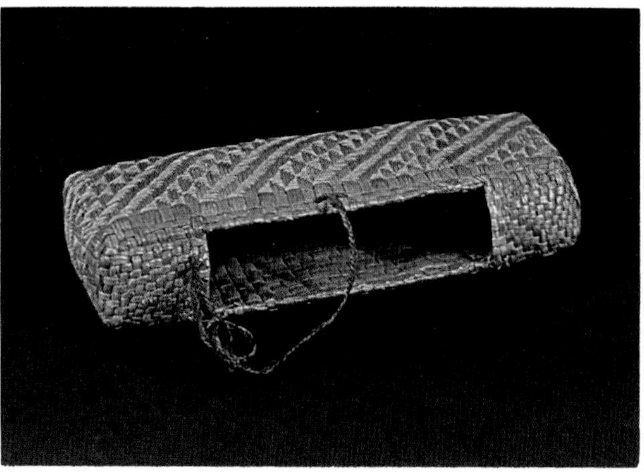
Figure 456. — Basket, Stockholm 1799.2.43.

Figure 457. — Basket (detail), Stockholm 1799.2.43.

Figure 458. — Basket, Vienna 130.

Figure 459. — Basket, Vienna 131.

Figure 460. — Fly whisk, Vienna 89.

Figure 461. — Fly whisk, Göttingen OZ 149.

61. Basket of pandanus (flat with four pockets). Lost.
    Evidence: Leverian Museum depiction.

62-63. Two baskets, Oxford (86, 91). Missing.
    Evidence: Forster collection, second voyage.
    Literature: Gathercole, n.d. [1970].

64-65. Two baskets, Göttingen.
    Evidence: Purchased from London dealer Humphrey in 1782.

66-72. Seven baskets, Göttingen.
    Evidence: Forster collection, second voyage.

73-? Several baskets. Lost.
    Evidence: Leverian Museum.

Fly Whisks

Fly whisks collected on Cook's voyages had quite varied handles, ranging from delicate wood or bone handles, through incised handles inlaid with ivory pieces, to recycled objects, such as a spear point, that probably had *mana* in their own right. Apparently they were carried by chiefs (rather than by ceremonial attendants, as in Samoa) as a visual symbol of status.

Figure 462. — Fly whisk, Greenwich L15/94/c.

1-2. Two fly whisks with incised wood handles inlaid with ivory pieces, Vienna (89 [exhibited],[7] 144). Lengths of handles 33.2 cm, 28.5 cm. Figure 460.
Evidence: Leverian Museum.
Literature: Moschner, 1955, pp. 221-222.

3. Fly whisk with straight wood handle, Göttingen (OZ 149). Length 50.5 cm. Figure 461.
Evidence: Purchased from London dealer Humphrey in 1782.

4. Fly whisk with bone handle, Berne (TAH 33).
Evidence: Webber collection, third voyage.
Literature: Henking, 1957, p. 352; Kaeppler, 1977.

5. Fly whisk with straight wood handle, Oxford (101). Length 53 cm.
Evidence: Forster collection, second voyage.
Literature: Gathercole, n.d. [1970]; Kaeppler, 1971, p. 215.

6. Fly whisk with straight wood handle, Florence (195).
Evidence: Circumstantial. Cook voyage collection from various sources.
Literature: Giglioli, 1893, pp. 210-211; Kaeppler, 1977.

7. Fly whisk made from a spear point, Greenwich (L15/94/c). Total length 45 cm, length of handle 26 cm. Figure 462.
Evidence: Circumstantial. Part of "Cook collection," but source unknown.

[7]Given by Paulaho, the highest Tongan chief (Tu'i Tonga), to Captain Cook.

8. Fly whisk with curved wooden handle, Edinburgh (1956.1009). Length 36 cm. Figure 463.
Evidence: Given by Mrs. Cook to Sir John Pringle.

9. Fly whisk with curved wooden handle, Cambridge (22.938). Total length 48 cm.
Evidence: Leverian Museum.

10. Fly whisk, Christchurch (E 149.154).
Evidence: Circumstantial. Worden Hall Collection. See Appendix II, this volume.

11-12. Two fly whisks (with old "Cook Voyage" labels), Dublin (1882.3694 and 3696 [both exhibited]). "Flapper from Otaheiti 21" and "Flapper, Friendly Isles." Lengths 57 cm, 43 cm. Figure 464.
Evidence: Circumstantial. Thought to be part of Cook voyage collection given to Trinity College, Dublin, by Patten or King.

13. Fly whisk with broken zigzag handle,[8] Vienna (145). Length of handle 10.5 cm.
Evidence: Leverian Museum. Figure 465.
Literature: Moschner, 1955, pp. 223-224.

Food Hooks

Hooks with a flat disk above them were used inside the house to hang food out of the reach of rats, either from above or from below.

1. Food hook with disk, Stockholm (1799.2.9). Diameter of disk 32 cm, length of hook 16.5 cm. Figure 466.
Evidence: Sparrman collection, second voyage.
Literature: Söderström, 1939, p. 40.

[8]The provenance for this fly whisk is unknown. The attachment of fibers is similar to Tongan attachments; however, the zigzag handle is more appropriate to Tahiti.

Figure 463. — Fly whisk, Edinburgh 1956.1009.

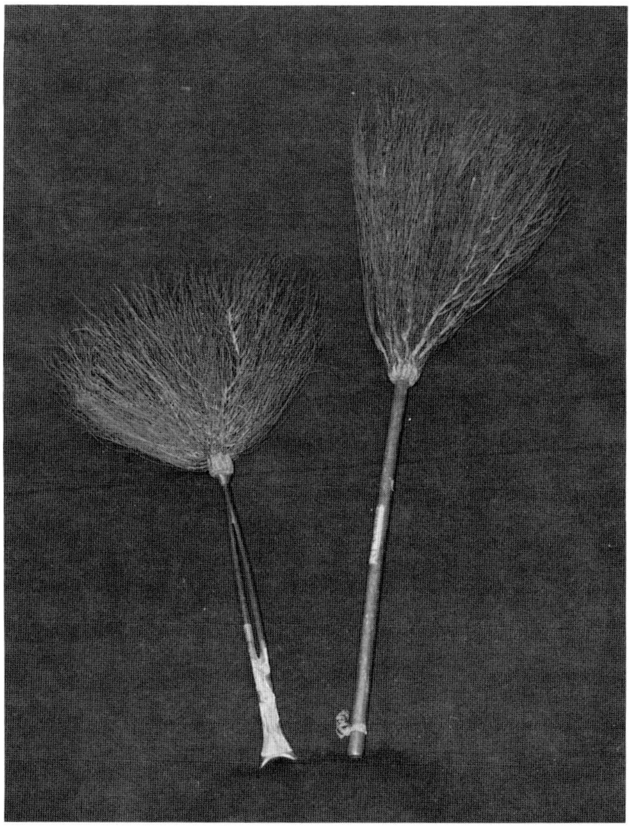

Figure 464. — Two fly whisks, Dublin 1882.3694, 1882.3696.

2. Food hook with disk, Ortiz collection, Geneva. Figures 467, 468.
   Evidence: Circumstantial. Probably Leverian Museum.

3. Ivory hook (broken), Vienna (147). Length 4 cm. Figure 469.
   Evidence: Leverian Museum.
   Literature: Moschner, 1955, p. 230.

4. Food hook with disk, Göttingen.
   Evidence: Purchased from London dealer Humphrey in 1782.

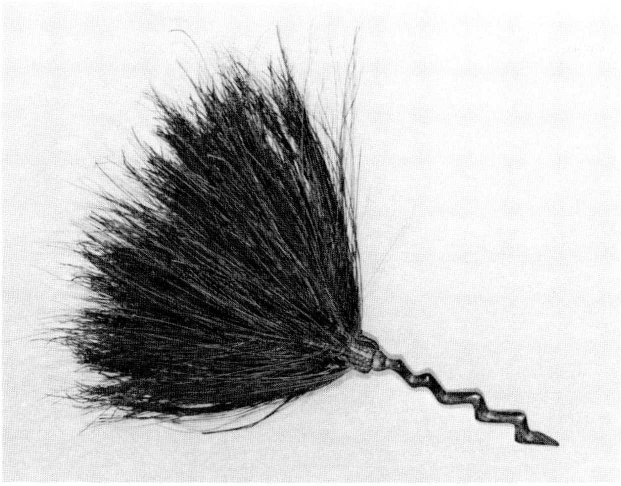

Figure 465. — Fly whisk, Vienna 145.

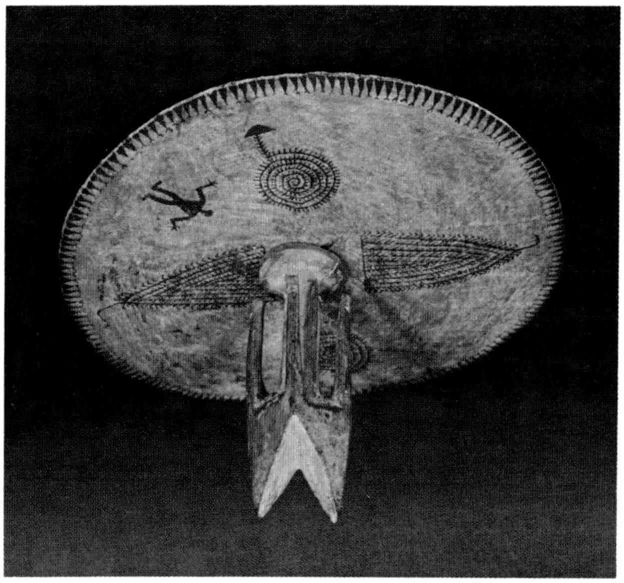

Figure 466. — Food hook, Stockholm 1799.2.9.

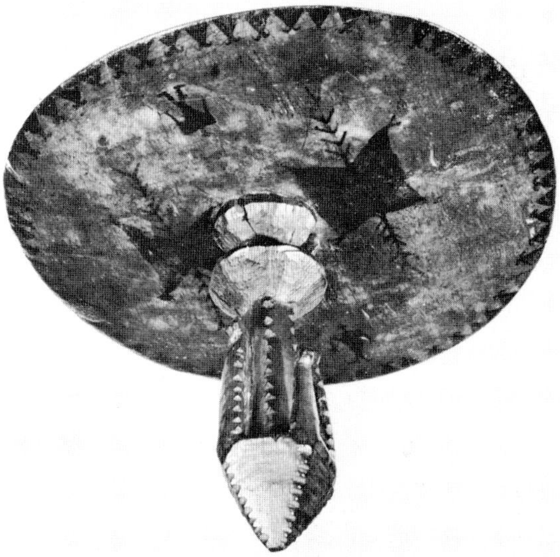

Figure 467. — Food hook, Ortiz collection.

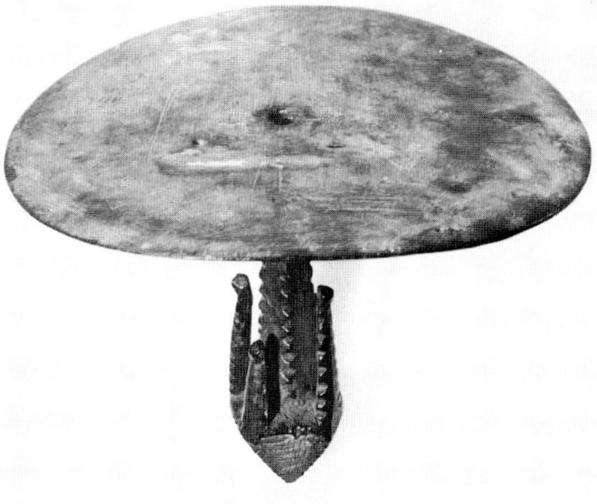

Figure 468. — Food hook (top view), Ortiz collection.

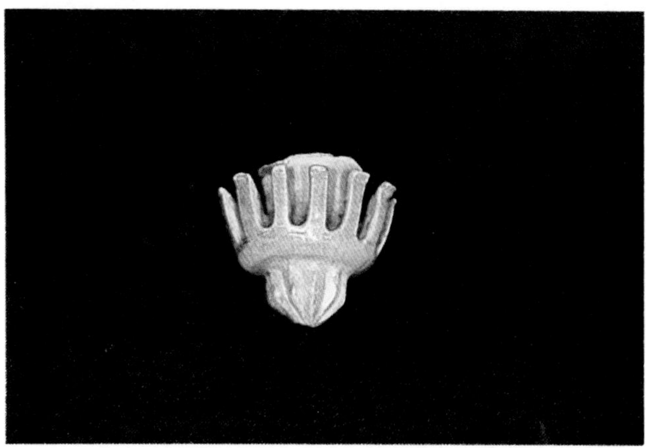
Figure 469. — Ivory hook, Vienna 147.

5. Disk for a food hook (hook missing), Oxford (93).
   Evidence: Forster collection, second voyage.
   Literature: Gathercole, n.d. [1970].
6. Food hook (disk missing), Wellington (FE 330).
   Evidence: Probably given by Banks to Bullock's Museum. Depicted in British Library Add. Ms. 23,920.110.
   Literature: Kaeppler, 1974a, p. 79.

Figure 470. — Two food pounders, Cambridge 22.929, 25.378.

Figure 471. — Wooden vessel, British Museum 1971.Oc5.1.

Food Pounders

Wooden food pounders collected in Tonga on Cook's voyages were usually thought to be Tahitian pounders[9] or Tongan hand clubs. They are certainly Tongan, however, and were used to pound starchy foods to make a pudding called *faikakai.*

1. Wood food pounder, Cambridge (22.929). Height 25.5 cm. Figure 470.
   Evidence: Leverian Museum.
2. Wood food pounder, Oxford (80). Height 31 cm.
   Evidence: Forster collection, second voyage.
   Literature: Gathercole, n.d. [1970].
3. Wood food pounder, Wörlitz (15). Height 28.1 cm, diameter 9.9 cm.
   Evidence: Forster collection, second voyage.
   Literature: Germer, 1975, p. 90.
4. Wood food pounder, Göttingen (OZ 81). Height 29 cm, diameter 10.7 cm.
   Evidence: Forster collection, second voyage.
   Literature: Urban, 1966, pp. 42, 47-48.

[9] A pounder in the British Museum (TAH 19) is very similar to those listed here. It is certainly Tongan but has no accession information and thus cannot be attributed to Cook's voyages.

Figure 472. — Wooden vessel, Hewett collection.

5. Wood food pounder, Cambridge (25.378). Figure 470.
   Evidence: Pennant collection of Cook voyage objects from various sources.
6. Wood food pounder, Vienna (37). Height 33 cm, diameter 9.5 cm.
   Evidence: Leverian Museum.
   Literature: Moschner, 1955, p. 153.

Wooden Kava Vessels

Wooden vessels similar to those used today for making *kava* were probably used for this purpose in the 18th century as well. Forster's remarks seem to indicate that they were also used for food, but this is unlikely.

1. Wooden vessel, British Museum (1971.0c5.1). Diameter 49 cm, height 14 cm. Figure 471.
   Evidence: Circumstantial. Probably Leverian Museum.
2. Wooden vessel (with patina of *kava* sediment), Göttingen (OZ 409).
   Evidence: Forster collection, second voyage.
   Literature: Urban, 1966, p. 47.
3. Wooden vessel, Oxford (65). Diameter 42 cm.
   Evidence: Forster collection, second voyage.
   Literature: Gathercole, n.d. [1970].

Pottery Vessels

Although no pottery from Tonga collected on Cook's vessels can be located today, no doubt some vessels were taken to England, for Cook collected two pots at Tongatapu and there is reference to at least one in the Leverian Museum.

1. Pottery vessel. Lost.
   Evidence: Leverian Museum.
   Literature: Kaeppler, 1973, p. 221.

Wooden Oil Dishes

Carved wooden vessels for holding oil are not characteristic of Polynesia. Yet those collected in Tonga during Cook's voyages include some superb examples of pre-European wood carving and finishing. Although they may have been made in Tonga, the stimulus for their use and development was certainly from Fiji. It is possible that some of the vessels listed here were used for holding food or other purposes.

1. Large double wooden vessel (for oil), John Hewett collection. Length 101.5 cm, diameter 34 cm. Figure 472.
   Evidence: Leverian Museum.
2. Small double wooden vessel (for oil), Vienna (51). Length 29 cm, height 4 cm. Figure 473.
   Evidence: Leverian Museum.
   Literature: Moschner, 1955, pp. 179-180.

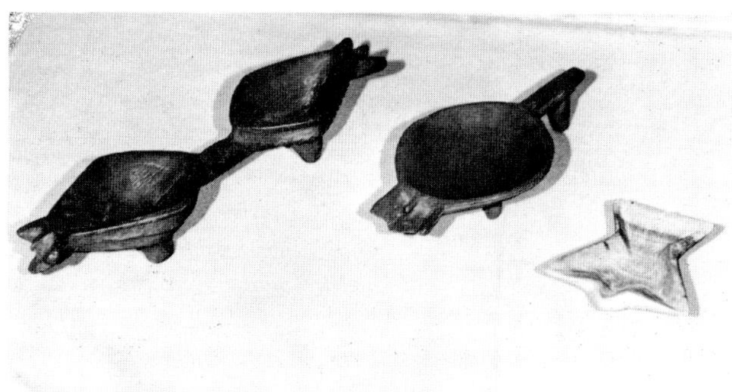

Figure 473. — Three wooden vessels, Vienna 51, 52, 53.

3. Small wooden vessel (for oil), Ortiz collection, Geneva.
   Evidence: Leverian Museum.
4. Small wooden vessel (for oil), Vienna (52). Length 22.5 cm, height 4.5 cm. Figure 473.
   Evidence: Leverian Museum.
   Literature: Moschner, 1955, p. 180.
5. Bird-shaped wooden vessel (for oil), Vienna (53). Length 10 cm, width 9.5 cm. Figure 473.
   Evidence: Leverian Museum.
   Literature: Moschner, 1955, p. 180.
6. Bird-shaped wooden vessel (for oil). Lost.
   Evidence: Depicted in British Library Add. Ms. 23,920.110 (Fig. 474).
7. Large double-pointed wooden vessel (for food ?), Vienna (132).[10] Length 63 cm, width 41 cm, height 13 cm. Figure 475.
   Evidence: Leverian Museum.
   Literature: Moschner, 1955, pp. 177-178.
8. Small double-pointed wooden vessel (for food ?), John Hewett collection. Length 27.5 cm, width 13.5 cm, height 6 cm.
   Evidence: Leverian Museum.

[10] These double-pointed vessels are usually attributed to Tahiti. In my view, a Tongan provenance is more likely.

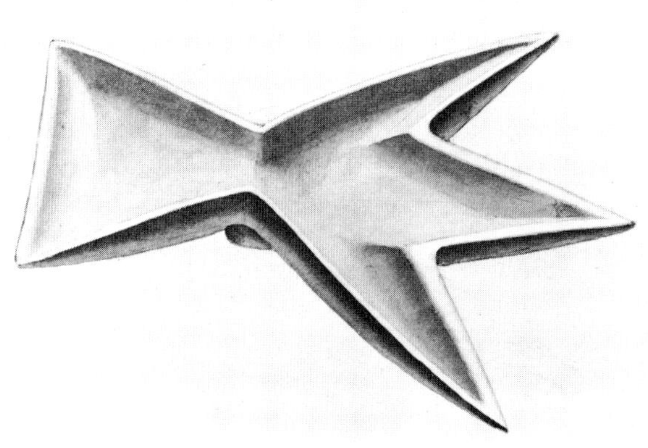

Figure 474. — Drawing of wooden vessel, British Library Add. Ms. 23,920.110.

Figure 475. — Wooden vessel, Vienna 132.

9. Large double-pointed wooden vessel (for food ?), Ortiz collection, Geneva. Figure 476.
   Evidence: Leverian Museum.

Neck Rests

Carved wooden neck rests are not widespread in Polynesia, but they are characteristic of the Society Islands and Tonga. Although those collected on Cook's voyages in Tonga have their own distinctive style, it is likely that their fabrication was because of Fijian influence. The forms of 18th century neck rests were quite varied, and may reflect the importance of the specific pieces of wood used in the manufacture. In the 19th century only two standardized forms survived.

1. Neck rest with four feet and ivory inlay, John Hewett collection. Length 83.5 cm, height 23 cm. Figure 477.
   Evidence: Leverian Museum.
2. Neck rest with four feet and ivory inlay, Dublin (1882.3642). Length 50 cm, height 12 cm. Figure 478.
   Evidence: Circumstantial. Thought to be part of the Cook voyage collection given to Trinity College, Dublin, by Patten or King. An old illegible label is attached (? Pillow Friendly Isles 76 or 16).
   Literature: Freeman, 1949.
3. Neck rest with four feet (two inset with ivory) and incised top edges, British Museum (NN). Length 79.5 cm, height 17 cm.
   Evidence: Circumstantial. "Cook voyage" label "Pillow from the Friendly Islands."
4. Neck rest with four feet, Wörlitz (4). Length 58.2 cm, height at midpoint 13.6 cm.
   Evidence: Forster collection, second voyage.
   Literature: Germer, 1975, pp. 65, 89.

5-6. Two neck rests with four feet, Oxford (94, 95). Lengths 72 cm, 56 cm.
   Evidence: Forster collection, second voyage.
   Literature: Gathercole, n.d. [1970].
7. Neck rest with four feet, Göttingen (OZ 347).
   Evidence: Forster collection, second voyage.
8. Neck rest with four feet, Vienna (50). Length 60 cm, height 9.5 cm.
   Evidence: Leverian Museum.
   Literature: Moschner, 1955, p. 226.
9. Neck rest with four feet, Leningrad (505-1). Length 52 cm.
   Evidence: Given by Captain Clerke to Governor of Kamchatka. Third voyage.
   Literature: Rozina, 1966, p. 248; Kaeppler, 1977.
10. Neck rest with four feet, Göttingen (OZ 348).
   Evidence: Purchased from London dealer Humphrey in 1782.
11. Neck rest with four feet, Stockholm (RM 367). Length 48 cm.
   Evidence: Sparrman collection, second voyage.
   Literature: Söderström, 1939, pp. 44-45.
12. Neck rest with four feet, Cambridge (25.379).
   Evidence: Pennant collection of Cook voyage objects from various sources.
13. Neck rest with four feet, Auckland (31872).
   Evidence: Circumstantial. Probably Leverian Museum.
14. Neck rest with four feet. Lost.
   Evidence: Depicted in British Library Add. Ms. 23,920.109; second voyage.
15. Neck rest with four legs, Dublin (1880.1647). Length 49 cm, height 15 cm. Figure 479.
   Evidence: Circumstantial. Thought to be part of the Cook voyage collection given to Trinity College, Dublin, by Patten or King.
   Literature: Freeman, 1949.

Figure 476. — Wooden vessel, Ortiz collection.

Figure 477. — Neck rest, Hewett collection.

16. Neck rest with four legs, Berne (FR 9).
    Evidence: Webber collection, third voyage.
    Literature: Henking, 1957, p. 336; Kaeppler, 1977.

17. Neck rest with four legs, Florence (263).
    Evidence: Circumstantial. Cook voyage collection from various sources. Possibly the neck rest depicted in British Library, Add. Ms. 23,920.108 (Fig. 480). If so, it probably came from Banks.
    Literature: Giglioli, 1893, p. 207; Kaeppler, 1977.

18. Neck rest with five legs, Vienna (6). Length 122 cm, height 17 cm. Figure 481.
    Evidence: Leverian Museum.
    Literature: Moschner, 1955, p. 226.

19. Neck rest with three legs, Greenwich (L15/92/c). Length 83 cm, height 14 cm. Figure 482.
    Evidence: Collected by William Griffin on the *Resolution* on the third voyage.

20. Neck rest with three legs, Exeter (E 1227). Length 65 cm. Figure 483.
    Evidence: Leverian Museum.

21. Neck rest with three legs, Vienna (7). Length 50.5 cm, height 9.5 cm.
    Evidence: Leverian Museum.
    Literature: Moschner, 1955, pp. 225-226.

22. Neck rest with three legs, Göttingen.
    Evidence: Purchased from London dealer Humphrey in 1782.

23. Neck rest with two extended legs, Florence (264).
    Evidence: Circumstantial. Cook voyage collection from various sources.
    Literature: Giglioli, 1893, p. 207; Kaeppler, 1977.

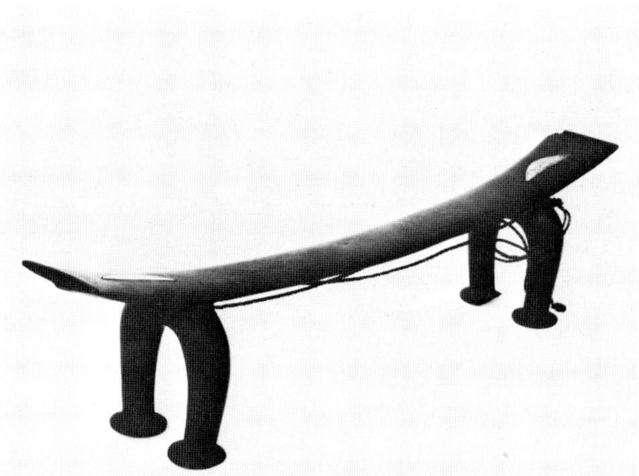

Figure 478. — Neck rest, Dublin 1882.3642.

Figure 479. — Neck rest, Dublin 1880.1647.

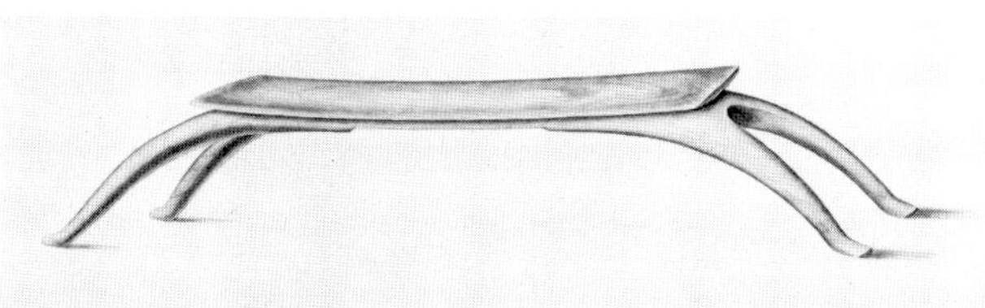

Figure 480. — Drawing by Cleveley, British Library Add. Ms. 23,920.108.

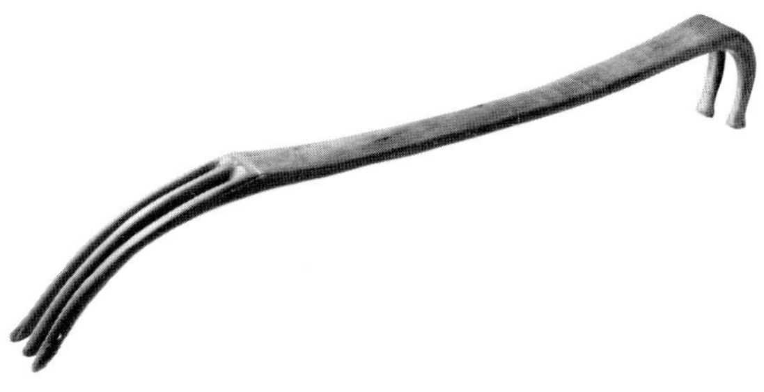

Figure 481. — Neck rest, Vienna 6.

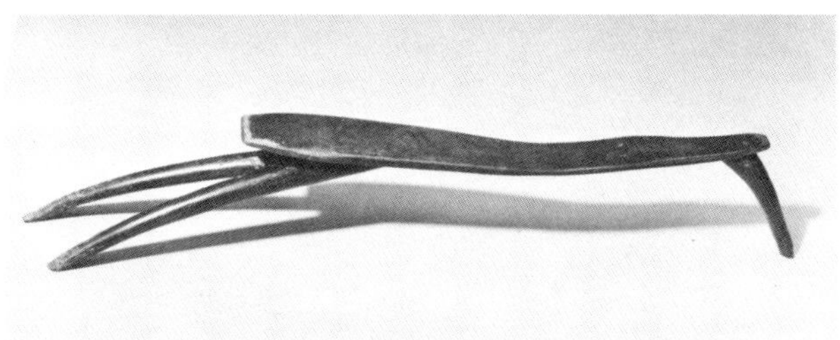
Figure 482.— Neck rest, Greenwich L15/92/c.

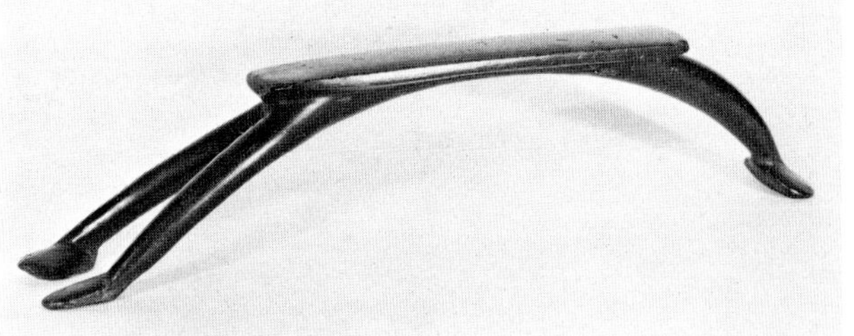
Figure 483.— Neck rest, Exeter E 1227.

Nose Flutes

Tongan nose flutes from Cook's voyages are usually attributed to Tahiti. The provenance is easily corrected because Tahiti nose flutes have one end open, while Tongan nose flutes have both ends closed by natural nodes in the bamboo. Four pitches are used which vary slightly from flute to flute (see Moyle, 1976, pp. 69-70).

⛵1-2. Two nose flutes, Göttingen (OZ 407 exhibited). Length 52 cm. Figure 484.
Evidence: Forster collection, second voyage.

⛵3-4. Two nose flutes, Vienna (149, 150). Lengths 54 cm, 39.5 cm. Figure 485.
Evidence: Leverian Museum.
Literature: Moschner, 1955, pp. 240-242.

5. Nose flute, Oxford (82). Length 54 cm.
Evidence: Forster collection, second voyage.
Literature: Gathercole, n.d. [1970].

6. Nose flute, Berne (TAH 40).
Evidence: Webber collection, third voyage.
Literature: Henking, 1957, pp. 353-354; Kaeppler, 1977.

7. Nose flute, British Museum (NN).
Evidence: Circumstantial. "Cook collection" label "Nose flutes of the Friendly Isles."

8. Nose flute, Christchurch (E 149.158).
Evidence: Circumstantial. Worden Hall collection. See Appendix II, this volume.

Panpipes

Panpipes collected in Tonga on Cook's voyages usually have nine or ten bamboo tubes bound in a raft with similar intervalic relationships among the pipes, which are placed in a definite order. Three important pitch relationships are incorporated in the instrument at two slightly different pitch levels (see Kaeppler, 1974b, pp. 110-111).

⛵1-2. Two panpipes, Stockholm (1799.2.35). Length of largest pipe of panpipe exhibited 19 cm. Figure 486.
Evidence: Sparrman collection, second voyage.
Literature: Söderström, 1939, p. 44; Kaeppler, 1974b, p. 106.

⛵3. Panpipe, London School of Economics. Length 28.5 cm. Figure 487.
Evidence: Leverian Museum.
Literature: Kaeppler, 1974b, p. 106.

4. Panpipe (some pipes missing), Vienna (90). Length 21.2 cm.
Evidence: Leverian Museum.
Literature: Moschner, 1955, pp. 238-239; Kaeppler, 1974b, p. 106.

5. Panpipe, Oxford (84). Length 24 cm.
Evidence: Forster collection, second voyage.
Literature: Gathercole, n.d. [1970]; Kaeppler, 1974b, p. 105.

6. Panpipe, Wörlitz (9). Length 23.9 cm.
Evidence: Forster collection, second voyage.
Literature: Germer, 1975, pp. 82, 90; Kaeppler, 1974b, p. 105.

7. Panpipe, Göttingen. Length 26.5 cm.
Evidence: Forster collection, second voyage.
Literature: Kaeppler, 1974b, p. 105.

8. Panpipe, British Museum (NN). Length 35.6 cm.
Evidence: Given by Banks to Sir John Pringle for analysis by Joshua Steele in 1775. Second voyage. Label "Cook coll."
Literature: Steele, 1775; Kaeppler, 1974b, p. 104.

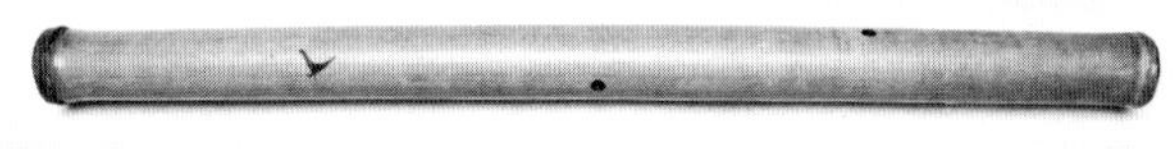
Figure 484.— Nose flute, Göttingen OZ 407.

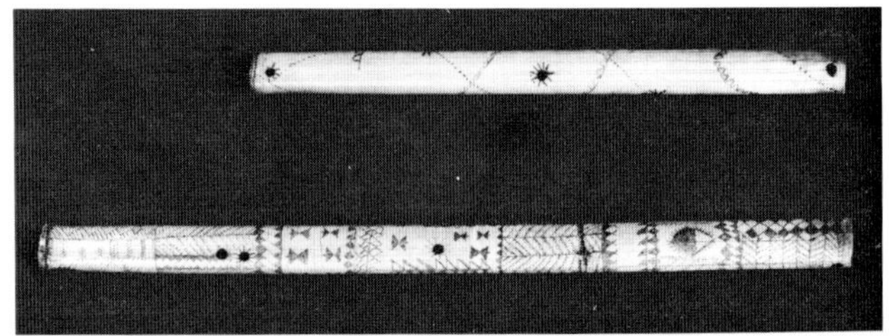
Figure 485.— Two nose flutes, Vienna 149, 150.

Figure 486. — Panpipes, Stockholm 1799.2.35.

9. Panpipe. Lost (? British Museum).
   Evidence: Given by Captain Furneaux to Sir John Pringle for analysis by Joshua Steele in 1774. Second voyage.
   Literature: Steele, 1775; Kaeppler, 1974b, p. 104.
10. Panpipe, Edinburgh (1956.1008). Length 29 cm.
    Evidence: Given by Mrs. Cook to Sir John Pringle.
    Literature: Kaeppler, 1974b, p. 105.
11. Panpipe, Göttingen. Length 22 cm.
    Evidence: Purchased from London dealer Humphrey in 1782.
    Literature: Kaeppler, 1974b, p. 106.
12. Panpipe, Berne (FR 2). Missing.
    Evidence: Webber collection, third voyage.
    Literature: Kaeppler, 1974b, p. 106; 1977.

13-14. Two panpipes, Florence (252, 253).
    Evidence: Circumstantial. Cook voyage collection from various sources.
    Literature: Giglioli, 1893, p. 217; Kaeppler, 1974b, p. 105; 1977.

15. Panpipe, Dublin (1882.3665). Missing.
    Evidence: Circumstantial. Thought to be part of Cook voyage collection from Patten or King.
    Literature: Freeman, 1949; Kaeppler, 1974b, p. 106.

Ankle Rattle

Rattles made of seeds were used in some Tongan dances. The cut seeds were strung on fiber and tied around the ankle. Only one has been located.

1. Ankle rattle, Berne (FR 23).
   Evidence: Webber collection, third voyage.
   Literature: Kaeppler, 1977.

Dance Paddles

Paddles used in the dance *me'etu'upaki* were collected on the second and third voyages. The dance was seen only on the third voyage and Forster describes his second voyage paddle as "a Spatule of wood to mix up their paste of breadfruit with"—perhaps a secondary use for a broken paddle.

1. Dance paddle (mended with sennit), Oxford (81). Length 73 cm.
   Evidence: Forster collection, second voyage.
   Literature: Gathercole, n.d. [1970]; Kaeppler, 1971, p. 218.

2-3. Two dance paddles, Florence (240-241).
   Evidence: Circumstantial. Cook voyage collection from various sources.
   Literature: Giglioli, 1893, pp. 218-219; Kaeppler, 1977.

Figure 487. — Panpipe, London School of Economics.

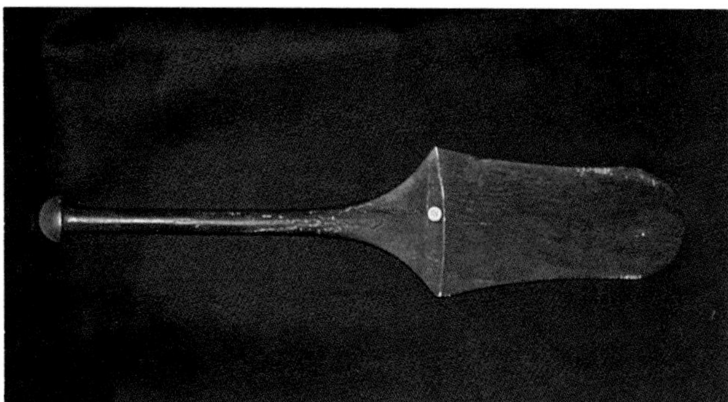

Figure 488.— Dance paddle, Dublin 1894.55.

4. Dance paddle, Christchurch (E 149.155).
   Evidence: Circumstantial. Worden Hall collection. See Appendix II, this volume.

5-7. Three broken dance paddles, Göttingen.
   Evidence: Forster collection (?), second voyage.

8. Dance paddle, Göttingen (OZ 134).
   Evidence: Purchased from London dealer Humphrey in 1782.

9. Dance paddle, Dublin (1894.55). Length 88.5 cm, width of blade 19.5 cm. Figure 488.
   Evidence: Circumstantial. Thought to be part of the Cook voyage collection given to Trinity College, Dublin, by Patten or King.

Tools

Tongan tools collected on Cook's voyages include adzes, basalt chisels, shark tooth incising tools, rasps, and thatching needles.

1. Hafted adz, Glasgow (E 366a). Length of handle 60 cm, length of blade 34 cm. Figure 489.
   Evidence: Circumstantial. Cook voyage collection from various sources. See Appendix III, this volume.

2-3. Two hafted adzes, Göttingen (OZ 358 exhibited). Figure 490.
   Evidence: Forster collection, second voyage.

4. Hafted adz, Wellington (FE 375). Length 37 cm.
   Evidence: Leverian Museum.
   Literature: Kaeppler, 1974a, p. 79.

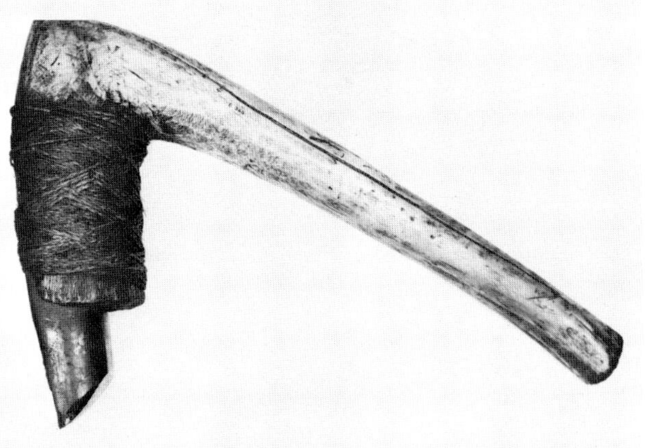

Figure 489.— Hafted adz, Glasgow E 366a.

5. Hafted adz, Christchurch (E 149.156).
   Evidence: Circumstantial. Worden Hall collection. See Appendix II, this volume.

6. Hafted basalt chisel, Stockholm (1799.2.10). Length 14 cm. Figure 491.
   Evidence: Sparrman collection, second voyage.
   Literature: Söderström, 1939, p. 40.

7. Shark tooth incising tool, Exeter (E 1228). Length 19 cm. Figure 492.
   Evidence: Leverian Museum.

8. Shark tooth incising tool, Vienna (40). Length 16.3 cm.
   Evidence: Leverian Museum.
   Literature: Moschner, 1955, pp. 163-164.

9-10. Two shark tooth incising tools, Dublin (1882.3885 [exhibited] and 3886). Lengths 14.5 cm, 12.5 cm. Figure 493.
   Evidence: Circumstantial. Thought to be part of the Cook voyage collection given to Trinity College, Dublin, by Patten and King.
   Literature: Freeman, 1949.

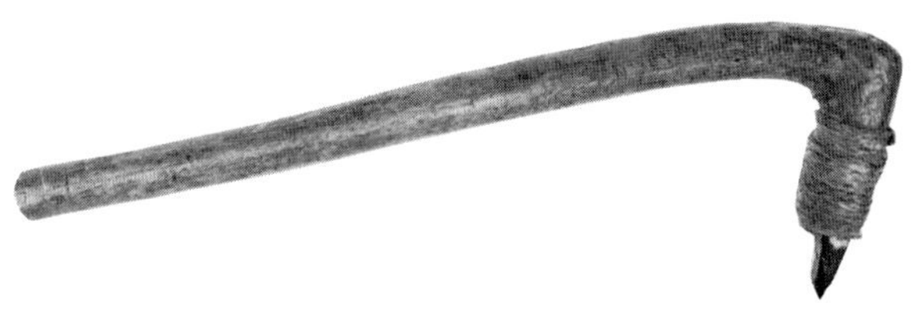

Figure 490.— Hafted adz, Göttingen OZ 358.

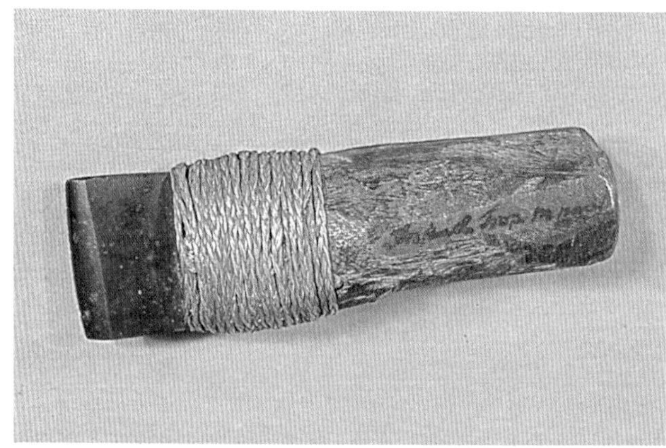

Figure 491.— Hafted chisel, Stockholm 1799.2.10.

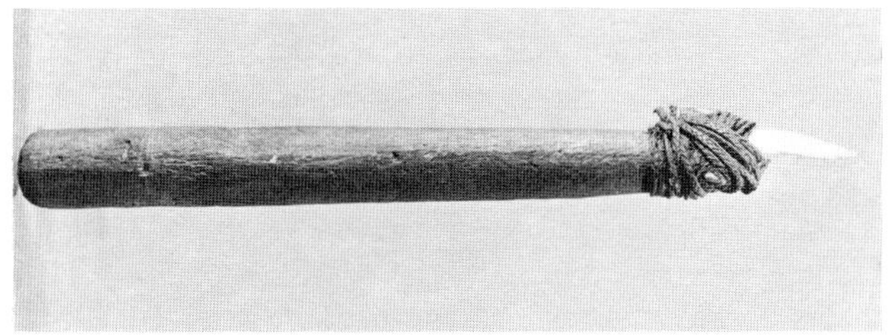

Figure 492.— Shark tooth incising tool, Exeter E 1228.

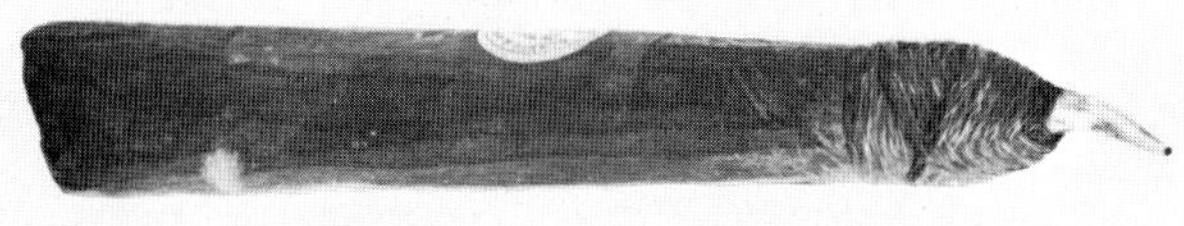

Figure 493.— Shark tooth incising tool, Dublin 1882.3885.

11. Shark tooth incising tool, Oxford (174). Length 19 cm.
    Evidence: Forster collection, second voyage.
    Literature: Gathercole, n.d. [1970]; Kaeppler, 1971, pp. 215-216.
12. Nail mounted in a handle of bone (a nail from the voyage of Tasman or Wallis mounted in the indigenous manner and used as an incising tool), Oxford (101a). Length 9.5 cm.
    Evidence: Forster collection, second voyage.
    Literature: Gathercole, n.d. [1970]; Kaeppler, 1971, pp. 216-217.

Rasps or Files

Rasps made of a piece of wood, covered with sharkskin or skin from the stingray, were used in Tonga (among other things) to grate sandalwood used for the scenting of coconut oil. Usually attributed to Tahiti, such files may also have been used there. However, there is more documentary evidence for a Tongan provenance for those collected on Cook's voyages. Thus, although they are attributed to Tonga in this Catalogue, some of them may, in fact, be from the Society Islands. I do not know how to distinguish them by place of origin, nor can I find any documents that would enable me to do so.

1-4. Four rasps, Vienna (113, 114, 115 [exhibited], 116). Lengths 36 cm, 33 cm, 22.5 cm, 21 cm. Figure 494.
    Evidence: Leverian Museum.
    Literature: Moschner, 1955, pp. 167-168.
5. Rasp, Dublin (1882.3887). Length 27.5 cm. Figure 495.
    Evidence: Circumstantial. Thought to be part of the Cook voyage collection given to Trinity College, Dublin, by Patten or King.
    Literature: Freeman, 1949.
6. Rasp, Cambridge (22.937).
    Evidence: Leverian Museum.
7. Rasp, Oxford (96). Length 33 cm.
    Evidence: Forster collection, second voyage.
    Literature: Gathercole, n.d. [1970].
8. Rasp, Florence (255).
    Evidence: Circumstantial. Cook voyage collection from various sources.
    Literature: Giglioli, 1893, p. 211; Kaeppler, 1977.

Thatching Needles

Thatching needles were apparently used in both Tonga and the Society Islands. Again, because I do not know how to differentiate between them, they are all listed here.

1. Wood thatching needle, Vienna (126). Length 37.5 cm. Figure 496.
    Evidence: Leverian Museum.
    Literature: Moschner, 1955, p. 170.
2-3. Two thatching needles of wood and bone, Göttingen.
    Evidence: Purchased from London dealer Humphrey in 1782.
4. Bone thatching needle, Florence (205).
    Evidence: Circumstantial. Cook voyage collection from various sources.
    Literature: Giglioli, 1893, p. 188; Kaeppler, 1977.

Canoe Paddles

1. Canoe paddle, Stockholm (1799.2.36). Length 115.5 cm, width of blade 28 cm. Figure 497.
    Evidence: Sparrman collection, second voyage.
    Literature: Söderström, 1939, pp. 43-44.

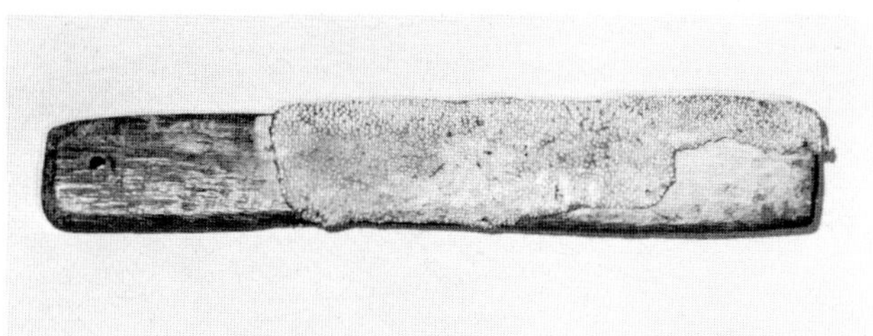

Figure 494.— Rasp, Vienna 115.

Figure 495.— Rasp, Dublin 1882.3887.

Figure 496. — Thatching needle, Vienna 126.

2. Canoe paddle, Göttingen.
   Evidence: Purchased from London dealer Humphrey in 1782.
3. Canoe paddle, Oxford (69). Missing.
   Evidence: Forster collection, second voyage.
   Literature: Gathercole, n.d. [1970].
4. Canoe paddle, Exeter (E 1215). Missing.
   Evidence: Leverian Museum.
5. Canoe paddle, Dublin (1894.416). Length 150 cm.
   Evidence: Circumstantial. Thought to be part of Cook voyage collection given to Trinity College, Dublin, by Patten or King.

Fishing Equipment

Fishing equipment apparently collected in Tonga on Cook's voyages includes fishnets, octopus lures, fishhooks of "Western Polynesian" type, and fishhooks of the classic Tongan type. The fishnets are usually given a provenance of "Otaheiti," but they seem more likely to have come from Tonga. The nets are made of *olongā* fiber, have stone or coral weights, and *hau* wood floats. They were placed nets, rather than throwing nets.

1. Fishnet, Oxford (60). Width 127 cm.
   Evidence: Forster collection, second voyage.
   Literature: Gathercole, n.d. [1970].
2. Fishnet, Göttingen.
   Evidence: Forster collection, second voyage.
3. Fishnet, Sydney (H 144). Said to be 34 feet 6 inches in length and 4 feet 3 inches in depth.
   Evidence: Cook collection exhibited at Colonial and Indian Exhibition.
   Literature: Mackrell, 1886; Appendix I, this volume.

Figure 498. — Octopus lure, Vienna 49.

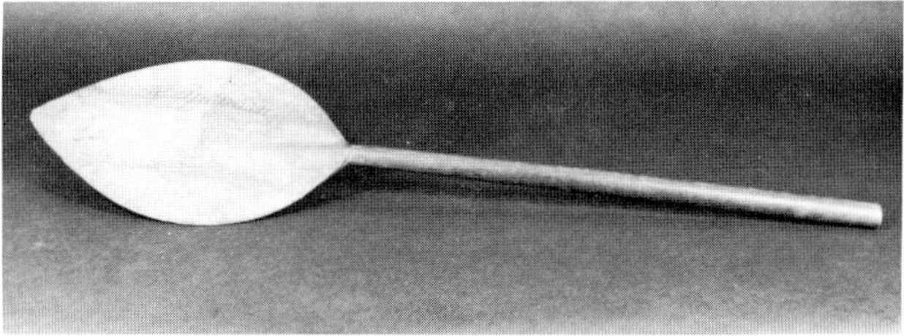

Figure 497. — Canoe paddle, Stockholm 1799.2.36.

4. Fishnet, Florence (203).
   Evidence: Circumstantial. Cook voyage collection from various sources.
   Literature: Giglioli, 1893, pp. 228-229; Kaeppler, 1977.

Octopus Lures

1. Octopus lure, Vienna (49). Length of lure (without stick) 8.5 cm. Figure 498.
   Evidence: Leverian Museum.
   Literature: Moschner, 1955, p. 191.
2. Octopus lure, Dublin (1882.3896). Total length 26 cm. Figure 287.
   Evidence: Circumstantial. Thought to be part of Cook voyage collection given to Trinity College, Dublin, by Patten or King.
   Literature: Freeman, 1949.
3. Octopus lure, Oxford (63). Total length 16 cm.
   Evidence: Forster collection, second voyage.
   Literature: Gathercole, n.d. [1970].
4. Octopus lure, Göttingen.
   Evidence: Purchased from London dealer Humphrey in 1782.
5. Octopus lure, Wörlitz (3). Length 9.7 cm.
   Evidence: Forster collection, second voyage.
   Literature: Germer, 1975, p. 89.

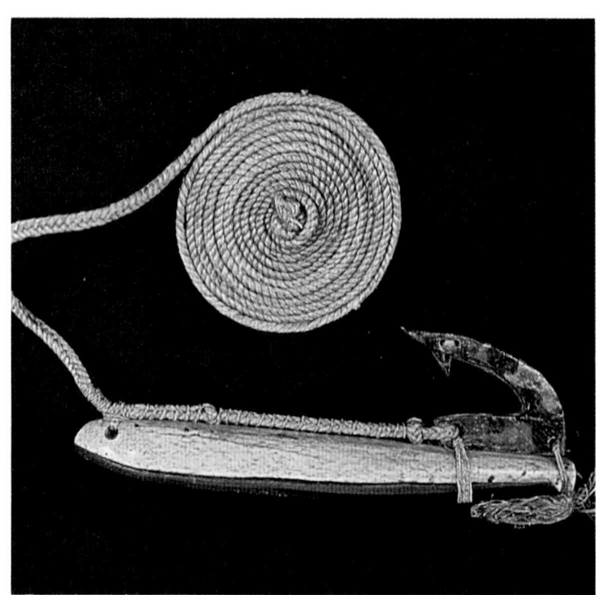

Figure 499. — Fishhook, Stockholm 1799.2.19.

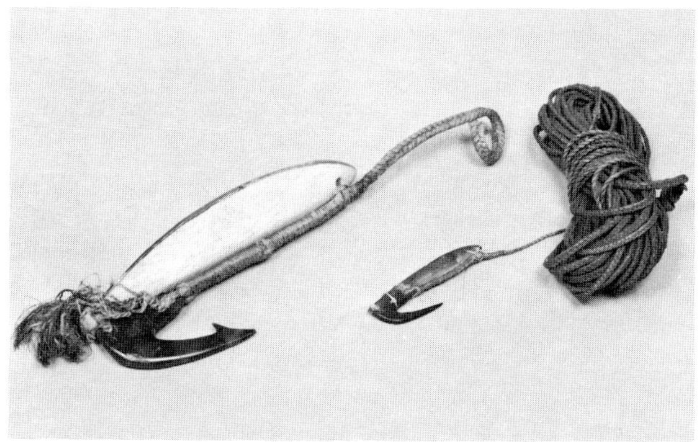

Figure 500.— Two fishhooks, Edinburgh 1956.1010, 1956.1011.

Fishhooks

Fishhooks of classic Tongan style, apparently used for taking bonito, were made of a bone shank, faced with black pearl shell, and pointed with turtle shell—usually having an inner barb, but occasionally unbarbed. Unbarbed points became recycled decorative elements added to necklaces (see above).

1. Fishhook, Stockholm (1799.2.19). Length 15.5 cm. Figure 499.
Evidence: Sparrman collection, second voyage.
Literature: Söderström, 1939, pp. 40-41.

2. Fishhook, Edinburgh (1956.1011). Length 14.5 cm. Figure 500.
Evidence: Given by Mrs. Cook to Sir John Pringle.

3-5. Three fishhooks, Vienna (99-101).
Evidence: Leverian Museum.
Literature: Moschner, 1955, p. 184.

6. Fishhook, Berne (FR 29).
Evidence: Webber collection, third voyage.
Literature: Henking, 1957, p. 343; Kaeppler, 1977.

7. Fishhook, Abbotsford (home of Sir Walter Scott).
Evidence: Circumstantial. Probably Leverian Museum.
Literature: Kaeppler, 1974a, p. 85.

8-12. Five fishhooks, Oxford (64). Lengths from 14 cm to 16 cm.
Evidence: Forster collection, second voyage.
Literature: Gathercole, n.d. [1970].

13. Fishhook, Florence (198). Missing.
Evidence: Circumstantial. Cook voyage collection from various sources.
Literature: Giglioli, 1895, pp. 142-143; Kaeppler, 1977.

14. Fishhook, Rome.
Evidence: Circumstantial. Cook voyage collection from various sources.
Literature: Giglioli, 1895, pp. 142-143; Kaeppler, 1977.

15-16. Two fishhooks (one with wood shank), Göttingen.
Evidence: Purchased from London dealer Humphrey in 1782.

17. Fishhook, Sydney (H 127). Length 14 cm.
Evidence: Cook collection exhibited at Colonial and Indian Exhibition.
Literature: Mackrell, 1886; Appendix I, this volume.

18. Fishhook, Wörlitz (1). Length 13.4 cm.
Evidence: Forster collection, second voyage.
Literature: Germer, 1975, p. 89.

19-24. Six fishhooks, Wellington.
Evidence: Circumstantial. Bullock's Museum from Leverian Museum or Banks.
Literature: Kaeppler, 1974a, p. 80.

Fishhooks of "West Polynesian" Type

A second type of composite fishhook was apparently collected in Tonga and was depicted by Cleveley (Fig. 501). The type has parallels in Samoa and similar examples are known from Central Polynesia.

1-3. Three fishhooks, Vienna (47, 102, 108 [latter two exhibited]). Lengths 8 cm, 10 cm, 3.2 cm. Figure 502.
Evidence: Leverian Museum.
Literature: Moschner, 1955, pp. 185-188.

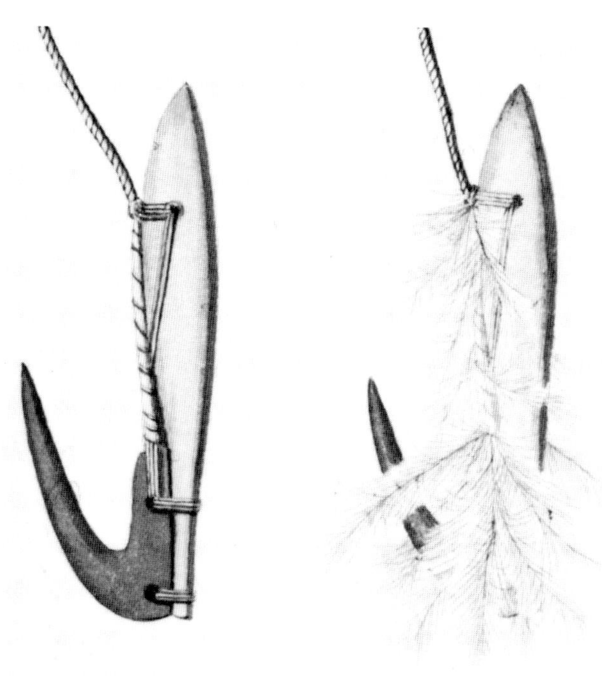

Figure 501.— Drawing by Cleveley, British Library Add. Ms. 23,920.111.

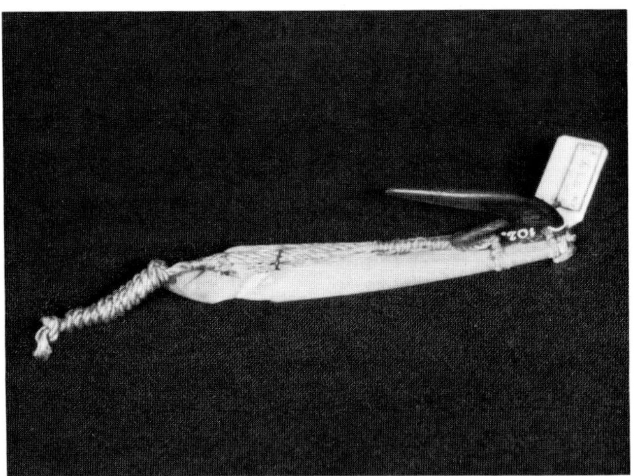

Figure 502. — Fishhook, Vienna 102.

4. Fishhook, Edinburgh (1956.1010). Length 6 cm. Figure 500.
   Evidence: Given by Mrs. Cook to Sir John Pringle.

5-7. Three fishhooks, Berne (TAH 28, 29, 30).
   Evidence: Webber collection, third voyage.
   Literature: Henking, 1957, pp. 356-357; Kaeppler, 1977.

8-9. Two fishhooks, Göttingen.
   Evidence: Purchased from London dealer Humphrey in 1782.

10-13. Four fishhooks, Sydney (H 129, 131, 132, 134). Lengths 8.5 cm, 9.5 cm, 7 cm, 7.5 cm.
   Evidence: Cook collection exhibited at Colonial and Indian Exhibition.
   Literature: Mackrell, 1886; Appendix I, this volume.

14-15. Two fishhooks, Florence.
   Evidence: Circumstantial. Cook voyage collection from various sources.
   Literature: Giglioli, 1895, pp. 85-88; Kaeppler, 1977.

16. Fishhook, Wörlitz (2). Length 9 cm.
   Evidence: Forster collection, second voyage.
   Literature: Germer, 1975, p. 89.

17-18. Two fishhooks. Unidentified.
   Evidence: Depicted in British Library Add. Ms. 23,920.111 (Fig. 501).

Fishhook Parts

1. Turtle shell point, Bishop Museum (1970.221.02). Length 5.1 cm.
   Evidence: Leverian Museum.

2. Shell shank, Vienna (48). Length 12.5 cm.
   Evidence: Leverian Museum.
   Literature: Moschner, 1955, p. 185.

Amusements

Amusements during the 18th century in Tonga included various kinds of athletic exercises, boxing, pigeon-snaring, and shooting rats with bow and arrow. Although a "quarter staff used in athletic exercises" was listed in the Leverian Museum sale catalogue, nothing has been found that would answer this description that can be traced to Cook's voyages. A number of bows and arrows have been located. Tongan bows have a deep groove carved on one long side of the bow in which one arrow was carried. Arrows are made of a long reed, pointed with hard wood.

1-2. Bow and arrow, Stockholm (1799.2.39 & 40). Length of bow 210 cm, length of arrow 185 cm.
   Evidence: Sparrman collection, second voyage.
   Literature: Söderström, 1939, pp. 36-40.

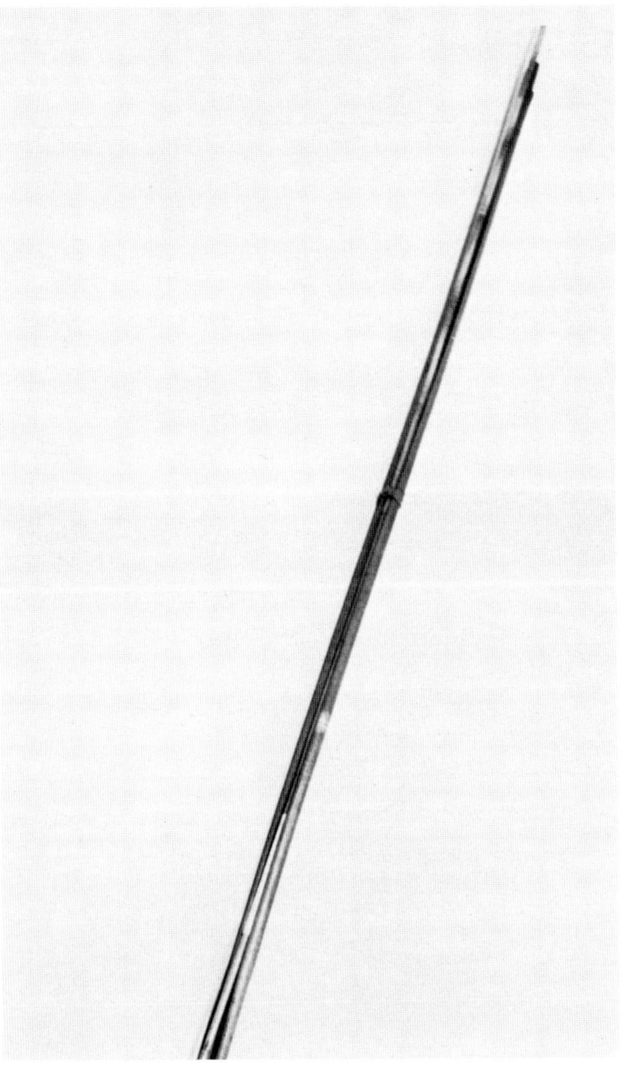

Figure 503. — Bow and arrow (detail), Oxford 67.

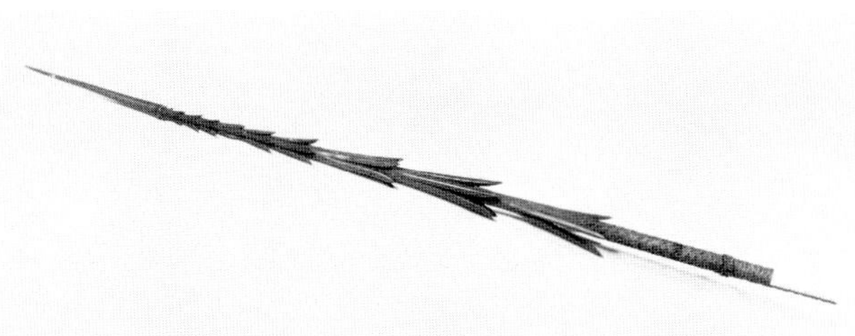

Figure 504. — Barbed spear, Oxford 68.

3-4. Bow and arrow, Oxford (67). Length of bow 205 cm, arrow point missing. Figure 503.
Evidence: Forster collection, second voyage. Probably the bow and arrow depicted in Cook, 1777, Plate 21 (Fig. 430). A fiber wrapping to hold the arrow in the groove which is shown in the lithograph is still extant on the bow.
Literature: Gathercole, n.d. [1970].

5-7. Bow and three arrows, Göttingen.
Evidence: Purchased from London dealer Humphrey in 1782.
Literature: Plischke, 1957, p. 209.

8-10. Bow and two arrows, Florence (26).
Evidence: Circumstantial. Cook voyage collection from various sources.
Literature: Giglioli, 1893, pp. 215-217; Kaeppler, 1977.

11-12. Two bows, Cape Town (SAM 1984).
Evidence: Thought to have arrived in Cape Town in 1775, second voyage.
Literature: Bax, 1970, p. 146.

Spears

Spears collected in Tonga on Cook's voyages were of two types—a fishing spear with three or four tines bound on one end, and a weapon either carved with barbed points and/or with barbs lashed on in rings. The Greenwich fly whisk is a recycled spear point (see Fig. 462).

Figure 505. — Reception for Captain Cook, British Library Add. Ms. 15,513.8.

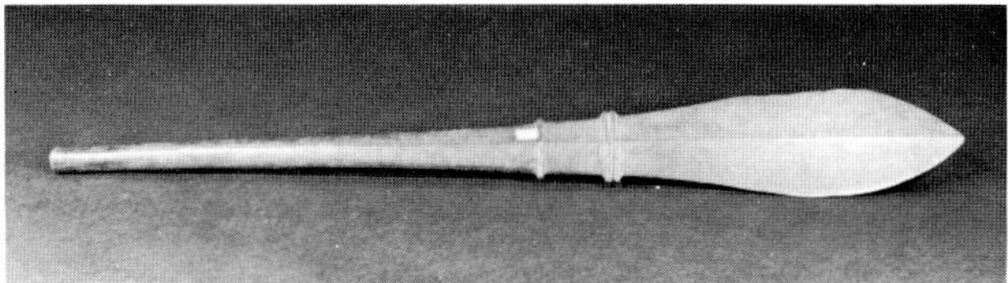

Figure 506. — Club, Stockholm 1799.2.38.

1. Fishing spear, Göttingen.
   Evidence: Purchased from London dealer Humphrey in 1782.
2. Barbed spear, Oxford (68). Length 304 cm. Figure 504.
   Evidence: Forster collection, second voyage. Probably the spear depicted in two views in Cook, 1777, Plate 21 (Fig. 430).
   Literature: Gathercole, n.d. [1970].
3. Barbed spear, Vienna (153).
   Evidence: Leverian Museum.
   Literature: Moschner, 1955, p. 141 (attributed to Hawaii).
4. Barbed spear, Göttingen.
   Evidence: Purchased from London dealer Humphrey in 1782.

Clubs

Tongan clubs were the most numerous type of artifacts collected on Cook's voyages. Quite a number can be located, but many have lost their association with Cook's voyages. More than 50 clubs from the Leverian Museum alone have lost their association with the voyages and are unidentified today. Because they are so numerous, Tongan clubs are particularly useful for studies of change in the short period between Cook's second and third voyage.[11] At a reception for Cook in Ha'apai, club fighting was apparently used for entertainment (Fig. 505).

1-2. Two clubs, Stockholm (1799.2.37 and 38 [exhibited]). Lengths 84.5 cm, 116.7 cm. Figure 506.
   Evidence: Sparrman collection, second voyage.
   Literature: Söderström, 1939, pp. 34-36.

3. Club, Cambridge (27.1382). Length 97 cm. Figure 507.
   Evidence: Leverian Museum.

4-12. Nine clubs, Exeter (E 1205, 1206, 1207, 1208, 1209, 1210, 1211, 1212, 1217 [all exhibited]). Lengths 116 cm, 108 cm, 89 cm, 86.5 cm, 94 cm, 94.5 cm, 110 cm, 72 cm, 116 cm. Figures 508-517.
   Evidence: Leverian Museum.

[11] Clubs attributed to Cook's voyages without convincing documentation or traditions have not been included, for example, those in the Oldman collection (31862, 31863 in Auckland).

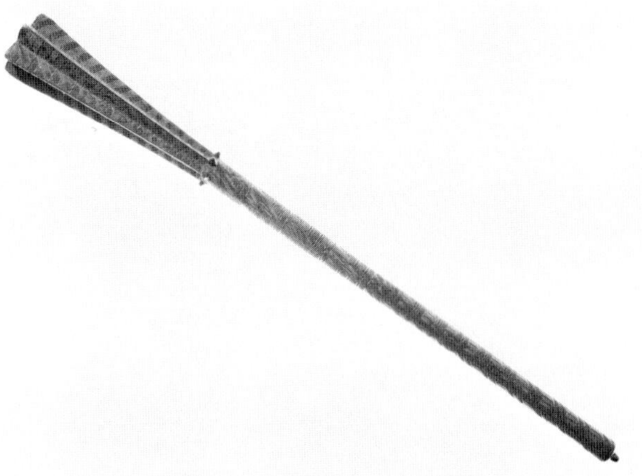

Figure 507. — Club, Cambridge 27.1382.

13. Club, Greenwich (L15/92/A). Length 84.5 cm. Figure 518.
   Evidence: Collected by William Griffin on the *Resolution,* third voyage.

14-23. Ten clubs, Oxford (70-79).
   Evidence: Forster collection, second voyage.
   Literature: Gathercole, n.d. [1970].

24-25. Two clubs, Wörlitz (7, 8). Lengths 101.8 cm, 100.5 cm.
   Evidence: Forster collection, second voyage.
   Literature: Germer, 1975, p. 90.

26-34. Nine (?) clubs, Göttingen.
   Evidence: Forster collection, second voyage.

35-36. Two clubs, Rupert Furneaux collection.
   Evidence: Collected by Captain Furneaux, second voyage.
   Literature: Furneaux, 1960, p. 180.

37-45. Nine clubs, Greenwich (L15/70/A-G, /71/A-B).
   Evidence: Circumstantial. Said to have been presented by Captain Cook to Neil Malcolm of Poltalloch before he left on his third voyage (Anon., 1958).

46. Club, British Museum (NN).
   Evidence: Circumstantial. Said to be the club depicted in the official account of the second voyage (Cook, 1777, Plate 21 [Fig. 430]).

47. Club, Cambridge (1914.79).
   Evidence: Sandwich collection. Given by Cook, second voyage.

48. Club, Cambridge (25.426).
   Evidence: Pennant collection of Cook voyage objects from various sources.

49. Club. Lost.
   Evidence: Depicted in a drawing pasted in Pennant's copy of Cook's voyages in the Dixson Library. Probably second voyage (Fig. 519).

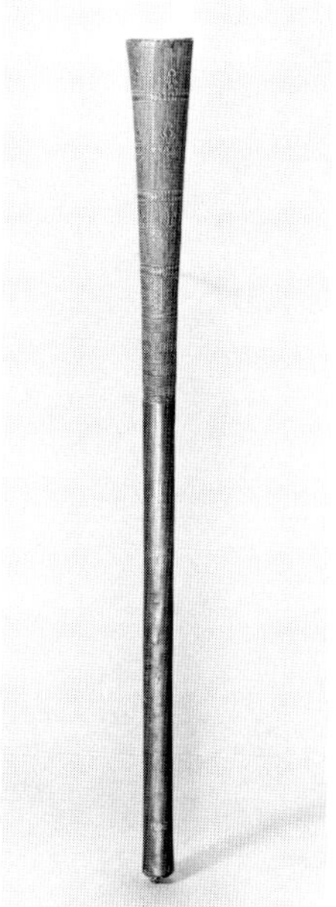

Figure 508. — Club, Exeter 1208.

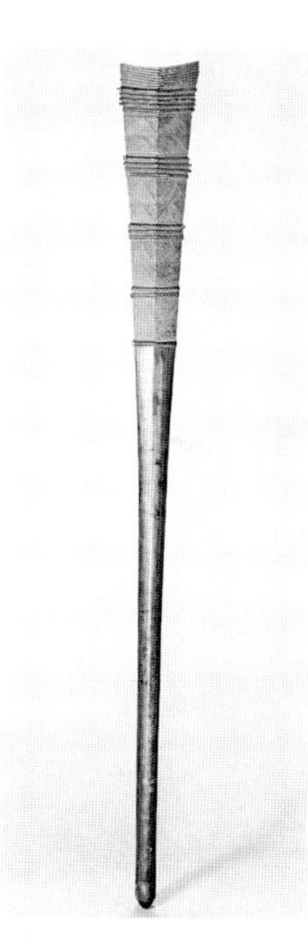

Figure 509. — Club, Exeter 1205.

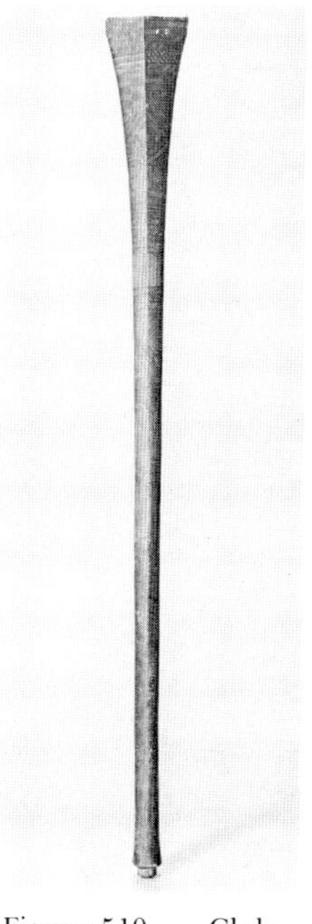

Figure 510. — Club, Exeter 1206.

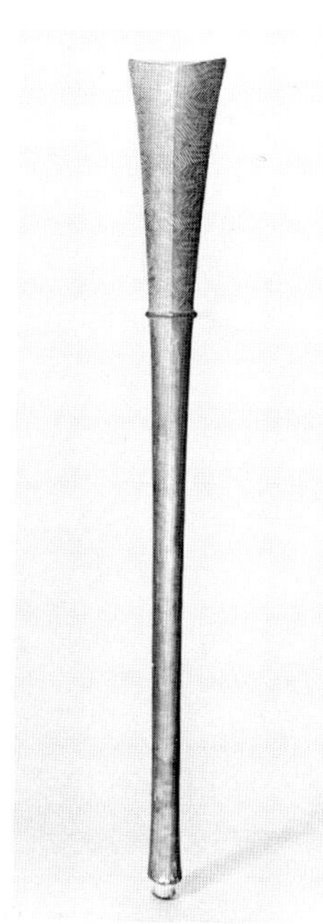

Figure 511. — Club, Exeter 1207.

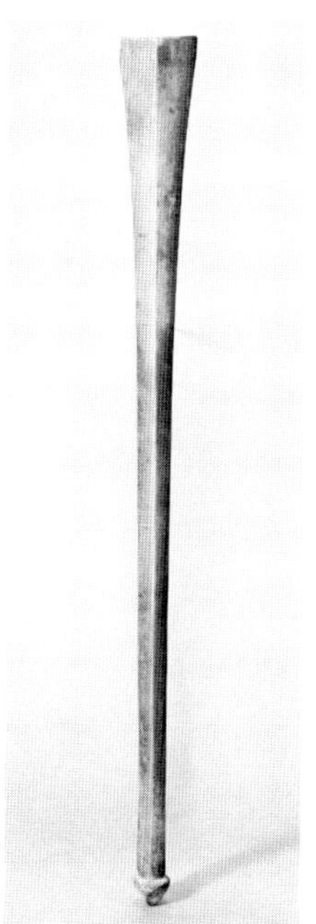

Figure 512. — Club, Exeter 1210.

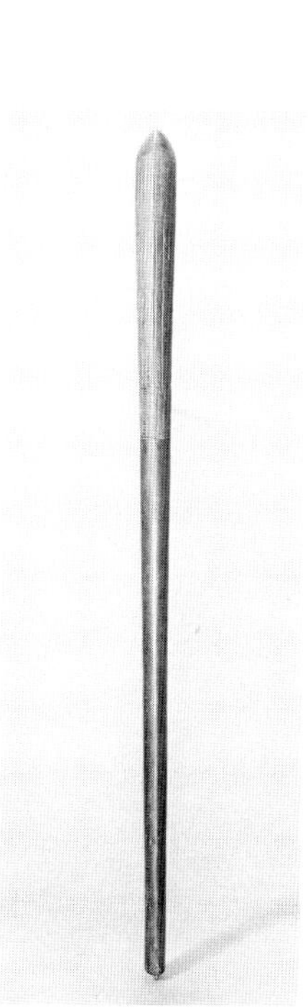

Figure 513. — Club, Exeter 1209.

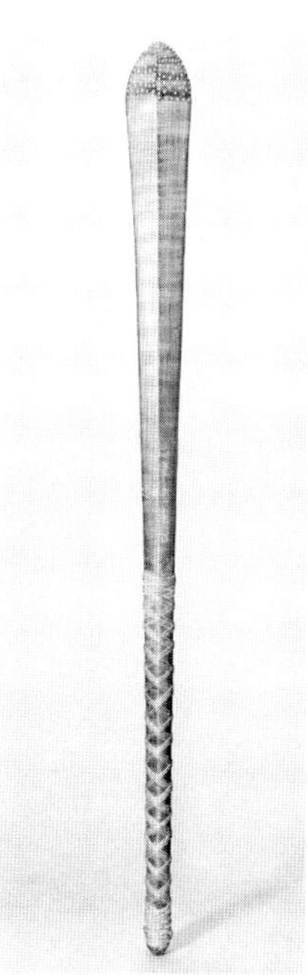

Figure 514. — Club, Exeter 1217.

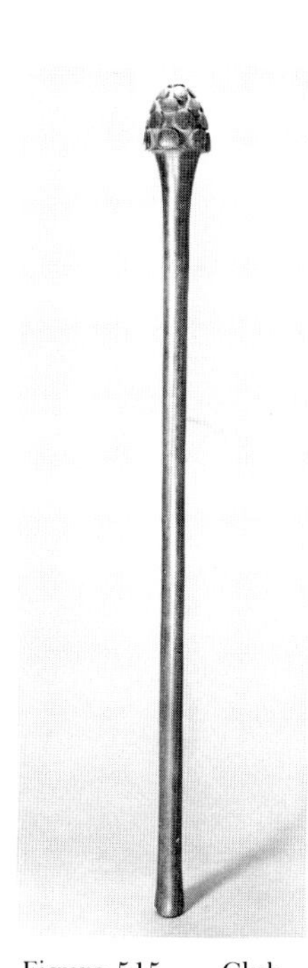

Figure 515. — Club, Exeter 1211.

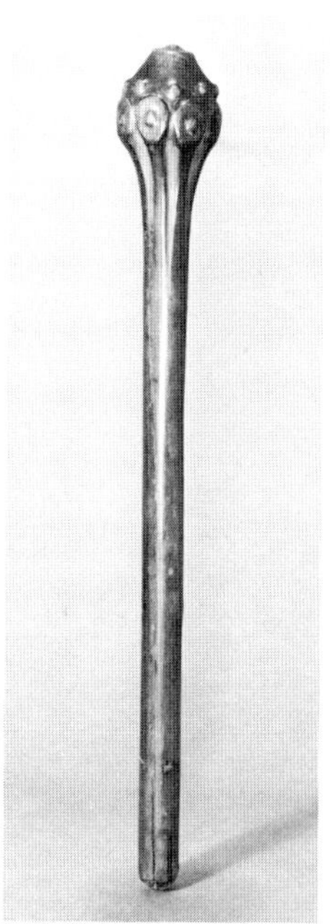

Figure 516. — Club, Exeter 1212.

Figure 517. — Club (detail), Exeter 1208.

50. Club, Berne (FR 8). Length 97 cm.
Evidence: Webber collection, third voyage.
Literature: Henking, 1957, p. 337; Kaeppler, 1977.

51. Club, British Museum (1932.10-8.1).
Evidence: Collected by James Ward, Midshipman on the *Resolution*. Third voyage.

52-53. Two clubs, Stockholm (1848.1.15 and 16). Lengths 87 cm, 80 cm.
Evidence: "Banks collection."

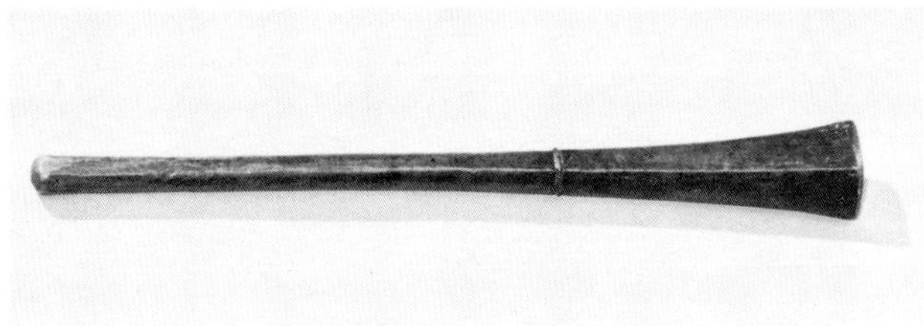

Figure 518. — Club, Greenwich L15/92/A.

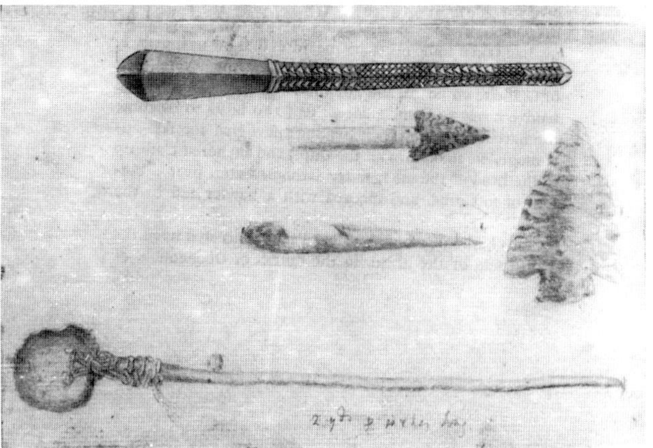

Figure 519. — Artifacts from Tonga and Tierra del Fuego, Dixson Library.

54-60. Seven clubs, Vienna (31-36, 38).
Evidence: Leverian Museum.
Literature: Moschner, 1955, pp. 147-153, 248-249.

61-66. Six clubs, Florence.
Evidence: Circumstantial. Cook voyage collection from various sources.
Literature: Giglioli, 1893, pp. 211-215; Kaeppler, 1977.

67-71. Five clubs, Göttingen.
Evidence: Purchased from London dealer Humphrey in 1782.

72. Club, Glasgow (E 565). Length 119 cm.
Evidence: Circumstantial. Cook voyage collection from various sources. A label "N," thought to designate Cook voyage pieces is still attached (Fig. 520). See Appendix III, this volume.

Figure 520. — Label on Tongan club, Glasgow E 565.

73. Club, Wellington (FE 339).
    Evidence: Probably Leverian Museum.
    Literature: Kaeppler, 1974, p. 79.
74. Club, Wellington (FE 3663). Length 137 cm.
    Evidence: Bequeathed by Mrs. Cook to her sister Margaret's granddaughter, whose daughter married S. J. Long.
75-81. Seven clubs, British Museum (ST. 851-852).
    Evidence: Circumstantial. From the sale of William H. Pepys, said to be from Cook's voyages.
82. Club, Christchurch (E149.148).
    Evidence: Circumstantial. Worden Hall collection. See Appendix II, this volume.
    Literature: Duff, 1969, Plate 85.
83-84. Two clubs, London School of Economics, on loan from the Cuming Museum (C 3175, 3189).
    Evidence: Circumstantial. Said to be from Cook's voyages. Probably Leverian Museum.

85-86. Two clubs. Lost.
    Evidence: Depicted in the Catalogue of the Colonial and Indian Exhibition.
    Literature: Mackrell, 1886; Appendix I, this volume.

87-? Several clubs, Dublin (1894?). Unidentifiable with available documentation.
    Evidence: Circumstantial. Thought to be part of the Cook voyage collections given to Trinity College, Dublin, by Patten and King.
    Literature: Freeman, 1949; Ball, 1894 [1895].

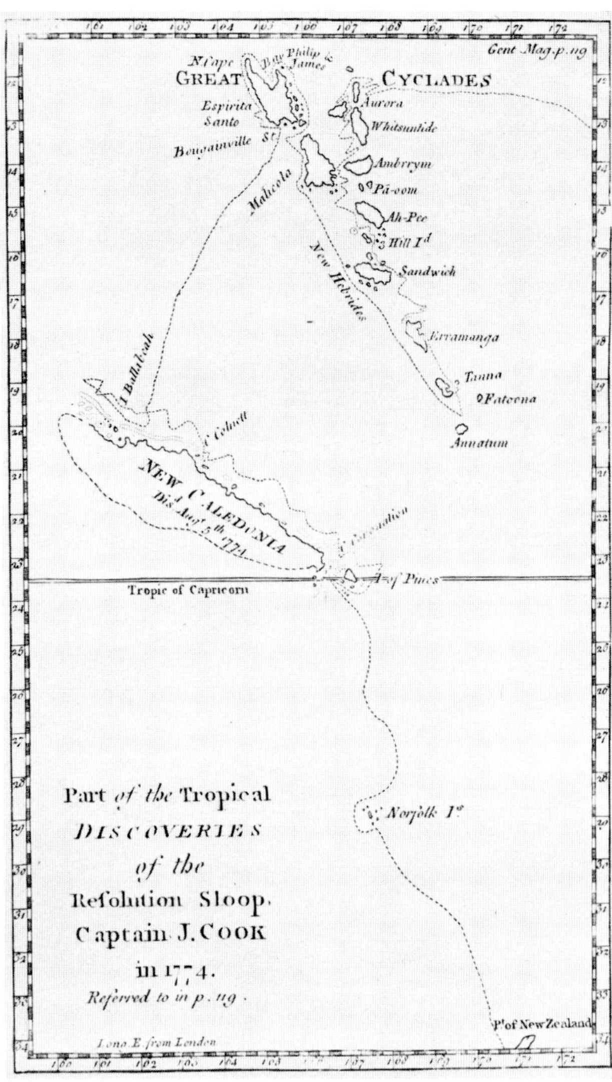

Figure 521.— Chart of New Caledonia and New Hebrides (56).

NEW CALEDONIA

During his second Pacific voyage Cook spent two weeks in New Caledonia, including eight days in the Balad area, where he participated in a ritual exchange of gifts, but apparently not many ethnographic specimens were collected. Cook himself was incapacitated by food poisoning (Douglas, 1970, p. 182). There were no overtly hostile clashes between Cook's men and the New Caledonians. Indeed, instead of using them against the voyagers, the men brought their weapons to sell, "but all the others came empty in respect to refreshments, but brought with them some arms such as clubs, darts, etc. which they exchanged away" (Beaglehole, 1961, p. 531). They appear to have exchanged little else for, with few exceptions, New Caledonian objects in Cook voyage collections are weapons.

Hat

Hodges's well-known picture of a New Caledonia man (Fig. 522) depicts a hat that was probably at one time in the Oxford collection. It appears to be the same hat that was also depicted in the plate of artifacts from New Caledonia (Cook, 1777, Plate 20 [Fig. 523])—objects which probably belonged to the Forsters.

1. "A cap with feathers & ferns," Oxford (155). Missing.
   Evidence: Forster collection.
   Literature: Gathercole, n.d. [1970].

Combs

1. Comb, Vienna (9). Length 30 cm. Figure 524.
   Evidence: Leverian Museum.
   Literature: Moschner, 1955, p. 219.

2-3. Two combs, Oxford (150). Lengths 27 cm, 20.5 cm.
   Evidence: Forster collection.
   Literature: Gathercole, n.d. [1970].

4. Comb, Stockholm (1799.2.47). Length 27 cm.
   Evidence: Sparrman collection.
   Literature: Söderström, 1939, pp. 60-61.

Figure 522.— Man of New Caledonia, *Atlas* to Cook's second voyage (28).

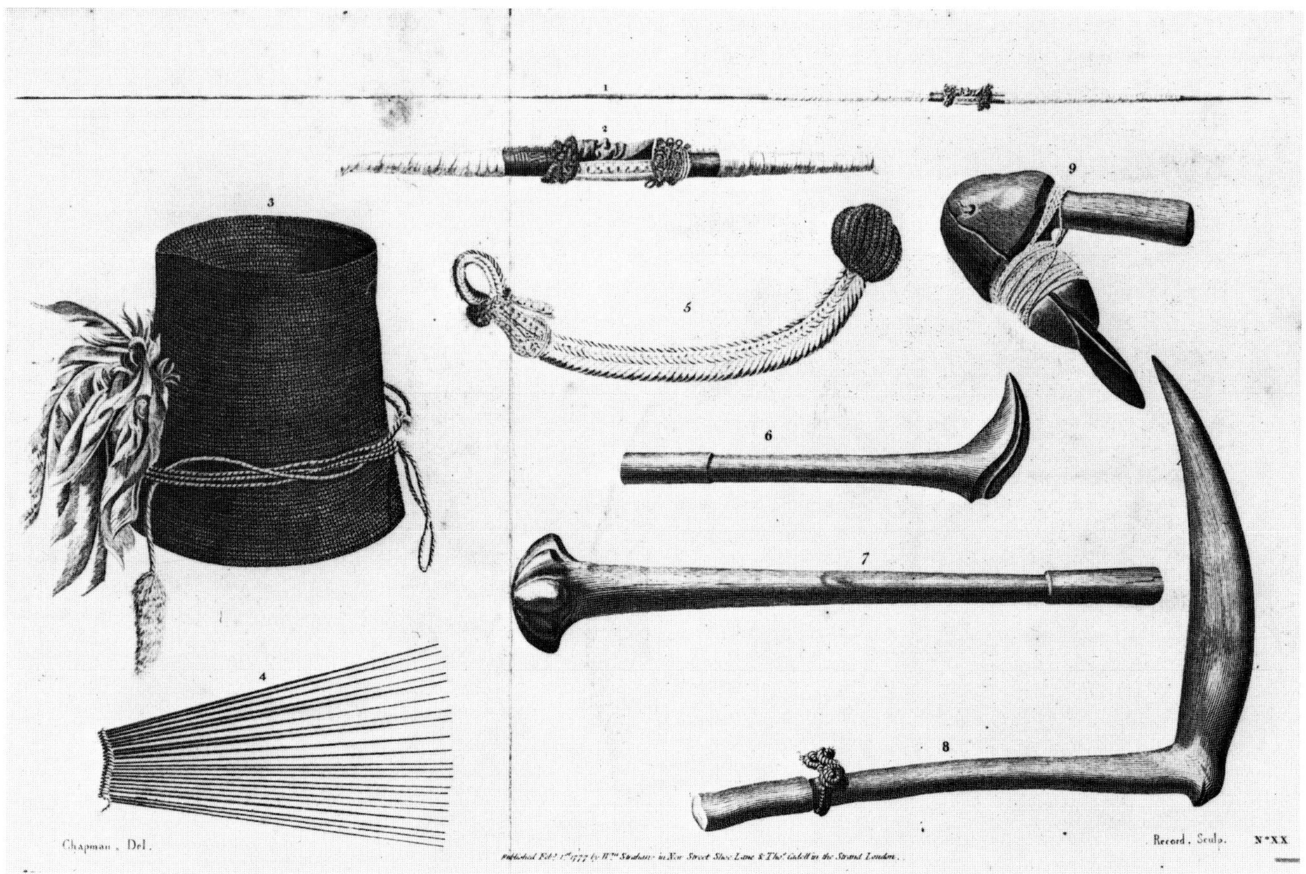

Figure 523. — Artifacts from New Caledonia, *Atlas* to Cook's second voyage (28).

5-6. Two combs, Sydney (H 108, 109). Lengths 40 cm, 27 cm.
Evidence: Cook voyage collection exhibited at the Colonial and Indian Exhibition.
Literature: Mackrell, 1886; Appendix I, this volume.

7-8. Two combs, Florence (206).
Evidence: Circumstantial. Cook voyage collection from various sources.
Literature: Giglioli, 1893, pp. 203-204; Kaeppler, 1977.

9-10. Two combs, Göttingen.
Evidence: Purchased from London dealer Humphrey in 1782.

Ornaments

Two ornaments in the Florence collection may be from New Caledonia. They were attributed by Giglioli to New Zealand and Hawaii, but this is unlikely. They are listed here as New Caledonian, but because of lack of comparative material, this should not be regarded as final.

1-2. Two ornaments of shell and dog teeth, Florence (211, 53).
Evidence: Cook voyage collection from various sources.
Literature: Giglioli, 1893, p. 189; 1895, p. 79; Kaeppler, 1977.

Spear Throwers

A spear thrower was depicted by Hodges being carried as an attachment to a hat (Fig. 522).

1. Spear thrower, Sydney (H 119). Length 22 cm. Figure 525.
Evidence: Cook collection exhibited at Colonial and Indian Exhibition.
Literature: Mackrell, 1886; Appendix I, this volume.

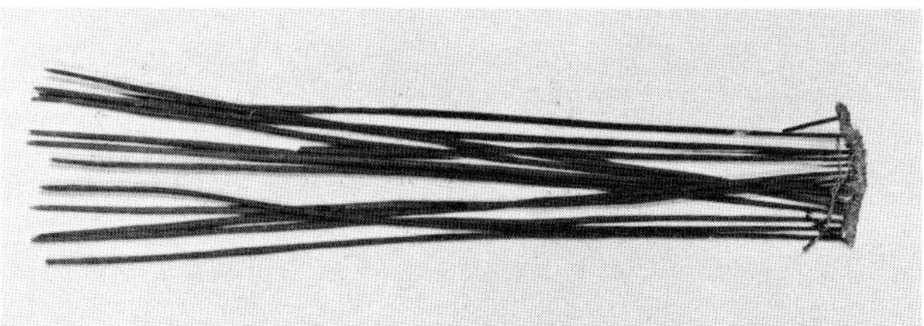

Figure 524. — Comb, Vienna 9.

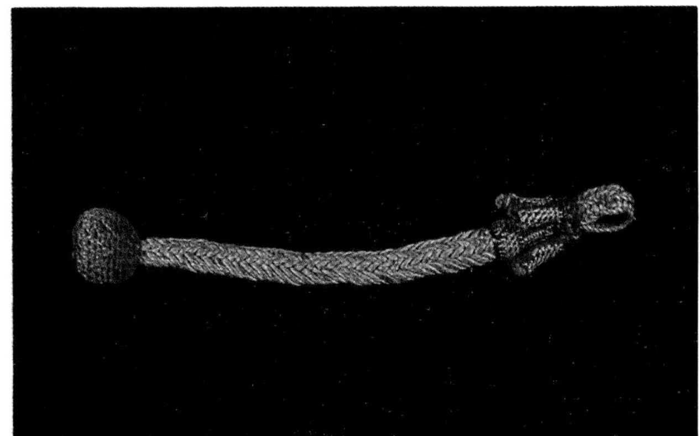

Figure 525. — Spear thrower, Sydney H 119.

2. Spear thrower, Vienna (3). Length 21.5 cm.
   Evidence: Leverian Museum.
   Literature: Moschner, 1955, p. 155.

3. Spear thrower, Oxford (160). Missing.
   Evidence: Forster collection.
   Literature: Gathercole, n.d. [1970].

4. Spear thrower, Göttingen.
   Evidence: Purchased from London dealer Humphrey in 1782.

Spears

1-2. Two spears (one carved, one plain), Oxford (161-162). Missing.
   Evidence: Forster collection. Perhaps the spear depicted in Figure 523.
   Literature: Gathercole, n.d. [1970].

3. Spear, Göttingen.
   Evidence: Purchased from London dealer Humphrey in 1782.

Slings

1. Sling (attributed to New Caledonia by Forster, but perhaps from New Hebrides), Oxford. Length 230 cm.
   Evidence: Forster collection.
   Literature: Gathercole, n.d. [1970].

2-3. Two slings (provenance questionable: New Caledonia or New Hebrides), Göttingen.
   Evidence: Forster and Humphrey collections.

4. Sling, Florence (154).
   Evidence: Circumstantial. Cook voyage collection from various sources.
   Literature: Giglioli, 1893, pp. 233-234; Kaeppler, 1977.

Figure 526. — Bag for sling stones, Sydney H 115.

Bags for Sling Stones

1. Bag for sling stones, Sydney (H 115). Length 20.5 cm, height 13 cm, ties 40 cm. Figure 526.
   Evidence: Cook collection exhibited at Colonial and Indian Exhibition.
   Literature: Mackrell, 1886; Appendix I, this volume.

2. Bag for sling stones, Oxford (164). Missing.
   Evidence: Forster collection.
   Literature: Gathercole, n.d. [1970].

3. Bag for sling stones, Göttingen.
   Evidence: Forster collection.

Sling Stones

1-6. Six sling stones, Oxford (164). Lengths 5 to 6 cm.
   Evidence: Forster collection.
   Literature: Gathercole, n.d. [1970].

7-?. Sling stones, Göttingen.
   Evidence: Forster and Humphrey collections.

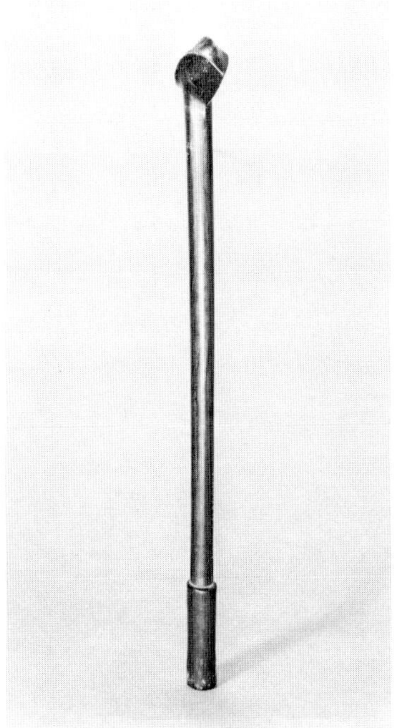

Figure 527. — Club, Exeter E 1214.

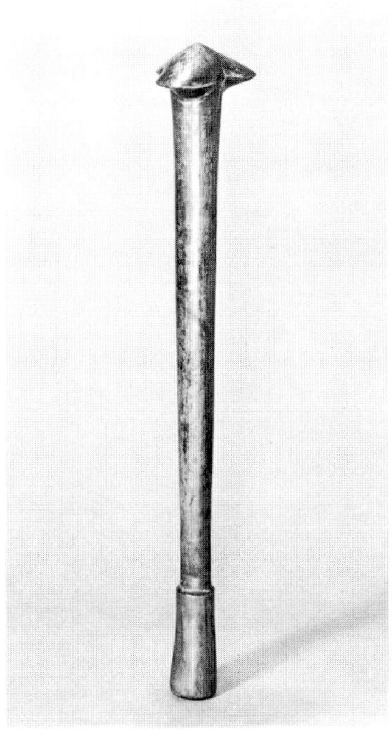

Figure 528. — Club, Exeter E 1218.

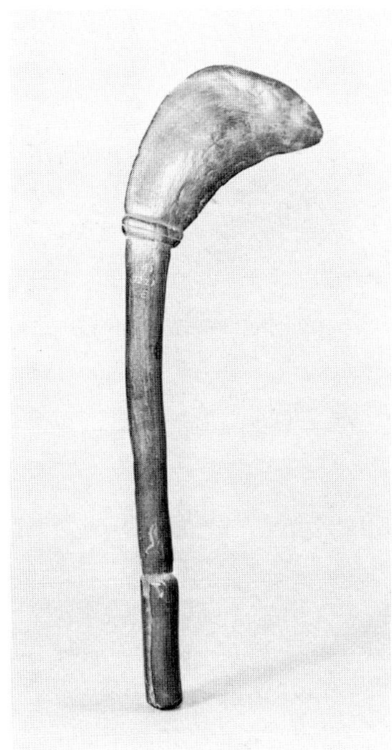

Figure 529. — Club, Exeter E 1221.

Figure 530. — Club, Stockholm 1799.2.48.

Clubs

New Caledonia clubs were beautifully carved and finished in hard wood. The several styles were not only effective, but aesthetically pleasing.

1-3. Three clubs, Exeter (E 1214, 1218, 1221, all exhibited). Lengths 76 cm, 65 cm, 61 cm. Figures 527, 528, 529.
Evidence: Leverian Museum.

4-5. Two clubs, Stockholm (1799.2.49, 1799.2.48[1] [exhibited]). Lengths 57.5 cm, 70 cm. Figure 530.
Evidence: Sparrman collection.
Literature: Söderström, 1939, pp. 58-61.

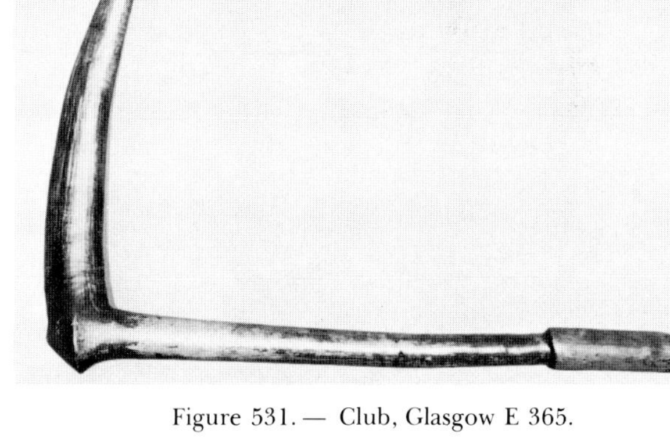

Figure 531. — Club, Glasgow E 365.

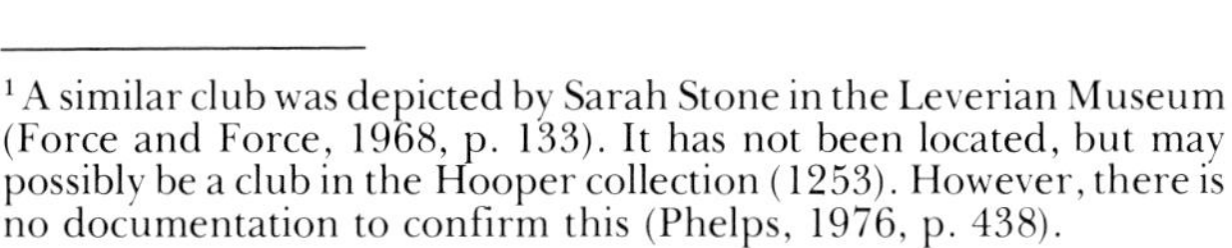

[1] A similar club was depicted by Sarah Stone in the Leverian Museum (Force and Force, 1968, p. 133). It has not been located, but may possibly be a club in the Hooper collection (1253). However, there is no documentation to confirm this (Phelps, 1976, p. 438).

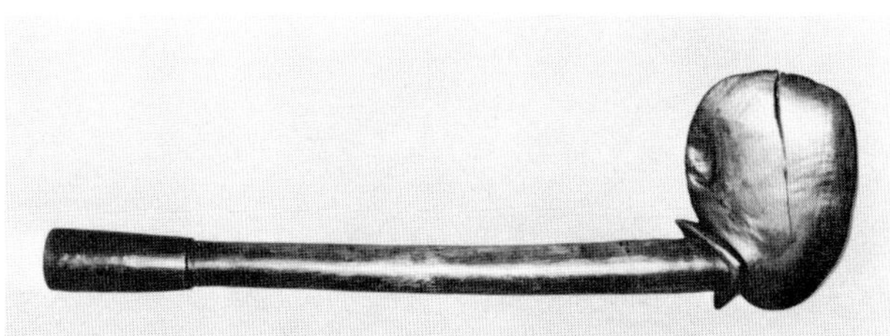

Figure 532. — Club, Glasgow E 364.

6-9. Four clubs, Glasgow (E 362, 363, 364 [exhibited], 365 [exhibited]). Lengths 83 cm, 67 cm, 63.5 cm, 63 cm. Figures 531, 532.
Evidence: Cook voyage collection from various sources. One club (E 365) is remarkably similar to one depicted in Plate 20 of the official account of Cook's second voyage (Fig. 523) and it is likely that Forster (the owner of the objects depicted) gave it to Dr. Hunter.

10-13. Four clubs, Oxford (156-159). Three missing.[2]
Evidence: Forster collection.
Literature: Gathercole, n.d. [1970].

14. Club, Göttingen.
Evidence: Purchased from London dealer Humphrey in 1782.

15-16. Two clubs, Cambridge (22.985, 22.986).
Evidence: Leverian Museum.

17-18. Two clubs, Vienna (4, 5). Lengths 68.5 cm, 76.5 cm.
Evidence: Leverian Museum.[3]
Literature: Moschner, 1955, pp. 153-155.

19-20. Two clubs, Sydney (H 147, 148). Lengths 69 cm, 75 cm.
Evidence: Cook collection exhibited at the Colonial and Indian Exhibition.
Literature: Mackrell, 1886; Appendix I, this volume.

Other Objects

Other objects were depicted in a plate in the official account of the second voyage (Fig. 523) which have not been located. These include two clubs and an adz.

[2] In my view the identification of the bird-headed club is unlikely.

[3] Several other clubs from the Leverian Museum have not been located.

NEW HEBRIDES

Exploring the group of islands that Quiros had named Australia Del Espiritu Santo, and which had been visited by Bougainville in 1768, Cook, during his second voyage, made three landings—at Malekula, Erromanga, and Tanna—and renamed the archipelago the New Hebrides (Fig. 521). Cook's ships were not well received, except at Tanna, and there was open warfare at Malekula and Erromanga.[1] It is likely that most of the objects other than weapons came from Tanna.

Figure 533.— Necklace, Stockholm 1799.2.41.

Ornaments[2]

1. Necklace of turtle shell links, Stockholm (1799.2.41). Length 93 cm. Figure 533.
Evidence: Sparrman collection.
Literature: Söderström, 1939, pp. 64-65.

2. Armlet of coconut shell, Oxford (148). Diameter 8.5 cm. Figure 534.
Evidence: Forster collection.
Literature: Gathercole, n.d. [1970].

3. Armlet of coconut shell, Göttingen.
Evidence: Purchased from London dealer Humphrey in 1782.

4. Armlet of coconut shell. Lost.
Evidence: Leverian Museum depiction.

[1] Because of the small number of objects collected, it is difficult to confirm provenances assigned to such things as slings, spear throwers, spears, and bows and arrows. A final analysis will have to be made by a specialist in Melanesian weaponry.

[2] See under Tonga for shell armlets with an uncertain provenance.

Figure 534. — Armlet, Oxford 148.

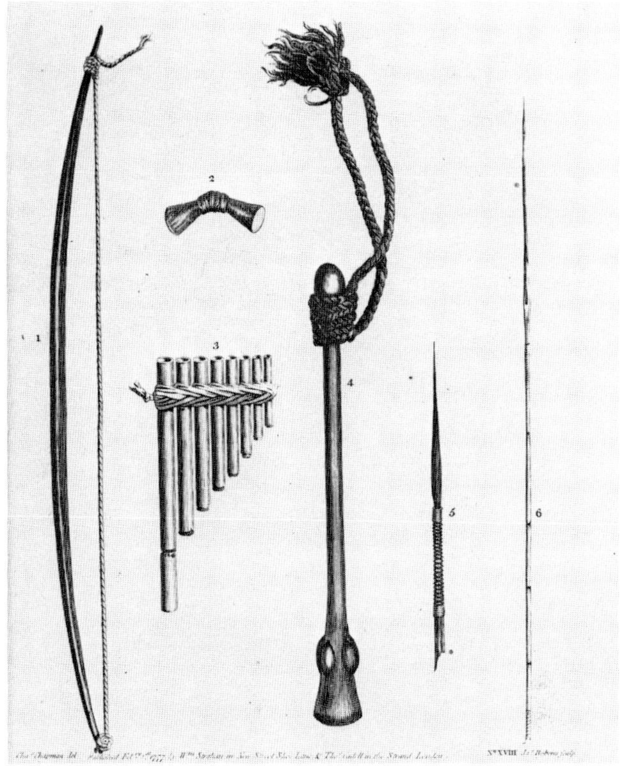

Figure 535. — Artifacts from New Hebrides, *Atlas* to Cook's second voyage (28).

5. Nose stone, Oxford (149). Missing.
   Evidence: Forster collection. Probably the one depicted in the official account of the second voyage (Cook, 1777, Plate 18 [Fig. 535]). See also Figure 536 for a nose stone being worn.
   Literature: Gathercole, n.d. [1970].
6. Greenstone ornament (attributed to the New Hebrides by Forster), Oxford (153). Missing.
   Evidence: Forster collection.
   Literature: Gathercole, n.d. [1970].
7. Boar tusk ornament (attributed to Tahiti, but probably from New Hebrides), Vienna (148).
   Evidence: Leverian Museum.
8. Comb of turtle shell, Stockholm (1799.2.42). Length 18.4 cm. Figure 537.
   Evidence: Sparrman collection.
   Literature: Söderström, 1939, p. 65.

Musical Instruments

1. Panpipe, Sydney (H 112). Length 19 cm. Figure 538.
   Evidence: Cook collection exhibited at the Colonial and Indian Exhibition.
   Literature: Mackrell, 1886; Appendix I, this volume.
2. Panpipe, Vienna (1). Length 11.3 cm.
   Evidence: Leverian Museum.
   Literature: Moschner, 1955, pp. 239-240.

Figure 536. — Man from Tanna, *Atlas* to Cook's second voyage (28).

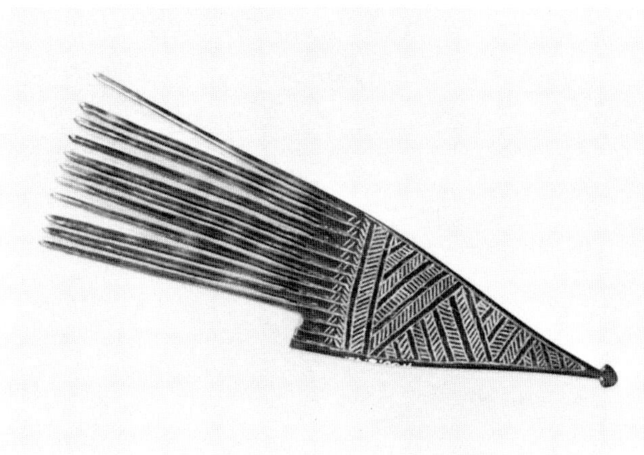

Figure 537.— Comb, Stockholm 1799.2.42.

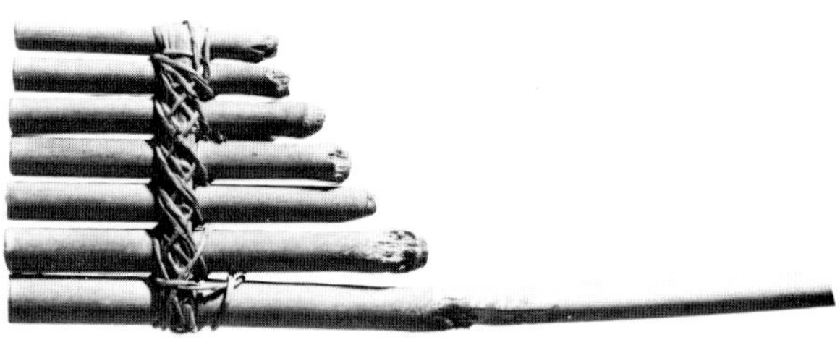

Figure 538.— Panpipe, Sydney H 112.

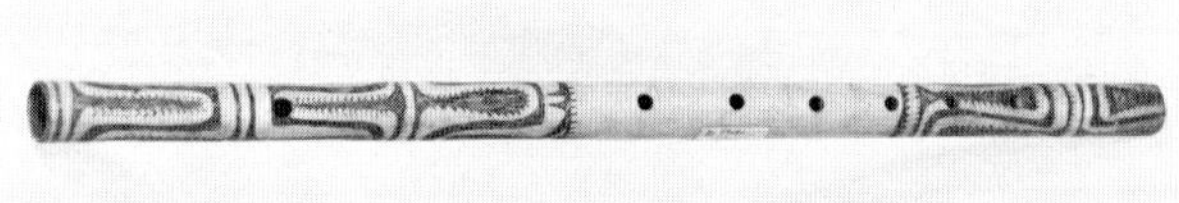

Figure 539.— Flute, Saffron Walden 1964.23.

Figure 540.— Neck rest, Vienna 8.

3-4. Two panpipes (one attributed to Tonga), Oxford (85, 154). Lengths 14 cm, 13 cm.
Evidence: Forster collection. Probably depicted in the official account of the second voyage (Cook, 1777, Plate 18 [Fig. 535]).
Literature: Gathercole, n.d. [1970].

5. Flute, Saffron Walden (1964.23). Length 38 cm. Figure 539.
Evidence: Leverian Museum.

6. Flute (attributed to Tonga), Oxford (83). Length 41 cm.
Evidence: Forster collection.
Literature: Gathercole, n.d. [1970].

Adz Blade

1. Stone adz blade (attributed to New Hebrides), Cambridge (25.408). Missing.
Evidence: Pennant collection of Cook voyage objects from various sources.

Neck Rest

A neck rest now in Vienna has traditionally been attributed to the New Hebrides. This provenance seems unlikely—and it may, in fact, be from Africa.

1. Neck rest, Vienna (8). Length 14 cm. Figure 540.
Evidence: Leverian Museum.
Literature: Moschner, 1955, p. 225.

Digging Sticks

1-2. Two digging sticks, Göttingen.
Evidence: Forster collection.

There are also in the Göttingen collection some sticks and tubes which may be from the New Hebrides—I do not know their use.

Figure 541.— Club, Cambridge 22.987.

Figure 542. — View in Malekula, British Library Add. Ms. 15,743.3.

Clubs

1. Club, Cambridge (22.987). Length 82 cm. Figure 541.
   Evidence: Leverian Museum. Similar to the club depicted by Hodges in British Library Add. Ms. 15,743.3 (Fig. 542).

2. Club with Janus-head carving, Oxford (142). Length 76 cm. Figure 543.
   Evidence: Forster collection.
   Literature: Gathercole, n.d. [1970].

3. Club. Location unknown.
   Evidence: Depicted in the official account of the second voyage (Cook, 1777, Plate 18 [Fig. 535]).

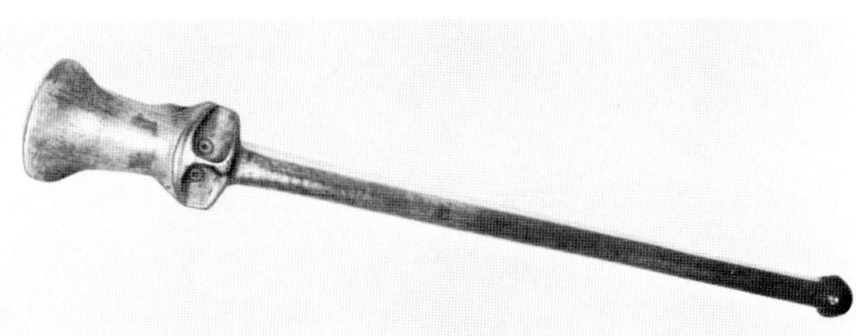

Figure 543. — Club, Oxford 142.

Bows and Arrows

1-11. Two bows (missing) and nine arrows, Oxford (143, 144, 151, 152).
   Evidence: Forster collection. Probably includes the bow and arrow depicted in the official account of the second voyage (Cook, 1777, Plate 18 [Fig. 535]).
   Literature: Gathercole, n.d. [1970].

12-17. Two bows and four arrows, Göttingen.
   Evidence: Purchased from London dealer Humphrey in 1782.

18-19. Two fishing arrows, Stockholm (1799.2.45 and 46).
   Evidence: Sparrman collection.
   Literature: Söderström, 1939, pp. 63-64.

Other Weapons

1. Sling, Stockholm (1799.2.50).
   Evidence: Sparrman collection.
   Literature: Söderström, 1939, pp. 61-62.

2. Spear thrower, Oxford (147). Missing.
   Evidence: Forster collection.
   Literature: Gathercole, n.d. (1970), p. 21.

3. Spear, Stockholm (1799.2.44). Length 217 cm.
   Evidence: Sparrman collection.
   Literature: Söderström, 1939, pp. 62-63.

4-5. Two spears, Oxford (145-146). Missing.
   Evidence: Forster collection.
   Literature: Gathercole, n.d. (1970), p. 21.

AUSTRALIA (NEW HOLLAND)

On Cook's first voyage quite some time was spent at Botany Bay and the eastern part of Australia between April 19, 1770, when Australia was sighted, and August, 1770, shortly after Cook took possession of the eastern coast of Australia in the name of the King (Fig. 28). There appears to have been little trading of artificial curiosities. On one occasion, however, 40 or 50 lances and fish spears were taken from their houses—the English leaving things in return. There were some descriptions of ornaments, household objects and weapons and some drawings by Parkinson (Figs. 544, 545), but apparently few of these were collected. Only a very small number of Australian objects can be traced to Cook's voyages.[1] Cook's third voyage visited Tasmania (Van Diemen's Land) and Webber made drawings of a man and a woman with a child, but no ethnographic objects can be traced to this encounter.

1-3. Three fish spears (fish "gigs"), Cambridge (1914.1-3). Figure 546.
   Evidence: Sandwich collection given by Captain Cook.

4. Lance or javelin, Cambridge (1914.4).
   Evidence: Sandwich collection, given by Captain Cook.

5. Spear shaft, Stockholm (1848.1.60).
   Evidence: "Banks collection." Provenance uncertain. Attributed to New Holland in the original catalogue of the collection.
   Literature: Rydén, 1965, p. 94.

6. Shield, British Museum.
   Evidence: Circumstantial. Said to be "almost certainly obtained at Botany Bay in 1770," but on what grounds this claim is made is unknown.
   Literature: Anon., 1970, p. 4.

Figure 544. — Two men of Australia, Plate 27 of Parkinson's journal.

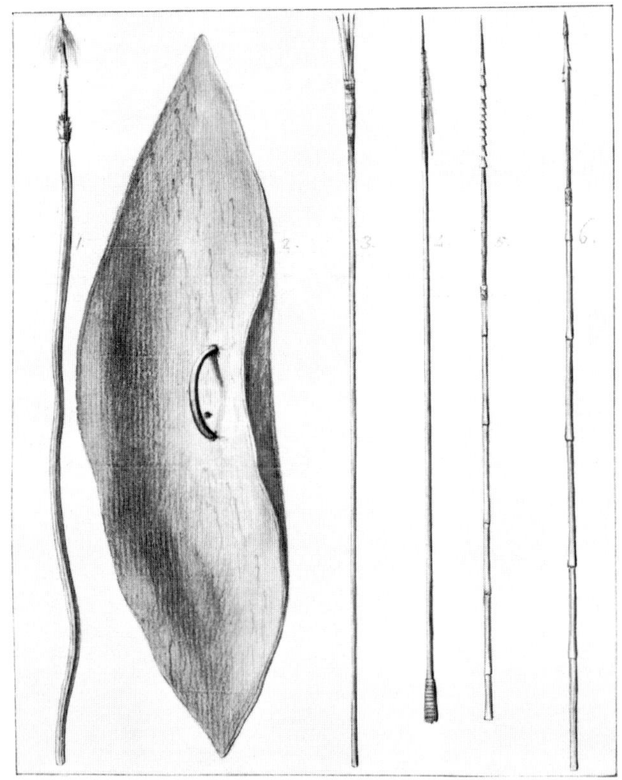

Figure 545. — Artifacts from Australia, New Zealand and New Guinea, British Library Add. Ms. 23,920.35.

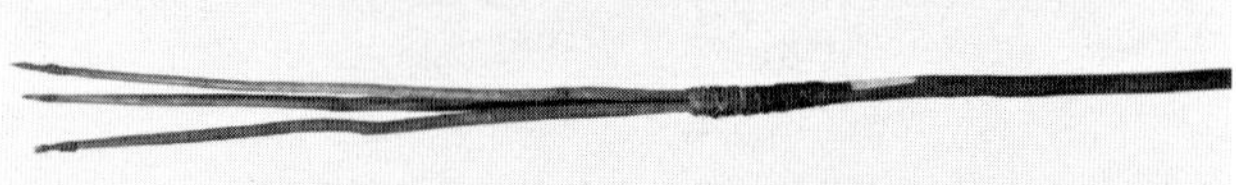

Figure 546. — Fish spear, Cambridge 1914.1.

[1] The objects in the Calvert collection (listed in Anon., 1970, p. 4), in the Australian Museum, Sydney, cannot be traced to Cook.

PACIFIC OBJECTS: PROVENANCE UNKNOWN

A number of objects which can be traced to collection on Cook's voyages cannot be assigned as to area of origin with any certainty. This is either because they cannot be found, they were not examined for this study, or similar objects were made and used in more than one area visited by Cook.

Textiles

1-4. Four mats, Stockholm (1848.1.12,1848.1.21, 1848.1.43, 1848.1.50). Probably Tahitian or Tongan, but not examined.
Evidence: "Banks collection."
Literature: Rydén, 1965, pp. 78, 92-94.

5-6. Two small pieces of bark cloth, Stockholm (1848.1.25 a and b). Probably Tahitian or Tongan, but not examined.
Evidence: "Banks collection."
Literature: Rydén, 1965, pp. 77-78.

7-8. Two pieces of cordage, Stockholm (1848.1.24, 1848.1.47).
Evidence: "Banks collection."
Literature: Rydén, 1965, pp. 94, 91-92.

Fishhooks

1-6. Six fishhooks, Wellington (FE 3001, 3002, 3003, 3013, 3014, 3025). Not examined.
Evidence: Circumstantial. Given by Queen Victoria to the Imperial Institute in a box containing articles "brought by Captain Cook from Otaheti."

7-16. Ten Polynesian fishhooks, Wellington.
Evidence: Circumstantial. Bullock's Museum from the Leverian Museum and Banks.
Literature: Kaeppler, 1974, p. 80.

17. Fishhook, Cambridge (25.425). (Not located and no provenance assigned).
Evidence: Pennant collection.

18-? Fishhooks, Göttingen.
Evidence: Forster and Humphrey collections.

Other Objects

1. "A piece of the perfume-wood." Oxford (43). Missing. Attributed to Tahiti, but likely to be Tongan sandalwood.
Evidence: Forster collection, second voyage.
Literature: Gathercole, n.d. [1970].

2. Candlenuts, Oxford (44). Attributed to Tahiti, but equally likely to be Tongan.
Evidence: Forster collection, second voyage.
Literature: Gathercole, n.d. [1970].

3. Candlenuts, Göttingen. Could be from Tahiti, Tonga, or Hawaii.
Evidence: Purchased from London dealer Humphrey in 1782.

4. Candlenuts. Location unknown. Could be from Tahiti, Tonga, or Hawaii.
Evidence: Leverian Museum depiction.[1]

[1] Possibly a string of candlenuts now in the British Museum.

NOOTKA SOUND (KING GEORGE SOUND)

Cook's ships left Hawaii on February 2, 1778, and set their course for North America, which they sighted on March 7th. They cruised until March 29, when they discovered Nootka Sound. The Spanish (under Perez in 1774) and the English (under Sir Francis Drake in 1579) both claimed the area, but it is unlikely that either of these navigators was actually in Nootka Sound. Cook named the area King George Sound after King George of England, but it was equally well known in Europe as Nootka Sound. The inhabitants, according to Samwell, "were not unacquainted with Iron" (Beaglehole, 1967, Pt. 2, p. 1088), but this was probably traded into the area from the north. Cook's ships spent about one month in Nootka Sound while the ships were repaired so that they could withstand the expedition to the north to look for a Northwest Passage. A great deal of trading was done and the largest number of objects collected by Cook's voyage on the Northwest Coast of America is from the Nootka Sound area. Although stylistically the tribal origin of some of the objects may be other than Nootka, all objects which appear to have been collected in the Nootka Sound area will be grouped together here. Objects which appear to be from the Tlingit are included under Prince William Sound.

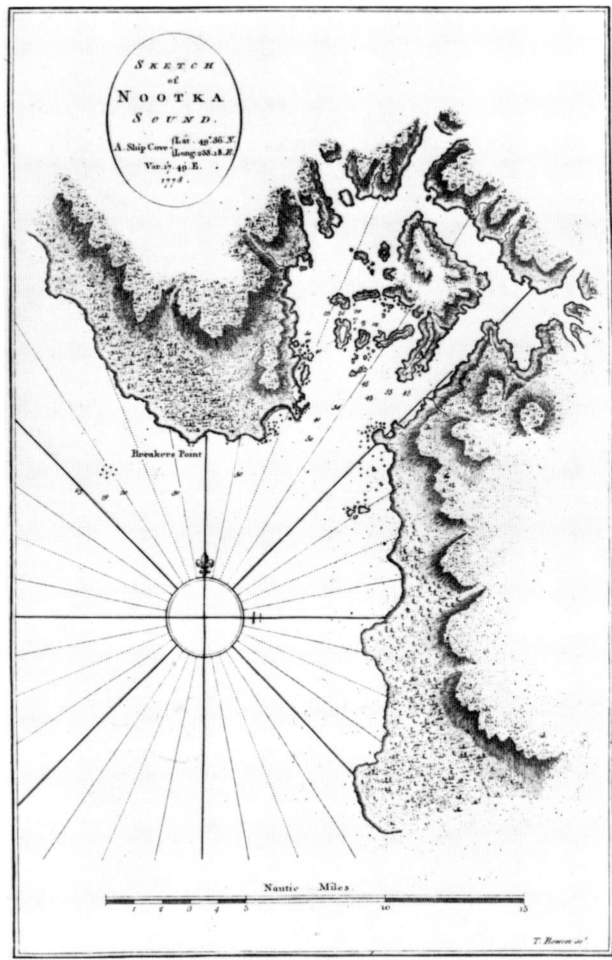

Figure 547.— Chart of Nootka Sound (60).

Cloaks

Seven cloaks can be traced to Cook's third voyage that may have been collected in Nootka Sound.[1] None of the cloaks has the characteristic stylization usually associated with "classic" Northwest Coast cloaks, which apparently was derived from 19th century Chilkat cloaks.

1. Cloak, Vienna (218). Dimensions 132 cm by 64 cm (without fringe), fringe 45 cm. Figures 548, 549.
   Evidence: Leverian Museum.
   Literature: Feest, 1968, p. 117.
2. Cloak, Berne (NS 23). Dimensions 147 cm by 94.5 cm (without fringe).
   Evidence: Webber collection.
   Literature: Henking, 1957, pp. 378-379 (attributed to New Zealand); Kaeppler, 1977.
3. Cloak, Florence (42b). Dimensions 145 cm by 82 cm (without fringe).
   Evidence: Cook voyage collection from various sources.
   Literature: Giglioli, 1895, pp. 104-105; Kaeppler, 1977.

4-6. Three cloaks, Dublin.
   Evidence: Thought to be part of the Cook collection given to Trinity College, Dublin, by Capt. King.
   Literature: Gunther, 1972, p. 208.

7. Cloak. Location unknown.
   Evidence: Leverian Museum depiction.

[1] Several cloaks in the British Museum (NWC 49, 50, 51, 52, 53, 54) are in the so-called "Cook-Banks collection," but there is no documentation to confirm the attribution.

Capes

Circular capes[2] were also collected in Nootka Sound, and were depicted by Webber (Fig. 550).

1. Cape, Florence (230).
   Evidence: Cook voyage collection from various sources.
   Literature: Giglioli, 1895, pp. 105-106; Kaeppler, 1977.
2. Cape, Dublin.
   Evidence: Circumstantial. Thought to be part of Cook voyage collection given to Trinity College, Dublin, by Capt. King.
   Literature: Gunther, 1972, p. 209.
3. Cape. Location unknown.
   Evidence: Leverian Museum depiction.

[2] A similar cape, formerly in the Hooper collection (1534) and now in the National Museum of Canada (?), was attributed to Cook's voyages by Hooper (Phelps, 1976, p. 445), but this cannot be verified.

Figure 548.— Cloak, Vienna 218.

Figure 549. — Cloak (detail), Vienna 218.

Figure 550. — A Woman of Nootka Sound, engraving after Webber.

Figure 551. — Basketry hat, Liverpool R.I.75.

Figure 552. — Basketry hat, Edinburgh 1956.658.

Other Clothing: Said to be from Nootka Sound.

1. Sea otter cloak, Berne (discarded?).
   Evidence: Webber collection.
   Literature: Kaeppler, 1977.
2. Skin garment said to be decorated with dried hoofs, Cambridge (22.983). Missing.
   Evidence: Leverian Museum.

3-4. Two fiber aprons, Florence (231-232). One missing.[3]
   Evidence: Cook voyage collection from various sources.
   Literature: Giglioli, 1895, p. 107; Kaeppler, 1977.

Hats

The classic hats from the Nootka Sound area are decorated with whale fishing scenes. Several of these were collected on Cook's voyage.[4] Other hats traditionally attributed to Nootka Sound will be included below—it being more likely that they were collected in Prince William Sound.

1. Hat (with whale fishery scene), Liverpool (R.I.75). Height 21 cm. Figure 551.
   Evidence: Original Cook voyage collection in Bullock's Museum.
   Literature: Kaeppler, 1974a, pp. 71, 84.
2. Hat (with whale fishery scene), Edinburgh (1956.658). Height 21 cm. Figure 552.
   Evidence: Circumstantial. Probably from the Leverian Museum.

3-4. Two hats (with whale fishery scenes), Florence (312, 313).
   Evidence: Cook voyage collection from various sources.
   Literature: Giglioli, 1895, pp. 107-108; Kaeppler, 1977.

5. Hat (with whale fishery scene), Dublin (1882.3876).
   Evidence: Circumstantial. Thought to be part of Cook voyage collection given to Trinity College, Dublin, by Captain King.
   Literature: Vaughan and Murray-Oliver, 1974, p. 91.

[3]Gunther does not question this attribution (1972, p. 209) so I have included them here. I suspect, however, that they are Tahitian.

[4]Two such hats in the British Museum (NWC 6 and 7) are attributed to Cook's voyage, but there are no documents to confirm the attribution.

Figure 553. — Comb, de Menil collection.

Combs

Wooden combs were characteristic of the Nootka and several were collected.[5]

1. Comb, de Menil collection.[6] Height 17.5 cm, width 12.1 cm. Figure 553.
   Evidence: Leverian Museum.
   Literature: Holm and Reid, 1975, No. 12.
2. Comb, Sydney (H110). Height 16.5 cm, width 7.5 cm.
   Evidence: Cook voyage collection exhibited at the Colonial and Indian Exhibition.
   Literature: Mackrell, 1886; Appendix I, this volume.

3-4. Two combs, Florence (159, 160).
   Evidence: Cook voyage collection from various sources.
   Literature: Giglioli, 1895, pp. 110-111; Kaeppler, 1977.

5. Comb, Cambridge (25.370).
   Evidence: Pennant collection of Cook voyage objects from various sources.

6-8. Three combs. Location unknown.
   Evidence: Leverian Museum depictions.

[5]Two combs in the British Museum (NWC 104, 105) are attributed to Cook's voyage, but this cannot be confirmed.

[6]Exhibited only during part of the exhibition.

Bracelets

Bracelets were made of shaped mountain goat horn, and sometimes inlaid with dentalium shells.

1. Bracelet, Florence (81b).
   Evidence: Cook voyage collection from various sources.
   Literature: Giglioli, 1895, p. 110; Kaeppler, 1977.
2. Bracelet (said to be made of deer hoof), Dublin.
   Evidence: Thought to be part of the Cook collection given to Trinity College, Dublin, by Captain King.
   Literature: Vaughan and Murray-Oliver, 1974, p. 91.

3-4. Two bracelets. Location unknown.
   Evidence: Leverian Museum depictions.

Ceremonial Weapons

A number of ceremonial implements, some of them traditionally known as "slave killers," were collected on Cook's voyage.[7]

[7]Several ceremonial weapons in the British Museum (NWC 97, 98, 99, 100 ["slave killers"] and NWC 93, 94, 95 [stone wedge-shaped implements]) are attributed to Cook's voyage, but this cannot be confirmed by documentation. Several ceremonial weapons from the Leverian Museum also cannot be located.

Figure 554. — Weapon, Vienna 211.

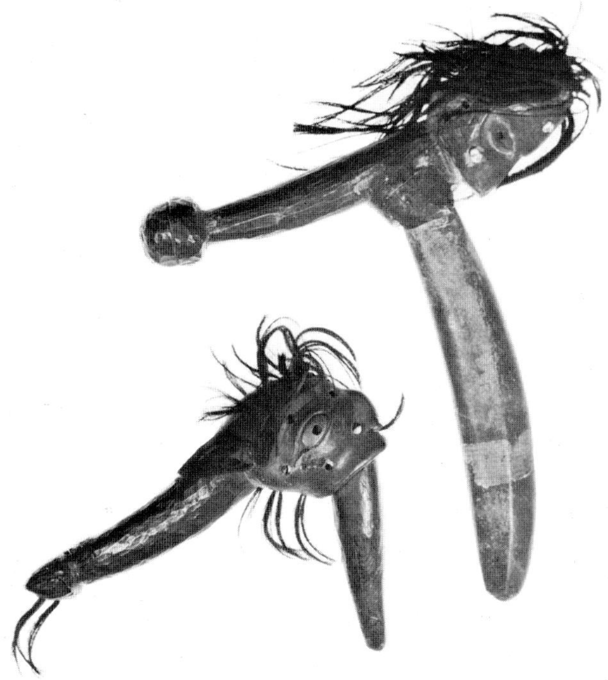

Figure 555. — Two weapons, Cambridge 22.949, 25.371.

⛵1. Ceremonial weapon (wood with stone "tongue"), Vienna (211). Length 37.5 cm. Figure 554.
   Evidence: Leverian Museum.
   Literature: Feest, 1968, p. 109.

⛵2. Ceremonial weapon (wood with wooden "tongue"), Cambridge (22.949). Length 30 cm, tongue 15 cm. Figures 555, 556, 557.
   Evidence: Leverian Museum.

3. Ceremonial weapon (wood with stone "tongue"), Exeter (E 1223). Lost.
   Evidence: Leverian Museum.
4. Ceremonial weapon (wood with stone "tongue"), Leipzig (NA 1064).
   Evidence: Circumstantial, probably Leverian Museum.
5. Ceremonial weapon (wood with stone "tongue"), Berne (AL 9).
   Evidence: Webber collection.
   Literature: Henking, 1957, p. 368; Kaeppler, 1977.
6. Ceremonial weapon (wood with stone "tongue"), Florence (155).
   Evidence: Cook voyage collection from various sources.
   Literature: Giglioli, 1895, pp. 118-119; Kaeppler, 1977.

Figure 556.— Weapon (detail), Cambridge 22.949.

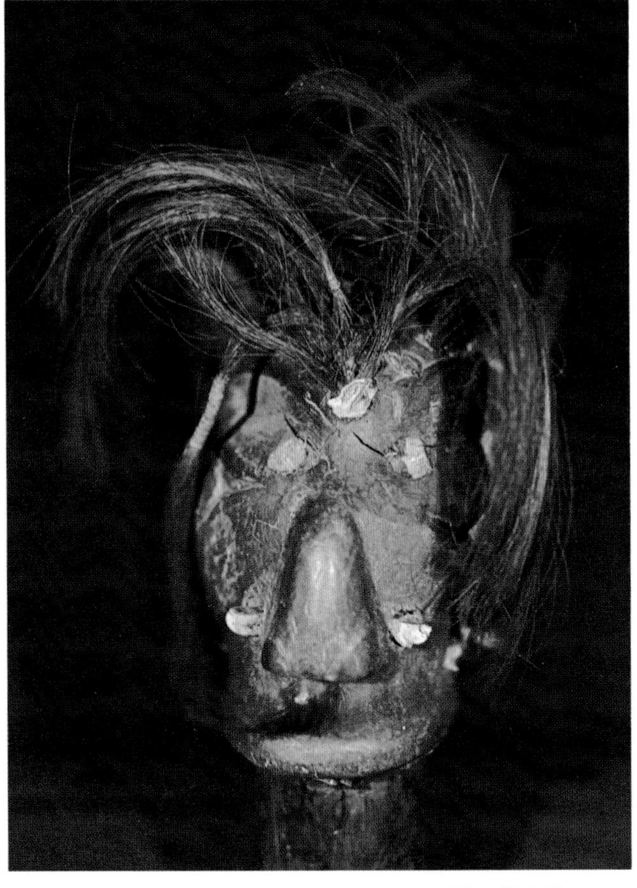

Figure 557.— Weapon (detail), Cambridge 22.949.

7. Ceremonial weapon (wood with stone "tongue"), Cambridge (25.371). Figure 555.
   Evidence: Pennant collection from various sources.

⛵8. Ceremonial weapon (wooden hand holding a ball), Bennet collection. Length 33 cm. Figure 558.
   Evidence: Leverian Museum.

⛵9. Ceremonial weapon (stone image), Hauberg collection. Length 35.5 cm. Figure 559.
   Evidence: Leverian Museum.

⛵10-11. Two weapons (stone wedge shaped implements), Vienna (209 and 210 [exhibited]). Lengths 26 cm, 30 cm. Figure 560.
   Evidence: Leverian Museum.
   Literature: Feest, 1968, pp. 108-109.

12. Weapon (stone wedge shaped implement), Wellington (FE 338).
   Evidence: Circumstantial, probably Leverian Museum.
   Literature: Kaeppler, 1974a, p. 80.

13. Weapon (stone wedge shaped implement), Florence (146).
   Evidence: Cook voyage collection from various sources.
   Literature: Giglioli, 1895, pp. 119-120; Kaeppler, 1977.

Bone Clubs

Bone clubs, usually carved with the head of a bird, were collected, probably in Nootka Sound. They were often compared with the *patu* of the Maori.

⛵1-2. Two bone clubs, Cambridge (21.567.1 [exhibited] and 22.954). Lengths 60 cm, 57 cm, widths 8 cm, 7.5 cm. Figures 561, 562.
   Evidence: Leverian Museum.

3-4. Two bone clubs, Vienna (212, 227). Lengths 52 cm, 49.5 cm.
   Evidence: Leverian Museum.
   Literature: Feest, 1968, p. 109.

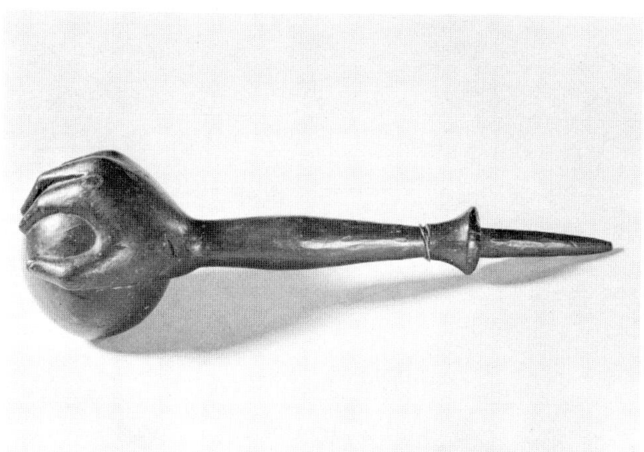

Figure 558. — Ceremonial weapon, Bennet collection.

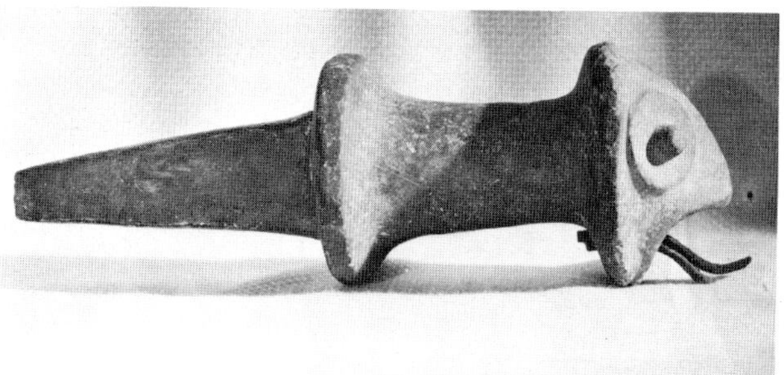

Figure 560. — Stone weapon, Vienna 210.

5. Bone club (without bird head), Exeter (E 1222). Length 55 cm, width 8 cm.
   Evidence: Leverian Museum.

6-7. Two bone clubs, Florence (242, 242b).
   Evidence: Cook voyage collection from various sources.
   Literature: Giglioli, 1895, pp. 116-118; Kaeppler, 1977.

8. Bone club, British Museum (NWC 42).[8]
   Evidence: Circumstantial. Noted "Capt. Cook Nootka Sound" in the same handwriting as other objects from the Pepys sale which appear to have a Cook provenance.

Figure 559. — Ceremonial weapon, Hauberg collection.

[8]Three other bone clubs in the British Museum (NWC 40, 41, 47) have been attributed to Cook's voyages, but there seems to be no document to support this.

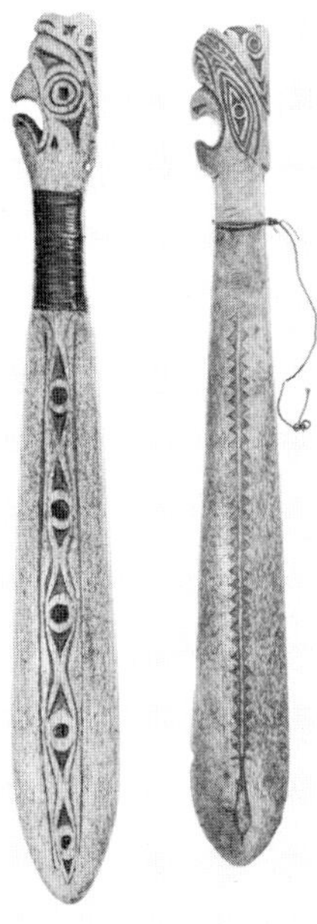

Figure 561. — Two bone clubs, Cambridge 21.567.1, 22.954.

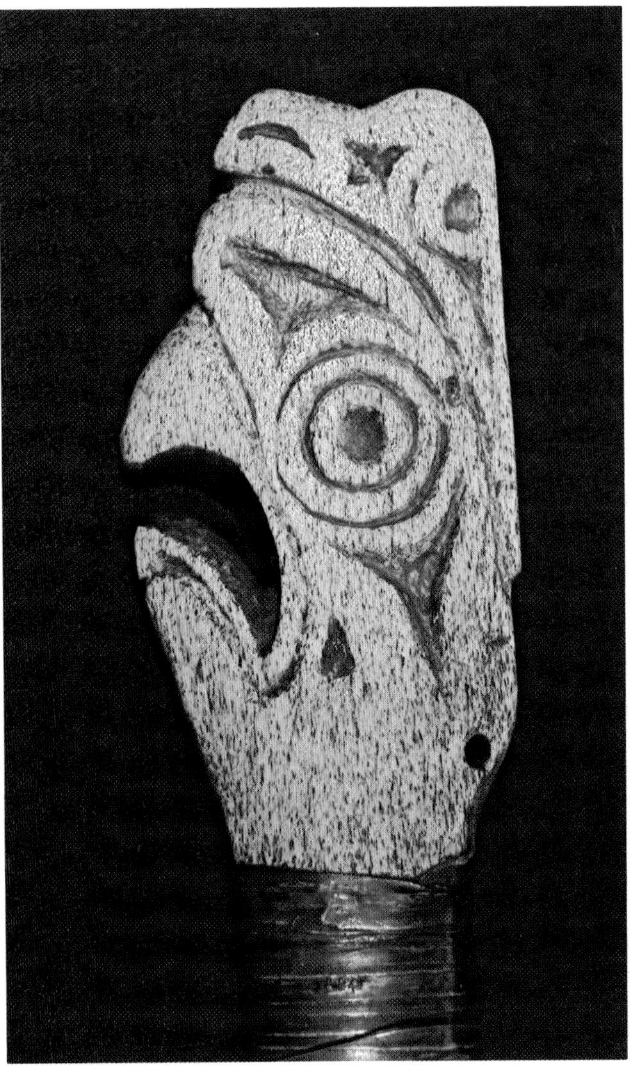

Figure 562. — Bone club (detail), Cambridge 21.567.1.

Figure 563. — Mask, Vienna 223.

Masks

Several masks were collected in Nootka Sound in both animal and human form.[9] The human masks are especially interesting because apparently there was little paint, and the eyes do not have the "classic" pointed stylization more characteristic of the 19th century masks.

1. Human mask, Vienna (223). Height 20.7 cm, width 17.3 cm. Figure 563.
   Evidence: Leverian Museum.
   Literature: Feest, 1968, pp. 119-120.
2. Human mask, de Menil collection.[10] Height 26 cm. Figure 564.
   Evidence: Leverian Museum.
   Literature: Holm and Reid, 1975, No. 87.
3. Human mask, Berne (AL 11).
   Evidence: Webber collection.
   Literature: Henking, 1957, p. 367; Kaeppler, 1977.
4. Human mask, Florence (176).
   Evidence: Cook voyage collection from various sources.
   Literature: Giglioli, 1895, pp. 121-122; Kaeppler, 1977.
5. Human head, Cape Town (SAM 2361). Height 27 cm, width 22 cm. Figure 565.
   Evidence: Said to have arrived in Cape Town in 1780.
   Literature: Bax, 1970, p. 146.
6. Bird mask, Vienna (222). Length 22.7 cm, height 11 cm, width 16.4 cm. Figure 566.
   Evidence: Leverian Museum.
   Literature: Feest, 1968, pp. 118-119.

[9] Two human masks in the British Museum (NWC 57, 58) and some animal masks (NWC 71) are attributed to Cook's voyages, but apparently there is no documentary evidence for this attribution. Several masks from the Leverian Museum have also not been located.

[10] Exhibited for only part of the exhibition.

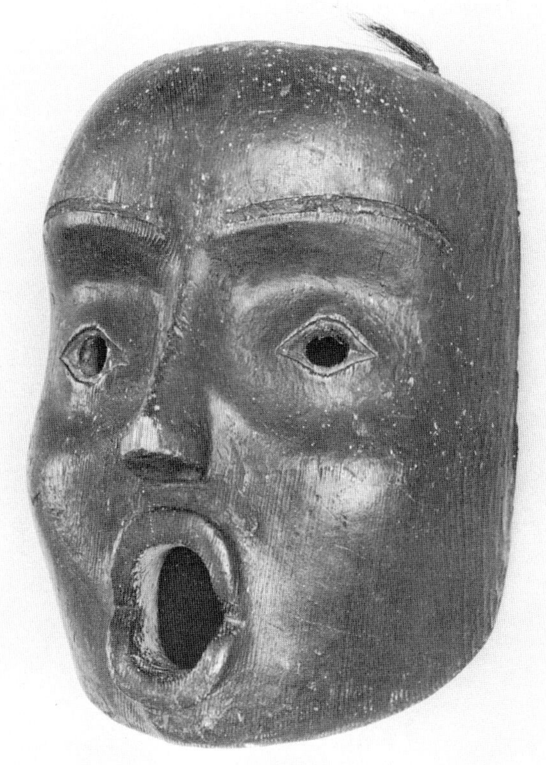

Figure 564. — Mask, de Menil collection.

Figure 565. — Human head, Cape Town SAM 2361.

7. Bird mask, British Museum (NWC 55).
   Evidence: Circumstantial. Said to be the one depicted in drawings in the British Library, for example, Add. Ms. 23,921.86 and Add. Ms. 17,277.19 (Fig. 567).

8. Wolf mask, Bennet collection. Length 26 cm, width 12.5 cm, height 11.5 cm. Figure 568.
   Evidence: Leverian Museum.

9. Forehead ornament or mask, Florence (171).
   Evidence: Cook voyage collection from various sources.
   Literature: Giglioli, 1895, pp. 122-123; Kaeppler, 1977.

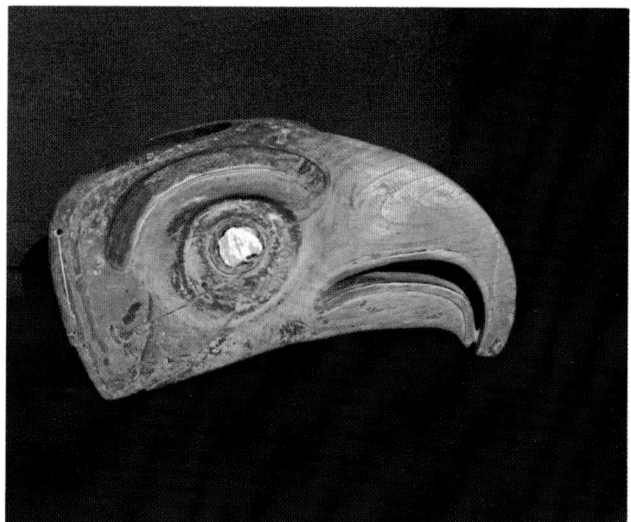

Figure 566. — Bird mask, Vienna 222.

Figure 567. — Artifact drawing by John Webber, British Library Add. Ms. 17,277.19.

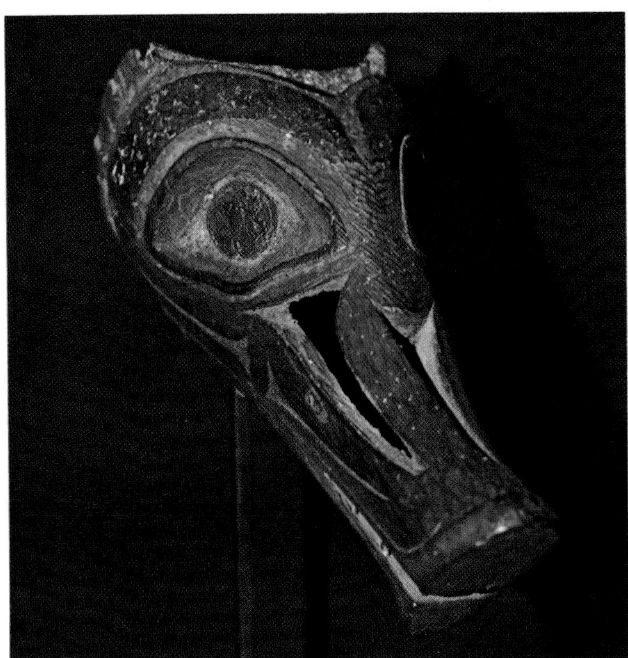

Figure 568. — Wolf mask, Bennet collection.

Rattles

Rattles collected in Nootka Sound are of two types, those in the form of a bird,[11] which apparently were made by the Nootka, and a rounded form with a handle, which seems to be more characteristic of the Salish.

[11]Two rattles in the British Museum (NWC 28 and 29) are attributed to Cook's voyage, but there seems to be no documentary evidence to confirm this. Several rattles in the Leverian Museum also cannot be located.

1. Double bird rattle, Cambridge (22.948). Length 35 cm, width 20 cm. Figure 569.
   Evidence: Leverian Museum.

2. Bird rattle, Vienna (224). Length 46 cm. Figure 570.
   Evidence: Leverian Museum.
   Literature: Feest, 1968, pp. 123-124.

3. Bird rattle, Glasgow (E 369). Length 49 cm, width at wing tips 23 cm, height 18.5 cm. Figures 571, 572.
   Evidence: Cook voyage collection from various sources. See Appendix III, this volume.

4. Bird rattle, Dublin (1882.3659). Length 47 cm, height 18 cm, width 10 cm. Figure 573.
   Evidence: Thought to be part of Cook voyage collection given to Trinity College, Dublin, by Capt. King. An old label remains: "Instrument from King Georges Sound. Probably used in their dances 116."

5. Rounded rattle (probably Salish), Cape Town (SAM 5330). Figure 574.
   Evidence: Said to have arrived in Cape Town in 1780.
   Literature: Bax, 1970, p. 146.

6-7. Two rattles (probably Salish). Location unknown.
   Evidence: Leverian Museum depiction.

Figure 569. — Double bird rattle, Cambridge 22.948.

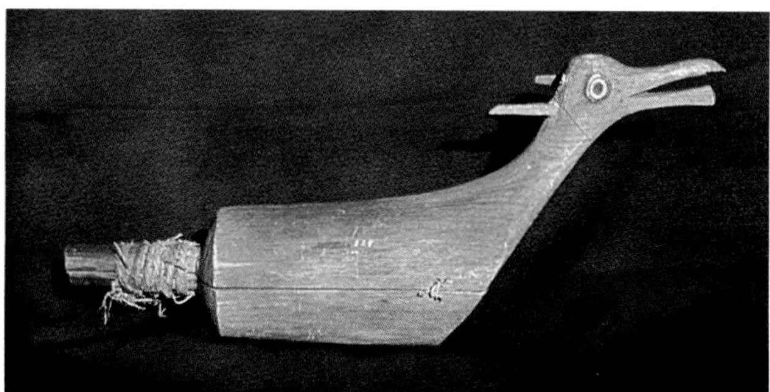

Figure 570. — Bird rattle, Vienna 224.

Figure 573. — Bird rattle, Dublin 1882.3659.

Figure 571. — Bird rattle, Glasgow E 369.

Figure 574. — Rattle, Cape Town SAM 5330.

Figure 572. — Bird rattle (detail), Glasgow E 369.

Whistles or Flutes

1. Part of a wooden flute, Cambridge (25.410). Not located.
   Evidence: Pennant collection of Cook voyage objects from various sources.

Human Images

Although described in the accounts of Cook's voyages, it appears that few human images were collected in Nootka Sound.

1. Image of mother and child, British Museum (NWC 62). Height 16 cm, width 6.8 cm. Figure 575.
   Evidence: Leverian Museum.
2. Image. Location unknown.
   Evidence: Leverian Museum depiction.

Figure 575.— Wood sculpture of mother and child, British Museum NWC 62.

Figure 576.— Bowl with human images, British Museum 1971.AM5.1.

Figure 577.— Bowl (detail), British Museum 1971.AM5.1.

Bowls

Bowls with human and animal images are superb pieces of sculptured form. They have a simplicity and style that must have changed very rapidly, for bowls in later collections are considerably different.

1. Bowl with human images,[12] British Museum (1971.AM5.1). Length 19.8 cm, diameter of bowl 10 cm. Figures 576, 577, 578.
   Evidence: Leverian Museum.

2-3. Two bowls with bird heads (large and small), Cambridge (22.946 [exhibited], 22.947). Lengths 72 cm, 22.5 cm, widths 23 cm, 10 cm. Figures 579, 580.
   Evidence: Leverian Museum.

4. Bowl with beaver image, Greenwich (L15/95/). Length 34 cm, width 19 cm. Figure 581.
   Evidence: Circumstantial. Traditionally said to be from Cook's voyage but source unknown.
   Literature: Vaughan and Murray-Oliver, 1974, p. 93.

5. Bowl with animal image. Location unknown.
   Evidence: Leverian Museum depiction.

[12]The workmanship of this bowl is so very similar to the image of mother and child above that they look as though they could have been made by the same artist.

Figure 578. — Bowl (detail), British Museum 1971.AM5.1.

Figure 579. — Bowl with bird head, Cambridge 22.946.

Bone Beaters

Beaters for pounding bark fibers were made of whalebone.

1. Bone beater, Glasgow (E 370). Length 25.5 cm, cross section 4 cm. Figure 582.
   Evidence: Circumstantial. Cook voyage collection from various sources. See Appendix III, this volume.
2. Bone beater, Edinburgh (1956.657). Length 28 cm. Figure 583.
   Evidence: Given by Mrs. Cook to Sir John Pringle.
3. Bone beater, Berne (AL 48).
   Evidence: Webber collection.
   Literature: Henking, 1957, p. 369; Kaeppler, 1977.
4. Bone beater, Göttingen.
   Evidence: Purchased from London dealer Humphrey in 1782.
5. Bone beater, Vienna (123). Missing.
   Evidence: Leverian Museum.

6-7. Two bone beaters, Wellington (FE 331, 332).
   Evidence: Circumstantial. Probably from the Leverian Museum.
   Literature: Kaeppler, 1974a, p. 80.

8. Bone beater, British Museum.
   Evidence: Circumstantial. Noted "Capt. Cook."

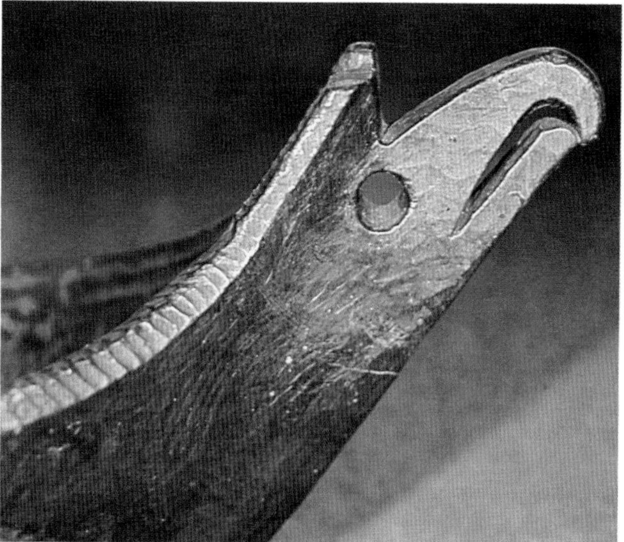

Figure 580. — Bowl (detail), Cambridge 22.946.

Figure 581. — Bowl with beaver image, Greenwich L15/95.

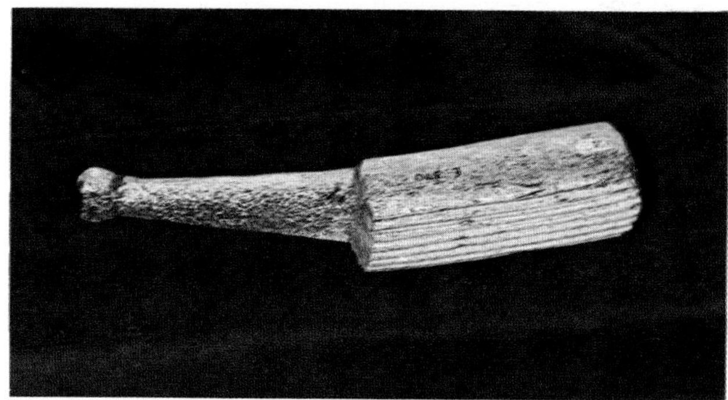

Figure 582. — Bone beater, Glasgow E 370.

Figure 583. — Bone beater, Edinburgh 1956.657.

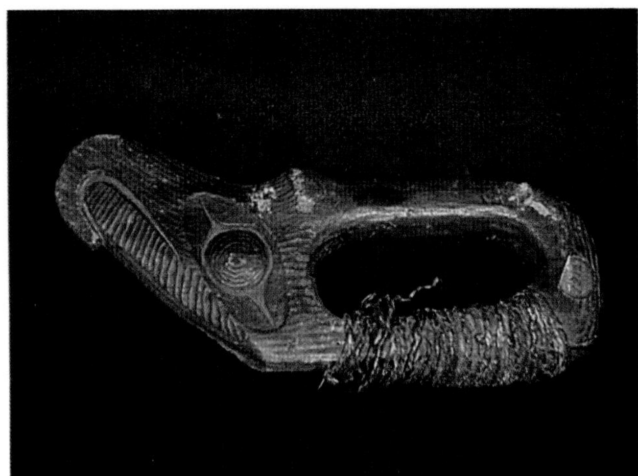

Figure 584. — Plane, Exeter E 1232.

Woodworking Tools

Woodworking tools included planes, knives, and awls, often with metal blades which were probably traded in from the north, and ultimately from Russia.

1. Plane (with metal blade), Exeter (E 1232). Length 24.5 cm, width 8.5 cm. Figure 584.
   Evidence: Leverian Museum.

2. Scraper (with metal blade), Berne (AL 10).
   Evidence: Webber collection.
   Literature: Henking, 1957, p. 368; Kaeppler, 1977.

3. Knife (with metal blade), Exeter (E 1234). Length 15.5 cm.
   Evidence: Leverian Museum.

4. Wooden awl, Exeter (E 1233). Length 14.5 cm.
   Evidence: Leverian Museum.

Arrow Cases

Carved wooden boxes for arrows were carved with abstract designs and sometimes inlaid with animal teeth.

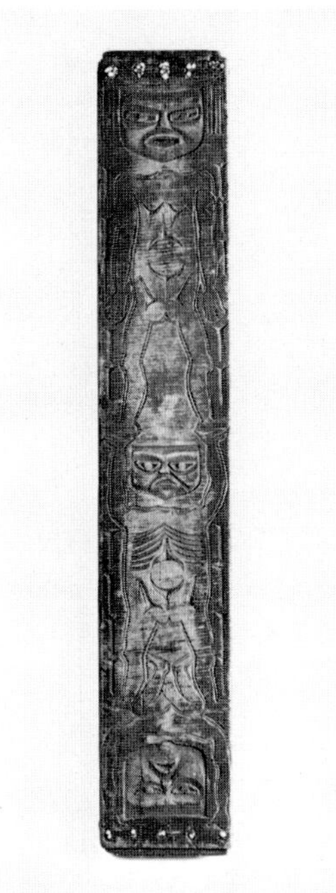

Figure 585. — Wooden arrow case, Vienna 215.

1-2. Two wooden arrow cases, Vienna (215 [exhibited], 216). Lengths 93 cm, 98 cm, widths 16 cm, 10.5 cm, heights 3.3 cm, 2.2 cm. Figure 585.
   Evidence: Leverian Museum.
   Literature: Feest, 1968, pp. 107-108.

3. Arrow case, Göttingen.
   Evidence: Purchased from London dealer Humphrey in 1782.

Bows and arrows, spears, harpoons, and fishhooks are difficult to assign area provenances—especially when they have not been studied in minute detail. Thus, instead of trying to sort out the area provenances, which apparently even North American Indian specialists have difficulty agreeing upon, they will be listed below in a Northwest Coast unlocalized section.

Figure 586. — Cloak (detail), Leningrad.

Cloaks

Cloaks probably collected in Prince William Sound[2] include the six now in Leningrad. Four of these cloaks were made of the usual cedar bark and mountain goat wool, while two are made of bird skins with a netting technique[3] (Gunther, 1972, p. 262).

1-6. Six cloaks, Leningrad (2520-4, 5, 6, 7, 8, 9). Figure 586.
Evidence: Given by Capt. Clerke to Governor of Kamchatka.
Literature: Rozina, 1966, p. 246; Kaeppler, 1977; Gunther, 1972, pp. 208, 260-262.

Garments of Whale Intestines

Rain garments or "foul weather frocks" are mentioned in early museum catalogues and were depicted by Webber (Fig. 587). None can be traced to Cook's voyage today. They were probably discarded because of decay.

[2]A sealskin dress in Bullock's Museum was attributed to Prince William Sound (Bullock, 1801, p. 8) but cannot be located.

[3]There is also a possibility that these cloaks are from the Aleut.

PRINCE WILLIAM SOUND AND COOK INLET

Following the American coast northward, the next major area visited by Cook's ships was Prince William Sound and Cook Inlet (or Cook's River). The ethnographic specimens collected in this area are very mixed and include objects of Eskimo,[1] probably Tlingit, and Athabaskan origin, and Cook remarks that "none of these people lived in the bay where we had anchored" (Beaglehole, 1967, Pt. 1, p. 351). Some of these 18th century objects have no known counterparts in museum collections and it is difficult to say from which tribe they actually originated. They are listed together here, but any information as to locality will be pointed out. Few specimens in museum collections that have associations with Cook's voyages can be localized to the Prince William Sound/Cook Inlet area, and most of these are unique or rare objects that were unrecognized as to area provenance, date, or historical associations.

[1]Gunther specifies the Eskimo of this area as Chugach (1972, p. 182*ff*).

Figure 587. — A man of Prince William Sound, engraving after Webber.

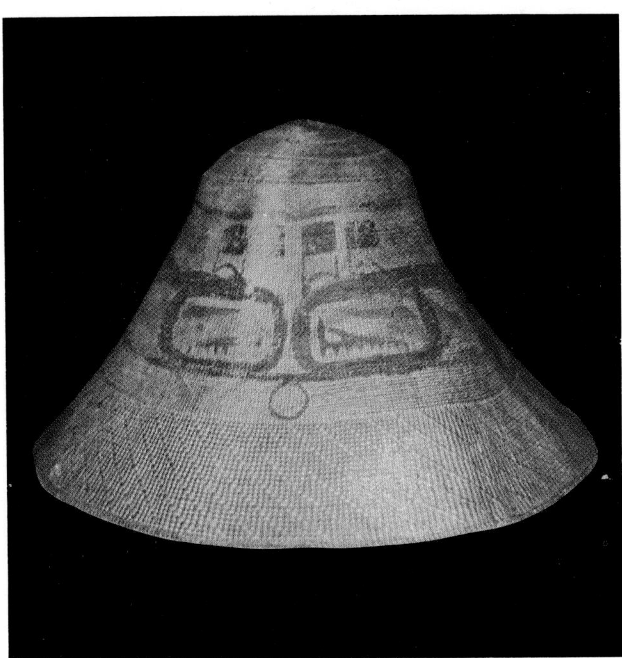

Figure 588.— Basketry hat, Vienna 219.

1. Garment of intestines, Berne (AL 1). Discarded.
   Evidence: Webber collection.
   Literature: Henking, 1957, pp. 376-377; Kaeppler, 1977.

2. Garment of intestines. Lost.
   Evidence: Leverian Museum depiction.

Woven Hats

High-crowned conical basketry hats were mentioned in Cook voyage literature and depicted by Webber (Fig. 587). Although hats in museum collections are difficult to localize, and are almost invariably attributed to Nootka Sound, it seems more likely that those listed here were collected farther north, and may be Tlingit.

⛵1-2. Two hats, Vienna (219 [exhibited], 220). Heights 14 cm, 14.5 cm. Figure 588.
   Evidence: Leverian Museum.
   Literature: Feest, 1968, p. 116.

3-4. Two hats, Florence (184, 193).
   Evidence: Cook voyage collection from various sources.
   Literature: Giglioli, 1895, pp. 108-109; Kaeppler, 1977.

5. Ring section from the top of a hat, Vienna (225).
   Evidence: Leverian Museum.

Seal Head Hats

Headgear in the shape of a seal's head was worn by the Eskimo as a headdress "decoy" while seal hunting. They were carved of wood and worn on top of the head (that is, not as a mask). One was depicted by Webber in British Library Add. Ms. 17,277.19 (Fig. 567), but none can be traced by documentation to Cook's voyage.[4]

1. Seal headgear. Location unknown.
   Evidence: Leverian Museum depiction, which may be the same object depicted by Webber and possibly now in the British Museum (NWC 11), but this cannot be confirmed.

Armor

Armor made of slats of wood was mentioned in the accounts of Cook's voyage in Prince William Sound. It is probably Tlingit.

⛵1. Armor (of wood and painted with human faces), Cambridge (22.950). Height 53 cm, width 49 cm. Faces 4.5 cm by 3.5 cm. Figure 589.
   Evidence: Leverian Museum.

Quiver

A superb quiver was collected in Prince William Sound, and is apparently Athabaskan. A similar quiver was depicted by Webber in a watercolor now in the British Library (Add. Ms. 15,514.5 [Fig. 590]), but it has not been located.

⛵1. Quiver, Cambridge (22.981). Length 82 cm. Figure 591.
   Evidence: Leverian Museum.

Human Images

Human images carved in ivory or wood and dressed in skin clothing were described from Prince William Sound, and two have been located.

⛵1. Bone figure with skin clothing and ornaments typical of Prince William Sound, Cambridge (21.567.2). Height 19 cm. Figure 592.
   Evidence: Leverian Museum.

2. Wood image with skin clothing, Berne (AL 11).
   Evidence: Webber collection.
   Literature: Henking, 1957, p. 367; Kaeppler, 1977.

[4]The seal headgear in Göttingen is sometimes attributed to Cook's voyage, but this is incorrect—it having come from the Baron von Asch collection.

Figure 589. — Armor, Cambridge 22.950.

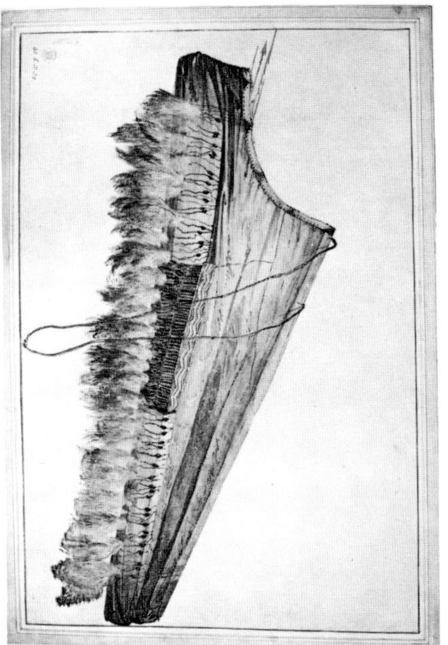

Figure 590. — Drawing of quiver by John Webber, British Library Add. Ms. 15,514.5.

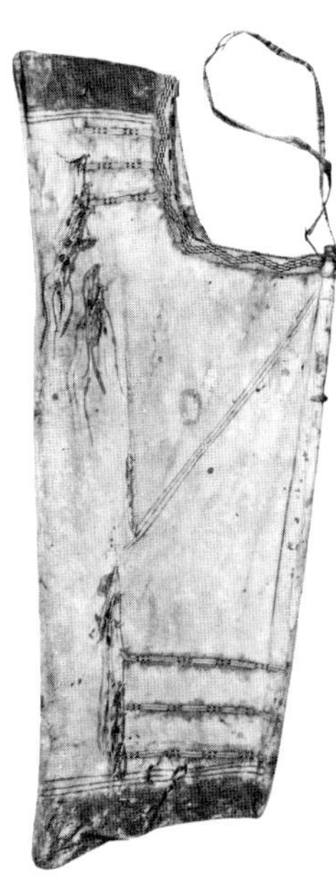

Figure 591. — Quiver, Cambridge 22.981.

Figure 592. — Bone figure, Cambridge 21.567.2.

Horn Bowls and Scoops

Containers of various kinds were made of mountain sheep horn. Often decorated with incising, one side is usually elongated into a squared-off handle, giving the container a very elegant shape. In style, they appear to be Athabaskan.[5]

1-2. Two horn scoops, Cambridge (22.951a [missing], b [exhibited]). The handle still retains its "4" label which indicates its placement in the Leverian Museum and keyed it to the *Companion* of the Museum of 1790.[6] Length 22.5 cm, width 8.5 cm. Figure 593.
Evidence: Leverian Museum.

3. Horn scoop, Sydney (H56). Length 27.5 cm, width 14.5 cm, height 12.5 cm.
Evidence: Part of Cook voyage collection exhibited at Colonial and Indian Exhibition.
Literature: Mackrell, 1886; Appendix I, this volume.

Figure 593. — Horn scoop, Cambridge 22.951b.

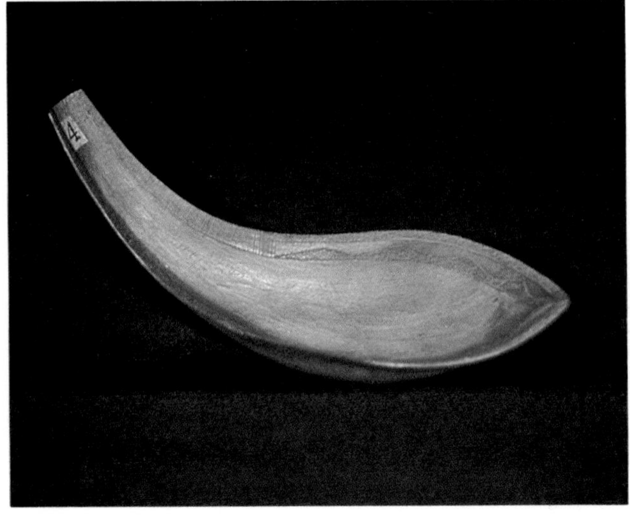

[5]A horn scoop in the British Museum (NWC 33) has been attributed to Cook's voyages (Gunther, 1972, p. 234), but this cannot be confirmed by documentation.

[6]Displayed in the Kahili Room.

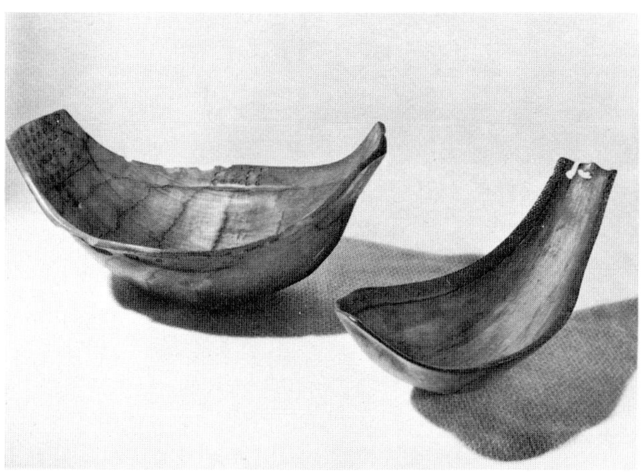

Figure 594.— Horn bowl and scoop, Vienna 232, 233.

4-5. Horn bowl and scoop, Vienna (232, 233). Lengths 23.2 cm, 24.8 cm, widths 10.8 cm, 16.7 cm. Figure 594.
Evidence: Leverian Museum.
Literature: Feest, 1968, pp. 112-113.

6. Horn scoop. Location unknown.
Evidence: Leverian Museum depiction.

Figure 595.— Basket, Vienna 57.

Other Containers

1-2. Two baskets (possibly Tlingit), Vienna (221, 57). Heights 15 cm, 33 cm, diameters 18 cm, 26 cm. Figure 595.
Evidence: Leverian Museum.
Literature: Feest, 1968, p. 114.

3. Wooden bowl (possibly from Prince William Sound), Vienna (134). Height 7 cm, diameter 14 cm.
Evidence: Leverian Museum.

Labrets and Other Ornaments

Cook and his men were surprised by the ornaments worn in a slit of the lower lip. A number of them were collected and mentioned in early museums such as the Leverian, but today cannot be traced. Other ornaments and wearing apparel were also mentioned in accounts of the voyage and in early museums but few can be located.

1. Leather fringing with quill work (attributed to Eastern Canada) may be Athabaskan, collected at Prince William Sound, Wellington (FE 3665).
Evidence: Bequeathed by Mrs. Cook to the granddaughter of her sister Margaret, whose daughter married S. J. Long.

2. Dagger with sheath (possibly Athabaskan), Cambridge (25.412). Missing.
Evidence: Pennant collection of Cook voyage objects from various sources.

OONALASKA (UNALASKA OR THE ALEUTIAN ISLANDS)

According to Samwell in his account of the Aleuts of Unalaska, "Our People barter their Otaheite cloth and that of the Sandwich Islands for the Darts & other manufactures of these Indians who are fond of these articles" (Beaglehole, 1967, Pt. 2, p. 1122). Only a few objects, however, are singled out for description and few can be traced today to Cook's voyage.

Figure 596.— A man of Unalaska, engraving after Webber.

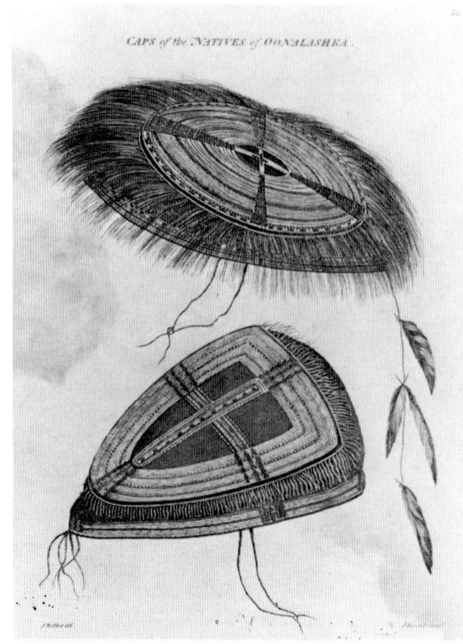

Figure 597.— Caps from Unalaska, engraving after Webber.

Eyeshades and Caps

Cook gives a good description of their eyeshades and Webber made several drawings of them (Fig. 596).

> Some of them wear boots and all of them a kind of oval snouted Cap made of wood, with a rim to admet the head: these are dyed with green and other Colours, and round the upper part of the rim, are stuck the long bristles of some sea animal on which are strung glass beads and on the front is a small image or two made out of bone. . . . The men wear a sort of bonnet, the front of which is like a scoop; it is made of wood hollowed out very thin; it hath no crown, but a circular hole to receive the head, for which reason one would think it designed to shade the face from the Sun, but as their luminary does not, I apprehend, often trouble them, I rather think it is intended to confine the hood of the upper garment close to the head. In some their chief pride seems to lie in these caps, they not only paint them with different colours, but ornament them with glass beads, got undoubtedly from the Russians, for I know of no other nation that could visit them (Beaglehole, 1967, Pt. 1, p. 459-460).

Depiction of these eyeshades by Webber include an unpainted drawing in the British Library (Add. Ms. 15,514.5) and eyeshades being worn, including the drawing in Add. Ms. 23,921.95, which depicts the eyeshade now in the British Museum.

1. Eyeshade or visor, British Museum (NWC 3). Length 42.5 cm.
   Evidence: Possibly from the Leverian Museum and depicted by Webber.
2. Bone figure from a visor, Göttingen.
   Evidence: Purchased from London dealer Humphrey in 1782.

3-4. Two caps. Location unknown.
   Evidence: Depiction by Webber in British Library Add. Ms. 15,514.30 and engraved for the official account of the third voyage (Fig. 597).

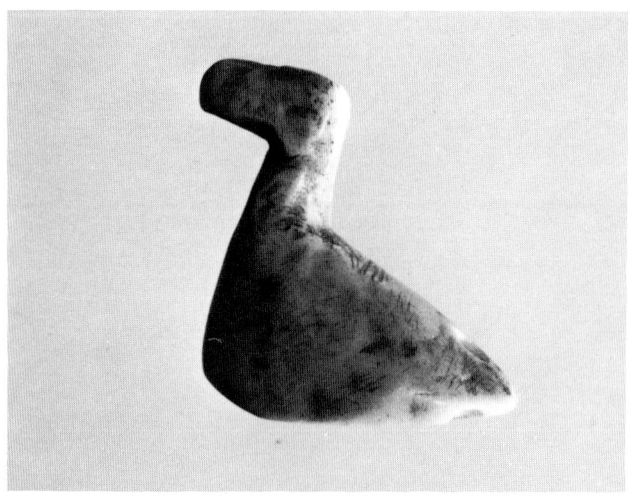

Figure 598.— Ivory bird, Sydney H 151.

Ivory Birds

Small ivory birds, possibly gaming pieces, were probably collected in Unalaska.

1. Ivory bird, Sydney (H 151). Length of base 2 cm, height 2.3 cm. Figure 598.
   Evidence: Part of Cook collection exhibited at the Colonial and Indian Exhibition.
   Literature: Mackrell, 1886; Appendix I, this volume.
2. Ivory bird, Göttingen.
   Evidence: Purchased from London dealer Humphrey in 1782.
3. Ivory bird, Dunedin.
   Evidence: Given by Mrs. Cook to her cousin who was the great grandmother of a Mrs. Hawker who gave it to Otago Museum. Figure 418.

4-7. Four ivory birds. Location unknown.
   Evidence: Part of Cook collection exhibited at Colonial and Indian Exhibition.
   Literature: Mackrell, 1886; Appendix I, this volume.

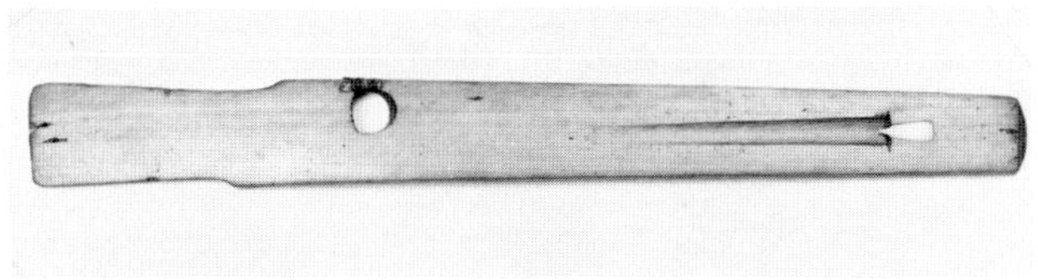

Figure 599. — Spear thrower, Edinburgh UC 244.

Spear Throwers

Characteristic of the Aleut was the use of a board or throwing stick for propelling their projectiles. They were often decorated with ivory images and a bone peg to hold the end of the spear.[1]

1. Spear thrower, Edinburgh (UC 244). Length 47 cm. Figure 599.
   Evidence: Circumstantial. Attributed to Cook's voyage in an early catalogue made before the collection came to the Royal Scottish Museum.
2. Spear thrower, Cambridge (22.962).
   Evidence: Leverian Museum.
3. Spear thrower, Vienna (235).
   Evidence: Leverian Museum.
4. Spear thrower, Göttingen.
   Evidence: Purchased from London dealer Humphrey in 1782.
5. Spear thrower, Berne (AL 4).
   Evidence: Webber collection.
   Literature: Henking, 1957, pp. 387-388; Kaeppler, 1977.
6. Spear thrower, Florence (554).
   Evidence: Cook voyage collection from various sources.
   Literature: Giglioli, 1895, pp. 138-139; Kaeppler, 1977.

[1]In Museum collections these spear throwers are often attributed to Nootka Sound or Prince William Sound; however, I have listed them together here.

ST. LAWRENCE BAY: NORTHEAST COAST OF ASIA

Traveling up the coast of Unalaska, Cook's ships passed through Bering Strait and into St. Lawrence Bay. They landed on the coast of Asia and traded with the Chukchi.

Quiver

Undoubtedly the most important piece collected from this area was the embroidered quiver now in Cambridge. The quiver was described by Cook:

> They gave us . . . some of their cloathing and a few Arrows, but nothing we had to offer them would induce them to part with a Spear or a Bow. . . . The Arrows they carried in a lather quiver slung over the left Shoulder; some of the quivers were extremely beautiful, being made of red leather on which was very neat embroidery and other ornaments" (Beaglehole, 1967, Pt. 1, pp. 411-412).

Figure 600. — A view of the Chukchi, British Library Add. Ms. 15,514.16.

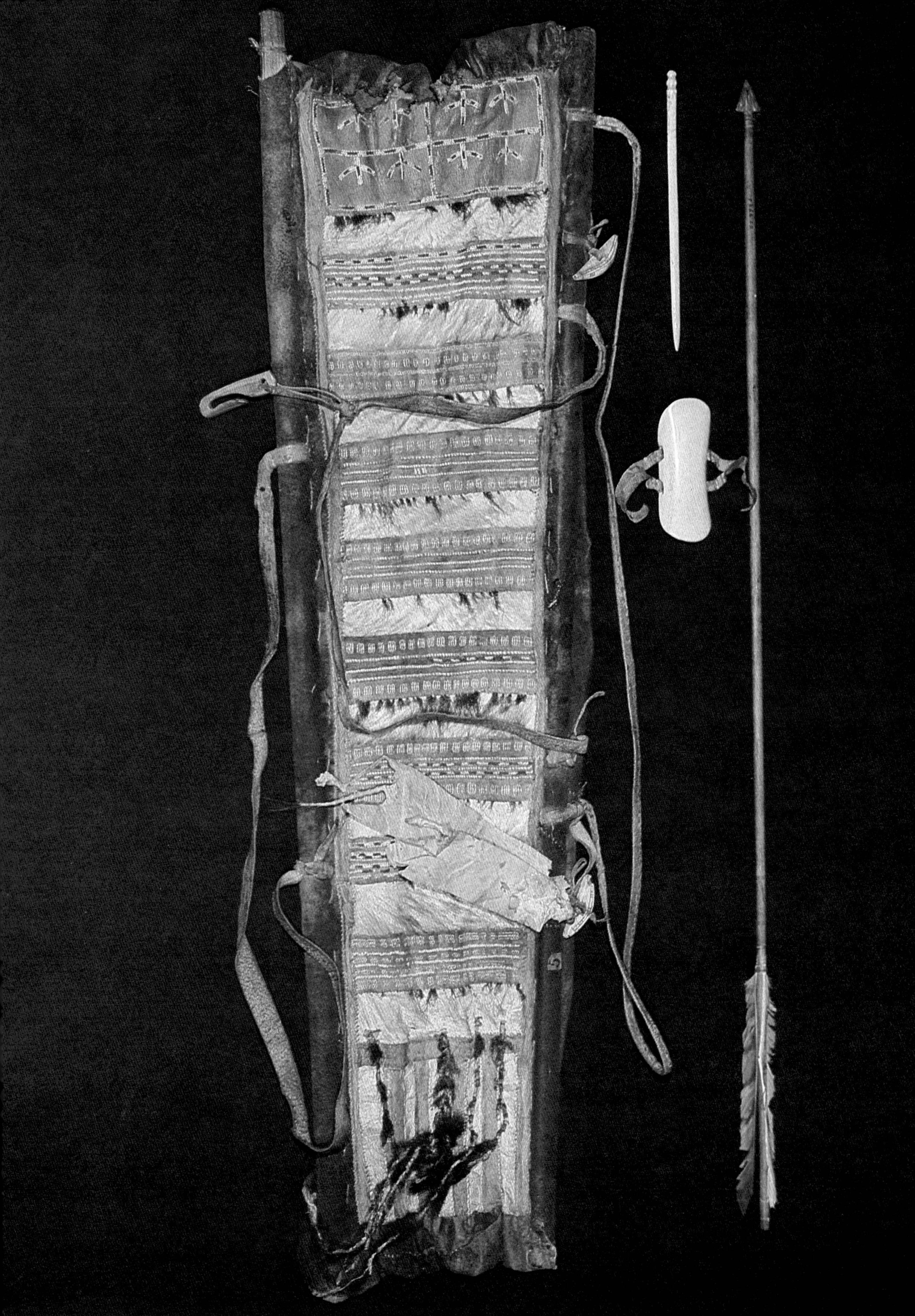

Webber made drawings in this area which depict the men wearing their embroidered quivers (British Library Add. Ms. 23,921.101 and 15,514.16 [Fig. 600]; and engraved in the *Atlas,* Plate 51). One of these quivers, which must have been collected by Cook on August 10, 1778, became part of the Leverian collection.[1]

1. Quiver ornamented with porcupine quill, squirrel skin, ermine, and ivory pieces, with an ivory wrist guard, Cambridge (22.958a, b). Length 78 cm, width 22 cm. Figure 601.
   Evidence: Leverian Museum. The "5" label is still attached that keyed the object to its description in the 1790 *Companion* to the Leverian Museum. Remnants of another label "6756" indicate its lot number when it was sold at the Leverian auction in 1806.

[1]These quivers are very rare in Museum collections. The only other one of which I am aware that was collected in the 18th century is in the Baron von Asch collection in the Institut für Völkerkunde, Göttingen.

Figure 603. — Costume design for *Omai* by P. J. de Loutherbourg.

KAMCHATKA

After the death of Cook, Captain Clerke again continued to explore the far north, calling at Kamchatka where they met with Major Behm the Governor of the area. During their stay in Kamchatka, King and others traveled by dog sledge and "no boys could be more pleas'd than we were in being carryed down to the boat by Dogs. We had all a separate Carriage. . . . The mode of traveling was so curious to us that we enjoy'd it prodigiously" (Beaglehole, 1967, Pt. 1, pp. 652 and 663). King was so taken with these sledges that

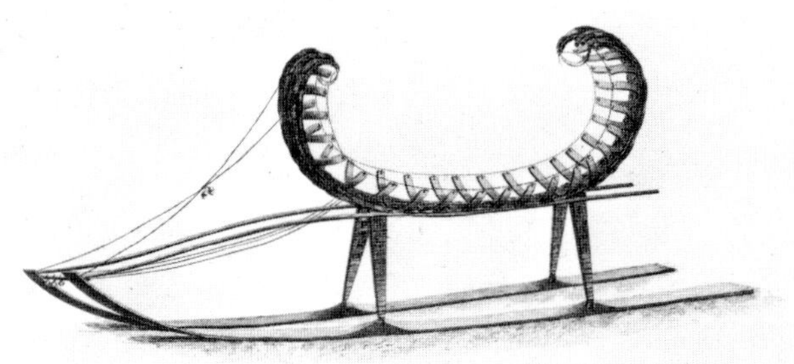

Figure 602. — A sledge of Kamchatka, engraving after Webber.

Figure 604. — Detail of a view in Kamchatka, engraving after Webber.

Figure 601. — (Opposite page) Quiver and ivory wrist guard, Cambridge 22.958a.

Figure 605. — Container, Vienna 133.

he took one home and presented it to Ashton Lever's Museum. Unfortunately it cannot be located today, but it was depicted by Webber (Fig. 602).

King was also given a "magnificent Kamtschadale dress . . . worn by the principal *Toions* of the country, on occasions of great ceremony" (Beaglehole, 1967, Pt. 1, p. 669n). What happened to this dress is unknown, but it may have been used for a model for Loutherbourg's stage costume for *Omai* (see Fig. 603).

In the collection of artificial curiosities that Joseph Banks gave to the British Museum, objects from Kamchatka were included, and in 1782 Banks also gave "a vest and a pair of boots, which belonged to the King of Tsutsky." Unfortunately, these objects cannot be identified.

Containers

The only object that can be located today that appears to have been collected in Kamchatka on Cook's voyage is a container which is similar to those depicted by Webber (Fig. 604).

1. Container, Vienna (133). Height 7 cm, diameter 15 cm. Figure 605.
   Evidence: Leverian Museum.

NORTHWEST COAST OF AMERICA AND NORTHEAST COAST OF ASIA

A large number of weapons and fishing and hunting implements, as well as a few paddles and canoe models, were collected in the northern areas of America and Asia. There is disparity in the provenances assigned in museum collections and evidently no definitive work has been done on area provenances of these objects. Therefore, they are listed here together to facilitate further work on the subject.

Bows and Arrows

1-3. Bow and two arrows, Vienna (252, 253, 254). Missing. Possibly from St. Lawrence Bay.
Evidence: Leverian Museum.

4-6. Bow and two arrows, Cape Town (SAM 2192, 2197). Possibly Eskimo.
Evidence: Thought to have arrived in Cape Town in 1780.
Literature: Bax, 1970, p. 146.

7-15. Bow and eight arrows, Berne (AL 5.10, A1 5.1-8). Possibly Prince William Sound.
Evidence: Webber collection.
Literature: Henking, 1957, pp. 370-373; Kaeppler, 1977.

16-28. Thirteen arrows, Sydney (H 158-170).
Evidence: Part of Cook collection exhibited at Colonial and Indian Exhibition.
Literature: Mackrell, 1886; Appendix I, this volume.

29. Bow, Florence (262).
Evidence: Cook voyage collection from various sources.
Literature: Giglioli, 1895, pp. 114-115; Kaeppler, 1977.

30-? Bows and arrows, Göttingen.
Evidence: Purchased from London dealer Humphrey in 1782.

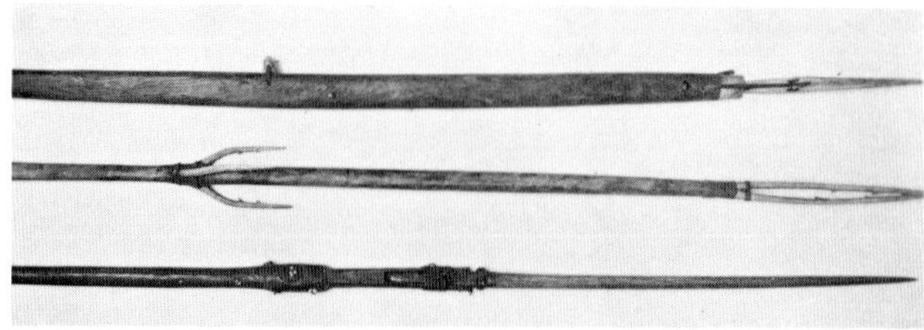

Figure 606. — Three spears, Vienna 228, 229, 132.

Arrow Straightener

1. Straightener for arrow shafts (mussel shell with wood handle), Wellington (FE 3668).
   Evidence: Bequeathed by Mrs. Cook to the granddaughter of her sister Margaret, whose daughter married S. J. Long.

Spears

1-3. Three spears including an extraordinary lance with an ivory head and shaft inlaid with seal teeth, Vienna (228, 229, 132). Figure 606.
   Evidence: Leverian Museum.
   Literature: Feest, 1968, p. 108.

4. Spear (for flying birds), Berne (AL 7).
   Evidence: Webber collection.
   Literature: Henking, 1957, pp. 373-374; Kaeppler, 1977.

Fish Spears (Fish "Gigs")

1. Fish spear, Vienna (234). Possibly Aleut.
   Evidence: Leverian Museum.

2-4. Two fish spears and a barbed point, Göttingen.
   Evidence: Purchased from London dealer Humphrey in 1782.

Harpoons and Harpoon Parts

1. Harpoon head, Edinburgh (1956.656). Figure 607.
   Evidence: Given by Mrs. Cook to Sir John Pringle.

2-4. Three harpoon parts, Vienna (217, 229, 230).
   Evidence: Leverian Museum.

Figure 607.— Harpoon head, Edinburgh 1956.656.

Figure 608.— Halibut hook, Vienna 231.

5-7. Three harpoons (one with complete bladder) and a harpoon head of shell in wood, Cambridge (22.956, 22.957, 27.1633).
   Evidence: Leverian Museum.

8. Harpoon (lacking point), Cambridge (25.389).
   Evidence: Pennant collection of Cook voyage objects from various sources.

9-17. Five harpoons, three harpoon parts and a sheath, Berne (AL 6a-e, AL 14).
   Evidence: Webber collection.
   Literature: Henking, 1957, pp. 369-370, 374-376; Kaeppler, 1977.

18. Harpoon head, Exeter (E 1235).
   Evidence: Leverian Museum.

19-20. Harpoon head, Göttingen.
   Evidence: Purchased from London dealer Humphrey in 1782.

21-32. Twelve harpoons and harpoon parts, Florence.
   Evidence: Cook voyage collection from various sources.
   Literature: Giglioli, 1895, p. 112*ff;* Kaeppler, 1977.

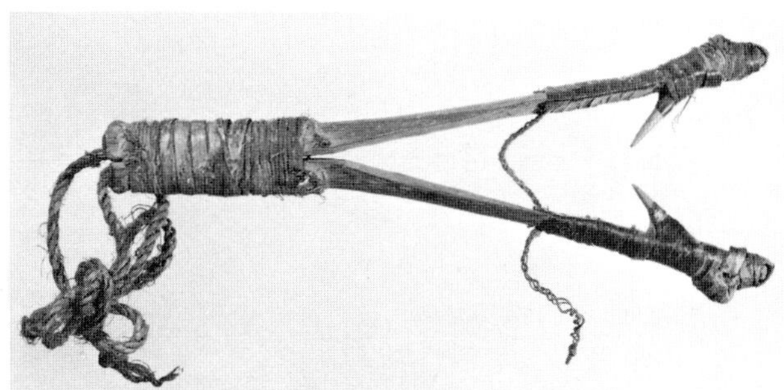

Figure 609.— Halibut hook, Sydney H 106.

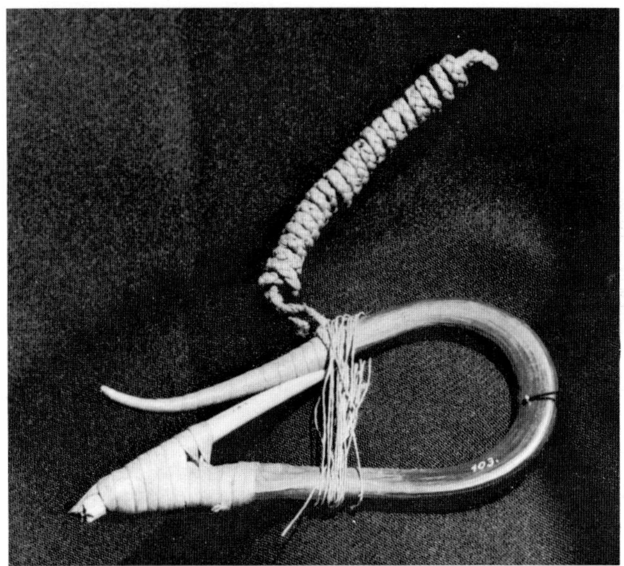

Figure 610.— Halibut hook, Vienna 103.

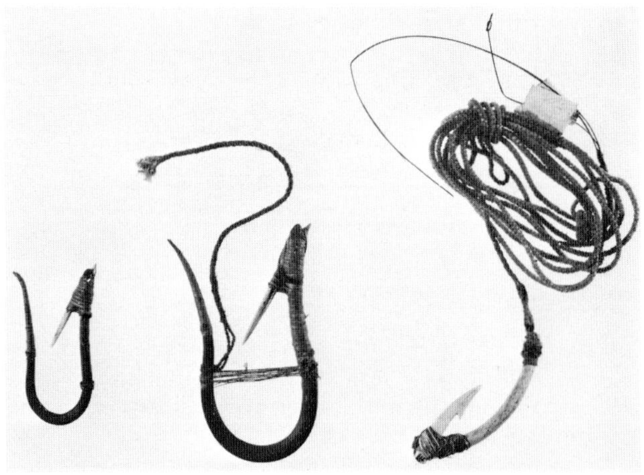

Figure 611.— Three fishhooks, Wellington.

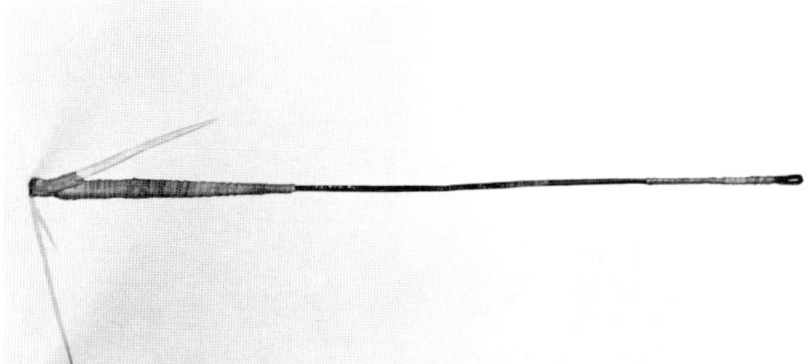

Figure 612.— Fishhook, Cambridge 22.952.

Fishing Equipment

1. Halibut hook with carved shank, Vienna (231). Length 37 cm. Figure 608.
   Evidence: Leverian Museum.
   Literature: Feest, 1968, pp. 109-110.

2. Halibut hook, Sydney (H 106). Figure 609.
   Evidence: Part of Cook collection exhibited at the Colonial and Indian Exhibition.
   Literature: Mackrell, 1886; Appendix I, this volume.

3. Halibut hook with bent C-shaped shank and bone point, Vienna (103). Length 14.2 cm. Figure 610.
   Evidence: Leverian Museum.
   Literature: Feest, 1968, p. 110.

4-6. Three fishhooks, Wellington. Figure 611.
   Evidence: Circumstantial. From Leverian Museum and/or Bullock's Museum.
   Literature: Kaeppler, 1974a, p. 80.

7-9. Three fishhooks, Cambridge (22.953a, b, c).
   Evidence: Leverian Museum.

10. Fishhook, Göttingen.
   Evidence: Purchased from London dealer Humphrey in 1782.

11-12. Two fishhooks (long flexible shank with bone points), Cambridge (22.952a, b). Figure 612.
   Evidence: Leverian Museum.

13. Fishhook, Cape Town (SAM 1899). Figure 613.
   Evidence: Thought to have arrived in Cape Town in 1780.
   Literature: Bax, 1970 p. 146.

14. Fishline, Vienna (237). Possibly Aleut.
   Evidence: Leverian Museum.

Figure 613.— Fishhook, Cape Town SAM 1899.

15. Fishline, Berne (AL 2a, b).
    Evidence: Webber collection.
    Literature: Henking, 1957, p. 377; Kaeppler, 1977.

16. Fishhook, British Museum (1944.Am2-139).
    Evidence: Circumstantial. Said to have been given by Mrs. Cook to Ann Gates, who gave it to Ann Smith, who gave it to Jane Backhouse. Beasley collection.

Canoe Models

1. Canoe model, Cambridge (22.955). Not located.
   Evidence: Leverian Museum.

2-3. Two canoe models, Vienna (238 [possibly Eskimo], 238a).
   Evidence: Leverian Museum.

4. Canoe model, Göttingen.
   Evidence: Purchased from London dealer Humphrey in 1782.

Canoe Paddles

1-3. Three canoe paddles, Florence (one said to be Nootka [256], two said to be Chukchi).
   Evidence: Cook voyage collection from various sources.
   Literature: Giglioli, 1895, pp. 111-112, 134-135; Kaeppler, 1977.

4. Canoe paddle (provenance unknown), Truro.
   Evidence: Circumstantial. Labeled from Cook's voyages from H. Cuming (who did have Cook voyage objects, mainly from the Leverian Museum).

TERRA DEL FUEGO (TIERRA DEL FUEGO)

Tierra del Fuego was visited by Cook's ships on his first and second voyages. Objects were collected by Banks on the first voyage and the Forsters on the second voyage, but few of these can be traced today. A number of drawings from the voyages depict houses, people, and a few objects (British Library Add. Ms. 23,920.16, 17 [Figs. 614, 615]).

Necklaces

1. Necklace of shells, Cambridge (1914.77).
   Evidence: Pennant collection of Cook voyage objects from various sources.

2. Necklace of shells, Oxford (168). Missing.
   Evidence: Forster collection, second voyage.
   Literature: Gathercole, n.d. [1970].

3. Necklace of shells, Göttingen.
   Evidence: Purchased from London dealer Humphrey in 1782.

4. Necklace of shells. Not located.
   Evidence: Leverian Museum depiction.

5-? Necklaces of shells. Location unknown.
   Evidence: Depicted in British Library Add. Ms. 23,920.20 (Fig. 616).

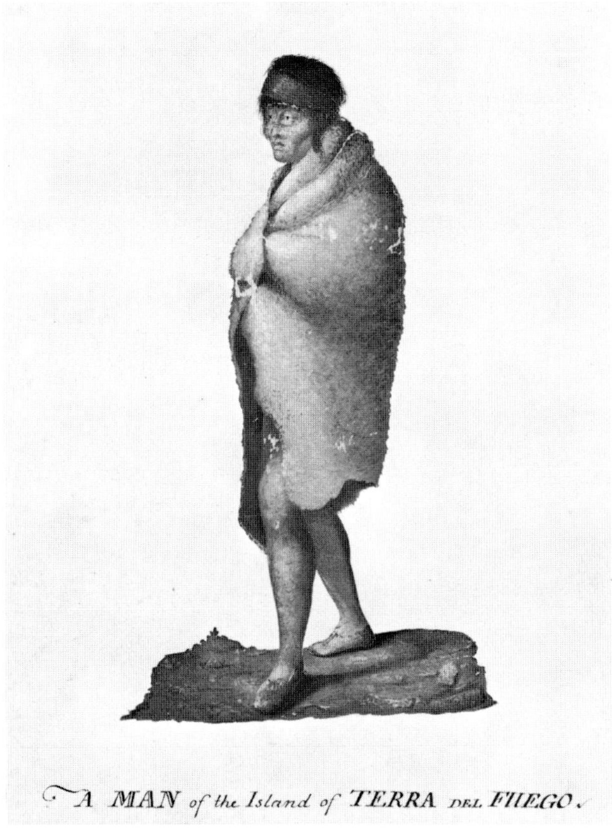

Figure 614. — A man from Tierra del Fuego, British Library Add. Ms. 23,920.16.

Figure 615. — A woman from Tierra del Fuego, British Library Add. Ms. 23,920.17.

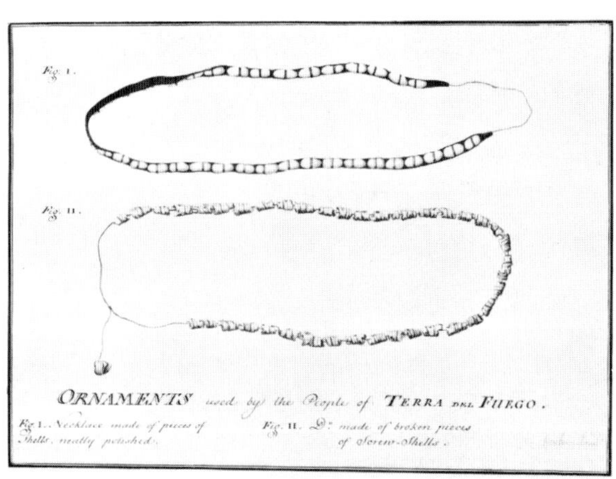

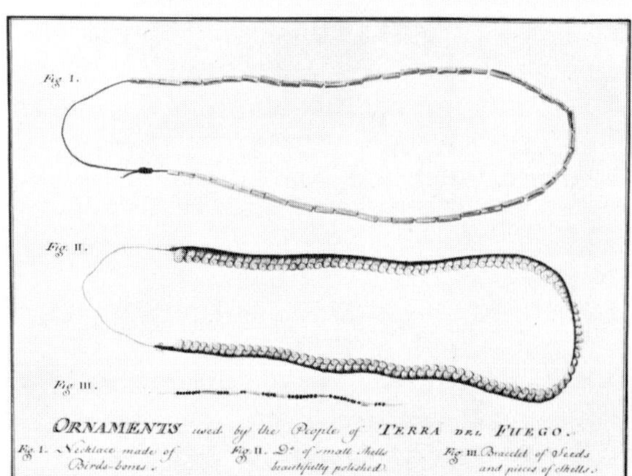

Figure 616. — Ornaments from Tierra del Fuego, British Library Add. Ms. 23,920.20.

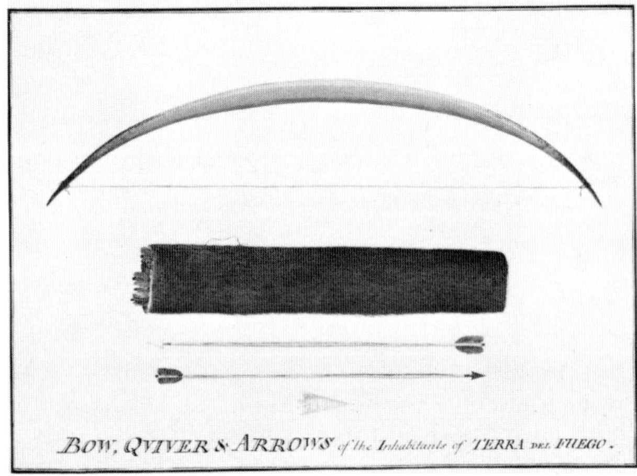

Figure 617. — Artifacts from Tierra del Fuego, British Library Add. Ms. 23,920.21.

Clothing

Clothing was depicted by Buchan, but only one reference can be found to clothing in a museum collection.

1. Sealskin coat, Oxford (165). Missing.
   Evidence: Forster collection, second voyage.
   Literature: Gathercole, n.d. [1970].

Weapons

A number of weapons were collected and depicted. Bows are triangular in cross section and arrows have tanged heads made of finely chipped glass or flint.

1-5. Bow and four arrow shafts, Stockholm (1848.1.65, 1848.1.51-54).
   Evidence: "Banks collection," probably from first voyage.
   Literature: Rydén, 1965, pp. 94-96.

6. Bow, Cambridge (1914.98).
   Evidence: Pennant collection of Cook voyage objects from various sources.

7. Bow (and arrows ?), Göttingen.
   Evidence: Forster collection, second voyage.

8. Spear point ("a piece of jagged bone"), Oxford (167). Missing.
   Evidence: Forster collection, second voyage. Perhaps the "harpoon head" depicted in a drawing pasted in Pennant's copy of Cook's voyages in the Dixson Library (Fig. 519).
   Literature: Gathercole, n.d. [1970].

9. Spear point, Göttingen.
   Evidence: Purchased from London dealer Humphrey in 1782.

10. Spear, Oxford (166). Missing.
   Evidence: Forster collection, second voyage.
   Literature: Gathercole, n.d. [1970].

11. Arrowhead. Location unknown.
   Evidence: Depicted in drawing pasted in Pennant's copy of Cook's voyages in the Dixson Library (Fig. 519).

12. Sling (?), Göttingen.
   Evidence: Purchased from London dealer Humphrey in 1782.

13. Quiver (attributed to Northwest Coast of America but see British Library Add. Ms. 23,920.21 [Fig. 617]), Cambridge (25.380).
   Evidence: Pennant collection of Cook voyage objects from various sources.

Appendix I
The Cook Collection
Exhibited at the Colonial and Indian Exhibition

The Colonial and Indian Exhibition, held in London in 1886, included a "Collection of Relics of the late Captain James Cook, R.N., FRS.," which was exhibited by Mr. John Mackrell at the request of the Government of New South Wales, Australia. The collection originally belonged to Mrs. James Cook and included not only ethnographic specimens, but portraits and memorabilia. Mrs. Cook's cousin, Rear Admiral Isaac Smith, sailed on Cook's first and second voyages and resided with Mrs. Cook until he died in 1831. Mrs. Cook's children died before she did, and many of her relics were inherited by Isaac Smith's descendants including his great nephew, John Mackrell—who organized the exhibition in question. Apparently when Mackrell decided to organize the exhibition, he borrowed other artificial curiosities and memorabilia from Cook's voyages from other relatives of Mrs. Cook. These included Rev. Bennett, Miss Bennett, and Mrs. Thomas Langton—all children of Rev. Frederick Bennett, whose maternal great grandfather, Charles Smith, was Mrs. Cook's first cousin. Mackrell also borrowed objects from William Adams and Henry Adams, who descend from Mrs. Cook's cousin Ursula Cragg (sister of Isaac Smith), whose daughter Mary married Dr. P. James Adams.[1] Two clubs were also loaned by Mrs. C. R. Smith, who was probably also related to Isaac Smith.

A Catalogue of the exhibition lists the items exhibited and to whom they belonged in 1886. In 1887 the Government of New South Wales purchased those parts of the collection that belonged to Mackrell, Rev. Bennett, Miss Bennett, Mrs. Langton, and Mrs. Place (who is not identified). The ethnographic objects are now in the Australian Museum, Sydney, and the memorabilia in the Mitchell Library. These items are listed in the Catalogue and can be specifically identified by comparison with photographs taken at the 1886 exhibition that are part of a copy of the Catalogue in the John Hewett collection (Figs. 618-622). William Adams also gave his memorabilia, but the items that belonged to Henry Adams and Mrs. C. R. Smith were retained by their owners.

In 1967 some of the objects that belonged to Henry Adams, then the property of L. Rickman-Adams, were sold by Christie's auction house. The illustrated Catalogue and the Tongan ivory image were purchased by John Hewett. Five pieces of bark cloth were purchased by Maggs (rare book dealer) and their location is unknown. Four ivory birds (from N. W. Coast America) and a Tongan ivory piece were purchased by Binney—and sold again at Christie's in 1973; their location is unknown to me. Two ornament pieces of ivory and turtle shell (probably Hawaiian) and an animal tooth were purchased at the 1967 sale by Yalkire (?) and are now in the collection of Jean-Jacques Laurent, Tahiti. Four gourds (not from the Pacific) that belonged to Henry Adams and are depicted in the Catalogue were given to the Dominion Museum (now National Museum), Wellington, by a descendant of the Adams family, along with some Pacific bark cloth and mats. One of the Wellington mats appears to be part of a mat in Sydney (H 98) that belonged to Mr. Mackrell.

Finally, the location of the two Tongan clubs that belonged to Mrs. C. R. Smith is unknown—they are depicted in Figure 620.

The ethnographic specimens from Cook collection exhibited at the Colonial and Indian Exhibition now in the Australian Museum, Sydney, are as follows:

[1] Information from Mitchell Library, Sydney, and Betty McFadgen, Wellington. See also Kaeppler, 1971, pp. 196-197. One of the objects (the New Zealand bowenite ornament [Fig. 337]) was referred to in 1791 while it was still in Mrs. Cook's collection (Raspe, 1791, p. vi).

Figure 618. — Photograph of the Colonial and Indian Exhibition.

Hawaii

Feather cape H104
Wicker helmet H141
Feather *lei* H87
Ivory turtles (3) H151
Nose whistle H118
Shark tooth knife H111
Shark tooth ring H150
Sample of cloak foundation H114
Bark cloth (15 small pieces)

Society Islands

Gorget H105
Nose flute H143
Shell apron from mourning dress H149
Shell clappers from mourning dress H46
Hafted adz H146
Netting shuttle with hair H153
Fishhook H136
Bark cloth (11 small pieces and three larger ones) H97, 99, 103

Tonga

Necklaces H116, 117, 152
Ivory image H151
Ornament H119
Basket H102
Comb H109
Fishnet H144
Fishhooks (5) H127, 129, 131, 132, 134
Mat H98

New Zealand

Cloak H103
Greenstone ornaments H156, 63
Patu onewa H85
Ornament of twisted flax H222
Adz blades (4) H81, 82, 83, 356
Fishhook H137

New Caledonia

Bag for sling stone H115
Spear thrower H119
Clubs (2) H147, 148
Comb H108

New Hebrides

Panpipe H112

Figure 619. — Photograph of the Colonial and Indian Exhibition.

Figure 620. — Photograph of the Colonial and Indian Exhibition.

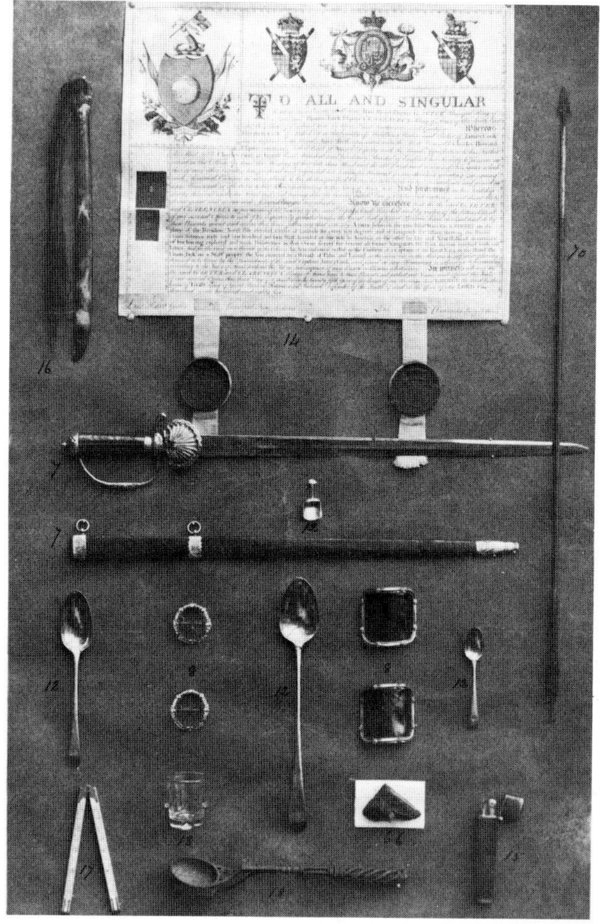

Figure 621. — Photograph of the Colonial and Indian Exhibition.

Northwest Coast of America
- Horn scoop H56
- Ivory bird H151
- Comb H110
- Fishing implement H106

Without Provenance
- Arrows and heads (13) H158-170

Other ethnographic specimens exhibited at the Colonial and Indian Exhibition are now located as follows:

Wellington
- Three pandanus mats (probably from Tonga) FE5250-5252
- Two pieces of Hawaiian bark cloth, FE5246-5247
- Three pieces of plain bark cloth (probably from Tahiti) FE5248, 5249
- Four gourds (not Pacific)

John Hewett Collection
- Ivory image

Jean-Jacques Laurent Collection
- Two ornament pieces and an animal tooth

Location Unknown
- Four ivory birds and a Tongan ivory piece
- Five pieces of bark cloth
- Two Tongan clubs

Figure 622. — Photograph of the Colonial and Indian Exhibition.

Appendix II
The Worden Hall Collection

Worden Hall, an estate at Faringdon, near Preston, Lancashire, England, contained a large private collection of curiosities, including a group of objects thought to have come from Cook's voyages. The collector of these objects is not known; however, they are accompanied by a manuscript list entitled "Some account of the Curiosities," in which the objects from Hawaii and the Northwest Coast of America are designated "new discovered." The objects derive mainly from places visited on Cook's third voyage (including the Hottentots), and those objects from this collection that have been located conform to the type and style of objects known to have come from Cook's voyages. In the 1940's the contents of Worden Hall were dispersed and a number of objects on the list of curiosities were purchased by K. A. Webster and given by him to the Christchurch Museum. A few other objects, including a New Zealand *heitiki* (with red sealing-wax eyes), were also acquired, which are not on the list of curiosities. In the Catalogue above I have included only the objects so far located that are on the manuscript list. The list follows:

SOME ACCOUNT OF THE CURIOSITIES

1. The flat wooden-like Shovel—is called the pagi—and is brandished in the hand in the War Dance—At the friendly Islands in the South Seas.
2. A net—worn by the Women of the same Islands.
3. The reed Flute, played on with the Nose—by the women of the same Islands.
4. A Carved War Club—from the same Islands.
5. A fly flapper—from the same Islands.
6. The reed pipe—from friendly Islands.
7. The Combs—from the same.
8. The Baskets from the Island of Tanna—one of the friendly Isles.
9. The feathered Wreath or Wra—worn by the Women, round the Neck, of the Sandwich Islands—new discovered—in the South Seas.
10. The Matting—from New Zealand.
11. A bracelet made of Hog's Tusks—worn by the Women of the Sandwich Islands.
12. Another, made of Bones—small—and flat—from the same.
13. Large fishing hook—from the same.
14. Small fishing hooks—from same.
15. The several pieces of coloured Cloth—from the Sandwich Islands.
16. The White Cloth from Otahaita.
17. The bone Weapon of War—from King Georges Sound—America—new discovered.
18. The Wooden Figure—from the same.
19. The inlaid horn Bracelet—from the same.
20. Whale bladder Jacket from same.
21. Small Figure of Bone from same.
22. Green Stone being the head of a Hatchet from Same.
23. Bow & Arrows poisoned (as sayd)—from the Hottentots.
24. The braided hair from Otahaita.
25. Two Captain's Commissions—from the King of Tanjore East Indies—done on leaves.
26. A Hatchet from Otahaita.
27. An Ancient Corn pipe—found in Wales . . .

The objects now in Christchurch are the following:

Hawaii

Boar tusk bracelet. No. 11 of the list
Turtle shell bracelet. No. 12
Pieces of bark cloth. No. 15

New Zealand

Piece of a flax cloak. No. 10

Tonga

Dance paddle. No. 1
Club. No. 4
Basket. No. 8
Fly whisk. No. 5
Nose flute. No. 3

Provenance Not Confirmed

Hafted adz No. 26. Listed as Tahiti, identified by Duff as Tonga [listed in Catalogue above as Tonga].

Bark cloth No. 16. Listed as Tahiti, identified by Duff as Tonga [listed in Catalogue above as Tahiti because Tongan collections do not usually include white bark cloth].

Appendix III
Cook Voyage Objects in Glasgow, Greenwich, and Wellington

The information on these three collections was not presented in detail above, and thus is included here.

GLASGOW

The individual objects in the Cook voyage collection in Glasgow cannot be documented by actual traceable links. However, the objects that have strong circumstantial evidence, including attribution and appropriate type and style, are included here and in the Catalogue above. (See also chapter on Ethnography and Cook's Voyages above.)

Hawaii

Drum (E 367). Attributed to Cook on Robertson list. Probably the drum purchased by John Hunter at Samwell's sale.

Hafted adz (E 366b). On Robertson list. (Probably "P" of Laskey's list [1813].)

Tahiti

Three hafted adzes (E 366c, d, e). On Robertson list. (Probably "P" of Laskey's list [1813].)

New Zealand

Taiaha (E 331). On Robertson list. (Probably "L" of Laskey's list [1813].)

Two whalebone clubs (E 563). Presented by Captain King (Probably "C" of Laskey's list [1813]).

Tonga

Basket (E 355). On Robertson list. An old parchment label attached "No. 21 A Provision Basket from Amsterdam Island."

Hafted adz (E 366a). On Robertson list. (Probably "P" of Laskey's list [1813].)

Club (E 565). "N" label attached—which, according to Laskey (1813) probably indicates a Cook voyage provenance.

Easter Island

Dance paddle (E 348). Presented by Captain King.

Austral Islands

Carved wood object (E 349). Presented by Captain King.

New Caledonia

Four clubs (E 362, 363, 364, 365). On Robertson list. Possibly presented by the Forsters—E 365 is much like the object depicted in the New Caledonia plate of the official account of the second voyage (Fig. 523). Most of the objects on these plates belonged to the Forsters (Probably "B" of Laskey's list [1813]).

Northwest Coast

Bird rattle (E 369). On Robertson list. (Probably "E" of Laskey's list [1813].)

Bone beater (E 370). On Robertson list. (Probably "F" of Laskey's list [1813].)

At least five other objects were purchased at Samwell's sale by John Hunter, but have not yet been located or identified.

Hawaii

Kahili with human bone handle.

Bark cloth

Barbed spear (probably "G" or "H" of Laskey's list [1813]).

Tahiti

White bark cloth.

New Zealand

Patu onewa (probably "C" of Laskey's list [1813]).

NATIONAL MARITIME MUSEUM, GREENWICH[1]

Collected by William Griffin, cooper of HMS *Resolution* (see Griffin papers, Dixson Library, Sydney).

Hawaiian spear L15(92)B

Tongan neckrest L15(92)C

Tongan club L15(92)A

From collection of Henry A. Baron, whose wife, Mary Cook Jenkins, was great granddaughter of Cook's sister Margaret (see also under Wellington).

Tahitian food pounder L15(94)A

From Bradley family through Charlotte Cook, who married T. Bradley about 1812.

Hawaii (?) shark tooth implement

Presented by Captain Cook to Neil Malcolm of Poltalloch shortly before leaving for his third voyage. Sold at auction in September, 1958 (see Anon., 1958).

New Zealand *kotiate* L15(74)

Tonga—nine clubs L15(70)A-G, L15(71)A-B

From Cook's voyages by "tradition."

Nootka Sound bowl L15(95)

New Zealand *tewhatewha* L15(88)

Tongan fly whisk L15(94)C

[1]Compiled with the help of Rina Prentice.

NATIONAL MUSEUM OF NEW ZEALAND, WELLINGTON[2]

From the A. G. Long collection—bequeathed by Mrs. Cook to Indiana Jenkins (nee Fleck, granddaughter of Cook's sister Margaret) who gave them to her daughter Hannah who married S. J. Long (see also under Greenwich).

Hawaiian hafted adz FE3667

Society Islands plain bark cloth FE3669

Tongan club FE3663

Length of plaited sennit (no provenance)

Northwest Coast of America shaft straightener FE3668

Northwest Coast of America leather fringe with quillwork FE3665

From the Adams collection—bequeathed by Mrs. Cook to children of her cousin, Mrs. Ursula Cragg, one of whom married Dr. P. James Adams (see Colonial and Indian Exhibition).

Hawaiian bark cloth (two pieces) FE5246-5247

Society Islands bark cloth (three pieces) FE5248-5249

Tongan pandanus mats (three pieces) FE5250-5552

Four gourds (no provenance)

From the Webster collection, two pieces identified by early depictions.

New Zealand *wahaika* (wood hand club) depicted in British Library Add. Ms. 15,508.24.

New Zealand "godstick" depicted in British Library Add. Ms. 15,508.26 (Fig. 238).

From the Imperial Institute, a collection which had been in the possession of Queen Victoria and given to the Imperial Institute (now Commonwealth Institute) by Edward VII (see also the New Zealand *heitiki,* in Catalogue above, that belongs to H.M. Queen Elizabeth, and probably came from this same collection). A paper with the collection said, "This box contains articles brought by Captain Cook from Otaheti." But, according to Betty McFadgen, there is no proof that it all came from one source. I have not examined all these pieces. The objects that I have examined from New Zealand and the other Pacific Islands are entirely in keeping in type and style with other objects collected on Cook's voyages. All the objects derive from areas visited on the first and second voyages, and it is conceivable that they were personal gifts from Cook to King George III. Therefore, I have included them in this Catalogue.

There are also nine pieces from North America in the collection. I have not examined these pieces, but they do not appear to be of the same type collected on third voyage, and, since there are no Hawaiian pieces in this collection, I suspect that these American pieces are not from Cook's voyage. Thus, I have not included them in the Catalogue, but the entire Imperial Institute Collection is listed here.

[2]Compiled from lists supplied by Betty McFadgen.

North America

Two arrow shafts FE2994
Ornament of quill work FE2995
Ornament of quill work FE2996
Crystal arrowhead FE2997
Two pairs of moccasins, quill work FE2998
Leather pouch with quill work FE2999
Leather knife sheath with quill work FE3015
Headband, feathers, and quill work FE3016
Two cloth sashes with beads and tassels FE3017

Pacific Islands

Fishhook FE3001
Fishhook FE3002
Fishhook FE3003
Eyeshade, Tahiti FE3004
Basalt food pounder, Tahiti FE3006
Hafted adz, Tahiti FE3007
Tapa beater FE3008
Tattoo mallet FE3009
Tattoo comb FE3010
Fishhook FE3013
Fishhook FE3014
Head rest, Tahiti FE3018
Comb, Tonga FE3019
Two fiber skirts FE3020
Fiber skirt FE3021
Three pieces plain tapa FE3022
Six small ear pendants, Tahiti (pearls, shells, stone) FE3023
Two shell necklaces FE3024
Shell fishhook FE3025

New Zealand

Patu onewa, stone club ME7849
Putorino, flute ME7850
Comb ME7851
Cloak ME7852
Cloak ME7853
Paua cloak pin ME7854
Dentalium necklaces ME7855
Nguru, flute ME11809
Fishhook and sinker ME12118
Fishhook and sinker ME12119

The National Museum also has other collections attributed to Cook's voyages, but since their documentation is either nonexistent or unlikely, I have not included them. These are:

1. Nine objects from the Oldman collection—undocumented.
2. Five pieces of bark cloth and matting from the Turnbull collection—undocumented.
3. A Tongan club from the Royal United Services Institute, at one time in a case with "Cook relics." There are photographs of this club and others taken when on exhibit in the Royal United Services Institute (photographs in the Mitchell Library, Sydney). However, because many of the pieces come from areas not visited on Cook's voyages, the documentation on all of the objects is suspect.

Finally, the Lord St. Oswald collection in the National Museum has previously been studied and the documentation published (Kaeppler, 1974a), and need not be repeated here. The objects with Cook voyage provenance from the St. Oswald collection have been included in this Catalogue.

References Cited

Anonymous

1774. *A Catalogue . . . of Natural and Artificial Curiosities . . . from . . . New-Discovered Islands in the South Seas . . . Exhibited in Mr. Pinchbeck's Repository.*

1776. *A Catalogue of . . . Natural and Artificial Rarities . . . from the New-Discovered Islands in the South-Seas. . . . Property of Mr. Samuel Jackson . . . by Auction . . . March 14.*

1781. *A Catalogue of . . . Rarities from the New-Discovered Places in the South Seas . . . Property of an Officer Belonging to . . . the* Discovery . . . *by Auction June 14.*

1786. *A Catalogue of the Portland Museum . . . the Property of the Duchess of Portland, Deceased . . . Sold by Auction . . . April 24.* [By Lightfoot?]

1794. [Obituary of Anna Blackburne.] *Gentleman's Mag.* 64:180.

1808. *Part V of the Remainder of the Stock in Trade of Mr. Jacob Forster . . . June 28.*

1958. *At Poltalloch House . . . Catalogue of Antique Furniture and Plenishing . . . by Auction . . . September 17-19.*

1970. *Catalogue of Items Included in the Captain Cook Bi-Centenary Exhibition Entitled "Cook, Banks and Australia."* Sydney and Melbourne, April-May.

Ball, V.

1894 [1895?]. *Collection of Weapons, etc. . . . from the South Sea Islands . . . in Trinity College, Dublin.* Dublin: Science and Art Mus.

Barrow, T.

1964. *The Decorative Arts of the New Zealand Maori.* Wellington and Auckland: Reed.

1969. *Maori Wood Sculpture of New Zealand.* Rutland, Vermont and Tokyo: Tuttle.

1972. *Art and Life in Polynesia.* London: Pall Mall Press.

Bax, D.

1970. "Zuid-Afrika's eerste openbare verzameling op het gebied van kunst en etnologie, 1764-1821." *Verhandelingen der Koninklike Nederlande Akademie van Wetenschappen, Afd. Letterkunde (Nuwe reeks)* 75(3):145-147.

Beaglehole, J. C.

1955-1967. *The Journals of Captain James Cook on His Voyages of Discovery.* 3 vols. Cambridge.

Brigham, William T.

1898. "Report of a Journey Around the World Undertaken to Examine Various Ethnological Collections." *B. P. Bishop Mus. Occ. Pap.* 1(1):1-72.

1899. "Hawaiian Feather Work." *Mem. B. P. Bishop Mus.* 1(1):1-81.

1903. "Additional Notes on Hawaiian Feather Work." *Mem. B. P. Bishop Mus.* 1(5):437-453; 7(1):1-69.

1911. "Ka Hana Kapa: The Making of Bark-Cloth in Hawaii." *Mem. B. P. Bishop Mus.* 3:1-276.

1913. "Report of a Journey Around the World to Study Matters Relating to Museums." *B. P. Bishop Mus. Occ. Pap.* 5(5):151-320.

1918. "Additional Notes on Hawaiian Feather Work." (2nd Suppl.) *Mem. B. P. Bishop Mus.* 7(1):1-69.

Brock, C. H.

1973. "Dr. Hunter's South Seas Curiosities." *Scottish Arts Rev.* 14(2):6-9, 37-38.

Buck, Peter H. (Te Rangi Hiroa)

1957. *Arts and Crafts of Hawaii.* Bishop Mus. Spec. Publ. 45. Honolulu.

Bullock, William

1801. *A Catalogue of the Liverpool Museum.* 3rd ed. Liverpool.

1809. *A Companion to the Liverpool Museum.* 7th ed. Bath.

1810. *A Companion to Mr. Bullock's Museum.* 9th ed. London.

Chalmers-Hunt, J. M.

1976. *Natural History Auctions 1700-1972.* London: Sotheby Parke Bernet.

Christie's

1793. *A Catalogue of the . . . Collection . . . of Mr. John Webber, R.A. . . . Sold by Auction . . . June 14.*

1972. *African, American and Oceanic Sculpture, Tibetan and Nepalese Ritual Art, Indian and Kashmir Bronze and Stone Sculpture . . . at Auction . . . March 27.* London: White Bros.

Cook, James

1777. *A Voyage towards the South Pole and Round the World . . .* Resolution *and* Adventure, *1772-1775.* London.

Cox, J. Halley, with William H. Davenport

1974. *Hawaiian Sculpture.* Honolulu: Univ. Hawaii Press.

Coxe, Peter

1812. *A Catalogue of All the Valuable Drawings, Sketches, Sea-Views, and Studies of That Celebrated Artist James Philip de Loutherbourg.* London.

Cranstone, B. A. L., and H. J. Gowers

1968. "The Tahitian Mourner's Dress: A Discovery and a Description." *British Mus. Quart.* 32(3-4):138-144.

Dance, S. Peter

1971. "The Cook Voyages and Conchology." *J. Conchology* 26:354-379.

1972. "The Cook Voyages and Conchology: A Supplementary Note." *J. Conchology* 27:357-358.

De Barde, Chevalier

1814. *A Descriptive Catalogue of the . . . Large Water Color Drawings by de Barde . . . at Mr. Bullock's Museum.* London: Whittingham and Rowland.

Dodge, Ernst S.

1969. "The Cook Ethnographical Collections." In Roger Duff (Ed.) *No Sort of Iron.* Christchurch: Art Galleries and Museums Assoc. New Zealand.

Douglas, Bronwen

1970. "A Contact History of the Balad People of New Caledonia 1774-1845." *J. Polynesian Soc.* 79(2):180-200.

Duff, Roger

1969. *No Sort of Iron.* Christchurch: Art Galleries and Museums Assoc. New Zealand.

Edge-Partington Library

1934. *Books, Maps and Pictures Relating to Australia, New Zealand and the Pacific: A Catalogue of the Library of the Late James Edge-Partington.* Pts. 1, 2. London: Francis Edwards.

Ellis, Annie Raine

1907. *The Early Diary of Frances Burney 1768-1778.* 2 vols. London: George Bell and Sons.

Feest, Christian

1968. *Indianer Nordamerikas.* Vienna: Mus. für Völkerkunde.

Force, Roland W., and Maryanne Force

1968. *Art and Artifacts of the 18th Century: Objects in the Leverian Museum as Painted by Sarah Stone.* Honolulu: Bishop Mus. Press.

1971. *The Fuller Collection of Pacific Artifacts.* New York and Washington: Praeger.

Forster, George

1777. *A Voyage round the World in His Britannic Majesty's Sloop* Resolution *Commanded by Capt. James Cook . . .* London.

Freeman, J. D.

1949. "The Polynesian Collection of Trinity College, Dublin, and the National Museum of Ireland." *J. Polynesian Soc.* 58(1):1-18.

Furneaux, Rupert

1960. *Tobias Furneaux: Circumnavigator.* London: Cassell.

Gathercole, Peter

[n.d.] (1970). *From the Islands of the South Seas 1773-4: An Exhibition of a Collection Made on Capn. Cook's Second Voyage . . . by J. R. Forster.* Oxford: Pitt Rivers Mus.

1976. "A Maori Shell Trumpet at Cambridge." In G. de Sieveking, I. H. Longworth, and K. E. Wilson (eds.), *Problems in Economic and Social Archaeology,* pp. 187-199. London: Duckworth.

Germer, Ernst

1975. "Zu Georg Forsters Polynesien-Sammlung von Wörlitz." In *Georg Forster: Naturforscher, Weltreisender, Humanist und Revolutionär,* pp. 61-88. Wörlitz: Staatliche Schlösser und Gärten.

Gianetti, M.

1785. *Elogy of Captain James Cook.* Florence: Cambiagi.

Giglioli, Enrico H.

1893, 1895. "Appunti intorno ad una Collezione etnografica fatta durante il terzo Viaggio di Cook." *Archivio l'Antropologia e la Etnologia* 23:173-242; 25:57-143.

Greene, Richard

1786. *A . . . Catalogue of the Curiosities, Natural and Artificial, in the Lichfield Museum.* 3rd ed. Lichfield: John Jackson.

Gunther, Erna

1972. *Indian Life on the Northwest Coast of North America: As Seen by the Early Explorers and Fur Traders during the Last Decades of the Eighteenth Century.* Chicago: Univ. Chicago Press.

Hawkesworth, John

1773. *An Account of the Voyages Undertaken . . . for Making Discoveries in the Southern Hemisphere.* 3 vols. London.

Henking, Karl H.

1957. "Die Südsee- und Alaskasammlung Johann Wäber: Beschreibender Katalog." *Jahrbuch Bernischen Historischen Mus.* 1955-1956. 35, 36:325-389.

Holm, Bill, and Bill Reid

1975. *Indian Art of the Northwest Coast.* Houston: Rice Univ.

Humphrey, George

1779. *A Catalogue of the . . . Museum of Mr. George Humphrey . . . Sold by Auction . . . April 15.*

Kaeppler, Adrienne L.

1971. "Eighteenth Century Tonga: New Interpretations of Tongan Society and Material Culture at the Time of Captain Cook." *Man: J. Royal Anthropological Inst.* 6(2):204-220. Pls. 1-6.

1972. "The Use of Documents in Identifying Ethnographic Specimens from the Voyages of Captain Cook." *J. Pacific History* 7:195-200.

1973. "Pottery Sherds from Tungua, Ha'apai; and Remarks on Pottery and Social Structure in Tonga." *J. Polynesian Soc.* 82(2):218-222.

1974a. "Cook Voyage Provenance of the 'Artificial Curiosities' of Bullock's Museum." *Man: J. Royal Anthropological Inst.* 9(1):68-92.

1974b. "A Study of Tongan Panpipes with a Speculative Interpretation." *Ethnos* 39(1-4):102-128.

1975a. "An Eighteenth Century Kāhili from Kaua'i." *Archaeology on Kaua'i* 4(2):3-9.

1975b. *The Fabrics of Hawaii: Bark Cloth.* World's Heritage of Woven Fabrics. Vol. 14. Leigh-on-Sea, England.

1977. (Ed.) Cook Voyage Artifacts in Leningrad, Berne, and Florence Museums. In press. Honolulu: Bishop Mus. Press.

Forthcoming. Captain James Cook, Sir Ashton Lever and Miss Sarah Stone: A Study of Art and Artifacts of the 18th Century in the Leverian Museum.

Keevil, J. J.

1933. "William Anderson, 1748-1778: Master Surgeon, Royal Navy." *Ann. Medical History* (n.s.) 5(6):511-524.

Kooijman, Simon

1972. *Tapa in Polynesia.* B. P. Bishop Mus. Bull. 234. Honolulu.

Laskey, J.

1813. *A General Account of the Hunterian Museum, Glasgow.* Glasgow: Smith.

Leverian Museum

1790. *A Companion to the Museum.* London.

1806. *Catalogue of the Leverian Museum . . . the Sale of the Entire Collection.* London: Hayden.

Linneaus, Carl

1735. *Systema Naturae.*

Mackrell, John (Exhibitor)

1886. *A Catalogue of the Collection of Relics of the Late Captain James Cook, R.N., F.R.S., at the Colonial and Indian Exhibition* (The New South Wales Exhibit). London.

Mead, S. M.

1969. *Traditional Maori Clothing: A Study of Technological and Functional Change.* Wellington.

Medway, David G.

1976. "Extant Types of New Zealand Birds from Cook's Voyages." *Notornis* 23(1):44-60; 23(2):120-137.

Moschner, Irmgard

1955. "Die Wiener Cook-Sammlung: Südsee-Teil." *Archiv für Völkerkunde* 10:136-253.

1957. "Die Rindenstoffe der Wiener Cook-Sammlung." *Archiv für Völkerkunde* 12:144-171.

Moyle, Richard M.

1976. "Tongan Musical Instruments." *Galpin Soc. J.* 29:64-83.

Murray-Oliver, Anthony

1975. *Captain Cook's Hawaii as Seen by His Artists.* Wellington: Millwood.

O'Keeffe, [Mr.]

1785. *. . . Omai or, A Trip round the World.* London: Cadell.

Paget, Hugh

1970. *To the South There is a Great Land: Captain Cook, Sir Joseph Banks and Australia.* Sydney: The Australian.

Phelps, Steven

1976. *Art and Artefacts of the Pacific, Africa and the Americas: The James Hooper Collection.* London: Hutchinson.

Plischke, Hans

1929. "Kukailimoku: Ein Kriegsgott von Hawaii." *Abh. der Gesell. der Wiss. zu Göttingen, Phil.-Hist. Kl.* (N.F.) 24(1):1-40.

1931. "Tahitische Trauergewänder." *Abh. der Gesell. der Wiss. zu Göttingen, Phil.-Hist. Kl.* (N.F.) 24(2):1-47.

1939. "Ein Brust-Schmuck von Tonga-tabu und die Verarbeitung von Walknochen in Polynesien." *Nachr. der Gesell. der Wiss. zu Göttingen, Phil.-Hist. Kl.* (N.F.) 2:121-138.

1957. "Bogen und Pfeil auf den Tonga-Inseln und in Polynesien." *Göttinger Völkerkunde Studien* 2:207-225.

1959. "Bogen und Pfeil auf den Marquesas-Inseln." *Zeit. Ethnologie* 84(1):19-24.

Raspe, Rudolf Erich

1791. *A Descriptive Catalogue of a General Collection of Ancient and Modern Engraved Gems.* London: Tassie and Murray.

Robertson, George

1948. *The Discovery of Tahiti: A Journal of the Second Voyage of H.M.S.* Dolphin . . . *1766 . . . 1768.* London: Hakluyt Soc. (Ser. 2, No. 98).

Rose, Roger

In press. "On the Origin and Diversity of 'Tahitian' Fly Whisks." In *The Visual Art of Oceania.* Honolulu: Univ. Press Hawaii.

Rozina, L. G.

1966. "The James Cook Collection in the Museum of Anthropology and Ethnography" (title translated from Russian). *Sbornik Mus. Antropologii i Etnografii* 23:234-253.

Rydén, S.

1965. *The Banks Collection: An Episode in 18th-Century Anglo-Swedish Relations.* Monogr. Ser., Publ. 8. Göteborg: Ethnographical Mus. Sweden, Stockholm.

Sharp, Andrew

1968. *Voyages of Abel Janszoon Tasman.* London: Clarendon.

Shaw, Alexander

1787. *A Catalogue of the Different Specimens of Cloth, Collected in the Three Voyages of Captain Cook.* London.

Shawcross, F. Wilfred

1970. "The Cambridge University Collection of Maori Artifacts Made on Captain Cook's First Voyage." *J. Polynesian Soc.* 79(3):305-348.

Sherborn, C. Davies

1905. "Note on the 'Museum Humfredianum.' " *Ann. and Mag. of Natural History* 16, Ser. 7, pp. 262-264.

Söderström, Jan

1939. *A. Sparrman's Ethnographical Collection from James Cook's 2nd Expedition (1772-1775).* Ethnographical Mus. Sweden, n.s., Publ. 6. Stockholm.

Sotheby and Co.

1969. *Catalogue of Primitive Art and Indian Sculpture: The Property of the Trustees of the Warwick Castle Resettlement . . . Day of Sale . . . 8th December.* London.

Steele, Joshua

1775. "Account of a Musical Instrument . . . Brought from the Isle of Amsterdam . . . in 1774: A Letter to Sir John Pringle." *Philosophical Trans. Royal Soc.* 65:67-78.

Thorpe, W. W.

1931. "Tangiwai Ear-Drop Collected by Captain Cook." *New Zealand J. Science and Technology* (Wellington) 7(3):181.

Urban, Manfred

1966. "Polynesische Stössel." *Jahrbuch des Museums für Völkerkunde zu Leipzig* 22:40-56.

Vaughan, Thomas, and A. A. St. C. M. Murray-Oliver

1974. *Captain Cook, R.N., the Resolute Mariner: An International Record of Oceanic Discovery.* Portland: Oregon Historical Soc.

Warner, Oliver (Editor)

1955. *An Account of the Discovery of Tahiti: From the Journal of George Robertson, Master of H.M.S.* Dolphin. London: Folio Soc.

Wernhart, Karl R.

1972. "Deux anciens *tapas* de Tahiti." *J. Soc. Océanistes* 28(34):82-85.

Whitehead, P. J. P.

1969. "Zoological Specimens from Captain Cook's Voyages." *J. Soc. Bibliography Natural History* 5:161-201.

Photo Credits

Grateful acknowledgment is made for photographs furnished by the following:

British Museum
Figures 61, 165, 215, 236, 237, 239, 258, 261, 283, 299, 334, 343, 367, 405, 409, 442, 453.

British Library
Pages v, vi. Figures 50, 154, 163, 206, 207, 208, 212, 216, 224, 225, 226, 238, 240, 248, 254, 265, 272, 280, 282, 284, 285, 292, 294, 295, 303, 333, 335, 344, 354, 371, 381, 392, 393, 394, 395, 396, 397, 401, 411, 443, 454, 474, 480, 501, 505, 542, 545, 567, 590, 600, 614, 615, 616, 617.

London School of Economics
Figure 487.

Merseyside County Museum, Liverpool
Figures 372, 551.

National Maritime Museum, Greenwich
Figures 31, 266, 462, 482, 518, 581.

Pitt Rivers Museum, Oxford
Figures 217, 235, 259, 320, 386, 390, 391, 408, 426, 503, 504, 534, 543.

Royal Albert Memorial Museum, Exeter
Figures 173, 186, 273, 304, 317, 355, 483, 492, 508, 509, 510, 511, 512, 513, 514, 515, 516, 527, 528, 529.

Royal Scottish Museum, Edinburgh
Figures 105, 106, 463, 500, 583, 599, 607.

Saffron Walden Museum, Essex
Figures 122, 539.

University Museum of Archaeology and Ethnology, Cambridge
Figures 77, 170, 176, 198, 199, 228, 229, 233, 252, 253, 255, 267, 349, 365, 379, 428, 470, 507, 541, 546, 555, 561, 569, 579, 585, 589, 612.

Bearnes Sales Rooms, Torquay
Figures 103, 104, 112, 558.

John Hewett, London
Figures 618, 619, 620, 621, 622.

National Museum of Ireland, Dublin
Figures 434, 478, 479, 493.

Etnografiska Museet, Stockholm
Figures 326, 327.

Institut für Völkerkunde der Universität, Göttingen
Figures 133, 134, 137, 138, 139, 148, 190, 222, 241, 242, 244, 245, 260, 340, 399, 400, 433, 439, 444, 461, 484, 490.

Museum für Völkerkunde, Berlin
Figure 58.

Museum für Völkerkunde, Vienna
Figures 113, 132, 149, 151, 172, 191, 193, 196, 234, 276, 288, 305, 324, 366, 375, 481, 485, 540, 548, 554, 560, 594, 605, 606.

George Ortiz, Geneva
Figures 467, 468, 476.

South African Museum, Cape Town
Figures 87, 185, 219, 308, 361, 362, 363, 565, 574, 613.

National Museum, Wellington
Figures 99, 188, 370, 611.

Otago Museum, Dunedin
Figure 418.

A. R. Merritt, Christchurch
Figure 33.

The Australian Museum, Sydney
Figures 66, 75, 88, 93, 94, 95, 96, 180, 417, 440, 451, 538, 598, 609.

National Library of Australia, Canberra
Figures 41, 42, 603.

State Library of New South Wales, Sydney
Dixson Library—Figures 264, 286, 519.
Mitchell Library—Figure 221.

Field Museum of Natural History, Chicago
Figure 331.

Menil Foundation, Houston
Figures 553, 564.

John Hauberg, Seattle
Figure 559.

Marilyn Weidner
Figure 64.

Bishop Museum—Benjamin W. Patnoi and Lynne Gilliland
Frontispiece. Page xii. Figures 1, 2, 3, 4, 5, 6, 7, 8, 9, 10, 15, 16, 17, 18, 19, 20, 21, 22, 23, 24, 25, 26, 27, 28, 29, 30, 32, 34, 35, 36, 37, 38, 39, 40, 43, 44, 45, 46, 47, 48, 49, 51, 52, 54, 55, 72, 73, 89, 90, 98, 130, 150, 164, 167, 182, 184, 194, 205, 209, 210, 213, 214, 220, 243, 246, 247, 251, 306, 307, 314, 321, 322, 323, 329, 337, 353, 364, 398, 412, 415, 423, 430, 431, 432, 521, 522, 523, 525, 526, 535, 536, 544, 547, 550, 587, 596, 597, 602, 604.

Bishop Museum—Peter Gilpin
Figures 168, 211.

Bishop Museum—John Cotton Wright
—Front, back, and inside covers, and all remaining photographs.

THIS VOLUME WAS COMPOSED IN
BASKERVILLE TYPE
AND PRINTED
BY
EDWARD ENTERPRISES, INC.
HONOLULU, HAWAII

ORGANIZED AND DESIGNED
BY
GENEVIEVE A. HIGHLAND
SADIE J. DOYLE
ADRIENNE L. KAEPPLER
CHARLES TAKETA
JOHN COTTON WRIGHT